A
WORLD OF
IDEAS

ESSENTIAL READINGS
FOR
COLLEGE WRITERS

ALSO WRITTEN OR EDITED
BY
LEE A. JACOBUS

Improving College Reading, Sixth Edition, 1992

Aesthetics and the Arts, 1968

Issues and Response, 1968, 1972

Developing College Reading, Fourth Edition, 1990

Seventeen from Everywhere:
Short Stories from around the World, 1971

Poems in Context (with William Moynihan), 1974

John Cleveland: A Critical Study, 1975

The Humanities through the Arts (with F. David Martin),
Fourth Edition, 1990

The Sentence Book, Third Edition, 1989

The Paragraph and Essay Book, 1977

Sudden Apprehension:
Aspects of Knowledge in Paradise Lost, 1976

Longman Anthology of American Drama, 1982

Humanities: The Evolution of Values, 1986

Writing as Thinking, 1989

The Bedford Introduction to Drama, Second Edition, 1992

Shakespeare and the Dialectic of Certainty, 1992

FOURTH EDITION

A
WORLD OF
IDEAS

ESSENTIAL READINGS
FOR
COLLEGE WRITERS

LEE A. JACOBUS
University of Connecticut

BEDFORD BOOKS
OF ST. MARTIN'S PRESS
Boston

For Bedford Books

Publisher: Charles H. Christensen
Associate Publisher/General Manager: Joan E. Feinberg
Managing Editor: Elizabeth M. Schaaf
Developmental Editor: Ellen M. Kuhl
Production Editor: Lori Chong
Copyeditor: Deborah Fogel
Text Design: Anna Post George
Portraits: Anatoly Dverin; Lyrl C. Ahern and Bill Ogden of PC & F, Inc.
Cover Design: Steve Snider
Cover Art: Tom Phillips, *Dante in His Study,* 1978. © Tom Phillips/VAGA,
  New York/DACS, London 1993

Acknowledgments

Aristotle, "The Aim of Man." From *The Nichomachean Ethics,* translated by Martin
  Ostwald. Copyright © 1962 by the Bobbs-Merrill Company, Inc. Reprinted
  by permission of the publisher.
Ruth Benedict, "The Pueblos of New Mexico." From *Patterns of Culture* by Ruth
  Benedict. Copyright 1934 by Ruth Benedict; copyright © renewed 1961 by
  Ruth Valentine. Reprinted by permission of Houghton Mifflin Co. All rights
  reserved.
Franz Boas, "Stability of Culture." From *Anthropology and Modern Life* by Franz
  Boas. Reprinted by permission of Dover Publications, Inc.
Rachel Carson, "Elixirs of Death." From *Silent Spring* by Rachel Carson. Copyright
  © 1962 by Rachel L. Carson; © renewed 1990 by Roger Christie. Reprinted by
  permission of Houghton Mifflin Co. All rights reserved.

*Acknowledgments and copyrights are continued at the back of the book on pages
  705–706, which constitute an extension of the copyright page.*

PREFACE

When I describe this book to friends, I often say that it includes selections from Plato, Aristotle, Darwin, Wollstonecraft, Douglass, Freud, Kuhn, Gould, and no one less important. Although that may be a mild exaggeration, it is very close to the truth. When the first edition of *A World of Ideas* was published, the notion that students in first-year composition courses ought to be able to read and write about challenging works by great thinkers was a radical one. I expected that the choice of selections in this book would appeal to a small minority of people who, like me, regard the first college composition course as a chance (for too many students, alas, the only chance) to introduce some of the significant ideas of our culture. To my delight, there were more of us than I had thought, and each year our ranks appear to be swelling.

In preparing the fourth edition of *A World of Ideas,* I have benefited from the suggestions of hundreds of users of earlier editions. Their concern for this book is that it remain strong and centered on the tradition of important ideas. To that end, I have chosen selections by authors who have had a strong impact on our thinking. As I once wrote to a student who was curious about my choice of selections, this is called *A World of Ideas,* not *The World of Ideas*. In other words, I always thought of the first edition not as complete and finished but rather as part of a work in progress. This fourth edition continues that progression, and I feel it amplifies much of what appeared in earlier editions while still serving the fundamental purpose of the book: to present college students with a representative sampling of important ideas examined by men and women who have shaped our thought.

All of the selections in this volume are of the highest quality. Each was chosen for its importance, range of thought, and capacity

v

to sustain discussion and stimulate good writing. Unlike most composition anthologies that include such figures, this one does not offer two pages of Bacon, four pages of Kuhn, and a page-and-a-half of Aristotle. Instead, every writer is represented by as complete a selection as is practicable, averaging about fifteen pages in length. The selections are not edited to fit, but instead all of the arguments are developed completely as the authors wrote them. Developing a serious idea takes time. Most students respect the fact that the further you read in the work of an important thinker, the better is your grasp of its ideas.

New in This Edition

The fourth edition includes new selections by four authors who appeared in earlier editions: Aristotle, Frederick Douglass, Simone Weil, and Thomas S. Kuhn. In the case of Aristotle the selection "The Aim of Man" from *The Nichomachean Ethics,* popular in an earlier edition, is now included in the Philosophy section. Simone Weil's new selection on the dignity of labor establishes her credentials as a thinker on important aspects of economics, especially as they affect the worker. Frederick Douglass is represented by a new selection from the *Narrative* showing the effects of slavery on slave and slaveholder alike. Thomas S. Kuhn, famous for redefining the term "paradigm," is represented by a selection that directs our attention to scientific paradigms and their role in thought.

Of the thirty-five selections, fourteen are new. In addition to those authors for whom new selections have been chosen are Catharine A. MacKinnon in the section on Politics, Robert B. Reich in the Economics section, Erich Fromm in Psychology, Rachel Carson in Science, and René Descartes in Philosophy. Essays by Franz Boas, Ruth Benedict, Margaret Mead, Claude Lévi-Strauss, and Clifford Geertz comprise a new Part Six, Anthropology, which concerns itself with the nature of culture and poses the following questions: How can one culture understand another? Is there such a thing as an objective analysis of other cultures? At the same time this section raises important issues about the diversity of human behavior and the attitudes people have toward those of different cultures.

Continuing the emphasis of past editions on critical thinking, this edition offers a number of new features designed to help students analyze ideas and develop ideas of their own. The book begins with an introduction to critical reading that demonstrates a range of methods students can adopt to participate in an active dialogue with the passage. The dialogue is one of the keys to critical reading, since it demands an active, questioning approach to the text. This emphasis on critical reading is developed further in the appendix, "Writing About Ideas," which has been overhauled for this edition. Finally, the group of questions following each selection includes a new category: "Connections." "Connections" questions, too, emphasize critical reading by asking the reader to connect the passage with a selection by another writer, either in the same section or in another section. The variety of connections is extraordinary—Nietzsche with Benedict, Freud with Horney, Jefferson with Douglass, and many more conjunctions. The questions are designed to promote inquiry into exciting and powerful ideas.

A Text for Readers and Writers

Emphasis on Critical Thinking. This book has always been predicated on the interactions of student and teacher, student and student, and student and author. The suggestions for reading and annotating selections highlight critical thinking by focusing on questions and by establishing a dialogue with the text. The emphasis on critical thinking is even greater in this fourth edition, in which all questions and writing assignments are based on a critical approach to the material.

"Evaluating Ideas: An Introduction to Critical Reading" concentrates on techniques that students can use to make the ideas of great thinkers meaningful. Because this is, and always has been, a reader for writers, I try to emphasize ways in which the text can be read in order to develop ideas for writing. The best method for developing such ideas is annotating the text carefully—establishing both a dialogue with the text and a system for retrieving ideas formulated during that dialogue. In this section, I offer an example of a portion of Machiavelli's essay on "The Qualities of the Prince" in an annotated form. The annotations are discussed for their own usefulness and for techniques by which similar annotations can be developed while reading other essays in the book. Annotation is the key to critical reading.

At the back of the book, "Writing About Ideas: An Introduction to Rhetoric" explains how a reader can apply the procedures of annotation in order to perform the critical thinking that results in a good written response to the ideas in any of the selections in the book. This section relies on the annotations of the Machiavelli selection expounded in "Evaluating Ideas: An Introduction to Critical Reading." A sample essay on Machiavelli, using all of the techniques taught in the context of reading and writing, gives students an idea of how they might write their own material. In addition, this section helps students understand how they can put to work some of the basic rhetorical principles discussed throughout the book.

Central Questions for Each Part.   This edition continues the third edition's highly praised focus on broad and timeless questions in each section, for example: What determines our psychological identity? How are our psychology and our sexuality connected? Must the need for a stable social order conflict with the need for individual liberty? Each individual essay in every part of the book addresses the issues raised in the questions for that part, although all the essays also develop their own important issues.

Introductions for Each Selection.   Each selection is preceded by a detailed introduction to the life and work of the author, as well as comments about the selection's primary ideas. The most interesting rhetorical achievements of the selection are also identified and discussed, with an eye toward helping the student discover how rhetorical techniques can achieve specific effects. These essays all offer useful models for writing: Douglass representing narrative; Machiavelli and Darwin, example; Bacon and Daly, enumeration; Kuhn and Reich, cause and effect. They are the kinds of models that beginning writers find useful: models of thought and models of structure—in other words, the materials of invention and arrangement.

Suggestions for Discussion and Writing.   At the end of each essay is a group of discussion questions designed for use inside or outside the classroom. While they focus on key issues and ideas, they are also designed to stimulate a general discussion and critical thinking. Suggestions for writing that help the student practice some of the rhetorical strategies employed by the author follow. These suggestions range from personal responses to complete essays that involve research and comparison or contrast with other essays in the anthology.

Instructor's Manual.   I have also prepared an extensive manual, *Resources for Teaching A World of Ideas,* that contains further background on the selections, examples from my own classroom responses to the authors, and more suggestions for classroom discussion as well as student writing assignments. A sentence outline for each selection has been carefully prepared by Carol Verburg, Ellen Troutman, and Ellen Darion and can be photocopied and handed out to students. The idea came from Darwin's own phrase outlines preceding each chapter of *On the Origin of Species*. These outlines may be used to go over the more difficult selections. A sentence outline offers guidance for the cautious student. At the end of the manual, I have provided brief bibliographies for all thirty-five authors. These bibliographies can be photocopied and distributed to those students who wish to explore the primary selections in more depth.

Acknowledgments

I remain grateful to Michael Bybee at the University of Oregon. He was so concerned that I include Asian thinkers in this book that he sent me many fascinating pieces to read, all of which he had taught to his own students in conjunction with the second edition. As a result of our mutual concern, this edition contains two important selections, one by Lao-Tzu and another by Siddhārtha Gautama, the Buddha, as interpreted by Buddhist monks.

Like its predecessors, this edition is indebted to a great many creative people at Bedford Books, whose support is both lavish and invaluable. I want to thank Charles H. Christensen, whose close attention to detail is striking. I appreciated as always the support of Joan E. Feinberg. My editor, Ellen Kuhl, was brilliant in making sure that the project developed in a timely manner. Lori Chong, the production editor, also helped with innumerable important details and suggestions. Deborah Fogel, my copyeditor, found ways to tighten and sharpen the prose. Ellen Darion contributed the sentence outlines for each new selection in the instructor's manual. In addition were some very important staff and researchers: Mark Reimold, Andrea Goldman, Beth Castrodale, Jonathan Burns, Mary Beth McNulty, and Beth Chapman; I felt I had a personal relationship with all of them. Outside Bedford Books, I relied upon the ingenious Nevil Parker of Storrs. I want to thank Anatoly Dverin and Lyrl Ahern and Bill Ogden of PC & F, Incorporated, for their wonderful portraits, which have added a special human touch to the book. I also want to thank the students—quite a few of them—who wrote me directly about their experience reading the first three editions. I have paid attention to all that they said and I am warmed by their regard for the high quality of the material in this book.

Earlier editions named the hundreds of users of this book who sent their comments and encouragement. I would like to thank them again (you know who you are). In addition, the following professors were generous with the criticism, praise, and detailed recommendations for this fourth edition:

Sandra Adickes, Ph.D., Winona State University; Linda C. Badley, Middle Tennessee State University; Linda Bannister, Loyola Marymount University; James E. Barcus, Baylor University; Craig Barrow, University of Tennessee at Chattanooga; Libby Bay, Rockland Community College; Adrien P. Beaudoin, Florida Community College at Jacksonville; Bonnie C. Bedford, Wilkes University; David Bergdahl, Ohio University; Barbara Biasiolli, St. Mary's University; Kevin Binfield, University of Nebraska–Lincoln; Jennings Blackmon, Pittsburg State University; Jani Blake, Mountain View College; Billy T. Boyar, Wharton County Junior College; Carol Breslin, Gwynedd-Mercy College; William Buchanan, Grand Valley State University; Allison E. Carey, University of Florida; Martha C. Carpentier, Seton Hall University; Dennis Chaldecott, San Jose State University; Kurt Cline, State University of New York College at Cortland; John C. Cobb, Princeton University; Linda Currivan, University of Hawaii Leeward Community College; John R. Darling, Sacramento City College; Donna Davidson, College of the Canyons; Lynn Deming, New Mexico Institute of Mining and Technology; Loretta Denner, Santa Rosa Junior College; Robert F. Denton, Valdosta State College; Beth Doriani, Northwestern College; Sally Doud, Virginia Commonwealth University; Alexander Dunlop, Auburn University; Claire Eby, University of Connecticut; Gary Eddy, Winona State University; Bashir El-Beshti, Wake Forest University; Charles Ess, Drury College; John M. Ferrone, Iowa State University; Stephen L. Fisher, Emory and Henry College; Kaye Fredericks, University of Hawaii at Manoa; Mary Free, Florida International University; Jean Glazier, California State University–San Bernardino; James A. Glynn, Bakersfield College; Janet E. Goebel, Indiana University of Pennsylvania; Leonard Goldberg, Gettysburg College; Stuart Goodman, Duke University; David Gould, University of Connecticut; Joe Green, Dixie College; Lauralee Guibault, Lakeland College; A. Waller Hastings, Northern State University; Lucretia Hediger-Crawford, Lakeland College; Donald W. Heidt, College of the Canyons; Mike Hood, Belmont Abbey College; Barbara Huff Huddleston, School of the Ozarks; Evanne Jardine, Santa Barbara City College; Raymonda Johnson, City College of Chicago Harold Washington College; Arthur C. Johnston, Towson State University; Mark G. Jones, University of Florida; David H. Karrfalt, Edinboro University of Pennsylvania; James Kastely, University of Hawaii at Manoa; Jane Kaufman, University of Akron; Robert Kelley, Santa Rosa Junior College; Kathryn Kimball, Drew University; Carolyn Kyler, Washington and Jefferson College; Frank V. LaFerriere, Los Angeles City College; John Lamb, Lewis University; Robert N. Lawson, Washburn University of Topeka; Linda Leff, Oklahoma State University; Rosemary Lyons-Chase, Columbia–Greene Community College; Loralee MacPike, California State University–San Bernardino; Tony Markham, South Dakota School of Mines and Technology; Richard Marranca, Union County College; Jean B. McDonald, Miami–Dade Community College; George C. McLoone, Northern Virginia Community College; Jane Melbourne, Lynchburg College; Thomas Moore, Western Washington University; Eugene Nable, College of New Rochelle School of New Resources; Sharon Nell, Drury College; Joseph O'Brien, State University of New York College at Geneseo; C. Sue Poor, Wharton County Junior College; L. V. Quintana, San Diego Mesa College; Will Rawn, Northern Montana College; David Robinson, Georgia Southern College; James Rodgers, Lawrence Technological University; Jennifer Rosson, Texas Tech University; J. Rubenstein, University of Cincinnati; Robert E. Ryan, Clark College; Barbara Schaffer, De Paul University; Julia Scott, Santa Barbara City College; Alvin J. Seltzer, Pennsylvania State University Ogontz Campus; Lantz Simpson, Santa Monica College; Robert A. Smart, Bradford College; John Smith, Northern Montana College; Reiner Smolinski, Georgia State University; Ed Stieve, Nova University; Dale Sullivan, University of Nebraska–Kearney; Andrew Tadie, Seattle University; Zeynep Tenger, Berry College; Raymond G. Terhorst, University of Maryland Baltimore County; Ted Thompson, Joliet Junior College; Shirley D. Vatz, University of North Carolina at Greens boro; Margreta von Pein, Pace University and Columbia–Greene Community College; Joel Westerholm, Northwestern College; Stephen R. Whited, Lakeland College; Rev. Michael A. Williams, S.J., Spring Hill College; Deborah S. Wilson, Illinois State University; William B. Woolum, Lane Community College; Michael Wutz, Weber State College; J. W. Yarbrough, South Dakota State University; Rose Yesu, Massasoit Community College; Bin Zhu, Boston University; Mary Jane Zimmerman, Seattle Central Community College; Edward J. Zimmermann, Canisius College.

CONTENTS

xiii

*Jefferson justifies the right of the colonies to dissolve their bonds
with a tyrannical monarchy and to construct a free nation of
independent souls in its stead.*

*In this excerpt from one of the first great works of feminism,
Wollstonecraft argues that the laws, property rights, and class
distinctions of her day are mechanisms of control that deny
women their liberty and demean their lives.*

*This selection from the most influential nineteenth-century
work by an African American reveals how an indomitable
human spirit reacts to a government-sanctioned system that
treats some people as chattel.*

*A man who lived by his ideals, Thoreau explains how and
why it is not only reasonable but also sometimes essential to
disobey unjust laws imposed by the state.*

*King, a minister and civil rights leader, advocates nonviolent
action as a means of changing the unconscionable practices of
a discriminatory social order.*

CATHARINE A. MacKINNON   Sexual Harassment
and Sexual Politics   **141**

A prominent law professor speaks out on the legal and political consequences of sexual harassment. For MacKinnon, this issue parallels that of racial discrimination and has the same political implications: the oppression of a social group by those in power.

PART TWO

IDEAS IN THE WORLD OF ECONOMICS

SHOULD WE JUDGE A SOCIETY'S ECONOMIC STRUCTURE BY ITS EFFECT ON THE INDIVIDUAL LIBERTY OF ITS MEMBERS?
–159–

KARL MARX   The Communist Manifesto   **165**

The chief critic of laissez-faire capitalism traces the dehumanizing progress of the nineteenth-century bourgeois economic structure and heralds its downfall at the hands of a united international proletariat.

THORSTEIN VEBLEN   Pecuniary Emulation   **193**

Casting a cold eye on the predatory, consumption-driven society of his time, Veblen, a sociologist and economist, posits that envy and hunger for esteem are the primary psychological spurs to economic success.

JOHN MAYNARD KEYNES   The End of
Laissez-Faire   **209**

In the aftermath of the First World War, an architect of contemporary economic policies predicts that the raw money-making energies of capitalism will have to be harnessed by nationalist interests and tempered by social conscience.

PART THREE

**IDEAS IN THE
WORLD OF PSYCHOLOGY**

WHAT DETERMINES OUR PSYCHOLOGICAL
IDENTITY? HOW ARE OUR PSYCHOLOGY
AND OUR SEXUALITY CONNECTED?
–269–

PART FOUR

IDEAS IN THE
WORLD OF SCIENCE

CAN WE KNOW THE SECRETS
OF NATURE? HOW CAN WE MAKE
OUR KNOWLEDGE USEFUL?
–379–

PART FIVE

IDEAS IN THE WORLD OF PHILOSOPHY

HOW CAN WE TELL THE GOOD
FROM THE BAD? HOW CAN WE
KNOW WHAT IS TRUE?
–475–

A
WORLD OF
IDEAS

ESSENTIAL READINGS
FOR
COLLEGE WRITERS

EVALUATING IDEAS

An Introduction to Critical Reading

THE SELECTIONS in this book demand a careful and attentive reading. The authors, whose works have changed the way we view our world, our institutions, and ourselves, make every effort to communicate their views with clarity and style. But their views are complex and subtle, and as a result we must train ourselves to read sensitively, responsively, and critically. Critical reading is basic for approaching the essays in this book. Indeed, it is basic for approaching any reading material that deserves serious attention.

Reading critically means reading actively: questioning the premises of the argument, speculating on the ways in which evidence is used, comparing the statements of one writer with those of another, and holding an inner dialogue with the author. These skills differ completely from the passive reception we employ when we watch television or read lightweight materials. Being an active, participating reader makes it possible to derive the most from good books.

Critical reading involves most of the following processes:

- *Prereading:* Developing a sense of what the piece is about and what its general purposes seem to be.

- *Annotating:* Using a pencil or a pen to mark those passages that seem important enough to return to later. Annotations establish a dialogue between you and the author.

- *Questioning:* Raising issues that you feel need to be taken into consideration. These may be issues that you believe the author has treated either well or badly and that you feel are important. Questioning can be part of the annotation process.

1

- *Reviewing:* Rereading your annotations and underlinings in order to grasp the entire "picture" of what you've just read. Sometimes writing a summary of the piece as you review will make the meaning even clearer.

- *Forming your own ideas:* The final step consists of reviewing what you have read, developing your own views on the issues, and evaluating the way that the writer presents the issues.

THE PROCESS OF CRITICAL READING

Prereading

Before you read a particular selection, you may find it useful to turn to the beginning of the part in which it appears. There you will find an introduction discussing the broader issues and questions central to all the selections in the part that may help you to focus your thoughts and formulate your opinions as you read the essays themselves.

Begin any selection in this book by reading its headnote. Each headnote supplies historical background on the writer, sets the intellectual stage for the ideas discussed in the essay, and comments on the writer's main points. The second part of each headnote also introduces the main rhetorical or stylistic methods that the writers use to communicate their thoughts. In the process of reading the headnote, you will develop an overview that helps prepare you for reading the essay.

This kind of preparation is typical of critical reading. It makes the task of reading more delightful, useful, and much easier. A review of the headnote to Niccolò Machiavelli and part of his essay "The Qualities of the Prince" will illustrate the usefulness of such preparation. This essay appears in the part on politics, so the content can already be expected to be political. The introduction to Machiavelli provides the following points, each followed here by the number of the paragraph in which it appears.

Machiavelli was an Italian aristocrat in Renaissance Italy. (1)

Machiavelli describes the qualities necessary for a prince—that is, any ruler—to maintain power. (2)

A weak Italy was prey to the much stronger France at this time. (2)

Machiavelli recommends securing power by whatever means necessary and maintaining it. (3)

His concern for moralizing or acting out of high moral principle is not great. (3)

He supports questionable means of becoming and remaining prince. (3)

Machiavelli does not fret over the means used to achieve his ends and sometimes advocates repression, imprisonment, and torture. (3)

Machiavelli has been said to have a cynical view of human nature. (4)

His rhetorical method is to discuss both sides of an issue: cruelty and mercy; liberality and stinginess. (6)

He uses aphorisms to persuade the reader that he is saying something wise and true. (7)

With these observations in mind, the reader knows that the selection following will be concerned with politics in Renaissance Italy. The question of ends versus means is central to Machiavelli's discussion, and he does not display the highest ideals regarding the general goodness of people. Yet, because of Machiavelli's rhetorical methods, particularly his use of aphorism, the reader can expect that Machiavelli's argument will be exceptionally persuasive.

Thus, as a critical reader, you will be well advised to keep track of these basic statements from the headnote. You need not accept all of them, but you should certainly be alert to the issues that will probably be central to your experience of the essay. Remember: it is just as reasonable to question the headnote as it is to question the essay itself.

Before reading the essay in detail, you might develop an overview of its meaning by scanning it quickly. In the case of "The Qualities of the Prince," note the subheadings, such as "On Those Things for Which Men, and Particularly Princes, Are Praised or Blamed." Checking each of the subheadings before you read the entire piece might provide you with a map or guide to the essay.

Annotating and Questioning

The annotations you make as you read a text establish a dialogue between you and the author. You can underline or highlight important statements that you feel help clarify the author's position. They may be statements to which you will want to refer later. Think of them as serving one overriding purpose: to make it possible for you to review the piece and understand its key points without having to reread it entirely.

Your dialogue with the author will be most visible in the margins of the essay, which is one reason the margins in this book are so generous. Take issue with key points or note your assent—the more you annotate, the more you free your imagination to develop your own ideas. My own personal methods involve both notations of agreement and of disagreement. I annotate thoroughly, so that after a quick second glance I know what the author is saying as well as what I thought of the essay when I read it closely. My annotations help me keep the major points fresh in my mind.

Annotation keeps track both of what the author says and of what our responses are. No one can reduce annotation to a formula—we all do it differently—but it is not a passive act. Reading with a pencil or a pen in hand should become second nature. Without annotations, you often have to reread entire sections of an essay in order to remember the gist of an argument that may once have been clear and understandable but after a time lapse has become part of the fabric of the prose and thus is "invisible." Annotation is the conquest of the invisible; it provides a quick view of the main points.

When you annotate:

- Read with a pen or a pencil.

- Underline key sentences—for example, definitions and statements of purpose.

- Underline key words that appear often.

- Note the topic of paragraphs in the margins.

- Ask questions in the margins.

- Make notes in the margins to remind you to work up ideas later.

- Mark passages you might want to quote in your essay.

- Keep track of points with which you disagree.

Some sample annotations follow, again from the second essay in the book, Niccolò Machiavelli's "The Qualities of the Prince." A sixteenth-century text in translation, *The Prince* is challenging to work with. My annotations appear in the form of underlinings and marginal comments and questions. Only the first few paragraphs appear here, but the entire essay is annotated in my copy of the book.

A Prince's Duty Concerning Military Matters

The prince's profession should be war.

A prince, therefore, must not have any other object nor any other thought, nor must he take anything as his profession but war, its institutions, and its discipline; because that is the only profession which befits one who commands; and it is of such importance that not only does it maintain those who were born princes, but many times it enables men of private station to rise to that position; and, on the other hand, it is evident that when princes have given more thought to personal luxuries than to arms, they have lost their state. And the first way to lose it is to neglect this art; and the way to acquire it is to be well versed in this art.

Examples

Being disarmed makes you despised. Is this true?

Francesco Sforza became Duke of Milan from being a private citizen because he was armed; his sons, since they avoided the inconveniences of arms, became private citizens after having been dukes. For, among the other bad effects it causes, being disarmed makes you despised; this is one of those infamies a prince should guard himself against, as will be treated below: for between an armed and an unarmed man there is no comparison whatsoever, and it is not reasonable for an armed man to obey an unarmed man willingly, nor that an unarmed man should be safe among armed servants; since, when the former is suspicious and the latter are contemptuous, it is impossible for them to work well together. And therefore, a prince who does not understand military matters, besides the other misfortunes already noted, cannot be esteemed by his own soldiers, nor can he trust them.

Training action/mind

Knowledge of terrain

Two benefits

He must, therefore, never raise his thought from this exercise of war, and in peacetime he must train himself more than in time of war; this can be done in two ways: one by action, the other by the mind. And as far as actions are concerned, besides keeping his soldiers well disciplined and trained, he must always be out hunting, and must accustom his body to hardships in this manner; and he must also learn the nature of the terrain, and know how mountains slope, how valleys open, how plains lie, and understand the nature of rivers and swamps; and he should devote much attention to such activities. Such knowledge is useful in two ways: first, one learns to know one's own country and can better understand how to defend it; second, with the knowledge and experience of the terrain, one can easily comprehend the characteristics of any other terrain that it is necessary to explore for the first time; for the hills, valleys, plains, rivers, and swamps of Tuscany, for instance, have certain similarities to those of other provinces; so that by knowing the lay of the land in one province one can easily understand it in others. And a prince who lacks this ability lacks the most important quality in a leader; because this skill teaches you to find the enemy, choose a campsite, lead troops, organize them for battle, and besiege towns to your own advantage.

[There follow the examples of Philopoemon, who was always observing terrain for its military usefulness, and a recommendation that princes read histories and learn from them. Three paragraphs are omitted.]

On Those Things for Which Men, and Particularly Princes, Are Praised or Blamed

Now there remains to be examined what should be the methods and procedures of a prince in dealing with his subjects and friends. And because I know that many have written about this, I am afraid that writing about it again I shall be thought of as presumptuous, since in discussing this material I depart radically from the procedures of others. But since my intention is to write something useful for anyone who understands it, it seemed more suitable to me to search after the effectual truth of the matter rather than its imagined one. And many writers have imagined for themselves republics and principalities that have never been seen nor known to exist in reality; for there is such a gap between how one lives and how one ought to live that anyone who abandons what is done for what ought to be done learns his ruin rather than his preservation: for a man who wishes to make a vocation of being good at all times will come to ruin among so many who are not good. Hence it is necessary for a prince who wishes to maintain his position to learn how not to be good, and to use this knowledge or not to use it according to necessity.

Leaving aside, therefore, the imagined things concerning a prince, and taking into account those that are true, I say that all men, when they are spoken of, and particularly princes, since they are placed on a higher level, are judged by some of these qualities which bring them either <u>blame or praise.</u> And this is why one is considered generous, another miserly (to use a Tuscan word, since "avaricious" in our language is still used to mean one who wishes to acquire by means of theft; we call "miserly" one who excessively avoids using what he has); one is considered a giver, the other rapacious; one cruel, another merciful; one treacherous, another faithful; one effeminate and cowardly, another bold and courageous; one humane, another haughty; one lascivious, another chaste; one trustworthy, another cunning; one harsh, another lenient; one serious, another frivolous; one religious, another unbelieving; and the like. And I know that everyone will admit that it would be a very praiseworthy thing to find in a prince, of the qualities mentioned above, those that are held to be good, but since it is neither possible to have them nor to observe them all completely, because human nature does not permit it, <u>a prince must be prudent enough to know how to escape the bad reputation of those vices that would lose the state for him, and must protect himself from those that will not lose it for him, if this is possible;</u> but if he cannot, he need not concern himself unduly if he ignores these less serious vices. And, moreover, he need not worry about incurring the bad reputation of those vices without which it would be difficult to hold his state; since, carefully taking everything into account, <u>one will discover that something which appears to be a virtue, if pursued, will end in his destruction;</u> while some other thing which seems to be a vice, if pursued, will result in his safety and his well-being.

Note the Prince's reputation.

Prince must avoid reputation for the worst vices.

Some vices may be needed to hold the state. True?

Some virtues may end in destruction.

Reviewing

The process of review, which takes place after a careful reading, is much more useful if you have annotated and underlined the text well. To a large extent, the review process can be devoted to accounting for the primary ideas that have been uncovered by your annotations and underlinings. For example, reviewing the Machiavelli annotations shows that the following ideas are crucial to Machiavelli's thinking:

> The prince's profession should be war, so the most successful princes are probably experienced in the military.
>
> If they do not pay attention to military matters, princes will lose their power.
>
> Being disarmed makes the prince despised.
>
> The prince should be in constant training.
>
> The prince needs a sound knowledge of terrain.
>
> Machiavelli says he tells us what is true, not what ought to be true.
>
> Those who are always good will come to ruin among those who are not good.
>
> To remain in power, the prince must learn how not to be good.
>
> The prince should avoid the worst vices in order not to harm his reputation.
>
> To maintain power, some vices may be necessary.
>
> Some virtues may end in destruction.

Putting Machiavelli's ideas in this raw form does an injustice to his skill as a writer, but annotation is designed to result in such summary statements. We can see that there are some constant themes, such as the insistence that the prince be a military person. As the headnote tells us, in Machiavelli's day Italy was a group of rival city-states and France, a larger, united nation, was invading these states one by one. Machiavelli dreamed that one powerful prince, such as his favorite, Cesare Borgia, could fight the French and save Italy. He emphasized the importance of the military because he lived in an age in which war was a constant threat.

Machiavelli anticipates the complaints of pacifists—those who argue against war—by telling us that those who remain unarmed are despised. To demonstrate his point, he gives us examples of those who lost their positions as princes because they avoided being armed. He clearly expects these examples to be persuasive.

A second important theme pervading Machiavelli's essay is his view on moral behavior. For Machiavelli, being in power is much more important than being virtuous. He is quick to admit that vice is not desirable and that the worst vices will do harm to the prince's reputation. But he also says that the prince need not worry about the "less serious" vices. Moreover, he need not worry about incurring the bad reputation of those vices without which it would be difficult to hold his state. In the same spirit, he tells us that there are some virtues that might lead to the destruction of the prince.

Forming Your Own Ideas

One of the most important reasons for critically reading texts of the kind that appear in this book is to enable you to develop your own critical positions on issues that writers raise. Identifying and clarifying the main ideas is only the first step; the next step in critical reading is evaluating those ideas.

For example, you might ask whether, as most people have suggested, Machiavelli's ideas have any relevance for today. After all, he wrote four hundred years ago and times have changed. You might feel that Machiavelli is relevant strictly to the Italian Renaissance, or, alternatively, that his principles are timeless and that every age can learn from them. Most people treat Machiavelli as if he were a political philosopher whose views are useful anytime and anywhere.

If you agree with the majority, then you may want to examine his ideas to see if you can accept them. Consider just two of those ideas and their implications:

Should rulers always be members of the military? Should they always be armed?

Should rulers ignore virtue and practice vice when it is convenient?

Should the ruler of a nation first demonstrate competence as a military leader? In his commentary on government, Lao-Tzu offers different advice because his assumptions are that the ruler ought to respect the rights of individuals. For Lao-Tzu the waging of war is an annoying, essentially wasteful activity. On the other hand, Machiavelli never once questions the usefulness of war: to him, it is basic to government. As a critical reader, you can take issue with such an assumption, and in doing so you will deepen your understanding of Machiavelli.

If we were to follow Machiavelli's advice, then we would choose presidents on the basis of whether or not they had been good military leaders. Among those we would not have chosen from our country's history might be Thomas Jefferson, Abraham Lincoln, and Franklin Delano Roosevelt. Those who were high-ranking military men include George Washington, Ulysses S.

Grant, and Dwight D. Eisenhower. If you followed Machiavelli's rhetorical technique of using examples to convince your audience, you could choose from either group to prove your case.

Of course, there are examples from other nations. It has been common since the 1930s to see leaders of certain nations always dressed in their military uniforms: Benito Mussolini (Italy); Adolf Hitler (Germany); Joseph Stalin (Russia); Idi Amin (Uganda); Muammar al-Qaddafi (Libya). These are all tyrants who have tormented their citizens and their neighbors. That gives us something to think about. Should a president dress in full military regalia all the time? Is that a good image for the ruler of a free nation?

Do you want a ruler, then, who is usually virtuous, but embraces vice when it is necessary? This is a very difficult question to answer. When Jimmy Carter swore to the American people that he would never lie to them, many Americans were skeptical. They thought that politics was essentially a game of careful and judicious lying—at least at times. In other words, these Americans were already committed to Machiavelli's position.

These are only a few of the questions that are raised by my annotations in the few pages from Machiavelli examined here. There are many other issues that could be uncovered by these annotations and many more from subsequent pages of the essay. Critical reading can be a powerful means by which to open what you read to discovery and discussion.

Once you begin a line of questioning, the ways in which you think about a passage begin expanding. You find yourself with more ideas of your own that have grown in response to those you have been reading about. Reading critically, in other words, gives you an enormous return on your investment of time. If you have the chance to investigate your responses to the assumptions and underlying premises of passages such as Machiavelli's, you will be able to refine your thinking even further. For example, if you agree with Machiavelli that rulers should be successful military leaders for whom small vices may be useful at times, and you find yourself in a position to argue with someone who feels Machiavelli is mistaken in this view, then you will have a good opportunity to evaluate the soundness of your thinking. You will have a chance to see your own assumptions and arguments tested.

In many ways, this entire book is about such opportunities. The essays that follow offer you powerful ideas from great thinkers. They invite you to participate in their thoughts, exercise your own knowledge and assumptions, and arrive at your own conclusions. Basically, that is the meaning of education.

PART ONE

IDEAS IN THE WORLD OF POLITICS

MUST THE NEED FOR A STABLE SOCIAL ORDER CONFLICT WITH THE NEED FOR INDIVIDUAL LIBERTY?

Lao-Tzu

Niccolò Machiavelli

Thomas Jefferson

Mary Wollstonecraft

Frederick Douglass

Henry David Thoreau

Martin Luther King, Jr.

Catharine A. MacKinnon

INTRODUCTION

THE EIGHT SELECTIONS in this part cover a range of political ideas that extend from ancient China to the modern United States. The issues that concern writers on politics are multitudinous, but at their root are questions that relate to the balance between individual freedoms and the exercise of power by the state.

Power and its effects upon the individual have always been topics of first interest to politicians. The delicate balance between the needs of individuals to assert their rights and the needs of a strong government to maintain the order and stability that make individual freedom meaningful has never been easy to achieve—in any culture or in any age.

Lao-Tzu, the founder of Taoism, one of the three major Chinese religions, advocated a complex form of inactivity. His writings, *Tao-te Ching,* loosely translated as "The Way of Power," concern questions of governance and the role of the individual. Because his ideas are centered in a mysticism that is intensely antimaterialistic, they are not easy for the Western mind to grasp. Yet they have been influential in China for almost twenty-five hundred years.

Niccolò Machiavelli was a practical man of the Renaissance, with very little that could be called mystical in his concerns for power and its effect on the individual. His name has become a synonym for political cunning. Yet his motives in recommending a ruthless wielding of power on the part of his prince derived largely from his fear that a weak ruler would lose his state to France or to another powerful, plundering nation. Therefore, to a large extent, Machiavelli ignores questions of independence and liberty. However, underlying his discussion is the conviction that a strong prince will in the long run guarantee the peace and happiness of the citizen for whom independence is otherwise irrelevant.

In an important way, Thomas Jefferson declared his independence from the paternalism of British government. He broke away from the concept of government as a family, in which Britain was the mother country and its colonies were the children. In the Declaration of Independence, Jefferson piles offense upon offense, indignity upon indignity, to make us feel the dread weight of British paternalism and the presumptions that went with it. No child could be expected to remain docile in the face of the complaints Jefferson leveled against Britain.

Mary Wollstonecraft, like Jefferson, suffered at the hands of a paternalistic government, but in her case the structure of society— no matter where the seat of government rested—militated against her because she was a woman. Just as Jefferson felt the weight of colonization, Wollstonecraft felt that women were colonized and exploited without ever being able to attain the full independence that should be guaranteed to all citizens. One of the first, and still among the most influential and eloquent writers in favor of women's independence, Mary Wollstonecraft shows how a society can praise freedom while at the same time denying it to half of its citizens.

The question of freedom is central, too, in the excerpt from Frederick Douglass's *Narrative of the Life of Frederick Douglass, an American Slave*. According to the policy and laws of the United States in the early nineteenth century, Douglass was doomed to remain a slave until the day he died. One of the most touching moments in Douglass's memoir is when he tells the young boys helping him learn to read that although they will someday be free men, he must remain a slave for his whole life. The awful irony for anyone who has read Thomas Jefferson is that independence was still not a completely meaningful term in the 1830s, when Douglass grew up. Douglass records the circumstances of life under a government that enforced slave laws—both in the North and in the South—at the same time as it advocated independence.

The question of how the individual should react in the face of a government whose laws are vicious is taken up by Henry David Thoreau. His refusal to pay taxes that he knew would be used in a war against Mexico—a war he felt was immoral and dishonorable—brought him into conflict with the law. He realized that he would have to pay a penalty for his views, and he was willing to do so. The problem he faced in 1849 has arisen for governments around the world and is still an issue today.

The laws in the United States have often resulted in conflicts with individual conscience. The laws colluded to harm the individual not only by supporting slavery but also by refusing to grant women the vote, by upholding Jim Crow laws that enforced second-class citizenship for blacks, and by extending the Vietnam War, which was the subject of a nationwide protest based on the kinds of questions of conscience raised by Thoreau.

For fighting against the Jim Crow laws, Martin Luther King, Jr., went to jail. While there, he wrote a letter to clergymen who he felt should be firmly on his side in support of equality and freedom. His letter was in the tradition of many other such letters from prison, and its effect is still powerful.

Catharine A. MacKinnon addresses the legal issues involved in sexual harassment, behavior that some people do not yet recognize as having political consequences. However, just as racial injustice and racially motivated laws have political consequences, so too does sexual harassment. Reviewing the background of harassment and its effects on women, MacKinnon demonstrates that it operates much as racial discrimination functions in the writing of Martin Luther King. King's concern was with the law—he wrote while imprisoned for a legal offense—just as MacKinnon's concern is for the law, because ultimately, the force of politics in a democracy is felt in the interpretation and implementation of its laws.

The writers in this part of the book share striking qualities of endurance in their work. They have been and will be read for centuries, both because their causes are important and because their way of presenting their beliefs is effective. Each of these writers is a capable rhetorician, using fundamental techniques to express his or her ideas in ways that affect our thoughts and our feelings.

Further, none of the central ideas presented in these selections can be said to be totally original with the writer. And each writer was well aware of this fact. The power that inheres in these essays comes not so much from the originality of the ideas as from an appropriate and convincing combination of style, energy, and commitment on the part of the writers. These writers convince us that what they are saying is of immense importance and that they feel strongly the emotions that are related to, and aroused by, the ideas they present. It is the depth of their commitment to such ideas, their capacity to involve us in them, and the rhetorical conviction with which they present them that compel us to respond as we do.

LAO-TZU

Thoughts from the
Tao-te Ching

*L*AO-TZU *(604?–531? B.C.) is a name that means "Master Lao"*
or "Old Master." The man who bore this title was named Li Erh and
is traditionally said to have been born in the state of Ch'u in 604 B.C.,
making him a contemporary of Confucius. He was employed as librarian
and historian in the royal court. However, he was also a metaphysician
and thinker who inspired many of his contemporaries. Tradition holds
that near the end of his life, when he decided to leave the court of the
Chou dynasty, where he lived and worked his entire life, he was
persuaded by the keeper of the city gate to write his thoughts down for
him—and others—to keep. The keeper of the gate feared that Lao-
Tzu was heading into a self-imposed exile and that no one would ever
know what he had thought. Fortunately, Lao-Tzu agreed to his request,
and after he left Ch'u he was never seen again.

Legends have grown up around Lao-Tzu. For example, he was
said to have gestated more than fifty years in his mother's womb so
that when he was born he was already white-haired and venerable. He
was said to have lived as long as two hundred years. He was the founder
of Taoism, which began apparently not as a religion but as a kind of
philosophy. The term Tao *is very difficult to translate into English,*
but it has been interpreted to mean "the way." Yet the "way" has
been interpreted in two senses. One is as a path, since the Chinese
written character for Tao *is related to the concept of path. The second*
way is as a method—as in "the way to gain enlightenment." Both
meanings are clearly implied in the text, and both successfully interpret
it.

Translated by D. C. Lau.

Yet the text of the Tao-te Ching *is problematic because of its many ambiguities. Carefully annotated editions of the text are often interrupted by commentary that explains why it is so difficult to be absolutely sure what Lao-Tzu means at a given moment. Sometimes the text seems to be purposely ambiguous—a rhetorical device that promotes examination and careful speculation on the part of the reader. This ambiguity may annoy a reader who is used to having ideas clearly spelled out and explained. Lao-Tzu seems to treat ideas like seeds to be planted in the mind of a listener, to take root and grow as the soil will permit.*

To modern American readers, Lao-Tzu's formulations seem "laid-back." *He seems the very opposite of those materialistic and grasping people who sacrifice everything for amassing money and goods. Lao-Tzu takes the view that such things are leaden weights of the soul, that they are meaningless and trivial, and that the truly free and enlightened person will regard them as evil.*

Because of its antimaterialist doctrine, the Tao-te Ching *can be baffling to the modern mind—which may indicate the extent to which people today are committed to a materialist philosophy. Lao-Tzu's antimaterialism led him to recommend that politicians practice judicious inactivity. Lao-Tzu saw the busy hustling of the politicians and businessmen of his day—most of whom were oppressively materialistic—as a form of destructive and useless activity. They were busy, humming with action, but all to no purpose. Therefore, the logical analysis of the situation produced the antidote: inactivity.*

For many of us, inactivity is almost impossible to imagine. To do nothing implies laziness, "dropping out." But Lao-Tzu did not counsel sloth: instead he was concerned to avoid the useless busyness that he felt distracted people from the true course of enlightenment.

What enlightenment is may be difficult to determine. Those who possess it know what it is; those who do not can hardly hope to imagine it. It may be likened to a state of spiritual peacefulness, a sense of fulfillment. But whatever it may be, it is certainly impossible to achieve if spiritual matters are not put first and if one is enmeshed in the coils of desire for material goods.

The result of Lao-Tzu's political philosophy is to minimize the power of the state—especially the power of the state to oppress the people. Lao-Tzu takes the question of the freedom of the individual into account in a very complex way by asserting that the wise leader will provide the people with what they need, but not annoy them with promises of what they do not need. By keeping people "innocent of knowledge and free from desire" the sage ruler will have a population that will not want what it cannot have. Discontent, as Lao-Tzu interprets it, derives from desiring wrong things or from permitting the clever to act. As he says, "Do that which consists in taking no action, and order will prevail." On the surface such a statement seems almost naive; yet, on reflection it possesses remarkable wisdom.

LAO-TZU'S RHETORIC

To the Western reader, the Tao-te Ching may at first glance appear to be poetry. Instead of using thoroughly developed ideas, Lao-Tzu uses a traditional Chinese form that resembles the aphorism, a compressed statement weighty with meaning. For this reason, one of the jobs of the reader is to mull over what has been said. Virtually every statement requires thought and reflection. Therefore, the act of reading becomes an act of intense cooperation with the text.

The most profitable way to read this text is with other people to see in how many different ways it can be interpreted. Your own act of analysis should be measured by your patience and your willingness to think a statement through to see what lies beneath the surface. Take, for example, one of the opening statements:

> Not to honor men of worth will keep the people from contention; not to value goods which are hard to come by will keep them from theft; not to display what is desirable will keep them from being unsettled of mind.
>
> Therefore in governing the people, the sage empties their minds but fills their bellies, weakens their wills but strengthens their bones.

Not honoring men of worth means not assuming that wealth is the measure of a person's goodness or value. Not valuing goods that are hard to come by will obviously prevent theft, since the thief would hardly steal that which others do not value. And not showing things that are desirable to people who cannot have them will definitely promote their peace of mind. We know all these things, and it is probably easy to agree with Lao-Tzu that his recipe for contentedness in the state would work. On the other hand, it is also probable that most Westerners would not want to try this recipe or would find it hard to follow. The reasons for making that choice are important to examine.

If the text resembles poetry—and it does so very closely in many passages—it may also be true that it should be read like poetry. Every line should be read for innuendo, subtle interpretation, and possible hidden meaning. Lao-Tzu was very serious in what he had to say. He felt he was contributing to the spiritual enlightenment of the ruling sage, although he had no real hope that his message would be put into action.

Later ages, however, have seen the significance of his thinking, and today Lao-Tzu has far more readers than he could have imagined. People have seen that much of what he said is reasonable and desirable, and that although it may be impossible for entire states to follow his thinking, it may be possible for individuals to heed his philosophy.

Thoughts from the Tao-te Ching

III

Not to honor men of worth will keep the people from contention; not to value goods which are hard to come by will keep them from theft; not to display what is desirable will keep them from being unsettled of mind.

Therefore in governing the people, the sage empties their minds but fills their bellies, weakens their wills but strengthens their bones. He always keeps them innocent of knowledge and free from desire, and ensures that the clever never dare to act.

Do that which consists in taking no action, and order will prevail.

XIII

Favor and disgrace are things that startle;   4
High rank[1] is, like one's body, a source of great trouble.

What is meant by saying that favor and disgrace are things that startle? Favor when it is bestowed on a subject serves to startle as much as when it is withdrawn. This is what is meant by saying that favor and disgrace are things that startle. What is meant by saying that high rank is, like one's body, a source of great trouble? The reason I have great trouble is that I have a body. When I no longer have a body, what trouble have I?

---

[1]It is probable that the word *kuei* ("high rank") here has crept in by mistake, since, as it stands, this line has one word more than the first. If this is the case, then the line should be translated: "Great trouble is like one's body." This brings it into line with the explanation that follows where "high rank" is not, in fact, mentioned. [Translator's note]

Hence he who values his body more than dominion over the empire can be entrusted with the empire. He who loves his body more than dominion over the empire can be given the custody of the empire.

XVII

The best of all rulers is but a shadowy presence to his subjects.
Next comes the ruler they love and praise;
Next comes one they fear;
Next comes one with whom they take liberties.
When there is not enough faith, there is lack of good faith.   8
Hesitant, he does not utter words lightly.
When his task is accomplished and his work done
The people all say, "It happened to us naturally."

XVIII

When the great way falls into disuse
There are benevolence and rectitude;
When cleverness emerges
There is great hypocrisy;
When the six relations[2] are at variance
There are filial children;
When the state is benighted
There are loyal ministers.

XIX

Exterminate the sage, discard the wise,
And the people will benefit a hundredfold;
Exterminate benevolence, discard rectitude,
And the people will again be filial;
Exterminate ingenuity, discard profit,
And there will be no more thieves and bandits.
These three, being false adornments, are not enough   12
And the people must have something to which they can attach
    themselves:

---

[2]The six relations, according to Wang Pi, are father and son, elder and younger brother, husband and wife. [Translator's note]

Exhibit the unadorned and embrace the uncarved block,
Have little thought of self and as few desires as possible.

XXVI

The heavy is the root of the light;
The still is the lord of the restless.
Therefore the gentleman when traveling all day
Never lets the heavily laden carts out of his sight.
It is only when he is safely behind walls and watch-towers
That he rests peacefully and is above worries.
How, then, should a ruler of ten thousand chariots
Make light of his own person in the eyes of the empire?
If light, then the root is lost;
If restless, then the lord is lost.

XXVII

One who excels in traveling leaves no wheel tracks;   16
One who excels in speech makes no slips;
One who excels in reckoning uses no counting rods;
One who excels in shutting uses no bolts yet what he has shut
     cannot be opened;
One who excels in tying uses no cords yet what he has tied
     cannot be undone.
Therefore the sage always excels in saving people, and so aban-
dons no one; always excels in saving things, and so abandons nothing.
This is called following one's discernment.
Hence the good man is the teacher the bad learns from;
And the bad man is the material the good works on.
Not to value the teacher
Nor to love the material
Though it seems clever, betrays great bewilderment.
This is called the essential and the secret.   20

XXIX

Whoever takes the empire and wishes to do anything to it I see
will have no respite. The empire is a sacred vessel and nothing
should be done to it. Whoever does anything to it will ruin it;
whoever lays hold of it will lose it.

Hence some things lead and some follow;
Some breathe gently and some breathe hard;
Some are strong and some are weak;
Some destroy and some are destroyed.
Therefore the sage avoids excess, extravagance, and arrogance.

XXX

One who assists the ruler of men by means of the way does 24
not intimidate the empire by a show of arms.
This is something which is liable to rebound.
Where troops have encamped
There will brambles grow;
In the wake of a mighty army
Bad harvests follow without fail.
One who is good aims only at bringing his campaign to a
conclusion and dare not thereby intimidate. Bring it to a conclusion
but do not boast; bring it to a conclusion but do not brag; bring it
to a conclusion but do not be arrogant; bring it to a conclusion but
only when there is no choice; bring it to a conclusion but do not
intimidate.
A creature in its prime doing harm to the old
Is known as going against the way.
That which goes against the way will come to an early end.

XLVI

When the way prevails in the empire, fleet-footed horses are 28
relegated to plowing the fields; when the way does not prevail in
the empire, war-horses breed on the border.
There is no crime greater than having too many desires;
There is no disaster greater than not being content;
There is no misfortune greater than being covetous.
Hence in being content, one will always have enough.

XLIX

The sage has no mind of his own. He takes as his own the
mind of the people.
Those who are good I treat as good. Those who are not good 32
I also treat as good. In so doing I gain in goodness. Those who are

of good faith I have faith in. Those who are lacking in good faith I also have faith in. In so doing I gain in good faith.

The sage in his attempt to distract the mind of the empire seeks urgently to muddle it. The people all have something to occupy their eyes and ears, and the sage treats them all like children.

LIV

What is firmly rooted cannot be pulled out;
What is tightly held in the arms will not slip loose;
Through this the offering of sacrifice by descendants will never
        come to an end.
Cultivate it in your person
And its virtue will be genuine;
Cultivate it in the family
And its virtue will be more than sufficient;
Cultivate it in the hamlet
And its virtue will endure;
Cultivate it in the state
And its virtue will abound;
Cultivate it in the empire
And its virtue will be pervasive.

Hence look at the person through the person; look at the family   36
through the family; look at the hamlet through the hamlet; look at the state through the state; look at the empire through the empire.

How do I know that the empire is like that? By means of this.

LVII

Govern the state by being straightforward; wage war by being crafty; but win the empire by not being meddlesome.

How do I know that it is like that? By means of this.

The more taboos there are in the empire   40
The poorer the people;
The more sharpened tools the people have
The more benighted the state;
The more skills the people have
The further novelties multiply;
The better known the laws and edicts
The more thieves and robbers there are.
Hence the sage says,
I take no action and the people are transformed of themselves;
I prefer stillness and the people are rectified of themselves;

I am not meddlesome and the people prosper of themselves;
I am free from desire and the people of themselves become
    simple like the uncarved block.

LVIII

When the government is muddled
The people are simple;
When the government is alert
The people are cunning.
It is on disaster that good fortune perches;
It is beneath good fortune that disaster crouches.
Who knows the limit? Does not the straightforward exist? The   44
straightforward changes again into the crafty, and the good changes
again into the monstrous. Indeed, it is long since the people were
perplexed.
Therefore the sage is square-edged but does not scrape,
Has corners but does not jab,
Extends himself but not at the expense of others,
Shines but does not dazzle.

LX

Governing a large state is like boiling a small fish.³
When the empire is ruled in accordance with the way,
The spirits lose their potencies.
Or rather, it is not that they lose their potencies,
But that, though they have their potencies, they do not harm
    the people,
It is not only they who, having their potencies, do not harm
    the people,
The sage, also, does not harm the people.
As neither does any harm, each attributes the merit to the other.

LXI

A large state is the lower reaches of a river—   48
The place where all the streams of the world unite.

---

³This is because a small fish can be spoiled simply by being handled. [Translator's note]

In the union of the world,
The female always gets the better of the male by stillness.
Being still, she takes the lower position.
Hence the large state, by taking the lower position, annexes
    the small state;
The small state, by taking the lower position, affiliates itself to
    the large state.
Thus the one, by taking the lower position, annexes;   52
The other, by taking the lower position, is annexed.
All that the large state wants is to take the other under its
    wing;
All that the small state wants is to have its services accepted
    by the other.
If each of the two wants to find its proper place,
It is meet that the large should take the lower position.

LXV

Of old those who excelled in the pursuit of the way did not
use it to enlighten the people but to hoodwink them. The reason
why the people are difficult to govern is that they are too clever.
    Hence to rule a state by cleverness
    Will be to the detriment of the state;
    Not to rule a state by cleverness
    Will be a boon to the state.
    These two are models.
    Always to know the models
    Is known as mysterious virtue.
    Mysterious virtue is profound and far-reaching,
    But when things turn back it turns back with them.
    Only then is complete conformity realized.

LXVI

The reason why the River and the Sea are able to be king of 56
the hundred valleys is that they excel in taking the lower position.
Hence they are able to be king of the hundred valleys.
    Therefore, desiring to rule over the people,
    One must in one's words humble oneself before them;
    And, desiring to lead the people,
    One must, in one's person, follow behind them.
    Therefore the sage takes his place over the people yet is no
burden; takes his place ahead of the people yet causes no obstruction.

That is why the empire supports him joyfully and never tires of doing so.

It is because he does not contend that no one in the empire is in a position to contend with him.

LXVIII

One who excels as a warrior does not appear formidable;   60
One who excels in fighting is never roused in anger;
One who excels in defeating his enemy does not join issue;
One who excels in employing others humbles himself before
     them.
This is known as the virtue of non-contention;
This is known as making use of the efforts of others;
This is known as matching the sublimity of heaven.

LXXV

The people are hungry:
It is because those in authority eat up too much in taxes
That the people are hungry.
The people are difficult to govern:
It is because those in authority are too fond of action
That the people are difficult to govern.
The people treat death lightly:
It is because the people set too much store by life
That they treat death lightly.
It is just because one has no use for life that one is wiser than
the man who values life.

LXXX

Reduce the size and population of the state. Ensure that even   64
though the people have tools of war for a troop or a battalion they
will not use them; and also that they will be reluctant to move to
distant places because they look on death as no light matter.

Even when they have ships and carts, they will have no use
for them; and even when they have armor and weapons, they will
have no occasion to make a show of them.

Bring it about that the people will return to the use of the
knotted rope,

Will find relish in their food
And beauty in their clothes,
Will be content in their abode
And happy in the way they live.

Though adjoining states are within sight of one another, and
the sound of dogs barking and cocks crowing in one state can be
heard in another, yet the people of one state will grow old and die
without having had any dealings with those of another.

QUESTIONS FOR CRITICAL READING

1. What is Lao-Tzu's first concern for the people? What must the ruler provide them with if they are to be happy?
2. To what extent is the happiness of the individual taken into account by Lao-Tzu?
3. Does Lao-Tzu regard the people as inferior? Does he seem paternalistic toward them?
4. What are Lao-Tzu's views on the empire and its value? Does he feel the empire is of great or little significance?
5. Which statements made in this selection do you feel support a materialist view of experience? Can they be resolved with Lao-Tzu's overall thinking in the selection?
6. Would you describe Lao-Tzu's position as one that recommends following a mean, a middle way between excesses?
7. To what extent is Lao-Tzu in favor of military action? What seem to be his views about the military?
8. The term "sage" is used frequently in the selection. Does Lao-Tzu use it as a form of praise, or is it a form of dispraise? Is the sage good or bad?

WRITING ASSIGNMENTS

1. The term "the way" is used often in this selection. Write a short essay that defines what Lao-Tzu seems to mean by the term. If you were a politician and had the responsibility of governing a state, how would you follow the way that is implied in Lao-Tzu's statements? Is the way restrictive? Difficult? Open to interpretation? How well do you think it would work?
2. Write a brief essay that examines the following statements from the perspective of a young person today:

>   There is no crime greater than having too many desires;
>   There is no disaster greater than not being content;
>   There is no misfortune greater than being covetous.

To what extent do you agree with these statements, and to what extent do you feel they are statements that have a political importance? Does the United States, as you interpret it, seem to agree with these views, or does it disagree? What are the most visible political consequences of our nation's position regarding these ideas?

3. Some people have asserted that the American political system benefits the people most when the following views of Lao-Tzu are carefully followed:

> Hence the sage says,
> I take no action and the people are transformed of themselves;
> I prefer stillness and the people are rectified of themselves;
> I am not meddlesome and the people prosper of
>   themselves;
> I am free from desire and the people of themselves become
>   simple like the uncarved block.

In a brief essay, decide to what extent American leaders do follow these precepts. Whether you feel they do or not, do you think that they should follow these precepts? What are the likely results of their being put into practice?

4. Some of the statements Lao-Tzu makes are so packed with meaning that it would take pages to explore them. One example is "It is on disaster that good fortune perches." Take this statement as the basis of a short essay and, in reference to a personal disaster that you know about, explain the significance of this statement.

5. What does Lao-Tzu imply about the obligation of the state to the individual it governs, and about the obligation of the individual to the state? Is one much more important than the other? Using the texts in this selection, establish what you feel is the optimum balance in the relationship between the two.

6. **CONNECTIONS** Compare Lao-Tzu's view of government with that of Machiavelli in the next selection. Consider what seem to be the ultimate purposes of government, what seem to be the obligations of the leader to the people being led, and what seems to be the main work of the state.

NICCOLÒ MACHIAVELLI
The Qualities of the Prince

NICCOLÒ MACHIAVELLI (1469–1527) was an aristocrat whose fortunes wavered according to the shifts in power in Florence. Renaissance Italy was a collection of powerful city-states, which were sometimes volatile and unstable. When Florence's famed Medici princes were returned to power in 1512 after eighteen years of banishment, Machiavelli did not fare well. He was suspected of crimes against the state and imprisoned. Even though he was not guilty, he had to learn to support himself as a writer instead of continuing his career in civil service.

His works often contrast two forces: luck (one's fortune) and character (one's virtues). His own character outlasted his bad luck in regard to the Medicis, and he was returned to a position of responsibility. The Prince (1513), his most celebrated work, was a general treatise on the qualities the prince (i.e., ruler) must have to maintain his power. In a more particular way, it was directed at the Medicis to encourage them to save Italy from the predatory incursions of France and Spain, whose troops were nibbling at the crumbling Italian principalities and who would, in time, control much of Italy.

The chapters presented here contain the core of the philosophy for which Machiavelli became famous. His instructions to the prince are curiously devoid of any high-sounding moralizing or any encouragement to be good as a matter of principle. Machiavelli recommends a very practical course of action for the prince: secure power; secure it by practical, simple, and effective means. It may be that Machiavelli fully expects that the prince will use his power for good ends—certainly he does not recommend tyranny. But he also supports questionable means

From *The Prince*. Translated by Peter Bondanella and Mark Musa.

that will achieve the final end of becoming and remaining the prince. Machiavelli believes that there is a conflict between the ends and the means used to achieve them, and he certainly does not fret over the possible problems that may accompany the use of "unpleasant" means, such as punishment of upstarts, or the use of repression, imprisonment, and torture.

Machiavelli's view of human nature has come under criticism for its cynicism. He suggests that a perfectly good person would not last long in any high office because that person would have to compete with the mass of people, who, he says, are basically bad. Machiavelli constantly tells us that he is describing the world as it really is, not as it should be. He implies that if the prince operated as if the world were as it ought to be, he would not last very long. Perhaps Machiavelli is correct, but people have long resented the way he approves of cunning, deceit, and outright lying as means of staying in power.

The contrast with Lao-Tzu's opinions in the Tao-te Ching *is instructive. Lao-Tzu's advice issues from a detached view of a universal ruler; Machiavelli's advice is very personal, embodying a set of directives for a specific prince. Machiavelli expounds upon a litany of actions that must be taken; Lao-Tzu, on the other hand, advises that judicious inaction will produce the best results.*

MACHIAVELLI'S RHETORIC

Machiavelli's approach is less poetic than Lao-Tzu's, and because he is so pragmatic in his approach—he is writing for a limited and temporal audience—he seems less to be dispensing universal wisdom. While Lao-Tzu's tone is almost biblical, Machiavelli's is that of a how-to book, relevant to a particular time and a particular place. Yet like Lao-Tzu, Machiavelli is brief and to the point. Each segment of the discussion is terse and economical. Nothing is wasted.

Machiavelli announces his primary point clearly; he usually refers to a historical precedent (or several) to support his point; then he explains why his position is the best one by appealing to both common sense and historical experience. In those cases in which he suspects the reader will not share his view wholeheartedly, he suggests an alternate argument, then explains why it is wrong. This is a very forceful way of presenting one's views. It gives the appearance of fairness and thoroughness—and, as we learn from reading Machiavelli, he is very much concerned with appearances. His method also gives his work fullness, a quality that makes us forget how brief it really is.

One of his rhetorical methods is to discuss opposites, including both

*sides of an issue. From the first he explores a number of oppositions—
the art of war and the art of life, liberality and stinginess, cruelty and
clemency, the fox and the lion. The method is simplicity itself, but it
is important because it employs one of the basic techniques of rhetoric—
the strategy of comparison, in which we perform one of the mind's
favorite tasks, comparison and contrast.*

*The aphorism is another of Machiavelli's rhetorical weapons. An
aphorism is a saying—or a sentence that sounds like a saying—which
has been accepted as true. Familiar examples are "A penny saved is a
penny earned" and "There is no fool like an old fool." Machiavelli
tells us: To be feared is much safer than to be loved; any man who
tries to be good all the time is bound to come to ruin among the great
number who are not good.*

*Such definite statements have several important qualities. One is
that they are pithy—they seem to say a great deal in a few words.
Another is that they appear to contain a great deal of wisdom, in part
because they are delivered with such certainty, and in part because they
have the ring of other aphorisms that we accept as true. Finally, because
they sound like aphorisms, we tend to accept them much more readily
than perhaps we should. Language that has the appearance of truth is
much more likely to be accepted as conveying truth than any other
language. This may be why the speeches of contemporary politicians
(modern versions of the prince) are often sprinkled with such expressions.
Machiavelli's rhetorical technique is still reliable, still effective, and
still worth studying.*

The Qualities of the Prince

A Prince's Duty Concerning Military Matters

A prince, therefore, must not have any other object nor any
other thought, nor must he take anything as his profession but war,
its institutions, and its discipline; because that is the only profession
which befits one who commands; and it is of such importance that
not only does it maintain those who were born princes, but many
times it enables men of private station to rise to that position; and,
on the other hand, it is evident that when princes have given more
thought to personal luxuries than to arms, they have lost their state.
And the first way to lose it is to neglect this art; and the way to
acquire it is to be well versed in this art.

Francesco Sforza[1] became Duke of Milan from being a private citizen because he was armed; his sons, since they avoided the inconveniences of arms, became private citizens after having been dukes. For, among the other bad effects it causes, being disarmed makes you despised; this is one of those infamies a prince should guard himself against, as will be treated below: for between an armed and an unarmed man there is no comparison whatsoever, and it is not reasonable for an armed man to obey an unarmed man willingly, nor that an unarmed man should be safe among armed servants; since, when the former is suspicious and the latter are contemptuous, it is impossible for them to work well together. And therefore, a prince who does not understand military matters, besides the other misfortunes already noted, cannot be esteemed by his own soldiers, nor can he trust them.

He must, therefore, never raise his thought from this exercise of war, and in peacetime he must train himself more than in time of war; this can be done in two ways: one by action, the other by the mind. And as far as actions are concerned, besides keeping his soldiers well disciplined and trained, he must always be out hunting, and must accustom his body to hardships in this manner; and he must also learn the nature of the terrain, and know how mountains slope, how valleys open, how plains lie, and understand the nature of rivers and swamps; and he should devote much attention to such activities. Such knowledge is useful in two ways: first, one learns to know one's own country and can better understand how to defend it; second, with the knowledge and experience of the terrain, one can easily comprehend the characteristics of any other terrain that it is necessary to explore for the first time; for the hills, valleys, plains, rivers, and swamps of Tuscany,[2] for instance, have certain similarities to those of other provinces; so that by knowing the lay of the land in one province one can easily understand it in others. And a prince who lacks this ability lacks the most important quality in a leader; because this skill teaches you to find the enemy, choose a campsite, lead troops, organize them for battle, and besiege towns to your own advantage.

Philopoemon, Prince of the Achaeans,[3] among the other praises   4

---

[1]*Francesco Sforza (1401–1466)*   Became duke of Milan in 1450. He was, like most of Machiavelli's examples, a skilled diplomat and soldier. His court was a model of Renaissance scholarship and achievement.

[2]*Tuscany*   Florence is in the region known as Tuscany.

[3]*Philopoemon (252?–182 B.C.), Prince of the Achaeans*   Philopoemon, from the city-state of Megalopolis, was a Greek general noted for skillful diplomacy. He

given to him by writers, is praised because in peacetime he thought of nothing except the means of waging war; and when he was out in the country with his friends, he often stopped and reasoned with them: "If the enemy were on that hilltop and we were here with our army, which of the two of us would have the advantage? How could we attack them without breaking formation? If we wanted to retreat, how could we do this? If they were to retreat, how could we pursue them?" And he proposed to them, as they rode along, all the contingencies that can occur in an army; he heard their opinions, expressed his own, and backed it up with arguments; so that, because of these continuous deliberations, when leading his troops no unforeseen incident could arise for which he did not have the remedy.

But as for the exercise of the mind, the prince must read histories and in them study the deeds of great men; he must see how they conducted themselves in wars; he must examine the reasons for their victories and for their defeats in order to avoid the latter and to imitate the former; and above all else he must do as some distinguished man before him has done, who elected to imitate someone who had been praised and honored before him, and always keep in mind his deeds and actions; just as it is reported that Alexander the Great imitated Achilles; Caesar, Alexander; Scipio, Cyrus.[4] And anyone who reads the life of Cyrus written by Xenophon then realizes how important in the life of Scipio that imitation was to his glory and how much, in purity, goodness, humanity, and generosity, Scipio conformed to those characteristics of Cyrus that Xenophon had written about.

Such methods as these a wise prince must follow, and never in peaceful times must he be idle; but he must turn them diligently to his advantage in order to be able to profit from them in times of adversity, so that, when Fortune changes, she will find him prepared to withstand such times.

On Those Things for Which Men, and Particularly Princes, Are Praised or Blamed

Now there remains to be examined what should be the methods and procedures of a prince in dealing with his subjects and friends.

---

led the Achaeans, a group of Greek states that formed the Achaean League, in several important expeditions, notably against Sparta. His cruelty in putting down a Spartan uprising caused him to be reprimanded by his superiors.

[4]***Cyrus (585?–529 B.C.)***   Cyrus II (the Great), Persian emperor. Cyrus and the

And because I know that many have written about this, I am afraid
that by writing about it again I shall be thought of as presumptuous,
since in discussing this material I depart radically from the procedures of others. But since my intention is to write something useful
for anyone who understands it, it seemed more suitable to me to
search after the effectual truth of the matter rather than its imagined
one. And many writers have imagined for themselves republics and
principalities that have never been seen nor known to exist in reality;
for there is such a gap between how one lives and how one ought
to live that anyone who abandons what is done for what ought to
be done learns his ruin rather than his preservation: for a man who
wishes to make a vocation of being good at all times will come to
ruin among so many who are not good. Hence it is necessary for
a prince who wishes to maintain his position to learn how not to
be good, and to use this knowledge or not to use it according to
necessity.

Leaving aside, therefore, the imagined things concerning a   8
prince, and taking into account those that are true, I say that all
men, when they are spoken of, and particularly princes, since they
are placed on a higher level, are judged by some of these qualities
which bring them either blame or praise. And this is why one is
considered generous, another miserly (to use a Tuscan word, since
"avaricious" in our language is still used to mean one who wishes
to acquire by means of theft; we call "miserly" one who excessively
avoids using what he has); one is considered a giver, the other
rapacious; one cruel, another merciful; one treacherous, another
faithful; one effeminate and cowardly, another bold and courageous;
one humane, another haughty; one lascivious, another chaste; one
trustworthy, another cunning; one harsh, another lenient; one serious, another frivolous; one religious, another unbelieving; and the
like. And I know that everyone will admit that it would be a very
praiseworthy thing to find in a prince, of the qualities mentioned
above, those that are held to be good, but since it is neither possible
to have them nor to observe them all completely, because human
nature does not permit it, a prince must be prudent enough to know
how to escape the bad reputation of those vices that would lose the
state for him, and must protect himself from those that will not
lose it for him, if this is possible; but if he cannot, he need not

---

other figures featured in this sentence—Alexander the Great (356–323 B.C.); Achilles,
hero of Homer's *Iliad*; Julius Caesar (100–44 B.C.); and Scipio Africanus, legendary
Roman general—are all examples of politicians who were also great military geniuses.
Xenophon (434?–355? B.C.) was one of the earliest Greek historians; he chronicled
the lives and military exploits of Cyrus and his son-in-law Darius.

concern himself unduly if he ignores these less serious vices. And, moreover, he need not worry about incurring the bad reputation of those vices without which it would be difficult to hold his state; since, carefully taking everything into account, one will discover that something which appears to be a virtue, if pursued, will end in his destruction; while some other thing which seems to be a vice, if pursued, will result in his safety and his well-being.

On Generosity and Miserliness

Beginning, therefore, with the first of the above-mentioned qualities, I say that it would be good to be considered generous; nevertheless, generosity used in such a manner as to give you a reputation for it will harm you; because if it is employed virtuously and as one should employ it, it will not be recognized and you will not avoid the reproach of its opposite. And so, if a prince wants to maintain his reputation for generosity among men, it is necessary for him not to neglect any possible means of lavish display; in so doing such a prince will always use up all his resources and he will be obliged, eventually, if he wishes to maintain his reputation for generosity, to burden the people with excessive taxes and to do everything possible to raise funds. This will begin to make him hateful to his subjects, and, becoming impoverished, he will not be much esteemed by anyone; so that, as a consequence of his generosity, having offended many and rewarded few, he will feel the effects of any slight unrest and will be ruined at the first sign of danger; recognizing this and wishing to alter his policies, he immediately runs the risk of being reproached as a miser.

A price, therefore, unable to use this virtue of generosity in a manner which will not harm himself if he is known for it, should, if he is wise, not worry about being called a miser; for with time he will come to be considered more generous once it is evident that, as a result of his parsimony, his income is sufficient, he can defend himself from anyone who makes war against him, and he can undertake enterprises without overburdening his people, so that he comes to be generous with all those from whom he takes nothing, who are countless, and miserly with all those to whom he gives nothing, who are few. In our times we have not seen great deeds accomplished except by those who were considered miserly; all others were done away with. Pope Julius II,[5] although he made use

---

[5]***Pope Julius II (1443–1513)***   Giuliano della Rovere, pope from 1503 to 1513. Like many of the popes of the day, Julius II was also a diplomat and a general.

of his reputation for generosity in order to gain the papacy, then decided not to maintain it in order to be able to wage war; the present King of France[6] has waged many wars without imposing extra taxes on his subjects, only because his habitual parsimony has provided for the additional expenditures; the present King of Spain,[7] if he had been considered generous, would not have engaged in nor won so many campaigns.

Therefore, in order not to have to rob his subjects, to be able to defend himself, not to become poor and contemptible, and not to be forced to become rapacious, a prince must consider it of little importance if he incurs the name of miser, for this is one of those vices that permits him to rule. And if someone were to say: Caesar with his generosity came to rule the empire, and many others, because they were generous and known to be so, achieved very high positions; I reply: you are either already a prince or you are on the way to becoming one; in the first instance such generosity is damaging; in the second it is very necessary to be thought generous. And Caesar was one of those who wanted to gain the principality of Rome; but if, after obtaining this, he had lived and had not moderated his expenditures, he would have destroyed that empire. And if someone were to reply: there have existed many princes who have accomplished great deeds with their armies who have been reputed to be generous; I answer you: a prince either spends his own money and that of his subjects or that of others; in the first case he must be economical; in the second he must not restrain any part of his generosity. And for that prince who goes out with his soldiers and lives by looting, sacking, and ransoms, who controls the property of others, such generosity is necessary; otherwise he would not be followed by his troops. And with what does not belong to you or to your subjects you can be a more liberal giver, as were Cyrus, Caesar, and Alexander; for spending the wealth of others does not lessen your reputation but adds to it; only the spending of your own is what harms you. And there is nothing that uses itself up faster than generosity, for as you employ it you lose the means of employing it, and you become either poor or despised or, in order to escape poverty, rapacious and hated. And above all other things a prince must guard himself against being despised and hated; and generosity leads you to both one and the

---

[6]*present King of France*   Louis XII (1462–1515). He entered Italy on a successful military campaign in 1494.

[7]*present King of Spain*   Ferdinand V (1452–1516). A studied politician; he and Queen Isabella (1451–1504) financed Christopher Columbus's voyage to the New World in 1492.

other. So it is wiser to live with the reputation of a miser, which produces reproach without hatred, than to be forced to incur the reputation of rapacity, which produces reproach along with hatred, because you want to be considered as generous.

On Cruelty and Mercy and Whether It Is Better to Be Loved Than to Be Feared or the Contrary

Proceeding to the other qualities mentioned above, I say that every prince must desire to be considered merciful and not cruel; nevertheless, he must take care not to misuse this mercy. Cesare Borgia[8] was considered cruel; nonetheless, his cruelty had brought order to Romagna,[9] united it, restored it to peace and obedience. If we examine this carefully, we shall see that he was more merciful than the Florentine people, who, in order to avoid being considered cruel, allowed the destruction of Pistoia.[10] Therefore, a prince must not worry about the reproach of cruelty when it is a matter of keeping his subjects united and loyal; for with a very few examples of cruelty he will be more compassionate than those who, out of excessive mercy, permit disorders to continue, from which arise murders and plundering; for these usually harm the community at large, while the executions that come from the prince harm one individual in particular. And the new prince, above all other princes, cannot escape the reputation of being called cruel, since new states are full of dangers. And Virgil, through Dido, states: "My difficult condition and the newness of my rule make me act in such a manner, and to set guards over my land on all sides."[11]

Nevertheless, a prince must be cautious in believing and in acting, nor should he be afraid of his own shadow; and he should proceed in such a manner, tempered by prudence and humanity, so that too much trust may not render him imprudent nor too much distrust render him intolerable.

From this arises an argument: whether it is better to be loved than to be feared, or the contrary. I reply that one should like to

---

[8]*Cesare Borgia (1476–1507)* He was known for his brutality and lack of scruples, not to mention his exceptionally good luck. He was a firm ruler, son of Pope Alexander VI.

[9]*Romagna* Region northeast of Tuscany; includes the towns of Bologna, Ferrara, Ravenna, and Rimini. Borgia united it as his base of power in 1501.

[10]*Pistoia* (also known as Pistoria). A town near Florence, disturbed in 1501 by a civil war that could have been averted by strong repressive measures.

[11]The quotation is from the *Aeneid* (II. 563–564), the greatest Latin epic poem, written by Virgil (70–19 B.C.). Dido was a woman general who ruled Carthage.

be both one and the other; but since it is difficult to join them together, it is much safer to be feared than to be loved when one of the two must be lacking. For one can generally say this about men: that they are ungrateful, fickle, simulators and deceivers, avoiders of danger, greedy for gain; and while you work for their good they are completely yours, offering you their blood, their property, their lives, and their sons, as I said earlier, when danger is far away; but when it comes nearer to you they turn away. And that prince who bases his power entirely on their words, finding himself stripped of other preparations, comes to ruin; for friendships that are acquired by a price and not by greatness and nobility of character are purchased but are not owned, and at the proper moment they cannot be spent. And men are less hesitant about harming someone who makes himself loved than one who makes himself feared because love is held together by a chain of obligation which, since men are a sorry lot, is broken on every occasion in which their own self-interest is concerned; but fear is held together by a dread of punishment which will never abandon you.

A prince must nevertheless make himself feared in such a manner that he will avoid hatred, even if he does not acquire love; since to be feared and not to be hated can very well be combined; and this will always be so when he keeps his hands off the property and the women of his citizens and his subjects. And if he must take someone's life, he should do so when there is proper justification and manifest cause; but, above all, he should avoid the property of others; for men forget more quickly the death of their father than the loss of their patrimony. Moreover, the reasons for seizing their property are never lacking; and he who begins to live by stealing always finds a reason for taking what belongs to others; on the contrary, reasons for taking a life are rarer and disappear sooner.

But when the prince is with his armies and has under his command a multitude of troops, then it is absolutely necessary that he not worry about being considered cruel; for without that reputation he will never keep an army united or prepared for any combat. Among the praiseworthy deeds of Hannibal[12] is counted this: that, having a very large army, made up of all kinds of men, which he commanded in foreign lands, there never arose the slightest dissention, neither among themselves nor against their prince, both during his good and his bad fortune. This could not have arisen

16

---

[12]**Hannibal (247–183 B.C.)**   An amazingly inventive military tactician who led the Carthaginian armies against Rome for more than fifteen years. He crossed the Alps from Gaul (France) in order to surprise Rome. He was noted for use of the ambush and for "inhuman cruelty."

from anything other than his inhuman cruelty, which, along with his many other abilities, made him always respected and terrifying in the eyes of his soldiers; and without that, to attain the same effect, his other abilities would not have sufficed. And the writers of history, having considered this matter very little, on the one hand admire these deeds of his and on the other condemn the main cause of them.

And that it be true that his other abilities would not have been sufficient can be seen from the example of Scipio, a most extraordinary man not only in his time but in all recorded history, whose armies in Spain rebelled against him; this came about from nothing other than his excessive compassion, which gave to his soldiers more liberty than military discipline allowed. For this he was censured in the senate by Fabius Maximus,[13] who called him the corruptor of the Roman militia. The Locrians,[14] having been ruined by one of Scipio's officers, were not avenged by him, nor was the arrogance of that officer corrected, all because of his tolerant nature; so that someone in the senate who tried to apologize for him said that there were many men who knew how not to err better than they knew how to correct errors. Such a nature would have, in time, damaged Scipio's fame and glory if he had maintained it during the empire; but, living under the control of the senate, this harmful characteristic of his not only concealed itself but brought him fame.

I conclude, therefore, returning to the problem of being feared and loved, that since men love at their own pleasure and fear at the pleasure of the prince, a wise prince should build his foundation upon that which belongs to him, not upon that which belongs to others: he must strive only to avoid hatred, as has been said.

How a Prince Should Keep His Word

How praiseworthy it is for a prince to keep his word and to live by integrity and not by deceit everyone knows; nevertheless, one sees from the experience of our times that the princes who have accomplished great deeds are those who have cared little for keeping their promises and who have known how to manipulate the minds

---

[13]***Fabius Maximus (?–203 B.C.)***   Roman general who fought Hannibal. He was jealous of the younger Roman general Scipio.

[14]***Locrians***   Inhabitants of Locri, an Italian town settled by the Greeks in 683 B.C.

of men by shrewdness; and in the end they have surpassed those who laid their foundations upon honesty.

You must, therefore, know that there are two means of fighting: one according to the laws, the other with force; the first way is proper to man, the second to beasts; but because the first, in many cases, is not sufficient, it becomes necessary to have recourse to the second. Therefore, a prince must know how to use wisely the natures of the beast and the man. This policy was taught to princes allegorically by the ancient writers, who described how Achilles and many other ancient princes were given to Chiron[15] the Centaur to be raised and taught under his discipline. This can only mean that, having a half-beast and half-man as a teacher, a prince must know how to employ the nature of the one and the other; and the one without the other cannot endure.

Since, then, a prince must know how to make good use of the nature of the beast, he should choose from among the beasts the fox and the lion; for the lion cannot defend itself from traps and the fox cannot protect itself from wolves. It is therefore necessary to be a fox in order to recognize the traps and a lion in order to frighten the wolves. Those who play only the part of the lion do not understand matters. A wise ruler, therefore, cannot and should not keep his word when such an observance of faith would be to his disadvantage and when the reasons which made him promise are removed. And if men were all good, this rule would not be good; but since men are a sorry lot and will not keep their promises to you, you likewise need not keep yours to them. A prince never lacks legitimate reasons to break his promises. Of this one could cite an endless number of modern examples to show how many pacts, how many promises have been made null and void because of the infidelity of princes; and he who has known best how to use the fox has come to a better end. But it is necessary to know how to disguise this nature well and to be a great hypocrite and a liar: and men are so simpleminded and so controlled by their present necessities that one who deceives will always find another who will allow himself to be deceived.

I do not wish to remain silent about one of these recent instances. Alexander VI[16] did nothing else, he thought about nothing else, except to deceive men, and he always found the occasion to do this. And there never was a man who had more forcefulness in his

---

[15]**Chiron** A mythical figure, a centaur (half man, half horse). Unlike most centaurs, he was wise and benevolent; he was also a legendary physician.

[16]**Alexander VI (1431–1503)** Roderigo Borgia, pope from 1492 to 1503. He was Cesare Borgia's father and a corrupt but immensely powerful pope.

oaths, who affirmed a thing with more promises, and who honored his word less; nevertheless, his tricks always succeeded perfectly since he was well acquainted with this aspect of the world.

Therefore, it is not necessary for a prince to have all of the above-mentioned qualities, but it is very necessary for him to appear to have them. Furthermore, I shall be so bold as to assert this: that having them and practicing them at all times is harmful; and appearing to have them is useful; for instance, to seem merciful, faithful, humane, forthright, religious, and to be so; but his mind should be disposed in such a way that should it become necessary not to be so, he will be able and know how to change to the contrary. And it is essential to understand this: that a prince, and especially a new prince, cannot observe all those things by which men are considered good, for in order to maintain the state he is often obliged to act against his promise, against charity, against humanity, and against religion. And therefore, it is necessary that he have a mind ready to turn itself according to the way the winds of Fortune and the changeability of affairs require him; and, as I said above, as long as it is possible, he should not stray from the good, but he should know how to enter into evil when necessity commands.

A prince, therefore, must be very careful never to let anything 24 slip from his lips which is not full of the five qualities mentioned above: he should appear, upon seeing and hearing him, to be all mercy, all faithfulness, all integrity, all kindness, all religion. And there is nothing more necessary than to seem to possess this last quality. And men in general judge more by their eyes than their hands; for everyone can see but few can feel. Everyone sees what you seem to be, few perceive what you are, and those few do not dare to contradict the opinion of the many who have the majesty of the state to defend them; and in the actions of all men, and especially of princes, where there is no impartial arbiter, one must consider the final result.[17] Let a prince therefore act to seize and to maintain the state; his methods will always be judged honorable and will be praised by all; for ordinary people are always deceived by appearances and by the outcome of a thing; and in the world there is nothing but ordinary people; and there is no room for the few, while the many have a place to lean on. A certain prince[18] of the present day, whom I shall refrain from naming, preaches nothing but peace and faith, and to both one and the other he is entirely

---

[17]The Italian original, *si guarda al fine,* has often been mistranslated as "the ends justify the means," something Machiavelli never wrote. [Translators' note]

[18]*A certain prince* Probably King Ferdinand V of Spain (1452–1516).

opposed; and both, if he had put them into practice, would have cost him many times over either his reputation or his state.

On Avoiding Being Despised and Hated

But since, concerning the qualities mentioned above, I have spoken about the most important, I should like to discuss the others briefly in this general manner: that the prince, as was noted above, should think about avoiding those things which make him hated and despised; and when he has avoided this, he will have carried out his duties and will find no danger whatsoever in other vices. As I have said, what makes him hated above all else is being rapacious and a usurper of the property and the women of his subjects; he must refrain from this; and in most cases, so long as you do not deprive them of either their property or their honor, the majority of men live happily; and you have only to deal with the ambition of a few, who can be restrained without difficulty and by many means. What makes him despised is being considered changeable, frivolous, effeminate, cowardly, irresolute; from these qualities a prince must guard himself as if from a reef, and he must strive to make everyone recognize in his actions greatness, spirit, dignity, and strength; and concerning the private affairs of his subjects, he must insist that his decision be irrevocable; and he should maintain himself in such a way that no man could imagine that he can deceive or cheat him.

That prince who projects such an opinion of himself is greatly esteemed; and it is difficult to conspire against a man with such a reputation and difficult to attack him, provided that he is understood to be of great merit and revered by his subjects. For a prince must have two fears: one, internal, concerning his subjects; the other, external, concerning foreign powers. From the latter he can defend himself by his good troops and friends; and he will always have good friends if he has good troops; and internal affairs will always be stable when external affairs are stable, provided that they are not already disturbed by a conspiracy; and even if external conditions change, if he is properly organized and lives as I have said and does not lose control of himself, he will always be able to withstand every attack, just as I said that Nabis the Spartan[19] did. But concerning his subjects, when external affairs do not change, he has to fear that

---

[19]***Nabis the Spartan***   Tyrant of Sparta from 207 to 192 B.C., routed by Philopoemon and the Achaean League.

they may conspire secretly: the prince secures himself from this by avoiding being hated or despised and by keeping the people satisfied with him; this is a necessary matter, as was treated above at length. And one of the most powerful remedies a prince has against conspiracies is not to be hated by the masses; for a man who plans a conspiracy always believes that he will satisfy the people by killing the prince; but when he thinks he might anger them, he cannot work up the courage to undertake such a deed; for the problems on the side of the conspirators are countless. And experience demonstrates that conspiracies have been many but few have been concluded successfully; for anyone who conspires cannot be alone, nor can he find companions except from amongst those whom he believes to be dissatisfied; and as soon as you have uncovered your intent to one dissatisfied man, you give him the means to make himself happy, since he can have everything he desires by uncovering the plot; so much is this so that, seeing a sure gain on the one hand and one doubtful and full of danger on the other, if he is to maintain faith with you he has to be either an unusually good friend or a completely determined enemy of the prince. And to treat the matter briefly, I say that on the part of the conspirator there is nothing but fear, jealousy, and the thought of punishment that terrifies him; but on the part of the prince there is the majesty of the principality, the laws, the defenses of friends and the state to protect him; so that, with the good will of the people added to all these things, it is impossible for anyone to be so rash as to plot against him. For, where usually a conspirator has to be afraid before he executes his evil deed, in this case he must be afraid, having the people as an enemy, even after the crime is performed, nor can he hope to find any refuge because of this.

One could cite countless examples on this subject; but I want to satisfy myself with only one which occurred during the time of our fathers. Messer Annibale Bentivogli, prince of Bologna and grandfather of the present Messer Annibale, was murdered by the Canneschi[20] family, who conspired against him; he left behind no heir except Messer Giovanni,[21] then only a baby. As soon as this murder occurred, the people rose up and killed all the Canneschi. This came about because of the good will that the house of the Bentivogli enjoyed in those days; this good will was so great that with Annibale dead, and there being no one of that family left in the city who could rule Bologna, the Bolognese people, having

---

[20]*Canneschi* Prominent family in Bologna.

[21]*Giovanni Bentivoglio (1443–1508)* Former tyrant of Bologna. In sequence he was a conspirator against, then a conspirator with, Cesare Borgia.

heard that in Florence there was one of the Bentivogli blood who was believed until that time to be the son of a blacksmith, went to Florence to find him, and they gave him the control of that city; it was ruled by him until Messer Giovanni became of age to rule.

I conclude, therefore, that a prince must be little concerned 28 with conspiracies when the people are well disposed toward him; but when the populace is hostile and regards him with hatred, he must fear everything and everyone. And well-organized states and wise princes have, with great diligence, taken care not to anger the nobles and to satisfy the common people and keep them contented; for this is one of the most important concerns that a prince has.

QUESTIONS FOR CRITICAL READING

1. The usual criticism of Machiavelli is that he advises his prince to be unscrupulous. Does this seem to be the case in this excerpt?
2. Is Machiavelli correct when he asserts that the great majority of people are not good? Does our government assume that to be true, too?
3. Politicians—especially heads of state—are the contemporary counterparts of the prince. Should successful heads of state show skill in war to the same extent Machiavelli's prince must?
4. Clarify the advice Machiavelli gives concerning liberality and stinginess. Is this still good advice?
5. Are modern politicians likely to succeed by following all or most of Machiavelli's recommendations?

WRITING ASSIGNMENTS

1. In speaking of the prince's military duties Machiavelli says, "being disarmed makes you despised." Take a stand on this issue. If possible, choose an example or instance to strengthen your argument. Is it possible that in modern society being defenseless is an advantage?
2. Find evidence within this excerpt to demonstrate that Machiavelli's attitude toward human nature is accurate. Remember that the usual criticism of Machiavelli is that he is cynical—that he thinks the worst of people rather than the best. Find quotations from the excerpt that would support either or both of these views; then use them as the basis for an essay analyzing just what Machiavelli's views on human nature are.
3. By referring to current events and current leaders—either local, national, or international—decide whether or not Machiavelli's advice to the prince would be useful to the modern politician. Consider whether the advice is completely useless, completely reliable, or

whether its value depends upon specific conditions. Establish first exactly what the advice is; show how it is applicable or inapplicable for specific politicians; then critique its general usefulness.

4. Probably the chief ethical issue raised by *The Prince* is the question of whether or not the desired ends justify the means that need to be used to achieve them. Write an essay in which you take a stand on this question. Begin by defining the issue: What does the concept "the ends justify the means" actually mean? What are the difficulties in accepting the idea that unworthy means may achieve worthy ends? If possible, use some historical or personal examples to give your argument substance. Carefully analyze Machiavelli's references to circumstances in which questionable means were (or should have been) used to achieve worthy ends. Is it possible for politicians to concern themselves only with ends and ignore the means entirely?

5. **CONNECTIONS** One of Machiavelli's most controversial statements is: "A man who wishes to make a vocation of being good at all times will come to ruin among so many who are not good." What would Lao-Tzu say in response to this statement? Do you feel that the American political environment in the current decade supports this statement? Or do you feel that in our time such a statement is irrelevant?

THOMAS JEFFERSON
The Declaration of Independence

THOMAS JEFFERSON *(1743–1826), an exceptionally accomplished and well-educated man, is probably best known for writing the Declaration of Independence. He composed the work under the eyes of Benjamin Franklin, John Adams, and the Continental Congress, which spent two and a half days going over every word. The substance of the document was developed in committee, but Jefferson, because of the grace of his style, was chosen to do the actual writing. The result is one of the most memorable statements in American history.*

Jefferson had a long and distinguished career. He received a classical education and went on to become a lawyer. By the time he took a seat in the House of Burgesses, which governed Virginia, that colony was already on a course toward revolution. His pamphlet "A Summary View of the Rights of British America" (1774) first brought him to the attention of those who were agitating for independence.

Jefferson's services to Virginia were considerable. In addition to serving in the House of Burgesses, he became governor (1779) and founded the University of Virginia (1819). Many details of the design of the university's buildings reflect Jefferson's considerable skill as an architect. His one book, Notes on Virginia *(1782), is sometimes personal, sometimes public, sometimes scientific, sometimes haphazard. He discusses slavery, racial differences, the effects of the environment on people, and some of his own feelings about revolution while describing his home state, its geography and its people.*

Jefferson's services to the nation include being the first secretary of state (1790–1793), second vice-president (1797–1801), and third president (1801–1809). During his presidency he negotiated the Louisiana Purchase, buying 828,000 square miles of land west of the Mississippi from France for only $15 million. He was sympathetic to the *efforts of the French to throw off their monarchy, but when Napoleon extended French influence into the rest of Europe by waging war, Jefferson was careful to keep the United States neutral.*

Jefferson's training in the classics and his wide reading of contemporary authors helped him become a gifted stylist. His work has balance and eloquence as well as clarity. The Declaration of Independence says little that was not familiar or widely understood at the time, but what it does *say, it says in a memorable fashion.*

JEFFERSON'S RHETORIC

Jefferson is notable for a number of interesting techniques. One is the periodic sentence, which was especially typical of the age. The first sentence of the Declaration of Independence is periodic, that is, it is long and carefully balanced, and the main point comes at the end. Such sentences are not popular today, although an occasional periodic sentence can still be powerful in contemporary prose. That first sentence says (in paraphrase): When one nation must sever its relations with a parent nation . . . and stand as an independent nation itself . . . the causes ought to be explained. The entire paragraph is taken up by this one sentence. Moreover, the main body of the Declaration of Independence is devoted to listing the "causes," so we see that the most important element of the sentence comes at the end.

The periodic sentence demands certain qualities of balance and parallelism that all good writers should heed. The first sentence in paragraph 2 demonstrates both qualities. The balance is achieved by making each part of the sentence about the same length. The parallelism is achieved by using certain key linking words in repetition (they are in roman type in the analysis below). Note how the "truths" mentioned in the first clause are enumerated in the succession of noun clauses beginning with "that"; "Rights" are enumerated in the final clause.

> *We hold these truths to be self-evident,*
> > that *all men are created equal,*
> > that *they are endowed by their Creator with certain*
> > *unalienable Rights,*
> > that *among these are Life, Liberty and the pursuit of Happiness.*

Parallelism is one of the greatest stylistic techniques available to a writer sensitive to rhetoric. It is a natural technique—many untrained writers and speakers develop it on their own.

One benefit of parallelism is that it creates a natural link to the useful device of enumeration, or the list. Many writers use this technique very effectively by establishing their purpose from the outset: "There are three important issues I wish to address. . . ."; and then numbering them: "First, I want to say. . . . Second. . . ," and so on. Like any technique, this can of course become tiresome, but if used judiciously, it is authoritative and powerful. Jefferson devotes paragraphs 3–29 to enumerating the "causes" he mentions in paragraph 1. Each one constitutes a separate paragraph; thus, each has separate weight and importance. Each begins with "He" or "For" and is therefore in parallel structure. The technique of repetition of the same words at the beginning of successive lines is called anaphora. *Jefferson's use of anaphora here is one of the best known and most effective in all literature. The "He" referred to is Britain's King George III (1738–1820), who is never mentioned by name. Congress is opposed not to a personality but to the sovereign of a nation that is oppressing the United States and a tyrant who is not dignified by being named. The "For" introduces grievous acts the king has given his assent to; these are offenses against the colonies.*

None of the causes is developed in any detail. We do not have specific information about what trade was cut off by the British, what taxes were imposed without consent, how King George waged war or abdicated government in the colonies. Presumably, Jefferson's audience knew the details. What he did, in listing all the causes in twenty-seven paragraphs, was to point out how many there were. And all are so serious that one alone could cause a revolution. The effect of Jefferson's enumeration is to illustrate the patience of the colonies up to this point and to tell the world that the colonies have finally lost patience, on account of the reasons listed. The Declaration of Independence projects the careful meditations and decisions of exceptionally calm, patient, and—above all—reasonable people. The periodicity of the sentences and the balance of their parallelism underscores thoughtfulness, grace, learning, and, ultimately, wisdom.

The Declaration of Independence

In Congress, July 4, 1776

The Unanimous Declaration of the Thirteen United States of America

When in the Course of human events, it becomes necessary for one people to dissolve the political bands which have connected them with another, and to assume among the Powers of the earth, the separate and equal station to which the Laws of Nature and of Nature's God entitle them, a decent respect to the opinions of mankind requires that they should declare the causes which impel them to the separation.

We hold these truths to be self-evident, that all men are created equal, that they are endowed by their Creator with certain unalienable Rights, that among these are Life, Liberty and the pursuit of Happiness. That to secure these rights, Governments are instituted among Men, deriving their just powers from the consent of the governed. That whenever any Form of Government becomes destructive of these ends, it is the Right of the People to alter or to abolish it, and to institute new Government, laying its foundation on such principles and organizing its powers in such form, as to them shall seem most likely to effect their Safety and Happiness. Prudence, indeed, will dictate that Governments long established should not be changed for light and transient causes; and accordingly all experience hath shown, that mankind are more disposed to suffer, while evils are sufferable, than to right themselves by abolishing the forms to which they are accustomed. But when a long train of abuses and usurpations, pursuing invariably the same Object evinces a design to reduce them under absolute Despotism, it is their right, it is their duty, to throw off such Government, and to provide new Guards for their future security.— Such has been the patient sufferance of these Colonies; and such is now the necessity which constrains them to alter their former Systems of Government. The history of the present King of Great Britain is a history of repeated injuries and usurpations, all having in direct object the establishment of an absolute Tyranny over these States. To prove this, let Facts be submitted to a candid world.

He has refused his Assent to Laws, the most wholesome and necessary for the public good.

He has forbidden his Governors to pass Laws of immediate 4 and pressing importance, unless suspended in their operation till his Assent should be obtained; and when so suspended, he has utterly neglected to attend to them.

He has refused to pass other laws for the accommodation of large districts of people, unless those people would relinquish the right of Representation in the Legislature, a right inestimable to them and formidable to tyrants only.

He has called together legislative bodies at places unusual, uncomfortable, and distant from the depository of their Public Records, for the sole purpose of fatiguing them into compliance with his measures.

He has dissolved Representative Houses repeatedly, for opposing with manly firmness his invasions on the rights of the people.

He has refused for a long time, after such dissolutions, to cause 8 others to be elected; whereby the Legislative Powers, incapable of Annihilation, have returned to the People at large for their exercise; the State remaining in the mean time exposed to all the dangers of invasion from without, and convulsions within.

He has endeavoured to prevent the population of these States;[1] for that purpose obstructing the Laws for Naturalization of Foreigners; refusing to pass others to encourage their migration hither, and raising the conditions of new Appropriations of Lands.

He has obstructed the Administration of Justice, by refusing his Assent to Laws for establishing Judiciary Powers.

He has made Judges dependent on his Will alone, for the tenure of their offices, and the amount and payment of their salaries.

He has erected a multitude of New Offices, and sent hither swarms of Officers to harass our People, and eat out their substance.

He has kept among us, in times of peace, Standing Armies without the Consent of our legislature.

He has affected to render the Military independent of and superior to the Civil Power.

He has combined with others to subject us to a jurisdiction foreign to our constitution, and unacknowledged by our laws; giving his Assent to their acts of pretended Legislation:

For quartering large bodies of armed troops among us:

For protecting them, by a mock Trial, from Punishment for any Murders which they should commit on the Inhabitants of these States:

For cutting off our Trade with all parts of the world:

For imposing taxes on us without our Consent:

For depriving us in many cases, of the benefits of Trial by Jury:

For transporting us beyond Seas to be tried for pretended offences:

For abolishing the free System of English Laws in a neighbouring Province, establishing therein an Arbitrary government, and enlarging its Boundaries so as to render it at once an example and fit instrument for introducing the same absolute rule into these Colonies:

For taking away our Charters, abolishing our most valuable Laws, and altering fundamentally the Forms of our Governments:

For suspending our own Legislatures, and declaring themselves invested with Power to legislate for us in all cases whatsoever.

He has abdicated Government here, by declaring us out of his Protection and waging War against us.

---

[1]*prevent the population of these States*   This meant limiting emigration to the Colonies, thus controlling their growth.

He has plundered our seas, ravaged our Coasts, burnt our towns, and destroyed the lives of our people.

He is at this time transporting large armies of foreign mercenaries to compleat the works of death, desolation and tyranny, already begun with circumstances of Cruelty & perfidy scarcely paralleled in the most barbarous ages, and totally unworthy the Head of a civilized nation.

He has constrained our fellow Citizens taken Captive on the high Seas to bear Arms against their Country, to become the executioners of their friends and Brethren, or to fall themselves by their Hands.   28

He has excited domestic insurrections amongst us, and has endeavoured to bring on the inhabitants of our frontiers, the merciless Indian Savages, whose known rule of warfare, is an undistinguished destruction of all ages, sexes and conditions.

In every stage of these Oppressions We have Petitioned for Redress in the most humble terms: Our repeated Petitions have been answered only by repeated injury. A Prince, whose character is thus marked by every act which may define a Tyrant, is unfit to be the ruler of a free People.

Nor have We been wanting in attention to our British brethren. We have warned them from time to time of attempts by their legislature to extend an unwarrantable jurisdiction over us. We have reminded them of the circumstances of our emigration and settlement here. We have appealed to their native justice and magnanimity, and we have conjured them by the ties of our common kindred to disavow these usurpations, which, would inevitably interrupt our connections and correspondence. They too have been deaf to the voice of justice and of consanguinity. We must, therefore, acquiesce in the necessity, which denounces our Separation, and hold them, as we hold the rest of mankind, Enemies in War, in Peace Friends.

We, therefore, the Representatives of the United States of America, in General Congress, Assembled, appealing to the Supreme Judge of the world for the rectitude of our intentions, do, in the Name, and by Authority of the good People of these Colonies, solemnly publish and declare, That these United Colonies are, and of Right ought to be Free and Independent States, that they are Absolved from all Allegiance to the British Crown, and that all political connection between them and the State of Great Britain, is and ought to be totally dissolved; and that as Free and Independent States, they have full Power to levy War, conclude Peace, contract Alliances, establish Commerce, and to do all other Acts and Things which Independent States may of right do. And for the support of   32 this Declaration, with a firm reliance on the Protection of Divine Providence, we mutually pledge to each other our Lives, our Fortunes and our sacred Honor.

QUESTIONS FOR CRITICAL READING

1. What are the laws of nature Jefferson refers to in paragraph 1?
2. What do you think Jefferson feels is the function of government (para. 2)?
3. What does Jefferson have to say about women? Is there any way you can determine his views from reading this document?
4. Find at least one use of parallel structure in the Declaration. What key terms are repeated as a means of guaranteeing that structure?
5. Which of the causes listed in paragraphs 3–29 are the most serious? Is any one of them trivial? Is any one serious enough to cause a revolution?
6. What do you consider to be the most graceful sentence in the entire Declaration? Where is it placed in the Declaration? Do you think it was put there consciously, as a means of attracting attention?
7. In what ways do the king's desires for stable government interfere with Jefferson's sense of his own independence? Is he talking about his independence as a citizen?

WRITING ASSIGNMENTS

1. Jefferson defines the unalienable rights of a citizen as "Life, Liberty and the pursuit of Happiness." Do you think these are indeed unalienable rights? In the course of answering this question—using careful parallelism of any sort you like—be certain that you define each of these terms both for yourself and for our time.
2. Write an essay containing at least three periodic sentences (underline them) in which you discuss what you feel the function of government should be. You may first want to establish what you think Jefferson's view of it is, then compare or contrast it with your own.
3. Jefferson envisioned a government that would make it possible for its citizens to have the rights of life, liberty, and the pursuit of happiness. Has Jefferson's revolutionary vision been achieved in America? Begin with a definition of your key terms: "life," "liberty," and "the pursuit of happiness." Then, taking each in turn and using any examples available—drawn from current events, your own experience, American history—take a clear and well-argued stand on whether the nation has achieved Jefferson's goal.
4. Slavery was legal in America in 1776, and Jefferson reluctantly owned

slaves. He had a plan to grant gradual emancipation to the slaves but never presented it to Congress because he realized that Congress would never approve it. Jefferson and Franklin financed a plan to buy slaves and return them to Africa, where they founded the nation of Liberia. To what degree, if any, does the practice of slavery by the people who wrote the Declaration of Independence invalidate it? Take a stand on this question and defend it. You may wish to read the relevant chapters on Jefferson and slavery in Merrill D. Peterson's *Thomas Jefferson and the New Nation* (1970).

5. What kind of government does Jefferson seem to prefer? How different would he make his government from that of the king against whom he is reacting? Is he talking about an entirely different system or about the same system, but with a different kind of "prince" at the head? How would Jefferson protect the individual against the whim of the state, while also protecting the state against the whim of the individual?

6. **CONNECTIONS**   Write an essay in which you examine to what extent Jefferson agrees or disagrees with Lao-Tzu's conception of human nature and the ways in which a government should function. Does Jefferson seem to share Lao-Tzu's commitment to judicious inactivity? Is there any evidence that the king subscribes to it? What, for you, are the most important similarities and differences between Jefferson's views and those of Lao-Tzu?

7. **CONNECTIONS**   What principles does Jefferson share with Mary Wollstonecraft? Compare the fundamental demands of the Declaration of Independence with the issues Wollstonecraft holds sacred in "Pernicious Effects Which Arise from the Unnatural Distinctions Established in Society." What might Jefferson's reaction have been to Wollstonecraft's essay? Write a hypothetical response to her from Jefferson.

MARY WOLLSTONECRAFT

Pernicious Effects Which
Arise from the
Unnatural Distinctions
Established in Society

MARY WOLLSTONECRAFT (1759–1797) was born into relatively
simple circumstances, with a father whose heavy drinking and spending
eventually ruined the family and left her and her sisters to support
themselves. She became a governess, a teacher, and eventually a writer.
Her views were among the most enlightened of her day, particularly
regarding women and women's rights, giving her the reputation of being
a very forward-looking feminist, even for our time. Her thinking,
however, is comprehensive and not limited to a single issue.

She was known to the American patriot Thomas Paine (1737–
1809), to Dr. Samuel Johnson (1709–1784), and to the English philoso-
pher William Godwin (1756–1836), whom she eventually married. Her
views on marriage were remarkable for her time; among other things, she
felt it unnecessary to marry a man in order to live happily with him. Her
first liaison, with an American, Gilbert Imlay, gave her the opportunity
to travel and learn something about commerce and capitalism at first hand.
Her second liaison, with Godwin, brought her into the intellectual circles
of her day. She married Godwin when she was pregnant and died in
childbirth. Her daughter, Mary, married the poet Percy Bysshe Shelley
and wrote the novel Frankenstein *(1818).*

The excitement generated by the French Revolution (1789–1799)
caused Wollstonecraft to react against the very conservative view put for-
ward by the philosopher Edmund Burke. Her pamphlet A Vindication
of the Rights of Men *(1790) was well received. She followed it with*
Vindication of the Rights of Woman *(1792), which was translated*
into French.

From *Vindication of the Rights of Woman.*

She sees feminism in political terms. The chapter reprinted here concentrates on questions of property, class, and law. As a person committed to the revolutionary principles of liberty, equality, and fraternity, Wollstonecraft links the present condition of women to the political and social structure of her society. Her aim is to point up the inequities in treatment of women—which her society simply did not perceive—and to attempt to rectify them.

WOLLSTONECRAFT'S RHETORIC

Mary Wollstonecraft was writing for an audience that did not necessarily appreciate brief, exact expression. Rather, they appreciated a more luxuriant and leisurely style than we do today. As a result, her prose can sometimes seem wordy to a modern audience. However, she handles imagery carefully (especially in the first paragraph) without overburdening her prose. She uses an approach that she calls "episodical observations" (para. 12). These are anecdotes—personal stories—and apparently casual cataloguings of thoughts on a number of related issues. She was aware that her structure was not tight, that it did not develop a specific argument, and that it did not force the reader to accept or reject her position. She also considered this a wise approach, since it was obvious to her that her audience was completely prejudiced against her view. To attempt to convince them of her views was to invite total defeat.

Instead, she simply puts forward several observations that stand by themselves as examples of the evils she condemns. Even those who stand against her will see that there is validity to her claims; and they will not be so threatened by her argument as to become defensive before they have learned something new. She appeals always to the higher intellectual capacities of both men and women, directing her complaints, too, against both men and women. This balance of opinion, coupled with a range of thought-provoking examples, makes her views clear and convincing.

Also distinctive in this passage is the use of metaphor, a figure of speech that implies comparison without using "like" or "as." The second sentence of paragraph 1 is particularly heavy with metaphor: "For it is in the most polished society that noisome reptiles and venomous serpents lurk under the rank herbage; and there is voluptuousness pampered by the still sultry air, which relaxes every good disposition before it ripens into virtue." The metaphor presents society as a garden in which the grass is decaying and dangerous serpents are lurking. Good disposition—character—is a plant that might ripen, but—continuing the metaphor—it ripens into virtue, not just a fruit. A favorite source of metaphors for Wollstonecraft is drapery (dressmaking). When she uses one of these metaphors she is usually reminding the reader that drapery gives a new shape to things, that it sometimes hides the truth, and that it ought not to put a false appearance on what it covers.

One of her rhetorical techniques that can be easily copied is that of literary allusion. By alluding to important literary works and writers—such as Greek mythology, William Shakespeare, Jean Jacques Rousseau, and Samuel Johnson—she not only demonstrates her learning but also shows that she respects her audience, which she presumes shares her learning. She does not show off by overquoting or by referring to very obscure writers. She balances it perfectly, even by transforming folk aphorisms into "homely proverbs" such as, "whoever the devil finds idle he will employ."

Wollstonecraft's experiences with her difficult father gave her knowledge of unfortunate gambling tables and card games, another source of allusions. She draws further on personal experience—shared by some of her audience—when she talks about the degradation felt by a woman of intelligence forced to act the governess—a glorified servant—in a well-to-do family. Wollstonecraft makes excellent uses of these allusions, never overdoing them, always giving them just the right touch.

Pernicious Effects Which Arise from the Unnatural Distinctions Established in Society

From the respect paid to property flow, as from a poisoned fountain, most of the evils and vices which render this world such a dreary scene to the contemplative mind. For it is in the most polished society that noisome reptiles and venomous serpents lurk under the rank herbage; and there is voluptuousness pampered by the still sultry air, which relaxes every good disposition before it ripens into virtue.

One class presses on another; for all are aiming to procure respect on account of their property: and property, once gained, will procure the respect due only to talents and virtue. Men neglect the duties incumbent on man, yet are treated like demi-gods; religion is also separated from morality by a ceremonial veil, yet men wonder that the world is almost, literally speaking, a den of sharpers or oppressors.

There is a homely proverb, which speaks a shrewd truth, that whoever the devil finds idle he will employ. And what but habitual idleness can hereditary wealth and titles produce? For man is so constituted that he can only attain a proper use of his faculties by exercising them, and will not exercise them unless necessity of some kind first set the wheels in motion. Virtue likewise can only be acquired by the discharge of relative duties; but the importance of these sacred duties will scarcely be felt by the being who is cajoled out of his humanity by the flattery of sycophants.[1] There must be more equality established in society, or morality will never gain ground, and this virtuous equality will not rest firmly even when founded on a rock, if one half of mankind be chained to its bottom by fate, for they will be continually undermining it through ignorance or pride.

It is vain to expect virtue from women till they are in some   4 degree independent of men; nay, it is vain to expect that strength of natural affection which would make them good wives and mothers. Whilst they are absolutely dependent on their husbands they will be cunning, mean, and selfish, and the men who can be gratified by the fawning fondness of spaniel-like affection have not much delicacy, for love is not to be bought, in any sense of the words; its silken wings are instantly shrivelled up when anything beside a return in kind is sought. Yet whilst wealth enervates men, and women live, as it were, by their personal charms, how can we expect them to discharge those ennobling duties which equally require exertion and self-denial? Hereditary property sophisticates[2] the mind, and the unfortunate victims to it, if I may so express myself, swathed from their birth, seldom exert the locomotive faculty of body or mind; and, thus viewing everything through one medium, and that a false one, they are unable to discern in what true merit and happiness consist. False, indeed, must be the light when the drapery of situation hides the man, and makes him stalk in masquerade, dragging from one scene of dissipation to another the nerveless limbs that hang with stupid listlessness, and rolling round the vacant eye which plainly tells us that there is no mind at home.

I mean, therefore, to infer[3] that the society is not properly

---

[1]*sycophants* Toadies or false flatterers.
[2]*sophisticates* Ruins or corrupts.
[3]*infer* Imply.

organized which does not compel men and women to discharge their respective duties, by making it the only way to acquire that countenance from their fellow-creatures which every human being wishes some way to attain. The respect, consequently, which is paid to wealth and mere personal charms, is a true north-east blast that blights the tender blossoms of affection and virtue. Nature has wisely attached affections to duties to sweeten toil, and to give that vigour to the exertions of reason which only the heart can give. But the affection which is put on merely because it is the appropriated insignia of a certain character, when its duties are not fulfilled, is one of the empty compliments which vice and folly are obliged to pay to virtue and the real nature of things.

To illustrate my opinion, I need only observe that when a woman is admired for her beauty, and suffers herself to be so far intoxicated by the admiration she receives as to neglect to discharge the indispensable duty of a mother, she sins against herself by neglecting to cultivate an affection that would equally tend to make her useful and happy. True happiness, I mean all the contentment and virtuous satisfaction that can be snatched in this imperfect state, must arise from well regulated affections; and an affection includes a duty. Men are not aware of the misery they cause and the vicious weakness they cherish by only inciting women to render themselves pleasing; they do not consider that they thus make natural and artificial duties clash by sacrificing the comfort and respectability of a woman's life to voluptuous notions of beauty when in nature they all harmonize.

Cold would be the heart of a husband, were he not rendered unnatural by early debauchery, who did not feel more delight at seeing his child suckled by its mother, than the most artful wanton tricks could ever raise; yet this natural way of cementing the matrimonial tie and twisting esteem with fonder recollections, wealth leads women to spurn. To preserve their beauty and wear the flowery crown of the day, which gives them a kind of right to reign for a short time over the sex, they neglect to stamp impressions on their husbands' hearts that would be remembered with more tenderness when the snow on the head began to chill the bosom than even their virgin charms. The maternal solicitude of a reasonable affectionate woman is very interesting, and the chastened dignity with which a mother returns the caresses that she and her child receive from a father who has been fulfilling the serious duties of his station, is not only a respectable but a beautiful sight. So singular indeed are my feelings, and I have endeavored not to catch factitious ones, that after having been fatigued with the sight of insipid grandeur and the slavish ceremonies that with cumbrous pomp supplied the place of domestic affections, I have turned to some other scene to relieve my eye by resting it on the refreshing green everywhere scattered by nature. I have then viewed with pleasure a woman nursing her children, and discharging the duties of her station with, perhaps, merely a servant maid to take off her hands the servile part of the household business. I have seen her prepare herself and children, with only the luxury of cleanliness, to receive her husband, who returning weary home in the evening found smiling babes and a clean hearth. My heart has loitered in the midst of the group, and has even throbbed with sympathetic emotion, when the scraping of the well known foot has raised a pleasing tumult.

Whilst my benevolence has been gratified by contemplating   8 this artless picture, I have thought that a couple of this description, equally necessary and independent of each other, because each ful-filled the respective duties of their station, possessed all that life could give. Raised sufficiently above abject poverty not to be obliged to weigh the consequence of every farthing they spend, and having sufficient to prevent their attending to a frigid system of economy, which narrows both heart and mind, I declare, so vulgar[4] are my conceptions, that I know not what is wanted to render this the happiest as well as the most respectable situation in the world, but a taste for literature, to throw a little variety and interest into social converse, and some superfluous money to give to the needy and to buy books. For it is not pleasant when the heart is opened by compassion and the head active in arranging plans of usefulness, to have a prim urchin continually twitching back the elbow to prevent the hand from drawing out an almost empty purse, whispering at the same time some prudential maxim about the priority of justice.

Destructive, however, as riches and inherited honours are to the human character, women are more debased and cramped, if possible, by them than men, because men may still, in some degree, unfold their faculties by becoming soldiers and statesmen.

As soldiers, I grant, they can now only gather, for the most part, vainglorious laurels, whilst they adjust to a hair the European balance, taking especial care that no bleak northern nook or sound incline the beam.[5] But the days of true heroism are over, when a citizen fought for his country like a Fabricius[6] or a Washington,

---

[4]*vulgar* Common.

[5]*incline the beam* The metaphor is of the balance—the scale that representa-tions of blind justice hold up. Wollstonecraft's point is that in her time soldiers fought to prevent the slightest changes in a balance of power that grew ever more delicate, not in heroic wars with heroic consequences.

[6]*Fabricius (fl. 282 B.C.)* Gaius Fabricius, a worthy Roman general and states-

and then returned to his farm to let his virtuous fervour run in a more placid, but not a less salutary, stream. No, our British heroes are oftener sent from the gaming table than from the plough[7] and their passions have been rather inflamed by hanging with dumb suspense on the turn of a die, than sublimated by panting after the adventurous march of virtue in the historic page.

The statesman, it is true, might with more propriety quit the faro bank, or card table, to guide the helm, for he has still but to shuffle and trick.[8] The whole system of British politics, if system it may courteously be called, consisting in multiplying dependents and contriving taxes which grind the poor to pamper the rich; thus a war, or any wild goose chase, is, as the vulgar use the phrase, a lucky turn-up of patronage for the minister, whose chief merit is the art of keeping himself in place. It is not necessary then that he should have bowels for[9] the poor, so he can secure for his family the odd trick. Or should some show of respect, for what is termed with ignorant ostentation an Englishman's birthright, be expedient to bubble the gruff mastiff[10] that he has to lead by the nose, he can make an empty show very safely by giving his single voice and suffering his light squadron to file off to the other side. And when a question of humanity is agitated he may dip a sop in the milk of human kindness to silence Cerberus,[11] and talk of the interest which his heart takes in an attempt to make the earth no longer cry for vengeance as it sucks in its children's blood, though his cold hand may at the very moment rivet their chains by sanctioning the abominable traffic. A minister is no longer a minister than while he can carry a point which he is determined to carry. Yet it is not necessary that a minister should feel like a man, when a bold push might shake his seat.

But, to have done with these episodical observations, let me   12
return to the more specious slavery which chains the very soul of woman, keeping her for ever under the bondage of ignorance.

The preposterous distinctions of rank, which render civilization

---

man known for resistance to corruption.

[7]*from the plough*   Worthy Roman heroes were humble farmers, not gamblers.

[8]*shuffle and trick*   The upper class spent much of its time gambling: faro is a high-stakes card game. Wollstonecraft is ironic when she says the statesman has "still but to shuffle and trick," but she connects the "training" of faro with the practice of politics in a deft, sardonic fashion. She is punning on the multiple meanings of *shuffle*—to mix up a deck of cards and to move oneself or one's papers about slowly and aimlessly—and *trick*—to win one turn of a card game and to do a devious deed.

[9]*bowels for*   Feelings for; sense of pity.

[10]*to bubble the gruff mastiff*   This means to fool even a guard dog.

[11]*Cerberus*   The guard dog of Hades, the Greek hell or underworld.

a curse by dividing the world between voluptuous tyrants and cunning envious dependents, corrupt, almost equally, every class of people, because respectability is not attached to the discharge of the relative duties of life, but to the station, and when the duties are not fulfilled the affections cannot gain sufficient strength to fortify the virtue of which they are the natural reward. Still there are some loopholes out of which a man may creep, and dare to think and act for himself; but for a woman it is a herculean task, because she has difficulties peculiar to her sex to overcome which require almost superhuman powers.

A truly benevolent legislator always endeavors to make it the interest of each individual to be virtuous; and thus private virtue becoming the cement of public happiness, an orderly whole is consolidated by the tendency of all the parts towards a common centre. But, the private or public virtue of woman is very problematical; for Rousseau, and a numerous list of male writers, insist that she should all her life be subjected to a severe restraint, that of propriety. Why subject her to propriety—blind propriety, if she be capable of acting from a nobler spring, if she be an heir of immortality? Is sugar always to be produced by vital blood? Is one half of the human species, like the poor African slaves, to be subject to prejudices that brutalize them, when principles would be a surer guard, only to sweeten the cup of man? Is not this indirectly to deny woman reason? for a gift is a mockery, if it be unfit for use.

Women are, in common with men, rendered weak and luxurious by the relaxing pleasures which wealth procures; but added to this they are made slaves to their persons, and must render them alluring that man may lend them his reason to guide their tottering steps aright. Or should they be ambitious, they must govern their tyrants by sinister tricks, for without rights there cannot be any incumbent duties. The laws respecting woman, which I mean to discuss in a future part, make an absurd unit of a man and his wife;[12] and then, by the easy transition of only considering him as responsible, she is reduced to a mere cypher.

The being who discharges the duties of its station is independent; and, speaking of women at large, their first duty is to themselves as rational creatures, and the next in point of importance, as citizens, is that which includes so many, of a mother. The rank in life which dispenses with their fulfilling this duty necessarily degrades them by making them mere dolls. Or, should they turn

---

[12]***absurd unit of a man and his wife***   In English law man and wife were legally one; the man spoke for both.

to something more important than merely fitting drapery upon a smooth block, their minds are only occupied by some soft platonic attachment; or, the actual management of an intrigue may keep their thoughts in motion; for when they neglect domestic duties, they have it not in their own power to take the field and march and counter-march like soldiers, or wrangle in the senate to keep their faculties from rusting.

I know that, as a proof of the inferiority of the sex, Rousseau has exultingly exclaimed, How can they leave the nursery for the camp![13] And the camp has by some moralists been termed the school of the most heroic virtues; though, I think, it would puzzle a keen casuist[14] to prove the reasonableness of the greater number of wars that have dubbed heroes. I do not mean to consider this question critically; because, having frequently viewed these freaks of ambition as the first natural mode of civilization, when the ground must be torn up, and the woods cleared by fire and sword, I do not choose to call them pests; but surely the present system of war has little connection with virtue of any denomination, being rather the school of *finesse* and effeminacy than of fortitude.

Yet if defensive war, the only justifiable war, in the present advanced state of society, where virtue can show its face and ripen amidst the rigours which purify the air on the mountain's top, were alone to be adopted as just and glorious, the true heroism of antiquity might again animate female bosoms. But fair and softly, gentle reader, male or female, do not alarm thyself, for though I have compared the character of a modern soldier with that of a civilized woman, I am not going to advise them to turn their distaff[15] into a musket, though I sincerely wish to see the bayonet converted into a pruning-hook. I only recreated an imagination, fatigue by contemplating the vices and follies which all proceed from a feculent[16] stream of wealth that has muddied the pure rills of natural affection, by supposing that society will some time or other be so constituted, that man must necessarily fulfill the duties of a citizen or be despised, and that while he was employed in any of the departments of civil life, his wife, also an active citizen, should be equally intent to manage her family, educate her children, and assist her neighbours.

---

[13]*leave the nursery for the camp!*   Rousseau's Émile complains that women cannot leave a nursery to go to war.

[14]*casuist*   One who argues closely, persistently, and sometimes unfairly.

[15]*distaff*   Instrument to wind wool in the act of spinning, notoriously a job only "fit for women."

[16]*feculent*   Filthy, polluted; related to *feces*.

But, to render her really virtuous and useful, she must not, if she discharge her civil duties, want, individually, the protection of civil laws; she must not be dependent on her husband's bounty for her subsistence during his life or support after his death—for how can a being be generous who has nothing of its own? or virtuous, who is not free?

The wife, in the present state of things, who is faithful to her husband, and neither suckles nor educates her children, scarcely deserves the name of a wife, and has no right to that of a citizen. But take away natural rights, and duties become null.

Women then must be considered as only the wanton solace of men when they become so weak in mind and body that they cannot exert themselves, unless to pursue some frothy pleasure or to invent some frivolous fashion. What can be a more melancholy sight to a thinking mind than to look into the numerous carriages that drive helter-skelter about this metropolis in a morning full of pale-faced creatures who are flying from themselves. I have often wished, with Dr. Johnson,[17] to place some of them in a little shop with half a dozen children looking up to their languid countenances for support. I am much mistaken if some latent vigour would not soon give health and spirit to their eyes, and some lines drawn by the exercise of reason the blank cheeks, which before were only undulated by dimples, might restore lost dignity to the character, or rather enable it to attain the true dignity of its nature. Virtue is not to be acquired even by speculation, much less by the negative supineness that wealth naturally generates.

Besides, when poverty is more disgraceful than even vice, is not morality cut to the quick? Still to avoid misconstruction, though I consider that women in the common walks of life are called to fulfill the duties of wives and mothers, by religion and reason, I cannot help lamenting that women of a superior cast have not a road open by which they can pursue more extensive plans of usefulness and independence. I may excite laughter by dropping a hint which I mean to pursue some future time, for I really think that women ought to have representatives, instead of being arbitrarily governed without having any direct share allowed them in the deliberations of government.

But, as the whole system of representation is now in this country only a convenient handle for despotism, they need not complain,

[20]

---

[17]***Dr. Samuel Johnson (1709–1784)***   The greatest lexicographer and one of the most respected authors of England's eighteenth century. He was known to Mary Wollstonecraft and to her sister, Eliza, a teacher. The reference is to an item published in his *Rambler*, essay 85.

for they are as well represented as a numerous class of hard-working mechanics, who pay for the support of royalty when they can scarcely stop their children's mouths with bread. How are they represented whose very sweat supports the splendid stud of an heir apparent, or varnishes the chariot of some female favourite who looks down on shame? Taxes on the very necessaries of life enable an endless tribe of idle princes and princesses to pass with stupid pomp before a gaping crowd, who almost worship the very parade which costs them so dear. This is mere gothic grandeur, something like the barbarous useless parade of having sentinels on horseback at Whitehall,[18] which I could never view without a mixture of contempt and indignation.

How strangely must the mind be sophisticated when this sort   24
of state impresses it! But, till these monuments of folly are levelled by virtue, similar follies will leaven the whole mass. For the same character, in some degree, will prevail in the aggregate of society; and the refinements of luxury, or the vicious repinings of envious poverty, will equally banish virtue from society, considered as the characteristic of that society, or only allow it to appear as one of the stripes of the harlequin coat worn by the civilized man.

In the superior ranks of life every duty is done by deputies, as if duties could ever be waived, and the vain pleasures which consequent idleness forces the rich to pursue appear so enticing to the next rank that the numerous scramblers for wealth sacrifice everything to tread on their heels. The most sacred trusts are then considered as sinecures, because they were procured by interest, and only sought to enable a man to keep *good company*. Women in particular, all want to be ladies. Which is simply to have nothing to do, but listlessly to go they scarcely care where, for they cannot tell what.

But what have women to do in society? I may be asked, but to loiter with easy grace; surely you would not condemn them all to suckle fools and chronicle small beer![19] No. Women might certainly study the art of healing, and be physicians as well as nurses. And midwifery, decency seems to allot to them, though I am afraid the word midwife in our dictionaries will soon give place to *accoucheur*,[20] and one proof of the former delicacy of the sex be effaced from the language.

They might also study politics, and settle their benevolence on

---

[18]***sentinels on horseback at Whitehall***   This is a reference to the expensive piece of showmanship which continues to our day: the changing of the guard at Whitehall.

[19]***chronicle small beer!***   *Othello* (II.i.158). This means to keep the household accounts.

[20]**accoucheur**   Male version of the female midwife.

the broadest basis; for the reading of history will scarcely be more useful than the perusal of romances, if read as mere biography; if the character of the times, the political improvements, arts, &c., be not observed. In short, if it be not considered as the history of man; and not of particular men, who filled a niche in the temple of fame, and dropped into the black rolling stream of time, that silently sweeps all before it, into the shapeless void called—eternity. For shape, can it be called, "that shape hath none"?[21]

Business of various kinds they might likewise pursue, if they   28 were educated in a more orderly manner, which might save many from common and legal prostitution. Women would not then marry for a support, as men accept of places under government, and neglect the implied duties; nor would an attempt to earn their own subsistence—a most laudable one!—sink them almost to the level of those poor abandoned creatures who live by prostitution. For are not milliners and mantua-makers[22] reckoned the next class? The few employments open to women, so far from being liberal, are menial; and when a superior education enables them to take charge of the education of children as governesses, they are not treated like the tutors of sons, though even clerical tutors are not always treated in a manner calculated to render them respectable in the eyes of their pupils, to say nothing of the private comfort of the individual. But as women educated like gentlewomen are never designed for the humiliating situation which necessity sometimes forces them to fill, these situations are considered in the light of a degradation; and they know little of the human heart, who need to be told that nothing so painfully sharpens sensibility as such a fall in life.

Some of these women might be restrained from marrying by a proper spirit or delicacy, and others may not have had it in their power to escape in this pitiful way from servitude; is not that government then very defective, and very unmindful of the happiness of one half of its members, that does not provide for honest, independent women, by encouraging them to fill respectable stations? But in order to render their private virtue a public benefit, they must have a civil existence in the state, married or single; else we shall continually see some worthy woman, whose sensibility has been rendered painfully acute by undeserved contempt, droop like "the lily broken down by a plowshare."

---

[21]*"that shape hath none"*   The reference is to *Paradise Lost* (II.667) by John Milton (1608–1674); it is an allusion to death.

[22]*milliners and mantua-makers*   Dressmakers, usually women (as tailors were usually men).

It is a melancholy truth—yet such is the blessed effect of civilization!—the most respectable women are the most oppressed; and, unless they have understandings far superior to the common run of understandings, taking in both sexes, they must, from being treated like contemptible beings, become contemptible. How many women thus waste life away the prey of discontent, who might have practiced as physicians, regulated a farm, managed a shop, and stood erect, supported by their own industry, instead of hanging their heads surcharged with the dew of sensibility, that consumes the beauty to which it at first gave lustre; nay, I doubt whether pity and love are so near akin as poets feign, for I have seldom seen much compassion excited by the helplessness of females, unless they were fair; then, perhaps pity was the soft handmaid of love, or the harbinger of lust.

How much more respectable is the woman who earns her own bread by fulfilling any duty, than the most accomplished beauty!—beauty did I say?—so sensible am I of the beauty of moral loveliness, or the harmonious propriety that attunes the passions of a well-regulated mind, that I blush at making the comparison; yet I sigh to think how few women aim at attaining this respectability by withdrawing from the giddy whirl of pleasure, or the indolent calm that stupefies the good sort of women it sucks in.

Proud of their weakness, however, they must always be protected, guarded from care, and all the rough toils that dignify the mind. If this be the fiat of fate, if they will make themselves insignificant and contemptible, sweetly to waste "life away," let them not expect to be valued when their beauty fades, for it is the fate of the fairest flowers to be admired and pulled to pieces by the careless hand that plucked them. In how many ways do I wish, from the purest benevolence, to impress this truth on my sex; yet I fear that they will not listen to a truth that dear-bought experience has brought home to many an agitated bosom, nor willingly resign the privileges of rank and sex for the privileges of humanity, to which those have no claim who do not discharge its duties. 32

Those writers are particularly useful, in my opinion, who make man feel for man, independent of the station he fills, or the drapery of factitious sentiments. I then would fain[23] convince reasonable men of the importance of some of my remarks; and prevail on them to weigh dispassionately the whole tenor of my observations. I appeal to their understandings; and, as a fellow-creature, claim, in the name of my sex, some interest in their hearts. I entreat them

---

[23]*fain* Happily.

to assist to emancipate their companion, to make her a *help meet* for them!

Would men but generously snap our chains, and be content with rational fellowship instead of slavish obedience, they would find us more observant daughters, more affectionate sisters, more faithful wives, more reasonable mothers—in a word, better citizens. We should then love them with true affection, because we should learn to respect ourselves; and, the peace of mind of a worthy man would not be interrupted by the idle vanity of his wife, nor the babes sent to nestle in a strange bosom, having never found a home in their mother's.

QUESTIONS FOR CRITICAL READING

1. Who is the audience for Wollstonecraft's writing? Is she writing more for men than for women? Is it clear from what she says that she has an explicit audience with specific qualities?
2. Analyze paragraph 1 carefully for the use of imagery, especially metaphor. What are the actual effects of these images? Are they overdone?
3. Wollstonecraft begins by attacking property, or the respect paid to it. What does she mean? Does she sustain that line of thought throughout the piece?
4. In paragraph 12, Wollstonecraft speaks of the "bondage of ignorance" in which women are held. Clarify precisely what she means by that expression.
5. In paragraph 30, Wollstonecraft says that people who are treated as if they were contemptible will become contemptible. Is this a political or a psychological judgment?
6. What is the substance of Wollstonecraft's complaint concerning the admiration of women for their beauty?

WRITING ASSIGNMENTS

1. Throughout the chapter Wollstonecraft attacks the unnatural distinctions made between men and women. Establish carefully what those unnatural distinctions are, why they are unnatural, and whether or not such distinctions persist to the present day. By contrast, establish what some natural distinctions between men and women are and whether or not Wollstonecraft has taken them into consideration.
2. References are made throughout the piece to prostitution and to the debaucheries of men. Paragraph 7 specifically refers to the "wanton tricks" of prostitutes. What is Wollstonecraft's attitude toward men in regard to sexuality and their attitudes toward women—both the

women of the brothels and the women with whom they live? Find explicit passages in the piece that you can quote and analyze in an effort to examine her views.

3. In paragraph 2, Wollstonecraft complains that "the respect due only to talents and virtue" is instead being given to people on account of their property. Further, she says in paragraph 9 that riches are "destructive . . . to the human character." Determine carefully, by means of reference to and analysis of specific passages, just what Wollstonecraft means by such statements. Then, use your own anecdotes or "episodical observations" to take a stand on whether these are views you yourself can hold for our time. Are riches destructive to character? Is too much respect paid to those who possess property? If possible, use metaphor, or allusion—literary or personal.

4. In paragraph 4, Wollstonecraft speaks of "men who can be gratified by the fawning fondness of spaniel-like affection" from their women. Search through the essay for other instances of similar views and analyze them carefully. Establish exactly what the men she describes want their women to be like. What do men today want their women to be like? Have today's men changed very much in their expectations? Why? Why not? Use personal observations where possible in answering this question.

5. The question of what roles women ought to have in society is addressed in paragraphs 26, 27, and 28. What are those roles? Why are they defined in terms of work? Do you agree that they are, indeed, the roles that women should assume? Would you include more roles? Do women in our time have greater access to those roles? Consider the question of what women actually did in Wollstonecraft's time and what they do today.

6. **CONNECTIONS** Compare Wollstonecraft's views on the ways in which women are victims of prejudice with the views of Martin Luther King, Jr. How much do women of Wollstonecraft's time have in common with the conditions of African Americans as described by King? What political issues are central to the efforts of both groups to achieve justice and equal opportunity? Might Wollstonecraft have seen herself in the same kind of struggle as King, or would she have drawn sharp distinctions?

FREDERICK DOUGLASS

From *Narrative of the Life of Frederick Douglass, an American Slave*

FREDERICK DOUGLASS (1818–1895) *was born into slavery in Maryland; he died not only a free man but a man who commanded the respect of his country, his government, and hosts of supporters. His owner's wife, Mrs. Hugh Auld, was a Northerner and did not know about the state law forbidding slaves to learn to read and write. This was a lucky accident, indeed: Mrs. Auld taught Douglass enough so that he could begin his own education—and escape to freedom.*

However, it did not take Mrs. Auld long to become much like the slaveowners around her. Douglass tells us that her behavior grew to be even more vicious than the behavior of other slaveowners he knew. The touching point of the excerpt here is that slavery had a negative effect on slave and slaveholder alike. Mrs. Auld unwittingly set Douglass on his path to freedom by implying that he could learn to read. In the process both suffered the consequences of a political system that was inherently oppressive and unjust.

The rest of the Narrative *is filled with stories about Douglass growing up as a slave. He had little connection with his family. His mother, Harriet Bailey, was not able to be close with him, nor was he ever to know who his father was. He records not only the beatings he witnessed as a slave but also the conditions under which he lived and the struggles he felt within himself to be a free man. He himself survived brutal beatings and torture by a professional slave "breaker."*

Since the institution of slavery was legal in the South, police officers in the North were obliged to return runaways. A slave was property. In every sense, Douglass was a person for whom the concept of independence was a kind of imaginative flight of fancy. The entire weight of the government sat on him to make sure he had few, if any, rights.

His description of how he managed to keep his spirits up in this dreadful situation is extraordinary.

After publication of an early version of his life, to avoid capture he spent two years on a speaking tour of Great Britain and Ireland. Douglass then returned to the United States and became the editor of the North Star, *an abolitionist paper in Rochester, New York. One of his chief concerns was for the welfare of the slaves who had managed to secure their freedom. When John Brown invited him to participate in the raid at Harpers Ferry, Virginia, Douglass was famous throughout the North. He refused Brown's invitation because he believed that such an act would not benefit the antislavery cause. When the Civil War began, there were no plans to free the slaves, but Douglass managed to get Lincoln's ear and helped convince the president that it would further the war effort to free them; in 1863 Lincoln delivered the Emancipation Proclamation.*

The years after the war and Lincoln's death were not good for freed slaves. Terrorist groups in both the North and the South worked to keep them from enjoying freedom, and training programs for ex-slaves that might have been effective were never fully instituted. During this time Douglass worked in various capacities for the government—as U.S. minister to Haiti (1889–1891), as assistant secretary of the Santo Domingo Commission, and as an official in Washington, D.C. He was the first African American to become a national figure and to have powerful influence with the government.

DOUGLASS'S RHETORIC

Douglass was basically self-taught, but he knew enough to read the powerful writers of his day. He was a commanding speaker in an age in which eloquence was valued and speakers rewarded handsomely. This excerpt from the Narrative—*Chapters 6, 7, and 8—is notable for its plainness of style. It is direct and clear. The use of the first-person narrative is as simple as one could wish, yet the feelings projected are sincere and moving.*

Douglass's structure is the chronological narrative, telling events in the order in which they occurred. He begins his story at the point of meeting a new mistress, a woman from whom he might have expected kindness. Because she was new to the concept of slavery, she behaved in ways that were unusual, and Douglass remarks on her attitude. Douglass does not interrupt himself with flashbacks or leaps forward in time but tells the story as it happened. At critical moments, he slows the narrative down to describe people or incidents in unusual detail.

By today's standards, Douglass may seem slightly formal. His sentences are often longer than those of modern writers, although they

are always carefully balanced and punctuated by briefer sentences. De-
spite his long paragraphs, heavy with example and description, after
a century and a half, his work remains immediate and moving. No
modern reader will have difficulty responding to what Frederick Doug-
lass has to say. His views on freedom, justice, government, and the
economy are as accessible and as powerful now as when they were
written.

From *Narrative of the Life of Frederick Douglass, an American Slave*

My new mistress proved to be all she appeared when I first met her at the door,—a woman of the kindest heart and finest feelings. She had never had a slave under her control previously to myself, and prior to her marriage she had been dependent upon her own industry for a living. She was by trade a weaver; and by constant application to her business, she had been in a good degree preserved from the blighting and dehumanizing effects of slavery. I was utterly astonished at her goodness. I scarcely knew how to behave towards her. She was entirely unlike any other white woman I had ever seen. I could not approach her as I was accustomed to approach other white ladies. My early instruction was all out of place. The crouching servility, usually so acceptable a quality in a slave, did not answer when manifested toward her. Her favor was not gained by it; she seemed to be disturbed by it. She did not deem it impudent or unmannerly for a slave to look her in the face. The meanest slave was put fully at ease in her presence, and none left without feeling better for having seen her. Her face was made of heavenly smiles, and her voice of tranquil music.

But, alas! this kind heart had but a short time to remain such. The fatal poison of irresponsible power was already in her hands, and soon commenced its infernal work. That cheerful eye, under the influence of slavery, soon became red with rage; that voice, made all of sweet accord, changed to one of harsh and horrid discord; and that angelic face gave place to that of a demon.

Very soon after I went to live with Mr. and Mrs. Auld, she very kindly commenced to teach me the A, B, C. After I had learned this, she assisted me in learning to spell words of three or four letters. Just at this point of my progress, Mr. Auld found out

what was going on, and at once forbade Mrs. Auld to instruct me
further, telling her, among other things, that it was unlawful, as
well as unsafe, to teach a slave to read. To use his own words,
further, he said, "If you give a nigger an inch, he will take an ell.[1]
A nigger should know nothing but to obey his master—to do as
he is told to do. Learning would *spoil* the best nigger in the world.
Now," said he, "if you teach that nigger (speaking of myself) how
to read, there would be no keeping him. It would forever unfit
him to be a slave. He would at once become unmanageable, and
of no value to his master. As to himself, it could do him no good,
but a great deal of harm. It would make him discontented and
unhappy." These words sank deep into my heart, stirred up sentiments within that lay slumbering, and called into existence an entirely new train of thought. It was a new and special revelation,
explaining dark and mysterious things, with which my youthful
understanding had struggled, but struggled in vain. I now understood what had been to me a most perplexing difficulty—to wit,
the white man's power to enslave the black man. It was a grand
achievement, and I prized it highly. From that moment, I understood the pathway from slavery to freedom. It was just what I
wanted, and I got it at a time when I the least expected it. Whilst
I was saddened by the thought of losing the aid of my kind mistress,
I was gladdened by the invaluable instruction which, by the merest
accident, I had gained from my master. Though conscious of the
difficulty of learning without a teacher, I set out with high hope,
and a fixed purpose, at whatever cost of trouble, to learn how to
read. The very decided manner with which he spoke, and strove
to impress his wife with the evil consequences of giving me instruction, served to convince me that he was deeply sensible of the truths
he was uttering. It gave me the best assurance that I might rely
with the utmost confidence on the results which, he said, would
flow from teaching me to read. What he most dreaded, that I most
desired. What he most loved, that I most hated. That which to him
was a great evil, to be carefully shunned, was to me a great good,
to be diligently sought; and the argument which he so warmly
urged, against my learning to read, only served to inspire me with
a desire and determination to learn. In learning to read, I owe almost
as much to the bitter opposition of my master, as to the kindly aid
of my mistress. I acknowledge the benefit of both.

I had resided but a short time in Baltimore before I observed   4
a marked difference, in the treatment of slaves, from that which I
had witnessed in the country. A city slave is almost a freeman,

---

[1] *ell*   A measure about a yard in length.

compared with a slave on the plantation. He is much better fed and clothed, and enjoys privileges altogether unknown to the slave on the plantation. There is a vestige of decency, a sense of shame, that does much to curb and check those outbreaks of atrocious cruelty so commonly enacted upon the plantation. He is a desperate slave-holder, who will shock the humanity of his nonslaveholding neighbors with the cries of his lacerated slave. Few are willing to incur the odium attaching to the reputation of being a cruel master; and above all things, they would not be known as not giving a slave enough to eat. Every city slaveholder is anxious to have it known of him, that he feeds his slaves well; and it is due to them to say, that most of them do give their slaves enough to eat. There are, however, some painful exceptions to this rule. Directly opposite to us, on Philpot Street, lived Mr. Thomas Hamilton. He owned two slaves. Their names were Henrietta and Mary. Henrietta was about twenty-two years of age, Mary was about fourteen; and of all the mangled and emaciated creatures I ever looked upon, these two were the most so. His heart must be harder than stone, that could look upon these unmoved. The head, neck, and shoulders of Mary were literally cut to pieces. I have frequently felt her head, and found it nearly covered with festering sores, caused by the lash of her cruel mistress. I do not know that her master ever whipped her, but I have been an eye-witness to the cruelty of Mrs. Hamilton. I used to be in Mr. Hamilton's house nearly every day. Mrs. Hamilton used to sit in a large chair in the middle of the room, with a heavy cowskin always by her side, and scarce an hour passed during the day but was marked by the blood of one of these slaves. The girls seldom passed her without her saying, "Move faster, you *black gip!*" at the same time giving them a blow with the cowskin over the head or shoulders, often drawing the blood. She would then say, "Take that, you *black gip!*"—continuing, "If you don't move faster, I'll move you!" Added to the cruel lashings to which these slaves were subjected, they were kept nearly half-starved. They seldom knew what it was to eat a full meal. I have seen Mary contending with the pigs for the offal thrown into the street. So much was Mary kicked and cut to pieces, that she was oftener called *"pecked"* than by her name.

I lived in Master Hugh's family about seven years. During this time, I succeeded in learning to read and write. In accomplishing this, I was compelled to resort to various stratagems. I had no regular teacher. My mistress, who had kindly commenced to instruct me, had, in compliance with the advice and direction of her husband, not only ceased to instruct, but had set her face against my being instructed by any one else. It is due, however, to my mistress to say of her, that she did not adopt this course of treatment immediately. She at first lacked the depravity indispensable to shutting me up in mental darkness. It was at least necessary for her to have some training in the exercise of irresponsible power, to make her equal to the task of treating me as though I were a brute.

My mistress was, as I have said, a kind and tender-hearted woman; and in the simplicity of her soul she commenced, when I first went to live with her, to treat me as she supposed one human being ought to treat another. In entering upon the duties of a slaveholder, she did not seem to perceive that I sustained to her the relation of a mere chattel, and that for her to treat me as a human being was not only wrong, but dangerously so. Slavery proved as injurious to her as it did to me. When I went there, she was a pious, warm, and tender-hearted woman. There was no sorrow or suffering for which she had not a tear. She had bread for the hungry, clothes for the naked, and comfort for every mourner that came within her reach. Slavery soon proved its ability to divest her of these heavenly qualities. Under its influence, the tender heart became stone, and the lamblike disposition gave way to one of tiger-like fierceness. The first step in her downward course was in her ceasing to instruct me. She now commenced to practise her husband's precepts. She finally became even more violent in her opposition than her husband himself. She was not satisfied with simply doing as well as he had commanded; she seemed anxious to do better. Nothing seemed to make her more angry than to see me with a newspaper. She seemed to think that here lay the danger. I have had her rush at me with a face made all up of fury, and snatch from me a newspaper, in a manner that fully revealed her apprehension. She was an apt woman; and a little experience soon demonstrated, to her satisfaction, that education and slavery were incompatible with each other.

From this time I was most narrowly watched. If I was in a separate room any considerable length of time, I was sure to be suspected of having a book, and was at once called to give an account of myself. All this, however, was too late. The first step had been taken. Mistress, in teaching me the alphabet, had given me the *inch,* and no precaution could prevent me from taking the *ell.*

The plan which I adopted, and the one by which I was most 8 successful, was that of making friends of all the little white boys whom I met in the street. As many of these as I could, I converted into teachers. With their kindly aid, obtained at different times and in different places, I finally succeeded in learning to read. When I was sent to errands, I always took my book with me, and by going one part of my errand quickly, I found time to get a lesson before my return. I used also to carry bread with me, enough of which was always in the house, and to which I was always welcome; for I was much better off in this regard than many of the poor white children in our neighborhood. This bread I used to bestow upon the hungry little urchins, who, in return, would give me that more valuable bread of knowledge. I am strongly tempted to give the names of two or three of those little boys, as a testimonial of the gratitude and affection I bear them; but prudence forbids;—not that it would injure me, but it might embarrass them; for it is almost an unpardonable offence to teach slaves to read in this Christian country. It is enough to say of the dear little fellows, that they lived on Philpot Street, very near Durgin and Bailey's ship-yard. I used to talk this matter of slavery over with them. I would sometimes say to them, I wished I could be as free as they would be when they got to be men. "You will be free as soon as you are twenty-one, *but I am a slave for life!* Have not I as good a right to be free as you have?" These words used to trouble them; they would express for me the liveliest sympathy, and console me with the hope that something would occur by which I might be free.

I was now about twelve years old, and the thought of being *a slave for life* began to bear heavily upon my heart. Just about this time, I got hold of a book entitled "The Columbian Orator." Every opportunity I got, I used to read this book. Among much of other interesting matter, I found in it a dialogue between a master and his slave. The slave was represented as having run away from his master three times. The dialogue represented the conversation which took place between them, when the slave was retaken the third time. In this dialogue, the whole argument in behalf of slavery was brought forward by the master, all of which was disposed of by the slave. The slave was made to say some very smart as well as impressive things in reply to his master—things which had the desired though unexpected effect; for the conversation resulted in the voluntary emancipation of the slave on the part of the master.

In the same book, I met with one of Sheridan's[2] mighty speeches on and in behalf of Catholic emancipation. These were choice documents to me. I read them over and over again with unabated interest. They gave tongue to interesting thoughts of my own soul, which had frequently flashed through my mind, and died away for want of utterance. The moral which I gained from the dialogue was the power of truth over the conscience of even a slaveholder. What I got

---

[2] *James Brinsley Sheridan (1751–1816)*   Irish dramatist and orator.

from Sheridan was a bold denunciation of slavery, and a powerful vindication of human rights. The reading of these documents enabled me to utter my thoughts, and to meet the arguments brought forward to sustain slavery; but while they relieved me of one difficulty, they brought on another even more painful than the one of which I was relieved. The more I read, the more I was led to abhor and detest my enslavers. I could regard them in no other light than a band of successful robbers, who had left their homes, and gone to Africa, and stolen us from our homes, and in a strange land reduced us to slavery. I loathed them as being the meanest as well as the most wicked of men. As I read and contemplated the subject, behold! that very discontentment which Master Hugh had predicted would follow my learning to read had already come, to torment and sting my soul to unutterable anguish. As I writhed under it, I would at times feel that learning to read had been a curse rather than a blessing. It had given me a view of my wretched condition, without the remedy. It opened my eyes to the horrible pit, but to no ladder upon which to get out. In moments of agony, I envied my fellow-slaves for their stupidity. I have often wished myself a beast. I preferred the condition of the meanest reptile to my own. Any thing, no matter what, to get rid of thinking! It was this everlasting thinking of my condition that tormented me. There was no getting rid of it. It was pressed upon me by every object within sight or hearing, animate or inanimate. The silver trump of freedom had roused my soul to eternal wakefulness. Freedom now appeared, to disappear no more forever. It was heard in every sound, and seen in every thing. It was ever present to torment me with a sense of my wretched condition. I saw nothing without seeing it, I heard nothing without hearing it, and felt nothing without feeling it. It looked from every star, it smiled in every calm, breathed in every wind, and moved in every storm.

I often found myself regretting my own existence, and wishing myself dead; and but for the hope of being free, I have no doubt but that I should have killed myself, or done something for which I should have been killed. While in this state of mind, I was eager to hear any one speak of slavery. I was a ready listener. Every little while, I could hear something about the abolitionists.[3] It was some time before I found what the word meant. It was always used in such connections as to make it an interesting word to me. If a slave ran away and succeeded in getting clear, or if a slave killed his master, set fire to a barn, or did any thing very wrong in the mind

---

[3]*abolitionists*   Those who actively opposed slavery.

of a slaveholder, it was spoken of as the fruit of *abolition*. Hearing
the word in this connection very often, I set about learning what
it meant. The dictionary afforded me little or no help. I found it
was "the act of abolishing"; but then I did not know what was to
be abolished. Here I was perplexed. I did not dare to ask any one
about its meaning, for I was satisfied that it was something they
wanted me to know very little about. After a patient waiting, I got
one of our city papers, containing an account of the number of
petitions from the north, praying for the abolition of slavery in the
District of Columbia, and of the slave trade between the States.
From this time I understood the words *abolition* and *abolitionist,* and
always drew near when that word was spoken, expecting to hear
something of importance to myself and fellow-slaves. The light
broke in upon me by degrees. I went one day down on the wharf
of Mr. Waters; and seeing two Irishmen unloading a scow of stone,
I went, unasked, and helped them. When we had finished, one of
them came to me and asked me if I were a slave. I told him I was.
He asked, "Are ye a slave for life?" I told him that I was. The good
Irishman seemed to be deeply affected by the statement. He said
to the other that it was a pity so fine a little fellow as myself should
be a slave for life. He said it was a shame to hold me. They both
advised me to run away to the north; that I should find friends
there, and that I should be free. I pretended not to be interested in
what they said, and treated them as if I did not understand them;
for I feared they might be treacherous. White men have been known
to encourage slaves to escape, and then, to get the reward, catch
them and return them to their masters. I was afraid that these
seemingly good men might use me so; but I nevertheless remembered their advice, and from that time I resolved to run away. I
looked forward to a time at which it would be safe for me to escape.
I was too young to think of doing so immediately; besides, I wished
to learn how to write, as I might have occasion to write my own
pass. I consoled myself with the hope that I should one day find a
good chance. Meanwhile, I would learn to write.

    The idea as to how I might learn to write was suggested to me   12
by being in Durgin and Bailey's ship-yard, and frequently seeing
the ship carpenters, after hewing, and getting a piece of timber
ready for use, write on the timber the name of that part of the ship
for which it was intended. When a piece of timber was intended
for the larboard side, it would be marked thus—"L." When a piece
was for the starboard side, it would be marked thus—"S." A piece
for the larboard side forward, would be marked thus—"L.F." When
a piece was for starboard side forward, it would be marked thus—
"S.F." For larboard aft, it would be marked thus—"L.A." For

starboard aft, it would be marked thus—"S.A." I soon learned the names of these letters, and for what they were intended when placed upon a piece of timber in the ship-yard. I immediately commenced copying them, and in a short time was able to make the four letters named. After that, when I met with any boy who I knew could write, I would tell him I could write as well as he. The next word would be, "I don't believe you. Let me see you try it." I would then make the letters which I had been so fortunate as to learn, and ask him to beat that. In this way I got a good many lessons in writing, which it is quite possible I should never have gotten in any other way. During this time, my copy-book was the board fence, brick wall, and pavement; my pen and ink was a lump of chalk. With these, I learned mainly how to write. I then commenced and continued copying the Italics in Webster's Spelling Book, until I could make them all without looking on the book. By this time, my little Master Thomas had gone to school, and learned how to write, and had written over a number of copy-books. These had been brought home, and shown to some of our near neighbors, and then laid aside. My mistress used to go to class meeting at the Wilk Street meeting-house every Monday afternoon, and leave me to take care of the house. When left thus, I used to spend the time in writing in the spaces left in Master Thomas's copy-book, copying what he had written. I continued to do this until I could write a hand very similar to that of Master Thomas. Thus, after a long, tedious effort for years, I finally succeeded in learning how to write.

In a very short time after I went to live at Baltimore, my old master's youngest son Richard died; and in about three years and six months after his death, my old master, Captain Anthony, died, leaving only his son, Andrew, and daughter, Lucretia, to share his estate. He died while on a visit to see his daughter at Hillsborough. Cut off thus unexpectedly, he left no will as to the disposal of his property. It was therefore necessary to have a valuation of the property, that it might be equally divided between Mrs. Lucretia and Master Andrew. I was immediately sent for, to be valued with the other property. Here again my feelings rose up in detestation of slavery. I had now a new conception of my degraded condition. Prior to this, I had become, if not insensible to my lot, at least partly so. I left Baltimore with a young heart overborne with sadness, and a soul full of apprehension. I took passage with Captain Rowe, in the schooner Wild Cat, and, after a sail of about twenty-four hours, I found myself near the place of my birth. I had now been absent from it almost, if not quite, five years. I, however, remembered the place very well. I was only about five years old when I left it, to go and live with my old master on Colonel Lloyd's plantation; so that I was now between ten and eleven years old.

We were all ranked together at the valuation. Men and women, old and young, married and single, were ranked with horses, sheep, and swine. There were horses and men, cattle and women, pigs and children, all holding the same rank in the scale of being, and were all subjected to the same narrow examination. Silvery-headed age and sprightly youth, maids and matrons, had to undergo the same indelicate inspection. At this moment, I saw more clearly than ever the brutalizing effects of slavery upon both slave and slaveholder.

After the valuation, then came the division. I have no language to express the high excitement and deep anxiety which were felt among us poor slaves during this time. Our fate for life was now to be decided. We had no more voice in that decision than the brutes among whom we were ranked. A single word from the white men was enough—against all our wishes, prayers, and entreaties—to sunder forever the dearest friends, dearest kindred, and strongest ties known to human beings. In addition to the pain of separation, there was the horrid dread of falling into the hands of Master Andrew. He was known to us all as being a most cruel wretch,—a common drunkard, who had, by his reckless misman-agement and profligate dissipation, already wasted a large portion of his father's property. We all felt that we might as well be sold at once to the Georgia traders, as to pass into his hands; for we knew that that would be our inevitable condition,—a condition held by us all in the utmost horror and dread.

I suffered more anxiety than most of my fellow-slaves. I had 16 known what it was to be kindly treated; they had known nothing of the kind. They had seen little or nothing of the world. They were in very deed men and women of sorrow, and acquainted with grief. Their backs had been made familiar with the bloody lash, so that they had become callous; mine was yet tender; for while at Baltimore I got few whippings, and few slaves could boast of a kinder master and mistress than myself; and the thought of passing out of their hands into those of Master Andrew—a man who, but a few days before, to give me a sample of his bloody disposition, took my little brother by the throat, threw him on the ground, and with the heel of his boot stamped upon his head till the blood gushed from his nose and ears—was well calculated to make me anxious as to my fate. After he had committed this savage outrage upon my brother, he turned to me, and said that was the way he meant to serve me one of these days,—meaning, I suppose, when I came into his possession.

Thanks to a kind Providence, I fell to the portion of Mrs. Lucretia, and was sent immediately back to Baltimore, to live again in the family of Master Hugh. Their joy at my return equalled their sorrow at my departure. It was a glad day to me. I had escaped a worse than lion's jaws. I was absent from Baltimore, for the purpose of valuation and division, just about one month, and it seemed to have been six.

Very soon after my return to Baltimore, my mistress, Lucretia, died, leaving her husband and child, Amanda; and in a very short time after her death, Master Andrew died. Now all the property of my old master, slaves included, was in the hands of strangers,—strangers who had had nothing to do with accumulating it. Not a slave was left free. All remained slaves, from the youngest to the oldest. If any one thing in my experience, more than another, served to deepen my conviction of the infernal character of slavery, and to fill me with unutterable loathing of slaveholders, it was their base ingratitude to my poor old grandmother. She had served my old master faithfully from youth to old age. She had been the source of all his wealth; she had peopled his plantation with slaves; she had become a great grandmother in his service. She had rocked him in infancy, attended him in childhood, served him through life, and at his death wiped from his icy brow the cold death-sweat, and closed his eyes forever. She was nevertheless left a slave—a slave for life—a slave in the hands of strangers; and in their hands she saw her children, her grandchildren, and her great-grandchildren, divided, like so many sheep, without being gratified with the small privilege of a single word, as to their or her own destiny. And, to cap the climax of their base ingratitude and fiendish barbarity, my grandmother, who was now very old, having outlived my old master and all his children, having seen the beginning and end of all of them, and her present owners finding she was of but little value, her frame already racked with the pains of old age, and complete helplessness fast stealing over her once active limbs, they took her to the woods, built her a little hut, put up a little mud-chimney, and then made her welcome to the privilege of supporting herself there in perfect loneliness; thus virtually turning her out to die! If my poor old grandmother now lives, she lives to suffer in utter loneliness; she lives to remember and mourn over the loss of children, the loss of grandchildren, and the loss of great-grandchildren. They are, in the language of the slave's poet, Whittier,[4]—

> Gone, gone, sold and gone
> To the rice swamp dank and lone,
> Where the slave-whip ceaseless swings,
> Where the noisome insect stings,
> Where the fever-demon strews
> Poison with the falling dews,
> Where the sickly sunbeams glare
> Through the hot and misty air:—
>> Gone, gone, sold and gone
>> To the rice swamp dank and lone,
>> From Virginia hills and waters—
>> Woe is me, my stolen daughters!

The hearth is desolate. The children, the unconscious children, who once sang and danced in her presence, are gone. She gropes her way, in the darkness of age, for a drink of water. Instead of the voices of her children, she hears by day the moans of the dove, and by night the screams of the hideous owl. All is gloom. The grave is at the door. And now, when weighed down by the pains and aches of old age, when the head inclines to the feet, when the beginning and ending of human existence meet, and helpless infancy and painful old age combine together—at this time, this most needful time, the time for the exercise of that tenderness and affection which children only can exercise towards a declining parent—my poor old grandmother, the devoted mother of twelve children, is left all alone, in yonder little hut, before a few dim embers. She stands—she sits—she staggers—she falls—she groans—she dies— and there are none of her children or grandchildren present, to wipe from her wrinkled brow the cold sweat of death, or to place beneath the sod her fallen remains. Will not a righteous God visit for these things?

In about two years after the death of Mrs. Lucretia, Master   20 Thomas married his second wife. Her name was Rowena Hamilton. She was the eldest daughter of Mr. William Hamilton. Master now lived in St. Michael's. Not long after his marriage, a misunderstanding took place between himself and Master Hugh; and as a means of punishing his brother, he took me from him to live with himself at St. Michael's. Here I underwent another most painful

---

[4]*John Greenleaf Whittier (1807–1892)*   New England abolitionist, journalist, and poet. The poem Douglass cites is "The Farewell" (1835).

separation. It, however, was not so severe as the one I dreaded at the division of property; for, during this interval, a great change had taken place in Master Hugh and his once kind and affectionate wife. The influence of brandy upon him, and of slavery upon her, had effected a disastrous change in the characters of both; so that, as far as they were concerned, I thought I had little to lose by the change. But it was not to them that I was attached. It was to those little Baltimore boys that I felt the strongest attachment. I had received many good lessons from them, and was still receiving them, and the thought of leaving them was painful indeed. I was leaving, too, without the hope of ever being allowed to return. Master Thomas had said he would never let me return again. The barrier betwixt himself and brother he considered impassable.

I then had to regret that I did not at least make the attempt to carry out my resolution to run away; for the chances of success are tenfold greater from the city than from the country.

I sailed from Baltimore for St. Michael's in the sloop Amanda, Captain Edward Dodson. On my passage, I paid particular attention to the direction which the steamboats took to go to Philadelphia. I found, instead of going down, on reaching North Point they went up the bay, in a north-easterly direction. I deemed this knowledge of the utmost importance. My determination to run away was again revived. I resolved to wait only so long as the offering of a favorable opportunity. When that came, I was determined to be off.

QUESTIONS FOR CRITICAL READING

1. What are the "dehumanizing effects of slavery"? Do they apply only to the slave, or also to the owner?
2. What does Douglass mean by the "fatal poison of irresponsible power"?
3. Why were the slave's circumstances better in a city than in the country?
4. Why did Mrs. Hamilton beat her slaves?
5. Which passage do you feel contains the best description in the essay? What is the purpose of the description, and what effect does it have on you?

WRITING ASSIGNMENTS

1. In paragraph 3, Douglass describes his experiences learning to read with Mrs. Auld. Why would literate slaves be such a problem for

slaveholders? Why would slaveowners consider ignorance an advantage in slaves? Mr. Auld explains that learning to read would make Douglass "forever unfit" to be a slave. Explain how Douglass's reading and learning promote a sense of liberty.

2. How did Mrs. Auld's personality change through the experience of owning slaves? Douglass assures us that she was "a kind and tenderhearted woman," but her behavior soon comes to resemble that of other slaveholders. How did her behavior alter, and what circumstances contributed to the change? Why does Douglass tell us about the changes?

3. What, on the whole, is Douglass's attitude toward white people? Examine his statements about them, and establish as far as possible his feelings regarding their character. Is he bitter about his slavery experiences?

4. How effective is the detailed description in the essay? Select the best descriptive passages and analyze them for their effectiveness in context. Why does Douglass lavish so much attention on such description? What does he hope to accomplish by it?

5. What is the most important political issue raised in the essay? Douglass never talks about the law, but he implies a great deal about justice. What is the political truth regarding the law in Maryland in this time? What is the relationship between politics and justice in this essay?

6. **CONNECTIONS** Which of the political writers in this section would Douglass most agree with: Lao-Tzu, Machiavelli, Wollstonecraft, or Jefferson? Which would the slaveholders agree with? What political ideals does Douglass hold? Do they seem to have their sources in any of these writers?

HENRY DAVID THOREAU
Civil Disobedience

HENRY DAVID THOREAU *(1817–1862) began keeping a journal when he graduated from Harvard in 1837. The journal was preserved and published, and it shows us the seriousness, determination, and elevation of moral values characteristic of all his work. He is best known for* Walden *(1854), a record of his departure from the warm congeniality of Concord, Massachusetts—and the home of his close friend, Ralph Waldo Emerson (1803–1882)—for the comparative "wilds" of Walden Pond, where he built a cabin, planted a garden, and lived simply.* Walden *tells of the deadening influence of ownership and extols the vitality and spiritual uplift that comes from living close to nature. It also argues that civilization's comforts sometimes rob a person of independence, integrity, and even conscience.*

Thoreau and Emerson were prominent among the group of writers and thinkers who were styled the Transcendentalists. They believed in something that transcended the limits of sensory experience; in other words, something that transcended materialism. Their philosophy was based on the works of Immanuel Kant (1724–1804), the German idealist philosopher; Samuel Taylor Coleridge (1772–1834), the English poet; and Johann Wolfgang von Goethe (1749–1832), the German dramatist and thinker. These writers praised human intuition and the capacity to see beyond the limits of common experience.

Their philosophical idealism carried over into the plainer social concerns of the day, expressing itself in works such as Walden *and "Civil Disobedience," which was published with the title "Resistance to Civil Government," in 1849, a year after the publication of* The Communist Manifesto. *Although Thoreau all but denies his idealism in "Civil Disobedience," it is obvious that after having spent a night in the Concord jail, he had realized he could not quietly accept his* government's behavior in regard to slavery. He had begun to feel that it was not only appropriate but imperative to disobey unjust laws.

In Thoreau's time the most flagrantly unjust laws were those that supported slavery. The Transcendentalists were strongly opposed to slavery and spoke out against it. Abolitionists in Massachusetts actively harbored escaped slaves and helped them move to Canada and freedom. The Fugitive Slave Act, enacted in 1850, the year after "Civil Disobedience" was published, made Thoreau a criminal because he refused to comply with Massachusetts civil authorities when in 1851 they began to return escaped slaves to the South as the law required.

"Civil Disobedience" has been much more influential in the twentieth century than it was in the nineteenth. Mohandas Gandhi (1869–1948) claimed that while he was editor of an Indian newspaper in South Africa, it helped to inspire his theories of nonviolent resistance. Gandhi eventually brought the British Empire to heel by implementing these theories, helping to win independence for India. In the 1960s, Martin Luther King, Jr., applied the same theories in the fight for racial equality in the United States. Thoreau's essay once again assumed great import during the latter days of the Vietnam War, when many young men resisted being drafted because they believed that the war was unjust.

"Civil Disobedience" was written after the Walden experience (which began on July 4, 1845, and ended September 6, 1847), when Thoreau quietly returned to Emerson's home. He also returned to "civilization" and discovered that his refusal to pay the Massachusetts poll tax—not a tax on voting but a "per head" tax imposed on all citizens to help support the Mexican War—landed him in the Concord jail. He spent just one day and one night there—his aunt paid the tax for him—but the experience was so extraordinary that he began examining it in his journal.

THOREAU'S RHETORIC

Thoreau's habit of writing in his journal lasted throughout his life, and though he intended to become a poet after college, he was soon convinced that one of the few ways he could hope to earn a living was by writing. However, he made more money from lecturing on the lyceum circuit. The lyceum, an institution in most New England towns, resembled a kind of adult education program, featuring important speakers such as the very successful Emerson and foreign lecturers. The fees were very reasonable, and in the absence of other popular entertainment, the lyceum was a popular proving ground for speakers interested in promoting their ideas.

Thus, "Civil Disobedience" went through three stages of development. First, its outlines were rough-hewn in the journal, where the main ideas appear, and where experiments in phrasing began. (Thoreau was a constant reviser.) In February 1848, "Civil Disobedience" was first delivered as a lecture at the Concord Lyceum. It urged people of conscience to actively resist a government that acted badly. It was finally written down for publication in Aesthetic Papers, a proper intellectual journal edited by Elizabeth Peabody (1804–1894), the sister-in-law of another important New England writer, Nathaniel Hawthorne (1804–1864). There it was refined again, and certain important details were added.

"Civil Disobedience" bears many of the hallmarks of the spoken lecture. For one thing, it is written in the first person and addresses an audience that Thoreau expects will share many of his sentiments but certainly not all his conclusions. His message is to some extent anarchistic, virtually denying government any authority or respect. Political conservatives generally take his opening quote, "That government is best which governs least," as a rallying cry to help reduce the interference of government in everyday affairs. Such conservatives usually mean by this a reduction in the government's capacity to tax wealth for unpopular causes. Communists, too, see the essay as offering support for their cause. But in fact what Thoreau opposes is quite simply any government that is not totally just, totally moral, and totally respectful of the individual.

The easiness of the pace of the essay also derives from its original form as a speech. Even such locutions as "But, to speak practically and as a citizen" (para. 3) obviously connect the essay with its origins. We can imagine that Thoreau himself was able to impart emphasis where it was demanded in the speech—although it is often said that he was certainly not an overwhelming orator. In fact, short and somewhat homely, he was an unprepossessing figure. Therefore, he was careful to ensure that his writing achieved what for some speakers might have been accomplished by means of gesture and theatrics.

Thoreau's language is marked by clarity. He speaks directly to every issue, stating his own position and recommending the position he feels his audience should accept as reasonable and moral people. One impressive achievement in this selection is Thoreau's capacity to shape memorable, virtually aphoristic statements that remain "quotable" generations later, beginning with his own quotation from the words of John L. O'Sullivan: "That government is best which governs least." Thoreau calls it a motto, as if it belonged on the great seal of a government, or on a coin. It contains an interesting and impressive rhetorical flourish; the device of repeating "govern" and almost rhyming "best" with "least."

His most memorable statements show considerable attention to the rhetorical qualities of balance, repetition, and pattern. "The only obligation which I have a right to assume is to do at any time what I think right" (para. 4) uses the word "right" in two senses: first as a matter of personal volition; second, as a matter of moral rectitude. One's rights, in other words, become the opportunity to do right. "For it matters not how small the beginning may seem to be: what is once well done is done forever" (para. 21) also relies on repetition for its effect, as well as balancing the concept of a beginning with its capacity to reach out into the future. The use of the rhetorical device of chiasmus, a crisscross relationship between key words, marks "Under a government which imprisons any unjustly, the true place for a just man is also a prison" (para. 22). Here is the pattern:

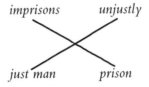

Such attention to phrasing is typical of speakers whose expressions must catch and retain the attention of listeners. They do not have the advantage of referring to a text, so the spoken words must be forceful.

Thoreau relies also on analogy, comparing men with machines, people with plants, even the citizen with states considering secession from the Union. His analogies are effective and thus worth examining in some detail. He draws on the analysis of circumstance throughout the essay, carefully examining government actions to determine their qualities and their results.

His questions include comments on politics (para. 1); on the Bible (para. 23); on Confucius (para. 24); and finally on his contemporary, Daniel Webster (1782–1852) (para. 41), demonstrating a wide range of influence but avoiding the pedantic tone that can come from using quotations too liberally or from citing obscure sources. Taken all in all, this essay is simple, direct, and uncluttered. Its influence is in part due to the clarity and grace that characterize Thoreau's writing at its best.

Civil Disobedience

I heartily accept the motto—"That government is best which governs least,"[1] and I should like to see it acted up to more rapidly and systematically. Carried out, it finally amounts to this, which also I believe—"That government is best which governs not at all"; and when men are prepared for it, that will be the kind of government which they will have. Government is at best but an expedient; but most governments are usually, and all governments are sometimes, inexpedient. The objections which have been brought against a standing army, and they are many and weighty, and deserve to prevail, may also at last be brought against a standing government. The standing army is only an arm of the standing government. The government itself, which is only the mode which the people have chosen to execute their will, is equally liable to be abused and perverted before the people can act through it. Witness the present Mexican war,[2] the work of comparatively a few individuals using the standing government as their tool; for in the outset the people would not have consented to this measure.

This American government—what is it but a tradition, a recent one, endeavoring to transmit itself unimpaired to posterity but each instant losing some of its integrity? It has not the vitality and force of a single living man; for a single man can bend it to his will. It is a sort of wooden gun to the people themselves. But it is not the less necessary for this; for the people must have some complicated machinery or other, and hear its din, to satisfy that idea of government which they have. Governments show thus how successfully men can be imposed on, even impose on themselves, for their own advantage. It is excellent, we must all allow. Yet this government never of itself furthered any enterprise but by the alacrity with which it got out of its way. *It* does not keep the country free. *It* does not settle the West. *It* does not educate. The character inherent in the American people has done all that has been accomplished;

---

[1] *. . . governs least* John L. O'Sullivan (1813–1895) wrote in the *United States Magazine and Democratic Review* (1837) that "all government is evil, and the parents of evil. . . . The best government is that which governs least." Thomas Jefferson wrote, "That government is best which governs the least, because its people discipline themselves." Both comments echo the *Tao-te Ching*.

[2] *the present Mexican war (1846–1848)* The war was extremely unpopular in New England because it was an act of a bullying government anxious to grab land from a weaker nation. The United States had annexed Texas in 1845, precipitating a welcome retaliation from Mexico.

and it would have done somewhat more if the government had not sometimes got in its way. For government is an expedient by which men would fain succeed in letting one another alone; and, as has been said, when it is most expedient the governed are most let alone by it. Trade and commerce, if they were not made of India-rubber, would never manage to bounce over the obstacles which legislators are continually putting in their way; and, if one were to judge these men wholly by the effects of their actions and not partly by their intentions, they would deserve to be classed and punished with those mischievous persons who put obstructions on the railroads.

But to speak practically and as a citizen, unlike those who call themselves no-government men, I ask for, not at once no government, but *at once* a better government. Let every man make known what kind of government would command his respect, and that will be one step toward obtaining it.

After all, the practical reason why, when the power is once in   4 the hands of the people, a majority are permitted, and for a long period continue, to rule is not because they are most likely to be in the right, nor because this seems fairest to the minority but because they are physically the strongest. But a government in which the majority rule in all cases cannot be based on justice, even as far as men understand it. Can there not be a government in which majorities do not virtually decide right and wrong but con-science?—in which majorities decide only those questions to which the rule of expediency is applicable? Must the citizen ever for a moment, or in the least degree, resign his conscience to the legisla-tor? Why has every man a conscience then? I think that we should be men first and subjects afterward. It is not desirable to cultivate a respect for the law, so much as for the right. The only obligation which I have a right to assume is to do at any time what I think right. It is truly enough said that a corporation has no conscience; but a corporation of conscientious men is a corporation *with* a conscience. Law never made men a whit more just; and, by means of their respect for it, even the well-disposed are daily made the agents of injustice. A common and natural result of an undue respect for law is that you may see a file of soldiers, colonel, captain, corporal, privates, powder-monkeys,[3] and all, marching in admi-rable order over hill and dale to the wars, against their wills, ay, against their common sense and consciences, which makes it very steep marching indeed and produces a palpitation of the heart. They have no doubt that it is a damnable business in which they are

---

[3] *powder-monkeys*   The boys who delivered gunpowder to cannons.

concerned; they are all peaceably inclined. Now, what are they? Men at all? or small movable forts and magazines at the service of some unscrupulous man in power? Visit the Navy-Yard,[4] and behold a marine, such a man as an American government can make, or such as it can make a man with its black arts—a mere shadow and reminiscence of humanity, a man laid out alive and standing, and already, as one may say, buried under arms with funeral accompaniments, though it may be—

> Not a drum was heard, not a funeral note,
> As his corse to the rampart we hurried;
> Not a soldier discharged his farewell shot
> O'er the grave where our hero we buried.[5]

The mass of men serve the state thus, not as men mainly, but as machines, with their bodies. They are the standing army, and the militia, jailers, constables, posse comitatus,[6] &c. In most cases there is no free exercise whatever of the judgment or of the moral sense; but they put themselves on a level with wood and earth and stones; and wooden men can perhaps be manufactured that will serve the purpose as well. Such command no more respect than men of straw or a lump of dirt. They have the same sort of worth only as horses and dogs. Yet such as these even are commonly esteemed good citizens. Others—as most legislators, politicians, lawyers, ministers, and office-holders—serve the state chiefly with their heads; and, as they rarely make any moral distinctions, they are as likely to serve the Devil, without *intending* it, as God. A very few, as heroes, patriots, martyrs, reformers in the great sense, and *men,* serve the state with their consciences also and so necessarily resist it for the most part; and they are commonly treated as enemies by it. A wise man will only be useful as a man and will not submit to be "clay" and "stop a hole to keep the wind away," but leave that office to his dust at least:

> I am too high-born to be propertied,
> To be a secondary at control,
> Or useful serving-man and instrument
> To any sovereign state throughout the world.[7]

---

[4]***Navy-Yard*** This is apparently the United States Naval yard at Boston.

[5]These lines are from "Burial of Sir John Moore at Corunna" (1817) by the Irish poet Charles Wolfe (1791–1823).

[6]***posse comitatus*** Literally, the power of the country; it means a law-enforcement group made up of ordinary citizens.

[7]***"clay," "stop a hole . . . wind away," I am too high-born. . . .*** These lines are from Shakespeare; the first is from *Hamlet,* V.i.236–237. The verse is from *King John,* V.ii.79–82.

He who gives himself entirely to his fellow-men appears to them useless and selfish; but he who gives himself partially to them is pronounced a benefactor and philanthropist.

How does it become a man to behave toward this American government today? I answer, that he cannot without disgrace be associated with it. I cannot for an instant recognize that political organization as *my* government which is the *slave's* government also.

All men recognize the right of revolution; that is, the right to 8 refuse allegiance to, and to resist the government when its tyranny or its inefficiency are great and unendurable. But almost all say that such is not the case now. But such was the case, they think, in the Revolution of '75. If one were to tell me that this was a bad government because it taxed certain foreign commodities brought to its ports, it is most probable that I should not make an ado about it, for I can do without them. All machines have their friction; and possibly this does enough good to counterbalance the evil. At any rate, it is a great evil to make a stir about it. But when the friction comes to have its machine, and oppression and robbery are organized, I say let us not have such a machine any longer. In other words, when a sixth of the population of a nation which has undertaken to be the refuge of liberty are slaves, and a whole country is unjustly overrun and conquered by a foreign army and subjected to military law, I think that it is not too soon for honest men to rebel and revolutionize. What makes this duty the more urgent is the fact that the country so overrun is not our own, but ours is the invading army.

Paley,[8] a common authority with many on moral questions, in his chapter on the "Duty of Submission to Civil Government," resolves all civil obligation into expediency; and he proceeds to say, "that so long as the interest of the whole society requires it, that is, so long as the established government cannot be resisted or charged without public inconveniency, it is the will of God that the established government be obeyed, and no longer. . . . This principle being admitted, the justice of every particular case of resistance is reduced to a computation of the quantity of the danger and grievance on the one side, and of the probability and expense of redressing it on the other." Of this, he says, every man shall judge for himself. But Paley appears never to have contemplated

---

[8]***William Paley (1743–1805)***   An English theologian who lectured widely on moral philosophy. Paley is famous for *A View of the Evidences of Christianity* (1794). "Duty of Submission to Civil Government Explained" is Chapter 3 of Book 6 of *The Principles of Moral and Political Philosophy* (1785).

those cases to which the rule of expediency does not apply, in which a people, as well as an individual, must do justice, cost what it may. If I have unjustly wrested a plank from a drowning man, I must restore it to him though I drown myself. This, according to Paley, would be inconvenient. But he that would save his life, in such a case, shall lose it. This people must cease to hold slaves and to make war on Mexico, though it cost them their existence as a people.

In their practice, nations agree with Paley; but does anyone think that Massachusetts does exactly what is right at the present crisis?

> A drab of state, a cloth-o'-silver slut,
> To have her train borne up, and her soul trail in the dirt.[9]

Practically speaking, the opponents to a reform in Massachusetts are not a hundred thousand politicians at the South but a hundred thousand merchants and farmers here, who are more interested in commerce and agriculture than they are in humanity, and are not prepared to do justice to the slave and to Mexico, *cost what it may.* I quarrel not with far-off foes but with those who, near at home, co-operate with, and do the bidding of, those far away, and without whom the latter would be harmless. We are accustomed to say that the mass of men are unprepared; but improvement is slow because the few are not materially wiser or better than the many. It is not so important that many should be as good as you as that there be some absolute goodness somewhere; for that will leaven the whole lump. There are thousands who are *in opinion* opposed to slavery and to the war who yet in effect do nothing to put an end to them; who, esteeming themselves children of Washington and Franklin, sit down with their hands in their pockets and say that they know not what to do, and do nothing; who even postpone the question of freedom to the question of free trade, and quietly read the prices-current along with the latest advices from Mexico after dinner and, it may be, fall asleep over them both. What is the price-current of an honest man and patriot today? They hesitate and they regret and sometimes they petition; but they do nothing in earnest and with effect. They will wait, well disposed, for others to remedy the evil, that they may no longer have it to regret. At most, they give only a cheap vote, and a feeble countenance and God-speed, to the right, as it goes by them. There are nine hundred and ninety-nine patrons

---

[9]*A drab. . . .*   From Cyril Tourneur (1575?–1626), *Revenger's Tragedy* (1607), IV.iv.70–72. "Drab" is an obsolete term for a prostitute. Thoreau quotes the lines to imply that Massachusetts is a "painted lady" with a defiled soul.

of virtue to one virtuous man. But it is easier to deal with the real possessor of a thing than with the temporary guardian of it.

All voting is a sort of gaming, like checkers or backgammon, with a slight moral tinge to it, a playing with right and wrong, with moral questions; and betting naturally accompanies it. The character of the voters is not staked. I cast my vote, perchance, as I think right; but I am not vitally concerned that that right should prevail. I am willing to leave it to the majority. Its obligation, therefore, never exceeds that of expediency. Even voting *for the right* is *doing* nothing for it. It is only expressing to men feebly your desire that it should prevail. A wise man will not leave the right to the mercy of chance, nor wish it to prevail through the power of the majority. There is but little virtue in the action of masses of men. When the majority shall at length vote for the abolition of slavery, it will be because they are indifferent to slavery, or because there is but little slavery left to be abolished by their vote. *They* will then be the only slaves. Only *his* vote can hasten the abolition of slavery who asserts his own freedom by his vote.

I hear of a convention to be held at Baltimore,[10] or elsewhere, for the selection of a candidate for the Presidency, made up chiefly of editors, and men who are politicians by profession; but I think, what is it to any independent, intelligent, and respectable man what decision they may come to? Shall we not have the advantage of his wisdom and honesty nevertheless? Can we not count upon some independent votes? Are there not many individuals in the country who do not attend conventions? But no: I find that the responsible man, so called, has immediately drifted from his position, and despairs of his country when his country has more reason to despair of him. He forthwith adopts one of the candidates thus selected as the only *available* one, thus proving that he is himself *available* for any purposes of the demagogue. His vote is of no more worth than that of any unprincipled foreigner or hireling native who may have been bought. O for a man who is a *man* and, as my neighbor says has a bone in his back which you cannot pass your hand through! Our statistics are at fault: the population has been returned too large. How many *men* are there to a square thousand miles in this country? Hardly one. Does not America offer any inducement for men to settle here? The American has dwindled into an Odd Fellow[11]—one who may be known by the development of his organ

12

---

[10]***Baltimore***   In 1848 the political environment was particularly intense; it was a seedbed for theoreticians of the Confederacy, which was only beginning to be contemplated seriously.

[11]***Odd Fellow***   The Independent Order of Odd Fellows, a fraternal and benevo-

of gregariousness and a manifest lack of intellect and cheerful self-reliance; whose first and chief concern, on coming into the world, is to see that the Almshouses are in good repair; and, before yet he has lawfully donned the virile garb, to collect a fund for the support of the widows and orphans that may be; who, in short, ventures to live only by the aid of the Mutual Insurance Company, which has promised to bury him decently.

It is not a man's duty, as a matter of course, to devote himself to the eradication of any, even the most enormous wrong; he may still properly have other concerns to engage him; but it is his duty, at least, to wash his hands of it and, if he gives it no thought longer, not to give it practically his support. If I devote myself to other pursuits and contemplations, I must first see, at least, that I do not pursue them sitting upon another man's shoulders. I must get off him first, that he may pursue his contemplations too. See what gross inconsistency is tolerated. I have heard some of my townsmen say, "I should like to have them order me out to help put down an insurrection of the slaves, or to march to Mexico—see if I would go"; and yet these very men have each directly by their allegiance and so indirectly, at least, by their money, furnished a substitute. The soldier is applauded who refuses to serve in an unjust war by those who do not refuse to sustain the unjust government which makes the war; is applauded by those whose own act and authority he disregards and sets at naught; as if the State were penitent to that degree that it hired one to scourge it while it sinned, but not to that degree that it left off sinning for a moment. Thus, under the name of Order and Civil Government, we are all made at last to pay homage to and support our own meanness. After the first blush of sin comes its indifference; and from immoral it becomes, as it were, *un*moral, and not quite unnecessary to that life which we have made.

The broadest and most prevalent error requires the most disinterested virtue to sustain it. The slight reproach to which the virtue of patriotism is commonly liable, the noble are most likely to incur. Those who, while they disapprove of the character and measures of a government, yield to it their allegiance and support, are undoubtedly its most conscientious supporters, and so frequently the most serious obstacles to reform. Some are petitioning the State to dissolve the Union, to disregard the requisitions of the President. Why do they not dissolve it themselves—the union between them-

---

lent secret society, founded in England in the eighteenth century and first established in the United States in 1819 in Baltimore.

selves and the State—and refuse to pay their quota into its treasury? Do not they stand in the same relation to the State that the State does to the Union? And have not the same reasons prevented the State from resisting the Union which have prevented them from resisting the State?

How can a man be satisfied to entertain an opinion merely, and enjoy *it?* Is there any enjoyment in it if his opinion is that he is aggrieved? If you are cheated out of a single dollar by your neighbor, you do not rest satisfied with knowing that you are cheated, or with saying that you are cheated, or even with petitioning him to pay you your due; but you take effectual steps at once to obtain the full amount and see that you are never cheated again. Action from principle, the perception and the performance of right, changes things and relations; it is essentially revolutionary and does not consist wholly with anything which was. It not only divides states and churches, it divides families; ay, it divides the *individual,* separating the diabolical in him from the divine.

Unjust laws exist: shall we be content to obey them, or shall we   16
endeavor to amend them and obey them until we have succeeded, or shall we transgress them at once? Men generally, under such a government as this, think that they ought to wait until they have persuaded the majority to alter them. They think that if they should resist the remedy would be worse than the evil. *It* makes it worse. Why is it not more apt to anticipate and provide for reform? Why does it not cherish its wise minority? Why does it cry and resist before it is hurt? Why does it not encourage its citizens to be on the alert to point out its faults and *do* better than it would have them? Why does it always crucify Christ and excommunicate Copernicus and Luther[12] and pronounce Washington and Franklin rebels?

One would think that a deliberate and practical denial of its authority was the only offence never contemplated by government; else why has it not assigned its definite, its suitable and proportionate penalty? If a man who has no property refuses but once to earn nine shillings for the State, he is put in prison for a period unlimited by any law that I know, and determined only by the discretion of those who placed him there; but if he should steal ninety times nine shillings from the State, he is soon permitted to go at large again.

If the injustice is part of the necessary friction of the machine

---

[12]***Nicolaus Copernicus (1473–1543) and Martin Luther (1483–1546)***   Copernicus revolutionized astronomy and the way humankind perceives the universe; Luther was a religious revolutionary who began the Reformation and created the first Protestant faith.

of government, let it go, let it go: perchance it will wear smooth—certainly the machine will wear out. If the injustice has a spring or a pulley or a rope or a crank exclusively for itself, then perhaps you may consider whether the remedy will not be worse than the evil; but if it is of such a nature that it requires you to be the agent of injustice to another, then I say break the law. Let your life be a counter friction to stop the machine. What I have to do is to see, at any rate, that I do not lend myself to the wrong which I condemn.

As for adopting the ways which the State has provided for remedying the evil, I know not of such ways. They take too much time, and a man's life will be gone. I have other affairs to attend to. I came into this world, not chiefly to make this a good place to live in, but to live in it, be it good or bad. A man has not everything to do, but something; and because he cannot do *every-thing,* it is not necessary that he should do *something* wrong. It is not my business to be petitioning the Governor or the Legislature any more than it is theirs to petition me; and if they should not hear my petition what should I do then? But in this case the State has provided no way: its very Constitution is the evil. This may seem to be harsh and stubborn and unconciliatory; but it is to treat with the utmost kindness and consideration the only spirit that can appreciate or deserves it. So is all change for the better, like birth and death, which convulse the body.

I do not hesitate to say that those who call themselves Abolition-ists should at once effectually withdraw their support, both in person and property, from the government of Massachusetts, and not wait till they constitute a majority of one before they suffer the right to prevail through them. I think that it is enough if they have God on their side, without waiting for that other one. Moreover, any man more right than his neighbors constitutes a majority of one already.

I meet this American government or its representative, the State government, directly and face to face once a year—no more—in the person of its tax-gatherer; this is the only mode in which a man situated as I am necessarily meets it; and it then says distinctly, Recognize me; and the simplest, the most effectual and, in the present posture of affairs, the indispensablest mode of treating with it on this head, of expressing your little satisfaction with and love for it, is to deny it then. My civil neighbor, the tax-gatherer, is the very man I have to deal with—for it is, after all, with men and not with parchment that I quarrel—and he has voluntarily chosen to be an agent of the government. How shall he ever know well what he is and does as an officer of the government, or as a man, until he is obliged to consider whether he shall treat me, his neighbor, for whom he has respect, as a neighbor and well-disposed man, or as a maniac and disturber of the peace, and see if he can get over this obstruction to his neighborliness without a ruder and more impetuous thought or speech corresponding with his action. I know this well, that if one thousand, if one hundred, if ten men whom I could name—if ten *honest* men only—ay, if *one* HONEST man in this State of Massachusetts, *ceasing to hold slaves,* were actually to withdraw from this copartnership and be locked up in the county jail therefor, it would be the abolition of slavery in America. For it matters not how small the beginning may seem to be: what is once well done is done forever. But we love better to talk about it: that we say is our mission. Reform keeps many scores of newspapers in its service but not one man. If my esteemed neighbor,[13] the State's ambassador, who will devote his days to the settlement of the question of human rights in the Council Chamber, instead of being threatened with the prisons of Carolina, were to sit down the prisoner of Massachusetts, that State which is so anxious to foist the sin of slavery upon her sister—though at present she can discover only an act of inhospitality to be the ground of a quarrel with her—the Legislature would not wholly waive the subject the following winter.

Under a government which imprisons any unjustly, the true place for a just man is also a prison. The proper place today, the only place which Massachusetts has provided for her freer and less desponding spirits is in her prisons, to be put out and locked out of the State by her own act, as they have already put themselves out by their principles. It is there that the fugitive slave and the Mexican prisoner on parole and the Indian come to plead the wrongs of his race should find them; on that separate but more free and honorable ground where the State places those who are not *with* her but *against* her—the only house in a slave State in which a free man can abide with honor. If any think that their influence would be lost there, and their voices no longer afflict the ear of the State, that they would not be as an enemy within its walls, they do not know by how much truth is stronger than error, nor how much more eloquently and effectively he can combat injustice who has experienced a little in his own person. Cast your whole vote, not a strip of paper merely, but your whole influence. A minority is

---

[13]*esteemed neighbor* Thoreau refers to Samuel Hoar (1778–1856), a Massachusetts congressman, who went to South Carolina to protest that state's practice of seizing black seamen from Massachusetts ships and enslaving them. South Carolina threatened Hoar and drove him out of the state. He did not secure the justice he demanded.

powerless while it conforms to the majority; it is not even a minority then; but it is irresistible when it clogs by its whole weight. If the alternative is to keep all just men in prison or give up war and slavery, the State will not hesitate which to choose. If a thousand men were not to pay their tax-bills this year, that would not be a violent bloody measure, as it would be to pay them, and enable the State to commit violence and shed innocent blood. This is, in fact, the definition of a peaceable revolution, if any such is possible. If the tax-gatherer or any other public officer asks me, as one has done, "But what shall I do?" my answer is, "If you really wish to do anything, resign your office." When the subject has refused allegiance and the officer has resigned his office, then the revolution is accomplished. But even suppose blood should flow. Is there not a sort of blood shed when the conscience is wounded? Through this wound a man's real manhood and immortality flow out, and he bleeds to an everlasting death. I see this blood flowing now.

I have contemplated the imprisonment of the offender rather than the seizure of his goods—though both will serve the same purpose—because they who assert the purest right, and consequently are most dangerous to a corrupt State, commonly have not spent much time in accumulating property. To such the State renders comparatively small service, and a slight tax is wont to appear exorbitant, particularly if they are obliged to earn it by special labor with their hands. If there were one who lived wholly without the use of money, the State itself would hesitate to demand it of him. But the rich man—not to make any invidious comparison—is always sold to the institution which makes him rich. Absolutely speaking, the more money, the less virtue; for money comes between a man and his objects and obtains them for him; and it was certainly no great virtue to obtain it. It puts to rest many questions which he would otherwise be taxed to answer; while the only new question which it puts is the hard but superfluous one, how to spend it. Thus his moral ground is taken from under his feet. The opportunities of living are diminished in proportion as what are called the "means" are increased. The best thing a man can do for his culture when he is rich is to endeavor to carry out those schemes which he entertained when he was poor. Christ answered the Herodians[14] according to their condition. "Show me the tribute-money," said he—and one took a penny out of his pocket—if you use money which has the image of Caesar on it, and which he has made current

---

[14]**Herodians** Followers of King Herod who were opposed to Jesus Christ (see Matthew 22:16).

and valuable, that is, if *you are men of the State* and gladly enjoy the advantages of Caesar's government, then pay him back some of his own when he demands it; "Render therefore to Caesar that which is Caesar's, and to God those things which are God's"—leaving them no wiser than before as to which was which; for they did not wish to know.

When I converse with the freest of my neighbors, I perceive   24
that whatever they may say about the magnitude and seriousness of the question, and their regard for the public tranquillity, the long and the short of the matter is that they cannot spare the protection of the existing government, and they dread the consequences to their property and families of disobedience to it. For my own part, I should not like to think that I ever rely on the protection of the State. But if I deny the authority of the State when it presents its tax-bill, it will soon take and waste all my property and so harass me and my children without end. This is hard. This makes it impossible for a man to live honestly, and at the same time comfortably, in outward respects. It will not be worth the while to accumulate property; that would be sure to go again. You must hire or squat somewhere and raise but a small crop and eat that soon. You must live within yourself and depend upon yourself always tucked up and ready for a start, and not have many affairs. A man may grow rich in Turkey even, if he will be in all respects a good subject of the Turkish government. Confucius[15] said: "If a state is governed by the principles of reason, poverty and misery are subjects of shame; if a state is not governed by the principles of reason, riches and honors are the subjects of shame." No; until I want the protection of Massachusetts to be extended to me in some distant Southern port, where my liberty is endangered, or until I am bent solely on building up an estate at home by peaceful enterprise, I can afford to refuse allegiance to Massachusetts and her right to my property and life. It costs me less in every sense to incur the penalty of disobedience to the State than it would to obey. I should feel as if I were worth less in that case.

Some years ago the State met me in behalf of the Church and commanded me to pay a certain sum toward the support of a clergyman whose preaching my father attended, but never I myself. "Pay," it said, "or be locked up in the jail." I declined to pay. But, unfortunately, another man saw fit to pay it. I did not see why the schoolmaster should be taxed to support the priest, and not the

---

[15]**Confucius (551–479 B.C.)**   The most important Chinese religious leader. His *Analects* (collection) treated not only religious but moral and political matters as well.

priest the schoolmaster; for I was not the State's schoolmaster, but I supported myself by voluntary subscription. I did not see why the lyceum should not present its tax-bill and have the State to back its demand, as well as the Church. However, at the request of the selectmen, I condescended to make some such statement as this in writing:—"Know all men by these presents, that I, Henry Thoreau, do not wish to be regarded as a member of any incorporated society which I have not joined." This I gave to the town clerk; and he has it. The State, having thus learned that I did not wish to be regarded as a member of that church, has never made a like demand on me since; though it said that it must adhere to its original presumption that time. If I had known how to name them, I should then have signed off in detail from all the societies which I never signed on to; but I did not know where to find a complete list.

I have paid no poll-tax[16] for six years. I was put into a jail once on this account, for one night; and, as I stood considering the walls of solid stone, two or three feet thick, the door of wood and iron, a foot thick, and the iron grating which strained the light, I could not help being struck with the foolishness of that institution which treated me as if I were mere flesh and blood and bones, to be locked up. I wondered that it should have concluded at length that this was the best use it could put me to and had never thought to avail itself of my services in some way. I saw that if there was a wall of stone between me and my townsmen, there was a still more difficult one to climb or break through before they could get to be as free as I was. I did not for a moment feel confined, and the walls seemed a great waste of stone and mortar. I felt as if I alone of all my townsmen had paid my tax. They plainly did not know how to treat me but behaved like persons who are underbred. In every threat and in every compliment there was a blunder; for they thought that my chief desire was to stand the other side of that stone wall. I could not but smile to see how industriously they locked the door on my meditations, which followed them out again without let or hindrance, and *they* were really all that was dangerous. As they could not reach me, they had resolved to punish my body; just as boys, if they cannot come at some person against whom they have a spite, will abuse his dog. I saw that the State was half-witted, that it was timid as a lone woman with her silver spoons, and that it did not know its friends from its foes, and I lost all my remaining respect for it and pitied it.

---

[16]***poll-tax***   A tax levied on every citizen living in a given area; poll means "head," so it is a tax per head. It was about $2 and was used to support the Mexican War.

Thus the State never intentionally confronts a man's sense, intellectual or moral, but only his body, his senses. It is not armed with superior wit or honesty but with superior physical strength. I was not born to be forced. I will breathe after my own fashion. Let us see who is the strongest. What force has a multitude? They only can force me who obey a higher law than I. They force me to become like themselves. I do not hear of *men* being *forced* to live this way or that by masses of men. What sort of life were that to live? When I meet a government which says to me, "Your money or your life," why should I be in haste to give it my money? It may be in a great strait and not know what to do: I cannot help that. It must help itself; do as I do. It is not worth the while to snivel about it. I am not responsible for the successful working of the machinery of society. I am not the son of the engineer. I perceive that, when an acorn and a chestnut fall side by side, the one does not remain inert to make way for the other, but both obey their own laws and spring and grow and flourish as best they can till one, perchance, overshadows and destroys the other. If a plant cannot live according to its nature, it dies; and so a man.

The night in prison was novel and interesting enough. The prisoners in their shirt-sleeves were enjoying a chat and the evening air in the doorway when I entered. But the jailer said, "Come, boys, it is time to lock up"; and so they dispersed, and I heard the sound of their steps returning into the hollow apartments. My room-mate was introduced to me by the jailer as "a first-rate fellow and a clever man." When the door was locked, he showed me where to hang my hat and how he managed matters there. The rooms were whitewashed once a month; and this one, at least, was the whitest, most simply furnished, and probably the neatest apartment in the town. He naturally wanted to know where I came from and what brought me there; and when I had told him, I asked him in my turn how he came there, presuming him to be an honest man, of course; and, as the world goes, I believe he was. "Why," said he, "they accuse me of burning a barn; but I never did it." As near as I could discover, he had probably gone to bed in a barn when drunk and smoked his pipe there; and so a barn burnt. He had the reputation of being a clever man, had been there some three months waiting for his trial to come on, and would have to wait as much longer; but he was quite domesticated and contented, since he got his board for nothing and thought that he was well treated.

He occupied one window, and I the other; and I saw that if

one stayed there long, his principal business would be to look out the window. I had soon read all the tracts that were left there and examined where former prisoners had broken out and where a grate had been sawed off and heard the history of the various occupants of that room; for I found that even here there was a history and a gossip which never circulated beyond the walls of the jail. Probably this is the only house in the town where verses are composed, which afterward printed in a circular form but not published. I was shown quite a long list of verses which were composed by some young men who had been detected in an attempt to escape, who avenged themselves by signing them.

I pumped my fellow-prisoner as dry as I could, for fear I should never see him again; but at length he showed me which was my bed and left me to blow out the lamp.

It was like travelling into a far country, such as I had never expected to behold, to lie there for one night. It seemed to me that I never had heard the town-clock strike before, nor the evening sounds of the village; for we slept with the windows open, which were inside the grating. It was to see my native village in the light of the Middle Ages, and our Concord was turned into a Rhine stream, and visions of knights and castles passed before me. They were the voices of old burghers that I heard in the streets. I was an involuntary spectator and auditor of whatever was done and said in the kitchen of the adjacent village-inn—a wholly new and rare experience to me. It was a closer view of my native town. I was fairly inside of it. I never had seen its institutions before. This is one of its peculiar institutions; for it is a shire town.[17] I began to comprehend what its inhabitants were about.

In the morning our breakfasts were put through the hole in the door, in small oblong-square tin pans, made to fit, and holding a pint of chocolate, with brown bread and an iron spoon. When they called for the vessels again, I was green enough to return what bread I had left; but my comrade seized it and said that I should lay that up for lunch or dinner. Soon after he was let out to work at haying in a neighboring field, whither he went every day, and would not be back till noon; so he bade me good-day, saying that he doubted if he should see me again.

When I came out of prison—for someone interfered and paid that tax—I did not perceive that great changes had taken place on the common, such as he observed who went in a youth and emerged

32

---

[17]***shire town*** A county seat, which means the town would have a court, county offices, and jails.

a tottering and gray-headed man; and yet a change had to my eyes come over the scene—the town and State and country—greater than any that mere time could effect. I saw yet more distinctly the State in which I lived. I saw to what extent the people among whom I lived could be trusted as good neighbors and friends; that their friendship was for summer weather only; that they did not greatly propose to do right; that they were a distinct race from me by their prejudices and superstitions, as the Chinamen and Malays are; that, in their sacrifices to humanity, they ran no risks, not even to their property; that, after all, they were not so noble but they treated the thief as he had treated them and hoped, by a certain outward observance and a few prayers, and by walking in a particular straight though useless path from time to time, to save their souls. This may be to judge my neighbors harshly; for I believe that many of them are not aware that they have such an institution as the jail in their village.

It was formerly the custom in our village, when a poor debtor came out of jail, for his acquaintances to salute him, looking through their fingers, which were crossed to represent the grating of a jail window, "How do ye do?" My neighbors did not thus salute me but first looked at me and then at one another as if I had returned from a long journey. I was put into jail as I was going to the shoemaker's to get a shoe which was mended. When I was let out the next morning I proceeded to finish my errand, and having put on my mended shoe, joined a huckleberry party who were impatient to put themselves under my conduct; and in half an hour—for the horse was soon tackled—was in the midst of a huckleberry field on one of our highest hills two miles off, and then the State was nowhere to be seen.

This is the whole history of "My Prisons."

I have never declined paying the highway tax, because I am   36 as desirous of being a good neighbor as I am of being a bad subject; and as for supporting schools I am doing my part to educate my fellow countrymen now. It is for no particular item in the tax-bill that I refuse to pay it. I simply wish to refuse allegiance to the State, to withdraw and stand aloof from it effectually. I do not care to trace the course of my dollar, if I could, till it buys a man or a musket to shoot one with—the dollar is innocent—but I am concerned to trace the effects of my allegiance. In fact, I quietly declare war with the State, after my fashion, though I will still make what use and get what advantage of her I can, as is usual in such cases.

If others pay the tax which is demanded of me from a sympathy with the State, they do but what they have already done in their own case, or rather they abet injustice to a greater extent than the State requires. If they pay the tax from a mistaken interest in the individual taxed, to save his property, or prevent his going to jail, it is because they have not considered wisely how far they let their private feelings interfere with the public good.

This, then, is my position at present. But one cannot be too much on his guard in such a case, lest his action be biassed by obstinacy or an undue regard for the opinions of men. Let him see that he does only what belongs to himself and to the hour.

I think sometimes, Why, this people mean well; they are only ignorant; they would do better if they knew how: why give your neighbors this pain to treat you as they are not inclined to? But I think again, this is no reason why I should do as they do or permit others to suffer much greater pain of a different kind. Again, I sometimes say to myself, When many millions of men, without heat, without ill will, without personal feeling of any kind, demand of you a few shillings only, without the possibility, such is their constitution, of retracting or altering their present demand, and without the possibility, on your side, of appeal to any other millions, why expose yourself to this overwhelming brute force? You do not resist cold and hunger, the winds and the waves, thus obstinately; you quietly submit to a thousand similar necessities. You do not put your head into the fire. But just in proportion as I regard this as not wholly a brute force but partly a human force, and consider that I have relations to those millions as to so many millions of men, and not of mere brute or inanimate things, I see that appeal is possible, first and instantaneously, from them to the Maker of them, and secondly, from them to themselves. But if I put my head deliberately into the fire, there is no appeal to fire or to the Maker of fire, and I have only myself to blame. If I could convince myself that I have any right to be satisfied with men as they are, and to treat them accordingly, and not according, in some respects, to my requisitions and expectations of what they and I ought to be, then, like a good Mussulman[18] and fatalist, I should endeavor to be satisfied with things as they are and say it is the will of God. And, above all, there is this difference between resisting this and a purely brute or natural

---

[18]***Mussulman*** Muslim; a follower of the religion of Islam.

force, that I can resist this with some effect; but I cannot expect, like Orpheus,[19] to change the nature of the rocks and trees and beasts.

I do not wish to quarrel with any man or nation. I do not wish   40
to split hairs, to make fine distinctions, or set myself up as better than my neighbors. I seek rather, I may say, even an excuse for conforming to the laws of the land. I am but too ready to conform to them. Indeed, I have reason to suspect myself on this head; and each year, as the tax-gatherer comes round, I find myself disposed to review the acts and position of the general and State governments, and the spirit of the people, to discover a pretext for conformity.

> We must affect our country as our parents;
> And if at any time we alienate
> Our love or industry from doing it honor,
> We must respect effects and teach the soul
> Matter of conscience and religion,
> And not desire of rule or benefit.[20]

I believe that the State will soon be able to take all my work of this sort out of my hands, and then I shall be no better a patriot than my fellow-countrymen. Seen from a lower point of view, the Constitution, with all its faults, is very good; the law and the courts are very respectable; even this State and this American government are, in many respects, very admirable and rare things, to be thankful for, such as a great many have described them; but seen from a point of view a little higher, they are what I have described them; seen from a higher still, and the highest, who shall say what they are, or that they are worth looking at or thinking of at all?

However, the government does not concern me much, and I shall bestow the fewest possible thoughts on it. It is not many moments that I live under a government, even in this world. If a man is thought-free, fancy-free, imagination-free, that which *is not* never for a long time appearing *to be* to him, unwise rulers or reformers cannot fatally interrupt him.

I know that most men think differently from myself; but those whose lives are by profession devoted to the study of these or kindred subjects content me as little as any. Statesmen and

---

[19]***Orpheus***   In Greek mythology Orpheus was a poet whose songs were so plaintive that they affected animals, trees, and even stones.

[20]***We must affect. . . .***   From George Peele (1558?–1597?), *The Battle of Alcazar* (acted 1588–1589, printed 1594), II.ii. Thoreau added these lines in a later printing of the essay. They emphasize the fact that one is disobedient to the state as one is to a parent—with love and affection and from a cause of conscience. Disobedience is not taken lightly.

legislators, standing so completely within the institution, never distinctly and nakedly behold it. They speak of moving society but have no resting-place without it. They may be men of a certain experience and discrimination and have no doubt invented ingenious and even useful systems, for which we sincerely thank them; but all their wit and usefulness lie within certain not very wide limits. They are wont to forget that the world is not governed by policy and expediency. Webster[21] never goes behind government and so cannot speak with authority about it. His words are wisdom to those legislators who contemplate no essential reform in the existing government; but for thinkers, and those who legislate for all time, he never once glances at the subject. I know of those whose serene and wise speculations on this theme would soon reveal the limits of his mind's range and hospitality. Yet, compared with the cheap professions of most reformers, and the still cheaper wisdom and eloquence of politicians in general, his are almost the only sensible and valuable words, and we thank Heaven for him. Comparatively, he is always strong, original, and, above all, practical. Still his quality is not wisdom but prudence. The lawyer's truth is not Truth but consistency, or a consistent expediency. Truth is always in harmony with herself and is not concerned chiefly to reveal the justice that may consist with wrong-doing. He well deserves to be called, as he has been called, the Defender of the Constitution. There are really no blows to be given by him but defensive ones. He is not a leader but a follower. His leaders are the men of '87.[22] "I have never made an effort," he says, "and never propose to make an effort; I have never countenanced an effort, and never mean to countenance an effort, to disturb the arrangement as originally made, by which the various States came into the Union." Still thinking of the sanction which the Constitution gives to slavery, he says, "Because it was a part of the original compact—let it stand." Notwithstanding his special acuteness and ability, he is unable to take a fact out of its merely political relations and behold it as it lies absolutely to be disposed of by the intellect—what, for instance, it behooves a man to do here in America today with regard to slavery but ventures, or is driven, to make some such desperate answer as the following, while professing to speak absolutely, and as a private man—from which what new and singu-

---

[21]*Daniel Webster (1782–1852)*   One of the most brilliant orators of his time. He was secretary of state from 1841 to 1843, which is why Thoreau thinks he cannot be a satisfactory critic of government.

[22]*men of '87*   The men who framed the Constitution in 1787.

lar code of social duties might be inferred? "The manner," says he, "in which the governments of those States where slavery exists are to regulate it, is for their own consideration, under their responsibility to their constituents, to the general laws of propriety, humanity, and justice, and to God. Associations formed elsewhere, springing from a feeling of humanity, or any other cause, have nothing whatever to do with it. They have never received any encouragement from me, and they never will."[23]

They who know of no purer sources of truth, who have traced up its stream no higher, stand, and wisely stand, by the Bible and the Constitution, and drink at it there with reverence and humility; but they who behold where it comes trickling into this lake or that pool gird up their loins once more and continue their pilgrimage toward its fountain-head.

No man with a genius for legislation has appeared in America. They are rare in the history of the world. There are orators, politicians, and eloquent men by the thousand; but the speaker has not yet opened his mouth to speak who is capable of settling the much-vexed questions of the day. We love eloquence for its own sake and not for any truth which it may utter or any heroism it may inspire. Our legislators have not yet learned the comparative value of free-trade and of freedom, of union, and of rectitude, to a nation. They have no genius or talent for comparatively humble questions of taxation and finance, commerce and manufacturers and agriculture. If we were left solely to the wordy wit of legislators in Congress for our guidance, uncorrected by the seasonable experience and the effectual complaints of the people, America would not long retain her rank among the nations. For eighteen hundred years, though perchance I have no right to say it, the New Testament has been written; yet where is the legislator who has wisdom and practical talent enough to avail himself of the light which it sheds on the science of legislation? 44

The authority of government, even such as I am willing to submit to—for I will cheerfully obey those who know and can do better than I, and in many things even those who neither know nor can do so well—is still an impure one: to be strictly just, it must have the sanction and consent of the governed. It can have no pure right over my person and property but what I concede to it. The progress from an absolute to a limited monarchy, from a limited monarchy to a democracy, is a progress toward a true respect for the individual. Even the Chinese philosopher[24] was wise

---

[23]These extracts have been inserted since the Lecture was read. [Thoreau's note]
[24]***Chinese philosopher*** Thoreau probably means Confucius.

enough to regard the individual as the basis of the empire. Is a democracy such as we know it the last improvement possible in government? Is it not possible to take a step further towards recognizing and organizing the rights of man? There will never be a really free and enlightened State until the State comes to recognize the individual as a higher and independent power, from which all its own power and authority are derived, and treats him accordingly. I please myself with imagining a State at last which can afford to be just to all men and to treat the individual with respect as a neighbor; which even would not think it inconsistent with its own repose if a few were to live aloof from it, not meddling with it, nor embraced by it, who fulfilled all the duties of neighbors and fellow-men. A State which bore this kind of fruit and suffered it to drop off as fast as it ripened would prepare the way for a still more perfect and glorious State, which also I have imagined but not yet anywhere seen.

QUESTIONS FOR CRITICAL READING

1. How would you characterize the tone of Thoreau's address? Is he chastising his audience? Is he praising it? What opinion do you think he has of his audience?
2. How well does Thoreau use irony? Choose an example and comment on its effectiveness. (One example is in paragraph 25.)
3. What do you think are Thoreau's views on the responsibility of a majority to a minority in the eyes of government?
4. What kind of person does Thoreau seem to be? Can you tell much about his personality? Do you think you would have enjoyed knowing him? If you could meet him, what would you talk about with him?
5. Are Thoreau's concepts of justice clear?
6. Is it possible that when Thoreau mentions the Chinese philosopher he means Lao-Tzu? Would Lao-Tzu agree that the empire is built upon the individual?
7. Do you feel that the government of Thoreau's time was built on the individual or on the individual's best interests? Do you think our current government is based on the individual's best interests?

WRITING ASSIGNMENTS

1. Find the quotations that best describe government. Once you have examined them carefully, write an essay that establishes the kind of government Thoreau seems to be referring to. Be sure to include the values of the government Thoreau refers to, the way it sees its

obligations to the governed, and the way it treats matters of justice and moral issues. Describe Thoreau's view of the American government of his time in enough detail to give a clear sense of the essay to someone who has not read it.

2. Compare the government of Thoreau's day with that of our own. How much are they alike? What specific qualities do the governments have in common? How do they differ? Do you believe that the United States government has improved since Thoreau's time? Would Thoreau retract some of the things he says if he were alive today?

3. According to Thoreau, what should the role of conscience be in government? What do you think Thoreau means by "conscience"? Is it possible for a government to act out of conscience? If a government did act out of conscience, how would it act? Does our government act out of conscience? Does any government that you know of act out of conscience?

4. Thoreau says: "Unjust laws exist: shall we be content to obey them, or shall we endeavor to amend them and obey them until we have succeeded, or shall we transgress them at once?" (para. 16). Answer Thoreau's question in an essay that focuses on issues that are of significance to you; be as practical and cautious as you feel you should be, and provide your own answer, not the one you feel Thoreau might have given. What forms would Thoreau's disobedience be likely to take? What would the limits of his actions be?

5. Describe clearly what being in jail taught Thoreau. What was life in jail like? Why did it have the effect it had on him? Is it unreasonable for Thoreau to have reacted so strongly to being in a local jail for only a single day?

6. **CONNECTIONS**   Establish which of the writers in Part One has most in common with Thoreau and which has least in common. Analyze passages from each, in relation to what Thoreau says in "Civil Disobedience." Ask yourself whether the writer you feel is most like Thoreau would have gone to jail as Thoreau did. Would that writer have disobeyed a law that was perceived as immoral? Would that person be doing the right thing?

7. **CONNECTIONS**   Thoreau admits (para. 41) that he is not much concerned with the government because he does not have to pay much attention to it. His life goes on regardless of the government. He also says that "the authority of government . . . is still an impure one: to be strictly just, it must have the sanction and consent of the governed" (para. 45). How would Jefferson have reacted to Thoreau's attitudes toward government? Would he have agreed with Thoreau's view that it is essentially unimportant to the individual? Does Thoreau's view that the success of a government depends on the sanction of the governed derive from Jefferson? Or did Jefferson have a different idea regarding the relationship between the government and the governed?

8. **CONNECTIONS**   Thoreau was especially sympathetic to the plight

of African-American slaves and would likely have shared the views of Frederick Douglass and Martin Luther King, Jr. What would his advice to them have been? Write an essay that takes into account the basic ideas of "Civil Disobedience" and applies them to the circumstances in which Douglass and King found themselves.

MARTIN LUTHER KING, Jr.

Letter from Birmingham Jail

MARTIN LUTHER KING, JR. *(1929–1968) was the most influential black civil rights leader in America for a period of more than fifteen years. He was an ordained minister with a doctorate in theology from Boston University. He worked primarily in the South, where he worked steadily to overthrow laws that promoted segregation and to increase the number of black voters registered in southern communities.*

The period from 1958 to 1968 marked the most active years in the United States for demonstrations and actions that opened up opportunities for black Americans. Many laws in the South hitherto prohibited blacks from sitting in certain sections of buses, from using facilities such as water fountains in bus stations, and from sitting at luncheon counters with whites. Such laws—patently unfair and insulting, not to mention unconstitutional—were not challenged by local authorities. Martin Luther King, Jr., who became famous for supporting a program to integrate buses in Montgomery, Alabama, was asked by the Southern Christian Leadership Conference to assist in the fight for civil rights in Birmingham, Alabama, where the SCLC meeting was to be held.

King was arrested as the result of a program of sit-ins at luncheon counters and wrote the letter printed here to a number of Christian ministers who had criticized his position. King had been arrested before and would be arrested again—resembling Thoreau somewhat in his attitude toward laws that did not conform to moral justice.

King, like Thoreau, was willing to suffer for his views, especially when he found himself faced with punitive laws denying civil rights. His is a classic case in which the officers of the government pled that they were dedicated to maintaining a stable civil society, even as they inhibited King's individual rights. In 1963, many of the good people to whom King addressed this letter firmly believed that peace and order

*might be threatened by granting blacks the true independence and freedom
that King insisted were their rights, and indeed were guaranteed under
the constitution. This is why King's letter, thirty years later, seems to
be aimed at an injustice that would have been more appropriate in
Douglass's time than in the time of John F. Kennedy.*

*Eventually, the causes King had promoted were victorious. His
efforts helped not only to change attitudes in the South but also to
spur legislation that has benefited all Americans. His views concerning
nonviolence spread throughout the world, and by the early 1960s he
had become famous as a man who stood for human rights and human
dignity virtually everywhere. He won the Nobel Peace Prize in 1964.*

*Although King himself was nonviolent, his program left both him
and his followers open to the threat of violence. The sit-ins and voter
registration programs spurred countless bombings, threats, and murders
by members of the white community. King's life was often threatened,
his home bombed, his followers harassed. He was assassinated at the
Lorraine Motel in Memphis, Tennessee, on April 4, 1968. But before
he died he saw—largely through his own efforts, influence, and example—the face of America change.*

KING'S RHETORIC

*The most obvious rhetorical tradition King assumes in this im-
portant work is that of the books of the Bible that were originally letters,
such as Paul's Epistle to the Ephesians and his several letters to the
Corinthians. Many of Paul's letters were written while he was in prison
in Rome. In each of those instances, Paul was establishing a moral
position far in advance of that of the citizens who received the letters;
at the same time Paul was carrying out the most important work of the
early Christian Church: spreading the Word to those who wished to
be Christians but who needed clarification and encouragement.*

*It is not clear that the churchmen who received the letter fully
appreciated the rhetorical tradition King assumed—but since they were
men who preached from the Bible they certainly should have understood
it. The general public, which is less acquainted or concerned with the
Bible, may have needed some reminding, and the text itself alludes to
the mission of Paul and to his communications to his people. King
assumes this rhetorical tradition not only because it is effective but
because it resonates with the deepest aspect of his calling: spreading the
gospel of Christ. Brotherhood was his message.*

*King's tone is one of utmost patience with his critics. He seems
bent on winning them over to his point of view, just as he seems*

confident that—because they are, like him, clergymen—their goodwill should help them see the justice of his views.

His method is that of careful reasoning, focusing on the substance of their criticism, particularly on their complaints that his actions were "unwise and untimely." King takes each of those charges in turn and carefully analyzes it against his position; then follows the clearest possible statement of his own views and why he feels they are worth adhering to. The "Letter from Birmingham Jail" is a model of close and reasonable analysis of a very complex situation. It succeeds largely because it remains concrete, treating one issue after another carefully, refusing to be caught up in passion or posturing. King above all remains grounded in logic, convinced that his arguments will in turn convince his audience.

Letter from Birmingham Jail

April 16, 1963

MY DEAR FELLOW CLERGYMEN:[1]

While confined here in the Birmingham city jail, I came across your recent statement calling my present activities "unwise and untimely." Seldom do I pause to answer criticism of my work and ideas. If I sought to answer all the criticisms that cross my desk, my secretaries would have little time for anything other than such correspondence in the course of the day, and I would have no time for constructive work. But since I feel that you are men of genuine good will and that your criticisms are sincerely set forth, I want to try to answer your statement in what I hope will be patient and reasonable terms.

I think I should indicate why I am here in Birmingham, since

---

[1]This response to a published statement by eight fellow clergymen from Alabama (Bishop C. C. J. Carpenter, Bishop Joseph A. Durick, Rabbi Hilton L. Grafman, Bishop Paul Hardin, Bishop Holan B. Harmon, the Reverend George M. Murray, the Reverend Edward V. Ramage and the Reverend Earl Stallings) was composed under somewhat constricting circumstances. Begun on the margins of the newspaper in which the statement appeared while I was in jail, the letter was continued on scraps of writing paper supplied by a friendly Negro trusty, and concluded on a pad my attorneys were eventually permitted to leave me. Although the text remains in substance unaltered, I have indulged in the author's prerogative of polishing it for publication. [King's note]

you have been influenced by the view which argues against "outsiders coming in." I have the honor of serving as president of the Southern Christian Leadership Conference, an organization operating in every southern state, with headquarters in Atlanta, Georgia. We have some eighty-five affiliated organizations across the South, and one of them is the Alabama Christian Movement for Human Rights. Frequently we share staff, educational, and financial resources with our affiliates. Several months ago the affiliate here in Birmingham asked us to be on call to engage in a nonviolent direct-action program if such were deemed necessary. We readily consented, and when the hour came we lived up to our promise. So I, along with several members of my staff, am here because I was invited here. I am here because I have organizational ties here.

But more basically, I am in Birmingham because injustice is here. Just as the prophets of the eighth century B.C. left their villages and carried their "thus saith the Lord" far beyond the boundaries of their home towns, and just as the Apostle Paul left his village of Tarsus[2] and carried the gospel of Jesus Christ to the far corners of the Greco-Roman world, so am I compelled to carry the gospel of freedom beyond my own home town. Like Paul, I must constantly respond to the Macedonian call for aid.[3]

Moreover, I am cognizant of the interrelatedness of all communities and states. I cannot sit idly by in Atlanta and not be concerned about what happens in Birmingham. Injustice anywhere is a threat to justice everywhere. We are caught in an inescapable network of mutuality, tied in a single garment of destiny. Whatever affects one directly, affects all indirectly. Never again can we afford to live with the narrow, provincial, "outside agitator" idea. Anyone who lives inside the United States can never be considered an outsider anywhere within its bounds.

You deplore the demonstrations taking place in Birmingham. But your statement, I am sorry to say, fails to express a similar concern for the conditions that brought about the demonstrations. I am sure that none of you would want to rest content with the superficial kind of social analysis that deals merely with effects and does not grapple with underlying causes. It is unfortunate that demonstrations are taking place in Birmingham, but it is even more

4

---

[2]*village of Tarsus*   Birthplace of St. Paul (?– A.D. 67), in Asia Minor, present-day Turkey, close to Syria.

[3]*the Macedonian call for aid*   The citizens of Philippi, in Macedonia (northern Greece), were among the staunchest Christians. Paul went to their aid frequently; he also had to resolve occasional bitter disputes within the Christian community there (see Philippians 2:2–14).

unfortunate that the city's white power structure left the Negro community with no alternative.

In any nonviolent campaign there are four basic steps: collection of the facts to determine whether injustices exist; negotiation; self-purification; and direct action. We have gone through all these steps in Birmingham. There can be no gainsaying the fact that racial injustice engulfs this community. Birmingham is probably the most thoroughly segregated city in the United States. Its ugly record of brutality is widely known. Negroes have experienced grossly unjust treatment in the courts. There have been more unsolved bombings of Negro homes and churches in Birmingham than in any other city in the nation. These are the hard brutal facts of the case. On the basis of these conditions, Negro leaders sought to negotiate with the city fathers. But the latter consistently refused to engage in good-faith negotiation.

Then, last September, came the opportunity to talk with leaders of Birmingham's economic community. In the course of the negotiations, certain promises were made by the merchants—for example, to remove the stores' humiliating racial signs. On the basis of these promises, the Reverend Fred Shuttlesworth and the leaders of the Alabama Christian Movement for Human Rights agreed to a moratorium on all demonstrations. As the weeks and months went by, we realized that we were the victims of a broken promise. A few signs, briefly removed, returned; the others remained.

As in so many past experiences, our hopes had been blasted, and the shadow of deep disappointment settled upon us. We had no alternative except to prepare for direct action, whereby we would present our very bodies as a means of laying our case before the conscience of the local and the national community. Mindful of the difficulties involved, we decided to undertake a process of self-purification. We began a series of workshops on nonviolence, and we repeatedly asked ourselves: "Are you able to accept blows without retaliating?" "Are you able to endure the ordeal of jail?" We decided to schedule our direct-action program for the Easter season, realizing that except for Christmas, this is the main shopping period of the year. Knowing that a strong economic-withdrawal program would be the by-product of direct action, we felt that this would be the best time to bring pressure to bear on the merchants for the needed change.

Then it occurred to us that Birmingham's mayoral election was coming up in March, and we speedily decided to postpone action until after election day. When we discovered that the Commissioner of Public Safety, Eugene "Bull" Connor, had piled up enough votes to be in the run-off, we decided again to postpone action until the day after the run-off so that the demonstrations could not be used to cloud the issues. Like many others, we waited to see Mr. Connor defeated, and to this end we endured postponement after postponement. Having aided in this community need, we felt that our direct-action program could be delayed no longer.

You may well ask, "Why direct action? Why sit-ins, marches, and so forth? Isn't negotiation a better path?" You are quite right in calling for negotiation. Indeed, this is the very purpose of direct action. Nonviolent direct action seeks to create such a crisis and foster such a tension that a community which has constantly refused to negotiate is forced to confront the issue. It seeks so to dramatize the issue that it can no longer be ignored. My citing the creation of tension as part of the work of the nonviolent resister may sound rather shocking. But I must confess that I am not afraid of the word "tension." I have earnestly opposed violent tension, but there is a type of constructive, nonviolent tension which is necessary for growth. Just as Socrates[4] felt that it was necessary to create a tension in the mind so that individuals could rise from the bondage of myths and half truths to the unfettered realm of creative analysis and objective appraisal, so must we see the need for nonviolent gadflies to create the kind of tension in society that will help men rise from the dark depths of prejudice and racism to the majestic heights of understanding and brotherhood.

The purpose of our direct-action program is to create a situation so crisis-packed that it will inevitably open the door to negotiation. I therefore concur with you in your call for negotiation. Too long has our beloved Southland been bogged down in a tragic effort to live in monologue rather than dialogue.

One of the basic points in your statement is that the action that I and my associates have taken in Birmingham is untimely. Some have asked: "Why didn't you give the new city administration time to act?" The only answer that I can give to this query is that the new Birmingham administration must be prodded about as much as the outgoing one, before it will act. We are sadly mistaken if we feel that the election of Albert Boutwell as mayor will bring the millennium[5] to Birmingham. While Mr. Boutwell is a much more

12

---

[4]***Socrates (470?–399 B.C.)***   The tension in the mind King refers to is created by the question-answer technique known as the Socratic method. By posing questions in the beginning of the paragraph, King shows his willingness to share Socrates' rhetorical techniques. Socrates was imprisoned and killed for his civil disobedience (see para. 21). He was the greatest of the Greek philosophers.

[5]***the millennium***   A reference to Revelation 20, according to which the Second

gentle person than Mr. Connor, they are both segregationists, dedicated to maintenance of the status quo. I have hoped that Mr. Boutwell will be reasonable enough to see the futility of massive resistance to desegregation. But he will not see this without pressure from devotees of civil rights. My friends, I must say to you that we have not made a single gain in civil rights without determined legal and nonviolent pressure. Lamentably, it is an historical fact that privileged groups seldom give up their privileges voluntarily. Individuals may see the moral light and voluntarily give up their unjust posture; but, as Reinhold Niebuhr[6] has reminded us, groups tend to be more immoral than individuals.

We know through painful experience that freedom is never voluntarily given by the oppressor; it must be demanded by the oppressed. Frankly, I have yet to engage in a direct-action campaign that was "well timed" in the view of those who have not suffered unduly from the disease of segregation. For years now I have heard the word "Wait!" It rings in the ear of every Negro with piercing familiarity. This "Wait" has almost always meant "Never." We must come to see, with one of our distinguished jurists, that "justice too long delayed is justice denied."[7]

We have waited for more than 340 years for our constitutional and God-given rights. The nations of Asia and Africa are moving with jetlike speed toward gaining political independence, but we still creep at horse-and-buggy pace toward gaining a cup of coffee at a lunch counter. Perhaps it is easy for those who have never felt the stinging darts of segregation to say, "Wait." But when you have seen vicious mobs lynch your mothers and fathers at will and drown your sisters and brothers at whim; when you have seen hate-filled policemen curse, kick, and even kill your black brothers and sisters; when you see the vast majority of your twenty million Negro brothers smothering in an airtight cage of poverty in the midst of an affluent society; when you suddenly find your tongue twisted and your speech stammering as you seek to explain to your

---

Coming of Christ will be followed by 1,000 years of peace, when the devil will be incapacitated. After this will come a final battle between good and evil, followed by the Last Judgment.

[6]***Reinhold Niebuhr (1892–1971)*** Protestant American philosopher who urged church members to put their beliefs into action against social injustice. He urged Protestantism to develop and practice a code of social ethics, and wrote in *Moral Man and Immoral Society* (1932) of the point King mentions here.

[7]***"justice too long delayed is justice denied"*** Chief Justice Earl Warren's expression in 1954 was adapted from English writer Walter Savage Landor's phrase "Justice delayed is justice denied."

six-year-old daughter why she can't go to the public amusement park that has just been advertised on television, and see tears welling up in her eyes when she is told that Funtown is closed to colored children, and see ominous clouds of inferiority beginning to form in her little mental sky, and see her beginning to distort her personality by developing an unconscious bitterness toward white people; when you have to concoct an answer for a five-year-old son who is asking, "Daddy, why do white people treat colored people so mean?"; when you take a cross-country drive and find it necessary to sleep night after night in the uncomfortable corners of your automobile because no motel will accept you; when you are humiliated day in and day out by nagging signs reading "white" and "colored"; when your first name becomes "nigger," your middle name becomes "boy' (however old you are) and your last name becomes "John," and your wife and mother are never given the respected title "Mrs."; when you are harried by day and haunted by night by the fact that you are a Negro, living constantly at tiptoe stance, never quite knowing what to expect next, and are plagued with inner fears and outer resentments; when you are forever fighting a degenerating sense of "nobodiness"—then you will understand why we find it difficult to wait. There comes a time when the cup of endurance runs over, and men are no longer willing to be plunged into the abyss of despair. I hope, sirs, you can understand our legitimate and unavoidable impatience.

You express a great deal of anxiety over our willingness to break laws. This is certainly a legitimate concern. Since we so diligently urge people to obey the Supreme Court's decision of 1954 outlawing segregation in the public schools, at first glance it may seem rather paradoxical for us consciously to break laws. One may well ask: "How can you advocate breaking some laws and obeying others?" The answer lies in the fact that there are two types of laws: just and unjust. I would be the first to advocate obeying just laws. One has not only a legal but a moral responsibility to obey just laws. Conversely, one has a moral responsibility to disobey unjust laws. I would agree with St. Augustine[8] that "an unjust law is no law at all."

Now, what is the difference between the two? How does one 16 determine whether a law is just or unjust? A just law is a manmade code that squares with the moral law or the law of God. An unjust law is a code that is out of harmony with the moral law.

---

[8]***St. Augustine (354–430)*** Early bishop of the Christian Church; great church authority who deeply influenced the spirit of Christianity for many centuries.

To put it in the terms of St. Thomas Aquinas:[9] An unjust law is a human law that is not rooted in eternal law and natural law. Any law that uplifts human personality is just. Any law that degrades human personality is unjust. All segregation statutes are unjust because segregation distorts the soul and damages the personality. It gives the segregator a false sense of superiority and the segregated a false sense of inferiority. Segregation, to use the terminology of the Jewish philosopher Martin Buber,[10] substitutes an "I-it" relationship for an "I-thou" relationship and ends up relegating persons to the status of things. Hence segregation is not only politically, economically, and sociologically unsound, it is morally wrong and sinful. Paul Tillich[11] has said that sin is separation. Is not segregation an existential expression of man's tragic separation, his awful estrangement, his terrible sinfulness? Thus it is that I can urge men to obey the 1954 decision of the Supreme Court, for it is morally right; and I can urge them to disobey segregation ordinances, for they are morally wrong.

Let us consider a more concrete example of just and unjust laws. An unjust law is a code that a numerical or power majority group compels a minority group to obey but does not make binding on itself. This is *difference* made legal. By the same token, a just law is a code that a majority compels a minority to follow and that it is willing to follow itself. This is *sameness* made legal.

Let me give another explanation. A law is unjust if it is inflicted on a minority that, as a result of being denied the right to vote, had no part in enacting or devising the law. Who can say that the legislature of Alabama which set up that state's segregation laws was democratically elected? Throughout Alabama all sorts of devious methods are used to prevent Negroes from becoming registered voters, and there are some counties in which, even though Negroes constitute a majority of the population, not a single Negro is registered. Can any law enacted under such circumstances be considered democratically structured?

---

[9]***St. Thomas Aquinas (1225–1274)***   The greatest of the medieval Christian philosophers and one of the greatest church authorities.

[10]***Martin Buber (1878–1965)***   Jewish theologian; *I and Thou* (1923) is his most famous book.

[11]***Paul Tillich (1886–1965)***   An important twentieth-century Protestant theologian who held that Christianity was reasonable and effective in modern life. Tillich saw sin as an expression of man's separation from God, from himself, and from his fellow man. King sees the separation of the races as a further manifestation of man's sinfulness. Tillich, who was himself driven out of Germany by the Nazis, stresses the need for activism and the importance of action in determining moral vitality, just as does King.

Sometimes a law is just on its face and unjust in its application. For instance, I have been arrested on a charge of parading without a permit. Now, there is nothing wrong in having an ordinance which requires a permit for a parade. But such an ordinance becomes unjust when it is used to maintain segregation and to deny citizens the First Amendment privilege of peaceful assembly and protest.

I hope you are able to see the distinction I am trying to point out. In no sense do I advocate evading or defying the law, as would the rabid segregationist. That would lead to anarchy. One who breaks an unjust law must do so openly, lovingly, and with a willingness to accept the penalty. I submit that an individual who breaks a law that conscience tells him is unjust, and who willingly accepts the penalty of imprisonment in order to arouse the conscience of the community over its injustice, is in reality expressing the highest respect for law. 20

Of course, there is nothing new about this kind of civil disobedience. It was evidenced subliminally in the refusal of Shadrach, Meshach, and Abednego to obey the laws of Nebuchadnezzar,[12] on the ground that a higher moral law was at stake. It was practiced superbly by the early Christians, who were willing to face hungry lions and the excruciating pain of chopping blocks rather than submit to certain unjust laws of the Roman Empire. To a degree, academic freedom is a reality today because Socrates practiced civil disobedience. In our own nation, the Boston Tea Party represented a massive act of civil disobedience.

We should never forget that everything Adolf Hitler did in Germany was "legal" and everything the Hungarian freedom fighters[13] did in Hungary was "illegal." It was "illegal" to aid and comfort a Jew in Hitler's Germany. Even so, I am sure that, had I lived in Germany at the time, I would have aided and comforted my Jewish brothers. If today I lived in a Communist country where certain principles dear to the Christian faith are suppressed, I would openly advocate disobeying that country's antireligious laws.

I must make two honest confessions to you, my Christian and Jewish brothers. First, I must confess that over the past few years I have been gravely disappointed with the white moderate. I have

---

[12]*Nebuchadnezzar (c. 630–562 B.C.)*   Chaldean king who twice attacked Jerusalem. He ordered Shadrach, Meshach, and Abednego to worship a golden image. They refused, were cast into a roaring furnace, and were saved by God (see Daniel 1:7–3:30).

[13]*Hungarian freedom fighters*   The Hungarians rose in revolt against Soviet rule in 1956. Russian tanks put down the uprising with great force that shocked the world. Many freedom fighters died, and many others escaped to the West.

almost reached the regrettable conclusion that the Negro's great stumbling block in his stride toward freedom is not the White Citizen's Counciler[14] or the Ku Klux Klanner, but the white moderate, who is more devoted to "order" than to justice; who prefers a negative peace which is the absence of tension to a positive peace which is the presence of justice; who constantly says, "I agree with you in the goal you seek, but I cannot agree with your methods of direct action"; who paternalistically believes he can set the timetable for another man's freedom; who lives by a mythical concept of time and who constantly advises the Negro to wait for a "more convenient season." Shallow understanding from people of good will is more frustrating than absolute misunderstanding from people of ill will. Lukewarm acceptance is much more bewildering than outright rejection.

I had hoped that the white moderate would understand that law and order exist for the purpose of establishing justice and that when they fail in this purpose they become the dangerously structured dams that block the flow of social progress. I had hoped that the white moderate would understand that the present tension in the South is a necessary phase of the transition from an obnoxious negative peace, in which the Negro passively accepted his unjust plight, to a substantive and positive peace, in which all men will respect the dignity and worth of human personality. Actually, we who engage in nonviolent direct action are not the creators of tension. We merely bring to the surface the hidden tension that is already alive. We bring it out in the open, where it can be seen and dealt with. Like a boil that can never be cured so long as it is covered up but must be opened with all its ugliness to the natural medicines of air and light, injustice must be exposed, with all the tension its exposure creates, to the light of human conscience and the air of national opinion, before it can be cured. 24

In your statement you assert that our actions, even though peaceful, must be condemned because they precipitate violence. But is this a logical assertion? Isn't this like condemning a robbed man because his possession of money precipitated the evil act of robbery? Isn't this like condemning Socrates because his unswerving commitment to truth and his philosophical inquiries precipitated the act by the misguided populace in which they made him drink hemlock? Isn't this like condemning Jesus because his unique God-conscious-

---

[14]***White Citizen's Counciler***   White Citizen's Councils organized in southern states in 1954 to fight school desegregation as ordered by the Supreme Court in May 1954. The councils were not as secret or violent as the Klan; they were also ineffective.

ness and never-ceasing devotion to God's will precipitated the evil act of crucifixion? We must come to see that, as the federal courts have consistently affirmed, it is wrong to urge an individual to cease his efforts to gain his basic constitutional rights because the quest may precipitate violence. Society must protect the robbed and punish the robber.

I had also hoped that the white moderate would reject the myth concerning time in relation to the struggle for freedom. I have just received a letter from a white brother in Texas. He writes: "All Christians know that the colored people will receive equal rights eventually, but it is possible that you are in too great a religious hurry. It has taken Christianity almost two thousand years to accomplish what it has. The teachings of Christ take time to come to earth." Such an attitude stems from a tragic misconception of time, from the strangely irrational notion that there is something in the very flow of time that will inevitably cure all ills. Actually, time itself is neutral; it can be used either destructively or constructively. More and more I feel that the people of ill will have used time much more effectively than have the people of good will. We will have to repent in this generation not merely for the hateful words and actions of the bad people, but for the appalling silence of the good people. Human progress never rolls in on wheels of inevitability; it comes through the tireless efforts of men willing to be co-workers with God, and without this hard work, time itself becomes an ally of the forces of social stagnation. We must use time creatively, in the knowledge that the time is always ripe to do right. Now is the time to make real the promise of democracy and transform our pending national elegy into a creative psalm of brotherhood. Now is the time to lift our national policy from the quicksand of racial injustice to the solid rock of human dignity.

You speak of our activity in Birmingham as extreme. At first I was rather disappointed that fellow clergymen would see my nonviolent efforts as those of an extremist. I began thinking about the fact that I stand in the middle of two opposing forces in the Negro community. One is a force of complacency, made up in part of Negroes who, as a result of long years of oppression, are so drained of self-respect and a sense of "somebodiness" that they have adjusted to segregation; and in part of a few middle-class Negroes who, because of a degree of academic and economic security and because in some ways they profit by segregation, have become insensitive to the problems of the masses. The other force is one of bitterness and hatred, and it comes perilously close to advocating violence. It is expressed in the various black nationalist groups that are springing up across the nation, the largest and best known being Elijah Muhammad's Muslim movement.[15] Nourished by the Negro's frustration over the continued existence of racial discrimination, this movement is made up of people who have lost faith in America, who have absolutely repudiated Christianity, and who have concluded that the white man is an incorrigible "devil."

I have tried to stand between these two forces, saying that we   28 need emulate neither the "do-nothingism" of the complacent nor the hatred and despair of the black nationalist. For there is the more excellent way of love and nonviolent protest. I am grateful to God that, through the influence of the Negro church, the way of nonviolence became an integral part of our struggle.

If this philosophy had not emerged, by now many streets of the South would, I am convinced, be flowing with blood. And I am further convinced that if our white brothers dismiss as "rabble-rousers" and "outside agitators" those of us who employ nonviolent direct action, and if they refuse to support our nonviolent efforts, millions of Negroes will, out of frustration and despair, seek solace and security in black nationalist ideologies—a development that would inevitably lead to a frightening racial nightmare.[16]

Oppressed people cannot remain oppressed forever. The yearning for freedom eventually manifests itself, and that is what has happened to the American Negro. Something within has reminded him of his birthright of freedom, and something without has reminded him that it can be gained. Consciously or unconsciously, he has been caught up by the *Zeitgeist,*[17] and with his black brothers of Africa and his brown and yellow brothers of Asia, South America, and the Caribbean, the United States Negro is moving with a sense of great urgency toward the promised land of racial justice. If one recognizes this vital urge that has engulfed the Negro community, one should readily understand why public demonstrations are taking place. The Negro has many pent-up resentments and latent frustrations, and he must release them. So let him march;

---

[15]*Elijah Muhammad's Muslim movement*   The Black Muslim movement, which began in the 1920s but flourished in the 1960s under its leader, Elijah Muhammad (1897–1975). Among notable figures who became Black Muslims were the poet Imamu Amiri Baraka (b. 1934), the world championship prizefighter Muhammad Ali (b. 1942), and the controversial reformer and religious leader Malcolm X (1925–1965). King saw their rejection of white society (and consequently brotherhood) as a threat.

[16]*a frightening racial nightmare*   The black uprisings of the 1960s in all major American cities, and the conditions that led to them, were indeed a racial nightmare. King's prophecy was quick to come true.

[17]*Zeitgeist*   German word for the intellectual, moral, and cultural spirit of the times.

let him make prayer pilgrimages to the city hall; let him go on freedom rides[18]—and try to understand why he must do so. If his repressed emotions are not released in nonviolent ways, they will seek expression through violence; this is not a threat but a fact of history. So I have not said to my people, "Get rid of your discontent." Rather, I have tried to say that this normal and healthy discontent can be channeled into the creative outlet of nonviolent direct action. And now this approach is being termed extremist.

But though I was initially disappointed at being categorized as an extremist, as I continued to think about the matter I gradually gained a measure of satisfaction from the label. Was not Jesus an extremist for love: "Love your enemies, bless them that curse you, do good to them that hate you, and pray for them which despitefully use you, and persecute you." Was not Amos an extremist for justice: "Let justice roll down like waters and righteousness like an ever-flowing stream." Was not Paul an extremist for the Christian gospel: "I bear in my body the marks of the Lord Jesus." Was not Martin Luther an extremist: "Here I stand; I cannot do otherwise, so help me God." And John Bunyan: "I will stay in jail to the end of my days before I make a butchery of my conscience." And Abraham Lincoln: "This nation cannot survive half slave and half free." And Thomas Jefferson:[19] "We hold these truths to be self-evident, that all men are created equal. . . ." So the question is not whether we will be extremists, but what kind of extremists we will be. Will we be extremists for hate or for love? Will we be extremists for the preservation of injustice or for the extension of justice? In that dramatic scene on Calvary's hill three men were crucified. We must never forget that all three were crucified for the same crime—the crime of extremism. Two were extremists for immorality, and thus fell below their environment. The other, Jesus Christ, was an extremist for love, truth, and goodness, and thereby rose above his environment. Perhaps the South, the nation, and the world are in dire need of creative extremists.

I had hoped that the white moderate would see this need.   32

---

[18]*freedom rides* In 1961 the Congress of Racial Equality (CORE) organized rides of whites and blacks to test segregation in southern buses and bus terminals with interstate passengers. More than 600 federal marshalls were needed to protect the riders, most of whom were arrested.

[19]*Amos, Old Testament prophet (8th century B.C.); Paul (?–A.D. 67); Martin Luther (1483–1546); John Bunyan (1628–1688); Abraham Lincoln (1809–1865); and Thomas Jefferson (1743–1826)* These figures are all noted for religious, moral, or political innovations that changed the world. Amos was a prophet who favored social justice; Paul argued against Roman law; Luther began the Reformation of the Christian Church; Bunyan was imprisoned for preaching the gospel according to

Perhaps I was too optimistic; perhaps I expected too much. I suppose I should have realized that few members of the oppressor race can understand the deep groans and passionate yearnings of the oppressed race, and still fewer have the vision to see that injustice must be rooted out by strong, persistent, and determined action. I am thankful, however, that some of our white brothers in the South have grasped the meaning of this social revolution and committed themselves to it. They are still all too few in quantity, but they are big in quality. Some—such as Ralph McGill, Lillian Smith, Harry Golden, James McBride Dabbs, Ann Braden, and Sarah Patton Boyle—have written about our struggle[20] in eloquent and prophetic terms. Others have marched with us down nameless streets of the South. They have languished in filthy, roach-infested jails, suffering the abuse and brutality of policemen who view them as "dirty nigger-lovers." Unlike so many of their moderate brothers and sisters, they have recognized the urgency of the moment and sensed the need for powerful "action" antidotes to combat the disease of segregation.

Let me take note of my other major disappointment. I have been so greatly disappointed with the white church and its leadership. Of course, there are some notable exceptions. I am not unmindful of the fact that each of you has taken some significant stands on this issue. I commend you, Reverend Stallings, for your Christian stand on this past Sunday, in welcoming Negroes to your worship service on a nonsegregated basis. I commend the Catholic leaders of this state for integrating Spring Hill College several years ago.

But despite these notable exceptions, I must honestly reiterate that I have been disappointed with the church. I do not say this as one of those negative critics who can always find something wrong with the church. I say this as a minister of the gospel, who loves the church; who was nurtured in its bosom; who has been sustained by its spiritual blessings and who will remain true to it as long as the cord of life shall lengthen.

When I was suddenly catapulted into the leadership of the bus protest in Montgomery, Alabama, a few years ago, I felt we would be supported by the white church. I felt that the white ministers, priests, and rabbis of the South would be among our strongest allies. Instead, some have been outright opponents, refusing to

---

his own understanding; Jefferson drafted the Declaration of Independence.

[20]***written about our struggle***   These are all prominent southern writers who expressed their feelings regarding segregation in the South. Some of them, like Smith and Golden, wrote very popular books with a wide influence. Some, like McGill and Smith, were severely rebuked by white Southerners.

understand the freedom movement and misrepresenting its leaders; all too many others have been more cautious than courageous and have remained silent behind the anesthetizing security of stained-glass windows.

In spite of my shattered dreams, I came to Birmingham with the hope that the white religious leadership of this community would see the justice of our cause and, with deep moral concern, would serve as the channel through which our just grievances could reach the power structure. I had hoped that each of you would understand. But again I have been disappointed. . . .

There was a time when the church was very powerful—in the time when the early Christians rejoiced at being deemed worthy to suffer for what they believed. In those days the church was not merely a thermometer that recorded the ideas and principles of popular opinion; it was a thermostat that transformed the mores of society. Whenever the early Christians entered a town, the people in power became disturbed and immediately sought to convict the Christians for being "disturbers of the peace" and "outside agitators." But the Christians pressed on, in the conviction that they were "a colony of heaven," called to obey God rather than man. Small in number, they were big in commitment. They were too God intoxicated to be "astronomically intimidated." By their effort and example they brought an end to such ancient evils as infanticide and gladiatorial contests.

Things are different now. So often the contemporary church is a weak, ineffectual voice with an uncertain sound. So often it is an archdefender of the status quo. Far from being disturbed by the presence of the church, the powerful structure of the average community is consoled by the church's silent—and often even vocal—sanction of things as they are.

But the judgment of God is upon the church as never before. If today's church does not recapture the sacrificial spirit of the early church, it will lose its authenticity, forfeit the loyalty of millions, and be dismissed as an irrelevant social club with no meaning for the twentieth century. Every day I meet young people whose disappointment with the church has turned into outright disgust.

Perhaps I have once again been too optimistic. Is organized religion too inextricably bound to the status quo to save our nation and the world? Perhaps I must turn my faith to the inner spiritual church, the church within the church, as the true *ekklesia*[21] and the

36

40

---

[21]**ekklesia** Greek word for "church"; it means not just the institution but the spirit of the church.

hope of the world. But again I am thankful to God that some noble souls from the ranks of organized religion have broken loose from the paralyzing chains of conformity and joined us as active partners in the struggle for freedom. They have left their secure congregations and walked the streets of Albany, Georgia, with us. They have gone down the highways of the South on torturous rides for freedom. Yes, they have gone to jail with us. Some have been dismissed from their churches, have lost the support of their bishops and fellow ministers. But they have acted in the faith that right defeated is stronger than evil triumphant. Their witness has been the spiritual salt that has preserved the true meaning of the gospel in these troubled times. They have carved a tunnel of hope through the dark mountain of disappointment.

I hope the church as a whole will meet the challenge of this decisive hour. But even if the church does not come to the aid of justice, I have no despair about the future. I have no fear about the outcome of our struggle in Birmingham, even if our motives are at present misunderstood. We will reach the goal of freedom in Birmingham and all over the nation, because the goal of America is freedom. Abused and scorned though we may be, our destiny is tied up with America's destiny. Before the pilgrims landed at Plymouth, we were here. Before the pen of Jefferson etched the majestic words of the Declaration of Independence across the pages of history, we were here. For more than two centuries our forebears labored in this country without wages; they made cotton king; they built the homes of their masters while suffering gross injustice and shameful humiliation—and yet out of a bottomless vitality they continued to thrive and develop. If the inexpressible cruelties of slavery could not stop us, the opposition we now face will surely fail. We will win our freedom because the sacred heritage of our nation and the eternal will of God are embodied in our echoing demands.

Before closing I feel impelled to mention one other point in your statement that has troubled me profoundly. You warmly commended the Birmingham police force for keeping "order" and "preventing violence." I doubt that you would have so warmly commended the police force if you had seen its dogs sinking their teeth into unarmed, nonviolent Negroes. I doubt that you would so quickly commend the policemen if you were to observe their ugly and inhumane treatment of Negroes here in the city jail; if you were to watch them push and curse old Negro women and young Negro girls; if you were to see them slap and kick old Negro men and young boys; if you were to observe them, as they did on two occasions, refuse to give us food because we wanted to sing our grace together. I cannot join you in your praise of the Birmingham police department.

It is true that the police have exercised a degree of discipline in handling the demonstrators. In this sense they have conducted themselves rather "nonviolently" in public. But for what purpose? To preserve the evil system of segregation. Over the past few years I have consistently preached that nonviolence demands that the means we use must be as pure as the ends we seek. I have tried to make clear that it is wrong to use immoral means to attain moral ends. But now I must affirm that it is just as wrong, or perhaps even more so, to use moral means to preserve immoral ends. Perhaps Mr. Connor and his policemen have been rather nonviolent in public, as was Chief Pritchett in Albany, Georgia, but they have used the moral means of nonviolence to maintain the immoral end of racial injustice. As T. S. Eliot[22] has said, "The last temptation is the greatest treason: To do the right deed for the wrong reason."

I wish you had commended the Negro sit-inners and demon-   44
strators of Birmingham for their sublime courage, their willingness to suffer, and their amazing discipline in the midst of great provocation. One day the South will recognize its real heroes. They will be the James Merediths,[23] with the noble sense of purpose that enables them to face jeering and hostile mobs, and with the agonizing loneliness that characterizes the life of the pioneer. They will be old, oppressed, battered Negro women, symbolized in a seventy-two-year-old woman in Montgomery, Alabama, who rose up with a sense of dignity and with her people decided not to ride segregated buses, and who responded with ungrammatical profundity to one who inquired about her weariness: "My feets is tired, but my soul is at rest." They will be the young high school and college students, the young ministers of the gospel and a host of their elders, courageously and nonviolently sitting in at lunch counters and willingly going to jail for conscience' sake. One day the South will know that when these disinherited children of God sat down at lunch

---

[22]***Thomas Stearns Eliot (1888–1965)***   Renowned as one of the twentieth century's major poets, Eliot was born in the United States, but in 1927 became a British citizen and a member of the Church of England. Many of his poems focused on religious and moral themes. These lines are from Eliot's play *Murder in the Cathedral,* about Saint Thomas à Becket (1118–1170), the archbishop of Canterbury, who was martyred for his opposition to King Henry II.

[23]***the James Merediths***   James Meredith (b. 1933) was the first black to become a student at the University of Mississippi. His attempt to register for classes in 1962 created the first important confrontation between federal and state authorities, when Governor Ross Barnett personally blocked Meredith's entry to the university. Meredith graduated in 1963 and went on to study law at Columbia University.

counters, they were in reality standing up for what is best in the American dream and for the most sacred values in our Judaeo-Christian heritage, thereby bringing our nation back to those great wells of democracy which were dug deep by the founding fathers in their formulation of the Constitution and the Declaration of Independence.

Never before have I written so long a letter. I'm afraid it is much too long to take your precious time. I can assure you that it would have been much shorter if I had been writing from a comfortable desk, but what else can one do when he is alone in a narrow jail cell, other than write long letters, think long thoughts, and pray long prayers?

If I have said anything in this letter that overstates the truth and indicates an unreasonable impatience, I beg you to forgive me. If I have said anything that understates the truth and indicates my having a patience that allows me to settle for anything less than brotherhood, I beg God to forgive me.

I hope this letter finds you strong in the faith. I also hope that circumstances will soon make it possible for me to meet each of you, not as an integrationist or a civil rights leader but as a fellow clergyman and a Christian brother. Let us all hope that the dark clouds of racial prejudice will soon pass away and the deep fog of misunderstanding will be lifted from our fear-drenched communities, and in some not too distant tomorrow the radiant stars of love and brotherhood will shine over our great nation with all their scintillating beauty.

Yours in the cause of
Peace and Brotherhood,
MARTIN LUTHER KING, JR.

QUESTIONS FOR CRITICAL READING

1. What is the definition of "nonviolent direct action"? In what areas of human experience is it best implemented? Is politics its best area of application? What are the four steps in a nonviolent campaign?
2. Is King optimistic about the future of race relations in America? What evidence in the letter points to optimism or pessimism?
3. Which paragraphs in the letter are the most persuasive? Why? Did any part of the letter actually change your thinking on an important issue? Which part? Why was your thinking changed?
4. What do you think is the best-written paragraph in the essay? Why?
5. King cites "tension" in paragraph 10 and elsewhere as a beneficial force. Do you agree? What kind of tension does he mean?

6. Was King an extremist (paras. 30–31)?
7. In his letter, to what extent does King consider the needs of women? Would he feel that issues of women's rights are unrelated to issues of racial equality?
8. What is King's judgment of how a government should function in relation to the needs of the individual? Does he feel, like Thoreau's "Chinese philosopher," that the empire is built on the individual?

WRITING ASSIGNMENTS

1. In paragraph 43, King says, "I have consistently preached that nonviolence demands that the means we use must be as pure as the ends we seek." What exactly does he mean by this? Define the ends he seeks and the means he approves. Do you agree with him on this point? If you have read the selection from Machiavelli, contrast their respective views. Which view seems more reasonable to you?
2. Write a brief letter protesting an injustice that you feel may not be entirely understood by people you respect. Clarify the nature of the injustice, the reasons that people hold an unjust view, and the reasons your views should be accepted. Consult King's letter and consciously use his techniques.
3. The first part of the letter is a defense of King's having come to Birmingham as a Christian to help his fellows gain their rights. He challenges the view that he is an outsider, using such expressions as "network of mutuality" and "garment of destiny." How effective is his argument? Examine the letter for expressions such as those just quoted that justify King's intervention on behalf of his brothers and sisters. If the logic of his position holds, in what other social areas might you justify exerting your own views on behalf of humankind? Would you expect your endeavors to be welcomed? Are there any areas in which you might consider it wrong to intervene?
4. In paragraphs 15–22, King discusses two kinds of laws, those that are morally right and those that are morally wrong. Analyze his argument carefully, establishing what you feel his views are. Which laws did King regard as morally right? Which laws did he consider morally wrong? Name some laws, if possible, that you have personal knowledge of. Take a stand on one or two current laws that you feel are morally wrong. Be sure to be fair in describing the laws and establishing their nature. Then explain why they are morally wrong. Would you feel justified in breaking these laws? Would you feel prepared, as King was, to pay the penalties demanded of one who breaks the law?
5. Compare King's letter with sections of Paul's letters to the faithful in the New Testament. Either choose a single letter, such as the Epistle to the Romans, or select passages from Romans, the two letters to the Corinthians, the Galatians, the Ephesians, the Thessalonians, or the Philippians. What positions did Paul and King hold in common

or opposition concerning brotherly love, the mission of Christ, the mission of the church, concern for the law, and the duties of the faithful? Inventory the New Testament and the letter carefully for concrete evidence of similar or contrary positions.

6. **CONNECTIONS**   To what extent might Martin Luther King's views about government coincide with those of Lao-Tzu? Is there a legitimate comparison to be made between King's policy of nonviolent resistance and Lao-Tzu's judicious inactivity? To what extent would King have agreed with Lao-Tzu's views? Would Lao-Tzu have supported King's position in his letter, or would he have interpreted events differently?

CATHARINE A. MacKINNON

Sexual Harassment
and Sexual Politics

*CATHARINE MACKINNON (b. 1946), a Yale Law School gradu-
ate and a legal scholar at the University of Michigan Law School, has
taught at Yale, Harvard, Stanford, UCLA, the University of Chicago,
and other university law schools. Her work in feminist legal studies
has resulted in profound changes in the general attitude of lawyers
toward cases of sexual harassment, largely because she connects sexual
harassment with the violation of civil rights statutes. Much of her work,
especially* Sexual Harassment of Working Women: A Case of
Sex Discrimination *(1979), has been used as the basis of judicial
decisions concerning harassment. With antipornography writer Andrea
Dworkin she drafted an ordinance in Minneapolis, now widely known
as the Dworkin-MacKinnon ordinance, which forbids the subordination
of women in pictures and words because it is a form of sex discrimination.
This ordinance has been challenged in the courts and struck down as a
violation of the First Amendment right to free speech.*

*For MacKinnon, the political question of gender dominance paral-
lels Frederick Douglass's discussion of the politics of slavery—most
Americans are familiar enough with the pictorial and literary depictions
of African Americans as stereotypical Sambos to understand the effect
such representations have on those who are oppressed. MacKinnon's
views on pornography and men's sexual dominance over women have
been controversial in the extreme, drawing fire from liberals, conservatives, and even feminist groups. Pornography and sexual harassment
are not her only concerns, however. Among her important books are*
Feminism Unmodified: Discourse on Life and Law *(1987) and*
Toward a Feminist Theory of the State *(1989), which interprets
the structure of contemporary government as the reflection of persistent
patterns of male domination.*

*MacKinnon's essay, "Sexual Harassment and Sexual Politics,"
examines the development in recent decades of legal precedents concerning
sexual harassment. Her specific subject is the sexual harassment of
women in the workplace, but she discusses the underlying issues in a
wide-ranging examination that considers the effect of the law on individuals and society. She concerns herself with the politics of gender discrimination—which is one of the ways she interprets the entire phenomenon
of harassment. Because the victims of sexual harassment are usually
women and because the legal cases that have helped shape local and
federal laws have almost uniformly concerned women victims, MacKinnon establishes that the offense is gender-based. A number of specific
instances, as she explains, contribute to forming our general view of
harassment in these terms.*

*Moreover, MacKinnon uncovers some hidden issues, such as the
general male attitude toward women and their sexuality. For MacKinnon, harassment is not only a form of exploitation but part of a pattern
of sexual politics that is interpreted differently by each gender. She
asserts that men generally assume that women are available sexually
and that they are defined in these terms. Men's views on what constitutes
sexual harassment differ generally and historically from those of women.
The question of what a woman means by withholding consensual sex
is understood differently by each gender, and sometimes those differences
color the outcome of legal cases.*

*One of the issues MacKinnon explores in this essay is how case
law affects legislation. Laws against sexual harassment have developed
recently in response to individual cases tried in court. She sees these
laws as coming after, rather than before, legal testing in the courts—
unlike many of the laws that we take for granted. As she tells us, "The
legal claim for sexual harassment marks the first time in history, to
my knowledge, that women have defined women's injuries in a law"
(para. 7).*

*MacKinnon's essay addresses the issue of sexual harassment partly
with examples and implied definitions. She frequently cites legal cases
to provide authority for her claims. Sexual harassment, she explains,
happens to women because of their gender. Originally, she says, it was
argued that sexual harassment could happen to men as well as women,
and therefore it was not a gender issue. MacKinnon answers this in
part by pointing to the numbers: the overwhelming number of plaintiffs
are women. The women who bring sexual harassment charges to court
must undergo unusual personal scrutiny into their own sexual history
and their character. When Clarence Thomas was nominated to the
Supreme Court, for example, legal professor Anita Hill made allegations of sexual harassment against him. The entire country watched the
daily television coverage that demonstrated the kind of personal pain*

both individuals suffer because of assumptions that personal character is a key to defining harassment. Such assumptions make a harassment trial an odious procedure, especially since, as MacKinnon argues, the plaintiff's background is probably irrelevant.

MACKINNON'S RHETORIC

Originally delivered as a speech, this essay was revised and published in a volume of MacKinnon's speeches and essays. In its revised form it contains numerous footnotes (most omitted here) that refer the reader to legal documents. On the one hand the essay aims to convince the reader of its authoritativeness and thoroughness by careful reference; at the same time, it aims to be engaging and to evoke the listener's responses to important and emotional issues.

MacKinnon is a lawyer, and the structure of the essay reflects that of a legal argument. Indeed, several arguments coexist. One is that sexual harassment is a crime of oppression against women and that its implications are fundamentally political. Another is that our views of harassment are shaped by our attitudes toward women as sexual beings. The victimization of women, she says, does not stop with harassment or rape but continues through hearings and trials, so that it takes an unusual amount of courage for a woman to bring charges.

Her special analytic approach is evident in her analysis of the quid pro quo argument (para. 19). She says that many people see sexual harassment charges as "incidents of quid pro quo." The Latin term means "this for that": in this context, sex in return for a special consideration. In other words, a woman is forced into yielding to her boss sexually in hopes of not being fired, or of getting a promotion or a raise. If he does not come through with the promise, then a charge is brought on the basis of an injury: the quo was not provided after receipt of the quid. In two cases she cites, one in business and one in education, men assume that since the woman had sex, she is not entitled to damages, because in their view sex is what women are for (para. 21). Further, there is the question of whether the "woman is valuable enough to hurt" (para. 22). In these thoughtful progressions, some of MacKinnon's disdain for what she sees as masculine politics begins to show.

Generally, MacKinnon's tone is serious and detached, much in the spirit of the language of the law. On the other hand, she does not resort to cliché or legalese. Her hope is that a general reader will understand her with ease. As it is, MacKinnon has made important contributions to the understanding of legal issues involved in sexual harassment.

What she does here is examine the progress we have made since sexual harassment laws were put into effect.

Sexual Harassment and Sexual Politics

Sexual harassment, the event, is not new to women. It is the law of injuries that it is new to. Sexual pressure imposed on someone who is not in an economic position to refuse it became sex discrimination in the midseventies, and in education soon afterward. It became possible to do something legal about sexual harassment because some women took women's experience of violation seriously enough to design a law around it, as if what happens to women matters. This was apparently such a startling way of proceeding that sexual harassment was protested as a feminist invention. Sexual harassment, the event, was not invented by feminists; the perpetrators did that with no help from us. Sexual harassment, the legal claim—the idea that the law should see it the way its victims see it—is definitely a feminist invention. Feminists first took women's experience seriously enough to uncover this problem and conceptualize it and pursue it legally. That legal claim is just beginning to produce more than a handful of reported cases. Ten years later, "[i]t may well be that sex harassment is the hottest present day Title VII issue."[1] It is time for a down-the-road assessment of this departure.

The law against sexual harassment is a practical attempt to stop a form of exploitation. It is also one test of sexual politics as feminist jurisprudence, of possibilities for social change for women through law. The existence of a law against sexual harassment has affected both the context of meaning within which social life is lived and the concrete delivery of rights through the legal system. The sexually harassed have been given a name for their suffering and an analysis that connects it with gender. They have been given a forum, legitimacy to speak, authority to make claims, and an avenue for possible relief. Before, what happened to them was all right. Now it is not.

---

[1] *Rabidue* v. *Osceola Refining*, 584 F. Supp. 419, 427 n. 29 (E.D. Mich. 1984). [MacKinnon's note]

This matters. Sexual abuse mutes victims socially through the violation itself. Often the abuser enforces secrecy and silence; secrecy and silence may be part of what is so sexy about sexual abuse. When the state also forecloses a validated space for denouncing and rectifying the victimization, it seals this secrecy and reinforces this silence. The harm of this process, a process that utterly precludes speech, then becomes all of a piece. If there is no right place to go to say, this hurt me, then a woman is simply the one who can be treated this way, and no harm, as they say, is done.

In point of fact, I would prefer not to have to spend all this energy getting the law to recognize wrongs to women as wrong. But it seems to be necessary to legitimize our injuries as injuries in order to delegitimize our victimization by them, without which it is difficult to move in more positive ways. The legal claim for sexual harassment made the events of sexual harassment illegitimate socially as well as legally for the first time. Let me know if you figure out a better way to do that.

At this interface between law and society, we need to remember that the legitimacy courts give they can also take. Compared with a possibility of relief where no possibility of relief existed, since women started out with nothing in this area, this worry seems a bit fancy. Whether the possibility of relief alters the terms of power that gives rise to sexual harassment itself, which makes getting away with it possible, is a different problem. Sexual harassment, the legal claim, is a demand that state authority stand behind women's refusal of sexual access in certain situations that previously were a masculine prerogative. With sexism, there is always a risk that our demand for self-determination will be taken as a demand for paternal protection and will therefore strengthen male power rather than undermine it. This seems a particularly valid concern because the law of sexual harassment began as case law, without legislative guidance or definition.

Institutional support for sexual self-determination is a victory; institutional paternalism reinforces our lack of self-determination. The problem is, the state has never in fact protected women's dignity or bodily integrity. It just says it does. Its protections have been both condescending *and* unreal, in effect strengthening the protector's choice to violate the protected at will, whether the protector is the individual perpetrator or the state. This does not seem to me a reason not to have a law against sexual harassment. It is a reason to demand that the promise of "equal protection of the laws" be *delivered upon* for us, as it is when real people are violated. It is also part of a larger political struggle to value women more than the male pleasure of using us is valued. Ultimately, though, the question of whether the use of the state for women helps or hurts can be answered only in practice, because so little real protection of the laws has ever been delivered.

The legal claim for sexual harassment marks the first time in history, to my knowledge, that women have defined women's injuries in a law. Consider what has happened with rape. We have never defined the injury of rape; men define it. The men who define it, define what they take to be this violation of women according to, among other things, what they think they don't do. In this way rape becomes an act of a stranger (they mean Black) committed upon a woman (white) whom he has never seen before. Most rapes are intraracial and are committed by men the women know. Ask a woman if she has ever been raped, and often she says, "Well . . . not really." In that silence between the well and the not really, she just measured what happened to her against every rape case she ever heard about and decided she would lose in court. Especially when you are part of a subordinated group, your own definition of your injuries is powerfully shaped by your assessment of whether you could get anyone to do anything about it, including anything official. You are realistic by necessity, and the voice of law is the voice in power. When the design of a legal wrong does not fit the wrong as it happens to you, as is the case with rape, that law can undermine your social and political as well as legal legitimacy in saying that what happened was an injury at all—even to yourself.

It is never too soon to worry about this, but it may be too 8 soon to know whether the law against sexual harassment will be taken away from us or turn into nothing or turn ugly in our hands. The fact is, this law is working surprisingly well for women by any standards, particularly when compared with the rest of sex discrimination law. If the question is whether a law designed from women's standpoint and administered through this legal system can do anything for women—which always seems to be a good question—this experience so far gives a qualified and limited yes.

It is hard to unthink what you know, but there was a time when the facts that amount to sexual harassment did not amount to sexual harassment. It is a bit like the injuries of pornography until recently. The facts amounting to the harm did not socially "exist," had no shape, no cognitive coherence; far less did they state a legal claim. It just happened to you. To the women to whom it happened, it wasn't part of anything, much less something big or shared like gender. It fit no known pattern. It was neither a regularity nor an irregularity. Even social scientists didn't study it, and they study anything that moves. When law recognized sexual harassment as a practice of sex discrimination, it moved it from the realm of "and then he . . . and then he . . . ," the primitive language in which sexual abuse lives inside a woman, into an experience with a form, an etiology, a cumulativeness—as well as a club.

The shape, the positioning, and the club—each is equally critical politically. Once it became possible to do something about sexual harassment, it became possible to know more about it, because it became possible for its victims to speak about it. Now we know, as we did not when it first became illegal, that this problem is commonplace. We know this not just because it has to be true, but as documented fact. Between a quarter and a third of women in the federal workforce report having been sexually harassed, many physically, at least once in the last two years. Projected, that becomes 85 percent of all women at some point in their working lives. This figure is based on asking women "Have you ever been sexually harassed?"—the conclusion—not "has this fact happened? has that fact happened?" which usually produces more. The figures for sexual harassment of students are comparable.

When faced with individual incidents of sexual harassment, the legal system's first question was, is it a personal episode? Legally, this was a way the courts inquired into whether the incidents were based on sex, as they had to be to be sex discrimination. Politically, it was a move to isolate victims by stigmatizing them as deviant. It also seemed odd to me that a relationship was either personal or gendered, meaning that one is not a woman personally. Statistical frequency alone does not make an event not personal, of course, but the presumption that sexual pressure in contexts of unequal power is an isolated idiosyncrasy to unique individual victims has been undermined both by the numbers and by their division by gender. Overwhelmingly, it is men who sexually harass women, a lot of them. Actually, it is even more accurate to say that men do this than to say that women have this done to them. This is a description of the perpetrators' behavior, not of the statisticians' feminism.

Sexual harassment has also emerged as a creature of hierarchy. It inhabits what I call hierarchies among men: arrangements in which some men are below other men, as in employer/employee and teacher/student. In workplaces, sexual harassment by supervisors of subordinates is common; in education, by administrators of lower-level administrators, by faculty of students. But it also happens among coworkers, from third parties, even by subordinates in the workplace, men who are women's hierarchical inferiors or peers. Basically, it is done by men to women regardless of relative position on the formal hierarchy. I believe that the reason sexual harassment was first established as an injury of the systematic abuse of power in hierarchies among men is that this is power men recognize. They comprehend from personal experience that something is held over your head if you do not comply. The lateral or reverse hierarchical examples suggest something beyond this, something men don't understand from personal experience because they take its advantages for granted: gender is also a hierarchy. The courts do not use this analysis, but some act as though they understand it.

Sex discrimination law had to adjust a bit to accommodate the realities of sexual harassment. Like many other injuries of gender, it wasn't written for this. For something to be based on gender in the legal sense means it happens to a woman as a woman, not as an individual. Membership in a gender is understood as the opposite of, rather than part of, individuality. Clearly, sexual harassment is one of the last situations in which a woman is treated without regard to her sex; it is because of her sex that it happens. But the social meaning attributed to women as a class, in which women are defined as gender female by sexual accessibility to men, is not what courts have considered before when they have determined whether a given incident occurred because of sex.

Sex discrimination law typically conceives that something happens because of sex when it happens to one sex but not the other. The initial procedure is arithmetic: draw a gender line and count how many of each are on each side in the context at issue, or, alternatively, take the line drawn by the practice or policy and see if it also divides the sexes. One by-product of this head-counting method is what I call the bisexual defense. Say a man is accused of sexually harassing a woman. He can argue that the harassment is not sex-based because he harasses both sexes equally, indiscriminately as it were. Originally it was argued that sexual harassment was not a proper gender claim because someone could harass both sexes. We argued that this was an issue of fact to be pleaded and proven, an issue of did he do this, rather than an issue of law, of whether he could have. The courts accepted that, creating this kamikaze defense. To my knowledge, no one has used the bisexual defense since. As this example suggests, head counting can provide a quick topography of the terrain, but it has proved too blunt to distinguish treatment whose meaning is based on gender from treatment that has other social hermeneutics, especially when only two individuals are involved.

Once sexual harassment was established as bigger than personal, the courts' next legal question was whether it was smaller than biological. To say that sexual harassment was biological seemed to me a very negative thing to say about men, but defendants seemed to think it precluded liability. Plaintiffs argued that sexual harassment is not biological in that men who don't do it have nothing wrong with their testosterone levels. Besides, if murder were found to have biological correlates, it would still be a crime. Thus, although the question purported to be whether the acts were based on sex, the implicit issue seemed to be whether the source of the impetus for doing the acts was relevant to their harmfulness.

Similarly structured was the charge that women who resented   16
sexual harassment were oversensitive. Not that the acts did not occur, but rather that it was unreasonable to experience them as harmful. Such a harm would be based not on sex but on individual hysteria. Again shifting the inquiry away from whether the acts are based on sex in the guise of pursuing it, away from whether they occurred to whether it should matter if they did, the question became whether the acts were properly harmful. Only this time it was not the perpetrator's drives that made him not liable but the target's sensitivity that made the acts not a harm at all. It was pointed out that too many people are victimized by sexual harassment to consider them all hysterics. Besides, in other individual injury law, victims are not blamed; perpetrators are required to take victims as they find them, so long as they are not supposed to be doing what they are doing.

Once these excuses were rejected, then it was said that sexual harassment was not really an employment-related problem. That became hard to maintain when it was her job the woman lost. If it was, in fact, a personal relationship, it apparently did not start and stop there, although this is also a question of proof, leaving the true meaning of the events to trial. The perpetrator may have thought it was all affectionate or friendly or fun, but the victim experienced it as hateful, dangerous, and damaging. Results in such cases have been mixed. Some judges have accepted the perpetrator's view; for instance, one judge held queries by the defendant such as "What am I going to get for this?" and repeated importunings to "go out" to be "susceptible of innocent interpretation."[2] Other judges, on virtually identical facts, for example, "When are you going to do something nice for me?"[3] have held for the plaintiff. For what it's worth, the judge in the first case was a man, in the second a woman.

That sexual harassment is sex-based discrimination seems to be legally established, at least for now. In one of the few recent

---

[2]*Scott v. Sears & Roebuck,* 605 F. Supp. 1047, 1051, 1055 (N.D. Ill. 1985). [MacKinnon's note]

[3]*Coley v. Consolidated Rail,* 561 F. Supp. 647, 648 (1982). [MacKinnon's note]

cases that reported litigating the issue of sex basis, defendants argued that a sex-based claim was not stated when a woman worker complained of terms of abuse directed at her at work such as "slut," "bitch," and "fucking cunt" and "many sexually oriented drawings posted on pillars and at other conspicuous places around the warehouse" with plaintiffs' initials on them, presenting her having sex with an animal. The court said: "[T]he sexually offensive conduct and language used would have been almost irrelevant and would have failed entirely in its crude purpose had the plaintiff been a man. I do not hesitate to find that but for her sex, the plaintiff would not have been subjected to the harassment she suffered." "Obvious" or "patently obvious" they often call it. I guess this is what it looks like to have proven a point.

Sexual harassment was first recognized as an injury of gender in what I called incidents of quid pro quo.[4] Sometimes people think that harassment has to be constant. It doesn't; it's a term of art in which once can be enough. Typically, an advance is made, rejected, and a loss follows. For a while it looked as if this three-step occurrence was in danger of going from one form in which sexual harassment can occur into a series of required hurdles. In many situations the woman is forced to submit instead of being able to reject the advance. The problem has become whether, say, being forced into intercourse at work will be seen as a failed quid pro quo or as an instance of sexual harassment in which the forced sex constitutes the injury.

I know of one reported case in employment and one in education 20 in which women who were forced to submit to the sex brought a sexual harassment claim against the perpetrator; so far only the education case has won on the facts. The employment case that lost on the facts was reversed on appeal. The pressures for sex were seen to state a claim without respect to the fact that the woman was not able to avoid complying. It is unclear if the unwanted advances constitute a claim, separate and apart from whether or not they are able to be resisted, which they should; or if the acts of forced sex would also constitute an environmental claim separate from any quid pro quo, as it seems to me they also should. In the education case, the case of Paul Mann, the students were allowed to recover punitive damages for the forced sex. If sexual harassment is not to be defined only as sexual attention imposed upon someone who is not in a position to refuse it, who refuses it, women who

---

[4] ***quid pro quo***   This for that; in this context, something given in return for sex.

are forced to submit to sex must be understood as harmed not less, but as much or more, than those who are able to make their refusals effective.

Getting recoveries for women who have actually been sexually violated by the defendant will probably be a major battle. Women being compensated in money for sex they *had* violates male meta-physics because in that system sex is what a woman is for. As one judge concluded, "[T]here does not seem to be any issue that the plaintiff did not desire to have relations with [the defendant], but it is also altogether apparent that she willingly had sex with him." Now what do you make of that? The woman was not physically forced at the moment of penetration, and since it is sex she must have willed it, is about all you can make of it. The sexual politics of the situation is that men do not see a woman who has had sex as victimized, whatever the conditions. One dimension of this problem involves whether a woman who has been violated through sex has any credibility. Credibility is difficult to separate from the definition of the injury, since an injury in which the victim is not believed to have been injured *because she has been injured* is not a real injury, legally speaking.

The question seems to be whether a woman is valuable enough to hurt, so that what is done to her is a harm. Once a woman has had sex, voluntarily or by force—it doesn't matter—she is regarded as too damaged to be further damageable, or something. Many women who have been raped in the course of sexual harassment have been advised by their lawyers not to mention the rape because it would destroy their credibility! The fact that abuse is long term has suggested to some finders of fact that it must have been tolerated or even wanted, although sexual harassment that becomes a condi-tion of work has also been established as a legal claim in its own right. I once was talking with a judge about a case he was sitting on in which Black teenage girls alleged that some procedures at their school violated their privacy. He told me that with their sexual habits they had no privacy to lose. It seemed he knew what their sexual habits were from evidence in the case, examples of the privacy violations.

The more aggravated an injury becomes, the more it ceases to exist. Why is incomprehensible to me, but how it functions is not. Our most powerful moment is on paper, in complaints we frame, and our worst is in the flesh in court. Although it isn't much, we have the most credibility when we are only the idea of us and our violation in their minds. In our allegations we construct reality to some extent; face to face, their angle of vision frames us irrevocably. In court we have breasts, we are Black, we are (in a word) women.

Not that we are ever free of that, but the moment we physically embody our complaint, and they can see us, the pornography of the process starts in earnest.

I have begun to think that a major reason that many women   24 do not bring sexual harassment complaints is that they know this. They cannot bear to have their personal account of sexual abuse reduced to a fantasy they invented, used to define them and to pleasure the finders of fact and the public. I think they have a very real sense that their accounts are enjoyed, that others are getting pleasure from the first-person recounting of their pain, and that is the content of their humiliation at these rituals. When rape victims say they feel sexually harassed in the adjudication, it is not exactly metaphor. I hear that they—in being publicly sexually humiliated by the legal system, as by the perpetrator—are pornography. The first time it happens, it is called freedom; the second time, it is called justice.

If a woman is sexually defined—meaning all women fundamentally, intensified by previous sexual abuse or identification as lesbian, indelible if a prostitute—her chances of recovery for sexual abuse are correspondingly reduced. I'm still waiting for a woman to win at trial against a man who forced her to comply with the sex. Suppose the male plaintiff in one sexual harassment case who rented the motel room in which the single sexual encounter took place had been a woman, and the perpetrator had been a man. When the relationship later went bad, it was apparently not a credibility problem for *him* at trial that he had rented the motel room. Nor was *his* sexual history apparently an issue. Nor, apparently, was it said when he complained he was fired because the relationship went bad, that he had "asked for" the relationship. That case was reversed on appeal on legal grounds, but he did win at trial. The best one can say about women in such cases is that women who have had sex but not with the accused may have some chance. In one case the judge did not believe the plaintiff's denial of an affair with another coworker, but did believe that she had been sexually harassed by the defendant. In another, the woman plaintiff actually had "linguistic intimacy" with another man at work, yet when she said that what happened to her with the defendant was sexual harassment, she was believed. These are miraculous. A woman's word on these matters is usually indivisible. In another case a woman accused two men of sexual harassment. She had resisted and refused one man to whom she had previously submitted under pressure for a long time. He was in the process of eliminating her from her job when the second man raped her. The first man's defense was that it went on so long, she must have liked it. The second man's defense was that he had heard that she had had sexual relations with the first man, so he felt this was something she was open to. This piggyback defense is premised on the class definition of woman as whore, by which I mean what men mean: one who exists to be sexually done to, to be sexually available on men's terms, that is, a woman. If this definition of women is accepted, it means that if a woman has ever had sex, forced or voluntary, she can't be sexually violated.

A woman can be seen in these terms by being a former rape victim or by the way she uses language. One case holds that the evidence shows "the allegedly harassing conduct was substantially welcomed and encouraged by plaintiff. She actively contributed to the distasteful working environment by her own profane and sexually suggestive conduct."[5] She swore, apparently, and participated in conversations about sex. This effectively made her harassment-proof. Many women joke about sex to try to defuse men's sexual aggression, to try to be one of the boys in hopes they will be treated like one. This is to discourage sexual advances, not to encourage them. In other cases, judges have understood that "the plaintiffs did not appreciate the remarks and . . . many of the other women did not either."[6]

The extent to which a woman's job is sexualized is also a factor. If a woman's work is not to sell sex, and her employer requires her to wear a sexually suggestive uniform, if she is repeatedly sexually harassed by the clientele, she may have a claim against her employer. Similarly, although "there may well be a limited category of jobs (such as adult entertainment) in which sexual harassment may be a rational consequence of such employment," one court was "simply not prepared to say that a female who goes to work in what is apparently a predominantly male workplace should reasonably expect sexual harassment as part of her job."[7] There may be trouble at some point over what jobs are selling sex, given the sexualization of anything a woman does.

Sexual credibility, that strange amalgam of whether your word 28 counts with whether or how much you were hurt, also comes packaged in a variety of technical rules in the sexual harassment

---

[5]*Gan* v. *Kepro Circuit Systems,* 28 FEP Cases 639, 641 (E.D. Mo. 1982). *See also Reichman* v. *Bureau of Affirmative Action,* 536 F. Supp. 1149, 1177 (M.D. Penn. 1982). [MacKinnon's note]

[6]*Morgan* v. *Hertz Corp.,* 542 F. Supp. 123, 128 (W.D. Tenn. 1981). [MacKinnon's note]

[7]*Pryor* v. *U.S. Gypsum Co.,* 585 F. Supp. 311, 316 n. 3 (W.D. Mo. 1984). [MacKinnon's note]

cases: evidence, discovery, and burden of proof. In 1982 the EEOC[8] held that if a victim was sexually harassed without a corroborating witness, proof was inadequate as a matter of law. (Those of you who wonder about the relevance of pornography, get this: if nobody watched, it didn't happen.) A woman's word, even if believed, was legally insufficient, even if the man had nothing to put against it other than his word and the plaintiff's burden of proof. Much like women who have been raped, women who have experienced sexual harassment say, "But I couldn't prove it." They mean they have nothing but their word. Proof is when what you say counts against what someone else says—for which it must first be believed. To say as a matter of law that the woman's word is per se legally insufficient is to assume that, with sexual violations uniquely, the defendant's denial is dispositive, is proof. To say a woman's word is no proof amounts to saying a woman's word is worthless. Usually all the man has is his denial. In 1983 the EEOC found sexual harassment on a woman's word alone. It said it was enough, without distinguishing or overruling the prior case. Perhaps they recognized that women don't choose to be sexually harassed in the presence of witnesses.

The question of prior sexual history is one area in which the issue of sexual credibility is directly posed. Evidence of the defendant's sexual harassment of other women in the same institutional relation or setting is increasingly being considered admissible, and it should be. The other side of the question is whether evidence of a victim's prior sexual history should not be. Perpetrators often seek out victims with common qualities or circumstances or situations—we are fungible[9] to them so long as we are similarly accessible—but victims do not seek out victimization at all, and their nonvictimized sexual behavior is no more relevant to an allegation of sexual force than is the perpetrator's consensual sex life, such as it may be.

So far the leading case, consistent with the direction of rape law, has found that the victim's sexual history with other individuals is not relevant, although consensual history with the individual perpetrator may be. With sexual harassment law, we are having to deinstitutionalize sexual misogyny step by step. Some defendants' counsel have even demanded that plaintiffs submit to an unlimited psychiatric examination, which could have a major practical impact on victims' effective access to relief. How much sexual denigration

---

[8]***EEOC***   Equal Employment Opportunity Commission.
[9]***fungible***   Possible substitute (one woman victim as a substitute for any other woman victim).

will victims have to face to secure their right to be free from sexual denigration? A major part of the harm of sexual harassment is the public and private sexualization of a woman against her will. Forcing her to speak about her sexuality is a common part of this process, subjection to which leads women to seek relief through the courts. Victims who choose to complain know they will have to endure repeated verbalizations of the specific sexual abuse they complain about. They undertake this even though most experience it as an exacerbation, however unavoidable, of the original abuse. For others, the necessity to repeat over and over the verbal insults, innuendos, and propositions to which they have been subjected leads them to decide that justice is not worth such indignity.

Most victims of sexual harassment, if the incidence data are correct, never file complaints. Many who are viciously violated are so ashamed to make that violation public that they submit in silence, although it devastates their self-respect and often their health, or they leave the job without complaint, although it threatens their survival and that of their families. If, on top of the cost of making the violation known, which is painful enough, they know that the entire range of their sexual experiences, attitudes, preferences, and practices are to be discoverable, few such actions will be brought, no matter how badly the victims are hurt. Faced with a choice between forced sex in their jobs or schools on the one hand and forced sexual disclosure for the public record on the other, few will choose the latter. This cruel paradox would effectively eliminate much progress in this area.

Put another way, part of the power held by perpetrators of 32 sexual harassment is the threat of making the sexual abuse public knowledge. This functions like blackmail in silencing the victim and allowing the abuse to continue. It is a fact that public knowledge of sexual abuse is often worse for the abused than the abuser, and victims who choose to complain have the courage to take that on. To add to their burden the potential of making public their entire personal life, information that has no relation to the fact or severity of the incidents complained of, is to make the law of this area implicitly complicit in the blackmail that keeps victims from exercising their rights and to enhance the impunity of perpetrators. In effect, it means open season on anyone who does not want her entire intimate life available to public scrutiny. In other contexts such private information has been found intrusive, irrelevant, and more prejudicial than probative. To allow it to be discovered in the sexual harassment area amounts to a requirement that women be further violated in order to be permitted to seek relief for having been violated. I also will never understand why a violation's severity, or even its likelihood of occurrence, is measured according to the character of the violated, rather than by what was done to them.

In most reported sexual harassment cases, especially rulings on law more than on facts, the trend is almost uniformly favorable to the development of this claim. At least, so far. This almost certainly does not represent social reality. It may not even reflect most cases in litigation. And there may be conflicts building, for example, between those who value speech in the abstract more than they value people in the concrete. Much of sexual harassment is words. Women are called "cunt," "pussy," "tits";[10] they are invited to a company party with "bring your own bathing suits (women, either half)";[11] they confront their tormentor in front of their manager with, "You have called me a fucking bitch," only to be answered, "No, I didn't. I called you a fucking cunt."[12] One court issued an injunction against inquiries such as "Did you get any over the weekend?"[13] One case holds that where "a person in a position to grant or withhold employment opportunities uses that authority to attempt to induce workers and job seekers to submit to sexual advances, prostitution, and pornographic entertainment, and boasts of an ability to intimidate those who displease him," sexual harassment (and intentional infliction of emotional distress) are pleaded. Sexual harassment can also include pictures; visual as well as verbal pornography is commonly used as part of the abuse. Yet one judge found, apparently as a matter of law, that the pervasive presence of pornography in the workplace did not constitute an unreasonable work environment because, "For better or worse, modern America features open displays of written and pictorial erotica. Shopping centers, candy stores and prime time television regularly display naked bodies and erotic real or simulated sex acts. Living in this milieu, the average American should not be legally offended by sexually explicit posters."[14] She did not say she was offended, she said she was discriminated against based on her sex. If the pervasiveness of an abuse makes it nonactionable, no inequality sufficiently institutionalized to merit a law against it would be actionable.

Further examples of this internecine conflict have arisen in edu-

---

[10]*Rabidue* v. *Osceola Refining,* 584 F. Supp. 423 (E.D. Mich. 1984). [MacKinnon's note]

[11]*Cobb* v. *Dufresne-Henry,* 603 F. Supp. 1048, 1050 (D. Vt. 1985). [MacKinnon's note]

[12]*McNabb* v. *Cub Foods,* 352 N.W. 2d 378, 381 (Minn. 1984). [MacKinnon's note]

[13]*Morgan* v. *Hertz Corp.,* 27 FEP Cases at 994. [MacKinnon's note]

[14]*Rabidue* v. *Osceola Refining,* 584 F. Supp. 419, 435 (E.D. Mich. 1984). [MacKinnon's note]

cation. At the Massachusetts Institute of Technology pornography used to be shown every year during registration. Is this *not* sexual harassment in education, as a group of women complained it was, because attendance is voluntary, both sexes go, it is screened in groups rather than individually, nobody is directly propositioned, and it is pictures and words? Or is it sexual harassment because the status and treatment of women, supposedly secured from sex-differential harm, are damaged, including that of those who do not attend, which harms individuals and undermines sex equality; therefore pictures and words are the media through which the sex discrimination is accomplished?

For feminist jurisprudence, the sexual harassment attempt suggests that if a legal initiative is set up right from the beginning, meaning if it is designed from women's real experience of violation, it can make some difference. To a degree women's experience can be written into law, even in some tension with the current doctrinal framework. Women who want to resist their victimization with legal terms that imagine it is not inevitable can be given some chance, which is more than they had before. Law is not everything in this respect, but it is not nothing either. Perhaps the most important lesson is that the mountain can be moved. When we started, there was absolutely no judicial precedent for allowing a sex discrimination suit for sexual harassment. Sometimes even the law does something for the first time.

QUESTIONS FOR CRITICAL READING

1. How would you define sexual harassment? Is it a gender offense?
2. Is pornography a form of sexual harassment? Are "sexually oriented drawings" in the workplace and abusive terms such as "slut" (para. 18) examples of sexual harassment?
3. Why is it difficult to get "recoveries for women who have actually been sexually violated" (para. 21)?
4. Do you agree that "the sexual politics of the situation is that men do not see a woman who has had sex as victimized, whatever the conditions" (para. 21)?
5. Is it still true that women are "publicly sexually humiliated by the legal system" when they bring charges of harassment or rape (para. 24)?
6. How relevant is "the question of prior sexual history" to charges of harassment or rape (paras. 29 and 30)? Is it equally relevant to both genders?
7. MacKinnon ends by expressing positive feelings about "women's real

experience" being "written into law, even in some tension with the current doctrinal framework" (para. 35). What does she mean by "current doctrinal framework"?

WRITING ASSIGNMENTS

1. What examples of sexual harassment have you witnessed either in the workplace or in education? What forms does sexual harassment take? How serious is it, and under what conditions do you feel charges should be brought in a court of law?

2. Do you have any reservations concerning MacKinnon's arguments? Do you feel there are circumstances or situations that she has not adequately considered that would cast new light on sexual harassment charges? Is there a fundamental social difference between the genders that might make their perception of harassment quite different? Are there legitimate biological differences that should be considered?

3. Defend or attack MacKinnon's contention that sexual harassment is a male form of political discrimination. Is harassment a tool of oppression used by men in an effort to keep women in a subservient position in the workplace?

4. Is MacKinnon justified in saying, "I also will never understand why a violation's severity, or even its likelihood of occurrence, is measured according to the character of the violated, rather than by what was done to them" (para. 32). Consider this statement in connection with a variety of other criminal violations, for example, murder, rape, robbery, or assault. Is it uniformly true that the violated person's character should have nothing to do with a decision about the fate of the violator?

5. **CONNECTIONS**   To what extent do the experiences of Frederick Douglass parallel the experiences of women who are victims of sexual harassment? Is the treatment of African-American slaves similar to the treatment described by the women plaintiffs referred to in MacKinnon's essay? To what extent are the circumstances of the two groups parallel?

6. **CONNECTIONS**   What are the differences and similarities between MacKinnon's and Mary Wollstonecraft's approaches to the condition of women? Does Wollstonecraft take the charge of political oppression any less seriously than does MacKinnon? Would Wollstonecraft agree with MacKinnon about the seriousness of sexual harassment?

PART TWO

IDEAS IN THE WORLD OF ECONOMICS

SHOULD WE JUDGE A SOCIETY'S
ECONOMIC STRUCTURE BY ITS
EFFECT ON THE INDIVIDUAL LIBERTY
OF ITS MEMBERS?

Karl Marx

Thorstein Veblen

John Maynard Keynes

John Kenneth Galbraith

Simone Weil

Robert B. Reich

INTRODUCTION

ECONOMIC SYSTEMS ARE to some extent political in nature, but they also extend beyond politics. Each person is affected by the economic circumstances of the society in which he or she lives. The great disputes in our time have been between various forms of state-controlled economies—such as communism and fascism—contending with various forms of capitalism. These economic disputes became political, and world wars resulted. For the time being capitalism seems to have eclipsed state-controlled economic systems, with both communism and fascism having given way to the free-market approach. Even China, the last stronghold of communism, has developed a free-market system to the extent that Chinese entrepreneurs and millionaires now regularly do big business with other nations. Japan and Germany, once authoritarian, have become major capitalist democracies.

The question of wealth and power is of universal interest. And to one extent or another, each of the writers in Part Two is concerned with the effects of an economic system on the lives of individuals in that society. In our time, a period of relative wealth, we are still beset with issues related to poverty, a condition that even an era of prosperity and economic growth cannot seem to alleviate.

Karl Marx's *Communist Manifesto* is a special kind of document that clarifies the relationship between a people's condition and the economic system in which they live. Marx saw that capitalism provided opportunities for the wealthy and powerful to take advantage of labor. He argued that because labor cannot efficiently sell its product, management can take advantage of labor and not only maintain control but also keep labor in perpetual economic bondage.

Himself a poor man, Marx knew poverty firsthand. One of his close associates, Friedrich Engels, who collaborated on portions of the *Manifesto,* was the son of a factory owner and so was able to observe closely how the rich can oppress the poor. For both of them, the economic system of capitalism produced a class struggle between the rich (bourgeoisie) and the laboring classes (proletariat).

Thorstein Veblen, in "Pecuniary Emulation," begins to question the powerful surge of middle-class materialism that manifested itself in enormous wealth and smug self-satisfaction in the late nineteenth and early twentieth centuries. *The Theory of the Leisure Class* (1899) is a careful analysis of nineteenth-century wealth and its power. Immense fortunes had been amassed by relatively few people, and the social order had been distorted by this wealth. Veblen was disturbed by the materialism of the culture and by the sacrifice of intellectual values to business interests and profits. The materialism Veblen condemned may have contributed to the major European wars of this century; and materialism is still widely regarded as a social problem because the wealth of the nation is so unevenly distributed.

Veblen portrayed the environment of nineteenth-century America as he knew it. He respected some of the doctrines of Marx, although he drew quite a different conclusion. His essay is indebted not only to Marx but also to Darwin in its emphasis on evolutionary changes of capitalism, and it points to Galbraith in its examination of the antithesis of poverty. Veblen wanted to know why people need to be wealthy—what drives them toward it. In essence, he investigated the motives that shape the lives of those living in a capitalist economy.

John Maynard Keynes is probably the best-known economist of the twentieth century. A lecturer at Cambridge University in England for many years, his most important early work involved an accurate and farsighted analysis of the economics of recovery after World War I. During the period of the Great Depression of the 1930s, his influence may have been greater in the United States than it was in Great Britain. President Franklin D. Roosevelt followed his advice to boost public spending, loosen credit restrictions, and promote a freer economic environment that could profit from expansion and growth. Keynes's theories are based on production and consumption and remain important factors in modern capitalism. Keynes held that permitting ambitious businesspeople to pursue their goals of wealth would benefit the entire community. His views, despite revisionist trends in recent years, are still central to economic policies in the West.

John Kenneth Galbraith's selection, "The Position of Poverty," dates from the middle of the twentieth century and addresses an issue that none of the earlier thinkers treated—the question of poverty. It is not that the earlier writers were unaware that poverty existed; after all, each mentions it in passing. Rather, these writers were concerned with the accumulation and preservation of wealth. Galbraith, in his study of the economics of contemporary America, also focuses on wealth; the title of his most famous book is *The Affluent Society* (1958). He is, however, interested in pointing toward something greater than the issue of getting and spending, something more important than affluence per se. His concern is with the allocation of the wealth that American society has produced. His fears that selfishness and waste will dominate the affluent society have led him to write about what he considers the most important social issue related to economics: poverty and its effects. If Keynes was correct in seeing wealth as appropriate subject matter for economic study, then Galbraith has pointed to the opposite of wealth as being equally worthy of close examination.

Although not a professional economist, Simone Weil, a mid-twentieth-century philosopher, has made important contributions to the practical side of economics. Her concerns have been shaped by personal experience in heavy industrial labor, and her sympathies lie with the common workers and their spiritual needs, which industry essentially ignores. "Prerequisite to Dignity of Labor" focuses on the human side of labor, ignoring its use as an element in capitalist equations and emphasizing instead the need for work to be spiritually rewarding. Weil's economic concerns focus on the inner life of the laborer.

Like Simone Weil, Robert B. Reich, formerly a lecturer at Harvard until he was appointed secretary of labor in the Clinton administration, is not a professional economist. However, he has taught courses in economics and published widely. His 1992 book, *The Work of Nations,* echoes the title of Adam Smith's eighteenth-century masterpiece of capitalist theory, *The Wealth of Nations.* While Reich's views on labor are distinct from Simone Weil's, his essay focuses on labor with the same intensity. His views consider how worldwide economic developments will affect labor in the next decades. According to Reich, labor falls into three groups—routine workers, in-person servers, and symbolic analysts—each of which will fare differently in the coming years.

Most of these economic theorists agree that a healthy economy can relieve the misery and suffering of a population. Most agree that wealth and plenty are preferable to impoverishment and want. But some are also concerned with the effects of materialism and greed on the spiritual life of a nation. Veblen saw a society in which spiritual values were withering; Galbraith sees a society with enormous power to bring about positive social change, the capacity to make positive moral decisions. But Galbraith, for all his optimism, reminds us that we have made very little progress in an area of economics that has been a focus of thought and action for a generation.

KARL MARX

The Communist Manifesto

KARL MARX *(1818–1883) was born in Germany to Jewish parents who converted to Lutheranism. A very scholarly man, Marx studied literature and philosophy, ultimately earning a doctorate in philosophy at the University of Jena. He was denied a university position and was forced to begin making a livelihood from journalism.*

Soon after beginning his journalistic career, Marx came into conflict with Prussian authorities because of his radical social views, and after a period of exile in Paris he was forced to live in Brussels. After several more forced moves, Marx found his way to London, where he finally settled in absolute poverty. His friend Friedrich Engels (1820–1895) contributed money to prevent his and his family's starvation; and Marx wrote the books for which he is famous while writing for and editing newspapers. His contributions to the New York Daily Herald *number over three hundred items between the years 1852 and 1862.*

Marx is best known for his theories of socialism, as expressed in The Communist Manifesto *(1848)—which, like much of his important work, was written with Engels's help—and in the three-volume* Das Kapital *(Capital), the first volume of which was published in 1867. In his own lifetime he was not well known, nor were his ideas widely debated. Yet he was part of an ongoing movement composed mainly of intellectuals. Vladimir Lenin (1870–1924) was a disciple whose triumph in the Russian Revolution of 1917 catapulted Marx to the forefront of world thought. Since 1917 Marx's thinking has been scrupulously analyzed, debated, and argued. Capitalist thinkers have*

Translated by Samuel Moore. Part III of *The Communist Manifesto*, "Socialist and Communist Literature," is omitted here.

found him unconvincing, whereas Communist thinkers have found him a prophet and keen analyst of social structures.

In England, Marx's studies concentrated on economics. His thought centered on the concept of an ongoing class struggle between those who owned property—the bourgeoisie—and those who owned nothing but whose work produced wealth—the proletariat. Marx was concerned with the forces of history, and his view of history was that it is progressive and, to an extent, inevitable. This view is very prominent in The Communist Manifesto, *particularly in his review of the overthrow of feudal forms of government by the bourgeoisie. He thought it inevitable that the bourgeoisie and the proletariat would engage in a class struggle, from which the proletariat would emerge victorious. In essence, Marx took a materialist position. He denied the providence of God in the affairs of humans and defended the view that economic institutions evolve naturally and that, in their evolution, they control the social order. Thus, communism was an inevitable part of the process, and in the* Manifesto *he was concerned to clarify the reasons for its inevitability.*

One of Marx's primary contentions was that capitalism is "not personal, it is a social power." In a sense, he focused on one of the problems of economics in relation to government. If capital is a social power, then using it to oppress the society is a fearful thing. It is true, as Marx says, that the "past dominates the present," since the accumulation of past capital determines how people will live in the present. Capitalist economists see capital as a personal power, but a power that, as John Kenneth Galbraith might say, should be used in a socially responsible way. When John Maynard Keynes advocated the end of laissez-faire economics—the kind that Marx complained of and the kind in which oppression of the poor was possible (perhaps inevitable)—he pointed to a new direction in capitalism that Marx could not have anticipated.

MARX'S RHETORIC

The selection included here omits one section, the least important for the modern reader. The first section has a relatively simple rhetorical structure that depends upon comparison. The title, "Bourgeois and Proletarians," tells us right away that the section will clarify the nature of each class and then go on to make some comparisons and contrasts. These concepts were by no means as widely discussed or thought about in 1848 as they are today, so Marx is careful to define his terms. At the same time, he establishes his theories regarding history by making further comparisons with class struggles in earlier ages.

Marx's style is simple and direct. He moves steadily from point to point, establishing his views on the nature of classes, on the nature of bourgeois society, on the questions of industrialism and its effects upon modern society. He considers wealth, worth, nationality, production, agriculture, and machinery. Each point is dealt with in turn, usually in its own paragraph.

The organization of the next section, "Proletarians and Communists" (paras. 60–133), is not, despite its title, comparative in nature. Rather, with the proletariat defined as the class of the future, Marx tries to show that the Communist cause is the proletarian cause. In the process, Marx uses a fascinating rhetorical strategy. He assumes that he is addressed by an antagonist—presumably a bourgeois or a proletarian who is in sympathy with the bourgeoisie. He then proceeds to deal with each popular complaint against communism. He shows that it is not a party separate from other workers' parties (para. 61). He clarifies the question of abolishing existing property relations (paras. 68–93). He emphasizes the antagonism between capital and wage labor (para. 76); he discusses the disappearance of culture (para. 94); he clarifies the questions of the family (para. 98) and of the exploitation of children (para. 101). He brings up the new system of public education (para. 102). He raises the touchy issue of the "community of women" (paras. 102–110), as well as the charge that Communists want to abolish nations (para. 111). He brushes aside religion (para. 116). When he is done with the complaints, he gives us a rhetorical signal: "But let us have done with the bourgeois objections to Communism" (para. 126).

The rest of the second section contains a brief summary, and then Marx presents his ten-point program (para. 131). The structure is simple, direct, and effective. In the process of answering the charges against communism, Marx is able to clarify exactly what it is and what it promises. In contrast to his earlier arguments, the ten points of his Communist program seem clear, easy, and (again by contrast) almost acceptable. While the style is not dashing (despite a few memorable lines), the rhetorical structure is extraordinarily effective for the purposes at hand.

In the last section (paras. 135–146), in which Marx compares the Communists with other reform groups such as those agitating for redistribution of land and other agrarian reforms, he indicates that the Communists are everywhere fighting alongside existing groups for the rights of people who are oppressed by their societies. As Marx says, "In short, the Communists everywhere support every revolutionary movement against the existing social and political order of things." Nothing could be a more plain and direct declaration of sympathies.

The Communist Manifesto

A specter is haunting Europe—the specter of Communism. All the Powers of old Europe have entered into a holy alliance to exorcise this specter; Pope and Czar, Metternich[1] and Guizot,[2] French Radicals[3] and German police-spies.

Where is the party in opposition that has not been decried as communistic by its opponents in power? Where the Opposition that has not hurled back the branding reproach of Communism against the more advanced opposition parties, as well as against its reactionary adversaries?

Two things result from this fact.

I. Communism is already acknowledged by all European Powers to be itself a Power. 4

II. It is high time that Communists should openly, in the face of the whole world, publish their views, their aims, their tendencies, and meet this nursery tale of the specter of Communism with a Manifesto of the party itself.

To this end, Communists of various nationalities have assembled in London and sketched the following Manifesto, to be published in the English, French, German, Italian, Flemish and Danish languages.

Bourgeois and Proletarians[4]

The history of all hitherto existing society is the history of class struggles.

Freeman and slave, patrician and plebeian, lord and serf, guild- 8 master and journeyman, in a word, oppressor and oppressed, stood

---

[1]***Prince Klemens von Metternich (1773–1859)*** Foreign minister of Austria (1809–1848) who had a hand in establishing the peace after the final defeat in 1815 of Napoleon (1769–1821); Metternich was highly influential in the crucial Congress of Vienna (1814–1815).

[2]***François Pierre Guizot (1787–1874)*** Conservative French statesman, author, and philosopher. Like Metternich, he was opposed to communism.

[3]***French Radicals*** Actually middle-class liberals who wanted a return to a republic in 1848 after the eighteen-year reign of Louis Philippe (1773–1850), the "citizen king."

[4]By bourgeoisie is meant the class of modern Capitalists, owners of the means of social production and employers of wage labor. By proletariat, the class of modern wage laborers who, having no means of production of their own, are reduced to selling their labor-power in order to live. [Engels's note]

in constant opposition to one another, carried on uninterrupted, now hidden, now open fight, a fight that each time ended, either in a revolutionary re-constitution of society at large, or in the common ruin of the contending classes.

In the earlier epochs of history we find almost everywhere a complicated arrangement of society into various orders, a manifold gradation of social rank. In ancient Rome we have patricians, knights, plebeians, slaves; in the Middle Ages, feudal lords, vassals, guild-masters, journeymen, apprentices, serfs; in almost all of these classes, again, subordinate gradations.

The modern bourgeois society that has sprouted from the ruins of feudal society, has not done away with class antagonisms. It has but established new classes, new conditions of oppression, new forms of struggle in place of the old ones.

Our epoch, the epoch of the bourgeoisie, possesses, however, this distinctive feature; it has simplified the class antagonisms. Society as a whole is more and more splitting up into two great hostile camps, into two great classes directly facing each other: Bourgeoisie and Proletariat.

From the serfs of the Middle Ages sprang the chartered burghers   12
of the earliest towns. From these burgesses the first elements of the bourgeoisie were developed.

The discovery of America, the rounding of the Cape,[5] opened up fresh ground for the rising bourgeoisie. The East Indian and Chinese markets, the colonization of America, trade with the colonies, the increase in the means of exchange and in commodities generally, gave to commerce, to navigation, to industry, an impulse never before known, and thereby, to the revolutionary element in the tottering feudal society, a rapid development.

The feudal system of industry, under which industrial production was monopolized by closed guilds, now no longer sufficed for the growing wants of the new market. The manufacturing system took its place. The guild-masters were pushed on one side by the manufacturing middle-class: division of labor between the different corporate guilds vanished in the face of division of labor in each single workshop.

Meantime the markets kept ever growing, the demand ever rising. Even manufacture no longer sufficed. Thereupon, steam and machinery revolutionized industrial production. The place of manufacture was taken by the giant, Modern Industry, the place

---

[5]***the Cape***   The Cape of Good Hope, at the southern tip of Africa. This was a main sea route for trade with India and the Orient. Europe profited immensely from the opening up of these new markets in the sixteenth century.

of the industrial middle-class, by industrial millionaires, the leaders of whole industrial armies, the modern bourgeois.

Modern industry has established the world market, for which the discovery of America paved the way. This market has given an immense development to commerce, to navigation, to communication by land. This development has, in its turn, reacted on the extension of industry; and in proportion as industry, commerce, navigation, railways extended, in the same proportion the bourgeoisie developed, increased its capital, and pushed into the background every class handed down from the Middle Ages.   16

We see, therefore, how the modern bourgeoisie is itself the product of a long course of development, of a series of revolutions in the modes of production and of exchange.

Each step in the development of the bourgeoisie was accompanied by a corresponding political advance of that class. An oppressed class under the sway of the feudal nobility, an armed and self-governing association in the medieval commune,[6] here independent urban republic (as in Italy and Germany), there taxable "third estate"[7] of the monarchy (as in France), afterwards, in the period of manufacture proper, serving either the semi-feudal or the absolute monarchy as a counterpoise against nobility, and, in fact, corner stone of the great monarchies in general, the bourgeoisie has at last, since the establishment of Modern Industry and of the world-market, conquered for itself, in the modern representative State, exclusive political sway. The executive of the modern State is but a committee for managing the common affairs of the whole bourgeoisie.

The bourgeoisie, historically, has played a most revolutionary part.

The bourgeoisie, wherever it has got the upper hand, has put an end to all feudal, patriarchal, idyllic relations. It has pitilessly torn asunder the motley feudal ties that bound man to his "natural superiors," and has left no other nexus between man and man than naked self-interest, than callous "cash payment." It has drowned the most heavenly ecstasies of religious fervor,[8] of chivalrous enthu-   20

---

⁶*the medieval commune*   Refers to the growth in the eleventh century of towns whose economy was highly regulated by mutual interest and agreement.

⁷*"third estate"*   The clergy was the first estate, the aristocracy the second estate, and the bourgeoisie the third estate.

⁸*religious fervor*   This and other terms in this sentence contain a compressed historical observation. "Religious fervor" refers to the Middle Ages; "chivalrous enthusiasm" refers to the rise of the secular state and to the military power of knights; "Philistine sentimentalism" refers to the development of popular arts and literature in the sixteenth, seventeenth, and eighteenth centuries. The word "Philis-

siasm, of Philistine sentimentalism, in the icy water of egotistical calculation. It has resolved personal worth into exchange value, and in place of the numberless indefeasible chartered freedoms, has set up that single, unconscionable freedom—Free Trade. In one word, for exploitation, veiled by religious and political illusions, it has substituted naked, shameless, direct, brutal exploitation.

The bourgeoisie has stripped of its halo every occupation hitherto honored and looked up to with reverent awe. It has converted the physician, the lawyer, the priest, the poet, the man of science, into its paid wage laborers.

The bourgeoisie has torn away from the family its sentimental veil, and has reduced the family relation to a mere money relation.

The bourgeoisie has disclosed how it came to pass that the brutal display of vigor in the Middle Ages, which reactionists so much admire, found its fitting complement in the most slothful indolence. It has been the first to show what man's activity can bring about. It has accomplished wonders far surpassing Egyptian pyramids, Roman aqueducts and Gothic cathedrals; it has conducted expeditions that put in the shade all former Exoduses of nations and crusades.

The bourgeoisie cannot exist without constantly revolutioniz- 24 ing the instruments of production, and thereby the relations of production, and with them the whole relations of society. Conservation of the old modes of production in unaltered form was, on the contrary, the first condition of existence for all earlier industrial classes. Constant revolutionizing of production, uninterrupted disturbance of all social conditions, everlasting uncertainty and agitation distinguish the bourgeois epoch from all earlier ones. All fixed, fast frozen relations, with their train of ancient and venerable prejudices and opinions, are swept away, all new formed ones become antiquated before they can ossify. All that is solid melts into the air, all that is holy is profaned, and man is at last compelled to face with sober senses, his real conditions of life, and his relations with his kind.

The need of a constantly expanding market for its products chases the bourgeoisie over the whole surface of the globe. It must nestle everywhere, settle everywhere, establish connections everywhere.

The bourgeoisie has through its exploitation of the world-market given a cosmopolitan character to production and consump-

---

tine" refers to those who were generally uncultured, that is, the general public. "Sentimentalism" is a code word for the encouragement of emotional response rather than rational thought.

tion in every country. To the great chagrin of reactionists, it has drawn from under the feet of industry the national ground on which it stood. All old-established national industries have been destroyed or are daily being destroyed. They are dislodged by new industries, whose introduction becomes a life and death question for all civilized nations, by industries that no longer work up indigenous raw material, but raw material drawn from the remotest zones; industries whose products are consumed, not only at home, but in every quarter of the globe. In place of the old wants, satisfied by the productions of the country, we find new wants, requiring for their satisfaction the products of distant lands and climes. In place of the old local and national seclusion and self-sufficiency, we have intercourse in every direction, universal interdependence of nations. And as in material, so also in intellectual production. The intellectual creations of individual nations become common property. National onesidedness and narrowmindedness become more and more impossible, and from the numerous national and local literatures there arises a world–literature.

The bourgeoisie, by the rapid improvement of all instruments of production, by the immensely facilitated means of communication, draws all, even the most barbarian nations into civilization. The cheap prices of its commodities are the heavy artillery with which it batters down all Chinese walls, with which it forces the barbarians' intensely obstinate hatred of foreigners to capitulate. It compels all nations, on pain of extinction, to adopt the bourgeois mode of production; it compels them to introduce what it calls civilization into their midst, i.e., to become bourgeois themselves. In a word, it creates a world after its own image.

The bourgeoisie has subjected the country to the rule of the 28 towns. It has created enormous cities, has greatly increased the urban population as compared with the rural and has thus rescued a considerable part of the population from the idiocy of rural life. Just as it has made the country dependent on the towns, so it has made barbarian and semi-barbarian countries dependent on civilized ones, nations of peasants on nations of bourgeois, the East on the West.

The bourgeoisie keeps more and more doing away with the scattered state of the population, of the means of production, and of property. It has agglomerated population, centralized means of production, and has concentrated property in a few hands. The necessary consequence of this was political centralization. Independent, or but loosely connected provinces, with separate interests, laws, governments, and systems of taxation, became lumped together in one nation, with one government, one code of laws, one national class interest, one frontier and one customs tariff.

The bourgeoisie, during its rule of scarce one hundred years, has created more massive and more colossal productive forces than have all preceding generations together. Subjection of Nature's forces to man, machinery, application of chemistry to industry and agriculture, steam-navigation, railways, electric telegraphs, clearing of whole continents for cultivation, canalization of rivers, whole populations conjured out of the ground—what earlier century had even a presentiment that such productive forces slumbered in the lap of social labor?

We see then: the means of production and of exchange on whose foundation the bourgeoisie built itself up, were generated in feudal society. At a certain stage in the development of these means of production and of exchange, the conditions under which feudal society produced and exchanged, the feudal organization of agriculture and manufacturing industry, in one word, the feudal relations of property became no longer compatible with the already developed productive forces; they became so many fetters. They had to burst asunder; they were burst asunder.

Into their place stepped free competition, accompanied by a 32 social and political constitution adapted to it, and by the economical and political sway of the bourgeois class.

A similar movement is going on before our own eyes. Modern bourgeois society with its relations of production, of exchange and of property, a society that has conjured up such gigantic means of production and of exchange, is like the sorcerer, who is no longer able to control the powers of the nether world whom he has called up by his spells. For many a decade past, the history of industry and commerce is but the history of the revolt of modern productive forces against modern conditions of production, against the property relations that are the conditions for the existence of the bourgeoisie and of its rule. It is enough to mention the commercial crises that by their periodical return put on its trial, each time more threateningly, the existence of the entire bourgeois society. In these crises a great part not only of the existing products, but also of the previously created productive forces, are periodically destroyed. In these crises there breaks out an epidemic that, in all earlier epochs, would have seemed an absurdity—the epidemic of overproduction. Society suddenly finds itself put back into a state of momentary barbarism; it appears as if a famine, a universal war of devastation, had cut off the supply of every means of subsistence; industry and commerce seem to be destroyed; and why? Because there is too much civilization, too much means of subsistence, too much industry, too much commerce. The productive forces at the disposal of society no longer tend to further the development of the conditions of the bourgeois property; on the contrary, they have become too powerful for these conditions by which they are fettered, and as soon as they overcome these fetters they bring disorder into the whole of bourgeois society, endanger the existence of bourgeois property. The conditions of bourgeois society are too narrow to comprise the wealth created by them. And how does the bourgeoisie get over these crises? On the one hand by enforced destruction of a mass of productive forces; on the other, by the conquest of new markets, and by the more thorough exploitation of the old ones. That is to say, by paving the way for more extensive and more destructive crises, and by diminishing the means whereby crises are prevented.

The weapons with which the bourgeoisie felled feudalism to the ground are now turned against the bourgeoisie itself.

But not only has the bourgeoisie forged the weapons that bring death to itself; it has also called into existence the men who are to wield those weapons—the modern working class—the proletarians.

In proportion as the bourgeoisie, i.e., capital, is developed, in 36 the same proportion is the proletariat, the modern working class, developed, a class of laborers who live only so long as they find work, and who find work only so long as their labor increases capital. These laborers, who must sell themselves piecemeal, are a commodity, like every other article of commerce, and are consequently exposed to all the vicissitudes of competition, to all the fluctuations of the market.

Owing to the extensive use of machinery and to division of labor, the work of the proletarians has lost all individual character, and, consequently, all charm for the workman. He becomes an appendage of the machine, and it is only the most simple, most monotonous and most easily acquired knack that is required of him. Hence, the cost of production of a workman is restricted almost entirely to the means of subsistence that he requires for his maintenance, and for the propagation of his race. But the price of a commodity, and also of labor, is equal to its cost of production. In proportion, therefore, as the repulsiveness of the work increases the wage decreases. Nay more, in proportion as the use of machinery and division of labor increases, in the same proportion the burden of toil increases, whether by prolongation of the working hours, by increase of the work enacted in a given time, or by increased speed of the machinery, etc.

Modern industry has converted the little workshop of the patri archal master into the great factory of the industrial capitalist. Masses of laborers, crowded into factories, are organized like soldiers. As privates of the industrial army they are placed under the command of a perfect hierarchy of officers and sergeants. Not only are they the slaves of the bourgeois class and of the bourgeois state, they are daily and hourly enslaved by the machine, by the overlooker, and, above all, by the individual bourgeois manufacturer himself. The more openly this despotism proclaims gain to be its end and aim, the more petty, the more hateful and the more embittering it is.

The less the skill and exertion or strength implied in manual labor, in other words, the more modern industry becomes developed, the more is the labor of men superseded by that of women. Differences of age and sex have no longer any distinctive social validity for the working class. All are instruments of labor, more or less expensive to use, according to their age and sex.

No sooner is the exploitation of the laborer by the manufac- 40
turer, so far at an end, that he receives his wages in cash, than he is set upon by the other portions of the bourgeoisie, the landlord, the shopkeeper, the pawnbroker, etc.

The lower strata of the middle class—the small trades-people, shopkeepers and retired tradesmen generally, the handicraftsmen and peasants—all these sink gradually into the proletariat, partly because their diminutive capital does not suffice for the scale on which Modern Industry is carried on, and is swamped in the competition with the large capitalists, partly because their specialized skill is rendered worthless by new methods of production. Thus the proletariat is recruited from all classes of the population.

The proletariat goes through various stages of development. With its birth begins its struggle with the bourgeoisie. At first the contest is carried on by individual laborers, then by the workpeople of a factory, then by the operatives of one trade, in one locality, against the individual bourgeois who directly exploits them. They direct their attacks not against the bourgeois conditions of production, but against the instruments of production themselves; they destroy imported wares that compete with their labor, they smash to pieces machinery, they set factories ablaze, they seek to restore by force the vanished status of the workman of the Middle Ages.

At this stage the laborers still form an incoherent mass scattered over the whole country, and broken up by their mutual competition. If anywhere they unite to form more compact bodies, this is not yet the consequence of their own active union, but of the union of the bourgeoisie, which class, in order to attain its own political ends, is compelled to set the whole proletariat in motion, and is moreover yet, for a time, able to do so. At this stage, therefore, the proletarians do not fight their enemies, but the enemies of their enemies, the remnants of absolute monarchy, the landowners, the non-industrial bourgeois, the petty bourgeoisie. Thus the whole historical movement is concentrated in the hands of the bourgeoisie, every victory so obtained is a victory for the bourgeoisie.

But with the development of industry the proletariat not only   44
increases in number; it becomes concentrated in greater masses, its strength grows and it feels that strength more. The various interests and conditions of life within the ranks of the proletariat are more and more equalized, in proportion as machinery obliterates all distinctions of labor, and nearly everywhere reduces wages to the same low level. The growing competition among the bourgeois, and the resulting commercial crisis, make the wages of the workers even more fluctuating. The unceasing improvement of machinery, ever more rapidly developing, makes their livelihood more and more precarious; the collisions between individual workmen and individual bourgeois take more and more the character of collisions between two classes. Thereupon the workers begin to form combinations (Trades' Unions)[9] against the bourgeois; they club together in order to keep up the rate of wages; they found permanent associations in order to make provision beforehand for these occasional revolts. Here and there the contest breaks out into riots.

Now and then the workers are victorious, but only for a time. The real fruit of their battle lies not in the immediate result but in the ever-expanding union of workers. This union is helped on by the improved means of communication that are created by modern industry, and that places the workers of different localities in contact with one another. It was just this contact that was needed to centralize the numerous local struggles, all of the same character, into one national struggle between classes. But every class struggle is a political struggle. And that union, to attain which the burghers of the Middle Ages with their miserable highways, required centuries, the modern proletarians, thanks to railways, achieve in a few years.

This organization of the proletarians into a class, and consequently into a political party, is continually being upset again by the competition between the workers themselves. But it ever rises up again, stronger, firmer, mightier. It compels legislative recogni-

---

[9]*combinations (Trades' Unions)*   The labor movement was only beginning in 1848. It consisted of trades' unions that started as social clubs but soon began agitating for labor reform. They represented an important step in the growth of socialism in Europe.

tion of particular interests of the workers by taking advantage of the divisions among the bourgeoisie itself. Thus the ten hours' bill in England[10] was carried.

Altogether collisions between the classes of the old society further, in many ways, the course of development of the proletariat. The bourgeoisie finds itself involved in a constant battle. At first with the aristocracy; later on, with those portions of the bourgeoisie itself whose interests have become antagonistic to the progress of industry; at all times, with the bourgeoisie of foreign countries. In all these battles it sees itself compelled to appeal to the proletariat, to ask for its help, and thus, to drag it into the political arena. The bourgeoisie itself, therefore, supplies the proletariat with its own elements of political and general education; in other words, it furnishes the proletariat with weapons for fighting the bourgeoisie.

Further, as we have already seen, entire sections of the ruling classes are, by the advance of industry, precipitated into the proletariat, or are at least threatened in their conditions of existence. These also supply the proletariat with fresh elements of enlightenment and progress. 48

Finally, in times when the class-struggle nears the decisive hour, the process of dissolution going on within the ruling class—in fact, within the whole range of an old society—assumes such a violent, glaring character that a small section of the ruling class cuts itself adrift and joins the revolutionary class, the class that holds the future in its hands. Just as, therefore, at an earlier period, a section of the nobility went over to the bourgeoisie, so now a portion of the bourgeoisie goes over to the proletariat, and in particular, a portion of the bourgeois ideologists, who have raised themselves to the level of comprehending theoretically the historical movements as a whole.

Of all the classes that stand face to face with the bourgeoisie today the proletariat alone is a really revolutionary class. The other classes decay and finally disappear in the face of modern industry; the proletariat is its special and essential product.

The lower middle class, the small manufacturer, the shopkeeper, the artisan, the peasant, all these fight against the bourgeoisie, to save from extinction their existence as fractions of the middle class. They are therefore not revolutionary, but conservative. Nay, more; they are reactionary, for they try to roll back the wheel of

---

[10]***the ten hours' bill in England***   This bill (1847) was an important labor reform. It limited the working day for women and children in factories to only ten hours; at the time it was common for some people to work sixteen hours a day. The bill's passage was a result of political division, not of benevolence on the managers' part.

history. If by chance they are revolutionary, they are so only in view of their impending transfer into the proletariat; they thus defend not their present, but their future interests; they desert their own standpoint to place themselves at that of the proletariat.

The "dangerous class," the social scum, that passively rotting 52 mass thrown off by the lowest layers of old society, may, here and there, be swept into the movement by a proletarian revolution; its conditions of life, however, prepare it far more for the part of a bribed tool of reactionary intrigue.

In the conditions of the proletariat, those of the old society at large are already virtually swamped. The proletarian is without property; his relation to his wife and children has no longer anything in common with the bourgeois family relations; modern industrial labor, modern subjection to capital, the same in England as in France, in America as in Germany, has stripped him of every trace of national character. Law, morality, religion, are to him so many bourgeois prejudices, behind which lurk in ambush just as many bourgeois interests.

All the preceding classes that got the upper hand sought to fortify their already acquired status by subjecting society at large to their conditions of appropriation. The proletarians cannot become masters of the productive forces of society, except by abolishing their own previous mode of appropriation, and thereby also every other previous mode of appropriation. They have nothing of their own to secure and to fortify; their mission is to destroy all previous securities for and insurances of individual property.

All previous historical movements were movements of minorities, or in the interest of minorities. The proletarian movement is the self-conscious, independent movement of the immense majority. The proletariat, the lowest stratum of our present society, cannot stir, cannot raise itself up without the whole superincumbent strata of official society being sprung into the air.

Though not in substance, yet in form, the struggle of the prole- 56 tariat with the bourgeoisie is at first a national struggle. The proletariat of each country must, of course, first of all settle matters with its own bourgeoisie.

In depicting the most general phases of the development of the proletariat, we traced the more or less veiled civil war, raging within existing society, up to the point where that war breaks out into open revolution, and where the violent overthrow of the bourgeoisie, lays the foundations for the sway of the proletariat.

Hitherto every form of society has been based, as we have already seen, on the antagonism of oppressing and oppressed classes. But in order to oppress a class, certain conditions must be assured to it under which it can, at least, continue its slavish existence. The serf, in the period of serfdom, raised himself to membership in the commune, just as the petty bourgeois, under the yoke of feudal absolutism, managed to develop into a bourgeois. The modern laborer, on the contrary, instead of rising with the progress of industry, sinks deeper and deeper below the conditions of existence of his own class. He becomes a pauper, and pauperism develops more rapidly than population and wealth. And here it becomes evident that the bourgeoisie is unfit any longer to be the ruling class in society, and to impose its conditions of existence upon society as an over-riding law. It is unfit to rule, because it is incompetent to assure an existence to its slave within his slavery, because it cannot help letting him sink into such a state that it has to feed him, instead of being fed by him. Society can no longer live under this bourgeoisie; in other words, its existence is no longer compatible with society.

The essential condition for the existence, and for the sway of the bourgeois class, is the formation and augmentation of capital; the condition for capital is wage labor. Wage labor rests exclusively on competition between the laborers. The advance of industry, whose involuntary promoter is the bourgeoisie, replaces the isolation of the laborers, due to competition, by their involuntary combination, due to association. The development of Modern Industry, therefore, cuts from under its feet the very foundation on which the bourgeoisie produces and appropriates products. What the bourgeoisie therefore produces, above all, are its own grave diggers. Its fall and the victory of the proletariat are equally inevitable.

Proletarians and Communists

In what relation do the Communists stand to the proletarians 60 as a whole?

The Communists do not form a separate party opposed to other working class parties.

They have no interests separate and apart from those of the proletariat as a whole.

They do not set up any sectarian principles of their own, by which to shape and mold the proletarian movement.

The Communists are distinguished from the other working 64 class parties by this only: 1. In the national struggles of the proletarians of the different countries, they point out and bring to the front the common interests of the entire proletariat, independently of all nationality. 2. In the various stages of development which the struggle of the working class against the bourgeoisie has to pass through, they always and everywhere represent the interests of the movement as a whole.

The Communists, therefore, are on the one hand practically the most advanced and resolute section of the working class parties of every country, that section which pushes forward all others; on the other hand, theoretically, they have over the great mass of the proletariat the advantage of clearly understanding the line of march, the conditions, and the ultimate general results of the proletarian movement.

The immediate aim of the Communists is the same as that of all the other proletarian parties: formation of the proletariat into a class, overthrow of the bourgeois of supremacy, conquest of political power by the proletariat.

The theoretical conclusions of the Communists are in no way based on ideas or principles that have been invented or discovered by this or that would-be universal reformer.

They merely express, in general terms, actual relations spring-   68
ing from an existing class struggle, from a historical movement going on under our very eyes. The abolition of existing property relations is not at all a distinctive feature of Communism.

All property relations in the past have continually been subject to historical change consequent upon the change in historical conditions.

The French Revolution, for example, abolished feudal property in favor of bourgeois property.

The distinguishing feature of Communism is not the abolition of property generally, but the abolition of bourgeois property. But modern bourgeois private property is the final and most complete expression of the system of producing and appropriating products, that is based on class antagonism, on the exploitation of the many by the few.

In this sense, the theory of the Communists may be summed   72
up in the single sentence: Abolition of private property.

We Communists have been reproached with the desire of abolishing the right of personally acquiring property as the fruit of a man's own labor, which property is alleged to be the groundwork of all personal freedom, activity and independence.

Hard won, self-acquired, self-earned property! Do you mean the property of the petty artisan and of the small peasant, a form of property that preceded the bourgeois form? There is no need to abolish that; the development of industry has to a great extent already destroyed it, and is still destroying it daily.

Or do you mean modern bourgeois private property?

But does wage labor create any property for the laborer? Not a bit. It creates capital, i.e., that kind of property which exploits wage labor, and which cannot increase except upon condition of getting a new supply of wage labor for fresh exploitation. Property, in its present form, is based on the antagonism of capital and wage labor. Let us examine both sides of this antagonism.

To be a capitalist is to have not only a purely personal, but a social status in production. Capital is a collective product, and only by the united action of many members, nay, in the last resort, only by the united action of all members of society, can it be set in motion.

Capital is therefore not a personal, it is a social power.

When, therefore, capital is converted into common property, into the property of all members of society, personal property is not thereby transformed into social property. It is only the social character of the property that is changed. It loses its class character.

Let us now take wage labor.

The average price of wage labor is the minimum wage, i.e., that quantum of the means of subsistence which is absolutely requisite to keep the laborer in bare existence as a laborer. What, therefore, the wage laborer appropriates by means of his labor, merely suffices to prolong and reproduce a bare existence. We by no means intend to abolish this personal appropriation of the products of labor, an appropriation that is made for the maintenance and reproduction of human life, and that leaves no surplus wherewith to command the labor of others. All that we want to do away with is the miserable character of this appropriation, under which the laborer lives merely to increase capital and is allowed to live only in so far as the interests of the ruling class require it.

In bourgeois society, living labor is but a means to increase accumulated labor. In Communist society accumulated labor is but a means to widen, to enrich, to promote the existence of the laborer.

In bourgeois society, therefore, the past dominates the present; in Communist society the present dominates the past. In bourgeois society, capital is independent and has individuality, while the living person is dependent and has no individuality.

And the abolition of this state of things is called by the bourgeois abolition of individuality and freedom! And rightly so. The abolition of bourgeois individuality, bourgeois independence and bourgeois freedom is undoubtedly aimed at.

By freedom is meant, under the present bourgeois conditions of production, free trade, free selling and buying.

But if selling and buying disappears, free selling and buying disappears also. This talk about free selling and buying, and all the other "brave words" of our bourgeoisie about freedom in general have a meaning, if any, only in contrast with restricted selling and buying, with the fettered traders of the Middle Ages, but have no meaning when opposed to the Communistic abolition of buying and selling, of the bourgeois conditions of production, and of the bourgeoisie itself.

You are horrified at our intending to do away with private property. But in your existing society private property is already done away with for nine-tenths of the population; its existence for the few is solely due to its non-existence in the hands of those nine-tenths. You reproach us, therefore, with intending to do away with a form of property, the necessary condition for whose existence is the non-existence of any property for the immense majority of society.

In one word, you reproach us with intending to do away with   88
your property. Precisely so: that is just what we intend.

From the moment when labor can no longer be converted into capital, money, or rent, into a social power capable of being monopolized, i.e., from the moment when individual property can no longer be transformed into bourgeois property, into capital, from that moment, you say, individuality vanishes.

You must, therefore, confess that by "individual" you mean no other person than the bourgeois, than the middle-class owner of property. This person must, indeed, be swept out of the way and made impossible.

Communism deprives no man of the power to appropriate the products of society: all that it does is to deprive him of the power to subjugate the labor of others by means of such appropriation.

It has been objected that upon the abolition of private property   92
all work will cease and universal laziness will overtake us.

According to this, bourgeois society ought long ago to have gone to the dogs through sheer idleness; for those of its members who work acquire nothing, and those who acquire anything do not work. The whole of this objection is but another expression of the tautology: that there can no longer be any wage labor when there is no longer any capital.

All objections urged against the Communistic mode of producing and appropriating material products have, in the same way, been urged against the Communistic modes of producing and appropriating intellectual products. Just as, to the bourgeois, the disappearance of class property is the disappearance of production itself, so the disappearance of class culture is to him identical with the disappearance of all culture.

That culture, the loss of which he laments, is, for the enormous majority, a mere training to act as a machine.

But don't wrangle with us so long as you apply, to our intended abolition of bourgeois property, the standard of your bourgeois notions of freedom, culture, law, etc. Your very ideas are but the outgrowth of the conditions of your bourgeois production and bourgeois property, just as your jurisprudence is but the will of your class made into a law for all, a will whose essential character and direction are determined by the economical conditions of existence of your class. 96

The selfish misconception that induces you to transform into eternal laws of nature and of reason the social forms springing from your present mode of production and form of property—historical relations that rise and disappear in the progress of production—this misconception you share with every ruling class that has preceded you. What you see clearly in the case of ancient property, what you admit in the case of feudal property, you are of course forbidden to admit in the case of your own bourgeois form of property.

Abolition of the family! Even the most radical flare up at this infamous proposal of the Communists.

On what foundation is the present family, the bourgeois family, based? On capital, on private gain. In its completely developed form this family exists only among the bourgeoisie. But this state of things finds its complement in the practical absence of the family among the proletarians, and in public prostitution.

The bourgeois family will vanish as a matter of course when its complement vanishes, and both will vanish with the vanishing of capital. 100

Do you charge us with wanting to stop the exploitation of children by their parents? To this crime we plead guilty.

But, you will say, we destroy the most hallowed of relations when we replace home education by social.

And your education! Is not that also social, and determined by the social conditions under which you educate; by the intervention, direct or indirect, of society by means of schools, etc.? The Communists have not invented the intervention of society in education; they do but seek to alter the character of that intervention, and to rescue education from the influence of the ruling class.

The bourgeois clap-trap about the family and education, about the hallowed correlation of parent and child, become all the more disgusting, the more, by the action of Modern Industry, all family 104 ties among the proletarians are torn asunder and their children transformed into simple articles of commerce and instruments of labor.

But you Communists would introduce community of women, screams the whole bourgeoisie chorus.

The bourgeois sees in his wife a mere instrument of production. He hears that the instruments of production are to be exploited in common, and, naturally, can come to no other conclusion, than that the lot of being common to all will likewise fall to the women.

He has not even a suspicion that the real point aimed at is to do away with the status of women as mere instruments of production.

For the rest, nothing is more ridiculous than the virtuous indig-   108
nation of our bourgeois at the community of women which, they pretend, is to be openly and officially established by the Communists. The Communists have no need to introduce community of women, it has existed almost from time immemorial.

Our bourgeois, not content with having the wives and daughters of their proletarians at their disposal, not to speak of common prostitutes, take the greatest pleasure in seducing each others' wives.

Bourgeois marriage is in reality a system of wives in common, and thus, at the most, what the Communists might possibly be reproached with, is that they desire to introduce, in substitution for a hypocritically concealed, an openly legalized community of women. For the rest, it is self-evident that the abolition of the present system of production must bring with it the abolition of the community of women springing from that system, i.e., of prostitution both public and private.

The Communists are further reproached with desiring to abolish countries and nationalities.

The working men have no country. We cannot take from them   112
what they don't possess. Since the proletariat must first of all acquire political supremacy, must rise to be the leading class of the nation, must constitute itself the nation, it is, so far, itself national, though not in the bourgeois sense of the word.

National differences and antagonisms between peoples are daily more and more vanishing, owing to the development of the bourgeoisie, to freedom of commerce, to the world-market, to uniformity in the mode of production and in the conditions of life corresponding thereto.

The supremacy of the proletariat will cause them to vanish still faster. United action, of the leading civilized countries at least, is one of the first conditions for the emancipation of the proletariat.

In proportion as the exploitation of one individual by another is put an end to, the exploitation of one nation by another will also be put an end to. In proportion as the antagonism between classes within the nation vanishes, the hostility of one nation to another will come to an end.

The charges against Communism made from a religious, a 116 philosophical, and generally, from an ideological standpoint, are not deserving of serious examination.

Does it require deep intuition to comprehend that man's ideas, views and conceptions, in one word, man's consciousness, changes with every change in the conditions of his material existence, in his social relations and in his social life?

What else does the history of ideas prove than that intellectual production changes in character in proportion as material production is changed? The ruling ideas of each age have ever been the ideas of its ruling class.

When people speak of ideas that revolutionize society they do but express the fact that within the old society the elements of a new one have been created, and that the dissolution of the old ideas keeps even pace with the dissolution of the old conditions of existence.

When the ancient world was in its last throes the ancient reli- 120 gions were overcome by Christianity. When Christian ideas succumbed in the 18th century to rationalist ideas, feudal society fought its deathbattle with the then revolutionary bourgeoisie. The ideas of religious liberty and freedom of conscience merely gave expression to the sway of free competition within the domain of knowledge.

"Undoubtedly," it will be said, "religious, moral, philosophical and judicial ideas have been modified in the course of historical development. But religion, morality, philosophy, political science, and law, constantly survived this change.

"There are, besides, eternal truths such as Freedom, Justice, etc., that are common to all states of society. But Communism abolishes eternal truths, it abolishes all religion and all morality, instead of constituting them on a new basis; it therefore acts in contradiction to all past historical experience."

What does this accusation reduce itself to? The history of all past society has consisted in the development of class antagonisms, antagonisms that assumed different forms at different epochs.

But whatever form they may have taken, one fact is common 124 to all past ages, viz., the exploitation of one part of society by the other. No wonder, then, that the social consciousness of past ages, despite all the multiplicity and variety it displays, moves within certain common forms, or general ideas, which cannot completely vanish except with the total disappearance of class antagonisms.

The Communist revolution is the most radical rupture with traditional property relations; no wonder that its development involves the most radical rupture with traditional ideas.

But let us have done with the bourgeois objections to Communism.

We have seen above that the first step in the revolution by the working class is to raise the proletariat to the position of ruling class, to win the battle of democracy.

The proletariat will use its political supremacy to wrest, by degrees, all capital from the bourgeoisie, to centralize all instruments of production in the hands of the State, i.e., of the proletariat organized as a ruling class; and to increase the total productive forces as rapidly as possible.   128

Of course, in the beginning, this cannot be effected except by means of despotic inroads on the rights of property, and on the conditions of bourgeois production; by means of measures, therefore, which appear economically insufficient and untenable, but which in the course of the movement outstrip themselves, necessitate further inroads upon the old social order, and are unavoidable as a means of entirely revolutionizing the mode of production.

These measures will of course be different in different countries.

Nevertheless in the most advanced countries the following will be pretty generally applicable:

1. Abolition of property in land and application of all rents of land to public purposes.
2. A heavy progressive or graduated income tax.
3. Abolition of all right of inheritance.
4. Confiscation of the property of all emigrants and rebels.
5. Centralization of credit in the hands of the State, by means of a national bank with State capital and an exclusive monopoly.
6. Centralization of the means of communication and transport in the hands of the State.
7. Extension of factories and instruments of production owned by the State; the bringing into cultivation of waste lands, and the improvement of the soil generally in accordance with a common plan.
8. Equal liability of all to labor. Establishment of industrial armies, especially for agriculture.
9. Combination of agriculture with manufacturing industries; gradual abolition of the distinction between town and country by a more equable distribution of the population over the country.
10. Free education for all children in public schools. Abolition of

children's factory labor in its present form. Combination of education with industrial production, etc., etc.

When, in the course of development, class distinctions have   132
disappeared, and all production has been concentrated in the hands of a vast association of the whole nation, the public power will lose its political character. Political power, properly so called, is merely the organized power of one class for oppressing another. If the proletariat during its contest with the bourgeoisie is compelled, by the force of circumstances, to organize itself as a class, if, by means of a revolution, it makes itself the ruling class, and, as such, sweeps away by force the old conditions of production, then it will, along with these conditions, have swept away the conditions for the existence of class antagonism, and of classes generally, and will thereby have abolished its own supremacy as a class.

In place of the old bourgeois society, with its classes and class antagonisms, we shall have an association in which the free development of each is the condition for the free development of all. . . .

Position of the Communists in Relation to the Various Existing Opposition Parties

[The preceding section] has made clear the relations of the Communists to the existing working class parties, such as the Chartists in England and the Agrarian Reforms[11] in America.

The Communists fight for the attainment of the immediate aims, for the enforcement of the momentary interests of the working class; but in the movement of the present they also represent and take care of the future of that movement. In France the Communists ally themselves with the Social-Democrats[12] against the conservative and radical bourgeoisie, reserving, however, the right to take up a critical position in regard to phrases and illusions traditionally handed down from the great Revolution.

In Switzerland they support the Radicals,[13] without losing sight   136

---

[11]*Agrarian Reforms*   Agrarian reform was a very important issue in America after the Revolution. The Chartists were a radical English group established in 1838; they demanded political and social reforms. They were among the more violent revolutionaries of the day. Agrarian reform, redistribution of the land, was slow to come, and the issue often sparked violence between social classes.

[12]*Social-Democrats*   In France in the 1840s, a group that proposed the ideal of labor reform through the establishment of workshops supplied with government capital.

[13]*Radicals*   By 1848, European Radicals, taking their name from the violent

of the fact that this party consists of antagonistic elements, partly of Democratic Socialists, in the French sense, partly of radical bourgeois.

In Poland they support the party that insists on an agrarian revolution, as the prime condition for national emancipation, that party which fomented the insurrection of Cracow in 1846.[14]

In Germany they fight with the bourgeoisie whenever it acts in a revolutionary way, against the absolute monarchy, the feudal squirearchy, and the petty bourgeoisie.

But they never cease for a single instant to instill into the working class the clearest possible recognition of the hostile antagonism between bourgeoisie and proletariat, in order that the German workers may straightway use, as so many weapons against the bourgeoisie, the social and political conditions that the bourgeoisie must necessarily introduce along with its supremacy, and in order that, after the fall of the reactionary classes in Germany, the fight against the bourgeoisie itself may immediately begin.

The Communists turn their attention chiefly to Germany, be-   140
cause that country is on the eve of a bourgeois revolution,[15] that is bound to be carried out under more advanced conditions of European civilization, and with a more developed proletariat, than that of England was in the seventeenth and of France in the eighteenth century, and because the bourgeois revolution in Germany will be but the prelude to an immediately following proletarian revolution.

In short, the Communists everywhere support every revolutionary movement against the existing social and political order of things.

In all these movements they bring to the front, as the leading question in each, the property question, no matter what its degree of development at the time.

Finally, they labor everywhere for the union and agreement of the democratic parties of all countries.

The Communists disdain to conceal their views and aims. They   144
openly declare that their ends can be attained only by the forcible

---

revolutionaries of the French Revolution (1789–1799), were a nonviolent group content to wait for change.

[14]*the insurrection of Cracow in 1846*   Cracow was an independent city in 1846. The insurrection was designed to join Cracow with Poland and to further large-scale social reforms.

[15]*on the eve of a bourgeois revolution*   Ferdinand Lassalle (1825–1864) developed the German labor movement and was in basic agreement with Marx, who was nevertheless convinced that Lassalle's approach was wrong. The environment in Germany seemed appropriate for revolution, in part because of its fragmented political structure and in part because no major revolution had yet occurred there.

overthrow of all existing social conditions. Let the ruling classes tremble at a Communistic revolution. The proletarians have nothing to lose but their chains. They have a world to win.

Working men of all countries, unite!

QUESTIONS FOR CRITICAL READING

1. Begin by establishing your understanding of the terms "bourgeois" and "proletarian." Is the distinction Marx makes clear? Are such terms applicable to American society today? Do you feel that you can be properly associated with one or the other of these groups?
2. Marx makes the concept of social class fundamental to his theories. Can "social class" be easily defined? Are social classes evident in our society? Are they engaged in a struggle of the sort Marx assumes?
3. What are Marx's views about the value of work in the society he describes?
4. Marx says that every class struggle is a political struggle. Do you agree?
5. Examine the first part and total the number of paragraphs devoted to the bourgeoisie and to the proletariat respectively. Which class gets more paragraphs? Why?
6. Is the modern proletariat a revolutionary class?
7. Is Marx's analysis of history clear? Try to summarize his views on the progress of history.
8. Is capital a social force, or is it a personal force? Do you think of your savings (either now or in the future) as belonging to you alone or as in some way belonging to your society?
9. What, in Marx's view, is the responsibility of a government that takes the *Manifesto* seriously enough to consider reshaping its economic system accordingly?

WRITING ASSIGNMENTS

1. Defend or attack Marx's statement: "The executive of the modern State is but a committee for managing the common affairs of the whole bourgeoisie." Is this generally true? Take three "affairs of the whole bourgeoisie" and test each one in turn.
2. Examine Marx's statements regarding women. Refer especially to paragraphs 39, 98, 105, and 110. Does he imply that his views are in conflict with his general society? After you have a list of his statements, see if you can establish exactly what he is recommending. Do you approve of his recommendations?
3. Marx's program of ten points is listed in paragraph 131. Using the

technique that Marx himself uses—taking each point in its turn, clarifying the problems with the point, and finally deciding for or against the point—evaluate his program. Which points do you feel are most beneficial to society? Which are detrimental to society? What is your overall view of the general worth of the program? Do you think it would be possible to put such a program into effect?

4. All Marx's views are predicated on the present nature of property ownership and the changes that communism will institute. He claims, for example, that a rupture with property relations "involves the most radical rupture with traditional ideas" (para. 125). And he discusses in depth his proposal for the rupture of property relations (paras. 68–93). Clarify traditional property relations—what can be owned and by whom—and then contrast with these the proposals Marx makes. Establish your own views as you go along. Include your reasons for taking issue or expressing agreement with Marx. What kinds of property relations do you see around you? What kinds are most desirable for a healthy society? Does Marx's approval worry you?

5. What is the responsibility of the state toward the individual in the kind of economic circumstances that Marx describes? How can one balance the independence of those individuals who have amassed great wealth and wish to operate freely against the independence of those who are poor and have no wealth to manipulate? What are the possibilities of abuse in such circumstances, and what are the remedies that a state can achieve through altering the economic system? What specific remedies does Marx suggest? Are they workable?

6. Do you feel that Marx's suggestions are desirable? Or that they are likely to produce the effects he desires? What do you see as impediments to the full success of his program? Critics sometimes complain about Marx's misunderstanding of human nature. Do you feel he has an adequate understanding of human nature?

7. **CONNECTIONS** Marx's philosophy differs from that of Robert B. Reich. How would Marx respond to Reich's analysis of the future of labor in the next few decades? Would Marx see signs of a coming class struggle in the distinctions Reich draws between the routine workers, the in-person servers, and the symbolic analysts? Does Reich's essay take any of Marx's theories into account?

THORSTEIN VEBLEN

Pecuniary Emulation

THORSTEIN VEBLEN (1857–1929) is one of America's most powerfully original thinkers in the areas of economics, business, and sociology. A product of the Scandinavian settlements of the Midwest, he was educated at Carleton College in Northfield, Minnesota, and was awarded a Ph.D. in philosophy at Yale University. One of the interesting ironies of his career is that, brilliant though he was, he did not immediately proceed to an academic appointment. He languished for seven years on his father's farm in Minnesota, reading—a fate similar to that of the great seventeenth-century English poet John Milton, who spent a period of time on his father's estate before moving into a worldly career.

The reasons that Veblen had been ignored by the academic world seem to have centered on his difficult personality and on his extremely unpopular views of the direction of the American economy and of the nation's overall social structure. He was profoundly critical of the dominance of business interests over the interests of social betterment. He castigated the nation for its slavish worship of the canons of consumption. The passage included here is from his most famous book, The Theory of the Leisure Class *(1899), in which he develops a fascinating view of America as a culture that delights in abundance, waste, and conspicuous consumption. Conspicuous consumption is economic showing off. As a modern slogan puts it approvingly, "If you've got it, flaunt it."*

Veblen felt that "flaunting it" was central to the American way of life, especially the way of life of the leisure class produced by the

From *The Theory of the Leisure Class.* The Portable Veblen.

American economics of abundance. He condemned conspicuous consumption as fundamentally wasteful and as risking an ultimate financial collapse and a terrible fate for those who were poor. Interestingly, Veblen died in the year in which the spiraling economy, inflated by waves of selfish enthusiasm and reckless speculation, crashed so resoundingly that much of the nation was plunged into a decade of poverty.

It is no wonder that such a telling critic should at first have been kept from the rewards of academic life: he was too savage a gadfly to be tolerated. Yet he eventually succeeded. He taught at the University of Chicago after completing graduate studies in economics at Cornell. He taught at the New School for Social Research in New York City, at Stanford University in California for a short time, and at the University of Missouri. But the sad fact is that he was never a popular teacher: he begrudged his students their grades, usually marking them all C. He was a classroom mumbler, a monotone dryasdust. Yet, he had one of the most sparkling minds of his generation. Those students who persisted and got through the dull classroom periods were rewarded with an experience so memorable that several of them later wrote of it in their memoirs.

Almost all of his many publications are of more interest now than they were while he was alive. His greatest fame was posthumous. It was after his death that his views began to be appreciated as those of a farseeing economics savant. One of his books, The Higher Learning in America *(1918), is a biting attack on the willingness of America's universities to be dominated by capitalist businesses. The subservience of the universities to the demands of profits, he argued, resulted in the universities' goals of producing passive, malleable, and acceptable workers for the needs of business and industry. Veblen would much rather have had the universities forsake the world of business and concentrate on the goals of thorough education, even if such a change in focus would have produced graduates likely to be uncomfortable in the then repressive structure of American business. His views are certainly as unwelcome today as they were in his own time.*

His "Pecuniary Emulation" discusses the question of the development of the urge to accumulate wealth. In Veblen's America, huge fortunes had been amassed by innumerable American tycoons, among them the group often known as robber barons, those who defied most common ethical principles of decency and fairness in order to make themselves almost unbelievably wealthy. Veblen saw these men as predatory and compared their behavior to that of savage beasts of the wilderness. This view in turn led him to the analogy with Darwinian evolution and the "survival of the fittest."

Veblen's study includes ideas of evolutionary progress in economics. Interestingly, Marx too had such views. Yet Veblen did not have Marx's interest in recommending communism as the final stage of evolution of the modern state. Rather, he wanted to show that the question of ownership is susceptible to analysis in evolutionary terms. That is, by examining its beginnings, one would be able to understand in depth people's drive (clearly evident in his own time) to accumulate far more wealth and goods than they could ever use.

Like many of his expressions, the term "pecuniary emulation" becomes clear as one progresses through the selection. People live in a social milieu; their behavior is understood and measured in terms of their neighbors. They emulate each other in their own social sphere; and when they indulge in pecuniary emulation, they are indulging in amassing money in order to be like their neighbors. As he says, "The currently accepted legitimate end of effort becomes the achievement of a favorable comparison with other men; and therefore the repugnance to futility to a good extent coalesces with the incentive of emulation" (para. 19). In other words, the desire for achievement and the fear of failure (repugnance to futility) derive largely from the emulation of others who have been successful and the need to compare oneself with them. As he says in the same paragraph: "Among the motives which lead men to accumulate wealth, the primacy, both in scope and intensity, therefore, continues to belong to this motive of pecuniary emulation."

The section analyzes the sociological implications of the drive toward wealth, resting primarily on a comparison of contemporary practices with those of the earliest forms of society. Veblen traces the development of the concept of individual property, distinguishes ownership from simple appropriation (for example, owning a river versus simply using it), and attempts an analysis of the need to accumulate more than can be consumed. Such accumulation is, after all, what wealth is. For Veblen it therefore represents an unusual and curious fact. His analysis is perhaps even more pertinent for us than it was for his contemporaries at the end of the century.

VEBLEN'S RHETORIC

Veblen argues a position based upon an entirely hypothetical construct: the primitive societies from which we developed. He hypothesizes an evolutionary development from a barbarian culture, as he puts it, to the current industrial model. His analysis is detailed, and his argument follows conclusively from his postulation.

Another uncommon quality is Veblen's use of unusual terminology, which does not become clear until relatively deep into the essay. Thus, "pecuniary emulation" is an opaque expression until one begins to sort out the terminology near the end of the essay. The same is true of the term "invidious comparison," which usually implies simply a comparison that casts the thing compared in a dark light (invidious means "obnoxious or repugnant"). But Veblen uses the term simply to suggest a profound difference. A man of wealth becomes wealthy in order to create an "invidious comparison" with neighbors: the wealthy man makes himself very different from his neighbor.

Finally, Veblen reveals a bit of crustiness—and probably some of the qualities that made him an unpopular teacher—in his delight in complex words. His use of language is not so brilliant as to cast him into the company of the English men of letters Matthew Arnold (1822–1888) and William Hazlitt (1778–1830), to name two who influenced him; but it is certainly compelling and demanding. His views are of great moment; he demands that we rise to his level, and he refuses to lower himself to ours. The result of this rhetorical approach to style is to set him apart, to make him appear more difficult than he is, and ultimately to reward the reader with a view of an interesting mind commanding an unusual vocabulary for the purposes of making people sit up and take notice. Veblen rewards these efforts with the product of insights that actually change the reader's way of thinking about social issues and about the drive toward the accumulation of wealth.

Pecuniary Emulation

In the sequence of cultural evolution the emergence of a leisure class coincides with the beginning of ownership. This is necessarily the case, for these two institutions result from the same set of economic forces. In the inchoate phase[1] of their development they are but different aspects of the same general facts of social structure.

It is as elements of social structure—conventional facts—that leisure and ownership are matters of interest for the purpose in hand. An habitual neglect of work does not constitute a leisure class; neither does the mechanical fact of use and consumption

---

[1] ***inchoate phase*** The early, languageless phase before things are codified, set up, and explained.

constitute ownership. The present inquiry, therefore, is not concerned with the beginning of indolence, nor with the beginning of the appropriation of useful articles to individual consumption. The point in question is the origin and nature of a conventional leisure class on the one hand and the beginnings of individual ownership as a conventional right or equitable claim on the other hand.

The early differentiation out of which the distinction between a leisure and a working class arises is a division maintained between men's and women's work in the lower stages of barbarism. Likewise the earliest form of ownership is an ownership of the women by the able-bodied men of the community. The facts may be expressed in more general terms, and truer to the import of the barbarian theory of life, by saying that it is an ownership of the woman by the man.

There was undoubtedly some appropriation of useful articles 4 before the custom of appropriating women arose. The usages of existing archaic communities in which there is no ownership of women is warrant for such a view. In all communities the members, both male and female, habitually appropriate to their individual use a variety of useful things; but these useful things are not thought of as owned by the person who appropriates and consumes them. The habitual appropriation and consumption of certain slight personal effects goes on without raising the question of ownership; that is to say, the question of a conventional, equitable claim to extraneous things.

The ownership of women begins in the lower barbarian stages of culture, apparently with the seizure of female captives. The original reason for the seizure and appropriation of women seems to have been their usefulness as trophies. The practice of seizing women from the enemy as trophies gave rise to a form of ownership-marriage, resulting in a household with a male head. This was followed by an extension of slavery to other captives and inferiors, besides women, and by an extension of ownership-marriage to other women than those seized from the enemy. The outcome of emulation under the circumstances of a predatory life, therefore, has been on the one hand a form of marriage resting on coercion, and on the other hand the custom of ownership. The two institutions are not distinguishable in the initial phase of their development; both arise from the desire of the successful men to put their prowess in evidence by exhibiting some durable result of their exploits. Both also minister to that propensity for mastery which pervades all predatory communities. From the ownership of women the concept of ownership extends itself to include the products of their industry, and so there arises the ownership of things as well as of persons.

In this way a consistent system of property in goods is gradually installed. And although in the latest stages of the development, the serviceability of goods for consumption has come to be the most obtrusive element of their value, still, wealth has by no means yet lost its utility as an honorific evidence of the owner's prepotence.[2]

Wherever the institution of private property is found, even in a slightly developed form, the economic process bears the character of a struggle between men for the possession of goods. It has been customary in economic theory, and especially among those economists who adhere with least faltering to the body of modernized classical doctrines, to construe this struggle for wealth as being substantially a struggle for subsistence. Such is, no doubt, its character in large part during the earlier and less efficient phases of industry. Such is also its character in all cases where the "niggardliness of nature" is so strict as to afford but a scanty livelihood to the community in return for strenuous and unremitting application to the business of getting the means of subsistence. But in all progressing communities an advance is presently made beyond this early stage of technological development. Industrial efficiency is presently carried to such a pitch as to afford something appreciably more than a bare livelihood to those engaged in the industrial process. It has not been unusual for economic theory to speak of the further struggle for wealth on this new industrial basis as a competition for an increase of the comforts of life—primarily for an increase of the physical comforts which the consumption of goods affords.

The end of acquisition and accumulation is conventionally held 8 to be the consumption of the goods accumulated—whether it is consumption directly by the owner of the goods or by the household attached to him and for this purpose identified with him in theory. This is at least felt to be the economically legitimate end of acquisition, which alone it is incumbent on the theory to take account of. Such consumption may of course be conceived to serve the consumer's physical wants—his physical comfort—or his so-called higher wants—spiritual, aesthetic, intellectual, or what not; the latter class of wants being served indirectly by an expenditure of goods, after the fashion familiar to all economic readers.

But it is only when taken in a sense far removed from its naïve meaning that consumption of goods can be said to afford the incentive from which accumulation invariably proceeds. The

---

[2]**prepotence** Superior power.

motive that lies at the root of ownership is emulation; and the same motive of emulation continues active in the further development of the institution to which it has given rise and in the development of all those features of the social structure which this institution of ownership touches. The possession of wealth confers honor; it is an invidious distinction. Nothing equally cogent can be said for the consumption of goods, nor for any other conceivable incentive to acquisition, and especially not for any incentive to the accumulation of wealth.

It is of course not to be overlooked that in a community where nearly all goods are private property the necessity of earning a livelihood is a powerful and ever-present incentive for the poorer members of the community. The need of subsistence and of an increase of physical comfort may for a time be the dominant motive of acquisition for those classes who are habitually employed at manual labor, whose subsistence is on a precarious footing, who possess little and ordinarily accumulate little; but it will appear in the course of the discussion that even in the case of these impecunious classes the predominance of the motive of physical want is not so decided as has sometimes been assumed. On the other hand, so far as regards those members and classes of the community who are chiefly concerned in the accumulation of wealth, the incentive of subsistence or of physical comfort never plays a considerable part. Ownership began and grew into a human institution on grounds unrelated to the subsistence minimum. The dominant incentive was from the outset the invidious distinction attaching to wealth, and, save temporarily and by exception, no other motive has usurped the primacy at any later stage of the development.

Property set out with being booty held as trophies of the successful raid. So long as the group had departed but little from the primitive communal organization, and so long as it still stood in close contact with other hostile groups, the utility of things or persons owned lay chiefly in an invidious comparison between their possessor and the enemy from whom they were taken. The habit of distinguishing between the interests of the individual and those of the group to which he belongs is apparently a later growth. Invidious comparison between the possessor of the honorific booty and his less successful neighbors within the group was no doubt present early as an element of the utility of the things possessed, though this was not at the outset the chief element of their value. The man's prowess was still primarily the group's prowess, and the possessor of the booty felt himself to be primarily the keeper of the honor of his group. This appreciation of exploit from the communal point of view is met with also at later stages of social growth, especially as regards the laurels of war.[3]

But so soon as the custom of individual ownership begins to   12
gain consistency, the point of view taken in making the invidious comparison on which private property rests will begin to change. Indeed, the one change is but the reflex of the other. The initial phase of ownership, the phase of acquisition by naïve seizure and conversion, begins to pass into the subsequent stage of an incipient organization of industry on the basis of private property (in slaves); the horde develops into a more or less self-sufficing industrial community; possessions then come to be valued not so much as evidence of successful foray, but rather as evidence of the prepotence of the possessor of these goods over other individuals within the community. The invidious comparison now becomes primarily a comparison of the owner with the other members of the group. Property is still of the nature of trophy, but, with the cultural advance, it becomes more and more a trophy of successes scored in the game of ownership carried on between the members of the group under the quasi-peaceable methods of nomadic life.

Gradually, as industrial activity further displaces predatory activity in the community's everyday life and in men's habits of thought, accumulated property more and more replaces trophies of predatory exploit as the conventional exponent of prepotence and success. With the growth of settled industry, therefore, the possession of wealth gains in relative importance and effectiveness as a customary basis of repute and esteem. Not that esteem ceases to be awarded on the basis of other, more direct evidence of prowess; not that successful predatory aggression or warlike exploit ceases to call out the approval and admiration of the crowd, or to stir the envy of the less successful competitors; but the opportunities for gaining distinction by means of this direct manifestation of superior force grow less available both in scope and frequency. At the same time opportunities for industrial aggression, and for the accumulation of property by the quasi-peaceable methods of nomadic industry, increase in scope and availability. And it is even more to the point that property now becomes the most easily recognized evidence of a reputable degree of success as distinguished from heroic or signal achievement. It therefore becomes the conventional basis of esteem. Its possession in some amount becomes necessary in order to attain any reputable standing in the community. It becomes indispensable to accumulate, to acquire property, in order

---

[3]*laurels of war*   The term is mildly ironic and refers to the honors or prizes of war. Veblen means a man's military exploits are especially significant in society.

to retain one's good name. When accumulated goods have in this way once become the accepted badge of efficiency, the possession of wealth presently assumes the character of an independent and definitive basis of esteem. The possession of goods, whether acquired aggressively by one's own exertion or passively by transmission through inheritance from others, becomes a conventional basis of reputability. The possession of wealth, which was at the outset valued simply as evidence of efficiency, becomes, in popular apprehension, itself a meritorious act. Wealth is now itself intrinisically honorable and confers honor on its possessor. By a further refinement, wealth acquired passively by transmission from ancestors or other antecedents presently becomes even more honorific than wealth acquired by the possessor's own effort; but this distinction belongs at a later stage in the evolution of the pecuniary culture and will be spoken of in its place.

Prowess and exploit may still remain the basis of award of the highest popular esteem, although the possession of wealth has become the basis of commonplace reputability and of a blameless social standing. The predatory instinct and the consequent approbation of predatory efficiency are deeply ingrained in the habits of thought of those peoples who have passed under the discipline of a protracted predatory culture. According to popular award, the highest honors within human reach may, even yet, be those gained by an unfolding of extraordinary predatory efficiency in war, or by a quasi-predatory efficiency in statecraft; but for the purposes of a commonplace decent standing in the community these means of repute have been replaced by the acquisition and accumulation of goods. In order to stand well in the eyes of the community, it is necessary to come up to a certain, somewhat indefinite, conventional standard of wealth; just as in the earlier predatory stage it is necessary for the barbarian man to come up to the tribe's standard of physical endurance, cunning, and skill at arms. A certain standard of wealth in the one case, and of prowess in the other, is a necessary condition of reputability, and anything in excess of this normal amount is meritorious.

Those members of the community who fall short of this, somewhat indefinite, normal degree of prowess or of property suffer in the esteem of their fellow-men; and consequently they suffer also in their own esteem, since the usual basis of self-respect is the respect accorded by one's neighbors. Only individuals with an aberrant temperment can in the long run retain their self-esteem in the face of the disesteem of their fellows. Apparent exceptions to the rule are met with, especially among people with strong religious convictions. But these apparent exceptions are scarcely real exceptions, since such persons commonly fall back on the putative approbation[4] of some supernatural witness of their deeds.

So soon as the possession of property becomes the basis of 16 popular esteem, therefore, it becomes also a requisite to that complacency which we call self-respect. In any community where goods are held in severalty[5] it is necessary, in order to his own peace of mind, that an individual should possess as large a portion of goods as others with whom he is accustomed to class himself; and it is extremely gratifying to possess something more than others. But as fast as a person makes new acquisitions, and becomes accustomed to the resulting new standard of wealth, the new standard forthwith ceases to afford appreciably greater satisfaction than the earlier standard did. The tendency in any case is constantly to make the present pecuniary standard the point of departure for a fresh increase of wealth; and this in turn gives rise to a new standard of sufficiency and a new pecuniary classification of one's self as compared with one's neighbors. So far as concerns the present question, the end sought by accumulation is to rank high in comparison with the rest of the community in point of pecuniary strength. So long as the comparison is distinctly unfavorable to himself, the normal, average individual will live in chronic dissatisfaction with his present lot; and when he has reached what may be called the normal pecuniary standard of the community, or of his class in the community, this chronic dissatisfaction will give place to a restless straining to place a wider and ever-widening pecuniary interval between himself and this average standard. The invidious comparison can never become so favorable to the individual making it that he would not gladly rate himself still higher relatively to his competitors in the struggle for pecuniary reputability.

In the nature of the case, the desire for wealth can scarcely be satiated in any individual instance, and evidently a satiation of the average or general desire for wealth is out of the question. However widely, or equally, or "fairly," it may be distributed, no general increase of the community's wealth can make any approach to satiating this need, the ground of which is the desire of everyone to excel everyone else in the accumulation of goods. If, as is sometimes assumed, the incentive to accumulation were the want of subsistence or of physical comfort, then the aggregate economic wants of a community might conceivably be satisfied at some point in the advance of industrial efficiency; but since the struggle is substantially

---

[4]*putative approbation*   Supposed approval.
[5]*held in severalty*   Owned by individuals, not shared with others.

a race for reputability on the basis of an invidious comparison, no approach to a definitive attainment is possible.

What has just been said must not be taken to mean that there are no other incentives to acquisition and accumulation than this desire to excel in pecuniary standing and so gain the esteem and envy of one's fellow-men. The desire for added comfort and security from want is present as a motive at every stage of the process of accumulation in a modern industrial community; although the standard of sufficiency in these respects is in turn greatly affected by the habit of pecuniary emulation. To a great extent this emulation shapes the methods and selects the objects of expenditure for personal comfort and decent livelihood.

Besides this, the power conferred by wealth also affords a motive to accumulation. That propensity for purposeful activity and that repugnance to all futility of effort which belong to man by virtue of his character as an agent do not desert him when he emerges from the naïve communal culture where the dominant note of life is the unanalyzed and undifferentiated solidarity of the individual with the group with which his life is bound up. When he enters upon the predatory stage, where self-seeking in the narrower sense becomes the dominant note, this propensity goes with him still, as the pervasive trait that shapes his scheme of life. The propensity for achievement and the repugnance to futility remain the underlying economic motive. The propensity changes only in the form of its expression and in the proximate objects to which it directs the man's activity. Under the régime of individual ownership the most available means of visibly achieving a purpose is that afforded by the acquisition and accumulation of goods; and as the self-regarding antithesis between man and man[6] reaches fuller consciousness, the propensity for achievement—the instinct of workmanship— tends more and more to shape itself into a straining to excel others in pecuniary achievement. Relative success, tested by an invidious pecuniary comparison with other men, becomes the conventional end of action. The currently accepted legitimate end of effort becomes the achievement of a favorable comparison with other men; and therefore the repugnance to futility to a good extent coalesces with the incentive of emulation. It acts to accentuate the struggle for pecuniary reputability by visiting with a sharper disapproval all shortcoming and all evidence of shortcoming in point of pecuniary success. Purposeful effort comes to mean, primarily, effort directed to or resulting in a more creditable showing of accumulated wealth.

---

[6]*antithesis between man and man* Vying or competition between men.

Among the motives which lead men to accumulate wealth, the primacy, both in scope and intensity, therefore, continues to belong to this motive of pecuniary emulation.

In making use of the term "invidious," it may perhaps be   20 unnecessary to remark, there is no intention to extol or depreciate, or to commend or deplore any of the phenomena which the word is used to characterize. The term is used in a technical sense as describing a comparison of persons with a view to rating and grading them in respect of relative worth or value—in an aesthetic or moral sense—and so awarding and defining the relative degrees of complacency with which they may legitimately be contemplated by themselves and by others. An invidious comparison is a process of valuation of persons in respect of worth.

QUESTIONS FOR CRITICAL READING

1. What is your interpretation of the term "pecuniary emulation"? What makes the term difficult to understand at first? Does Veblen achieve any advantage because of its complexity?
2. Veblen assumes that humanity has experienced a cultural evolution. Explain what he means by this and try to decide if he is right.
3. Veblen often refers to the "leisure class." What do you think he means by this term? Do you think there were many people who fit into this class? Do you think they were aware they were members of it?
4. At the end of this selection, Veblen says he is not judging but simply describing the facts. Does the essay bear out this claim?
5. What are Veblen's most valid criticisms of modern industrial economies? Are they any less valid today than they seem to have been in his day?
6. To what extent is Veblen interested in the possibility of government interference with the economic activities of individuals?
7. Which passages suggest that Veblen was aware of Karl Marx and *The Communist Manifesto*? Does Veblen seem to agree with Marx on any key issues?

WRITING ASSIGNMENTS

1. In paragraph 6, Veblen states that "wealth has by no means yet lost its utility as an honorific evidence of the owner's prepotence." He was referring to the culture of America in 1899. Is the statement any less true today? What signs do you see of the fact that wealth seems to impart a sense of potency or power to the wealthy? In what ways do the wealthy most use this power or potency?

2. In the early part of the essay, Veblen speculates about a barbarian way of life in which people appropriated objects, such as tools, but did not conceive of ownership until male warriors carried off women prisoners as booty. They then owned the women and regarded them as trophies. Examine Veblen's reasoning on this point by explaining his theories and then considering the evidence or reasons on which he bases them. Are his views convincing? Once you have determined what his theory is, offer your own views on the subject. How do you think humankind first began to develop the concept of ownership?

3. What would society be like today if the concept of individual ownership had never developed? What might have developed instead? Write an essay that describes a hypothetical society in which nothing could be owned by an individual and in which no individual would ever wish to own anything. Would such a society be possible? Would it be better or worse than the kind of society we have today? Would you want to live in it? Do you know of any such society either past or present?

4. One of Veblen's basic assumptions is that our economic system evolved through early phases to its present stage. What do you think these stages are? What do you suppose the next phase of economic and social evolution is likely to be for our "postindustrial" phase of development? What will our economic and social system be like in the next stage? How long do you think it will take to reach it?

5. In paragraph 13, Veblen says that, in the latest stages of industrial society, "the possession of wealth . . . becomes . . itself a meritorious act. Wealth is now itself intrinsically honorable and confers honor on its possessor. By a further refinement, wealth acquired passively by transmission from ancestors or other antecedents presently becomes even more honorific than wealth acquired by the possessor's own effort." To what extent is Veblen correct in his evaluation? Is it true that inherited wealth imparts greater honor than wealth acquired through labor? Remember that people who have made their own fortune are sometimes called *nouveau riche* and that the term is never meant as a compliment. Why do people use such a term for those who have acquired wealth? Why is inherited wealth thought to be so much more honorific than acquired wealth? Do you think that wealth should be honorific at all?

6. Veblen says, "A certain standard of wealth in the one case, and of prowess in the other, is a necessary condition of reputability, and anything in excess of this normal amount is meritorious" (para. 14). What is this standard in our society? He admits that it is "somewhat indefinite" (para. 15), but is it possible to discuss it well enough so that others can understand that it does indeed exist? What signs give evidence of it? In paragraph 15 he also says that when men fall in the esteem of others by not reaching the indefinite level, they also lose self-esteem. Moreover, "the usual basis of self-respect is the respect accorded by one's neighbors." Examine these points and show, by example and description, the extent to which Veblen is correct in describing the society you know.

7. Given that Veblen does not wholly approve of the behavior of many people who possess great wealth, what kinds of recommendations would he make to a government in order to bring reform into play? Does Veblen have faith in government's capacity to institute economic change, or does he believe that an economic system is beyond the power of a government's capacity for management?

8. **CONNECTIONS**   In paragraph 10, Veblen talks about the need to work on the part of the poor and the desire to accumulate wealth on the part of the rich. To what extent does Veblen take into account Marx's views on the potential struggle between these two classes of people? Analyze Veblen's essay for its awareness of and concern for the distinction of classes and the potential for economic struggle or dissatisfaction among the classes. Is Veblen as sensitive to the issues of class struggle as Marx?

9. **CONNECTIONS**   Veblen speaks a great deal about consumption of goods in the economy. Simone Weil hardly mentions the consumption of goods. Compare their essential views on the ways in which the structure of the economy affects the spiritual values of the workers. To what extent are their differing attitudes toward consumption of goods reflected in their concern for the spiritual well-being of workers?

JOHN MAYNARD KEYNES

The End of Laissez-Faire

JOHN MAYNARD KEYNES *(1883–1946) became one of the most influential economists in modern times after his extraordinary analyses of economic decisions following World War I. He advised the British government from this time until after World War II. His advice to the United States government was responsible for policies that helped to restore economic prosperity in postwar Europe.*

His first famous book, The Economic Consequences of the Peace *(1919), was written after he left his official position with the government in Britain during negotiations leading to the Treaty of Versailles. That document clarified the political and economic terms of the surrender of Germany and its allies at the end of World War I. Keynes was outraged by the plans demanding reparations from Germany for damages caused by the war, and he was especially appalled at the behavior of President Woodrow Wilson, whom he regarded as both ignorant and hypocritical. The publication of* The Economic Consequences of the Peace *immediately established him not only as the most original economic mind of his generation but also as a kind of prophet. He pointed out that the economic strictures imposed on Germany would produce economic collapse and social disorder. Like many others, he was fearful that Germany might become Communist—as Karl Marx predicted it would—as had Russia during a period of war and social upheaval.*

His views were prophetic, but his analysis of the situation in Germany was not completely accurate. He felt that the Treaty of Versailles had been motivated by political and military considerations

---

From *Essays in Persuasion.*

and that it had ignored the impact of economic issues. This he feared would lead to collapse, and to an extent it did. But the fact is that Britain and France had modified their demands for reparations, and the economic conditions of most Germans before the Great Depression of 1929 were not as bad as he had predicted they would be.

"The End of Laissez-Faire" was written before the Great Depression and in anticipation of important changes in the nature of modern democratic capitalism. With Great Britain and other European nations bearing immense debts after World War I, certain radical "socialist" moves, such as the nationalization of the mines, were being proposed in Britain as the socialist Labour party gained power.

Laissez-faire is a policy on the part of government to leave business alone to do what it will, including committing various abuses of the kind that Marx complained of. If a government will not regulate business, then government must let it go; Keynes realized that the period of unregulated business was over. Socialism implies complete control of an economic system and of business; although this occurred to a large degree in Britain after World War II, at the time Keynes wrote the country was not yet ready for such socialization. But the essay, as he said later, was prophetic.

One of his chief points was that the corporation served as an intermediate structure between the state and the individual, and thus corporate groups might best represent the interests of both. Certainly, as Keynes explained, the problems of the economy are beyond the power of the individual to control. Corporations are, he noted, "a mode of government," and a more manageable mode than the state itself. However, he also pointed out that management of corporations is rarely responsible to the owners of its capital, the shareholders, in a direct way. Indeed, corporations sometimes downplay the individual interest so that they appear to be socializing themselves.

Keynes, like Marx, Veblen, and Reich, saw an evolutionary pattern to economics. He expressed this in part by looking backward to the corporate structures of guilds and abbeys in the medieval period and forward to what he called a "natural line of evolution," with socialism winning out "against unlimited private profit." Keynes interpreted the kind of changes that were occurring as the end of laissez-faire but also as a continuation of some qualities of laissez-faire—those qualities that stimulated the growth of wealth, such as individual initiative.

KEYNES'S RHETORIC

Keynes's technique is based on a principle of separating issues into two parts. He begins the essay with a quick analysis of whether or not the policies of laissez-faire—doing economically as you will with regard only to personal profit—are a God-given right. Then he moves to the question of what the state ought to be doing in regard to managing an economic system. He refers to Jeremy Bentham's terms: Agenda and Non-Agenda. These translate into what government should do versus what it should not do. Then he moves to the proposition that people should begin to rely on "forms of Government within a Democracy" that can actually accomplish what is on the agenda. These forms center on the corporation. At that point (para. 3) the discussion focuses on two examples: first, the nature of the corporation, and the second, the distinctions between the social and the individual aspects of the agenda (para. 9).

Within each of these two relatively brief discussions, Keynes offers analyses of the economic situations he knows best. He examines socialism in some detail, then examines the state in relation to the individual. He sees that the powerful individual can serve society badly and that some kind of regulation may be essential. To Keynes, such regulation falls short of socialism. He is intent on assuring the reader that whatever government does, it should be something that the individual is not doing. In this way, government will have a chance of being effective without displacing individual initiative.

Keynes's primary rhetorical stance is analytic. He examines an element, weighs it, compares it with other elements, then makes a pronouncement on its value and potential effectiveness. His was one of the most comprehensive and farseeing minds of our time.

The End of Laissez-Faire

Let us clear from the ground the metaphysical or general principles upon which, from time to time, laissez-faire[1] has been founded. It is *not* true that individuals possess a prescriptive "natural liberty" in their economic activities. There is *no* "compact" conferring perpetual rights on those who Have or on those who Acquire. The world is *not* so governed from above that private and social interest always coincide. It is *not* so managed here below that in practice they coincide. It is *not* a correct deduction from the Principles of Economics that enlightened self-interest always operates in the pub-

---

[1]*laissez-faire* An economic environment in which government leaves businesses unregulated and unrestrained.

lic interest. Nor is it true that self-interest generally *is* enlightened;
more often individuals acting separately to promote their own ends
are too ignorant or too weak to attain even these. Experience does
not show that individuals, when they make up a social unit, are
always less clear-sighted than when they act separately.

We cannot, therefore, settle on abstract grounds, but must
handle on its merits in detail, what Burke[2] termed "one of the finest
problems in legislation, namely, to determine what the State ought
to take upon itself to direct by the public wisdom, and what it
ought to leave, with as little interference as possible, to individual
exertion." We have to discriminate between what Bentham,[3] in his
forgotten but useful nomenclature, used to term *Agenda* and *Non-
Agenda,* and to do this without Bentham's prior presumption that
interference is at the same time, "generally needless" and "generally
pernicious."[4] Perhaps the chief task of Economists at this hour is
to distinguish afresh the *Agenda* of Government from the *Non-
Agenda;* and the companion task of Politics is to devise forms of
Government within a Democracy which shall be capable of accomplishing the *Agenda.* I will illustrate what I have in mind by two
examples.

(1) I believe that in many cases the ideal size for the unit of
control and organization lies somewhere between the individual
and the modern State. I suggest, therefore, that progress lies in the
growth and the recognition of semiautonomous bodies within the
State—bodies whose criterion of action within their own field is
solely the public good as they understand it, and from whose deliberations motives of private advantage are excluded, though some
place it may still be necessary to leave, until the ambit of men's
altruism grows wider, to the separate advantage of particular
groups, classes, or faculties—bodies which in the ordinary course
of affairs are mainly autonomous within their prescribed limitations,
but are subject in the last resort to the sovereignty of the democracy
expressed through Parliament.

I propose a return, it may be said, towards mediaeval concep-   4

---

[2]***Edmund Burke (1729–1797)***   Anglo-Irish statesman who wrote *Reflections on
the French Revolution* (1790). His views were influential in causing Britain not to
support the Revolution.

[3]***Jeremy Bentham (1748–1832)***   English philosopher, whose *Introduction to the
Principles and Morals of Legislation* (1789) with its notion of "the greatest happiness
for the greatest number" was a major influence on English law in the midnineteenth
century.

[4]Bentham's *Manual of Political Economy,* published posthumously, in Bowring's
edition (1843). [Keynes's note]

tions of separate autonomies. But, in England at any rate, corporations are a mode of government which has never ceased to be important and is sympathetic to our institutions. It is easy to give examples, from what already exists, of separate autonomies which have attained or are approaching the mode I designate—the Universities, the Bank of England, the Port of London Authority, even perhaps the Railway Companies.

But more interesting than these is the trend of Joint Stock Institutions, when they have reached a certain age and size, to approximate to the status of public corporations rather than that of individualistic private enterprise. One of the most interesting and unnoticed developments of recent decades has been the tendency of big enterprise to socialize itself. A point arrives in the growth of a big institution—particularly a big railway or big public utility enterprise, but also a big bank or a big insurance company—at which the owners of the capital, i.e., the shareholders, are almost entirely dissociated from the management, with the result that the direct personal interest of the latter in the making of great profit becomes quite secondary. When this stage is reached, the general stability and reputation of the institution are more considered by the management than the maximum of profit for the shareholders. The shareholders must be satisfied by conventionally adequate dividends; but once this is secured, the direct interest of the management often consists in avoiding criticism from the public and from the customers of the concern. This is particularly the case if their great size or semimonopolistic position renders them conspicuous in the public eye and vulnerable to public attack. The extreme instance, perhaps, of this tendency in the case of an institution, theoretically the unrestricted property of private persons, is the Bank of England. It is almost true to say that there is no class of persons in the Kingdom of whom the Governor of the Bank of England thinks less when he decides on his policy than of his shareholders. Their rights, in excess of their conventional dividend, have already sunk to the neighborhood of zero. But the same thing is partly true of many other big institutions. They are, as time goes on, socializing themselves.

Not that this is unmixed gain. The same causes promote conservatism and a waning of enterprise. In fact, we already have in these cases many of the faults as well as the advantages of State Socialism. Nevertheless we see here, I think, a natural line of evolution. The battle of Socialism against unlimited private profit is being won in detail hour by hour. In these particular fields—it remains acute elsewhere—this is no longer the pressing problem. There is, for instance, no so-called important political question so really unimportant, so irrelevant to the reorganization of the economic life of Great Britain, as the Nationalization of the Railways.

It is true that many big undertakings, particularly Public Utility enterprises and other business requiring a large fixed capital, still need to be semisocialized. But we must keep our minds flexible regarding the forms of this semisocialism. We must take full advantage of the natural tendencies of the day, and we must probably prefer semiautonomous corporations to organs of the Central Government for which Ministers of State are directly responsible.

I criticize doctrinaire State Socialism, not because it seeks to   8 engage men's altruistic impulses in the service of Society, or because it departs from *laissez-faire,* or because it takes away from man's natural liberty to make a million, or because it has courage for bold experiments. All these things I applaud. I criticize it because it misses the significance of what is actually happening; because it is, in fact, little better than a dusty survival of a plan to meet the problems of fifty years ago, based on a misunderstanding of what some one said a hundred years ago. Nineteenth-century State Socialism sprang from Bentham, free competition, etc., and is in some respects a clearer, in some respects a more muddled, version of just the same philosophy as underlies nineteenth-century individualism. Both equally laid all their stress on freedom, the one negatively to avoid limitations on existing freedom, the other positively to destroy natural or acquired monopolies. They are different reactions to the same intellectual atmosphere.

(2) I come next to a criterion of *Agenda* which is particularly relevant to what it is urgent and desirable to do in the near future. We must aim at separating those services which are *technically social* from those which are *technically individual*. The most important *Agenda* of the State relate not to those activities which private individuals are already fulfilling, but to those functions which fall outside the sphere of the individual, to those decisions which are made by *no one* if the State does not make them. The important thing for Government is not to do things which individuals are doing already, and to do them a little better or a little worse; but to do those things which at present are not done at all.

It is not within the scope of my purpose on this occasion to develop practical policies. I limit myself, therefore, to naming some instances of what I mean from among those problems about which I happen to have thought most.

Many of the greatest economic evils of our time are fruits of risk, uncertainty, and ignorance. It is because particular individuals, fortunate in situation or in abilities, are able to take advantage of uncertainty and ignorance, and also because for the same reason big business is often a lottery, that great inequalities of wealth come about; and these same factors are also the cause of the Unemployment of Labor, or the disappointment of reasonable business expectations, and of the impairment of efficiency and production. Yet the cure lies outside the operations of individuals; it may even be to the interest of individuals to aggravate the disease. I believe that the cure for these things is partly to be sought in the deliberate control of the currency and of credit by a central institution, and partly in the collection and dissemination on a great scale of data relating to the business situation, including the full publicity, by law if necessary, of all business facts which it is useful to know. These measures would involve Society in exercizing directive intelligence through some appropriate organ of action over many of the inner intricacies of private business, yet it would leave private initiative and enterprise unhindered. Even if these measures prove insufficient, nevertheless they will furnish us with better knowledge than we have now for taking the next step.

My second example relates to Savings and Investment. I believe   12
that some co-ordinated act of intelligent judgment is required as to the scale on which it is desirable that the community as a whole should save, the scale on which these savings should go abroad in the form of foreign investments, and whether the present organization of the investment market distributes savings along the most nationally productive channels. I do not think that these matters should be left entirely to the chances of private judgment and private profits, as they are at present.

My third example concerns Population. The time has already come when each country needs a considered national policy about what size of Population, whether larger or smaller than at present or the same, is most expedient. And having settled this policy, we must take steps to carry it into operation. The time may arrive a little later when the community as a whole must pay attention to the innate quality as well as to the mere numbers of its future members.

These reflections have been directed towards possible improvements in the technique of modern Capitalism by the agency of collective action. There is nothing in them which is seriously incompatible with what seems to me to be the essential characteristic of Capitalism, namely the dependence upon an intense appeal to the money-making and money-loving instincts of individuals as the main motive force of the economic machine. Nor must I, so near to my end, stray towards other fields. Nevertheless, I may do well to remind you, in conclusion, that the fiercest contests and the most deeply felt divisions of opinion are likely to be waged in the coming years not round technical questions, where the arguments on either side are mainly economic, but round those which, for want of better words, may be called psychological or, perhaps, moral.

In Europe, or at least in some parts of Europe—but not, I think, in the United States of America—there is a latent reaction, somewhat widespread, against basing Society to the extent that we do upon fostering, encouraging, and protecting the money-motives of individuals. A preference for arranging our affairs in such a way as to appeal to the money-motive as little as possible, rather than as much as possible, need not be entirely *a priori,* but may be based on the comparison of experiences. Different persons, according to their choice of profession, find the money-motive playing a large or a small part in their daily lives, and historians can tell us about other phases of social organization in which this motive has played a much smaller part than it does now. Most religions and most philosophies deprecate, to say the least of it, a way of life mainly influenced by considerations of personal money profit. On the other hand, most men today reject ascetic notions and do not doubt the real advantages of wealth. Moreover it seems obvious to them that one cannot do without the money-motive, and that, apart from certain admitted abuses, it does its job well. In the result the average man averts his attention from the problem, and has no clear idea what he really thinks and feels about the whole confounded matter.

Confusion of thought and feeling leads to confusion of speech.   16 Many people, who are really objecting to Capitalism as a way of life, argue as though they were objecting to it on the ground of its inefficiency in attaining its own objects. Contrariwise, devotees of Capitalism are often unduly conservative, and reject reforms in its technique, which might really strengthen and preserve it, for fear that they may prove to be first steps away from Capitalism itself. Nevertheless a time may be coming when we shall get clearer than at present as to when we are talking about Capitalism as an efficient or inefficient technique, and when we are talking about it as desirable or objectionable in itself. For my part, I think that Capitalism, wisely managed, can probably be made more efficient for attaining economic ends than any alternative system yet in sight, but that in itself it is in many ways extremely objectionable. Our problem is to work out a social organization which shall be as efficient as possible without offending our notions of a satisfactory way of life.

The next step forward must come, not from political agitation or premature experiments, but from thought. We need by an effort of the mind to elucidate our own feelings. At present our sympathy and our judgment are liable to be on different sides, which is a painful and paralysing state of mind. In the field of action reformers will not be successful until they can steadily pursue a clear and definite object with their intellects and their feelings in tune. There is no party in the world at present which appears to me to be pursuing right aims by right methods. Material Poverty provides the incentive to change precisely in situations where there is very little margin for experiments. Material Prosperity removes the incentive just when it might be safe to take a chance. Europe lacks the means, America the will, to make a move. We need a new set of convictions which spring naturally from a candid examination of our own inner feelings in relation to the outside facts.

QUESTIONS FOR CRITICAL READING

1. Does the economic future seem to have been especially uncertain in 1926, when Keynes wrote this essay?
2. How would you explain the meaning of "laissez-faire" to someone unfamiliar with the term?
3. Why does Keynes feel it is beyond his scope to "develop practical policies"? What is one practical policy he might have developed?
4. Is a corporation a form of government? Should it be?
5. According to Keynes, what economic rights does an individual have in terms of making a great deal of money?
6. On which points do you find yourself in disagreement with Keynes? On which points do you agree with him?
7. What does Keynes mean by the terms *Agenda* and *Non-Agenda?*
8. Under what conditions does Keynes believe it is necessary for a nation to control the quantity and quality of its population (para. 13)?

WRITING ASSIGNMENTS

1. Keynes distinguishes between the role of government and the role of the individual in the economy. When he says that he does not want government to perform those functions that individuals are already performing, he implies that individuals are leaving undone much that would improve the economy. What would you recommend that your government do today that individuals are currently not doing? And how would the government's actions benefit the economy?
2. In paragraph 8, Keynes refers to man's "natural liberty to make a million." Do you believe that such a liberty exists and if so, that it is natural? What are the results of such a liberty, and how could any government guarantee it?

3. Which services are technically social and technically individual in economics? That is, what can you do as an individual that government either cannot or will not do? In what senses can these two services conflict, and how can such conflict create an unhealthy economic situation? Have you had any experience of such a conflict?

4. How do you feel about the nature of the corporation as a government of sorts? Do you think it is as good a development as Keynes seems to feel it is? Is this development in any way a substitute for government? In reading the business section of your newspaper, do you see evidence of corporate activity that can be in any way interpreted as governmental? Is the result desirable? Is it the result Keynes seems to have hoped for?

5. In paragraph 12, Keynes reminds us that the extent to which individuals save money affects the general health of the economy. He says he believes that "a co-ordinated act of intelligent judgment" is required to establish a national policy of savings. The United States has long been behind nations such as Japan in terms of the individual's goal to save. Do you feel that the government should intervene in the lives of individuals and determine how much they should save? How could any government achieve that end?

6. **CONNECTIONS**   Compare Keynes's views with those of Thorstein Veblen and Simone Weil. What aspects of economics attract the notice of all of them? Do their concerns for labor, for the owners of manufacturing resources, or for the health of the general economy overlap enough to regard them as comparable in their views? In what important ways do their views diverge?

7. **CONNECTIONS**   Karl Marx was especially opposed to the style of capitalism Keynes called laissez-faire, in which capitalists were free to exploit labor and economic conditions for their personal benefit. Do Keynes's views parellel those of Marx in *The Communist Manifesto?* Cite the main issues of agreement and disagreement and argue a case for or against Keynes as a potential follower of Karl Marx.

JOHN KENNETH GALBRAITH

The Position of Poverty

*J*OHN KENNETH GALBRAITH *(b. 1908) was born in Canada but has been an American citizen since 1937. He grew up on a farm in Ontario, which helps to explain his having taken his first university degree in agricultural science. It may also help to explain why, in his many books on subjects such as economics, the State Department, Indian art, and government, he has always been praised for helping a layperson understand complex concepts. Sometimes, of course, he has been criticized for oversimplifying issues, but on the whole, he has made a brilliant success of writing with wit and up-tempo humor about issues that are basically perplexing and sometimes troubling.*

Galbraith was professor of economics at Harvard University for many years. During the presidential campaigns of Adlai Stevenson in 1952 and 1956, he assisted the Democrats as a speechwriter and economics adviser. He performed the same tasks for John F. Kennedy in 1960. Kennedy appointed Galbraith ambassador to India, a post that he maintained for a little over two years, including the period during which India and China fought a border war. His experiences in India resulted in Ambassador's Journal: A Personal Account of the Kennedy Years *(1969). Kennedy called Galbraith his finest ambassadorial appointment.*

Galbraith's involvement with politics was somewhat unusual for an academic economist at that time. It seems to have stemmed from strongly held personal views on the social issues of his time. One of the most important contributions of his best-known and probably most significant book, The Affluent Society *(1958; rev. eds. 1969, 1976,*

From *The Affluent Society.*

1984), was its analysis of America's economic ambitions. He pointed out that at that time the welfare of the economy was entirely tied up in the measurement and growth of the gross national product. Economists and government officials concentrated on boosting output. He tried to help people see that, by itself, this goal was misdirected. The result, he said, would be a profusion of products that people really did not need and from which they would not benefit. It would result in creating artificial needs for things that had no ultimate value. Concentrating on bigger, more luxurious automobiles and building in a "planned obsolescence" that essentially put consumers in an economic squirrel cage seemed to him to be wasteful and ultimately destructive.

Galbraith suggested that America concentrate on genuine needs and satisfy them immediately. He was deeply concerned about the environment and suggested that clean air was a priority that took precedence over industry. He supported development of the arts and stressed the importance of improving housing across the nation. His effort was directed at trying to help Americans change certain basic values. He wished to help them give up the pursuit of useless consumer novelties and to substitute a program of genuine social development. The commitment to consumer products as the basis of the economy naturally argued against a redirection of effort toward the solution of social problems.

"The Position of Poverty" is interesting because it is among the few statements made by an economist about what the country can or should do about the poor. As Galbraith points out at the beginning of the selection, economists generally comment on the entire economy and pay only lip service to the problem of poverty. The result is that we do not understand the economics of poverty very well and therefore are not likely to make much progress in eliminating it from society.

Galbraith is so exceptionally clear in his essay that little commentary is needed to establish its importance. He is insightful in clarifying two kinds of poverty: case poverty and insular poverty. Case poverty is restricted to an individual and his or her family. Alcoholism, ignorance, mental deficiency, discrimination, or specific handicaps seem to be the causes of such poverty. It is an individual, not a group, disorder. Insular poverty affects a group in a given area—an "island" within the larger society. He points to poverty in Appalachia and in the slums of major cities, where most of the people in those "islands" are at or below the poverty level. Insular poverty is linked to the environment, and its causes are somehow derived from that environment.

Galbraith's analysis is perceptive and influential, and while little or no progress has been made in solving the problem of poverty since 1959, he assures us that there are steps that can be taken to help eradicate it. He also warns that such steps demand the nation's will, however, and that the nation may lack the will. As he wisely points out, the

cause of the impoverished is not likely to be a popular political issue
in 1958. Because the poverty-stricken are a minority, few politicians,
he reasons, would make them a campaign issue. Actually, he was
wrong. Kennedy in 1960, Lyndon Johnson in 1964, and Jimmy Carter
in 1976 made programs for the poor central among their governmental
concerns. Because of the war in Vietnam and other governmental policies, however, the 1960s and early 1970s were a time of staggering
inflation, wiping out any of the advances the poverty-stricken had made.
The extent to which this is true is observable instantly on reading the
selection; the income figures for 1959 seem so unbelievably low as to
conjure up the last century rather than the midtwentieth century.

GALBRAITH'S RHETORIC

The most important rhetorical achievement of the piece is its style.
This is an example of the elevated plain style: a clear, direct, and
basically simple approach to language that only occasionally admits a
somewhat learned vocabulary—as in the use of a very few words such
as "opulent," "unremunerative," and "ineluctable." The vast majority
of words he uses are ordinary ones.

He breaks the essay into six carefully numbered sections. In this
way he highlights its basic structure and subtly reminds us that he has
clearly separated its elements into related groups so that he can speak
directly to aspects of his subject rather than to the entire topic. This
rhetorical technique of division imparts clarity and confers a sense of
authority on the writer.

Galbraith relies on statistical information that the reader can examine if necessary. This information is treated in the early stages of the
piece as a prologue. Once such information has been given, Galbraith
draws some conclusions from it, proceeding in the manner of a logician
establishing premises and deriving the necessary conclusions. The subject
is sober and sobering, and so is the style. The issues are complex,
uncertain, and difficult, but the style is direct, confident, and essentially
simple. This is the secret of the success of the book from which this
selection comes. The Affluent Society *has been translated into well
over a dozen languages and has been a best-seller around the globe.
And despite the fact that the statistical information is outdated, it remains
an influential book. Its fundamental insights are such that it is likely
to be relevant to the economy of the United States for generations to
come.

The Position of Poverty

"The study of the causes of poverty," Alfred Marshall[1] observed at the turn of the century, "is the study of the causes of the degradation of a large part of mankind." He spoke of contemporary England as well as of the world beyond. A vast number of people both in town and country, he noted, had insufficient food, clothing and house-room; they were: "Overworked and undertaught, weary and careworn, without quiet and without leisure." The chance of their succor, he concluded, gave to economic studies, "their chief and their highest interest."

No contemporary economist would be likely to make such an observation about the United States. Conventional economic discourse makes obeisance to the continued existence of some poverty. "We must remember that we still have a great many poor people." In the nineteen-sixties, poverty promised, for a time, to become a subject of serious political concern. Then war came and the concern evaporated or was displaced. For economists of conventional mood, the reminders that the poor still exist are a useful way of allaying uneasiness about the relevance of conventional economic goals. For some people, wants must be synthesized. Hence, the importance of the goods to them is not *per se* very high. So much may be conceded. But others are far closer to physical need. And hence we must not be cavalier about the urgency of providing them with the most for the least. The sales tax may have merit for the opulent, but it still bears heavily on the poor. The poor get jobs more easily when the economy is expanding. Thus, poverty survives in economic discourse partly as a buttress to the conventional economic wisdom.

The privation of which Marshall spoke was, a half century ago, the common lot at least of all who worked without special skill. As a general affliction, it was ended by increased output which, however imperfectly it may have been distributed, nevertheless accrued in substantial amount to those who worked for a living. The result was to reduce poverty from the problem of a majority to that of a minority. It ceased to be a general case and became a special case. It is this which has put the problem of poverty into its peculiar modern form.

---

[1] *Alfred Marshall (1842–1924)*   An English economist whose *Principles of Economics* (1890) was long a standard text and is still relied on by some economists for its theories of costs, value, and distribution.

For poverty does survive. In part, it is a physical matter; those 4
afflicted have such limited and insufficient food, such poor clothing,
such crowded, cold and dirty shelter that life is painful as well as
comparatively brief. But just as it is far too tempting to say that,
in matters of living standards, everything is relative, so it is wrong
to rest everything on absolutes. People are poverty-stricken when
their income, even if adequate for survival, falls radically behind
that of the community. Then they cannot have what the larger
community regards as the minimum necessary for decency; and
they cannot wholly escape, therefore, the judgment of the larger
community that they are indecent. They are degraded for, in the
literal sense, they live outside the grades or categories which the
community regards as acceptable.

Since the first edition of this book appeared, and one hopes
however slightly as a consequence, the character and dimension of
this degradation have become better understood. There have also
been fulsome promises that poverty would be eliminated. The performance on these promises has been less eloquent.

The degree of privation depends on the size of the family, the
place of residence—it will be less with given income in rural areas
than in the cities—and will, of course, be affected by changes in
living costs. The Department of Health, Education and Welfare has
established rough standards, appropriately graded to family size,
location and changing prices, to separate the poor from the less
poor and the affluent. In 1972, a non-farm family of four was
deemed poor if it had an income of $4275; a couple living otherwise
than on a farm was called poor if it had less than $2724 and an
unattached individual if receiving less than $2109. A farm family
of four was poor with less than $3639; of two with less than $2315.[2]

By these modest standards, 24.5 million households, including
individuals and families, were poor in 1972 as compared with 13.4
million in 1959. Because of the increase in population, and therewith
in the number of households, in these years the reduction in the
number of poor households, as a proportion of all households, was
rather greater—from 24 percent in 1959 to 12 percent in 1972.[3]

One can usually think of the foregoing deprivation as falling 8
into two broad categories. First, there is what may be called *case
poverty*. This one encounters in every community, rural or urban,
however prosperous that community or the times. Case poverty is
the poor farm family with the junk-filled yard and the dirty children

---

[2]*Statistical Abstract of the United States, 1974*, p. 389. [Galbraith's note]
[3]*Statistical Abstract*, p. 389. [Galbraith's note]

playing in the bare dirt. Or it is the gray-black hovel beside the railroad tracks. Or it is the basement dwelling in the alley.

Case poverty is commonly and properly related to some characteristic of the individuals so afflicted. Nearly everyone else has mastered his environment; this proves that it is not intractable. But some quality peculiar to the individual or family involved—mental deficiency, bad health, inability to adapt to the discipline of industrial life, uncontrollable procreation, alcohol, discrimination involving a very limited minority, some educational handicap unrelated to community shortcoming, or perhaps a combination of several of these handicaps—has kept these individuals from participating in the general well-being.

Second, there is what may be called *insular* poverty—that which manifests itself as an "island" of poverty. In the island, everyone or nearly everyone is poor. Here, evidently, it is not easy to explain matters by individual inadequacy. We may mark individuals down as intrinsically deficient in social performance; it is not proper or even wise so to characterize an entire community. The people of the island have been frustrated by some factor common to their environment.

Case poverty exists. It has also been useful to those who have needed a formula for keeping the suffering of others from causing suffering to themselves. Since this poverty is the result of the deficiencies, including the moral shortcomings, of the persons concerned, it is possible to shift the responsibility to those involved. They are worthless and, as a simple manifestation of social justice, they suffer for it. Or, at a somewhat higher level of social perception and compassion, it means that the problem of poverty is sufficiently solved by private and public charity. This rescues those afflicted from the worst consequences of their inadequacy or misfortune; no larger social change or reorganization is suggested. Except as it may be insufficient in its generosity, the society is not at fault.

Insular poverty yields to no such formulas. In earlier times, 12 when agriculture and extractive industries were the dominant sources of livelihood, something could be accomplished by shifting the responsibility for low income to a poor natural endowment and thus, in effect, to God. The soil was thin and stony, other natural resources absent and hence the people were poor. And, since it is the undoubted preference of many to remain in the vicinity of the place of their birth, a homing instinct that operates for people as well as pigeons, the people remained in the poverty which heaven had decreed for them. It is an explanation that is nearly devoid of empirical application. Connecticut is very barren and stony and incomes are very high. Similarly Wyoming. West Virginia is well watered with rich mines and forests and the people are very poor. The South is much favored in soil and climate and similarly poor and the very richest parts of the South, such as the Mississippi-Yazoo Delta, have long had a well-earned reputation for the greatest deprivation. Yet so strong is the tendency to associate poverty with natural causes that even individuals of some modest intelligence will still be heard, in explanation of insular poverty, to say, "It's basically a poor country." "It's a pretty barren region."

Most modern poverty is insular in character and the islands are the rural and urban slums. From the former, mainly in the South, the southern Appalachians and Puerto Rico, there has been until recent times a steady flow of migrants, some white but more black, to the latter. Grim as life is in the urban ghetto, it still offers more hope, income and interest than in the rural slum. Largely in consequence of this migration, the number of poor farm families—poor by the standards just mentioned—declined between 1959 and 1973 from 1.8 million to 295,000. The decline in the far larger number of poor non-farm households in these years was only from 6.5 million to 4.5 million.[4]

This is not the place to provide a detailed profile of this poverty. More than half of the poor households are headed by a woman, although in total women head only 9 percent of families. Over 30 percent are black, another 10 percent are of Spanish origin. A very large proportion of all black households (31 percent in 1973 as compared with 8 percent of whites) fall below the poverty line. Especially on the farms, where the young have departed for the cities, a disproportionate number of the poor are old. More often than not, the head of the household is not in the labor force at all.

But the more important characteristic of insular poverty is forces, common to all members of the community, which restrain or prevent participation in economic life at going rates of return. These restraints are several. Race, which acts to locate people by their color rather than by the proximity to employment, is obviously one. So are poor educational facilities. (And this effect is further exaggerated when the poorly educated, endemically a drug on the labor market, are brought together in dense clusters by the common inadequacy of the schools available to blacks and the poor.) So is the disintegration of family life in the slum which leaves households in the hands of women. Family life itself is in some measure a manifestation of affluence. And so, without doubt, is

---

[4]U.S. Department of Commerce, *Current Population Reports,* "Consumer Income," Series P-60, No. 98 (Washington, D.C.: U.S. Government Printing Office, 1975). [Galbraith's note]

the shared sense of helplessness and rejection and the resulting demoralization which is the product of the common misfortune.

The most certain thing about this poverty is that it is not   16
remedied by a general advance in income. Case poverty is not
remedied because the specific individual inadequacy precludes employment and participation in the general advance. Insular poverty
is not directly alleviated because the advance does not remove the
specific frustrations of environment to which the people of these
islands are subject. This is not to say that it is without effect. If
there are jobs outside the ghetto or away from the rural slum, those
who are qualified, and not otherwise constrained, can take them
and escape. If there are no such jobs, none can escape. But it remains
that advance cannot improve the position of those who, by virtue
of self or environment, cannot participate.

With the transition of the very poor from a majority to a
comparative minority position, there has been a change in their
political position. Any tendency of a politician to identify himself
with those of the lowest estate usually brought the reproaches of
the well-to-do. Political pandering and demagoguery were naturally
suspected. But, for the man so reproached, there was the compensating advantage of alignment with a large majority. Now any politician who speaks for the very poor is speaking for a small and
generally inarticulate minority. As a result, the modern liberal politician regularly aligns himself not with the poverty-ridden members
of the community but with the far more numerous people who
enjoy the far more affluent income of (say) the modern trade union
member or the intellectual. Ambrose Bierce, in *The Devil's Dictionary,* called poverty "a file provided for the teeth of the rats of
reform."[5] It is so no longer. Reform now concerns itself with the
needs of people who are relatively well-to-do—whether the comparison be with their own past or with those who are really at the
bottom of the income ladder.

In consequence, a notable feature of efforts to help the very
poor is their absence of any very great political appeal.[6] Politicians
have found it possible to be indifferent where they could not be
derisory. And very few have been under a strong compulsion to
support these efforts.

The concern for inequality and deprivation had vitality only so

---

[5]***Ambrose Bierce (1842–1914?)***   A southern American writer noted for satirical
writings such as the one quoted.

[6]This was true of the Office of Economic Opportunity—the so-called poverty
program—and was ultimately the reason for its effective demise. [Galbraith's note]

long as the many suffered while a few had much. It did not survive as a decisive political issue in a time when the many had much even though others had much more. It is our misfortune that when inequality declined as an issue, the slate was not left clean. A residual and in some ways rather more hopeless problem remained.

An affluent society, that is also both compassionate and rational 20 would, no doubt, secure to all who needed it the minimum income essential for decency and comfort. The corrupting effect on the human spirit of unearned revenue has unquestionably been exaggerated as, indeed, have the character-building values of hunger and privation. To secure to each family a minimum income, as a normal function of the society, would help ensure that the misfortunes of parents, deserved or otherwise, were not visited on their children. It would help ensure that poverty was not self-perpetuating. Most of the reaction, which no doubt would be adverse, is based on obsolete attitudes. When poverty was a majority phenomenon, such action could not be afforded. A poor society, as this essay has previously shown, had to enforce the rule that the person who did not work could not eat. And possibly it was justified in the added cruelty of applying the rule to those who could not work or whose efficiency was far below par. An affluent society has no similar excuse for such rigor. It can use the forthright remedy of providing income for those without. Nothing requires such a society to be compassionate. But it no longer has a high philosophical justification for callousness.

The notion that income is a remedy for indigency has a certain forthright appeal.[7] As elsewhere argued, it would also ease the problems of economic management by reducing the reliance on production as a source of income. The provision of such a basic source of income must henceforth be the first and the strategic step in the attack on poverty.

But it is only one step. In the past, we have suffered from the supposition that the only remedy for poverty lies in remedies that allow people to look after themselves—to participate in the economy. Nothing has better served the conscience of people who wished to avoid inconvenient or expensive action than an appeal, on this issue, to Calvinist precept—"The only sound way to solve the problem of poverty is to help people help themselves." But this does not mean that steps to allow participation and to keep poverty from being self-perpetuating are unimportant. On the contrary. It

---

[7]As earlier noted, in the first edition, the provision of guaranteed income was discussed but dismissed as "beyond reasonable hope." [Galbraith's note]

requires that the investment in children from families presently afflicted be as little below normal as possible. If the children of poor families have first-rate schools and school attendance is properly enforced; if the children, though badly fed at home, are well nourished at school; if the community has sound health services, and the physical well-being of the children is vigilantly watched; if there is opportunity for advanced education for those who qualify regardless of means; and if, especially in the case of urban communities, housing is ample and housing standards are enforced, the streets are clean, the laws are kept, and recreation is adequate—then there is a chance that the children of the very poor will come to maturity without inhibiting disadvantage. In the case of insular poverty, this remedy requires that the services of the community be assisted from outside. Poverty is self-perpetuating partly because the poorest communities are poorest in the services which would eliminate it. To eliminate poverty efficiently, we must, indeed, invest more than proportionately in the children of the poor community. It is there that high quality schools, strong health services, special provision for nutrition and recreation are most needed to compensate for the very low investment which families are able to make in their own offspring.

The effect of education and related investment in individuals is to help them overcome the restraints that are imposed by their environment. These need also to be attacked even more directly—by giving the mobility that is associated with plentiful, good and readily available housing, by provision of comfortable, efficient and economical mass transport, by making the environment pleasant and safe, and by eliminating the special health handicaps that afflict the poor.

Nor is case poverty entirely resistant to such remedies. Much can be done to treat those characteristics which cause people to reject or be rejected by the modern industrial society. Educational deficiencies can be overcome. Mental deficiencies can be treated. Physical handicaps can be remedied. The limiting factor is not a lack of knowledge of what can be done. Overwhelmingly, it is a shortage of money.

It will be clear that, to a remarkable extent, the remedy for poverty leads to the same requirements as those for social balance. The restraints that confine people to the ghetto are those that result from insufficient investment in the public sector. And the means to escape from these constraints and to break their hold on subsequent generations just mentioned—better nutrition and health, better education, more and better housing, better mass transport, an environment more conducive to effective social participation—all, with rare exceptions, call for massively greater investment in the public sector. In recent years, the problems of the urban ghetto have been greatly discussed but with little resultant effect. To a certain extent, the search for deeper social explanations of its troubles has been motivated by the hope that these (together with more police) might lead to solutions that would somehow elide the problem of cost. It is an idle hope. The modern urban household is an extremely expensive thing. We have not yet taken the measure of the resources that must be allocated to its public tasks if it is to be agreeable or even tolerable. And first among the symptoms of an insufficient allocation is the teeming discontent of the modern ghetto.

A further feature of these remedies is to be observed. Their consequence is to allow participation in the economic life of the larger community—to make people and the children of people who are now idle productive. This means that they will add to the total output of goods and services. We see once again that even by its own terms the present preoccupation with the private sector of the economy as compared with the whole spectrum of human needs is inefficient. The parallel with investment in the supply of trained and educated manpower discussed above will be apparent.

But increased output of goods is not the main point. Even to the most intellectually reluctant reader, it will now be evident that enhanced productive efficiency is not the motif of this volume. The very fact that increased output offers itself as a by-product of the effort to eliminate poverty is one of the reasons. No one would be called up to write at such length on a problem so easily solved as that of increasing production. The main point lies elsewhere. Poverty—grim, degrading and ineluctable—is not remarkable in India. For few, the fate is otherwise. But in the United States, the survival of poverty is remarkable. We ignore it because we share with all societies at all times the capacity for not seeing what we do not wish to see. Anciently this has enabled the nobleman to enjoy his dinner while remaining oblivious to the beggars around his door. In our own day, it enables us to travel in comfort by Harlem and into the lush precincts of midtown Manhattan. But while our failure to notice can be explained, it cannot be excused. "Poverty," Pitt[8] exclaimed, "is no disgrace but it is damned annoying." In the contemporary United States, it is not annoying but it is a disgrace.

---

[8]***William Pitt, the Younger (1759–1806)*** British prime minister from 1783 to 1801 and, briefly, again in 1804 and 1805.

Q U E S T I O N S   F O R   C R I T I C A L   R E A D I N G

1. What is the fundamental difference between the attitude Alfred Marshall held toward the poor (para. 1) and the attitude contemporary economists hold?
2. Galbraith avoids a specific definition of poverty because he says it changes from society to society. How would you define poverty as it exists in our society? What are its major indicators?
3. According to Galbraith, what is the relationship of politics to poverty?
4. What, according to this essay, seem to be the causes of poverty?
5. Clarify the distinctions Galbraith makes between case poverty and insular poverty. Are they reasonable distinctions?
6. Does Galbraith oversimplify the issues of poverty in America?
7. Galbraith first published this piece in 1958. How much have attitudes toward poverty changed since then? What kinds of progress seem to have been made toward eradicating poverty?

W R I T I N G   A S S I G N M E N T S

1. In paragraph 4, Galbraith says, "People are poverty-stricken when their income, even if adequate for survival, falls radically behind that of the community. Then they cannot have what the larger community regards as the minimum necessary for decency; and they cannot wholly escape, therefore, the judgment of the larger community that they are indecent. They are degraded for, in the literal sense, they live outside the grades or categories which the community regards as acceptable." Examine what he says here and explain what he means. Is this an accurate description of poverty? Would you amend it? If so, in what ways? If you accept his description of poverty, what public policy would you recommend to deal with it? What would be the consequences of accepting Galbraith's description?
2. Galbraith points out some anomalies of poverty and place. For example, he notes that West Virginia is rich in resources but that its people have been notable for their poverty. Connecticut, on the other hand, is poor in resources, with stony, untillable land, and its people have been notable for their wealth. Some economists have also pointed out that, when the Americas were settled, South America had the gold, the lush tropics that yielded food and fruit for the asking, and that it held the promise of immense wealth. North America had a harsh climate, stubborn soil conditions, and dense forests that needed clearing. Yet North America has less poverty now than does South America. Write a brief essay in which you consider whether what is said above is too simplified to be useful. If it is not, what do you think is the reason for the economic distinctions that Galbraith and others point out?
3. What personal experiences have you had with poverty? Are you famil-

iar with examples of case poverty? If so, describe them in such a way as to help others understand them. Do you have any insight into the causes that produced the poverty? How could poor people in this category be rescued from poverty? What is their social situation in the community?

4. Examine the newspapers for the last several days and look through back issues of magazines such as *Time, Newsweek,* the *New Republic, The New Leader,* or *U.S. News & World Report.* How much attention does each pay to the question of poverty? Present a survey of the views you find and compare them with Galbraith's. How much agreement or disagreement is there? Would the level of the nation's concern with poverty please Galbraith?

5. Write a brief essay in which you delineate what you think is the current political attitude toward poverty. If possible, gather some recent statements made by politicians. Analyze them to see how closely they tally with Galbraith's concerns and views. Do any specific politicians act as spokespeople for the poor?

6. Galbraith says that the position of poverty has resulted from a dramatic change in our society, from a circumstance in which most people were poor and only a few were affluent to one in which most people are affluent and only a few are poor. Is Galbraith correct in this assessment? Interview your parents and grandparents and their friends. By this means, establish the validity of Galbraith's claim, and then explain what you feel are the problems the poor face as a result of their current minority status. If possible, during your interviews ask what feelings your parents and their friends have about the poverty-stricken. What feelings do you have? Are they shared by your friends?

7. **CONNECTIONS** How might Simone Weil respond to Galbraith's essay? Her concern is for the dignity of labor, his is to understand the position of poverty. How might their different interests connect in shared views about economics? Would Weil be sympathetic to Galbraith? Would he be sympathetic to her?

SIMONE WEIL

Prerequisite to Dignity of Labor

SIMONE WEIL *(1909–1943) was born in Paris and died in Kent, England. Weil (pronounced* Vay*) is a highly controversial figure in modern thought, ranking in some people's estimation among the most important thinkers of her generation. She has been praised by Jean-Paul Sartre, Albert Camus, and T. S. Eliot for the spiritual intensity of her life and her writing. She has been described in terms that are usually reserved for saints. A remarkably contradictory person, Weil was born a Jew yet felt herself to be a Christian. She nevertheless resisted baptism into the Christian faith. Her struggles with Judaism paralleled her struggles with the authoritative aspects of the Roman Catholic church. Always, her sympathies were with the weak. The tenets and practices of institutional religions were often at odds with her thinking.*

She was an intellectual who demanded of herself that she bring her life into accord with her beliefs. She was influenced by Marxist thought when she was at the Sorbonne, and in 1931 she began teaching philosophy at a girls' school near Lyon. Her activities as a supporter of unemployed workers caused a scandal and cost her her job. It was not the last time such activism caused her to lose a teaching post. In 1934, feeling that physical labor was an important part of spiritual life, Weil stopped teaching in order to work on farms and in factories. As an intellectual, she feared that remaining distant from labor would distort her thought. To experience life from the point of view of the working class, Weil spent two years working as a common laborer. Her efforts

---

From *La Condition Ouvrière*. Translated by Siân Miles.

produced insights into economic realities such as those she describes in the essay reprinted here.

By the time she left the Renault factory, Weil had begun to think of herself as a Christian. She had formed very close friendships among the French priesthood and frequently attended mass, although she never formally joined the Catholic church. Her religious beliefs led her to reevaluate her political views. One of her most important decisions came in 1936, after her factory experience, when she decided to take part in the Spanish civil war on the side of the antifascist Republicans, posing as a cook. Always frail in health, she was almost totally disabled when she was accidentally scalded with a pot of boiling oil. She was in Spain only two months. During her convalescence, she traveled to Portugal, then went to Italy where she found herself in the chapel of Santa Maria degli Angeli, where St. Francis of Assisi had often prayed. She found herself kneeling for the first time in her life—impressed, she said, by a spiritual force greater than herself. Her "Spiritual Autobiography," recording her religious views, is one of the most touching religious documents of the 1930s.

By 1939 Weil wrote largely about religious matters, while continuing to publish important essays on economics and other subjects. Her writings in this period, no matter what their subject, concerned themselves with spiritual fulfillment. Nowhere did she sense the need for increased spiritual awareness more than in areas of daily labor, especially the labor of factory workers, which she saw as repetitive, soul-sapping, and demoralizing. "Prerequisite to Dignity of Labor" was published in 1941 in Marseilles and in 1948 was included in a volume of collected essays on work and economics based on her experiences in the Renault automotive plant and other factories in Paris.

Weil's efforts were directed toward restoring the dignity due to labor by reestablishing its spiritual qualities and by arguing against the efficiency experts who then dictated the character and structure of factory experience. She protested the "taylorization" of labor, a growing trend based on The Principles of Scientific Management, *by Frederick Winslow Taylor. Taylor's views, published in 1911 and widely followed in the 1930s, recommended the cooperation of management and labor but also emphasized an absolute division between them in terms of status. Later interpreters used his thinking as a means of standardizing the work done in factories in the "conveyor-belt" fashion that Weil so deplored. By suppressing the special skills of individual trades in favor of regulated, simple (and meaningless) mechanical activities, Taylor-based systems robbed workers of their pride and denied them the development of individual talents.*

World War II forced Weil and her family out of France. They reached the United States in 1942, but Weil soon found herself anxious to take part in the French resistance. She returned to England to work for the Free French Ministry, but because she had fought for the Communists in Spain, she was not altogether trusted. Nevertheless, she persevered. She limited her diet to the rations of those living in occupied France in a symbolic gesture that eventually weakened her constitution. She died of tuberculosis and starvation at the age of thirty-four in 1943.

WEIL'S RHETORIC

Weil's essay is largely abstract. She does not provide descriptions of individual workers, working conditions in individual factories, or work on farms. She speaks more as a philosopher than as a laborer, although the reader knows that she has experienced hard factory labor firsthand. A less philosophical writer would use the modern journalistic techniques of following an individual worker through his or her tasks and then leave the job of judging the circumstances to the reader. However, Weil feels she treats a subject larger than the individual worker. She refers to the collective experience of labor and avoids limiting the significance of her message to our response to individuals.

Her opening paragraphs establish certain philosophical points, as when she says, "Existence is not an end in itself but merely the framework upon which all good . . . may be built" (para. 2). In this sense, her rhetorical position announces itself as totally distinct from that of most economists. Marx discusses the condition of labor and laborers, but as a materialist he does not approach Weil's concern for spiritual realization in the workplace. Veblen and Keynes may privately worry over spiritual issues, but such matters do not seem to have a clear place in their theorizing.

Weil thus distinguishes herself from the other economists in this section by focusing on the inner life of the worker. Eventually, she begins to ground the discussion by reference to certain images and symbols: "a squirrel in a cage" (para. 1); "slavery" (paras. 2 and 3); "revolution" (paras. 4–6); "beauty" (para. 8); "prayer" (paras. 9–11); religious "symbols" (paras. 12–18); " social inequality" (paras. 19–21); "the violation of the workers' attention" (para. 23). However, most of these subjects are fragile and spiritual in their own right. For example, her discourse on "intuitive attention" (para. 18) is almost completely theoretical. Consequently, the reader must imagine the conditions of work to which Weil only alludes.

The reader must also keep in mind that Weil knew what she was doing. When she took a nationwide examination for college, she placed first in France; another great French intellectual, Simone de Beauvoir, placed second that year. Her abstract approach can be unsettling, but *it also leaves room for the reader's personal experience to inform the essay. Weil's constant concern with God may seem out of place in a discussion of economic realities, but for her there was no higher reality. Perhaps if a saint had written about economics, it might have sounded like this essay.*

Prerequisite to Dignity of Labor

There is in all manual work and all work performed to order, that's to say in all real labor, an ineradicable element of constraint which would exist in even the most equitable of societies. The reason is that such work is governed by necessity and not by purpose. It is performed not for a result but because of a need, "since you've got to make a living" as people say whose existence is spent doing just that. It means exerting effort whose sole end is to secure no more than what one already has, while failure to exert such effort results in losing it. But in human effort, the only source of energy is desire. It is not in a person's nature to desire what he already has. Desire is a tendency, the start of a movement toward something, towards a point from which one is absent. If, at the very outset, this movement doubles back on itself towards its point of departure, a person turns round and round like a squirrel in a cage or a prisoner in a condemned cell. Constant turning soon produces revulsion. All workers, especially though not exclusively those who work under inhumane conditions, are easily the victims of revulsion, exhaustion, and disgust, and the strongest are often the worst affected.

Existence is not an end in itself but merely the framework upon which all good, both real and imagined, may be built. When all objectives vanish and existence appears starkly stripped of everything, it no longer bears any relation to what is good. Indeed it becomes evil. And it is precisely then, when existence is substituted for all absent ends, that it becomes an end in itself, the only object of desire. When desire is directed like that towards sheer naked evil, the soul lives in the same horror as when violent death is imminent. In the past, the state could last an entire lifetime, as for example when a man disarmed by his enemy's sword found his life spared. In exchange for his life, he would exhaust all his energies all day, every day, as a slave, with nothing on which to pin his hopes except the possibility of not being whipped or not being killed. The only good objective for him was existence itself. The ancients used to say that the day a man became a slave half his soul was taken from him.

A similar kind of slavery persists whenever people find themselves in the same position on the first and the last day of a month, of a year, or of twenty years' effort. The similarity lies in its being equally impossible for them to desire more than they already possess or to direct effort towards the acquisition of what is good. Effort is for survival. The unit of time is a day and they oscillate like a ball bouncing off two walls, from work to sleep, working so as to eat, eating so as to continue to work, and so on *ad nauseam*. In this sort of existence, everything is an intermediary, a means from which all finality is excluded. The manufactured object is a means. It will be sold. Who could invest in it his or her idea of the good? Material objects, tools, the worker's body, and even his soul are a means of manufacturing. Necessity is omnipresent, good nowhere. This is the sole reason for people's present loss of morale. It is the unchanging, essential working condition. We must look for the reasons why in the past there has been no similar demoralization.

The emptiness of such a life is only bearable either through   4 enormous physical strength, in which effort is scarcely perceived, or through total moral paralysis. In the absence of these, compensations are necessary. One is the hope, either for oneself or for one's children, of occupying a different position in society. Another, of the same sort, is mindless pleasure or violence. In both, illusion is substituted for objective. On Sunday, for example, people want to forget that they have to work, so they dress and spend as though they did not. Vanity has to be satisfied and illusions of power easily procured by abandon. Enjoyments of this sort act like a drug, and drugs are always a temptation to those who are suffering. Revolution itself is a similar sort of compensation. It is ambition transposed to the collective level, the wild ambition that all workers shall soar above the working condition itself.

Most revolutionary feeling, though initially a revolt against injustice, often becomes very rapidly, as it has done in the past, a workers' imperialism exactly analogous to national imperialism. Its aim is the total and unlimited domination of one collectivity over all humanity and all aspects of human life. The absurdity of it lies in the fact that under such a regime, the dominators, being themselves workers, would be unable to dominate. As a revolt against the injustices of society, the idea of revolution is right and proper. But as a revolt against the essential misery of the working condition it is misleading, for no revolution will get rid of the latter.

Belief in revolution holds the greater sway, however, since the misery of the working condition is more keenly felt than injustice itself. In people's minds, the one is rarely distinguished from the other. The phrase "opium of the people," which Marx used appropriately enough to describe religion when it had failed itself, applies essentially to revolution. The hope of a revolution to come satisfies a craving for adventure, of escaping from necessity, which again is a reaction against misery. In adolescence, this same craving is shown in a taste for crime fiction and a tendency towards delinquency. It was naive of the bourgeoisie to believe that all would be well if they transferred to the people the principle that governs the middle classes, namely the acquisition of wealth. They did as much as they could in this direction by introducing piecework and extending exchange between urban and rural areas. But all that did was increase dissatisfaction to the level of dangerous frustration, and the reason was simple. The acquisition of money as the object of desire and effort cannot take place under conditions within which it is impossible to become enriched. A small industrialist or businessman may enrich himself and become a big industrialist or a big businessman; a teacher, a writer, or a minister is rich or poor according to circumstance, but a worker who becomes rich ceases to be a worker and the same is nearly always true of a peasant. A worker cannot be smitten by the desire for money without wishing to escape, either with or without his companions, from the working condition.

The workers' universe excludes purpose. Purpose does not penetrate it except for very short periods always regarded as exceptional. The rapid development of new countries such as the United States and the USSR produces change at such a rate that from one day to the next it seems there are fresh expectations, more and more things to desire and to covet. This frenzied social reconstruction was the great attraction of Russian communism, by coincidence as it happened, since it had to do with the economic state of the country and not with revolution or Marxist doctrine. When a system of metaphysics is based on brief, temporary, and exceptional circumstances, as in the case of the American and the Russian, it is ill-founded. The family acquires purpose in the form of children to be brought up. But unless one aspires on their behalf to a different social position—rare as these social advances are—the prospect of children condemned to the same existence provides no relief from its painful emptiness. This emptiness weighs heavily, and it is felt and suffered by many of low intelligence and little culture. Those whose position in society protects them from it cannot judge fairly the actions of those who bear it all their lives. It does not kill but is perhaps as painful as hunger, possibly more painful. It might be literally true that bread is less necessary than the relief of such pain.

There is one form of relief and one only. Only one thing makes   8
monotony bearable and that is beauty, the light of the eternal. It is in respect of one thing only that human nature can bear for the soul's desire to be directed towards not what could be or will be, but towards what exists, and that is in respect of beauty. Everything beautiful is the object of desire, but one desires that it be not otherwise, that it be unchanged, that it be exactly what it is. One looks with desire at a clear, starry night and one desires exactly the sight before one's eyes. Since the people are forced to direct all their desires towards what they already possess, beauty is made for them and they for it. For other social classes, poetry is a luxury, but the people need poetry as they need bread. Not the poetry closed inside words: by itself that is no use to them. They need poetry to be the very substance of daily life. Such poetry can come from one source only and that is God. The poetry can only be religion. There is no stratagem, no procedure, no reform or reversal whereby purpose can enter the world in which workers are placed by the working condition itself. But this entire world may be connected to the one true purpose. It may be linked to God. The condition of the workers is one in which the hunger for purpose that is the very being of all people cannot be satisfied except by God. And it is their exclusive privilege. They alone possess it. In all other conditions of life, without exception, specific aims govern activity. And there is not a single aim, including the salvation of one or many souls, which may not act as a screen and hide God. The screen must be pierced through detachment. For workers, there is no screen. Nothing separates them from God. They have only to lift their heads. Therein lies the greatest difficulty for them. Unlike other people, they do not have too much of something which must be shed with effort. They have too little of something. They have too few intermediaries. Asking people to think of God and to offer him their pain and suffering is not help at all.

People go to church specifically to pray, yet we know they could not do so unless their attention were drawn through intermediaries towards God. The architecture of the church itself, the images which fill it, the words of the liturgy and prayer, the ritual gestures of the priest are all intermediaries. By fixing attention on them it is guided towards God. How much more necessary then is the provision of such intermediaries in a place where someone goes merely to make a living! In the workplace all thought is dragged down to earth. It is clearly not possible to put up religious pictures and suggest people look at them or recite prayers while working. The only perceptible objects of attention there are the materials, the tools, and the movements of work. If these very objects are not transformed into reflections of light, it is impossible for attention during work to be directed towards the source of all light. Nothing is more urgently needed than such a transformation. It is only possible if a reflective property is to be found in the matter that confronts working people. No concoction of arbitrary symbols will do. In truth there is no place for fiction, imagination, or dreams. Fortunately for us a reflective property does exist in matter which is like a mirror misted over by our breath. We have only to wipe the mirror to read in it symbols inscribed in matter through eternity.

Some are contained in the Gospels. Inside a room, if one wishes to think about spiritual death being a prerequisite of true rebirth, one needs words about the seed fertilized by death alone. A sower in the act of sowing, however, may, if he wishes, through his own movements and the sight of the seed entering the earth, direct his attention towards that truth without the help of a single word. If he does not reason around it but simply looks, the undiminished attention he pays to the accomplishment of his task reaches the very highest degree of intensity.

Religious attention is justly called the plenitude of attention. Plenitude of attention is nothing other than prayer. Similarly, the image of the alienation of the soul parched by Christ is like the shriveling of the branch cut off from the vine. In the great vineyards, pruning takes place over very many days. And likewise, contemplation of the inexhaustible truth it symbolizes can also continue day after day.

It should be easy to find shaped in the nature of things many other symbols which can transfigure not only labor generally but individual tasks themselves. Christ is the bronze serpent which shields from death those who look upon it. Yet our gaze must be uninterrupted, and in order for it to be so, the things which our needs and obligations force us to look at must reflect what they prevent us from seeing directly. If a church made by human beings can be full of symbols, how much more full must the universe be. It is infinitely full of them. We must read into them.

The image in the Good Friday hymn of the Cross compared to a scales could be an inexhaustible source of inspiration to those who carry burdens, pull levers, and who are by evening exhausted by the weight of things. On the scales a considerable weight placed close to the supporting point may be lifted by a relatively small weight placed at a great distance from it. The body of Christ was a very small weight, but with the distance existing between heaven and earth, he counterbalanced the universe. It is often unbearably heavy, and body and soul are bowed beneath its wearying weight. But the person who is connected to heaven may support that weight, and once he has seen the connection, will not be distracted from it by weariness, tedium, or disgust. He will be led back to it constantly.

In the fields, sun and sap are constant reminders of the greatest thing in the world—the fact that we live by solar energy alone. It feeds us, keeps us upright, activates our muscles, and operates all our bodily actions. In its different forms it is perhaps the only thing in the universe to act as a countervailing force to gravity. It is through it that trees rise, our arms lift burdens, and our motor power is driven. It comes from a source inaccessible to us and towards which we cannot move a single step. It flows down towards us always, and though bathed in it we can never seize it. Only the chlorophyll in plant life can capture it, to make with it our food. Provided that by our efforts the earth is properly prepared, solar energy through chlorophyll becomes solid and enters into us in bread, wine, oil, and fruit. All peasant labor consists in the tending of this power in plants, which is a perfect image of Christ.

The laws of mechanics that derive from geometry and govern our machines contain supernatural truths. The oscillation of alternating motion is an image of the earthly condition. Everything belonging to creatures is limited except the desire within us which is the mark of our origin. The yearnings which make us seek the unlimited here on earth are therefore for us the only source of crime and error. The good contained in things is finite and so is the evil. In a general way, a given cause will produce a given effect up to a certain point beyond which, if it continues to act, the effect is reversed. It is God who imposes limit on all things and by whom the sea is bounded. In God, there is but one eternal, unchanging act which, rebounding on itself, has no object outside itself. In creatures there exist only movements directed outside themselves but which, because of their limits, are constrained to oscillate. This oscillation is a pale reflection of exclusively divine self-orientation. In our machines, the image of this link is that between circular and alternating motion. The circle is also the source of mean proportionals. There is no other perfectly exact way of finding the mean proportional between a unit and a number which is not a square than by drawing a circle. The numbers incommensurable with the unit provide an image of our misery. The circle, which comes from outside in a manner which is transcendental with respect to the domain of numbers and provides the mean, is the image of the sole remedy for that misery. These truths and many others are contained in the simple image of a pulley determining the oscillating motion.

Only the most elementary knowledge of geometry is needed to understand these last truths, and the very rhythm of work, corresponding as it does to oscillation, helps the body to sense them. A human life span is a very short time, indeed, in which to contemplate them.

Many other symbols could be found, some more intimately   16
linked with individual workers' actions. In some cases merely by applying his attitude at work to everything else, a worker could experience the good life. Symbols might also be found for those with routine nonmanual jobs. For clerks, these might come from elementary arithmetic, for cashiers, from money and so forth; the stock is inexhaustible. From then on, much could be accomplished. These great images, linked to the ideas of science and general culture, could be passed on to adolescents as part of their studies. They could be used as themes for their celebrations and theatrical ventures. New high days and holidays could be centered around them, such as the eve of that great day when a little fourteen-year-old goes to work alone for the first time. By means of these symbols, men and women could live constantly surrounded by an atmosphere of supernatural poetry, as they did in medieval times, perhaps even better than then, for why limit hope for the good?

In this way workers would be rid of the often painful feeling of inferiority they experience and also the false confidence which slight contact with intellectualism puts in its place. Intellectuals, for their part, would be rid of their unwarranted snobbery and the equally suspect cult of fashionable ranting that sprang up a few years ago. All those who were able would unite on equal terms at the highest point of full attention, that's to say in the fullness of prayer. Those who were unable would at least know that such a point exists. They would see that the various paths leading up to that point, though separate at lower levels, as by the base of a mountain are all equally viable.

The only serious aim of schoolwork is to train the attention. Attention is the only faculty of the soul which gives access to God. Mental gymnastics rely on an inferior, discursive form of attention, which reasons. Properly directed, however, this attention may give rise in the soul to another, of the highest kind, which is intuitive attention. Pure, intuitive attention is the only source of perfectly beautiful art, truly original and brilliant scientific discovery, of philosophy which really aspires to wisdom, and of true, practical love of one's neighbor. This kind of attention when turned to God is true prayer. Just as symbols can enable one to think of God while one is digging or mowing, so only a method of transforming schoolwork into preparation for this superior attention would allow an adolescent solving a problem in geometry or doing a Latin translation to think of God. Without such a transformation, intellectual work for all its apparent independence remains nevertheless servile. In order to attain intuitive attention, those with leisure to do so must exercise to their very utmost the discursive faculties which, while they remain, act as an obstacle. For those whose social function requires them to use those faculties, there is probably no other method. For those whose faculties are almost completely paralyzed by the fatigue of long daily labor, the possible obstacle is much reduced and the necessary wearing-down minimal. For them, the very work which paralyzes, provided it be transformed into poetry, will lead to intuitive attention.

In our society, it is educational rather than economic differences that produce the illusion of social inequality. Marx, who is nearly always very powerful when describing evil, rightly denounced as degrading the separation of manual and intellectual labor. He did not know that, in all domains, opposites are unified on a plane transcending both. The meeting point of intellectual and manual work is contemplation, which is no work at all. In no society does the person in charge of a machine exercise the same kind of attention as a person working out a problem. If they wish, however, and if they have a method for doing so, each, in exercising the particular kind of attention required of them by society, can allow another kind to appear and develop. This other kind of attention overrides all social obligations and constitutes a direct link with God.

If students, young peasants, and workers could perceive all the various social functions as equal prerequisites to the emergence in the soul of one uniquely valuable faculty, as they perceive cogs in a perfectly straightforward machine, then equality would become a real thing. It would be the principle of both justice and order. It is only through a clear understanding of the supernatural meaning of each social function that the desirability of reform can be judged and injustice defined. Otherwise injustice will be seen inevitably and erroneously as suffering rooted in the nature of things, or undeserved suffering that results from our own crimes will be attributed to the human condition itself. Certain degrees of subordination and monotony are sufferings inherent in the very nature of work and inseparable from a corresponding supernatural meaning. Neither is degrading in itself, but anything added to them is both degrading and unjust. Anything which prevents poetry from crystalizing around that suffering is criminal. It is not sufficient to rediscover the lost source of the poetry; working conditions must themselves favor its continued existence. If they are unfavorable, they kill it.

Anything which is inextricably linked with either the desire for or the fear of change should be excluded from what is essentially a uniform existence and one which should be accepted as such. First, all physical suffering except that which the nature of the work makes unavoidable, for it is impossible to suffer without hoping for relief. Hardships can scarcely be more unendurable than in this social condition. Food, lodging, rest, and leisure should be such that a normal working day, taken in itself, should be free of physical suffering. Excess, too, is no less undesirable in this kind of life, for the desire for it is itself unlimited and implies a desire for a change of condition. All advertising and propaganda of all kinds, and anything designed to stimulate the desire for excess in both rural and urban workers, should be regarded as criminal. There may be individual flights from the working condition either through unsuitability or the possession of different skills, but for those who remain, there should be no improvement in individual well-being that is not at the same time seen as linked to the general. There should be no way for a worker to be afraid of getting too little or hope to get more than he needs. Security should be greater than in any other social condition and unaffected by the fluctuations of supply and demand.

The arbitrary in human life forces the defenseless soul both to hope and to fear. It should therefore be excluded as far as possible from work as should all unnecessary authority. A small peasant holding is thus better than a large one. It follows that big is bad where small is possible and that parts are better manufactured in a small workshop than under the orders of a factory foreman. In the Book of Job, death is praised since it prevents the slave from hearing his master's voice. Harm is done each time a commanding voice is raised when a practical arrangement could have been made quietly without it.

The worst outrage, however, is violation of the workers' attention. This is perhaps an example of a sin against the spirit, which is unforgivable if committed deliberately. It destroys that faculty of the soul which is the source of all spiritual action. The inferior kind of attention required by taylorized (conveyor-belt) work is incompatible with any other kind of attention since it drains the soul of all save a preoccupation with speed. This kind of work cannot be transformed and must be stopped. All technological problems should be viewed within the context of what will bring about the best working conditions. This is the most important standard to establish; the whole of society should be first constituted so that work does not demean those who perform it. It is not sufficient that they avoid suffering. Their joy must be desired also, not bought treats but the natural delights that do not cheapen the spirit of poverty. The supernatural poetry which should permeate all their lives could from time to time be concentrated in dazzling celebrations, as necessary in working life as milestones to the walker. Free working holidays like the old *tours de France* would satisfy the youthful appetite for seeing and learning. All should be done so that nothing essential is missing and the best among them may then possess in their daily lives the completeness artists seek to express in their art. If man's vocation is to achieve pure joy through suffering, workers are better placed than all others to accomplish it in the truest way.

QUESTIONS FOR CRITICAL READING

1. How do you interpret the key statement "Existence is not an end in itself but merely the framework upon which all good, both real and imagined, may be built" (para. 2)? How does this statement relate to work and the conditions of labor? Does it affect you personally?
2. What is the meaning of work "governed by necessity and not by purpose" (para. 1)?
3. Why does Weil say that revolution will not cure the "essential misery of the working condition" (para. 5)? Do you agree with her?
4. What is your reaction to Weil's assertion "A worker cannot be smitten by the desire for money without wishing to escape . . . from the working condition" (para. 6)?
5. In paragraph 9, Weil talks about the role of "intermediaries towards God." How effective are these intermediaries, and what is their relationship to work and workers? Do they make a positive contribution to spiritual well-being?
6. Weil considers the power in plants, which peasant farmers harness, and the laws of mechanics, which factory workers harness, to be aspects of God. How convincing is her analysis for you? Do the laws that "govern our machines contain supernatural truths" (para. 15)?
7. Do you agree with Weil's statement "The only serious aim of school-work is to train the attention"?

WRITING ASSIGNMENTS

1. Consider Weil's statement "Necessity is omnipresent, good nowhere. This is the sole reason for people's present loss of morale." She associates the loss of morale with modern working conditions in factories and likens certain forms of labor to slavery. Is her view still reasonable in the 1990s?
2. Simone Weil wrote in the 1930s and 1940s, before the era of consumer-

ism. How has the consumer society of the last thirty years changed the concept of the purpose of work? Although Weil says, "The family acquires purpose in the form of children to be brought up," many modern working couples have no children, and do not intend to have any. What is their purpose in work? How has the world changed since Weil's time?

3. The discussion of symbols appropriate for workers in paragraphs 12–18 begins with the comparison of the cross to a scale. Weil says that appropriate symbols are intermediaries that help workers interpret their acts as spiritually significant. Which symbols do you feel are most appropriate for modern labor, and what are the chances that such symbols can be effective in imparting spiritual significance to work?

4. In paragraph 21, Weil discusses the environment of the worker, insisting that any form of suffering while working is unnecessary and harmful. In regard to this she says, "All advertising and propaganda of all kinds, and anything designed to stimulate the desire for excess in both rural and urban workers, should be regarded as criminal." What are the effects of such advertising or propaganda? As far as possible, draw on your own experience.

5. **CONNECTIONS** Weil was influenced by Marx. What connections do you see between her views and those of Marx in *The Communist Manifesto*? To what extent is Marx interested in the spiritual well-being of workers? Does the ten-point program near the end of his essay mesh well with Weil's thinking? How much does Weil agree with Marx and in what ways are her views distinct? Would Weil agree with the Marxist recommendation of centralizing communication and transport in the hands of the state?

6. **CONNECTIONS** Robert B. Reich sees three kinds of workers in the labor force: routine workers, in-person servers, and symbolic analysts. Would Weil agree with Reich that the economic future of workers is bound up with their relationship to these groups? Is Weil any less interested in the spiritual well-being of the routine worker than in that of the symbolic analyst? How would she react to Reich's argument concerning the fate of labor in the next decade?

ROBERT B. REICH

Why the Rich Are Getting Richer and the Poor, Poorer

ROBERT B. REICH *(b. 1946), a lecturer in political economy at Harvard University and secretary of labor in the Clinton administration, holds a graduate degree from Yale Law School, and unlike his colleagues in the John F. Kennedy School of Government at Harvard, he does not hold a Ph.D. in economics. Nonetheless, he has written numerous books on economics and has been a prominent lecturer for a dozen years.* The Work of Nations *(1991), from which this essay comes, is the distillation of many years' analysis of modern economic trends.*

As a college student, Reich was an activist but not a radical. In 1968 he was a Rhodes scholar, studying at Oxford University with Bill Clinton and a number of others who are now influential American policymakers. Reich is a specialist in policy studies, that is, the relationship of governmental policy to the economic health of the nation. Unlike Keynes, who championed free trade and unlimited expansion, Reich questions the existence of free trade by pointing to the effect of government taxation on business enterprise. Taxation—like many governmental policies regarding immigration, tariffs, and money supply—directly shapes the behavior of most companies. Reich feels that government must establish and execute an industrial policy that will benefit the nation.

While organized labor groups, such as industrial unions, have rejected much of his theorizing about labor, Reich has developed a reputation as a conciliator who can see opposite sides of a question and resolve them. He is known for his denunciation of mergers, lawsuits, takeovers, and other deals that he believes simply churn money around rather than producing wealth. He feels that such maneuvers enrich a few predatory people but do not benefit labor in general. Indeed, the debt created by such deals harms labor in the long run.

In his book The Next American Frontier *(1983) Reich insists* that government, unions, and businesses must cooperate to create a workable program designed to improve the economy. Trusting to chance and free trade, he argues, will no longer do in the current economy. He has also said methods must change from the old assembly-line methods of mass production to what he calls "flexible production," involving smaller, customized runs of products for specific markets. This method also involves high technology and specialized methods.

Reich's The Work of Nations, whose title draws on Adam Smith's classic The Wealth of Nations (1798, rev. 1803), examines the borderless nature of contemporary corporations. Multinational corporations are a reality, and as he points out in the following essay, their flexibility makes it possible for them to thrive by moving manufacturing plants from nation to nation. The reasons for moving are sometimes connected to lower wages; however, they are even more often connected to the infrastructure of a given nation. Reliable roads, plentiful electricity, well-educated workers, low crime rates, and political stability are all elements that make a location attractive to a multinational corporation.

Because being a Rhodes scholar put him in contact with Bill Clinton, Reich has an unusual opportunity. Most professional economists spend their life thinking about the economy, not doing something about it. Like John Maynard Keynes, who was hired by Franklin Delano Roosevelt during the Depression, Reich has been given a chance as secretary of labor to help shape government policies from a cabinet position. Perhaps for this reason, it is especially important for us to examine his thinking on the role of labor in the economy.

REICH'S RHETORIC

The structure of "Why the Rich Are Getting Richer and the Poor, Poorer" is built on a metaphor: that of boats rising or falling with the tide. As Reich notes, "All Americans used to be in roughly the same economic boat" (para. 2), and when the economic tide rose, most people rose along with it. However, today "national borders no longer define our economic fate"; Reich therefore views Americans today as being in different boats, depending on their role in the economy, and his essay follows the fates of three distinct kinds of workers.

The first is the routine worker, essentially comparable to the worker whose spiritual fate interested Simone Weil. Examining this worker, he observes, "The boat containing routine producers is sinking rapidly." As he demonstrates, the need for routine production has declined in part because of improvements in production facilities. Much labor-intensive work has been replaced by machines. Modern factories often scramble to locate where production costs are lowest. People in other nations *work at a fraction of the hourly rate of American workers, and since factories are relatively cheap to establish, they can be easily moved.*

Reich continues the boat metaphor with "in-person servers." The boat that carries these workers, he says, "is sinking as well, but somewhat more slowly and unevenly" (para. 20). Workers in restaurants, retail outlets, car washes, and other personal service industries often work part-time and have little in the way of health or other benefits. Their jobs are imperiled by machines as well, although not as much as manufacturing jobs are. Although the outlook for such workers is buoyed by a declining population, which will reduce competition for their jobs, increased immigration may cancel this benefit.

Finally, Reich argues that the "vessel containing America's symbolic analysts is rising" (para. 28). This third group contains the population that identifies and solves problems and brokers ideas. It is this group in America that is thriving and exporting its talent overseas as well. Engineers, consultants, marketing experts, publicists, and those in entertainment fields all manage to cross national boundaries and prosper at a rate that is perhaps startling. "Almost everyone around the world is buying the skills and insights of Americans who manipulate oral and visual symbols" (para. 33). As a result of an expanding world market, symbolic analysts do not depend only on the purchasing power of routine and in-service workers. Instead, they rely on the same global web that dominates the pattern of corporate structure.

Reich's essay follows the fate of these three groups in turn to establish the pattern of change and expectation that will shape America's economic future. His metaphor is deftly handled, and he includes details, examples, facts, and careful references to support his position.

Why the Rich Are Getting Richer
and the Poor, Poorer

The division of labour is limited by the extent of the market.
ADAM SMITH,
*An Inquiry into the Nature
and Causes of the Wealth of Nations* (1776)

Regardless of how your job is officially classified (manufacturing, service, managerial, technical, secretarial, and so on), or the industry in which you work (automotive, steel, computer, advertising, finance, food processing), your real competitive position in the world economy is coming to depend on the function you perform in it. Herein lies the basic reason why incomes are diverging. The fortunes of routine producers are declining. In-person servers are also becoming poorer, although their fates are less clear-cut. But symbolic analysts—who solve, identify, and broker new problems—are, by and large, succeeding in the world economy.

All Americans used to be in roughly the same economic boat. Most rose or fell together as the corporations in which they were employed, the industries comprising such corporations, and the national economy as a whole became more productive—or languished. But national borders no longer define our economic fates. We are now in different boats, one sinking rapidly, one sinking more slowly, and the third rising steadily.

The boat containing routine producers is sinking rapidly. Recall that by midcentury routine production workers in the United States were paid relatively well. The giant pyramidlike organizations at the core of each major industry coordinated their prices and investments—avoiding the harsh winds of competition and thus maintaining healthy earnings. Some of these earnings, in turn, were reinvested in new plant and equipment (yielding ever-larger-scale economies); another portion went to top managers and investors. But a large and increasing portion went to middle managers and production workers. Work stoppages posed such a threat to high-volume production that organized labor was able to exact an ever-larger premium for its cooperation. And the pattern of wages established within the core corporations influenced the pattern throughout the national economy. Thus the growth of a relatively affluent middle class, able to purchase all the wondrous things produced in high volume by the core corporations.

But, as has been observed, the core is rapidly breaking down   4
into global webs which earn their largest profits from clever problem-solving, -identifying, and brokering. As the costs of transporting standard things and of communicating information about them continue to drop, profit margins on high-volume, standardized production are thinning, because there are few barriers to entry. Modern factories and state-of-the-art machinery can be installed almost anywhere on the globe. Routine producers in the United States, then, are in direct competition with millions of routine producers in other nations. Twelve thousand people are added to the world's population every hour, most of whom, eventually, will happily work for a small fraction of the wages of routine producers in America.[1]

---

[1]The reader should note, of course, that lower wages in other areas of the

The consequence is clearest in older, heavy industries, where high-volume, standardized production continues its ineluctable move to where labor is cheapest and most accessible around the world. Thus, for example, the Maquiladora factories cluttered along the Mexican side of the U.S. border in the sprawling shanty towns of Tijuana, Mexicali, Nogales, Agua Prieta, and Ciudad Juárez—factories owned mostly by Americans, but increasingly by Japanese—in which more than a half million routine producers assemble parts into finished goods to be shipped into the United States.

The same story is unfolding worldwide. Until the late 1970s, AT&T had depended on routine producers in Shreveport, Louisiana, to assemble standard telephones. It then discovered that routine producers in Singapore would perform the same tasks at a far lower cost. Facing intense competition from other global webs, AT&T's strategic brokers felt compelled to switch. So in the early 1980s they stopped hiring routine producers in Shreveport and began hiring cheaper routine producers in Singapore. But under this kind of pressure for ever lower high-volume production costs, today's Singaporean can easily end up as yesterday's Louisianan. By the late 1980s, AT&T's strategic brokers found that routine producers in Thailand were eager to assemble telephones for a small fraction of the wages of routine producers in Singapore. Thus, in 1989, AT&T stopped hiring Singaporeans to make telephones and began hiring even cheaper routine producers in Thailand.

The search for ever lower wages has not been confined to heavy industry. Routine data processing is equally footloose. Keypunch operators located anywhere around the world can enter data into computers, linked by satellite or transoceanic fiber-optic cable, and take it out again. As the rates charged by satellite networks continue to drop, and as more satellites and fiber-optic cables become available (reducing communication costs still further), routine data processors in the United States find themselves in ever more direct competition with their counterparts abroad, who are often eager to work for far less.

By 1990, keypunch operators in the United States were earning, at most, $6.50 per hour. But keypunch operators throughout the rest of the world were willing to work for a fraction of this. Thus, many potential American data-processing jobs were disappearing, and the wages and benefits of the remaining ones were in decline.   8

---

world are of no particular attraction to global capital unless workers there are sufficiently productive to make the labor cost of producing *each unit* lower there than in higher-wage regions. Productivity in many low-wage areas of the world has improved due to the ease with which state-of-the-art factories and equipment can be installed there. [Reich's note]

Typical was Saztec International, a $20-million-a-year data-processing firm headquartered in Kansas City, whose American strategic brokers contracted with routine data processors in Manila and with American-owned firms that needed such data-processing services. Compared with the average Philippine income of $1,700 per year, data-entry operators working for Saztec earn the princely sum of $2,650. The remainder of Saztec's employees were American problem-solvers and -identifiers, searching for ways to improve the worldwide system and find new uses to which it could be put.[2]

By 1990, American Airlines was employing over 1,000 data processors in Barbados and the Dominican Republic to enter names and flight numbers from used airline tickets (flown daily to Barbados from airports around the United States) into a giant computer bank located in Dallas. Chicago publisher R. R. Donnelley was sending entire manuscripts to Barbados for entry into computers in preparation for printing. The New York Life Insurance Company was dispatching insurance claims to Castleisland, Ireland, where routine producers, guided by simple directions, entered the claims and determined the amounts due, then instantly transmitted the computations back to the United States. (When the firm advertised in Ireland for twenty-five data-processing jobs, it received six hundred applications.) And McGraw-Hill was processing subscription renewal and marketing information for its magazines in nearby Galway. Indeed, literally millions of routine workers around the world were receiving information, converting it into computer-readable form, and then sending it back—at the speed of electronic impulses—whence it came.

The simple coding of computer software has also entered into world commerce. India, with a large English-speaking population of technicians happy to do routine programming cheaply, is proving to be particularly attractive to global webs in need of this service. By 1990, Texas Instruments maintained a software development facility in Bangalore, linking fifty Indian programmers by satellite to TI's Dallas headquarters. Spurred by this and similar ventures, the Indian government was building a teleport in Poona, intended to make it easier and less expensive for many other firms to send their routine software design specifications for coding.[3]

This shift of routine production jobs from advanced to developing nations is a great boon to many workers in such nations who

---

[2]John Maxwell Hamilton, "A Bit Player Buys Into the Computer Age," *New York Times Business World,* December 3, 1989, p. 14. [Reich's note]

[3]Udayan Gupta, "U.S.-India Satellite Link Stands to Cut Software Costs," *Wall Street Journal,* March 6, 1989, p. B2. [Reich's note]

otherwise would be jobless or working for much lower wages. These workers, in turn, now have more money with which to purchase symbolic-analytic services from advanced nations (often embedded within all sorts of complex products). The trend is also beneficial to everyone around the world who can now obtain high-volume, standardized products (including information and software) more cheaply than before.

But these benefits do not come without certain costs. In particu-   12
lar the burden is borne by those who no longer have good-paying routine production jobs within advanced economies like the United States. Many of these people used to belong to unions or at least benefited from prevailing wage rates established in collective bargaining agreements. But as the old corporate bureaucracies have flattened into global webs, bargaining leverage has been lost. Indeed, the tacit national bargain is no more.

Despite the growth in the number of new jobs in the United States, union membership has withered. In 1960, 35 percent of all nonagricultural workers in America belonged to a union. But by 1980 that portion had fallen to just under a quarter, and by 1989 to about 17 percent. Excluding government employees, union membership was down to 13.4 percent.[4] This was a smaller proportion even than in the early 1930s, before the National Labor Relations Act created a legally protected right to labor representation. The drop in membership has been accompanied by a growing number of collective bargaining agreements to freeze wages at current levels, reduce wage levels of entering workers, or reduce wages overall. This is an important reason why the long economic recovery that began in 1982 produced a smaller rise in unit labor costs than any of the eight recoveries since World War II—the low rate of unemployment during its course notwithstanding.

Routine production jobs have vanished fastest in traditional unionized industries (autos, steel, and rubber, for example), where average wages have kept up with inflation. This is because the jobs of older workers in such industries are protected by seniority; the youngest workers are the first to be laid off. Faced with a choice of cutting wages or cutting the number of jobs, a majority of union members (secure in the knowledge that there are many who are junior to them who will be laid off first) often have voted for the latter.

Thus the decline in union membership has been most striking

---

[4]*Statistical Abstract of the United States* (Washington, D.C.: U.S. Government Printing Office, 1989), p. 416, table 684. [Reich's note]

among young men entering the work force without a college education. In the early 1950s, more than 40 percent of this group joined
unions; by the late 1980s, less than 20 percent (if public employees
are excluded, less than 10 percent).[5] In steelmaking, for example,
although many older workers remained employed, almost half of
all routine steelmaking jobs in America vanished between 1974 and
1988 (from 480,000 to 260,000). Similarly with automobiles: During
the 1980s, the United Auto Workers lost 500,000 members—one-
third of their total at the start of the decade. General Motors alone
cut 150,000 American production jobs during the 1980s (even as
it added employment abroad). Another consequence of the same
phenomenon: the gap between the average wages of unionized and
nonunionized workers widened dramatically—from 14.6 percent
in 1973 to 20.4 percent by end of the 1980s.[6] The lesson is clear. If
you drop out of high school or have no more than a high school
diploma, do not expect a good routine production job to be awaiting
you.

Also vanishing are lower- and middle-level management jobs   16
involving routine production. Between 1981 and 1986, more than
780,000 foremen, supervisors, and section chiefs lost their jobs
through plant closings and layoffs.[7] Large numbers of assistant
division heads, assistant directors, assistant managers, and vice presidents also found themselves jobless. GM shed more than 40,000
white-collar employees and planned to eliminate another 25,000 by
the mid-1990s.[8] As America's core pyramids metamorphosed into
global webs, many middle-level routine producers were as obsolete
as routine workers on the line.

As has been noted, foreign-owned webs are hiring some Americans to do routine production in the United States. Philips, Sony,
and Toyota factories are popping up all over—to the self-congratula-
tory applause of the nation's governors and mayors, who have lured
them with promises of tax abatements and new sewers, among
other amenities. But as these ebullient politicians will soon discover,
the foreign-owned factories are highly automated and will become
far more so in years to come. Routine production jobs account for

---

[5] Calculations from Current Population Surveys by L. Katz and A. Revenga,
"Changes in the Structure of Wages: U.S. and Japan," National Bureau of Economic
Research, September 1989. [Reich's note]

[6] U.S. Department of Commerce, Bureau of Labor Statistics, "Wages of Unionized and Non-Unionized Workers," various issues. [Reich's note]

[7] U.S. Department of Labor, Bureau of Labor Statistics, "Reemployment Increases Among Displaced Workers," BLS News, USDL 86–414, October 14, 1986,
table 6. [Reich's note]

[8] Wall Street Journal, February 16, 1990, p. A5. [Reich's note]

a small fraction of the cost of producing most items in the United States and other advanced nations, and this fraction will continue to decline sharply as computer-integrated robots take over. In 1977 it took routine producers thirty-five hours to assemble an automobile in the United States; it is estimated that by the mid-1990s, Japanese-owned factories in America will be producing finished automobiles using only eight hours of a routine producer's time.[9]

The productivity and resulting wages of American workers who run such robotic machinery may be relatively high, but there may not be many such jobs to go around. A case in point: in the late 1980s, Nippon Steel joined with America's ailing Inland Steel to build a new $400 million cold-rolling mill fifty miles west of Gary, Indiana. The mill was celebrated for its state-of-the-art technology, which cut the time to produce a coil of steel from twelve days to about one hour. In fact, the entire plant could be run by a small team of technicians, which became clear when Inland subsequently closed two of its old cold-rolling mills, laying off hundreds of routine workers. Governors and mayors take note: your much-ballyhooed foreign factories may end up employing distressingly few of your constituents.

Overall, the decline in routine jobs has hurt men more than women. This is because the routine production jobs held by men in high-volume metal-bending manufacturing industries had paid higher wages than the routine production jobs held by women in textiles and data processing. As both sets of jobs have been lost, American women in routine production have gained more equal footing with American men—equally poor footing, that is. This is a major reason why the gender gap between male and female wages began to close during the 1980s.

The second of the three boats, carrying in-person servers, is   20
sinking as well, but somewhat more slowly and unevenly. Most in-person servers are paid at or just slightly above the minimum wage and many work only part-time, with the result that their take-home pay is modest, to say the least. Nor do they typically receive all the benefits (health care, life insurance, disability, and so forth) garnered by routine producers in large manufacturing corporations or by symbolic analysts affiliated with the more affluent threads of global webs.[10] In-person servers are sheltered from

[9]Figures from the International Motor Vehicles Program, Massachusetts Institute of Technology, 1989. [Reich's note]

[10]The growing portion of the American labor force engaged in in-person services, relative to routine production, thus helps explain why the number of Americans lacking health insurance increased by at least 6 million during the 1980s. [Reich's note]

the direct effects of global competition and, like everyone else, benefit from access to lower-cost products from around the world. But they are not immune to its indirect effects.

For one thing, in-person servers increasingly compete with former routine production workers, who, no longer able to find well-paying routine production jobs, have few alternatives but to seek in-person service jobs. The Bureau of Labor Statistice estimates that of the 2.8 million manufacturing workers who lost their jobs during the early 1980s, fully one-third were rehired in service jobs paying at least 20 percent less.[11] In-person servers must also compete with high school graduates and dropouts who years before had moved easily into routine production jobs but no longer can. And if demographic predictions about the American work force in the first decades of the twenty-first century are correct (and they are likely to be, since most of the people who will comprise the work force are already identifiable), most new entrants into the job market will be black or Hispanic men, or women—groups that in years past have possessed relatively weak technical skills. This will result in an even larger number of people crowding into in-person services. Finally, in-person servers will be competing with growing numbers of immigrants, both legal and illegal, for whom in-person services will comprise the most accessible jobs. (It is estimated that between the mid-1980s and the end of the century, about a quarter of all workers entering the American labor force will be immigrants.[12])

Perhaps the fiercest competition that in-person servers face comes from labor-saving machinery (much of it invented, designed, fabricated, or assembled in other nations, of course). Automated tellers, computerized cashiers, automatic car washes, robotized vending machines, self-service gasoline pumps, and all similar gadgets substitute for the human beings that customers once encountered. Even telephone operators are fast disappearing, as electronic sensors and voice simulators become capable of carrying on conversations that are reasonably intelligent and always polite. Retail sales workers—among the largest groups of in-person servers—are similarly imperiled. Through personal computers linked to television screens, tomorrow's consumers will be able to buy furniture, appliances, and all sorts of electronic toys from their living rooms— examining the merchandise from all angles, selecting whatever color, size, special features, and price seem most appealing, and

---

[11]U.S. Department of Labor, Bureau of Labor Statistics, "Reemployment Increases Among Disabled Workers," October 14, 1986. [Reich's note]

[12]Federal Immigration and Naturalization Service, *Statistical Yearbook* (Washington, D.C.: U.S. Government Printing Office, 1986, 1987). [Reich's note]

then transmitting the order instantly to warehouses from which the selections will be shipped directly to their homes. So, too, with financial transactions, airline and hotel reservations, rental car agreements, and similar contracts, which will be executed between consumers in their homes and computer banks somewhere else on the globe.[13]

Advanced economies like the United States will continue to generate sizable numbers of new in-person service jobs, of course, the automation of older ones notwithstanding. For every bank teller who loses her job to an automated teller, three new jobs open for aerobics instructors. Human beings, it seems, have an almost insatiable desire for personal attention. But the intense competition nevertheless ensures that the wages of in-person servers will remain relatively low. In-person servers—working on their own, or else dispersed widely amid many small establishments, filling all sorts of personal-care niches—cannot readily organize themselves into labor unions or create powerful lobbies to limit the impact of such competition.

In two respects, demographics will work in favor of in-person 24 servers, buoying their collective boat slightly. First, as has been noted, the rate of growth of the American work force is slowing. In particular, the number of young workers is shrinking. Between 1985 and 1995, the number of the eighteen- to twenty-four-year-olds will have declined by 17.5 percent. Thus, employers will have more incentive to hire and train in-person servers whom they might previously have avoided. But this demographic relief from the competitive pressures will be only temporary. The cumulative procreative energies of the postwar baby-boomers (born between 1946 and 1964) will result in a new surge of workers by 2010 or thereabouts.[14] And immigration—both legal and illegal—shows every sign of increasing in years to come.

Next, by the second decade of the twenty-first century, the number of Americans aged sixty-five and over will be rising precipitously, as the baby-boomers reach retirement age and live longer. Their life expectancies will lengthen not just because fewer of them will have smoked their way to their graves and more will have eaten better than their parents, but also because they will receive all sorts of expensive drugs and therapies designed to keep them

---

[13]See Claudia H. Deutsch, "The Powerful Push for Self-Service," *New York Times,* April 9, 1989, section 3, p. 1. [Reich's note]

[14]U.S. Bureau of the Census, Current Population Reports, Series P–23, no. 138, tables 2–1, 4–6. See W. Johnson, A. Packer, et al., *Workforce 2000: Work and Workers for the 21st Century* (Indianapolis: Hudson Institute, 1987). [Reich's note]

alive—barely. By 2035, twice as many Americans will be elderly as in 1988, and the number of octogenarians is expected to triple. As these decaying baby-boomers ingest all the chemicals and receive all the treatments, they will need a great deal of personal attention. Millions of deteriorating bodies will require nurses, nursing-home operators, hospital administrators, orderlies, home-care providers, hospice aides, and technicians to operate and maintain all the expensive machinery that will monitor and temporarily stave off final disintegration. There might even be a booming market for euthanasia specialists. In-person servers catering to the old and ailing will be in strong demand.[15]

One small problem: the decaying baby-boomers will not have enough money to pay for these services. They will have used up their personal savings years before. Their Social Security payments will, of course, have been used by the government to pay for the previous generation's retirement and to finance much of the budget deficits of the 1980s. Moreover, with relatively fewer young Americans in the population, the supply of housing will likely exceed the demand, with the result that the boomers' major investments—their homes—will be worth less (in inflation-adjusted dollars) when they retire than they planned for. In consequence, the huge cost of caring for the graying boomers will fall on many of the same people who will be paid to care for them. It will be like a great sump pump: in-person servers of the twenty-first century will have an abundance of health-care jobs, but a large portion of their earnings will be devoted to Social Security payments and income taxes, which will in turn be used to pay their salaries. The net result: no real improvement in their standard of living.

The standard of living of in-person servers also depends, indirectly, on the standard of living of the Americans they serve who are engaged in world commerce. To the extent that *these* Americans are richly rewarded by the rest of the world for what they contribute, they will have more money to lavish upon in-person services. Here we find the only form of "trickle-down" economics that has a basis in reality. A waitress in a town whose major factory has just been closed is unlikely to earn a high wage or enjoy much job security; in a swank resort populated by film producers and banking moguls, she is apt to do reasonably well. So, too, with nations. In-person servers in Bangladesh may spend their days performing roughly the same tasks as in-person servers in the United States, but have

---

[15]The Census Bureau estimates that by the year 2000, at least 12 million Americans will work in health services—well over 6 percent of the total work force. [Reich's note]

a far lower standard of living for their efforts. The difference comes in the value that their customers add to the world economy.

Unlike the boats of routine producers and in-person servers, however, the vessel containing America's symbolic analysts is rising. Worldwide demand for their insights is growing as the ease and speed of communicating them steadily increases. Not every symbolic analyst is rising as quickly or as dramatically as every other, of course; symbolic analysts at the low end are barely holding their own in the world economy. But symbolic analysts at the top are in such great demand worldwide that they have difficulty keeping track of all their earnings. Never before in history has opulence on such a scale been gained by people who have earned it, and done so legally.

Among symbolic analysts in the middle range are American scientists and researchers who are busily selling their discoveries to global enterprise webs. They are not limited to American customers. If the strategic brokers in General Motors' headquarters refuse to pay a high price for a new means of making high-strength ceramic engines dreamed up by a team of engineers affiliated with Carnegie Mellon University in Pittsburgh, the strategic brokers of Honda or Mercedes-Benz are likely to be more than willing.

So, too, with the insights of America's ubiquitous management consultants, which are being sold for large sums to eager entrepreneurs in Europe and Latin America. Also, the insights of America's energy consultants, sold for even larger sums to Arab sheikhs. American design engineers are providing insights to Olivetti, Mazda, Siemens, and other global webs; American marketers, techniques for learning what worldwide consumers will buy; American advertisers, ploys for ensuring that they actually do. American architects are issuing designs and blueprints for opera houses, art galleries, museums, luxury hotels, and residential complexes in the world's major cities; American commercial property developers, marketing these properties to worldwide investors and purchasers.

Americans who specialize in the gentle art of public relations are in demand by corporations, governments, and politicians in virtually every nation. So, too, are American political consultants, some of whom, at this writing, are advising the Hungarian Socialist Party, the remnant of Hungary's ruling Communists, on how to salvage a few parliamentary seats in the nation's first free election in more than forty years. Also at this writing, a team of American agricultural consultants is advising the managers of a Soviet farm collective employing 1,700 Russians eighty miles outside Moscow. As noted, American investment bankers and lawyers specializing in financial circumnavigations are selling their insights to Asians and Europeans who are eager to discover how to make large amounts of money by moving large amounts of money.

Developing nations, meanwhile, are hiring American civil engi-   32 neers to advise on building roads and dams. The present thaw in the Cold War will no doubt expand these opportunities. American engineers from Bechtel (a global firm notable for having employed both Caspar Weinberger and George Shultz for much larger sums than either earned in the Reagan administration) have begun helping the Soviets design and install a new generation of nuclear reactors. Nations also are hiring American bankers and lawyers to help them renegotiate the terms of their loans with global banks, and Washington lobbyists to help them with Congress, the Treasury, the World Bank, the IMF, and other politically sensitive institutions. In fits of obvious desperation, several nations emerging from communism have even hired American economists to teach them about capitalism.

Almost everyone around the world is buying the skills and insights of Americans who manipulate oral and visual symbols— musicians, sound engineers, film producers, makeup artists, directors, cinematographers, actors and actresses, boxers, scriptwriters, songwriters, and set designers. Among the wealthiest of symbolic analysts are Steven Spielberg, Bill Cosby, Charles Schulz, Eddie Murphy, Sylvester Stallone, Madonna, and other star directors and performers—who are almost as well known on the streets of Dresden and Tokyo as in the Back Bay of Boston. Less well rewarded but no less renowned are the unctuous anchors on Turner Broadcasting's Cable News, who appear daily, via satellite, in places ranging from Vietnam to Nigeria. Vanna White is the world's most-watched game-show hostess. Behind each of these familiar faces is a collection of American problem-solvers, -identifiers, and brokers who train, coach, advise, promote, amplify, direct, groom, represent, and otherwise add value to their talents.[16]

There are also the insights of senior American executives who occupy the world headquarters of global "American" corporations and the national or regional headquarters of global "foreign" corporations. Their insights are duly exported to the rest of the world through the webs of global enterprise. IBM does not export many machines from the United States, for example. Big Blue makes

---

[16]In 1989, the entertainment business summoned to the United States $5.5 billion in foreign earnings—making it among the nation's largest export industries, just behind aerospace. U.S. Department of Commerce, International Trade Commission, "Composition of U.S. Exports," various issues. [Reich's note]

machines all over the globe and services them on the spot. Its prime American exports are symbolic and analytic. From IBM's world headquarters in Armonk, New York, emanate strategic brokerage and related management services bound for the rest of the world. In return, IBM's top executives are generously rewarded.

The most important reason for this expanding world market and increasing global demand for the symbolic and analytic insights of Americans has been the dramatic improvement in worldwide communication and transportation technologies. Designs, instructions, advice, and visual and audio symbols can be communicated more and more rapidly around the globe, with ever-greater precision and at ever-lower cost. Madonna's voice can be transported to billions of listeners, with perfect clarity, on digital compact discs. A new invention emanating from engineers in Battelle's laboratory in Columbus, Ohio, can be sent almost anywhere via modem, in a form that will allow others to examine it in three dimensions through enhanced computer graphics. When face-to-face meetings are still required—and videoconferencing will not suffice—it is relatively easy for designers, consultants, advisers, artists, and executives to board supersonic jets and, in a matter of hours, meet directly with their worldwide clients, customers, audiences, and employees.

With rising demand comes rising compensation. Whether in 36 the form of licensing fees, fees for service, salaries, or shares in final profits, the economic result is much the same. There are also nonpecuniary rewards. One of the best-kept secrets among symbolic analysts is that so many of them enjoy their work. In fact, much of it does not count as work at all, in the traditional sense. The work of routine producers and in-person servers is typically monotonous; it causes muscles to tire or weaken and involves little independence or discretion. The "work" of symbolic analysts, by contrast, often involves puzzles, experiments, games, a significant amount of chatter, and substantial discretion over what to do next. Few routine producers or in-person servers would "work" if they did not need to earn the money. Many symbolic analysts would "work" even if money were no object.

At midcentury, when America was a national market dominated by core pyramid-shaped corporations, there were constraints on the earnings of people at the highest rungs. First and most obviously, the market for their services was largely limited to the borders of the nation. In addition, whatever conceptual value they might contribute was small relative to the value gleaned from large scale—and it was dependent on large scale for whatever income it was to summon. Most of the problems to be identified and solved had to do with enhancing the efficiency of production and improving the flow of materials, parts, assembly, and distribution. Inventors searched for the rare breakthrough revealing an entirely new product to be made in high volume; management consultants, executives, and engineers thereafter tried to speed and synchronize its manufacture, to better achieve scale efficiencies; advertisers and marketers sought then to whet the public's appetite for the standard item that emerged. Since white-collar earnings increased with larger scale, there was considerable incentive to expand the firm; indeed, many of America's core corporations grew far larger than scale economies would appear to have justified.

By the 1990s, in contrast, the earnings of symbolic analysts were limited neither by the size of the national market nor by the volume of production of the firms with which they were affiliated. The marketplace was worldwide, and conceptual value was high relative to value added from scale efficiencies.

There had been another constraint on high earnings, which also gave way by the 1990s. At midcentury, the compensation awarded to top executives and advisers of the largest of America's core corporations could not be grossly out of proportion to that of low-level production workers. It would be unseemly for executives who engaged in highly visible rounds of bargaining with labor unions, and who routinely responded to government requests to moderate prices, to take home wages and benefits wildly in excess of what other Americans earned. Unless white-collar executives restrained themselves, moreover, blue-collar production workers could not be expected to restrain their own demands for higher wages. Unless both groups exercised restraint, the government could not be expected to forbear from imposing direct controls and regulations.

At the same time, the wages of production workers could not 40
be allowed to sink too low, lest there be insufficient purchasing power in the economy. After all, who would buy all the goods flowing out of American factories if not American workers? This, too, was part of the tacit bargain struck between American managers and their workers.

Recall the oft-repeated corporate platitude of the era about the chief executive's responsibility to carefully weigh and balance the interests of the corporation's disparate stakeholders. Under the stewardship of the corporate statesman, no set of stakeholders—least of all white-collar executives—was to gain a disproportionately large share of the benefits of corporate activity; nor was any stakeholder—especially the average worker—to be left with a share that was disproportionately small. Banal though it was, this idea helped to maintain the legitimacy of the core American corporation in the eyes of most Americans, and to ensure continued economic growth.

But by the 1990s, these informal norms were evaporating, just as (and largely because) the core American corporation was vanishing. The links between top executives and the American production worker were fading: an ever-increasing number of subordinates and contractees were foreign, and a steadily growing number of American routine producers were working for foreign-owned firms. An entire cohort of middle-level managers, who had once been deemed "white collar," had disappeared; and, increasingly, American executives were exporting their insights to global enterprise webs.

As the American corporation itself became a global web almost indistinguishable from any other, its stakeholders were turning into a large and diffuse group, spread over the world. Such global stakeholders were less visible, and far less noisy, then national stakeholders. And as the American corporation sold its goods and services all over the world, the purchasing power of American workers became far less relevant to its economic survival.

Thus have the inhibitions been removed. The salaries and bene-   44
fits of America's top executives, and many of their advisers and consultants, have soared to what years before would have been unimaginable heights, even as those of other Americans have declined.

QUESTIONS FOR CRITICAL READING

1. What are symbolic analysts? Give some examples from your own experience.
2. What is the apparent relationship between higher education and the economic prospects of an educated worker?
3. To what extent do you agree or disagree with Reich's description and analysis of routine workers and in-service workers?
4. If Reich's analysis is correct, which gender or social groups are likely to be most harmed by modern economic circumstances in America? Which are most likely to benefit? Why?
5. Are symbolic analysts inherently more valuable to our society than routine or in-service workers? Why do symbolic analysts command so much more wealth?
6. Which of the three groups Reich mentions do you see as having the greatest potential for growth in the next thirty years?

WRITING ASSIGNMENTS

1. Judging from the views that Reich holds about the slowdown of the work force of all three groups of workers, what will the effect of increased immigration be on the American economy? Is immigration a hopeful sign? Is it a danger to the economy? How do most people seem to perceive the effect of increased immigration?

2. To what extent do you think Reich is correct about the economic success of symbolic analysts? He says, "Never before in history has opulence on such a scale been gained by people who have earned it, and done so legally" (para. 28). Do you see yourself as a symbolic analyst? How do you see your future in relation to the three economic groups Reich describes?

3. Reich says, "Few routine producers or in-person servers would 'work' if they did not need to earn the money. Many symbolic analysts would 'work' even if money were no object" (para. 36). Is this true? Examine your own experience—along with the experience of others you know—and defend or attack this view. How accurate do you consider Reich to be in his analysis of the way various workers view their work?

4. What changes in the American economy does this essay cover that have taken place in the last forty years? How have they affected the way Americans work and the work that Americans can expect to find? Do you feel your personal opportunities have been broadened or narrowed by the changes? Do you feel the changes have been good for the country or not?

5. Reich's view of the great success of Japanese corporations and of their presence as manufacturing giants in the United States and elsewhere is largely positive. He has pointed out elsewhere that Honda and other manufacturers in the United States provide jobs and municipal income that would otherwise go to other nations. What is your view of the presence of large Japanese corporations in the United States? What is your view of other nations' manufacturing facilities in the United States?

6. What do you feel is the greatest threat to social stability in the United States as a result of changes in the economy? Do the changes Reich describes have social as well as economic consequences? Do they foster or reduce social injustice?

7. Why are the rich getting richer and the poor poorer? Examine the kinds of differences between the rich and the poor that Reich describes. Is the process of increasing riches for the rich and increasing poverty for the poor inevitable, or will it begin to change in the near future?

8. **CONNECTIONS** To what extent is Reich concerned with the spiritual well-being of any of the three groups he describes? Would he be sympathetic to the concerns that dominate Simone Weil's essay on labor? Should he be? Should she have regarded workers as other than routine producers? Would her views be different if she had?

PART THREE

IDEAS IN THE WORLD OF PSYCHOLOGY

WHAT DETERMINES OUR PSYCHOLOGICAL IDENTITY? HOW ARE OUR PSYCHOLOGY AND OUR SEXUALITY CONNECTED?

Sigmund Freud
Carl Jung
Karen Horney
Erich Fromm
B. F. Skinner

P SYCHOLOGY has often been described as a science in its infancy; however, it has done an immense amount of growing in the twentieth century. All the psychologists in this part are modern, and indeed most of the exciting discoveries in psychology were made during their professional careers. The most important discovery is probably that of the unconscious mind, first discussed in the works of the American psychologist William James (1842–1910). But it was the work of Sigmund Freud around the turn of the century that most startled the world of psychology; it was he who began to suggest the functions of the unconscious mind as a repository of painful emotions and repressed thoughts. He also suggested means by which the unconscious mind could be apprehended— through the complex symbolic language of dreams and free-associating conversation with an analyst. Thus, his psychoanalytic methods are based upon the analysis of patients' dreams and of patients' free associations while lying on a couch and talking with a doctor.

One of Freud's most controversial theories is that nervous disorders are sexual in origin. He probably alarmed the psychological community most with his theories of infantile sexuality, which postulated that even infants have sexual urges and needs. He also developed certain theories concerning instincts that are natural to human beings. For a time, it was exceedingly controversial to suggest that humans, like other animals, had instincts. Freud, however, dared to assert that sexual needs, as well as the need for sustenance, were instinctive and that because people live in regulated communities, they are bound to experience conflicts between their instinctual and social needs.

What Sigmund Freud has to say in his essay on infantile sexuality seems fairly tame and perhaps even a bit obvious to us today. But it was a bombshell in its own day. People had always thought that children had no psychosexual awareness or drives until after puberty. Freud demonstrated that the sexual drive, which he had predicated as the strongest of psychic drives, was present even in the infant. His study was a pioneering effort that changed the nature of psychology entirely.

Freud's most distinguished follower was Carl Jung, who eventually broke away from Freud's influence and developed his own distinctive approach to psychology. Whereas Freud concentrated on the unique qualities of the individual's unconscious, Jung began to conceive of the unconscious as a repository of racial awareness, akin to the memory of the human species. In the process, he became aware of the feminine aspects of the personalities of his male patients and the masculine aspects of his female patients. His views in "Anima and Animus" are unsettling to many people, because they imply that all people have the psychological qualities of both sexes in their subconscious. One of the unnerving aspects of the split that Jung observed was the potential for each part of the psyche to be at war with the other. Jung's insights now guide a growing school of psychology that has been very productive in the fields of art criticism, literature, and psychiatry. Jung deepened our sense of the nature of the unconscious by pointing us in totally unexpected directions.

Karen Horney, a contemporary of both Freud and Jung, responded in her work to some of Freud's theories concerning the sexual development of women, one of which was that girls naturally developed penis envy when they realized that they lacked this anatomical feature. After reflecting on the behavior of primitive tribespeople, Horney theorized that the boot was actually on the other foot. She asserted that men are envious of the power of women to create a human life out of their bodies and that as a result, throughout history, men have ascribed extraordinary powers to female deities.

However, Horney did not necessarily disagree entirely with Freud. As her daughter, Marianne Horney Eckardt, put it: "Her early writing did focus on such topics as penis envy among other issues. Her observations concluded that penis envy and other feminine symptomatology did exist, but were determined by cultural factors rather than libidinal conflicts." In Dr. Eckardt's words, then, Horney's interest in feminine psychology as such centered more on the cultural than on the purely psychiatric.

Erich Fromm, originally of the Freudian school, eventually broke with Freud concerning the degree to which the unconscious determines behavior. Fromm concentrated on practical applications of psychology and observed that the environment plays a key role in the development of the psyche. Consequently, he concerned himself with the socioeconomic circumstances of the individual and with the role of culture in shaping behavior. He saw, too, that certain personality traits—neatness and promptness, for example—develop in response to the needs of the business environment in American culture. The importance of Fromm's work is that he sees the problems of psychology in relation to the larger social circumstances into which a person is born and raised. In other words, the primary psychological issues for Fromm are not necessarily the Oedipus complex or a neurosis that might be traced to childhood and the early years of development. Fromm was convinced that the individual's unconscious patterns of behavior are inherent to the extent that they are automatic—but he insisted that they derive from the culture, not primarily from the individual's early psychic experience, as Freud had assumed.

B. F. Skinner, a psychologist of a quite different school, assumed that human beings are like all animals: a product of the interaction between psychology and environment. He believed that in modern society, the price individuals pay for the freedom to do as they want may be too great and that people may have to surrender much of this freedom in order to achieve greater stability and happiness.

His theories are called behaviorist because they state that individuals adapt their behavior to the environment according to a pattern of rewards and punishments. If this is so—and Skinner's views have achieved widespread acceptance—the issues of sexuality and the psyche are deeply connected to the structure of society and the environmental rewards and punishments associated with both male and female behavior. Any balanced view of psychology must take these opinions into account.

Skinner was not concerned with sexuality in the essay included here. He saw the issues of psychology as based on environment, not on genetic or psychogenetic displacement, and so he tended to sidestep Freud, Jung, and Horney. Skinner's efforts were directed at producing what he felt was a higher level of scientific discourse, one illustrated by considerable laboratory experiment and detailed observation.

The quality of writing in these pieces varies not only because many are translations but also because not all of these writers were preoccupied with style. Yet they are worthy of note for their efforts toward clarifying complex and sometimes unyielding problems. In other words, these authors are all exceptionally skillful but not necessarily great writers. They write an expository prose that strives to communicate their position clearly and convincingly. None of them makes an emotional appeal; each relies on evidence, reasoning, and cautious conclusion.

SIGMUND FREUD
Infantile Sexuality

SIGMUND FREUD *(1856–1939) is, in the minds of many, the founder of modern psychiatry. He developed the psychoanalytic method, the examination of the mind using methods of dream analysis, the analysis of the unconscious through free association, and the correlation of findings with attitudes toward sexuality and sexual development. His theories changed the way people treated neurosis and most other mental disorders. Today his theories have spread all over the world.*

Freud was born in Freiberg, Moravia (now in Czechoslovakia), and moved to Vienna, Austria, when he was four. He lived and worked in Vienna until he was put under house arrest by the Nazis. He was released in 1938 and moved to London. The psychoanalytic movement of the twentieth century has often been described as a Viennese movement, or at least as a movement closely tied to the prosperity of the Viennese middle-class intellectuals of the time.

As a movement, psychoanalysis shocked most of the world by postulating a superego, which establishes high standards of behavior; an ego, which corresponds to the apparent personality; an id, which includes the deepest primitive forces of life; and an unconscious, into which thoughts and memories we cannot face are "repressed" or "sublimated." The origin of much mental illness, the theory presumes, lies in the inability of the mind to find a way to sublimate—express in harmless and often creative ways—the painful thoughts that have been repressed. Dreams and unconscious actions sometimes act as "releases" or harmless expressions of these thoughts and memories.

Difficult as some of these ideas were to accept, they did not cause

From *Three Essays on the Theory of Sexuality*. Translated by A. A. Brill.

quite the furor of the present excerpt, which is taken from Three Essays on the Theory of Sexuality *(1905, tr. 1953), a book that was hotly debated and sometimes violently rejected. At that time, Freud had become convinced by his work with neurotic patients that much of what disturbed them was bound up with their sexuality. That led him to review the research on infantile sexuality and add to it his own findings. It was also natural to his way of thinking to produce a theory of behavior built upon his researches.*

What infuriated people so much was the suggestion that tiny children, even infants, had a sexual life. That it should also figure in the psychological health of the adult was almost as serious. Most people rejected the idea out of hand because it did not square with what they already believed or with what they felt they observed. The typical Freudian habit of seeing psychoanalytic "meaning" in otherwise innocent gestures, such as thumbsucking and bed-wetting, was brought into play in his observations on the sexuality of infants. Freud had a gift for interpretation—analysis—of apparently meaningless events. Many still resent his capacity to find meaning in such events, in part because they do not accept Freud's view that the psychological being—the person—makes every word, gesture, and act "meaningful" to his whole being. For Freud there are no accidents, only unconscious intentions. When we understand those intentions, we begin to understand ourselves.

Freud believed that sexuality was perhaps the most powerful force in the psyche. He knew that middle-class propriety would be revolted by the concepts presented in this piece. It is doubtful that he expected the middle class to accept his views. Yet he remained absolutely convinced that his views were too important to be swept aside for fear that society might be offended.

FREUD'S RHETORIC

Because this treatise is not aimed at the general public, Freud is free to use language appropriate to address a general scientific community. He spares them no details regarding bodily functions; and he adds little color to an already graceful style. His rhetorical technique is quite simple: he establishes a theory, reviews the evidence that he and others have gathered, and then derives certain conclusions from his process.

One would not think of this piece as having a beginning, a middle, and a conclusion. Rather, it has independent sections that treat specific problems and observations. All of the sections come under the heading of infantile sexuality, and all relate to the Freud's general theory: there is a connection between infantile sexuality and mature sexuality, and it is revealed in the common amnesia (the forgetting or repressing from conscious memory) of experiences related to sexual awareness in both the infant and the hysteric patient.

Freud's rhetorical approach might best be called the process of evidence and inference. In this respect it is similar to the accepted methods of science in most fields. Evidence points to an inference, which then must be tested by analysis. Observe the process as you read Freud's work.

This method sounds very straightforward and artless, and Freud's writing is generally marked by those qualities. But there is one rhetorical technique of which he is the master: the memorable phrase. For example, the term "psychoanalysis," which was invented by Freud when he was thirty-nine, is now universally used. The term "Oedipus complex," the condition of wishing your same-sex parent dead so that you will be left to "marry" your opposite-sex parent, is also taken for granted now. "Penis envy," used in this selection, is known worldwide, as is the "castration complex." Freud changed both our language and our world.

Infantile Sexuality

The Neglect of the Infantile.   It is a part of popular belief about the sexual instinct that it is absent in childhood and that it first appears in the period of life known as puberty. This, though a common error, is serious in its consequences and is chiefly due to our ignorance of the fundamental principles of the sexual life. A comprehensive study of the sexual manifestations of childhood would probably reveal to us the essential features of the sexual instinct and would show us its development and its composition from various sources.

It is quite remarkable that those writers who endeavor to explain the qualities and reactions of the adult individual have given so much more attention to the ancestral period than to the period of the individual's own existence—that is, they have attributed more influence to heredity than to childhood. As a matter of fact, it might well be supposed that the influence of the latter period would be easier to understand, and that it would be entitled to more consideration than heredity. To be sure, one occasionally finds in medical literature notes on the premature sexual activities of small children, about erections and masturbation and even reactions resembling coitus, but these are referred to merely as exceptional occurrences, as curiosities, or as deterring[1] examples of premature perversity. No author has, to my knowledge, recognized the normality of the sexual instinct in childhood, and in the numerous writings on the development of the child the chapter on "Sexual Development" is usually passed over.

Infantile Amnesia.   The reason for this remarkable negligence I seek partly in conventional considerations, which influence writers because of their own bringing up, and partly to a psychic phenomenon which thus far has remained unexplained. I refer to the peculiar amnesia which veils from most people (not from all) the first years of their childhood, usually the first six or eight years. So far, it has not occurred to us that this amnesia should surprise us, though we have good reasons for it. For we are informed that during those years which have left nothing except a few incomprehensible memory fragments, we have vividly reacted to impressions, that we have manifested human pain and pleasure and that we have expressed love, jealousy and other passions as they then affected us. Indeed, we are told that we have uttered remarks which proved to grown-ups that we possessed understanding and a budding power of judgment. Still we know nothing of all this when we become older. Why does our memory lag behind all our other psychic activities? We really have reason to believe that at no time of life are we more capable of impressions and reproductions[2] than during the years of childhood.

On the other hand we must assume, or we may convince   4 ourselves through psychological observations on others, that the very impressions which we have forgotten have nevertheless left the deepest traces in our psychic life, and acted as determinants for our whole future development. We conclude therefore that we do not deal with a real forgetting of infantile impressions but rather with an amnesia similar to that observed in neurotics for later experiences, the nature of which consists in their being kept away from consciousness (repression). But what forces bring about this repression of the infantile impressions? He who can solve this riddle will also explain hysterical amnesia.[3]

We shall not, however, hesitate to assert that the existence of

---

[1]*deterring*   Frightening.

[2]*reproductions*   Imitations, such as mimicry.

[3]*hysterical amnesia*   The forgetfulness induced by psychological shock; Freud sees a connection between it and the fact that we forget most of our earliest experience, even though it is of crucial importance to our growth.

the infantile amnesia gives us a new point of comparison between the psychic states of the child and those of the psychoneurotic. We have already encountered another point of comparison when confronted by the fact that the sexuality of the psychoneurotic preserves the infantile character or has returned to it. May there not be an ultimate connection between the infantile and the hysterical amnesias?

The connection between infantile and hysterical amnesias is really more than a mere play of wit. Hysterical amnesia which serves the repression can only be explained by the fact that the individual already possesses a sum of memories which were withdrawn from conscious disposal and which by associative connection now seize that which is acted upon by the repelling forces of the repression emanating from consciousness. We may say that without infantile amnesia there would be no hysterical amnesia.

I therefore believe that the infantile amnesia which causes the individual to look upon his childhood as if it were a *prehistoric* time and conceals from him the beginning of his own sexual life—that this amnesia, is responsible for the fact that one does not usually attribute any value to the infantile period in the development of the sexual life. One single observer cannot fill the gap which has been thus produced in our knowledge. As early as 1896, I had already emphasized the significance of childhood for the origin of certain important phenomena connected with the sexual life, and since then I have not ceased to put into the foreground the importance of the infantile factor for sexuality.

The Sexual Latency Period of Childhood and Its Interruptions

The extraordinary frequent discoveries of apparently abnormal 8
and exceptional sexual manifestations in childhood, as well as the discovery of infantile reminiscences in neurotics, which were hitherto unconscious, allow us to sketch the following picture of the sexual behavior of childhood. It seems certain that the newborn child brings with it the germs of sexual feelings which continue to develop for some time and then succumb to a progressive suppression, which may in turn be broken through by the regular advances of the sexual development or may be checked by individual idiosyncrasies. Nothing is known concerning the laws and periodicity of this oscillating course of development. It seems, however, that the sexual life of the child mostly manifests itself in the third or fourth year in some form accessible to observation.

Sexual Inhibition.   It is during this period of total or at least partial latency[4] that the psychic forces develop which later act as inhibitions on the sexual life, and narrow its direction like dams. These psychic forces are loathing, shame, and moral and esthetic ideal demands. We may gain the impression that the erection of these dams in the civilized child is the work of education; and surely education contributes much to it. In reality, however, this development is organically determined and can occasionally be produced without the help of education. Indeed education remains properly within its assigned domain if it strictly follows the path laid out by the organic,[5] and only imprints it somewhat cleaner and deeper.

Reaction Formation and Sublimation.   What are the means that accomplish these very important constructions so important for the later personal culture and normality? They are probably brought about at the cost of the infantile sexuality itself. The influx of this sexuality does not stop even in this latency period, but its energy is deflected either wholly or partially from sexual utilization and conducted to other aims. The historians of civilization seem to be unanimous in the opinion that such deflection of sexual motive powers from sexual aims to new aims, a process which merits the name of *sublimation,*[6] has furnished powerful components for all cultural accomplishments. We will, therefore, add that the same process acts in the development of every individual, and that it begins to act in the sexual latency period.

We can also venture an opinion about the mechanisms of such sublimation. The sexual feelings of these infantile years would on the one hand be unusable, since the procreating functions are postponed—this is the chief character of the latency period; on the other hand, they would as such be perverse, as they would emanate from erogenous zones and from impulses which in the individual's course of development could only evoke a feeling of displeasure. They, therefore, awaken psychic counterforces (feelings of reaction), which build up the already mentioned psychical dams of disgust, shame and morality.

---

[4]*latency*   Period when sexual interests are not evident, as before puberty.

[5]*the organic*   Freud means that the organism—the person—comes to certain understandings as a factor of growth and development. Education must respect organic growth and try not to get "out of order" with it.

[6]*sublimation*   A psychological process whereby drives, such as the sexual drive, are transformed into different expressions, such as transforming a powerful sexual drive into a drive to make money or to excel in a given field.

The Interruptions of the Latency Period.   Without deluding ourselves   12
as to the hypothetical nature and deficient clearness of our understanding regarding the infantile period of latency and delay, we will
return to reality and state that such a utilization of the infantile
sexuality represents an ideal bringing up from which the development of the individual usually deviates in some measure, often
very considerably. A part of the sexual manifestation which has
withdrawn from sublimation occasionally breaks through, or a sexual activity remains throughout the whole duration of the latency
period until the reinforced breaking through of the sexual instinct
in puberty. In so far as they have paid any attention to infantile
sexuality, the educators behave as if they shared our views concerning the formation of the moral defense forces at the cost of sexuality.
They seem to know that sexual activity makes the child uneducable,
for they consider all sexual manifestations of the child as an "evil"
in the face of which little can be accomplished. We have, however,
every reason for directing our attention to those phenomena so
much feared by the educators, for we expect to find in them the
solution of the primary structure of the sexual instinct.

The Manifestations of Infantile Sexuality

Thumbsucking.   For reasons which we shall discuss later, we will
take as a model of the infantile sexual manifestations thumbsucking,
to which the Hungarian pediatrist, Lindner, has devoted an excellent
essay.

Thumbsucking, which manifests itself in the nursing baby and
which may be continued till maturity or throughout life, consists
in a rhythmic repetition of sucking contact with the mouth (the
lips), wherein the purpose of taking nourishment is excluded. A
part of the lip itself, the tongue, which is another preferable skin
region within reach, and even the big toe—may be taken as objects
for sucking. Simultaneously, there is also a desire to grasp things,
which manifests itself in a rhythmical pulling of the ear lobe and
which may cause the child to grasp a part of another person (generally the ear) for the same purpose. The pleasure-sucking is connected
with a full absorption of attention and leads to sleep or even to a
motor reaction in the form of an orgasm. Pleasure-sucking is often
combined with a rubbing contact with certain sensitive parts of the
body, such as the breast and external genitals. It is by this path that
many children go from thumbsucking to masturbation.

Lindner himself clearly recognized the sexual nature of this
activity and openly emphasized it. In the nursery, thumbsucking

is often treated in the same way as any other sexual "naughtiness" of the child. A very strong objection was raised against this view by many pediatrists and neurologists, which in part is certainly due to the confusion between the terms "sexual" and "genital." This contradiction raises the difficult question, which cannot be avoided, namely, in what general traits do we wish to recognize the sexual expression of the child. I believe that the association of the manifestations into which we have gained an insight through psychoanalytic investigation justifies us in claiming thumbsucking as a sexual activity. Through thumbsucking we can study directly the essential features of infantile sexual activities.

Autoerotism.   It is our duty here to devote more time to this manifestation. Let us emphasize the most striking character of this sexual activity which is, that the impulse is not directed to other persons but that the child gratifies himself on his own body; to use the happy term invented by Havelock Ellis, we will say that he is *autoerotic.*[7]   16

It is, moreover, clear that the action of the thumbsucking child is determined by the fact that he seeks a pleasure which he has already experienced and now remembers. Through the rhythmic sucking on a portion of the skin or mucous membrane, he finds gratification in the simplest way. It is also easy to conjecture on what occasions the child first experienced this pleasure which he now strives to renew. The first and most important activity in the child's life, the sucking from the mother's breast (or its substitute), must have acquainted him with this pleasure. We would say that the child's lips behaved like an *erogenous zone,* and that the stimulus from the warm stream of milk was really the cause of the pleasurable sensation. To be sure, the gratification of the erogenous zone was at first united with the gratification of the need for nourishment. The sexual activity leans first on one of the self-preservation functions and only later makes itself independent of it. He who sees a satiated child sink back from the mother's breast and fall asleep with reddened cheeks and blissful smile, will have to admit that this picture remains as typical of the expression of sexual gratification in later life. But the desire for repetition of sexual gratification is then separated from the desire for taking nourishment; a separation which becomes unavoidable with the appearance of teeth when the nourishment is no longer sucked but chewed. The child does not make

---

[7]***autoerotic***   English psychologist Havelock Ellis (1859–1939) used the term to refer to masturbatory behavior.

use of a strange object for sucking but prefers his own skin, because it is more convenient, because it thus makes himself independent of the outer world which he cannot control, and because in this way he creates for himself, as it were, a second, even if an inferior, erogenous zone. This inferiority of this second region urges him later to seek the same parts, the lips of another person. ("It is a pity that I cannot kiss myself," might be attributed to him.)

Not all children suck their thumbs. It may be assumed that it is found only in children in whom the erogenous significance of the lip-zone is constitutionally reinforced. If the latter is retained in some children, they develop into kissing epicures with a tendency to perverse kissing, or as men, they show a strong desire for drinking and smoking. But should repression come into play, they then show disgust for eating and evince hysterical vomiting. By virtue of the community of the lip-zone, the repression encroaches upon the instinct of nourishment. Many of my female patients showing disturbances in eating, such as *hysterical globus,*[8] choking sensations and vomiting have been energetic thumbsuckers in infancy.

In thumbsucking or pleasure-sucking, we are already able to observe the three essential characters of an infantile sexual manifestation. It has its origin in an *anaclitic*[9] relation to a physical function which is very important for life; it does not yet know any sexual object, that is, it is *autoerotic,* and its sexual aim is under the control of an *erogenous zone.* Let us assume for the present that these characteristics also hold true for most of the other activities of the infantile sexual instinct.

The Sexual Aim of the Infantile Sexuality

Characteristic Erogenous Zones. From the example of thumbsucking, we may gather a great many points useful for distinguishing an erogenous zone. It is a portion of skin or mucous membrane in which stimuli produce a feeling of pleasure of definite quality. There is no doubt that the pleasure-producing stimuli are governed by special conditions; as yet we do not know them. The rhythmic characters must play some part and this strongly suggests an analogy to tickling. It does not, however, appear so certain whether the character of the pleasurable feeling evoked by the stimulus can be designed as "peculiar," and in what part of this peculiarity the

20

---

[8]*hysterical globus* Abnormal reaction to putting things in the mouth.
[9]*anaclitic* Characterized by a strong emotional—but not sexual—dependence.

sexual factor consists. Psychology is still groping in the dark when it concerns matters of pleasure and pain, and the most cautious assumption is therefore the most advisable. We may perhaps later come upon reasons which seem to support the peculiar quality of the sensation of pleasure.

The erogenous quality may adhere most notably to definite regions of the body. As is shown by the example of thumbsucking, there are predestined erogenous zones. But the same example also shows that any other region of skin or mucous membrane may assume the function of an erogenous zone, hence it must bring along a certain adaptability for it. The production of the sensation of pleasure therefore depends more on the quality of the stimulus than on the nature of the bodily region. The thumbsucking child looks around on his body and selects any portion of it for pleasure-sucking, and becoming accustomed to this particular part, he then prefers it. If he accidentally strikes upon a predestined region, such as breast, nipple or genitals, it naturally gets the preference. A very analogous tendency to displacement is again found in the symptomatology of hysteria. In this neurosis, the repression mostly affects the genital zones proper, and they in turn transmit their excitability to the other zones which are usually dormant in adult life, but then behave exactly like genitals. But besides this, just as in thumbsucking, any other region of the body may become endowed with the excitation of the genitals and raised to an erogenous zone. Erogenous and hysterogenous zones show the same characters.[10]

The Infantile Sexual Aim.   The sexual aim of the infantile impulse consists in the production of gratification through the proper excitation of this or that selected erogenous zone. To have a desire for its repetition, this gratification must have been previously experienced, and we may be sure that nature has devised definite means so as not to leave this experience of gratification to mere chance. The arrangement which has fulfilled this purpose for the lip-zone, we have already discussed; it is the simultaneous connection of this part of the body with the taking of nourishment. We shall also meet other similar mechanisms as sources of sexuality. The state of desire for repetition of gratification can be recognized through a peculiar feeling of tension which in itself is rather of a painful character, and through a *centrally-conditioned* feeling of itching or sensitiveness

---

[10]Further reflection and evaluation of other observations lead me to attribute the quality of erotism to all parts of the body and inner organs. [Freud's note]

which is projected into the peripheral erogenous zone. The sexual aim may therefore be formulated by stating that the main object is to substitute for the projected feeling of sensitiveness in the erogenous zone that outer stimulus which removes the feeling of sensitiveness by evoking the feeling of gratification. This external stimulus consists usually in a manipulation which is analogous to sucking.

It is in full accord with our physiological knowledge, if the need happens to be awakened also peripherally, through an actual change in the erogenous zone. The action is puzzling only to some extent, as one stimulus seems to want another applied to the same place for its own abrogation.

The Masturbatic Sexual Manifestations

It is a matter of great satisfaction to know that there is nothing   24
further of great importance to learn about the sexual activity of the child, after the impulse of one erogenous zone has become comprehensible to us. The most pronounced differences are found in the action necessary for the gratification, which consists in sucking for the lip-zone, and which must be replaced by other muscular actions in the other zones, depending on their situation and nature.

The Activity of the Anal Zone.   Like the lip-zone, the anal zone is, through its position, adapted to produce an anaclisis of sexuality to other functions of the body. It should be assumed that the erogenous significance of this region of the body was originally very strong. Through psychoanalysis, one finds, not without surprise, the many transformations that normally take place in the sexual excitations emanating from here, and that this zone often retains for life a considerable fragment of genital irritability. The intestinal catarrhs[11] which occur quite frequently during infancy, produce sensitive irritations in this zone, and we often hear it said that intestinal catarrh at this delicate age causes "nervousness." In later neurotic diseases, they exert a definite influence on the symptomatic expression of the neurosis, placing at its disposal the whole sum of intestinal disturbances. Considering the erogenous significance of the anal zone which has been retained at least in transformation, one should not laugh at the hemorrhoidal influences to which the old medical

---

[11]*catarrhs*   Inflammations of the membrane.

literature attached so much weight in the explanation of neurotic states.

Children utilizing erogenous sensitiveness of the anal zone, can be recognized by their holding back of fecal masses until through accumulation there result violent muscular contractions; the passage of these masses through the anus is apt to produce a marked irritation of the mucous membrane. Besides the pain, this must also produce a sensation of pleasure. One of the surest premonitions of later eccentricity or nervousness is when an infant obstinately refuses to empty his bowel when placed on the chamber by the nurse, and controls this function at his own pleasure. It naturally does not concern him that he will soil his bed; all he cares for is not to lose the subsidiary pleasure in defecating. Educators have again shown the right inkling when they designate children who withhold these functions as naughty.

The content of the bowel which acts as a stimulus to the sexually sensitive surface of mucous membrane, behaves like the precursor of another organ which does not become active until after the phase of childhood. In addition, it has other important meanings to the nursling. It is evidently treated as an additional part of the body; it represents the first "donation," the disposal of which expresses the pliability while the retention of it can express the spite of the little being towards his environment. From the idea of "donation," he later derives the meaning of the "babe," which according to one of the infantile sexual theories, is supposed to be acquired through eating, and born through the bowel.

The retention of fecal masses, which is at first intentional in order to utilize them, as it were, for masturbatic excitation of the anal zone, is at least one of the roots of constipation so frequent in neurotics. The whole significance of the anal zone is mirrored in the fact that there are but few neurotics who have not their special scatologic[12] customs, ceremonies, etc., which they retain with cautious secrecy.

Real masturbatic irritation of the anal zone by means of the fingers, evoked through either centrally or peripherally supported itching, is not at all rare in older children.

The Activity of the Genital Zone.   Among the erogenous zones of the child's body, there is one which certainly does not play the first role, and which cannot be the carrier of the earliest sexual feeling, which, however, is destined for great things in later life. In both

---

[12]*scatologic* Pertaining to excrement, waste, or feces.

male and female, it is connected with the voiding of urine (penis, clitoris), and in the former, it is enclosed in a sack of mucous membrane, probably in order not to miss the irritations caused by the secretions which may arouse sexual excitement at an early age. The sexual activities of this erogenous zone, which belongs to the real genitals, are the beginning of the later "normal" sexual life.

Owing to the anatomical position, the overflowing of secretions, the washing and rubbing of the body, and to certain accidental excitements (the wandering of intestinal worms in the girl), it happens that the pleasurable feeling which these parts of the body are capable of producing makes itself noticeable to the child, even during the sucking age, and thus awakens a desire for repetition. When we consider the sum of all these arrangements and bear in mind that the measures for cleanliness hardly produce a different result than uncleanliness, we can scarcely ignore the fact that the infantile masturbation from which hardly anyone escapes, forms the foundation for the future primacy of this erogenous zone for sexual activity. The action of removing the stimulus and setting free the gratification consists in a rubbing contiguity with the hand or in a certain previously-formed pressure reflex, effected by the closure of the thighs. The latter procedure seems to be the more common in girls. The preference for the hand in boys already indicates what an important part of the male sexual activity will be accomplished in the future by the mastery impulse.

I can only make it clearer if I state that the infantile masturbation 32 should be divided into three phases. The first phase belongs to the nursing period, the second to the short flourishing period of sexual activity at about the fourth year, and only the third corresponds to the one which is often considered exclusively as masturbation of puberty.

Second Phase of Childhood Masturbation. Infantile masturbation seems to disappear after a brief time, but it may continue uninterruptedly till puberty and thus represent the first marked deviation from that development which is desirable for civilized man. At some time during childhood after the nursing period, the sexual instinct of the genitals re-awakens and continues active for some time until it is again suppressed, or it may continue without interruption. The possible relations are very diverse and can only be elucidated through a more precise analysis of individual cases. The details, however, of this *second* infantile sexual activity leave behind the profoundest (unconscious) impressions in the person's memory; if the individual remains healthy they determine his character and if he becomes sick after puberty, they determine the symptomatology of his neurosis. In the latter case, it is found that this sexual period is forgotten and the conscious reminiscences pointing to it are displaced; I have already mentioned that I would like to connect the normal infantile amnesia with this infantile sexual activity. By psychoanalytic investigation, it is possible to bring to consciousness the forgotten material and thereby to remove a compulsion which emanates from the unconscious psychic material.

The Return of Infantile Masturbation.   The sexual excitation of the nursing period returns during the designated years of childhood as a centrally determined tickling sensation demanding masturbatic gratification, or as a pollution-like process which, analogous to the pollution of maturity, may attain gratification without the aid of any action. The latter case is more frequent in girls and in the second half of childhood; its determinants are not well understood, but it often, though not regularly, seems to have as a basis a period of early active masturbation. The symptomatology of this sexual manifestation is poor; the genital apparatus is still undeveloped and all signs are therefore displayed by the urinary apparatus which is, so to say, the guardian of the genital apparatus. Most of the so-called bladder disturbances of this period are of sexual nature; whenever the *enuresis nocturna*[13] does not represent an epileptic attack, it corresponds to a pollution.

The return of the sexual activity is determined by inner and outer causes, which can be conjectured from the formation of the neurotic symptoms and can be definitely revealed by psychoanalytic investigations. The internal causes will be discussed later; the accidental outer causes attain at this time a great and permanent importance. As the first outer cause, there is the influence of seduction which prematurely treats the child as a sexual object; under conditions favoring impressions, this teaches the child the gratification of the genital zones and thus, usually forces it to repeat this gratification in masturbation. Such influences can come from adults or other children. I cannot admit that I overestimated its frequency or its significance in my contributions to the etiology[14] of hysteria, though I did not know then that normal individuals may have the same experiences in their childhood, and hence placed a higher value on seductions than on the factors found in the sexual constitution and development. It is quite obvious that no seduction is necessary to

---

[13]*enuresis nocturna*   Nighttime bed-wetting.
[14]*etiology*   The source or cause of something, especially of a disease.

awaken the sexual life of the child, that such an awakening may come on spontaneously from inner sources.

Polymorphous-Perverse Disposition. It is instructive to know that under the influence of seduction, the child may become polymorphous-perverse[15] and may be misled into all sorts of transgressions. This goes to show that the child carries along the adaptation for them in his disposition. The formation of such perversions meets but slight resistance because the psychic dams against sexual transgressions, such as shame, loathing and morality—which depend on the age of the child—are not yet erected or are only in the process of formation. In this respect, the child perhaps does not behave differently from the average uncultured woman in whom the same polymorphous-perverse disposition exists. Such a woman may remain sexually normal under usual conditions, but under the guidance of a clever seducer, she will find pleasure in every perversion and will retain it as her sexual activity. The same polymorphous or infantile disposition fits the prostitute for her professional activity, still it is absolutely impossible not to recognize in the uniform disposition to all perversions, as shown by an enormous number of prostitutes and by many women who do not necessarily follow this calling, a universal and primitive human tendency.

Partial Impulses. For the rest, the influence of seduction does not aid us in unravelling the original relations of the sexual instinct, but rather confuses our understanding of the same, inasmuch as it prematurely supplies the child with a sexual object at a time when the infantile sexual instinct does not yet evince any desire for it. We must admit, however, that the infantile sexual life, though mainly under the control of erogenous zones, also shows components which from the very beginning point to other persons as sexual objects. Among these, we may mention the impulses for looking, showing off, and for cruelty, which manifest themselves somewhat independently of the erogenous zones and only later enter into intimate relationship with the sexual life; but along with the erogenous sexual activity they are noticeable even in the infantile years, as separate and independent strivings. The little child is, above all, shameless, and during his early years, he evinces definite pleasure in displaying his body and especially his sex organs. A counterpart to this perverse desire, the curiosity to see other persons'

36

---

[15]*polymorphous-perverse*   Freud's term for a person whose sexual expression is oral, anal, and genital rather than the usual adult expression, essentially genital.

genitals, probably appears first in the later years of childhood when the hindrance of the feeling of shame has already reached a certain development. Under the influence of seduction, the looking perversion may attain great importance for the sexual life of the child. Still, from my investigations of the childhood years of normal and neurotic patients, I must conclude that the impulse for looking can appear in the child as a spontaneous sexual manifestation. Small children, whose attention has once been directed to their own genitals—usually by masturbation—are wont to progress in this direction without outside interference and to develop a vivid interest in the genitals of their playmates. As the occasion for the gratification of such curiosity is generally afforded during the gratification of both excrementitious needs, such children become *voyeurs*[16] and are zealous spectators at the voiding of urine and feces of others. After this tendency has been repressed, the curiosity to see the genitals of others (one's own or those of the other sex) remains as a tormenting desire which in some neurotic cases, furnishes the strongest motive-power for the formation of symptoms.

The cruelty component of the sexual instinct develops in the child with still greater independence of those sexual activities which are connected with erogenous zones. Cruelty is intimately related to the childish character, since the inhibition which restrains the mastery impulse before it causes pain to others—that is, the capacity for sympathy—develops comparatively late. As we know that a thorough psychological analysis of this impulse has not as yet been successfully done, we may assume that the feelings of cruelty emanate from the mastery impulse and appear at a period in the sexual life before the genitals have taken on their later role. This feeling then dominates a phase of the sexual life which we shall later describe as the pregenital organization. Children who are distinguished for evincing especial cruelty to animals and playmates may be justly suspected of an intensive and a premature sexual activity which emanates from the erogenous zones. But in a simultaneous prematurity of all sexual impulses, the erogenous sexual activity surely seems to be primary. The absence of the barrier of sympathy carries with it the danger that a connection formed in childhood between cruelty and the erogenous impulses will not be broken in later life.

An erogenous source of the passive impulse for cruelty (masochism) is found in the painful irritation of the gluteal region,[17]

---

[16]*voyeurs*   Those who get special pleasure from looking on, especially at something secret or private.

[17]*gluteal regions*   The buttocks, where children are spanked. Rousseau in his *Confessions* (1781, 1788) admits a certain pleasure in corporal punishment.

which is familiar to all educators since the confessions of J. J. Rousseau. This has justly caused them to demand that physical punishment, which is usually directed to this part of the body, should be withheld from all children in whom the libido might be forced into collateral roads by the later demands of cultural education.

Study of Infantile Sexual Investigation

Inquisitiveness.   About the same time as the sexual life of the child 40
reaches its first rich development, from the age of three to the age
of five, there appear the beginnings of that activity which are ascribed to the impulse for knowledge and investigation. The desire
for knowledge can neither be reckoned among the elementary instinctive components, nor can it be altogether subsumed under
sexuality. Its activity corresponds, on the one hand, to a sublimated
form of acquisition, and on the other hand, the energy with which
it works comes from the looking impulse. Its relation to the sexual
life, however, is of particular importance, for we have learned from
psychoanalysis that the inquisitiveness of children is directed to
sexual problems unusually early and in an unexpectedly intensive
manner; indeed, curiosity may perhaps first be awakened by sexual
problems.

The Riddle of the Sphinx.   It is not theoretical but practical interests,
which start the work of the child's investigation activity. The menace to the conditions of his existence through the actual or expected
arrival of a new child, the fear of losing the care and love which is
connected with this event, cause the child to become thoughtful
and sagacious.[18] Corresponding with the history of this awakening,
the first problem with which he occupies himself is not the question
as to the difference between the sexes, but the riddle: Where do
children come from? In a distorted form which can easily be unravelled, this is the same riddle which was proposed by the Theban
Sphinx.[19] The fact of the two sexes is usually first accepted by the
child without struggle and hesitation. It is quite natural for the male
child to presuppose in all persons he knows a genital like his own,

---

[18]*sagacious*   Shrewd, cunning.
[19]***Theban Sphinx***   The sphinx, with the face of a woman, body of a lion, and
wings of a bird, waited outside Thebes for years, killing all who passed by and
could not solve its riddle: "What walks on four legs in the morning, two legs in
the day, and three legs in the evening?" Oedipus answered the riddle: man, who
crawls in infancy, walks upright in his prime, and uses a cane in old age.

and to find it impossible to harmonize the lack of it with his conception of others.

The Castration Complex and Penis Envy.   This conviction is energetically adhered to by the boy and stubbornly defended against the contradictions which soon result, and is only given up after severe internal struggles (castration complex). The substitute formations of this lost penis on the part of the woman play a great role in the formation of many perversions.[20]

The assumption of the same (male) genital in all persons is the first of the remarkable and consequential infantile sexual theories. It is of little help to the child when biological science agrees with his preconceptions and recognizes the feminine clitoris as the real substitute for the penis. The little girl does not react with similar rejections when she sees the differently formed genital of the boy. She is immediately prepared to recognize it and soon becomes envious of the penis; this envy reaches its highest point in the consequentially important wish that she also should be a boy.

Birth Theories.   Many people can remember distinctly how intensely they interested themselves, in the prepubescent period, in the question of where children came from. The anatomical solutions at that time read very differently; the children come out of the breast or are cut out of the body, or the navel opens itself to let them out. Outside of analysis, one only seldom remembers this investigation from early childhood years, for it had long since merged into repression; its results, however, are thoroughly uniform. One gets children by eating something special (as in the fairy tale) or they are born through the bowel, like a passage. These infantile theories recall the structures in the animal kingdom, especially the *cloaca*[21] of those animals which are on a lower scale than mammals.

Sadistic Conception of the Sexual Act.   If the children at so tender an age witness the sexual act between adults, for which an occasion is furnished by the conviction of the adults that little children cannot

44

---

[20]One has the right to speak also of a castration complex in women. Male and female children form the theory that originally the woman, too, had a penis, which has been lost through castration. The conviction finally won (that the woman has no penis) often produces in the male a lasting depreciation of the other sex. [Freud's note]

[21]**cloaca**   All-purpose anal opening (as in a frog). The Latin word literally means a sewer.

understand anything sexual, they cannot help conceiving the sexual act as a kind of maltreating or overpowering; that is, it impresses them in a sadistic sense. Psychoanalysis teaches us also that such an early childhood impression contributes much to the disposition for a later sadistic displacement of the sexual aim. Besides this, children also occupy themselves with the problem of what the sexual act consists, or, as they grasp it, of what marriage consists, and seek the solution to the mystery usually in an intimacy carried on through the functions of urination and defecation.

The Typical Failure of the Infantile Sexual Investigation. It can be stated in general about infantile sexual theories that they are models of the child's own sexual constitution, and that despite their grotesque mistakes, they show more understanding of the sexual processes than is credited to their creators. Children also notice the pregnancy of their mother and know how to interpret it correctly. The stork fable is very often related before auditors who respond with a deep, but mostly mute suspicion. Inasmuch as two elements remain unknown to infantile sexual investigation, namely, the role of the fructifying semen and the existence of the female genital opening—precisely the same points in which the infantile organization is still backward—the effort of the infantile mind regularly remains fruitless and ends in a rejection, which not infrequently leaves a lasting injury to the desire for knowledge. The sexual investigation of these early childhood years is always conducted alone; it signifies the first step towards an independent orientation of the world, and causes a marked estrangement between the child and the persons of his environment who formerly enjoyed his full confidence.

QUESTIONS FOR CRITICAL READING

1. Freud begins with the question of the neglect of the infantile, the fact that most people paid little attention to the individual child's development (paras. 1–7). Explain what he means in these first seven paragraphs.
2. Children are said to go through a period of sexual latency. Clarify Freud's views on this question.
3. What kinds of sexual instincts are described in this selection? Are they recognizably sexual? Instinctual?
4. What are erogenous zones? Consult paragraph 20 and following.
5. Referring to paragraphs 42–43, clarify what Freud means by "castra-

tion complex" and "penis envy." What is their bearing on infantile sexuality?

6. What kind of audience would have found this work interesting and provocative? What kind would have found it repulsive? What kind would have found it unbelievable? Does Freud feel he must convince an unfriendly audience?

WRITING ASSIGNMENTS

1. Freud's complaint concerning the neglect of research and investigation into infantile behavior was written in 1905. Have things changed since then? What makes you feel that there is as much, less, or more neglect now than at that time? Do you feel that most people now accept Freud's views on infantile sexuality? Do you yourself accept his views?

2. Even the educated public of 1905 found the theories expressed in this work utterly unacceptable. They were revolted both by Freud's views and by his methods of research. What would be distressing, alarming, or revolting about this piece? What could possibly cause people to react violently to Freud's views? Are there still people who would have such a reaction?

3. Take an aspect of Freud's theories with which you disagree and present your own argument. You may resort to your own childhood memories or those of friends. Refer directly to the aspects of Freud's thinking that seem least convincing to you and explain your reasons for rejecting them.

4. In paragraph 18, Freud refers to "kissing epicures." Establish just what is meant by that term, then clarify such persons' behavior. Do such epicures exist today? What is their current behavior? Have you known any? You may wish to supplement your personal knowledge by conducting two or three interviews with people who do know such people. Be sure to try to connect your information with Freud's thoughts.

5. You may wish to offer your own theories concerning infantile sexuality. If so, you may use Freud's subject headings (where relevant to your theories) and rewrite the sections using your own thinking, and your own evidence to develop your own theories. Choose those subject headings that you feel are most important to your ideas. Headings such as "The Sexual Latency Period of Childhood and Its Interruptions," "Sexual Inhibition," and "The Sexual Aim of the Infantile Sexuality" may be of use to you. Naturally, you may make up your own headings if you wish.

6. The concepts of the castration complex and penis envy are both quite controversial. After establishing what Freud means by the terms, examine them to find out whether they are reasonable theories of behavior or whether they are not fully tenable. Moreover, consider the effect of holding such theories on matters related to social behavior—controversies related to feminism, for instance. Gather reactions from your

friends. Do their views support Freud's theories or not? Do their views matter to you?

7. Have you observed behavior in infants that suggests sexual awareness of the kind that Freud discusses? In Freud's time it was both repulsive and unthinkable to suggest that infants had any sexual awareness or feelings. Today's views may be a bit more relaxed, but general opinion probably still holds that infants are asexual. Based on your experience, is Freud right, or is general opinion right?

8. **CONNECTIONS** Freud and Jung were once closely joined as colleagues in the practice of psychotherapy. However, Jung had a falling out with Freud and developed his theories of archetypes and ceased promoting Freud's theories of infantile sexuality. What differences in method, ways of thought, or approach to psychology do you find most interesting when you compare the work of these two psychoanalysts?

9. **CONNECTIONS** What aspect of Freud's theories developed here would present the most difficulty for Erich Fromm to accept? What evidence does Freud give of social awareness or concern for the aspects of culture that Fromm feels shape the individual? Fromm was a follower of Freud. Are his views totally incompatible with those expressed by Freud in "Infantile Sexuality"?

CARL JUNG

Anima and Animus

CARL GUSTAV JUNG (1875–1961), probably Freud's most famous disciple, was a Swiss physician who collaborated with Freud from
1907 to 1912, when the two had a fundamental agreement concerning
the makeup of the unconscious. Jung was convinced that the unconscious
was composed of more than ego, superego, and id. He defined the
unconscious as a collection of archetypal images that could be inherited
by members of the same group. Experience clarified these images, but
the images in turn directed experience.

In his famous essay on the collective unconscious, for example, he
asserted that the great myths are expressions of the archetypes of actions
and heroes stored in the unconscious. The myths give expression to
these archetypes and help elucidate them for the individual and society.
Jung's view was that the individual must adapt to the archetypes that
reveal themselves in the myths in order to be psychically healthy.

The archetypes that Jung describes in this selection are subtle and
controversial. The anima is the female archetype that a man carries
always within his subconscious. Jung refers to it as an imago, a term
that has been interpreted in psychoanalysis as "primordial image" and
"archetype of the parent." An archetype is the basic pattern against
which all other similar experiences are measured; so the anima constitutes
an archetype against which the idea of woman is measured. But it is
also much more.

According to Jung, one's personality is not characterized by an
absolute unity. In fact, one has several personalities, including a mask
that one adopts and presents to the world. This mask hides some of the

---

From *Aspects of the Feminine*.

important truths about oneself, truths that might be embarrassing. The female part of a man (the anima) has its own demands and is shaped by the parental model (or a substitute in youth) of the mother. It must be accounted for in the construction of the persona—*the essential personality that one feels is one's own.*

The same is true of the animus in the case of women. The parental model provides the immediate archetype, although in many cases there may be other sources for the archetype. It makes significant demands on a woman and must be reckoned with and adapted to if the woman is to be healthy. Jung cites the characteristics of the animus in some detail in this selection and goes on to examine some of the problems that can arise when the animus is not properly balanced in relation to the persona.

Jung regarded the personality as a very complex structure, which balances the ego, the persona, the animus and anima, and possibly other archetypal images that may exist in the individual. Balancing these various segments of the personality is the job of the healthy person. When one segment becomes overpowering—for example, the animus in the personality of a woman—a pattern of psychic difficulties will be revealed. In other words, the animus can become dominant and overwhelm the personality of the woman. Much the same can happen in the case of a dominant anima in a man.

All of this leads to the curious problem of defining a person's "true personality." Jung attempted to do this, but his answer is not necessarily reassuring. He suggested that personalities are multiform, consisting of numerous "autonomous complexes." An autonomous complex is a self-directed component of the psyche. The ego, for example, is an autonomous complex, as is the anima. Jung reserves the term "self" for the collection of autonomous complexes that make up the conscious and the unconscious mind of any individual.

Like Freud, Jung agreed that the human psyche is composed of a conscious element, characterized best by the ego, and an unconscious element, filled with archetypal images and autonomous complexes. Jung asserted that "the unconscious is a psychological boundary-concept which covers all those psychic contents or processes which are not conscious, i.e., not related to the ego in a perceptible way." Jung described his proof of the evidence of the unconscious through his examination of patients, his use of hypnosis, and his experience with amnesiac hysterics. His lifetime of clinical work gave him the insights that he offers in this discussion.

The portrait that Jung painted of the archetype of men and women may not please all readers. In many ways he is profoundly traditional in his description of gender types, and for that reason some feminists have difficulty with this work. His description of the anima and the animus—as well as his clinical observations about the two sexes—*tend to sound conservative by modern standards. He made flat assertions concerning the basic nature of women and men and seemed to share his society's views about the way men and women should behave.*

JUNG'S RHETORIC

This subject is difficult, even for Jung, and he labors to avoid abstractions that would make his text more difficult to understand. The discussion reprinted here is drawn from a longer chapter in which Jung tries to clarify some of the more elusive ideas as he proceeds. For that reason, Jung is very patient in making his points, explaining them, and then illustrating them. Yet, despite his care, these knotty issues and fascinating ideas still require the reader's patience and attentiveness.

One of his primary techniques consists of defining his terms as he writes. For example, he opens by identifying what he means by personality, a definition that may turn out to surprise or alarm his readers. For instance, in this case he postulates two or even more personalities—indeed, he imagines a situation in which the ego may be confused over which is the "true" personality.

Jung then goes on to discuss the anima, relating it to the mother and reminding us that it is an autonomous complex, with many of the characteristics of a personality in its own right. Jung frequently illustrates his points by references to tribal behavior and tribal rites, because he sees in them a public recognition of the presence of the unconscious complexes. In tribal people, these complexes are accorded the status of spirits, but for Jung they are projections of the complexes that lie within each individual.

Jung also uses situations that are familiar to his readers. He discusses common patterns of marriage, but cites instances in which the imago of the mother is transferred to a man's wife. The pattern of behavior is described in enough detail so as to be verifiable (or not) in the mind of the reader. Therefore, although Jung works with a highly complex system of ideas, his efforts to be clear and lucid generally result in the reader's greater understanding.

Anima and Animus

It is probably no accident that our modern notions of "personal" and "personality" derive from the word *persona*. I can assert that my ego is personal or a personality, and in exactly the same sense I can say that my persona is a personality with which I identify myself more or less. The fact that I then possess two personalities is not so remarkable, since every autonomous or even relatively autonomous complex has the peculiarity of appearing as a personality, i.e., of being personified. This can be observed most readily in the so-called spiritualistic manifestations of automatic writing and the like. The sentences produced are always personal statements and are propounded in the first person singular, as though behind every utterance there stood an actual personality. A naïve intelligence at once thinks of spirits. The same sort of thing is also observable in the hallucinations of the insane, although these, more clearly than the first, can often be recognized as mere thoughts or fragments of thoughts whose connection with the conscious personality is immediately apparent to everyone.

The tendency of the relatively autonomous complex to direct personification also explains why the persona exercises such a "personal" effect that the ego is all too easily deceived as to which is the "true" personality.

Now, everything that is true of the persona and of all autonomous complexes in general also holds true of the anima. She likewise is a personality, and this is why she is so easily projected upon a woman. So long as the anima is unconscious she is always projected, for everything unconscious is projected. The first bearer of the soul-image is always the mother; later it is borne by those women who arouse the man's feelings, whether in a positive or a negative sense. Because the mother is the first bearer of the soul-image, separation from her is a delicate and important matter of the greatest educational significance. Accordingly among primitives we find a large number of rites designed to organize this separation. The mere fact of becoming adult, and of outward separation, is not enough; impressive initiations into the "men's house" and ceremonies of rebirth are still needed in order to make the separation from the mother (and hence form childhood) entirely effective.

Just as the father acts as a protection against the dangers of the 4 external world and thus serves his son as a model persona, so the mother protects him against the dangers that threaten from the darkness of his psyche. In the puberty rites, therefore, the initiate receives instruction about these things of "the other side," so that he is put in a position to dispense with his mother's protection.

The modern civilized man has to forgo this primitive but none-theless admirable system of education. The consequence is that the anima, in the form of the mother-imago, is transferred to the wife; and the man, as soon as he marries, becomes childish, sentimental, dependent, and subservient, or else truculent, tyrannical, hypersen-sitive, always thinking about the prestige of this superior masculin-ity. The last is of course merely the reverse of the first. The safeguard against the unconscious, which is what his mother meant to him, is not replaced by anything in the modern man's education; uncon-sciously, therefore, his ideal of marriage is so arranged that his wife has to take over the magical role of the mother. Under the cloak of the ideally exclusive marriage he is really seeking his mother's protection, and thus he plays into the hands of his wife's possessive instincts. His fear of the dark incalculable power of the unconscious gives his wife an illegitimate authority over him, and forges such a dangerously close union that the marriage is permanently on the brink of explosion from internal tension—or else, out of protest, he flies to the other extreme, with the same results.

I am of the opinion that it is absolutely essential for a certain type of modern man to recognize his distinction not only from the persona, but from the anima as well. For the most part our consciousness, in true Western style, looks outwards, and the inner world remains in darkness. But this difficulty can be overcome easily enough, if only we will make the effort to apply the same concentration and criticism to the psychic material which manifests itself, not outside, but in our private lives. So accustomed are we to keep a shamefaced silence about this other size—we even tremble before our wives, lest they betray us!—and, if found out, to make rueful confessions of "weakness," that there would seem to be only one method of education, namely, to crush or repress the weaknesses as much as possible or at least hide them from the public. But that gets us nowhere.

Perhaps I can best explain what has to be done if I use the persona as an example. Here everything is plain and straightfor-ward, whereas with the anima all is dark, to Western eyes anyway. When the anima continually thwarts the good intentions of the conscious mind, by contriving a private life that stands in sorry contrast to the dazzling persona, it is exactly the same as when a naïve individual, who has not the ghost of a persona, encounters the most painful difficulties in his passage through the world. There are indeed people who lack a developed persona—"Canadians who know not Europe's sham politeness''—blundering from one social solecism to the next, perfectly harmless and innocent, soulful bores or appealing children, or, if they are women, spectral Cassandras[1] dreaded for their tactlessness, eternally misunderstood, never knowing what they are about, always taking forgiveness for granted, blind to the world, hopeless dreamers. From them we can see how a neglected persona works, and what one must do to remedy the evil. Such people can avoid disappointments and an infinity of sufferings, scenes, and social catastrophes only by learning to see how men behave in the world. They must learn to understand what society expects of them; they must realize that there are factors and persons in the world far above them; they must know that what they do has a meaning for others, and so forth. Naturally all this is child's play for one who has a properly developed persona. But if we reverse the picture and confront the man who possesses a brilliant persona with the anima, and, for the sake of comparison, set him beside the man with no persona, then we shall see that the latter is just as well informed about the anima and her affairs as the former is about the world. The use which either makes of his knowledge can just as easily be abused, in fact it is more than likely that it will be.

The man with the persona is blind to the existence of inner   8 realities, just as the other is blind to the reality of the world, which for him has merely the value of an amusing or fantastic playground. But the fact of inner realities and their unqualified recognition is obviously the *sine qua non*[2] for a serious consideration of the anima problem. If the external world is, for me, simply a phantasm, how should I take the trouble to establish a complicated system of relationship and adaptation to it? Equally, the "nothing but fantasy" attitude will never persuade me to regard my anima manifestations as anything more than fatuous weakness. If, however, I take the line that the world is outside *and* inside, that reality falls to the share of both, I must logically accept the upsets and annoyances that come to me from inside as symptoms of faulty adaptation to the conditions of that inner world. No more than the blows rained on the innocent abroad can be healed by moral repression will it help him resignedly to catalogue his "weaknesses." Here are reasons, intentions, consequences, which can be tackled by will and understanding. Take, for example, the "spotless" man of honor and

---

[1]***Cassandra*** A prophetess of doom in Homer's *Iliad* and Aeschylus's *Agamemnon*.

[2]**sine qua non** Something absolutely essential and necessary.

public benefactor, whose tantrums and explosive moodiness terrify his wife and children. What is the anima doing here?

We can see it at once if we just allow things to take their natural course. Wife and children will become estranged; a vacuum will form about him. At first he will bewail the hard-heartedness of his family, and will behave if possible even more vilely than before. That will make the estrangement absolute. If the good spirits have not utterly forsaken him, he will after a time notice his isolation, and in his loneliness he will begin to understand how he caused the estrangement. Perhaps, aghast at himself, he will ask, "What sort of devil has got into me?"—without of course seeing the meaning of this metaphor. Then follow remorse, reconciliation, oblivion, repression, and, in next to no time, a new explosion. Clearly, the anima is trying to enforce a separation. This tendency is in nobody's interest. The anima comes between them like a jealous mistress who tries to alienate the man from his family. An official post or any other advantageous social position can do the same thing, but there we can understand the force of the attraction. Whence does the anima obtain the power to wield such enchantment? On the analogy with the persona there must be values or some other important and influential factors lying in the background like seductive promises. In such matters we must guard against rationalizations. Our first thought is that the man of honor is on the lookout for another woman. That might be—it might even be arranged by the anima as the most effective means to the desired end. Such an arrangement should not be misconstrued as an end in itself, for the blameless gentleman who is correctly married according to the law can be just as correctly divorced according to the law, which does not alter his fundamental attitude one iota. The old picture has merely received a new frame.

As a matter of fact, this arrangement is a very common method of implementing a separation—and of hampering a final solution. Therefore it is more reasonable not to assume that such an obvious possibility is the end-purpose of the separation. We would be better advised to investigate what is behind the tendencies of the anima. The first step is what I would call the objectivation of the anima, that is, the strict refusal to regard the trend towards separation as a weakness of one's own. Only when this has been done can one face the anima with the question, "Why do you want this separation?" To put the question in this personal way has the great advantage of recognizing the anima as a personality, and of making a relationship possible. The more personally she is taken the better.

To anyone accustomed to proceed purely intellectually and rationally, this may seem altogether too ridiculous. It would indeed be the height of absurdity if a man tried to have a conversation with his persona, which he recognized merely as a psychological means of relationship. But it is absurd only for the man who *has* a persona. If he has none, he is in this point no different from the primitive who, as we know, has only one foot in what we commonly call reality. With the other foot he stands in a world of spirits, which is quite real to him. Our model case behaves, in the world, like a modern European; but in the world of spirits he is the child of a troglodyte.[3] He must therefore submit to living in a kind of prehistoric kindergarten until he has got the right idea of the powers and factors which rule that other world. Hence he is quite right to treat the anima as an autonomous personality and to address personal questions to her.

I mean this as an actual technique. We know that practically   12 every one has not only the peculiarity, but also the faculty, of holding a conversation with himself. Whenever we are in a predicament we ask ourselves (or whom else?), "What shall I do?" either aloud or beneath our breath, and we (or who else?) supply the answer. Since it is our intention to learn what we can about the foundations of our being, this little matter of living in a metaphor should not bother us. We have to accept it as a symbol of our primitive backwardness (or of such naturalness as is still, mercifully, left to us) that we can, like the Negro, discourse personally with our "snake." The psyche not being a unity but a contradictory multiplicity of complexes, the dissociation required for our dialectics with the anima is not so terribly difficult. The art of it consists only in allowing our invisible partner to make herself heard, in putting the mechanism of expression momentarily at her disposal, without being overcome by the distaste one naturally feels at playing such an apparently ludicrous game with oneself, or by doubts as to the genuineness of the voice of one's interlocutor. This latter point is technically very important: we are so in the habit of identifying ourselves with the thoughts that come to us that we invariably assume we have made them. Curiously enough, it is precisely the most impossible thoughts for which we feel the greatest subjective responsibility. If we were more conscious of the inflexible universal laws that govern even the wildest and most wanton fantasy, we might perhaps be in a better position to see these thoughts above all others as objective occurrences, just as we see dreams, which nobody supposes to be deliberate or arbitrary inventions. It certainly requires the greatest objectivity and absence of prejudice to give

---

[3]*troglodyte* A prehistoric cave dweller.

the "other side" the opportunity for perceptible psychic activity. As a result of the repressive attitude of the conscious mind, the other side is driven into indirect and purely symptomatic manifestations, mostly of an emotional kind, and only in moments of overwhelming affectivity can fragments of the unconscious come to the surface in the form of thoughts or images. The inevitable accompanying symptom is that the ego momentarily identifies with these utterances, only to revoke them in the same breath. And, indeed, the things one says when in the grip of an affect sometimes seem very strange and daring. But they are easily forgotten, or wholly denied. This mechanism of deprecation and denial naturally has to be reckoned with if one wants to adopt an objective attitude. The habit of rushing in to correct and criticize is already strong enough in our tradition, and it is as a rule further reinforced by fear—a fear that can be confessed neither to oneself nor to others, a fear of insidious truths, of dangerous knowledge, of disagreeable verifications, in a word, fear of all those things that cause so many of us to flee from being alone with ourselves as from the plague. We say that it is egoistic or "morbid" to be preoccupied with oneself; one's own company is the worst, "it makes you melancholy"—such are the glowing testimonials accorded to our human makeup. They are evidently deeply ingrained in our Western minds. Whoever thinks in this way has obviously never asked himself what possible pleasure other people could find in the company of such a miserable coward. Starting from the fact that in a state of affect one often surrenders involuntarily to the truths of the other side, would it not be far better to make use of an affect so as to give the other side an opportunity to speak? It could therefore be said just as truly that one should cultivate the art of conversing with oneself in the setting provided by an affect, as though the affect itself were speaking without regard to our rational criticism. So long as the affect is speaking, criticism must be withheld. But once it has presented its case, we should begin criticizing as conscientiously as though a real person closely connected with us were our interlocutor. Nor should the matter rest there, but statement and answer must follow one another until a satisfactory end to the discussion is reached. Whether the result is satisfactory or not, only subjective feeling can decide. Any humbug is of course quite useless. Scrupulous honesty with oneself and no rash anticipation of what the other side might conceivably say are the indispensable conditions of this technique for educating the anima.

There is, however, something to be said for this characteristically Western fear of the other side. It is not entirely without justification, quite apart from the fact that it is real. We can understand at once the fear that the child and the primitive have of the great unknown. We have the same childish fear of our inner side, where we likewise touch upon a great unknown world. All we have is the affect, the fear, without knowing that this is a world-fear—for the world of affects is invisible. We have either purely theoretical prejudices against it, or superstitious ideas. One cannot even talk about the unconscious before many educated people without being accused of mysticism. The fear is legitimate in so far as our rational *Weltanschauung*[4] with its scientific and moral certitudes—so hotly believed in because so deeply questionable—is shattered by the facts of the other side. If only one could avoid them, then the emphatic advice of the Philistine to "let sleeping dogs lie" would be the only truth worth advocating. And here I would expressly point out that I am not recommending the above technique as either necessary or even useful to any person not driven to it by necessity. The stages, as I said, are many, and there are graybeards who die as innocent as babes in arms, and in this year of grace troglodytes are still being born. There are truths which belong to the future, truths which belong to the past, and truths which belong to no time.

I can imagine someone using this technique out of a kind of holy inquisitiveness, some youth, perhaps, who would like to set wings to his feet, not because of lameness, but because he yearns for the sun. But a grown man, with too many illusions dissipated, will submit to this inner humiliation and surrender only if forced, for why should he let the terrors of childhood again have their way with him? It is no light matter to stand between a day-world of exploded ideas and discredited values, and a night-world of apparently senseless fantasy. The weirdness of this standpoint is in fact so great that there is probably nobody who does not reach out for security, even though it be a reaching back to the mother who shielded his childhood from the terrors of night. Whoever is afraid must needs be dependent; a weak thing needs support. That is why the primitive mind, from deep psychological necessity, begot religious instruction and embodied it in magician and priest. *Extra ecclesiam nulla salus,*[5] is still a valid truth today—for those who can go back to it. For the few who cannot, there is only dependence upon a human being, a humbler and a prouder dependence, a weaker and a stronger support, so it seems to me, than any other. What can one say of the Protestant? He has neither church nor priest, but only God—and even God becomes doubtful.

---

[4]**Weltanschauung** A German term for a comprehensive understanding of the world, especially from a specific point of view.

[5]**Extra ecclesiam nulla salus** "There is no health outside the church."

The reader may ask in some consternation, "But what on earth does the anima do, that such double insurances are needed before one can come to terms with her?" I would recommend my reader to study the comparative history of religion so intently as to fill these dead chronicles with the emotional life of those who lived these religions. Then he will get some idea of what lives on the other side. The old religions with their sublime and ridiculous, their friendly and fiendish symbols did not drop from the blue, but were born of this human soul that dwells within us at this moment. All those things, their primal forms, live on in us and may at any time burst in upon us with annihilating force, in the guise of mass-suggestions against which the individual is defenseless. Our fearsome gods have only changed their names: they now rhyme with *ism*. Or has anyone the nerve to claim that the World War or Bolshevism was an ingenuous invention? Just as outwardly we live in a world where a whole continent may be submerged at any moment, or a pole be shifted, or a new pestilence break out, so inwardly we live in a world where at any moment something similar may occur, albeit in the form of an idea, but no less dangerous and untrustworthy for that. Failure to adapt to this inner world is a negligence entailing just as serious consequences as ignorance and ineptitude in the outer world. It is after all only a fraction of humanity, living mainly on that thickly populated peninsula of Asia which juts out into the Atlantic Ocean,[6] and calling themselves "cultured," who, because they lack all contact with nature, have hit upon the idea that religion is a peculiar kind of mental disturbance of undiscoverable purport. Viewed from a safe distance, say from central Africa or Tibet, it would certainly look as if this fraction had projected its own unconscious mental derangements upon nations still possessed of healthy instincts.

Because the things of the inner world influence us all the more 16 powerfully for being unconscious, it is essential for anyone who intends to make progress in self-culture (and does not all culture begin with the individual?) to objectivate the effects of the anima and then try to understand what contents underlie those effects. In this way he adapts to, and is protected against, the invisible. No adaptation can result without concessions to both worlds. From a consideration of the claims of the inner and outer worlds, or rather, from the conflict between them, the possible and the necessary follows. Unfortunately our Western mind, lacking all culture in this respect, has never yet devised a concept, nor even a name, for

---

[6]*peninsula . . . Atlantic Ocean* Europe.

the *union of opposites through the middle path,* that most fundamental item of inward experience, which could respectably be set against the Chinese concept of Tao. It is at once the most individual fact and the most universal, the most legitimate fulfillment of the meaning of the individual's life.

In the course of my exposition so far, I have kept exclusively to *masculine* psychology. The anima, being of feminine gender, is exclusively a figure that compensates the masculine consciousness. In woman the compensating figure is of a masculine character, and can therefore appropriately be termed the *animus.* If it was no easy task to describe what is meant by the anima, the difficulties become almost insuperable when we set out to describe the psychology of the animus.

The fact that a man naïvely ascribes his anima reactions to himself, without seeing that he really cannot identify himself with an autonomous complex, is repeated in feminine psychology, though if possible in even more marked form. This identification with an autonomous complex is the essential reason why it is so difficult to understand and describe the problem, quite apart from its inherent obscurity and strangeness. We always start with the naïve assumption that we are masters in our own house. Hence we must first accustom ourselves to the thought that, in our most intimate psychic life as well, we live in a kind of house which has doors and windows to the world, but that, although the objects or contents of this world act upon us, they do not belong to us. For many people this hypothesis is by no means easy to conceive, just as they do not find it at all easy to understand and to accept the fact that their neighbour's psychology is not necessarily identical with their own. My reader may think that the last remark is something of an exaggeration, since in general one is aware of individual differences. But it must be remembered that our individual conscious psychology develops out of an original state of unconsciousness and therefore of nondifferentiation (termed by Lévy-Bruhl[7] *participation mystique*). Consequently, consciousness of differentiation is a relatively late achievement of mankind, and presumably but a relatively small sector of the indefinitely large field of original identity. Differentiation is the essence, the *sine qua non* of consciousness. Everything unconscious is undifferentiated, and everything that happens unconsciously proceeds on the basis of nondifferentiation—that is to say, there is no determining whether it belongs or does not belong to

---

[7]**Lucien Lévy-Bruhl (1857–1939)**   French philosopher, psychologist, and ethnologist. He is especially well known for his studies of the psychology of preliterate peoples.

oneself. It cannot be established *a priori*[8] whether it concerns me, or another, or both. Nor does feeling give us any sure clues in this respect.

An inferior consciousness cannot *eo ipso*[9] be ascribed to women; it is merely different from masculine consciousness. But, just as a woman is often clearly conscious of things which a man is still groping for in the dark, so there are naturally fields of experience in a man which, for woman, are still wrapped in the shadows of nondifferentiation, chiefly things in which she has little interest. Personal relations are as a rule more important and interesting to her than objective facts and their interconnections. The wide fields of commerce, politics, technology, and science, the whole realm of the applied masculine mind, she relegates to the penumbra of consciousness; while, on the other hand, she develops a minute consciousness of personal relationships, the infinite nuances of which usually escape the man entirely.

We must therefore expect the unconscious of woman to show   20 aspects essentially different from those found in man. If I were to attempt to put in a nutshell the difference between man and woman in this respect, i.e., what it is that characterizes the animus as opposed to the anima, I could only say this: as the anima produces *moods,* so the animus produces *opinions;* and as the moods of a man issue from a shadowy background, so the opinions of a woman rest on equally unconscious prior assumptions. Animus opinions very often have the character of solid convictions that are not lightly shaken, or of principles whose validity is seemingly unassailable. If we analyze these opinions, we immediately come upon unconscious assumptions whose existence must first be inferred; that is to say, the opinions are apparently conceived *as though* such assumptions existed. But in reality the opinions are not thought out at all; they exist ready made, and they are held so positively and with so much conviction that the woman never has the shadow of a doubt about them.

One would be inclined to suppose that the animus, like the anima, personified itself in a single figure. But this, as experience shows, is true only up to a point, because another factor unexpectedly makes its appearance, which brings about an essentially different situation from that existing in a man. The animus does not appear as one person, but as a plurality of persons. In H. G. Wells' novel *Christina Alberta's Father*, the heroine, in all that she does or

---

[8]**a priori**   Beforehand.
[9]**eo ipso**   In and of itself.

does not do, is constantly under the surveillance of a supreme moral authority, which tells her with remorseless precision and dry matter-of-factness what she is doing and for what motives. Wells calls this authority a "Court of Conscience." This collection of condemnatory judges, a sort of College of Preceptors, corresponds to a personification of the animus. The animus is rather like an assembly of fathers or dignitaries of some kind who lay down incontestable, "rational," *ex cathedra*[10] judgments. On closer examination these exacting judgments turn out to be largely sayings and opinions scraped together more or less unconsciously from childhood on, and compressed into a canon of average truth, justice, and reasonableness, a compendium of preconceptions which, whenever a conscious and competent judgment is lacking (as not infrequently happens), instantly obliges with an opinion. Sometimes these opinions take the form of so-called common sense, sometimes they appear as principles which are like a travesty of education: "People have always done it like this," or "Everybody says it is like that."

It goes without saying that the animus is just as often projected as the anima. The men who are particularly suited to these projections are either walking replicas of God himself, who know all about everything, or else they are misunderstood word-addicts with a vast and windy vocabulary at their command, who translate common or garden reality into the terminology of the sublime. It would be insufficient to characterize the animus merely as a conservative, collective conscience; he is also a neologist who, in flagrant contradiction to his correct opinions, has an extraordinary weakness for difficult and unfamiliar words which act as a pleasant substitute for the odious task of reflection.

Like the anima, the animus is a jealous lover. He is an adept at putting, in place of the real man, an opinion about him, the exceedingly disputable grounds for which are never submitted to criticism. Animus opinions are invariably collective, and they override individuals and individual judgments in exactly the same way as the anima thrusts her emotional anticipations and projections between man and wife. If the woman happens to be pretty, these animus opinions have for the man something rather touching and childlike about them, which makes him adopt a benevolent, fatherly, professorial manner. But if the woman does not stir his sentimental side, and competence is expected of her rather than appealing helplessness and stupidity, then her animus opinions irritate the man to death, chiefly because they are based on nothing

---

[10]**ex cathedra**   From a seat of authority.

but opinion for opinion's sake, and "everybody has a right to his own opinions." Men can be pretty venomous here, for it is an inescapable fact that the animus always plays up the anima—and *vice versa*, of course—so that all further discussion becomes pointless.

In intellectual women the animus encourages a critical disputa- 24 tiousness and would-be highbrowism, which, however, consists essentially in harping on some irrelevant weak point and nonsensically making it the main one. Or a perfectly lucid discussion gets tangled up in the most maddening way through the introduction of a quite different and if possible perverse point of view. Without knowing it, such women are solely intent upon exasperating the man and are, in consequence, the more completely at the mercy of the animus. "Unfortunately I am always right," one of these creatures once confessed to me.

However, all these traits, as familiar as they are unsavory, are simply and solely due to the extraversion of the animus. The animus does not belong to the function of conscious relationship; his function is rather to facilitate relations with the unconscious. Instead of the woman merely associating opinions with external situations—situations which she ought to think about consciously—the animus, as an associative function, should be directed inwards, where it could associate the contents of the unconscious. The technique of coming to terms with the animus is the same in principle as in the case of the anima; only here the woman must learn to criticize and hold her opinions at a distance; not in order to repress them, but, by investigating their origins, to penetrate more deeply into the background, where she will then discover the primordial images, just as the man does in his dealings with the anima. The animus is the deposit, as it were, of all woman's ancestral experiences of man—and not only that, he is also a creative and procreative being, not in the sense of masculine creativity, but in the sense that he brings forth something we might call the λόγος σπερματικός, the spermatic word. Just as a man brings forth his work as a complete creation out of his inner feminine nature, so the inner masculine side of a woman brings forth creative seeds which have the power to fertilize the feminine side of the man. This would be the *femme inspiratrice*[11] who, if falsely cultivated, can turn into the worst kind of dogmatist and high-handed pedagogue—a regular "animus hound," as one of my women patients aptly expressed it.

A woman possessed by the animus is always in danger of losing her femininity, her adapted feminine persona, just as a man in like

---

[11]**femme inspiratrice** Inspirational woman.

circumstances runs the risk of effeminacy. These psychic changes of sex are due entirely to the fact that a function which belongs inside has been turned outside. The reason for this perversion is clearly the failure to give adequate recognition to an inner world which stands autonomously opposed to the outer world, and makes just as serious demands on our capacity for adaptation.

With regard to the plurality of the animus as distinguished from what we might call the "uni-personality" of the anima, this remarkable fact seems to me to be a correlate of the conscious attitude. The conscious attitude of woman is in general far more exclusively personal than that of man. Her world is made up of fathers and mothers, brothers and sisters, husbands and children. The rest of the world consists likewise of families, who nod to each other but are, in the main, interested essentially in themselves. The man's world is the nation, the state, business concerns, etc. His family is simply a means to an end, one of the foundations of the state, and his wife is not necessarily *the* woman for him (at any rate not as the woman means it when she says "my man"). The general means more to him than the personal; his world consists of a multitude of co-ordinated factors, whereas her world, outside her husband, terminates in a sort of cosmic mist. A passionate exclusiveness therefore attaches to the man's anima, and an indefinite variety to the woman's animus. Whereas the man has, floating before him, in clear outlines, the alluring form of a Circe or a Calypso, the animus is better expressed as a bevy of Flying Dutchmen[12] or unknown wanderers from over the sea, never quite clearly grasped, protean, given to persistent and violent motion. These personifications appear especially in dreams, though in concrete reality they can be famous tenors, boxing champions, or great men in faraway, unknown cities.

These two crepuscular figures from the dark hinterland of the psyche—truly the semigrotesque "guardians of the threshold," to use the pompous jargon of theosophy—can assume an almost inexhaustible number of shapes, enough to fill whole volumes. Their complicated transformations are as rich and strange as the world itself, as manifold as the limitless variety of their conscious correlate, the persona. They inhabit the twilight sphere, and we can just make out that the autonomous complex of anima and animus is essentially a psychological function that has usurped, or rather retained, a

---

[12]*Circe . . . Calypso . . . Flying Dutchmen* Circe and Calypso are temptresses in Homer's *Odyssey* who detained or trapped passing seamen. The Flying Dutchman is the captain of a legendary ghost ship; in his ship of the same name, he was condemned to sail the seas until Judgment Day.

"personality" only because this function is itself autonomous and undeveloped. But already we can see how it is possible to break up the personifications, since by making them conscious we convert them into bridges to the unconscious. It is because we are not using them purposefully as functions that they remain personified complexes. So long as they are in this state they must be accepted as relatively independent personalities. They cannot be integrated into consciousness while their contents remain unknown. The purpose of the dialectical process is to bring these contents into the light; and only when this task has been completed, and the conscious mind has become sufficiently familiar with the unconscious processes reflected in the anima, will the anima be felt simply as a function.

I do not expect every reader to grasp right away what is meant by animus and anima. But I hope he will at least have gained the impression that it is not a question of anything "metaphysical," but far rather of empirical facts which could equally well be expressed in rational and abstract language. I have purposely avoided too abstract a terminology because, in matters of this kind, which hitherto have been so inaccessible to our experience, it is useless to present the reader with an intellectual formulation. It is far more to the point to give him some conception of what the actual possibilities of experience are. Nobody can really understand these things unless he has experienced them himself. I am therefore much more interested in pointing out the possible ways to such experience than in devising intellectual formulae which, for lack of experience, must necessarily remain an empty web of words. Unfortunately there are all too many who learn the words by heart and add the experiences in their heads, thereafter abandoning themselves, according to temperament, either to credulity or to criticism. We are concerned here with a new questioning, a new—and yet age-old—field of psychological experience. We shall be able to establish relatively valid theories about it only when the corresponding psychological facts are known to a sufficient number of people. The first things to be discovered are always facts, not theories. Theory-building is the outcome of discussion among many.

QUESTIONS FOR CRITICAL READING

1. What is Jung's view of the makeup of the personality? Do you feel it is plausible?
2. How does Jung define the anima? How does he define the animus?

3. Are you in any way aware of possessing an anima or an animus? Can you detect its presence in others?

4. What is your sense of the unconscious? Have you ever become aware of possessing an unconscious? What can you tell about its nature?

5. Jung uses the term "the other side" in paragraph 13 and elsewhere. What does he seem to mean by it?

6. Is it reasonable to think that the behavior of primitive peoples can provide insights into the psyche? What is Jung's position?

7. Do you agree with Jung that the psyche is not a unity? What convinces you one way or the other?

8. How is the anima "a figure that compensates the masculine consciousness" (para. 17)? In what ways can the animus compensate the feminine consciousness?

WRITING ASSIGNMENTS

1. What is the archetype of the woman for you? Describe the most womanly female you can imagine, considering appearance, special qualities of behavior, effects on the environment and on other people, and kinds of functions that she might fulfill in society. Do you feel that your sense of the archetypal woman is shared by most of the people in your social group?

2. What is the archetype of the man for you? Follow the directions for writing assignment 1, but establish the ideal man rather than the ideal woman.

3. Judging from the films that you regard as classic—films being similar to the myths that ancient peoples believed in—what do you feel are your society's archetypes of male and female? Consider not only their appearance, but also how men and women act and relate to one another. Do you feel it is possible that your society projects its collective archetypes into its popular films? What insights into the psychic nature of the society can be gained by examining these projections?

4. One of the possible projections of the anima in Western culture is the witch, the female who possesses mysterious powers and communicates with spirits. Examine the typical pattern of the witch in order to connect it as well as you can to the model of the parent. How similar are the powers of witches to the powers of the mothers of small boys? Is it possible that the archetype of the witch is an expression of the anima?

5. Define the ways in which the anima and the animus seem to function in the psyches of men and women. What does Jung see the anima and the animus doing, and what kinds of problems can each cause? Examine in particular paragraph 20 and the following discussion concerning the way the animus expresses itself in women.

6. Jung asserts that the psyche is not a unity. His analysis of personality implies a multitude of personalities, as well as the presence of autono-

mous complexes, such as the animus and the anima. Examine your psyche as frankly as possible and determine whether or not there is evidence in your makeup of a multiplicity of personalities or expressions of personality. If you feel it is impossible to look at your psyche in this way, examine that of someone you know well, preferably someone your age.

7. In what sense can it be said that Jung's views are based on distinctions between the sexes apparent to him? Do you feel these distinctions are as prominent as he makes them out to be? Do you think that they are prominent enough to warrant his identification of the anima and the animus as significant parts of the psyche of every human being?

8. **CONNECTIONS**   Karen Horney reacted against Freud's theories, especially concerning penis envy. She does not speak specifically about her view of Jung. How do you think she would respond to Jung's view of the animus and anima? Would Horney find his theories congenial? What in each of their work seems to suggest that they would be compatible or incompatible?

9. **CONNECTIONS**   To what extent do Jung's concerns for archetypes of male and female help inform Mary Daly's vision of a patriarchal social order? Daly does not specifically refer to Jung (or any other psychologist); however, it may be possible to see that the forces of the anima and the animus are active in Daly's concerns in "The Qualitative Leap Beyond Patriarchal Religion." Establish Daly's awareness of archetypes or her use of them.

KAREN HORNEY

The Distrust Between the Sexes

KAREN HORNEY (1885–1952) was a distinguished psychiatrist who developed her career somewhat independently of the influence of Sigmund Freud. In her native Germany, she taught in the Berlin Psychoanalytic Institute from the end of World War I until 1932, a year before Hitler came to power. She was naturally influenced by Freud's work—as was every other psychoanalyst. But she found that, brilliant as it was, it did not satisfy her on important issues regarding female sexuality.

In Germany, Horney's early research was centered on questions about female psychology. This selection, first published in German in 1931, is part of these early studies. Horney's conclusion was that penis envy, like many other feminine psychological issues, was determined by cultural factors, and that these issues were not purely psychological or libidinal in origin. She thought Freud oversimplified female sexuality and that the truth, demonstrated through her own analysis, was vastly different. She began a significant theoretical shift that saw neurosis as a product of both psychological and cultural conflicts rather than of psychological stress alone.

In 1932, Horney emigrated to America, where she began writing a distinguished series of publications on neurosis. Her career in Chicago was remarkable. Not only did she found the American Institute for Psychoanalysis (1941) and the American Journal of Psychoanalysis, she also wrote such important books as The Neurotic Personality of Our Time (1937); New Ways in Psychoanalysis (1939); and Self-Analysis (1942). Her work was rooted in cultural studies, and one of

From *Feminine Psychology* (1967).

317

her principal arguments was that neuroses, including sexual problems, are caused by cultural influences and pressures that the individual simply cannot deal with. Freud thought the reverse, placing the causal force of neuroses in sexuality.

Her studies constantly brought her back to the question of interpersonal relations, and she saw neurotic patterns developed in childhood as the main cause of many failed relationships. The selection focuses particularly on the relationship that individuals establish with their mother or their father. Her insistence that childhood patterns affect adult behavior is consonant with Freudianism; however, her interpretations of those patterns are somewhat different. Unlike Freud, she looks toward anthropological studies of tribal behavior for help in interpreting the behavior of modern people.

Horney claims that the distrust between the sexes cannot be explained away as existing only in individuals; rather, it is a widespread phenomenon that must arise out of psychological forces present in men and women. She discusses a number of cultural practices in primitive peoples in an effort to suggest that even without modern cultural trappings, the two sexes suffer anxieties in their relationships. She also looks at the normal relationship of the individual in a family setting, showing that normal expectations of child-parent relations can sometimes be frustrated, with seriously harmful results.

In addition, she examines the nature of culture, reminding us that early societies were often matriarchal, that is, centered not on men and manly activities but on women. Her views about matriarchy, that the mystery of a woman is connected to her biologically creative nature, are quite suggestive in psychological terms. The envy as she sees it is on the part of men, who, to compensate for lacking the capacity to create life, spend their energies creating "state, religion, art, and science" (para. 14).

Horney speaks directly about sexual matters and about what she sees as male anxieties. She holds that there are distinct areas of conflict between men and women, and she contends that they are psychological in origin.

HORNEY'S RHETORIC

This is an expository essay, establishing the truth of hypothesis by pointing to a range of evidence from a variety of sources. Horney's view is that the distrust between the sexes is the result of cultural forces of which the individual is only dimly aware. In this sense, she aligns herself with the Freudians, who constantly point to influences on the individual that are subconscious in nature and, therefore, not part of the individual's self-awareness.

In a sense, her essay is itself an analysis of the relationship between men and women, with a look back at the history of culture. Her technique—a review of older societies—establishes that the current nature of the relationship between men and women is colored by the fact that modern society is dominated by patriarchal institutions. In ancient times, however, society may well have been matriarchal.

This selection was originally delivered as a lecture to the German Women's Medical Association in November 1930, and most of the audience was female. Consequently, the nature of the imagery, the frankness of the discourse, and the cultural focus concern issues that would have a distinct impact on women. On reading this essay, it becomes clear that Karen Horney is speaking with a particular directness that she might have modified for a mixed audience.

Her method of writing is analytical, as she says several times. She is searching for causes within the culture as well as within the individual. Her range of causal analysis includes the comparative study of cultures (ethnology) as well as personal psychology. Her capacity to call on earlier writers and cultures reveals her enormous scope of knowledge and also helps convince the reader of the seriousness of her inquiry.

The Distrust Between the Sexes

As I begin to talk to you today about some problems in the relationship between the sexes, I must ask you not to be disappointed. I will not concern myself primarily with the aspect of the problem that is most important to the physician. Only at the end will I briefly deal with the question of therapy. I am far more concerned with pointing out to you several psychological reasons for the distrust between the sexes.

The relationship between men and women is quite similar to that between children and parents, in that we prefer to focus on the positive aspects of these relationships. We prefer to assume that love is the fundamentally given factor and that hostility is an accidental and avoidable occurrence. Although we are familiar with slogans such as "the battle of the sexes" and "hostility between the sexes," we must admit that they do not mean a great deal. They make us overfocus on sexual relations between men and women, which can very easily lead us to a too one-sided view. Actually,

from our recollection of numerous case histories, we may conclude
that love relationships are quite easily destroyed by overt or covert
hostility. On the other hand we are only too ready to blame such
difficulties on individual misfortune, on incompatibility of the partners, and on social or economic causes.

The individual factors, which we find causing poor relations
between men and women, may be the pertinent ones. However,
because of the great frequency, or better, the regular occurrence of
disturbances in love relations, we have to ask ourselves whether
the disturbances in the individual cases might not arise from a
common background; whether there are common denominators
for this easily and frequently arising suspiciousness between the
sexes?

It is almost impossible to attempt within the framework of a   4
brief lecture to give you a complete survey of so large a field. I
therefore will not even mention such factors as the origin and effects
of such social institutions as marriage. I merely intend to select at
random some of the factors that are psychologically understandable
and pertain to the causes and effects of the hostility and tension
between the sexes.

I would like to start with something very commonplace—
namely, that a good deal of this atmosphere of suspiciousness is
understandable and even justifiable. It apparently has nothing to do
with the individual partner, but rather with the intensity of the
affects[1] and with the difficulty of taming them.

We know or may dimly sense, that these affects can lead to
ecstasy, to being beside oneself, to surrendering oneself, which
means a leap into the unlimited and the boundless. This is perhaps
why real passion is so rare. For like a good businessman, we are
loath to put all our eggs in one basket. We are inclined to be reserved
and ever ready to retreat. Be that as it may, because of our instinct
for self preservation, we all have a natural fear of losing ourselves
in another person. That is why what happens to love, happens to
education and psychoanalysis; everybody thinks he knows all about
them, but few do. One is inclined to overlook how little one gives
of oneself, but one feels all the more this same deficiency in the
partner, the feeling of "You never really loved me." A wife who
harbors suicidal thoughts because her husband does not give her
all his love, time, and interest, will not notice how much of her
own hostility, hidden vindictiveness, and aggression are expressed
through her attitude. She will feel only despair because of her abun-

---

[1]*affects* Feelings, emotions, or passions.

dant "love," while at the same time she will feel most intensely and see most clearly the lack of love in her partner. Even Strindberg[2] [who was a misogynist] defensively managed to say on occasion that he was no woman hater, but that women hated and tortured him.

Here we are not dealing with pathological phenomena at all. In pathological cases we merely see a distortion and exaggeration of a general and normal occurrence. Anybody, to a certain extent, will be inclined to overlook his own hostile impulses, but under pressure of his own guilty conscience, may project them onto the partner. This process must, of necessity, cause some overt or covert distrust of the partner's love, fidelity, sincerity, or kindness. This is the reason why I prefer to speak of distrust between the sexes and not of hatred; for in keeping with our own experience we are more familiar with the feeling of distrust.

A further, almost unavoidable, source of disappointment and   8 distrust in our normal love life derives from the fact that the very intensity of our feelings of love stirs up all of our secret expectations and longings for happiness, which slumber deep inside us. All our unconscious wishes, contradictory in their nature and expanding boundlessly on all sides, are waiting here for their fulfillment. The partner is supposed to be strong, and at the same time helpless, to dominate us and be dominated by us, to be ascetic and to be sensuous. He should rape us and be tender, have time for us exclusively and also be intensely involved in creative work. As long as we assume that he could actually fulfill all these expectations, we invest him with the glitter of sexual overestimation. We take the magnitude of such overvaluation for the measure of our love, while in reality it merely expresses the magnitude of our expectations. The very nature of our claims makes their fulfillment impossible. Herein lies the origin of the disappointments with which we may cope in a more or less effective way. Under favorable circumstances we do not even have to become aware of the great number of our disappointments, just as we have not been aware of the extent of our secret expectations. Yet there remain traces of distrust in us, as in a child who discovers that his father cannot get him the stars from the sky after all.

Thus far, our reflections certainly have been neither new nor specifically analytical and have often been better formulated in the past. The analytical approach begins with the question: What special

---

[2]*August Strindberg (1849–1912)*   A Swedish playwright and novelist whose dark portraits of women were influenced by his misogyny (hatred of women).

factors in human development lead to the discrepancy between expectations and fulfillment and what causes them to be of special significance in particular cases? Let us start with a general consideration. There is a basic difference between human and animal development—namely, the long period of the infant's helplessness and dependency. The paradise of childhood is most often an illusion with which adults like to deceive themselves. For the child, however, this paradise is inhabited by too many dangerous monsters. Unpleasant experiences with the opposite sex seem to be unavoidable. We need only recall the capacity that children possess, even in their very early years, for passionate and instinctive sexual desires similar to those of adults and yet different from them. Children are different in the aims of their drives, but above all, in the pristine integrity of their demands. They find it hard to express their desires directly, and where they do, they are not taken seriously. Their seriousness sometimes is looked upon as being cute, or it may be overlooked or rejected. In short, children will undergo painful and humiliating experiences of being rebuffed, being betrayed, and being told lies. They also may have to take second place to a parent or a sibling, and they are threatened and intimidated when they seek, in playing with their own bodies, those pleasures that are denied them by adults. The child is relatively powerless in the face of all this. He is not able to ventilate his fury at all, or only to a minor degree, nor can he come to grips with the experience by means of intellectual comprehension. Thus, anger and aggression are pent up within him in the form of extravagant fantasies, which hardly reach the daylight of awareness, fantasies that are criminal when viewed from the standpoint of the adult, fantasies that range from taking by force and stealing, to those about killing, burning, cutting to pieces, and choking. Since the child is vaguely aware of these destructive forces within him, he feels, according to the talion law,[3] equally threatened by the adults. Here is the origin of those infantile anxieties of which no child remains entirely free. This already enables us to understand better the fear of love of which I have spoke before. Just here, in this most irrational of all areas, the old childhood fears of a threatening father or mother are reawakened, putting us instinctively on the defensive. In other words, the fear of love will always be mixed with the fear of what we might do to the other person, or what the other person might do to us.

---

[3]*talion law*   Law which demands that the criminal be given the same punishment as was suffered by the victim—an eye for an eye.

A lover in the Aru Islands,[4] for example, will never make a gift of a lock of hair to his beloved, because should an argument arise, the beloved might burn it, thus causing the partner to get sick.

I would like to sketch briefly how childhood conflicts may affect the relationship to the opposite sex in later life. Let us take as an example a typical situation: The little girl who was badly hurt through some great disappointment by her father, will transform her innate instinctual wish to receive from the man, into a vindictive one of taking from him by force. Thus the foundation is laid for a direct line of development to a later attitude, according to which she will not only deny her maternal instincts, but will have only one drive, i.e., to harm the male, to exploit him, and to suck him dry. She has become a vampire. Let us assume that there is a similar transformation from the wish to receive to the wish to take away. Let us further assume that the latter wish was repressed due to anxiety from a guilty conscience; then we have here the fundamental constellation for the formation of a certain type of woman who is unable to relate to the male because she fears that every male will suspect her of wanting something from him. This really means that she is afraid that he might guess her repressed desires. Or by completely projecting onto him her repressed wishes, she will imagine that every male merely intends to exploit her, that he wants from her only sexual satisfaction, after which he will discard her. Or let us assume that a reaction formation of excessive modesty will mask the repressed drive for power. We then have the type of woman who shies away from demanding or accepting anything from her husband. Such a woman, however, due to the return of the repressed, will react with depression to the nonfulfillment of her unexpressed, and often unformulated, wishes. She thus unwittingly jumps from the frying pan into the fire, as does her partner, because a depression will hit him much harder than direct aggression. Quite often the repression of aggression against the male drains all her vital energy. The woman then feels helpless to meet life. She will shift the entire responsibility for her helplessness onto the man, robbing him of the very breath of life. Here you have the type of woman who, under the guise of being helpless and childlike, dominates her man.

These are examples that demonstrate how the fundamental attitude of women toward men can be disturbed by childhood

---

[4]***Aru Islands*** Islands in Indonesia that were especially interesting for modern anthropologists.

conflicts. In an attempt to simplify matters, I have stressed only one point, which, however, seems crucial to me—the disturbance in the development of motherhood.

I shall now proceed to trace certain traits of male psychology. 12 I do not wish to follow individual lines of development, though it might be very instructive to observe analytically how, for instance, even men who consciously have a very positive relationship with women and hold them in high esteem as human beings, harbor deep within themselves a secret distrust of them; and how this distrust relates back to feelings toward their mothers, which they experienced in their formative years. I shall focus rather on certain typical attitudes of men toward women and how they have appeared during various eras of history and in different cultures, not only as regards sexual relationships with women, but also, and often more so, in nonsexual situations, such as in their general evaluation of women.

I shall select some random examples, starting with Adam and Eve. Jewish culture, as recorded in the Old Testament, is outspokenly patriarchal. This fact reflects itself in their religion, which has no maternal goddesses; in their morals and customs, which allow the husband the right to dissolve the marital bond simply by dismissing his wife. Only by being aware of this background can we recognize the male bias in two incidents of Adam's and Eve's history. First of all, woman's capacity to give birth is partly denied and partly devaluated: Eve was made of Adam's rib and a curse was put on her to bear children in sorrow. In the second place, by interpreting her tempting Adam to eat of the tree of knowledge as a sexual temptation, woman appears as the sexual temptress, who plunges man into misery. I believe that these two elements, one born out of resentment, the other out of anxiety, have damaged the relationship between the sexes from the earliest times to the present. Let us follow this up briefly. Man's fear of woman is deeply rooted in sex, as is shown by the simple fact that it is only the sexually attractive woman of whom he is afraid and who, although he strongly desires her, has to be kept in bondage. Old women, on the other hand, are held in high esteem, even by cultures in which the young woman is dreaded and therefore suppressed. In some primitive cultures the old woman may have the decisive voice in the affairs of the tribe; among Asian nations also she enjoys great power and prestige. On the other hand, in primitive tribes woman is surrounded by taboos during the entire period of her sexual maturity. Women of the Arunta tribe are able to magically influence the male genitals. If they sing to a blade of grass and then point it at a man or throw it at him, he becomes ill or loses his genitals altogether. Women lure him to his doom. In a certain East African tribe, husband and wife do not sleep together, because her breath might weaken him. If a woman of a South African tribe climbs over the leg of a sleeping man, he will be unable to run; hence the general rule of sexual abstinence two to five days prior to hunting, warfare, or fishing. Even greater is the fear of menstruation, pregnancy, and childbirth. Menstruating women are surrounded by extensive taboos—a man who touches a menstruating woman will die. There is one basic thought at the bottom of all this: Woman is a mysterious being who communicates with spirits and thus has magic powers that she can use to hurt the male. He must therefore protect himself against her powers by keeping her subjugated. Thus the Miri in Bengal do not permit their women to eat the flesh of the tiger, lest they become too strong. The Watawela of East Africa keep the art of making fire a secret from their women, lest women become their rulers. The Indians of California have ceremonies to keep their women in submission; a man is disguised as a devil to intimidate the women. The Arabs of mecca exclude women from religious festivities to prevent familiarity between women and their overlords. We find similar customs during the Middle Ages—the Cult of the Virgin[5] side by side with the burning of witches; the adoration of "pure" motherliness, completely divested of sexuality, next to the cruel destruction of the sexually seductive woman. Here again is the implication of underlying anxiety, for the witch is in communication with the devil. Nowadays, with our more humane forms of aggression, we burn women only figuratively, sometimes with undisguised hatred, sometimes with apparent friendliness. In any case "The Jew must burn."[6] In friendly and secret autos-da-fé,[7] many nice things are said about women, but it is just unfortunate

---

[5]***Cult of the Virgin*** During the Medieval period (c. 700–1300), the Roman Catholic Church promoted a strong emotional attachment to the Virgin Mary, which resulted in the production of innumerable paintings and sculptures. Horney points out the irony of venerating the mother of God while tormenting human women by burning them at the stake.

[6]***"The Jew must burn."*** This is a quote from *Nathan the Wise* by the eighteenth-century German author Gotthold Ephraim Lessing, a humanist and a spokesman for enlightenment and rationality. The expression became a colloquialism. It meant no matter how worthy and well-intentioned his acts, by virtue of being a Jew, a man was guilty. [Translator's note]

[7]***autos-da-fé*** Literally, acts of faith. It was a term used to refer to the hearing at which the Holy Inquisition gave its judgment on a case of heresy, and its most common use is to refer to the burning of heretics at the stake.

that in her God–given natural state, she is not the equal of the male. Moebius[8] pointed out that the female brain weighs less than the male one, but the point need not be made in so crude a way. On the contrary, it can be stressed that woman is not at all inferior, only different, but that unfortunately she has fewer or none of those human or cultural qualities that man holds in such high esteem. She is said to be deeply rooted in the personal and emotional spheres, which is wonderful; but unfortunately, this makes her incapable of exercising justice and objectivity, therefore disqualifying her for positions in law and government and in the spiritual community. She is said to be at home only in the realm of eros. Spiritual matters are alien to her innermost being, and she is at odds with cultural trends. She therefore is, as Asians frankly state, a second–rate being. Woman may be industrious and useful but is, alas, incapable of productive and independent work. She is, indeed, prevented from real accomplishment by the deplorable, bloody tragedies of menstruation and childbirth. And so every man silently thanks his God, just as the pious Jew does in his prayers, that he was not created a woman.

Man's attitude toward motherhood is a large and complicated chapter. One is generally inclined to see no problem in this area. Even the misogynist is obviously willing to respect woman as a mother and to venerate her motherliness under certain conditions, as mentioned above regarding the Cult of the Virgin. In order to obtain a clearer picture, we have to distinguish between two attitudes: men's attitudes toward motherliness, as represented in its purest form in the Cult of the Virgin, and their attitude toward motherhood as such, as we encounter it in the symbolism of the ancient mother goddesses. Males will always be in favor of motherliness, as expressed in certain spiritual qualities of women, i.e, the nurturing, selfless, self-sacrificing mother; for she is the ideal embodiment of the woman who could fulfill all his expectations and longings. In the ancient mother goddesses, man did not venerate motherliness in the spiritual sense, but rather motherhood in its most elemental meaning. Mother goddesses are earthy goddesses, fertile like the soil. They bring forth new life and they nurture it. It was this life-creating power of woman, an elemental force, that filled man with admiration. And this is exactly the point where problems arise. For it is contrary to human nature to sustain appreciation without resentment toward capabilities that one does not

---

[8]***Paul Julius Möbius (1853–1907)*** German neurologist and student of the pathological traits of geniuses such as Rousseau, Goethe, Schopenhauer, and Nietzsche.

possess. Thus, a man's minute share in creating new life became, for him, an immense incitement to create something new on his part. He has created values of which he might well be proud. State, religion, art, and science are essentially his creations, and our entire culture bears the masculine imprint.

However, as happens elsewhere, so it does here; even the greatest satisfactions or achievements, if born out of sublimation, cannot fully make up for something for which we are not endowed by nature. Thus there has remained an obvious residue of general resentment of men against women. This resentment expresses itself, also in our times, in men's distrustful defensive maneuvers against the threat of women's invasion of their domains; hence their tendency to devalue pregnancy and childbirth and to overemphasize male genitality. This attitude does not express itself in scientific theories alone, but is also of far-reaching consequence for the entire relationship between the sexes, and for sexual morality in general. Motherhood, especially illegitimate motherhood, is very insufficiently protected by laws—with the one exception of a recent attempt at improvement in Russia. Conversely, there is ample opportunity for the fulfillment of the male's sexual needs. Emphasis on irresponsible sexual indulgence, and devaluation of women to an object of purely physical needs, are further consequences of this masculine attitude.

From Bachofen's[9] investigations we know that this state of the cultural supremacy of the male has not existed since the beginning of time, but that women once occupied a central position. This was the era of the so-called matriarchy, when law and custom were centered around the mother. Matricide was then, as Sophocles[10] showed in the *Eumenides,* the unforgivable crime, while patricide, by comparison, was a minor offense. Only in recorded historical times have men begun, with minor variations, to play the leading role in the political, economical, and judicial fields, as well as in the area of sexual morality. At present we seem to be going through a period of struggle in which women once more dare to fight for their equality. This is a phase, the duration of which we are not yet able to survey.

I do not want to be misunderstood as having implied that all

16

---

[9]*J. J. Bachofen (1815–1887)* One of the earliest German ethnologists who proposed, in 1861, that a pattern of matriarchy—in which the female was the dominant figure in society—had existed in the earliest societies.

[10]*Sophocles (496?–406 B.C.)* A great Greek tragedian. However, Horney is probably referring to Aeschylus (525–456 B.C.), who wrote the *Eumenides*, the play she mentions.

disaster results from male supremacy and that relations between the sexes would improve if women were given the ascendancy. However, we must ask ourselves why there should have to be any power struggle at all between the sexes. At any given time, the more powerful side will create an ideology suitable to help maintain its position and to make this position acceptable to the weaker one. In this ideology the differentness of the weaker one will be interpreted as inferiority, and it will be proven that these differences are unchangeable, basic, or God's will. It is the function of such an ideology to deny or conceal the existence of a struggle. Here is one of the answers to the question raised initially as to why we have so little awareness of the fact that there is a struggle between the sexes. It is in the interest of men to obscure this fact; and the emphasis they place on their ideologies has caused women, also, to adopt these theories. Our attempt at resolving these rationalizations and at examining these ideologies as to their fundamental driving forces, is merely a step on the road taken by Freud.[11]

I believe that my exposition shows more clearly the origin of resentment than the origin of dread, and I therefore want to discuss briefly the latter problem. We have seen that the male's dread of the female is directed against her as a sexual being. How is this to be understood? The clearest aspect of this dread is revealed by the Arunta tribe. They believe that the woman has the power to magically influence the male genital. This is what we mean by castration anxiety in analysis. It is an anxiety of psychogenic origin that goes back to feelings of guilt and old childhood fears. Its anatomical-psychological nucleus lies in the fact that during intercourse the male has to entrust his genitals to the female body, that he presents her with his semen and interprets this as a surrender of vital strength to the woman, similar to his experiencing the subsiding of erection after intercourse as evidence of having been weakened by the woman. Although the following idea has not been thoroughly worked through yet, it is highly probable, according to analytical and ethnological data, that the relationship to the mother is more strongly and directly associated with the fear of death than the relationship to the father. We have learned to understand the longing for death as the longing for reunion with the mother. In African fairy tales it is a woman who brings death into the world. The great mother goddesses also brought death and destruction. It is as though we were possessed by the idea that the one who gives

---

[11]***Sigmund Freud (1856–1939)***   See the introduction to his selection in this part.

life is also capable of taking it away. There is a third aspect of the male's dread of the female that is more difficult to understand and to prove, but that can be demonstrated by observing certain recurrent phenomena in the animal world. We can see that the male is quite frequently equipped with certain specific stimulants for attracting the female, or with specific devices for seizing her during sexual union. Such arrangements would be incomprehensible if the female animal possessed equally urgent or abundant sexual needs as does the male. As a matter of fact, we see that the female rejects the male unconditionally, after fertilization has occurred. Although examples taken from the animal world may be applied to human beings only with the greatest of caution, it is permissible, in this context, to raise the following question: Is it possible that the male is sexually dependent on the female to a higher degree than the woman is on him, because in women part of the sexual energy is linked to generative processes? Could it be that men, therefore, have a vital interest in keeping women dependent on them? So much for the factors that seem to be at the root of the great power struggle between men and women, insofar as they are of a psychogenic nature and related to the male.

That many-faceted thing called love succeeds in building bridges from the loneliness on this shore to the loneliness on the other one. These bridges can be of great beauty, but they are rarely built for eternity and frequently they cannot tolerate too heavy a burden without collapsing. Here is the other answer to the question posed initially of why we see love between the sexes more distinctly than we see hate—because the union of the sexes offers us the greatest possibilities for happiness. We therefore are naturally inclined to overlook how powerful are the destructive forces that continually work to destroy our chances for happiness.

We might ask in conclusion, how can analytical insights contribute to diminish the distrust between the sexes? There is no uniform answer to this problem. The fear of the power of the affects and the difficulty in controlling them in a love relationship, the resulting conflict between surrender and self-preservation, between the I and the Thou[12] is an entirely comprehensible, unmitigatable, and as it were, normal phenomenon. The same thing applies in essence to our readiness for distrust, which stems from unresolved childhood conflicts. These childhood conflicts, however, can vary greatly in intensity, and will leave behind traces of variable depth.

20

---

[12]***the I and the Thou***   A reference to Martin Buber's book *I and Thou*. Buber (1878–1965), a Jewish theologian and philosopher, is associated with modern existentialism.

Analysis not only can help in individual cases to improve the relationship with the opposite sex, but it can also attempt to improve the psychological conditions of childhood and forestall excessive conflicts. This, of course, is our hope for the future. In the momentous struggle for power, analysis can fulfill an important function by uncovering the real motives of this struggle. This uncovering will not eliminate the motives, but it may help to create a better chance for fighting the struggle on its own ground instead of relegating it to peripheral issues.

QUESTIONS FOR CRITICAL READING

1. Do you agree that there is hostility between the sexes?
2. What are some of the most important childhood experiences that can affect adult behavior toward the opposite sex?
3. This selection was originally a lecture delivered in Germany in 1930. To what extent do its concerns seem to be no longer relevant? To what extent are they still relevant?
4. Do you think this essay could promote better relations between men and women?
5. What kinds of expectations do women seem to have of men, and vice versa? Do these expectations tend to contribute to hostility in specific ways? Consider Horney's description of expectations in paragraph 8.
6. How do the examples of behavior in primitive cultures contribute to an understanding of the relationship between the sexes in our culture?
7. Is Horney pessimistic or optimistic about relationships between the sexes?

WRITING ASSIGNMENTS

1. In paragraph 9, Horney says that unpleasant experiences with the opposite sex are unavoidable. In your experience, is this true? What unpleasant experiences have you had with the opposite sex? What unpleasant experiences have you observed?
2. Horney mentions that the intensity of our feelings can stir up secret longings for, and expectations of, the opposite sex (para. 8). What kinds of secret expectations do you feel each sex might have about the other in a relationship? Why would such expectations remain secret? Does such secrecy contribute to problems? Does it contribute to hostility?
3. Deep in the essay, in paragraph 14, Horney talks about the possibility of envy contributing to the hostility between the sexes. She says, "For it is contrary to human nature to sustain appreciation without

resentment toward capabilities that one does not possess." Do you agree with her? Do you think envy may have something to do with the hostility between the sexes? Examine your own experience to see whether you recall instances of envy on your part toward a member of the opposite sex (or vice versa).

4. At one point, Horney says, "Man's fear of woman is deeply rooted in sex" (para. 13). Do you think this is true? Is woman's fear of man similarly rooted? Examine this question by comparing at least two, and preferably four, magazines for what they reveal about the psychology of men and women. Choose two men's magazines and two women's magazines. Compare their visual material, particularly photographs of members of the opposite sex. Also compare the fiction and look for signs of a specifically male or female form of fantasy. Compare the advertising to see how distinct the interests of men and women are—and try to relate these to psychological concerns.

5. Horney is very direct in her discussion of male dominance in society, saying not only that it exists but asking, "Could it be that men, therefore, have a vital interest in keeping women dependent on them?" (para. 18). Conduct an interview with one man and one woman. Find out whether they have the same or different feelings about this question. Ask them if they see an effort on the part of men to keep women dependent, and then ask them what form any such dependency takes. Do they agree? Where do you stand on this issue?

6. At one point, Horney discusses the question of how different men are from women. Write an essay in which you show the extent to which women are different from men. If possible, sample others' opinions and see if they feel that there are important differences. To what extent would differences between men and women contribute toward hostility?

7. **CONNECTIONS** How would you characterize Horney's disagreements with Freud and Jung? What are the issues that she most clearly targets, and what success do you feel she has achieved in her debate? Do you find that Horney agrees more with Erich Fromm, or is she in a camp all by herself? Isolate three or more specific issues from her discussion that might elucidate her position in relation to Freud, Jung, or Fromm.

ERICH FROMM

Love and Its Disintegration in Contemporary Western Society

Eʀɪᴄʜ Fʀᴏᴍᴍ *(1900–1980), born into a Jewish rabbinic family in Frankfurt, earned his Ph.D. at Heidelberg at the age of twenty-two; after establishing himself as an important psychoanalyst, he left Nazi Germany in 1934. He lectured from 1934 to 1941 at Columbia University and later took an academic appointment at Bennington College. At different times he lectured at Yale University and The New School for Social Research. In 1951 he joined the faculty at the National University of Mexico. From 1957 to 1961 he was professor at Michigan State University, and from 1962 until his death he was professor at New York University, dividing his time between New York and Mexico.*

His interest in politics and sociology led him to apply psychoanalytic theory to a wide range of important subjects. His first important book, Escape from Freedom *(1941), revealed some of the psychological anxieties people associate with freedom and set out to explain why totalitarian societies—such as those in Germany, Italy, and Japan— were so enthusiastically accepted. Throughout his life, Fromm's work was especially important for applying psychoanalytic theory to the practical matters of everyday life.*

Early in his career, he was considered an orthodox follower of Freud, and he accepted Freud's view of the importance of sexuality in human behavior. However, he soon became an innovator and revised Freud's theories in a number of areas. Fromm emphasized the social structure rather than the unconscious as a key force in shaping the individual character, noting that human beings, unlike other animals, are not driven entirely by instincts. Humans employ "reason, imagination, and self-awareness" throughout their lives. Fromm taught that the important elements in a person's life—the environment, the socioeco-

nomic circumstances, and especially the family—shape the character of the individual. He also explained that character traits inherent in individuals—such as promptness and neatness—satisfy the needs of the prevalent economic community. Such traits may change as the needs of society change, because society helps shape the individual.

Among his later views, Fromm held that character is dominated by two forces, necrophilia *(love of death) and* biophilia *(love of life). All personalities have both these qualities: what is important is which of these forces is dominant. The personality dominated by necrophilia may evidence sadomasochistic behavior, the desire to dominate and hurt others. Such behavior, which Fromm sees as a perversion, is linked to early childhood experiences. The opposite of necrophilia, biophilia, is marked by a love of life and a respect for living things. Mental health is linked to a well-developed sense of biophilia.*

Late in his career, Fromm examined the work of Karl Marx and saw in it a positive, humane philosophy. Fromm realized that for modern people Marx's thought is obscured by its application to Soviet Russian communism, although the Soviet system was essentially an authoritarian bureaucracy unlike anything Marx had hoped for. Marx, Fromm felt, was positive in his attitude toward humankind. He was both hopeful and optimistic about the capacity of people to improve their condition. Fromm's book Marx's Concept of Man *(1961) was one of several documents in which he attempted to clarify Marx's humanistic thought.*

The book for which Fromm is probably best known is The Art of Loving *(1956), the source of the selection presented here. In it Fromm asserts that love is the most important element in a well-balanced life. Many people, he says, already know this fact and seek love in their own lives. But they do not realize that love is a quality that can be cultivated, an art that can be perfected. For example, the love of one's neighbor is as important as the love of a husband or wife. Love permeates the life of the happy person. Love is affected by the social structure, by the demands of everyday life, and by the expectations of the larger society. His study of love in Western society naturally emphasizes the power of consumption in the style of capitalism that now dominates world economies.*

FROMM'S RHETORIC

Fromm's approach is marked by an allusive style. He refers to Freud and Marx in an almost casual manner, reminding the reader that these thinkers had a powerful effect on shaping modern thought. But he also grounds his discussion in comments on prevalent capitalist economic practices, emphasizing especially the commodification of love and human attachment to physical things. His rhetorical approach is analytical and careful, building his arguments on the basis of opinions that readers are invited to validate by comparison with their own experience.

Having established the power of contemporary capitalism in modern society, Fromm goes on to examine how an individual's senses of intimacy and self-worth are affected by social forces. He argues, in effect, that contemporary capitalism teaches people to value things over people—as evidenced in the relation of labor to capital in the market. Further, the functioning of capitalism demands workers who fit in and become, perhaps, automatons in order to do their jobs. Individuals thus lose their individuality. Finally, in paragraph 6, Fromm explains that the modern social structure can cause an individual to be "alienated from himself," a view to some extent consonant with Simone Weil's observations in "Prerequisite to Dignity of Labor."

According to Fromm, society teaches people to market "personality packages" but not to love. Team spirit may seem a positive concept until it is understood to be possibly inappropriate for a marriage (para. 9). His analysis of sexuality and love—and sexual technique—produces unexpected judgments that to some extent reduce the force of some of Freud's arguments, which are analyzed in paragraphs 12–14. As Fromm points out, Freud was himself influenced by the social structures of his time.

Fromm's most characteristic rhetorical technique is to list the patterns of neurotic love (paras. 16–31), beginning with mother-fixations, father-fixations, and other forms of "pseudo-love." He ends with a single paragraph reminding the reader of the need for maturity and communication in all love relationships. In essence, Fromm defines love in the modern age in terms of the pathology of love, the "wrong" loves that confound individuals and make it hard for them to achieve a true loving experience.

Love and Its Disintegration in Contemporary Western Society

If love is a capacity of the mature, productive character, it follows that the capacity to love in an individual living in any given culture depends on the influence this culture has on the character of the average person. If we speak about love in contemporary Western culture, we mean to ask whether the social structure of

Western civilization and the spirit resulting from it are conducive to the development of love. To raise the question is to answer it in the negative. No objective observer of our Western life can doubt that love—brotherly love, motherly love, and erotic love—is a relatively rare phenomenon, and that its place is taken by a number of forms of pseudo-love which are in reality so many forms of the disintegration of love.

Capitalistic society is based on the principle of political freedom on the one hand, and of the market as the regulator of all economic, hence social relations, on the other. The commodity market determines the conditions under which commodities are exchanged, the labor market regulates the acquisition and sale of labor. Both useful things and useful human energy and skill are transformed into commodities which are exchanged without the use of force and without fraud under the conditions of the market. Shoes, useful and needed as they may be, have no economic value (exchange value) if there is no demand for them on the market; human energy and skill are without exchange value if there is no demand for them under existing market conditions. The owner of capital can buy labor and command it to work for the profitable investment of his capital. The owner of labor must sell it to capitalists under the existing market conditions, unless he is to starve. This economic structure is reflected in a hierarchy of values. Capital commands labor; amassed things, that which is dead, are of superior value to labor, to human powers, to that which is alive.

This has been the basic structure of capitalism since its beginning. But while it is still characteristic of modern capitalism, a number of factors have changed which give contemporary capitalism its specific qualities and which have a profound influence on the character structure of modern man. As the result of the development of capitalism we witness an ever-increasing process of centralization and concentration of capital. The large enterprises grow in size continuously, the smaller ones are squeezed out. The ownership of capital invested in these enterprises is more and more separated from the function of managing them. Hundreds of thousands of stockholders "own" the enterprise; a managerial bureaucracy which is well paid, but which does not own the enterprise, manages it. This bureaucracy is less interested in making maximum profits than in the expansion of the enterprise, and in their own power. The increasing concentration of capital and the emergence of a powerful managerial bureaucracy are paralleled by the development of the labor movement. Through the unionization of labor, the individual worker does not have to bargain on the labor market by and for himself; he is united in big labor unions, also led by a powerful bureaucracy which represents him vis-à-vis the industrial colossi. The initiative has been shifted, for better or worse, in the fields of capital as well as in those of labor, from the individual to the bureaucracy. An increasing number of people cease to be independent, and become dependent on the managers of the great economic empires.

Another decisive feature resulting from this concentration of capital, and characteristic of modern capitalism, lies in the specific way of the organization of work. Vastly centralized enterprises with a radical division of labor lead to an organization of work where the individual loses his individuality, where he becomes an expendable cog in the machine. The human problem of modern capitalism can be formulated in this way:

Modern capitalism needs men who co-operate smoothly and in large numbers; who want to consume more and more; and whose tastes are standardized and can be easily influenced and anticipated. It needs men who feel free and independent, not subject to any authority or principle or conscience—yet willing to be commanded, to do what is expected of them, to fit into the social machine without friction; who can be guided without force, led without leaders, prompted without aim—except the one to make good, to be on the move, to function, to go ahead.

What is the outcome? Modern man is alienated from himself, from his fellow men, and from nature.[1] He has been transformed into a commodity, experiences his life forces as an investment which must bring him the maximum profit obtainable under existing market conditions. Human relations are essentially those of alienated automatons, each basing his security on staying close to the herd, and not being different in thought, feeling or action. While everybody tries to be as close as possible to the rest, everybody remains utterly alone, pervaded by the deep sense of insecurity, anxiety, and guilt which always results when human separateness cannot be overcome. Our civilization offers many palliatives which help people to be consciously unaware of this aloneness: first of all the strict routine of bureaucratized, mechanical work, which helps people to remain unaware of their most fundamental human desires, of the longing for transcendence and unity. Inasmuch as the routine alone does not succeed in this, man overcomes his unconscious despair by the routine of amusement, the passive consumption of sounds and sights offered by

---

[1]Cf. a more detailed discussion of the problem of alienation and of the influence of modern society on the character of man in *The Sane Society*, E. Fromm, Rinehart and Company, New York, 1955. [Fromm's note]

the amusement industry; furthermore by the satisfaction of buying ever new things, and soon exchanging them for others. Modern man is actually close to the picture Huxley describes in his *Brave New World:* well fed, well clad, satisfied sexually, yet without self, without any except the most superficial contact with his fellow men, guided by the slogans which Huxley formulated so succinctly, such as: "When the individual feels, the community reels"; or "Never put off till tomorrow the fun you can have today," or, as the crowning statement: "Everybody is happy nowadays." Man's happiness today consists in "having fun." Having fun lies in the satisfaction of consuming and "taking in" commodities, sights, food, drinks, cigarettes, people, lectures, books, movies—all are consumed, swallowed. The world is one great object for our appetite, a big apple, a big bottle, a big breast; we are the sucklers, the eternally expectant ones, the hopeful ones—and the eternally disappointed ones. Our character is geared to exchange and to receive, to barter and to consume; everything, spiritual as well as material objects, becomes an object of exchange and of consumption.

The situation as far as love is concerned corresponds, as it has to by necessity, to this social character of modern man. Automatons cannot love; they can exchange their "personality packages" and hope for a fair bargain. One of the most significant expressions of love, and especially of marriage with this alienated structure, is the idea of the "team." In any number of articles on happy marriage, the ideal described is that of the smoothly functioning team. This description is not too different from the idea of a smoothly functioning employee; he should be "reasonably independent," co-operative, tolerant, and at the same time ambitious and aggressive. Thus, the marriage counselor tells us, the husband should "understand" his wife and be helpful. He should comment favorably on her new dress, and on a tasty dish. She, in turn, should understand when he comes home tired and disgruntled, she should listen attentively when he talks about his business troubles, should not be angry but understanding when he forgets her birthday. All this kind of relationship amounts to is the well-oiled relationship between two persons who remain strangers all their lives, who never arrive at a "central relationship," but who treat each other with courtesy and who attempt to make each other feel better.

In this concept of love and marriage the main emphasis is on finding a refuge from an otherwise unbearable sense of aloneness. In "love" one has found, at last, a haven from aloneness. One forms   8 an alliance of two against the world, and this egoism *à deux*[2] is mistaken for love and intimacy.

The emphasis on team spirit, mutual tolerance, and so forth is a relatively recent development. It was preceded, in the years after the First World War, by a concept of love in which mutual sexual satisfaction was supposed to be the basis for satisfactory love relations, and especially for a happy marriage. It was believed that the reasons for the frequent unhappiness in marriage were to be found in that the marriage partners had not made a correct "sexual adjustment"; the reason for this fault was seen in the ignorance regarding "correct" sexual behavior, hence in the faulty sexual technique of one or both partners. In order to "cure" this fault, and to help the unfortunate couples who could not love each other, many books gave instructions and counsel concerning the correct sexual behavior, and promised implicitly or explicitly that happiness and love would follow. The underlying idea was that love is the child of sexual pleasure, and that if two people learn how to satisfy each other sexually, they will love each other. It fitted the general illusion of the time to assume that using the right techniques is the solution not only to technical problems of industrial production, but of all human problems as well. One ignored the fact that the contrary of the underlying assumption is true.

Love is not the result of adequate sexual satisfaction, but sexual happiness—even the knowledge of the so-called sexual technique—is the result of love. If aside from everyday observation this thesis needed to be proved, such proof can be found in ample material of psychoanalytic data. The study of the most frequent sexual problems—frigidity in women, and the more or less severe forms of psychic impotence in men—shows that the cause does not lie in a lack of knowledge of the right technique, but in the inhibitions which make it impossible to love. Fear of or hatred for the other sex are at the bottom of those difficulties which prevent a person from giving himself completely, from acting spontaneously, from trusting the sexual partner in the immediacy and directness of physical closeness. If a sexually inhibited person can emerge from fear or hate, and hence become capable of loving, his or her sexual problems are solved. If not, no amount of knowledge about sexual techniques will help.

But while the data of psychoanalytic therapy point to the fallacy of the idea that knowledge of the correct sexual technique leads to

---

[2] **à deux**   Double.

sexual happiness and love, the underlying assumption that love is the concomitant of mutual sexual satisfaction was largely influenced by the theories of Freud. For Freud, love was basically a sexual phenomenon. "Man having found by experience that sexual (genital) love afforded him his greatest gratification, so that it became in fact a prototype of all happiness to him, must have been thereby impelled to seek his happiness further along the path of sexual relations, to make genital eroticism the central point of his life."[3] The experience of brotherly love is, for Freud, an outcome of sexual desire, but with the sexual instinct being transformed into an impulse with "inhibited aim." "Love with an inhibited aim was indeed originally full of sensual love, and in man's unconscious mind is so still."[4] As far as the feeling of fusion, of oneness ("oceanic feeling"), which is the essence of mystical experience and the root of the most intense sense of union with one other person or with one's fellow men, is concerned, it was interpreted by Freud as a pathological phenomenon, as a regression to a state of an early "limitless narcissism."[5]

It is only one step further that for Freud love is in itself an irrational phenomenon. The difference between irrational love, and love as an expression of the mature personality does not exist for him. He pointed out in a paper on transference love,[6] that transference love is essentially not different from the "normal" phenomenon of love. Falling in love always verges on the abnormal, is always accompanied by blindness to reality, compulsiveness, and is a transference from love objects of childhood. Love as a rational phenomenon, as the crowning achievement of maturity, was, to Freud, no subject matter for investigation, since it had no real existence.

However, it would be a mistake to overestimate the influence of Freud's ideas on the concept that love is the result of sexual attraction, or rather that it is the *same* as sexual satisfaction, reflected in conscious feeling. Essentially the causal nexus proceeds the other way around. Freud's ideas were partly influenced by the spirit of the nineteenth century; partly they became popular through the prevailing spirit of the years after the First World War. Some of the factors which influenced both the popular and the Freudian concepts were, first, the reaction against the strict mores of the Victorian age. The second factor determining Freud's theories lies

12

---

[3]S. Freud, *Civilization and Its Discontents,* translated by J. Riviere, The Hogarth Press, Ltd., London, 1953, p. 69. [Fromm's note]

[4]Ibid., p. 69. [Fromm's note]

[5]Ibid., p. 21. [Fromm's note]

[6]Freud, *Gesamte Werke,* London, 1940–1952, Vol. X. [Fromm's note]

in the prevailing concept of man, which is based on the structure of capitalism. In order to prove that capitalism corresponded to the natural needs of man, one had to show that man was by nature competitive and full of mutual hostility. While economists "proved" this in terms of the insatiable desire for economic gain, and the Darwinists in terms of the biological law of the survival of the fittest, Freud came to the same result by the assumption that man is driven by a limitless desire for the sexual conquest of all women, and that only the pressure of society prevented man from acting on his desires. As a result men are necessarily jealous of each other, and this mutual jealousy and competition would continue even if all social and economic reasons for it would disappear.[7]

Eventually, Freud was largely influenced in his thinking by the type of materialism prevalent in the nineteenth century. One believed that the substratum of all mental phenomena was to be found in physiological phenomena; hence love, hate, ambition, jealousy were explained by Freud as so many outcomes of various forms of the sexual instinct. He did not see that the basic reality lies in the totality of human existence, first of all in the human situation common to all men, and secondly in the practice of life determined by the specific structure of society. (The decisive step beyond this type of materialism was taken by Marx in his "historical materialism," in which not the body, nor an instinct like the need for food or possession, serves as the key to the understanding of man, but the total life process of man, his "practice of life.") According to Freud, the full and uninhibited satisfaction of all instinctual desires would create mental health and happiness. But the obvious clinical facts demonstrate that men—and women—who devote their lives to unrestricted sexual satisfaction do not attain happiness, and very often suffer from severe neurotic conflicts or symptoms. The complete satisfaction of all instinctual needs is not only not a basis for happiness, it does not even guarantee sanity. Yet Freud's idea could only have become so popular in the period after the First World War because of the changes which had occurred in the spirit of capitalism, from the emphasis on saving to that on spending, from self-frustration as a means for economic success to consumption as the basis for an ever-widening market, and as the main satisfaction for the anxious, automatized individual. Not to

---

[7]The only pupil of Freud who never separated from the master, and yet who in the last years of his life changed his views on love, was Sándor Ferenczi. For an excellent discussion on this subject see *The Leaven of Love* by Izette de Forest, Harper & Brothers, New York, 1954. [Fromm's note]

postpone the satisfaction of any desire became the main tendency in the sphere of sex as well as in that of all material consumption. . . .

Love as mutual sexual satisfaction, and love as "teamwork" and as a haven from aloneness, are the two "normal" forms of the disintegration of love in modern Western society, the socially patterned pathology of love. There are many individualized forms of the pathology of love, which result in conscious suffering and which are considered neurotic by psychiatrists and an increasing number of laymen alike. Some of the more frequent ones are briefly described in the following examples.

The basic condition for neurotic love lies in the fact that one 16 or both of the "lovers" have remained attached to the figure of a parent, and transfer the feelings, expectations, and fear one once had toward father or mother to the loved person in adult life; the persons involved have never emerged from a pattern of infantile relatedness, and seek for this pattern in their affective demands in adult life. In these cases, the person has remained, affectively, a child of two, or of five, or of twelve, while intellectually and socially he is on the level of his chronological age. In the more severe cases, this emotional immaturity leads to disturbances in his social effectiveness; in the less severe ones, the conflict is limited to the sphere of intimate personal relationships.

Referring to our previous discussion of the mother- or father-centered personality, the following example for this type of neurotic love relation to be found frequently today deals with men who in their emotional development have remained stuck in an infantile attachment to mother. These are men who have never been weaned as it were from mother. These men still feel like children; they want mother's protection, love, warmth, care, and admiration; they want mother's unconditional love, a love which is given for no other reason than that they need it, that they are mother's child, that they are helpless. Such men frequently are quite affectionate and charming if they try to induce a woman to love them, and even after they have succeeded in this. But their relationship to the woman (as, in fact, to all other people) remains superficial and irresponsible. Their aim is to be loved, not to love. There is usually a good deal of vanity in this type of man, more or less hidden grandiose ideas. If they have found the right woman, they feel secure, on top of the world, and can display a great deal of affection and charm, and this is the reason why these men are often so deceptive. But when, after a while, the woman does not continue to live up to their phantastic expectations, conflicts and resentment start to develop. If the woman is not always admiring them, if she makes claims for a life of her own, if she wants to be loved and protected herself, and in extreme cases, if she is not willing to condone his love affair with other women (or even have an admiring interest in them), the man feels deeply hurt and disappointed, and usually rationalizes this feeling with the idea that the woman "does not love him, is selfish, or is domineering." Anything short of the attitude of a loving mother toward a charming child is taken as proof of a lack of love. These men usually confuse their affectionate behavior, their wish to please, with genuine love and thus arrive at the conclusion that they are being treated quite unfairly; they imagine themselves to be the great lovers and complain bitterly about the ingratitude of their love partner.

In rare cases such a mother-centered person can function without any severe disturbances. If his mother, in fact, "loved" him in an overprotective manner (perhaps being domineering, but without being destructive), if he finds a wife of the same motherly type, if his special gifts and talents permit him to use his charm and be admired (as is the case sometimes with successful politicians), he is "well adjusted" in a social sense, without ever reaching a higher level of maturity. But under less favorable conditions—and these are naturally more frequent—his love life, if not his social life, will be a serious disappointment; conflicts, and frequently intense anxiety and depression arise when this type of personality is left alone.

In a still more severe form of pathology the fixation to mother is deeper and more irrational. On this level, the wish is not, symbolically speaking, to return to mother's protecting arms, nor to her nourishing breast, but to her all-receiving—and all-destroying— womb. If the nature of sanity is to grow out of the womb into the world, the nature of severe mental disease is to be attracted by the womb, to be sucked back into it—and that is to be taken away from life. This kind of fixation usually occurs in relation to mothers who relate themselves to their children in this swallowing-destroying way. Sometimes in the name of love, sometimes of duty, they want to keep the child, the adolescent, the man, within them; he should not be able to breathe but through them; not be able to love, except on a superficial sexual level—degrading all other women; he should not be able to be free and independent but an eternal cripple or a criminal.

This aspect of mother, the destructive, engulfing one, is the 20 negative aspect of the mother figure. Mother can give life, and she can take life. She is the one to revive, and the one to destroy; she can do miracles of love—and nobody can hurt more than she. In religious images (such as the Hindu goddess Kali) and in dream symbolism the two opposite aspects of mother can often be found.

A different form of neurotic pathology is to be found in such cases where the main attachment is that to father.

A case in point is a man whose mother is cold and aloof, while his father (partly as a result of his wife's coldness) concentrates all his affection and interest on the son. He is a "good father," but at the same time authoritarian. Whenever he is pleased with the son's conduct he praises him, gives him presents, is affectionate; whenever the son displeases him, he withdraws, or scolds. The son, for whom father's affection is the only one he has, becomes attached to father in a slavish way. His main aim in life is to please father—and when he succeeds he feels happy, secure, and satisfied. But when he makes a mistake, fails, or does not succeed in pleasing father, he feels deflated, unloved, cast out. In later life such a man will try to find a father figure to whom he attaches himself in a similar fashion. His whole life becomes a sequence of ups and downs, depending on whether he has succeeded in winning father's praise. Such men are often very successful in their social careers. They are conscientious, reliable, eager—provided their chosen father image understands how to handle them. But in their relationships to women they remain aloof and distant. The woman is of no central significance to them; they usually have a slight contempt for her, often masked as the fatherly concern for a little girl. They may have impressed a woman initially by their masculine quality, but they become increasingly disappointing, when the woman they marry discovers that she is destined to play a secondary role to the primary affection for the father figure who is prominent in the husband's life at any given time; that is, unless the wife happens to have remained attached to her father—and thus is happy with a husband who relates to her as to a capricious child.

More complicated is the kind of neurotic disturbance in love which is based on a different kind of parental situation, occurring when parents do not love each other, but are too restrained to quarrel or to indicate any signs of dissatisfaction outwardly. At the same time, remoteness makes them also unspontaneous in their relationship to their children. What a little girl experiences is an atmosphere of "correctness," but one which never permits a close contact with either father or mother, and hence leaves the girl puzzled and afraid. She is never sure of what the parents feel or think; there is always an element of the unknown, the mysterious, in the atmosphere. As a result the girl withdraws into a world of her own, day-dreams, remains remote, and retains the same attitude in her love relationships later on.

Furthermore the withdrawal results in the development of in- 24 tense anxiety, a feeling of not being firmly grounded in the world, and often leads to masochistic tendencies as the only way to experience intense excitement. Often such women would prefer having the husband make a scene and shout, to his maintaining a more normal and sensible behavior, because at least it would take away the burden of tension and fear from them; not so rarely they unconsciously provoke such behavior, in order to end the tormenting suspense of affective neutrality.

Other frequent forms of irrational love are described in the following paragraphs, without going into an analysis of the specific factors in childhood development which are at their roots:

A form of pseudo-love which is not infrequent and is often experienced (and more often described in moving pictures and novels) as the "great love" is *idolatrous love*. If a person has not reached the level where he has a sense of identity, of I-ness, rooted in the productive unfolding of his own powers, he tends to "idolize" the loved person. He is alienated from his own powers and projects them into the loved person, who is worshiped as the *summum bonum*,[8] the bearer of all love, all light, all bliss. In this process he deprives himself of all sense of strength, loses himself in the loved one instead of finding himself. Since usually no person can, in the long run, live up to the expectations of her (or his) idolatrous worshiper, disappointment is bound to occur, and as a remedy a new idol is sought for, sometimes in an unending circle. What is characteristic for this type of idolatrous love is, at the beginning, the intensity and suddenness of the love experience. This idolatrous love is often described as the true, great love; but while it is meant to portray the intensity and depth of love, it only demonstrates the hunger and despair of the idolator. Needless to say it is not rare that two persons find each other in a mutual idolatry which, sometimes, in extreme cases, represents the picture of a *folie à deux*.[9]

Another form of pseudo-love is what may be called *"sentimental love."* Its essence lies in the fact that love is experienced only in phantasy and not in the here-and-now relationship to another person who is real. The most widespread form of this type of love is that to be found in the vicarious love satisfaction experienced by the

---

[8]**summum bonum** Highest good.
[9]**folie à deux** Double insanity.

consumer of screen pictures, magazine love stories, and love songs. All the unfulfilled desires for love, union, and closeness find their satisfaction in the consumption of these products. A man and a woman who in relation to their spouses are incapable of ever penetrating the wall of separateness are moved to tears when they participate in the happy or unhappy love story of the couple on the screen. For many couples, seeing these stories on the screen is the only occasion on which they experience love—not for each other, but together, as spectators of other people's "love." As long as love is a day dream, they can participate; as soon as it comes down to the reality of the relationship between two real people—they are frozen.

Another aspect of sentimental love is the abstractification of love in terms of time. A couple may be deeply moved by memories of their past love, although when this past was present no love was experienced—or the phantasies of their future love. How many engaged or newly married couples dream of their bliss of love to take place in the future, while at the very moment at which they live they are already beginning to be bored with each other? This tendency coincides with a general attitude characteristic of modern man. He lives in the past or in the future, but not in the present. He remembers sentimentally his childhood and his mother—or he makes happy plans for the future. Whether love is experienced vicariously by participating in the fictitious experiences of others, or whether it is shifted away from the present to the past or the future, this abstractified and alienated form of love serves as an opiate which alleviates the pain of reality, the aloneness and separateness of the individual.

Still another form of neurotic love lies in the use of *projective mechanisms* for the purpose of avoiding one's own problems, and being concerned with the defects and frailties of the "loved" person instead. Individuals behave in this respect very much as groups, nations, or religions do. They have a fine appreciation for even the minor shortcomings of the other person, and go blissfully ahead ignoring their own—always busy trying to accuse or to reform the other person. If two people both do it—as is so often the case—the relationship of love becomes transformed into one of mutual projection. If I am domineering or indecisive, or greedy, I accuse my partner of it, and depending on my character, I either want to cure him or to punish him. The other person does the same—and both thus succeed in ignoring their own problems and hence fail to undertake any steps which would help them in their own development.

Another form of projection is the projection of one's own problems on the children. First of all such projection takes place not infrequently in the wish for children. In such cases the wish for children is primarily determined by projecting one's own problem of existence on that of the children. When a person feels that he has not been able to make sense of his own life, he tries to make sense of it in terms of the life of his children. But one is bound to fail within oneself *and* for the children. The former because the problem of existence can be solved by each one only for himself, and not by proxy; the latter because one lacks in the very qualities which one needs to guide the children in their own search for an answer. Children serve for projective purposes also when the question arises of dissolving an unhappy marriage. The stock argument of parents in such a situation is that they cannot separate in order not to deprive the children of the blessings of a unified home. Any detailed study would show, however, that the atmosphere of tension and unhappiness within the "unified family" is more harmful to the children than an open break would be—which teaches them at least that man is able to end an intolerable situation by a courageous decision.

One other frequent error must be mentioned here. The illusion, namely, that love means necessarily the absence of conflict. Just as it is customary for people to believe that pain and sadness should be avoided under all circumstances, they believe that love means the absence of any conflict. And they find good reasons for this idea in the fact that the struggles around them seem only to be destructive interchanges which bring no good to either one of those concerned. But the reason for this lies in the fact that the "conflicts" of most people are actually attempts to avoid the *real* conflicts. They are disagreements on minor or superficial matters which by their very nature do not lend themselves to clarification or solution. Real conflicts between two people, those which do not serve to cover up or to project, but which are experienced on the deep level of inner reality to which they belong, are not destructive. They lead to clarification, they produce a catharsis from which both persons emerge with more knowledge and more strength. This leads us to emphasize again something said above.

Love is possible only if two persons communicate with each other from the center of their existence, hence if each one of them experiences himself from the center of his existence. Only in this "central experience" is human reality, only here is aliveness, only here is the basis for love. Love, experienced thus, is a constant challenge; it is not a resting place, but a moving, growing, working together; even whether there is harmony or conflict, joy or sadness, is secondary to the fundamental fact that two people experience themselves from the essence of their existence, that they are one with each other by being one with themselves, rather than by fleeing from themselves. There is only one proof for the presence of love: the depth of the relationship, and the aliveness and strength in each person concerned; this is the fruit by which love is recognized.

QUESTIONS FOR CRITICAL READING

1. Fromm begins by saying that love is a rare phenomenon in Western culture. Do you agree with him?
2. What hierarchy of values do you see as operative in capitalism? Do you agree that "amassed things, that which is dead, are of superior value to labor, to human powers, to that which is alive" (para. 2)?
3. What is someone's "personality package" (para. 7)?
4. Is the concept of marriage as "a smoothly functioning team" as problematic as Fromm seems to think?
5. Does Fromm believe that love is as irrational as Freud thought (para. 12)?
6. Do you think Fromm's descriptions of sentimental love are accurate? Are they fair?
7. Which of the neurotic forms of love (paras. 16–31) have you experienced or observed in others?

WRITING ASSIGNMENTS

1. Are you being prepared in college to become an automaton useful for the capitalist society that you will soon enter? In what ways are you being trained to "co-operate smoothly"? In what ways are your tastes standardized? In what ways does American education prepare you to "feel free and independent, not subject to any authority or principle or conscience—yet willing to be commanded . . . to fit into the social machine without friction" (para. 5)? Examine Fromm's assertions by analyzing the socialization of your immediate friends.
2. To what extent has love been commodified in our culture? How does the commodification of love affect relations between the genders? Does it help or harm women? Is there a direct connection between such commodification and modern capitalism, or would any economic system produce the same results?
3. Fromm says that "the obvious clinical facts demonstrate that men—and women—who devote their lives to unrestricted sexual satisfaction do not attain happiness, and very often suffer from severe neurotic conflicts or symptoms" (para. 14). Is this just propaganda, or does contemporary sexual behavior confirm Fromm's views? Give examples from your observation.

4. Fromm blames an "abstractification" of time for one kind of irrational love and describes married people looking to the future for their happiness (para. 28). To what extent do you think modern people live in the past and the future but not in the present? Examine the life of the college student in this respect.

5. Under what conditions is love possible in the modern world? Examine your own society and establish the necessary requirements for a loving relationship. Take into consideration Fromm's concerns and warnings. Ultimately, do you feel love is an attainable goal in today's world?

6. **CONNECTIONS** Compare Fromm's thoughts on love with Karl Marx's views on achieving satisfaction in the modern political world and with Simone Weil's views on achieving dignity for labor. How sympathetic is Fromm to their thinking?

B. F. SKINNER

What Is Man?

BURRHUS FREDERIC SKINNER *(1904–1990) was an experimental psychologist known for his theories of behaviorism. Behavioral psychology focuses on the ways in which animals and people respond to the myriad complexities of their physical and psychological environment. Skinner's thought has moved in interesting directions, particularly in dealing with the questions of freedom. To some extent, he holds, freedom is not entirely desirable in modern society. It is something that people can outgrow.*

Skinner's emphasis is on the reaction of the individual to the world in which he is placed, and to some extent Skinner sees the individual as a function of that world, as a person whose behavior is essentially created by reinforcement. Reinforcement may be aversive: punishment, such as a spanking, loss of a job, imprisonment. It may be positive: praise, a new job, greater privileges. The "contingencies of reinforcement," an expression he uses often in the present selection, can be aversive, positive, or both. Whatever form they take, they will create the personal behavior of most (if not all) individuals. In posing the question "What is man?" Skinner consciously raises questions that have been addressed by thinkers throughout the ages, from ancient Greek philosophers to modern theologians. In answering his question, he is trying to point the way to a new vision.

He calls his vision a scientific view of mankind. By calling it that he includes in his thinking the results of a considerable body of research into the behavior of lower animals as well as of human beings. He has studied the contingencies of reinforcement that have produced learning,

---

From *Beyond Freedom and Dignity* (1971).

which has, in turn, produced behavior of various sorts. To some extent, Skinner's scientific approach has postulated a view of the individual as not being the autonomous agent one would ordinarily assume. The "autonomous agent"—another of Skinner's key terms in this selection—feels able to do anything that free will dictates and as such seems to be free and independent. But Skinner points out that such freedom and independence are to some extent illusions. The culture, the family, the peer group, even the prejudices and ignorances of the individual—all combine as contingencies of reinforcement not only to reduce but actually to erase the autonomy of the individual. Autonomy" in this sense refers to the individual, personally controlled behavior that each person (as well as each squirrel, rat, and lower animal) feels he or she has.

Naturally, most people, adhering to a more traditional view of humankind, do not wholeheartedly endorse Skinner's views. Skinner seems heartless and, perhaps, merely scientific. Yet Skinner's claims suggest that he is most interested in pulling aside the veil of illusion that makes most of us feel we are free despite the limits we unconsciously impose on our freedom. As he points out, cultures have long agreed to maintain certain fictions in order to explain something about the forces that act on people. The ancient Greeks concerned themselves with the gods and with fate. The Christian view focuses on Jesus and God's providence. The eighteenth-century philosophers thought of the world in terms of a machine and believed that an ascertainable range of causes and effects controlled people's behavior. Skinner's view is different. He sees people as learning to adapt to an environment without even realizing that they do so. It is the invisible or unconscious aspects of this process of adaptation on which Skinner hopes to cast some light.

SKINNER'S RHETORIC

The most obvious rhetorical device Skinner uses is the rhetorical question: What is man? The rest of the essay is, quite logically, an answer to that question. In the first sentences of the first paragraph, Skinner shifts the ground of the discussion by establishing that the question must be answered by looking mainly not at the person but at the environment in which the person thrives. However, used to criticism of the simplified environmentalism that dominated nineteenth-century thought, he begins to clarify the entire nature of environment by examining the ways in which it assumes the function of direction, which had previously been thought to be the preserve of the individual. He then goes on to examine traits of character, which are generally thought to reside only within the individual, and shows how they, too, are dependent on the environment.

Skinner even calls into question the extent to which the world can be known (paras. 8–18) and clarifies the issues concerning words and the way they work to affect our sense of knowledge. From there, Skinner addresses the question of thinking, which he calls "the last stronghold of autonomous man." Skinner shows certain kinds of misunderstanding are buried in the "metaphor of storage" (paras. 23–29) in which it is assumed that a person can "possess" knowledge, his or her past, culture, even his or her character. This thinking leads to a consideration of the self (paras. 32–38) and to a rejection of low-grade views of man as a machine (paras. 39–41). In four paragraphs, Skinner discusses the question of direction and purpose in life (paras. 42–45), and then he springs an interesting trap. The essay to that point had been clearly predicting the doom of autonomous man, with whom the reader has been led to identify. But in the beginning of paragraph 46 he says, "It is only autonomous man who has reached a dead end. Man himself may be controlled by his environment, but it is an environment which is almost wholly of his own making."

The point Skinner wishes to make in answering the question he poses is that until we realize that the concept of autonomous man is a worn-out fiction, we will misunderstand our own nature. When Socrates insisted that we must know ourselves in order to function in the world, he raised the same issues Skinner addresses. But Skinner's answers to the most basic question—What is man?—are somewhat different from any we have heard before.

What Is Man?

As a science of behavior adopts the strategy of physics and biology, the autonomous agent[1] to which behavior has traditionally been attributed is replaced by the environment—the environment in which the species evolved and in which the behavior of the individual is shaped and maintained. The vicissitudes of "environmentalism" show how difficult it has been to make this change. That a man's behavior owes something to antecedent events and that the environment is a more promising point of attack than man himself has long been recognized. As Crane Brinton observed, "a program to change things not just to convert people" was a signifi-

---

[1] **autonomous agent** Skinner's term for the individual who feels he is a free agent directed by his own will and basically undirected by outside forces.

cant part of the English, French, and Russian revolutions.[2] It was Robert Owen,[3] according to Trevelyan, who first "clearly grasped and taught that environment makes character and that environment is under human control" or, as Gilbert Seldes[4] wrote, "that man is a creature of circumstance, that if you changed the environments of thirty little Hottentots and thirty little aristocratic English children, the aristocrats would become Hottentots, for all practical purposes, and the Hottentots little conservatives."

The evidence for a crude environmentalism is clear enough. People are extraordinarily different in different places, and possibly just because of the places. The nomad on horseback in Outer Mongolia and the astronaut in outer space are different people, but, as far as we know, if they had been exchanged at birth, they would have taken each other's place. (The expression "change places" shows how closely we identify a person's behavior with the environment in which it occurs.) But we need to know a great deal more before that fact becomes useful. What is it about the environment that produces a Hottentot? And what would need to be changed to produce an English conservative instead?

Both the enthusiasm of the environmentalist and his usually ignominious failure are illustrated by Owen's utopian experiment at New Harmony. A long history of environmental reform—in education, penology, industry, and family life, not to mention government and religion—has shown the same pattern. Environments are constructed on the model of environments in which good behavior has been observed, but the behavior fails to appear. Two hundred years of this kind of environmentalism has very little to show for itself, and for a simple reason. We must know how the environment works before we can change it to change behavior. A mere shift in emphasis from man to environment means very little.

Let us consider some examples in which the environment takes over the function and role of autonomous man. The first, often   4

---

[2]***revolutions***   The English "Glorious Revolution" of 1688 introduced a constitutional monarchy; the French Revolution of 1789 created a republic (for a time); the Russian Revolution of 1917 introduced Communist government.

[3]***Robert Owen (1771–1858)***   A Welsh industrialist and reformer who brought better living conditions and education to workers at his cotton mills in New Lanark, England, agitated for improved working conditions throughout England, and supported the new labor union movement. Owen's social thought can be seen in his book *A New View of Society* (1813). In 1825 he founded a utopian community in the United States, at New Harmony, Indiana, but it failed, and he lost most of his fortune.

[4]***. . . Gilbert Seldes***   Crane Brinton, G. M. Trevelyan, and Seldes are all writers on history, behavior, and thought.

said to involve human nature, is *aggression*. Men often act in such a way that they harm others, and they often seem to be reinforced by signs of damage to others. The ethologists[5] have emphasized contingencies of survival which would contribute these features to the genetic endowment of the species, but the contingencies of reinforcement in the lifetime of the individual are also significant, since anyone who acts aggressively to harm others is likely to be reinforced in other ways—for example, by taking possession of goods. The contingencies explain the behavior quite apart from any state or feeling of aggression or any initiating act by autonomous man.

Another example involving a so-called "trait of character" is *industry*. Some people are industrious in the sense that they work energetically for long periods of time, while others are lazy and idle in the sense that they do not. "Industry" and "laziness" are among thousands of so-called "traits." The behavior they refer to can be explained in other ways. Some of it may be attributed to genetic idiosyncrasies (and subject to change only through genetic measures), and the rest to environmental contingencies, which are much more important than is usually realized. Regardless of any normal genetic endowment, an organism will range between vigorous activity and complete quiescence depending upon the schedules on which it has been reinforced. The explanation shifts from a trait of character to an environmental history of reinforcement.

A third example, a "cognitive" activity, is *attention*. A person responds only to a small part of the stimuli impinging upon him. The traditional view is that he himself determines which stimuli are to be effective by "paying attention" to them. Some kind of inner gatekeeper is said to allow some stimuli to enter and to keep all others out. A sudden or strong stimulus may break through and "attract" attention, but the person himself seems otherwise to be in control. An analysis of the environmental circumstances reverses the relation. The kinds of stimuli which break through by "attracting attention" do so because they have been associated in the evolutionary history of the species or the personal history of the individual with important—e.g., dangerous—things. Less forceful stimuli attract attention only to the extent that they have figured in contingencies of reinforcement. We can arrange contingencies which ensure that an organism—even such a "simple" organism as a pigeon—will attend to one object and not to another, or to one property of an object, such as its color, and not to another, such

---

[5]***ethologists*** Those who study the formation and evolution of the human *ethos,* that is, the moral nature or guiding principles of a human group.

as its shape. The inner gatekeeper is replaced by the contingencies to which the organism has been exposed and which select the stimuli to which it reacts.

In the traditional view a person perceives the world around him and acts upon it to make it known to him. In a sense he reaches out and grasps it. He "takes it in" and possesses it. He "knows" it in the Biblical sense in which a man knows a woman. It has even been argued that the world would not exist if no one perceived it. The action is exactly reversed in an environmental analysis. There would, of course, be no perception if there were no world to be perceived, but an existing world would not be perceived if there were no appropriate contingencies. We say that a baby perceives his mother's face and knows it. Our evidence is that the baby responds in one way to his mother's face and in other ways to other faces or other things. He makes this distinction not through some mental act of perception but because of prior contingencies. Some of these may be contingencies of survival. Physical features of a species are particularly stable parts of the environment in which a species evolves. (That is why courtship and sex and relations between parent and offspring are given such a prominent place by ethologists.) The face and facial expressions of the human mother have been associated with security, warmth, food, and other important things, during both the evolution of the species and the life of the child.

We learn to perceive in the sense that we learn to respond to   8
things in particular ways because of the contingencies of which they are a part. We may perceive the sun, for example, simply because it is an extremely powerful stimulus, but it has been a permanent part of the environment of the species throughout its evolution and more specific behavior with respect to it could have been selected by contingencies of survival (as it has been in many other species). The sun also figures in many current contingencies of reinforcement: we move into or out of sunlight depending on the temperature; we wait for the sun to rise or set to take practical action; we talk about the sun and its effects; and we eventually study the sun with the instruments and methods of science. Our perception of the sun depends on what we do with respect to it. Whatever we do, and hence however we perceive it, the fact remains that it is the environment which acts upon the perceiving person, not the perceiving person who acts upon the environment.

The perceiving and knowing which arise from verbal contingencies are even more obviously products of the environment. We react to an object in many practical ways because of its color; thus, we pick and eat red apples of a particular variety but not green. It is clear that we can "tell the difference" between red and green, but something more is involved when we say that we *know* that one apple is red and the other green. It is tempting to say that knowing is a cognitive process altogether divorced from action, but the contingencies provide a more useful distinction. When someone asks about the color of an object which he cannot see, and we tell him that it is red, *we* do nothing about the object in any other way. It is the person who has questioned us and heard our answer who makes a practical response which depends on color. Only under verbal contingencies can a speaker respond to an isolated property to which a nonverbal response cannot be made. A response made to the property of an object without responding to the object in any other way is called *abstract*. Abstract thinking is the product of a particular kind of environment, not of a cognitive faculty.

As listeners we acquire a kind of knowledge from the verbal behavior of others which may be extremely valuable in permitting us to avoid direct exposure to contingencies. We learn from the experience of others by responding to what they say about contingencies. When we are warned against doing something or are advised to do something, there may be no point in speaking of knowledge, but when we learn more durable kinds of warnings and advice in the form of maxims or rules, we may be said to have a special kind of knowledge about the contingencies to which they apply. The laws of science are descriptions of contingencies of reinforcement, and one who knows a scientific law may behave effectively without being exposed to the contingencies it describes. (He will, of course, have very different feelings about the contingencies, depending on whether he is following a rule or has been directly exposed to them. Scientific knowledge is "cold," but the behavior to which it gives rise is as effective as the "warm" knowledge which comes from personal experience.)

Isaiah Berlin has referred to a particular sense of knowing, said to have been discovered by Giambattista Vico.[6] It is "the sense in which I know what it is to be poor, to fight for a cause, belong to a nation, to join or abandon a church or a party, to feel nostalgia, terror, the omnipresence of a god, to understand a gesture, a work of art, a joke, a man's character, that one is transformed or lying to oneself." These are the kinds of things one is likely to learn through direct contact with contingencies rather than from the verbal behavior of others, and special kinds of feelings are no doubt

---

[6]***Giovanni Battista Vico (1668–1744)*** Italian philosopher whose theories of history involve cycles of repetition of behavior. Sir Isaiah Berlin (b. 1909) is a British philosopher and historian of ideas.

associated with them, but, even so, the knowledge is not somehow directly given. A person can know what it is to fight for a cause only after a long history during which he has learned to perceive and to know that state of affairs called fighting for a cause.

The role of the environment is particularly subtle when what   12 is known is the knower himself. If there is no external world to initiate knowing, must we not then say that the knower himself acts first? This is, of course, the field of consciousness, or awareness, a field which a scientific analysis of behavior is often accused of ignoring. The charge is a serious one and should be taken seriously. Man is said to differ from the other animals mainly because he is "aware of his own existence." He knows what he is doing; he knows that he has had a past and will have a future; he "reflects on his own nature"; he alone follows the classical injunction "Know thyself." Any analysis of human behavior which neglected these facts would be defective indeed. And some analyses do. What is called "methodological behaviorism" limits itself to what can be publicly observed; mental processes may exist, but they are ruled out of scientific consideration by their nature. The "behaviorists" in political science and many logical positivists[7] in philosophy have followed a similar line. But self-observation can be studied, and it must be included in any reasonably complete account of human behavior. Rather than ignore consciousness, an experimental analysis of behavior has stressed certain crucial issues. The question is not whether a man can know himself but what he knows when he does so.

The problem arises in part from the indisputable fact of privacy: a small part of the universe is enclosed within a human skin. It would be foolish to deny the existence of that private world, but it is also foolish to assert that because it is private it is of a different nature from the world outside. The difference is not in the stuff of which the private world is composed, but in its accessibility. There is an exclusive intimacy about a headache, or heartache, or a silent soliloquy. The intimacy is sometimes distressing (one cannot shut one's eyes to a headache), but it need not be, and it has seemed to support the doctrine that knowing is a kind of possession.

The difficulty is that although privacy may bring the knower closer to what he knows, it interferes with the process through which he comes to know anything. As we saw in [an earlier chapter], the contingencies under which a child learns to describe his feelings

---

[7]*logical positivists* Twentieth-century thinkers who felt human knowledge was limited to only those things that could be known from observation.

are necessarily defective; the verbal community cannot use the procedures with which it teaches a child to describe objects. There are, of course, natural contingencies under which we learn to respond to private stimuli, and they generate behavior of great precision; we could not jump or walk or turn a handspring if we were not being stimulated by parts of our own body. But very little awareness is associated with this kind of behavior and, in fact, we behave in these ways most of the time without being aware of the stimuli to which we are responding. We do not attribute awareness to other species which obviously use similar private stimuli. To "know" private stimuli is more than to respond to them.

The verbal community specializes in self-descriptive contingencies. It asks such questions as: What did you do yesterday? What are you doing now? What will you do tomorrow? Why did you do that? Do you really want to do that? How do you feel about that? The answers help people to adjust to each other effectively. And it is because such questions are asked that a person responds to himself and his behavior in the special way called knowing or being aware. Without the help of a verbal community all behavior would be unconscious. Consciousness is a social product. It is not only *not* the special field of autonomous man, it is *not* within range of a solitary man.

And it is not within the range of accuracy of anyone. The 16 privacy which seems to confer intimacy upon self-knowledge makes it impossible for the verbal community to maintain precise contingencies. Introspective vocabularies are by nature inaccurate, and that is one reason why they have varied so widely among schools of philosophy and psychology. Even a carefully trained observer runs into trouble when new private stimuli are studied. (Independent evidence of private stimulation—for example, through physiological measures—would make it possible to sharpen the contingencies which generate self-observation and would, incidentally, confirm the present interpretation. Such evidence would not, as we noted in [an earlier chapter], offer any support for a theory which attributed human behavior to an observable inner agent.)

Theories of psychotherapy which emphasize awareness assign a role to autonomous man which is properly, and much more effectively, reserved for contingencies of reinforcement. Awareness may help if the problem is in part a lack of awareness, and "insight" into one's condition may help if one then takes remedial action, but awareness or insight alone is not always enough, and it may be too much. One need not be aware of one's behavior or the conditions controlling it in order to behave effectively—or ineffectively. On the contrary, as the toad's inquiry of the centipede demonstrates, constant self-observation may be a handicap. The accomplished pianist would perform badly if he were as clearly aware of his behavior as the student who is just learning to play.

Cultures are often judged by the extent to which they encourage self-observation. Some cultures are said to breed unthinking men, and Socrates[8] has been admired for inducing men to inquire into their own nature, but self-observation is only a preliminary to action. The extent to which a man *should* be aware of himself depends upon the importance of self-observation for effective behavior. Self-knowledge is valuable only to the extent that it helps to meet the contingencies under which it has arisen.

Perhaps the last stronghold of autonomous man is that complex "cognitive" activity called thinking. Because it is complex, it has yielded only slowly to explanation in terms of contingencies of reinforcement. When we say that a person *discriminates* between red and orange, we imply that discrimination is a kind of mental act. The person himself does not seem to be doing anything; he responds in different ways to red and orange stimuli, but this is the result of discrimination rather than the act. Similarly, we say that a person *generalizes*—say, from his own limited experience to the world at large—but all we see is that he responds to the world at large as he has learned to respond to his own small world. We say that a person *forms a concept or an abstraction,* but all we see is that certain kinds of contingencies of reinforcement have brought a response under the control of a single property of a stimulus. We say that a person *recalls* or *remembers* what he has seen or heard, but all we see is that the present occasion evokes a response, possibly in weakened or altered form, acquired on another occasion. We say that a person *associates* one word with another, but all we observe is that one verbal stimulus evokes the response previously made to another. Rather than suppose that it is therefore autonomous man who discriminates, generalizes, forms concepts or abstractions, recalls or remembers, and associates, we can put matters in good order simply by noting that these terms do not refer to forms of behavior.

A person may take explicit action, however, when he solves a   20 problem. In putting a jigsaw puzzle together he may move the pieces around to improve his chances of finding a fit. In solving an equation he may transpose, clear fractions, and extract roots to

---

[8]***Socrates (469?–399 B.C.)***   Greek philosopher. Socrates insisted upon rigorous self-examination no matter what the cost. He was put to death for "corrupting the youth" of Athens, which may indicate the problems inherent in promoting individualism in certain societies.

improve his chances of finding a form of the equation he has already learned how to solve. The creative artist may manipulate a medium until something of interest turns up. Much of this can be done covertly, and it is then likely to be assigned to a different dimensional system, but it can always be done overtly, perhaps more slowly but also often more effectively, and with rare exceptions it must have been learned in overt form. The culture promotes thinking by constructing special contingencies. It teaches a person to make fine discriminations by making differential reinforcement more precise. It teaches techniques to be used in solving problems. It provides rules which make it unnecessary to be exposed to the contingencies from which the rules are derived, and it provides rules for finding rules.

Self-control, or self-management, is a special kind of problem solving which, like self-knowledge, raises all the issues associated with privacy. We have discussed some techniques in connection with aversive control in [an earlier chapter]. It is always the environment which builds the behavior with which problems are solved, even when the problems are to be found in the private world inside the skin. None of this has been investigated in a very productive way, but the inadequacy of our analysis is no reason to fall back on a miracle-working mind. If our understanding of contingencies of reinforcement is not yet sufficient to explain all kinds of thinking, we must remember that the appeal to mind explains nothing at all.

In shifting control from autonomous man to the observable environment we do not leave an empty organism. A great deal goes on inside the skin, and physiology will eventually tell us more about it. It will explain why behavior is indeed related to the antecedent events of which it can be shown to be a function. The assignment is not always correctly understood. Many physiologists regard themselves as looking for the "physiological correlates" of mental events. Physiological research is regarded as simply a more scientific version of introspection. But physiological techniques are not, of course, designed to detect or measure personalities, ideas, attitudes, feelings, impulses, thoughts, or purposes. (If they were, we should have to answer a third question in addition to those raised in [an earlier chapter]: How can a personality, idea, feeling, or purpose affect the instruments of the physiologist?) At the moment neither introspection nor physiology supplies very adequate information about what is going on inside a man as he behaves, and since they are both directed inward, they have the same effect of diverting attention from the external environment.

Much of the misunderstanding about an inner man comes from

the metaphor of storage. Evolutionary and environmental histories change an organism, but they are not stored within it. Thus, we observe that babies suck their mothers' breasts, and we can easily imagine that a strong tendency to do so has survival value, but much more is implied by a "sucking instinct" regarded as something a baby possesses which enables it to suck. The concept of "human nature" or "genetic endowment" is dangerous when taken in that sense. We are closer to human nature in a baby than in an adult, or in a primitive culture than in an advanced, in the sense that environmental contingencies are less likely to have obscured the genetic endowment, and it is tempting to dramatize that endowment by implying that earlier stages have survived in concealed form: man is a naked ape, and "the paleolithic bull which survives in man's inner self still paws the earth whenever a threatening gesture is made on the social scene." But anatomists and physiologists will not find an ape, or a bull, or for that matter instincts. They will find anatomical and physiological features which are the product of an evolutionary history.

The personal history of the individual is also often said to be   24 stored within him. For "instinct" read "habit." The cigarette habit is presumably something more than the behavior said to show that a person possesses it; but the only other information we have concerns the reinforcers and the schedules of reinforcement which make a person smoke a great deal. The contingencies are not stores; they have simply left a changed person.

The environment is often said to be stored in the form of memories: to recall something we search for a copy of it, which can then be seen as the original thing was seen. As far as we know, however, there are no copies of the environment in the individual *at any time,* even when a thing is present and being observed. The products of more complex contingencies are also said to be stored; the repertoire acquired as a person learns to speak French is called a "knowledge of French."

Traits of character, whether derived from contingencies of survival or contingencies of reinforcement, are also said to be stored. A curious example occurs in Follett's *Modern American Usage:* "We say *He faced these adversities bravely,* aware without thought that the bravery is a property of the man, not of the facing; a brave act is poetic shorthand for the act of a person who shows bravery by performing it." But we call a man brave because of his acts, and he behaves bravely when environmental circumstances induce him to do so. The circumstances have changed his behavior; they have not implanted a trait or virtue.

Philosophies are also spoken of as things possessed. A man is said to speak or act in certain ways because he has a particular philosophy—such as idealism, dialectical materialism, or Calvinism.[9] Terms of this kind summarize the effect of environmental conditions which it would now be hard to trace, but the conditions must have existed and should not be ignored. A person who possesses a "philosophy of freedom" is one who has been changed in certain ways by the literature of freedom.

The issue has had a curious place in theology. Does man sin   28 because he is sinful, or is he sinful because he sins? Neither question points to anything very useful. To say that a man is sinful because he sins is to give an operational definition of sin. To say that he sins because he is sinful is to trace his behavior to a supposed inner trait. But whether or not a person engages in the kind of behavior called sinful depends upon circumstances which are not mentioned in either question. The sin assigned as an inner possession (the sin a person "knows") is to be found in a history of reinforcement. (The expression "God-fearing" suggests such a history, but piety, virtue, the immanence of God, a moral sense, or morality does not. As we have seen, man is not a moral animal in the sense of possessing a special trait or virtue; he has built a kind of social environment which induces him to behave in moral ways.)

These distinctions have practical implications. A recent survey of white Americans is said to have shown that "more than half blamed the inferior educational and economic status of blacks on 'something about Negroes themselves.'" The "something" was further identified as "lack of motivation," which was to be distinguished from *both* genetic and environmental factors. Significantly, motivation was said to be associated with "free will." To neglect the role of the environment in this way is to discourage any inquiry into the defective contingencies responsible for a "lack of motivation."

It is in the nature of an experimental analysis of human behavior that it should strip away the functions previously assigned to autonomous man and transfer them one by one to the controlling environment. The analysis leaves less and less for autonomous man to do. But what about man himself? Is there not something about a person

---

[9]*idealism, dialectical materialism, or Calvinism*   *Idealism* is the belief that reality is found in ideas rather than objects themselves; *dialectical materialism* is a Marxian belief in the conflict and resolution of powerful forces as well as a belief in material values and their reality; *Calvinism,* a strict Protestant religion, insists that people are totally depraved and that only a few will be saved by the grace of God. All these philosophies have strong adherents today.

which is more than a living body? Unless something called a self survives, how can we speak of self-knowledge or self-control? To whom is the injunction "Know thyself" addressed?

It is an important part of the contingencies to which a young child is exposed that his own body is the only part of his environment which remains the same *(idem)* from moment to moment and day to day. We say that he discovers his *identity* as he learns to distinguish between his body and the rest of the world. He does this long before the community teaches him to call things by name and to distinguish "me" from "it" or "you."

A self is a repertoire of behavior appropriate to a given set of contingencies. A substantial part of the conditions to which a person is exposed may play a dominant role, and under other conditions a person may report, "I'm not myself today," or, "I couldn't have done what you said I did, because that's not like me." The identity conferred upon a self arises from the contingencies responsible for the behavior. Two or more repertoires generated by different sets of contingencies compose two or more selves. A person possesses one repertoire appropriate to his life with his friends and another appropriate to his life with his family, and a friend may find him a very different person if he sees him with his family or his family if they see him with his friends. The problem of identity arises when situations are intermingled, as when a person finds himself with both his family and his friends at the same time.

Self-knowledge and self-control imply two selves in this sense. The self-knower is almost always a product of social contingencies, but the self that is known may come from other sources. The controlling self (the conscience or superego) is of social origin, but the controlled self is more likely to be the product of genetic susceptibilities to reinforcement (the id, or the Old Adam). The controlling self generally represents the interests of others, the controlled self the interests of the individual.

The picture which emerges from a scientific analysis *is* not of a body with a person inside, but of a body which *is* a person in the sense that it displays a complex repertoire of behavior. The picture is, of course, unfamiliar. The man thus portrayed is a stranger, and from the traditional point of view he may not seem to be a man at all. "For at least one hundred years," said Joseph Wood Krutch,[10] "we have been prejudiced in every theory, including economic

---

[10]***Joseph Wood Krutch (1893–1970)***   American critic and writer whose books and essays on nature were famed. His most famous book is *The Measure of Man* (1954). He also wrote *Henry David Thoreau* (1948), a highly regarded biography and appreciation.

determinism, mechanistic behaviorism, and relativism, that reduces the stature of man until he ceases to be man at all in any sense that the humanists of an earlier generation would recognize." Matson has argued that "the empirical behavioral scientist . . . denies, if only by implication, that a unique being, called Man, exists." "What is now under attack," said Maslow, "is the 'being' of man." C. S. Lewis[11] put it quite bluntly: Man is being abolished.

There is clearly some difficulty in identifying the man to whom these expressions refer. Lewis cannot have meant the human species, for not only is it not being abolished, it is filling the earth. (As a result it may eventually abolish itself through disease, famine, pollution, or a nuclear holocaust, but that is not what Lewis meant.) Nor are individual men growing less effective or productive. We are told that what is threatened is "man *qua*[12] man" or "man in his humanity," or "man as Thou not It," or "man as a person not a thing." These are not very helpful expressions, but they supply a clue. What is being abolished is autonomous man—the inner man, the homunculus,[13] the possessing demon, the man defended by the literatures of freedom and dignity.

His abolition has long been overdue. Autonomous man is a device used to explain what we cannot explain in any other way. He has been constructed from our ignorance, and as our understanding increases, the very stuff of which he is composed vanishes. Science does not dehumanize man, it de-homunculizes him, and it must do so if it is to prevent the abolition of the human species. To man *qua* man we readily say good riddance. Only by dispossessing him can we turn to the real causes of human behavior. Only then can we turn from the inferred to the observed, from the miraculous to the natural, from the inaccessible to the manipulable.

It is often said that in doing so we must treat the man who survives as a mere animal. "Animal" is a pejorative term, but only because "man" has been made spuriously honorific. Krutch has argued that whereas the traditional view supports Hamlet's exclamation, "How like a god!," Pavlov,[14] the behavioral scientist, em-

36

---

[11]*Abraham Maslow (1908–1970) and C. S. Lewis (1898–1963)* Widely known as writers on human values. Maslow, an American psychologist, based his thinking on a hierarchy of human needs, from survival at the bottom to self-actualization at the top. Lewis, an English critic and novelist, was one of the foremost twentieth-century spokesmen for orthodox Christian belief.

[12]*qua* As.

[13]*homunculus* A tiny man; in Goethe's *Faust,* a kind of possessing spirit.

[14]*Ivan Pavlov (1849–1936)* Russian physiologist who conditioned a dog to salivate upon the ringing of a bell. Much behaviorist psychology is based upon his experiments.

phasized "How like a dog!" But that was a step forward. A god is the archetypal pattern of an explanatory fiction, of a miracle-working mind, of the metaphysical. Man is much more than a dog, but like a dog he is within range of a scientific analysis.

It is true that much of the experimental analysis of behavior has been concerned with lower organisms. Genetic differences are minimized by using special strains; environmental histories can be controlled, perhaps from birth; strict regimens can be maintained during long experiments; and very little of this is possible with human subjects. Moreover, in working with lower animals the scientist is less likely to put his own responses to the experimental conditions among his data, or to design contingencies with an eye to their effect on him rather than on the experimental organism he is studying. No one is disturbed when physiologists study respiration, reproduction, nutrition, or endocrine systems in animals; they do so to take advantage of very great similarities. Comparable similarities in behavior are being discovered. There is, of course, always the danger that methods designed for the study of lower animals will emphasize only those characteristics which they have in common with men, but we cannot discover what is "essentially" human until we have investigated nonhuman subjects. Traditional theories of autonomous man have exaggerated species differences. Some of the complex contingencies of reinforcement now under investigation generate behavior in lower organisms which, if the subjects were human, would traditionally be said to involve higher mental processes.

Man is not made into a machine by analyzing his behavior in mechanical terms. Early theories of behavior, as we have seen, represented man as a push-pull automaton, close to the nineteenth-century notion of a machine, but progress has been made. Man is a machine in the sense that he is a complex system behaving in lawful ways, but the complexity is extraordinary. His capacity to adjust to contingencies of reinforcement will perhaps be eventually simulated by machines, but this has not yet been done, and the living system thus simulated will remain unique in other ways.

Nor is man made into a machine by inducing him to use ma-   40
chines. Some machines call for behavior which is repetitious and monotonous, and we escape from them when we can, but others enormously extend our effectiveness in dealing with the world around us. A person may respond to very small things with the help of an electron microscope and to very large things with radio-telescopes, and in doing so he may seem quite inhuman to those who use only their unaided senses. A person may act upon the environment with the delicate precision of a micromanipulator or

with the range and power of a space rocket, and his behavior may seem inhuman to those who rely only on muscular contractions. (It has been argued that the apparatus used in the operant laboratory misrepresents natural behavior because it introduces an external source of power, but men use external sources when they fly kites, sail boats, or shoot bows and arrows. They would have to abandon all but a small fraction of their achievements if they used only the power of their muscles.) People record their behavior in books and other media, and the use they make of the records may seem quite inhuman to those who can use only what they remember. People describe complex contingencies in the form of rules, and rules for manipulating rules, and they introduce them into electronic systems which "think" with a speed that seems quite inhuman to the unaided thinker. Human beings do all this with machines, and they would be less than human if they did not. What we now regard as machine-like behavior was, in fact, much commoner before the invention of these devices. The slave in the cotton field, the bookkeeper on his high stool, the student being drilled by a teacher—these were the machine-like men.

Machines replace people when they do what people have done, and the social consequences may be serious. As technology advances, machines will take over more and more of the functions of men, but only up to a point. We build machines which reduce some of the aversive features of our environment (grueling labor, for example) and which produce more positive reinforcers. We build them precisely because they do so. We have no reason to build machines to be reinforced by these consequences, and to do so would be to deprive ourselves of reinforcement. If the machines man makes eventually make him wholly expendable, it will be by accident, not design.

An important role of autonomous man has been to give human behavior direction, and it is often said that in dispossessing an inner agent we leave man himself without a purpose. As one writer has put it, "Since a scientific psychology must regard human behavior objectively, as determined by necessary laws, it must represent human behavior as unintentional." But "necessary laws" would have this effect only if they referred exclusively to antecedent conditions. Intention and purpose refer to selective consequences, the effects of which can be formulated in "necessary laws." Has life, in all the forms in which it exists on the surface of the earth, a purpose, and is this evidence of intentional design? The primate hand evolved *in order that* things might be more successfully manipulated, but its purpose is to be found not in a prior design but rather in the process of selection. Similarly, in operant conditioning the purpose of a skilled movement of the hand is to be found in the consequences which follow it. A pianist neither acquires nor executes the behavior of playing a scale smoothly because of a prior intention of doing so. Smoothly played scales are reinforcing for many reasons, and they select skilled movements. In neither the evolution of the human hand nor in the acquired use of the hand is any prior intention or purpose at issue.

The argument for purpose seems to be strengthened by moving back into the darker recesses of mutation. Jacques Barzun[15] has argued that Darwin and Marx both neglected not only human purpose but the creative purpose responsible for the variations upon which natural selection plays. It may prove to be the case, as some geneticists have argued, that mutations are not entirely random, but nonrandomness is not necessarily the proof of a creative mind. Mutations will not be random when geneticists explicitly design them in order that an organism will meet specific conditions of selection more successfully, and geneticists will then seem to be playing the role of the creative Mind in pre-evolutionary theory, but the purpose they display will have to be sought in their culture, in the social environment which has induced them to make genetic changes appropriate to contingencies of survival.

There is a difference between biological and individual purpose   44 in that the latter can be felt. No one could have felt the purpose in the development of the human hand, whereas a person can in a sense feel the purpose with which he plays a smooth scale. But he does not play a smooth scale *because* he feels the purpose of doing so; what he feels is a by-product of his behavior in relation to its consequences. The relation of the human hand to the contingencies of survival under which it evolved is, of course, out of reach of personal observation; the relation of the behavior to contingencies of reinforcement which have generated it is not.

A scientific analysis of behavior dispossesses autonomous man and turns the control he has been said to exert over to the environment. The individual may then seem particularly vulnerable. He is henceforth to be controlled by the world around him, and in large part by other men. Is he not then simply a victim? Certainly men

---

[15]*Jacques Barzun (b. 1907)*   A noted American scholar; Skinner is referring to his book *Darwin, Marx, and Wagner.*

have been victims, as they have been victimizers, but the word is too strong. It implies despoliation, which is by no means an essential consequence of interpersonal control. But even under benevolent control is the individual not at best a spectator who may watch what happens but is helpless to do anything about it? Is he not "at a dead end in his long struggle to control his own destiny"?

It is only autonomous man who has reached a dead end. Man himself may be controlled by his environment, but it is an environment which is almost wholly of his own making. The physical environment of most people is largely man-made. The surfaces a person walks on, the walls which shelter him, the clothing he wears, many of the foods he eats, the tools he uses, the vehicles he moves about in, most of the things he listens to and looks at are human products. The social environment is obviously man-made—it generates the language a person speaks, the customs he follows, the behavior he exhibits with respect to the ethical, religious, governmental, economic, educational, and psychotherapeutic institutions which control him. The evolution of a culture is in fact a kind of gigantic exercise in self-control. As the individual controls himself by manipulating the world in which he lives, so the human species has constructed an environment in which its members behave in a highly effective way. Mistakes have been made, and we have no assurance that the environment man has constructed will continue to provide gains which outstrip the losses, but man as we know him, for better or for worse, is what man has made of man.

This will not satisfy those who cry "Victim!" C. S. Lewis protested: ". . . the power of man to make himself what he pleases . . . means . . . the power of some men to make other men what they please." This is inevitable in the nature of cultural evolution. The controlling *self* must be distinguished from the controlled self, even when they are both inside the same skin, and when control is exercised through the design of an external environment, the selves are, with minor exceptions, distinct. The person who unintentionally or intentionally introduces a new cultural practice is only one among possibly billions who will be affected by it. If this does not seem like an act of self-control, it is only because we have misunderstood the nature of self-control in the individual.

When a person changes his physical or social environment "intentionally"—that is, in order to change human behavior, possibly including his own—he plays two roles: one as a controller, as the designer of a controlling culture, and another as the controlled, as the product of a culture. There is nothing inconsistent about this; it follows from the nature of the evolution of a culture, with or without intentional design.

The human species has probably not undergone much genetic change in recorded time. We have only to go back a thousand generations to reach the artists of the caves of Lascaux.[16] Features which bear directly on survival (such as resistance to disease) change substantially in a thousand generations, but the child of one of the Lascaux artists transplanted to the world of today might be almost indistinguishable from a modern child. It is possible that he would learn more slowly than his modern counterpart, that he could maintain only a smaller repertoire without confusion, or that he would forget more quickly; we cannot be sure. But we can be sure that a twentieth-century child transplanted to the civilization of Lascaux would not be very different from the children he met there, for we have seen what happens when a modern child is raised in an impoverished environment.

Man has greatly changed himself as a person in the same period of time by changing the world in which he lives. Something of the order of a hundred generations will cover the development of modern religious practices, and something of the same order of magnitude modern government and law. Perhaps no more than twenty generations will account for modern industrial practices, and possibly no more than four or five for education and psychotherapy. The physical and biological technologies which have increased man's sensitivity to the world around him and his power to change that world have taken no more than four or five generations.

Man has "controlled his own destiny," if that expression means anything at all. The man that man has made is the product of the culture man has devised. He has emerged from two quite different processes of evolution: the biological evolution responsible for the human species and the cultural evolution carried out by that species. Both of these processes of evolution may now accelerate because they are both subject to intentional design. Men have already changed their genetic endowment by breeding selectively and by changing contingencies of survival, and they may now begin to introduce mutations directly related to survival. For a long time men have introduced new practices which serve as cultural mutations, and they have changed the conditions under which practices are selected. They may now begin to do both with a clearer eye to the consequences.

Man will presumably continue to change, but we cannot say   52
in what direction. No one could have predicted the evolution of

---

[16]*caves of Lascaux*   Lascaux is in southwest France. The caves discovered there were painted with bison, elk, and other figures some 15,000 to 20,000 years ago. Other such caves have been found in Spain and elsewhere in France.

the human species at any point in its early history, and the direction of intentional genetic design will depend upon the evolution of a culture which is itself unpredictable for similar reasons. "The limits of perfection of the human species," said Étienne Cabet[17] in *Voyage en Icarie,* "are as yet unknown." But, of course, there are no limits. The human species will never reach a final state of perfection before it is exterminated—"some say in fire, some in ice," and some in radiation.

The individual occupies a place in a culture not unlike his place in the species, and in early evolutionary theory that place was hotly debated. Was the species simply a type of individual, and if so, in what sense could it evolve? Darwin himself declared species "to be purely subjective inventions of the taxonomist." A species has no existence except as a collection of individuals, nor has a family, tribe, race, nation, or class. A culture has no existence apart from the behavior of the individuals who maintain its practices. It is always an individual who behaves, who acts upon the environment and is changed by the consequences of his action, and who maintains the social contingencies which *are* a culture. The individual is the carrier of both his species and his culture. Cultural practices, like genetic traits, are transmitted from individual to individual. A new practice, like a new genetic trait, appears first in an individual and tends to be transmitted if it contributes to his survival as an individual.

Yet, the individual is at best a locus in which many lines of development come together in a unique set. His individuality is unquestioned. Every cell in his body is a unique genetic product, as unique as that classic mark of individuality, the fingerprint. And even within the most regimented culture every personal history is unique. No intentional culture can destroy that uniqueness, and, as we have seen, any effort to do so would be bad design. But the individual nevertheless remains merely a stage in a process which began long before he came into existence and will long outlast him. He has no ultimate responsibility for a species trait or a cultural practice, even though it was he who underwent the mutation or introduced the practice which became part of the species or culture. Even if Lamarck[18] had been right in supposing that the individual

---

[17]*Étienne Cabet (1788–1856)* A French communist thinker; his *Voyage en Icarie* (1840) offers a plan for a utopia, which he tried to put into practice in 1848. He purchased land on the Red River in Texas, then sent 1,500 settlers there. The experiment failed. He later took his "Icarians" to Nauvoo, Illinois, a former Mormon settlement. He withdrew from the community in 1856 after dissension.

[18]*Jean Baptiste Lamarck (1744–1829)* French scientist who thought that it was

could change his genetic structure through personal effort, we should have to point to the environmental circumstances responsible for the effort, as we shall have to do when geneticists begin to change the human endowment. And when an individual engages in the intentional design of a cultural practice, we must turn to the culture which induces him to do so and supplies the art or science he uses.

One of the great problems of individualism, seldom recognized as such, is death—the inescapable fate of the individual, the final assault on freedom and dignity. Death is one of those remote events which are brought to bear on behavior only with the aid of cultural practices. What we see is the death of others, as in Pascal's[19] famous metaphor: "Imagine a number of men in chains, all under sentence of death, some of whom are each day butchered in the sight of the others; those remaining see their own condition in that of their fellows, and looking at each other with grief and despair await their turn. This is an image of the human condition." Some religions have made death more important by picturing a future existence in heaven or hell, but the individualist has a special reason to fear death, engineered not by a religion but by the literatures of freedom and dignity. It is the prospect of personal annihilation. The individualist can find no solace in reflecting upon any contribution which will survive him. He has refused to act for the good of others and is therefore not reinforced by the fact that others whom he has helped will outlive him. He has refused to be concerned for the survival of his culture and is not reinforced by the fact that the culture will long survive him. In the defense of his own freedom and dignity he has denied the contributions of the past and must therefore relinquish all claim upon the future.

Science has probably never demanded a more sweeping change   56 in a traditional way of thinking about a subject, nor has there ever been a more important subject. In the traditional picture a person perceives the world around him, selects features to be perceived, discriminates among them, judges them good or bad, changes them to make them better (or, if he is careless, worse), and may be held responsible for his action and justly rewarded or punished for its consequences. In the scientific picture a person is a member of a species shaped by evolutionary contingencies of survival, displaying

---

possible for acquired characteristics to be passed on genetically to later generations.
   [19]**Blaise Pascal (1623–1662)**   French philosopher and scientist. He was generally enigmatic in his thought, particularly in his *Pensées* (1658), in which he begins to call all knowledge into doubt. Pascal was a devout Catholic, but the religious orthodoxy of his work is subject to debate.

behavioral processes which bring him under the control of the environment in which he lives, and largely under the control of a social environment which he and millions of others like him have constructed and maintained during the evolution of a culture. The direction of the controlling relation is reversed: a person does not act upon the world, the world acts upon him.

It is difficult to accept such a change simply on intellectual grounds and nearly impossible to accept its implications. The reaction of the traditionalist is usually described in terms of feelings. One of these, to which the Freudians have appealed in explaining the resistance to psychoanalysis, is wounded vanity. Freud himself expounded, as Ernest Jones[20] has said, "the three heavy blows which narcissism or self-love of mankind had suffered at the hands of science. The first was cosmological and was dealt by Copernicus;[21] the second was biological and was dealt by Darwin; the third was psychological and was dealt by Freud." (The blow was suffered by the belief that something at the center of man knows all that goes on within him and that an instrument called will power exercises command and control over the rest of one's personality.) But what are the signs or symptoms of wounded vanity, and how shall we explain them? What people *do* about such a scientific picture of man is call it wrong, demeaning, and dangerous, argue against it, and attack those who propose or defend it. They do so not out of wounded vanity but because the scientific formulation has destroyed accustomed reinforcers. If a person can no longer take credit or be admired for what he does, then he seems to suffer a loss of dignity or worth, and behavior previously reinforced by credit or admiration will undergo extinction. Extinction often leads to aggressive attack.

Another effect of the scientific picture has been described as a loss of faith or "nerve," as a sense of doubt or powerlessness, or as discouragement, depression, or despondency. A person is said to feel that he can do nothing about his own destiny. But what he feels is a weakening of old responses which are no longer reinforced. People are indeed "powerless" when long-established verbal repertoires prove useless. For example, one historian has complained that if the deeds of men are "to be dismissed as simply the product of material and psychological conditioning," there is nothing to

[20]***Ernest Jones (1879–1958)*** A follower of Freud. His book *Hamlet and Oedipus* (1949) applies Freud's theory to a literary classic, Shakespeare's *Hamlet*.

[21]***Nicolaus Copernicus (1473–1543)*** Polish astronomer who theorized that the earth revolved around the sun. His theory revolutionized astronomy and shook the foundations of Western thought.

write about; "change must be at least partially the result of conscious mental activity."

Another effect is a kind of nostalgia. Old repertoires break through, as similarities between present and past are seized upon and exaggerated. Old days are called the good old days, when the inherent dignity of man and the importance of spiritual values were recognized. Such fragments of outmoded behavior tend to be "wistful"—that is, they have the character of increasingly unsuccessful behavior.

These reactions to a scientific conception of man are certainly   60
unfortunate. They immobilize men of good will, and anyone concerned with the future of his culture will do what he can to correct them. No theory changes what it is a theory about. Nothing is changed because we look at it, talk about it, or analyze it in a new way. Keats drank confusion to Newton[22] for analyzing the rainbow, but the rainbow remained as beautiful as ever and became for many even more beautiful. Man has not changed because we look at him, talk about him, and analyze him scientifically. His achievements in science, government, religion, art, and literature remain as they have always been, to be admired as one admires a storm at sea or autumn foliage or a mountain peak, quite apart from their origins and untouched by a scientific analysis. What does change is our chance of doing something about the subject of a theory. Newton's analysis of the light in a rainbow was a step in the direction of the laser.[23]

The traditional conception of man if flattering; it confers reinforcing privileges. It is therefore easily defended and can be changed only with difficulty. It was designed to build up the individual as an instrument of countercontrol, and it did so effectively but in such a way as to limit progress. We have seen how the literatures of freedom and dignity, with their concern for autonomous man, have perpetuated the use of punishment and condoned the use of only weak nonpunitive techniques, and it is not difficult to demonstrate a connection between the unlimited right of the individual to pursue happiness and the catastrophes threatened by unchecked

---

[22]*Sir Isaac Newton (1642–1727)*   English scientist who invented differential and integral calculus and established the theory of gravity. His theories gave rise to a mechanical explanation of the universe in which all phenomena could be treated in terms of cause and effect. The English poet John Keats (1795–1821) reacted against Newton's analysis of the rainbow because he felt science was removing the romance and mystery from nature.

[23]*laser*   A highly focused beam of electrons; a form of light. (The word is an acronym for *l*ight *a*mplification by *s*timulated *e*mission of *r*adiation.)

breeding, the unrestrained affluence which exhausts resources and pollutes the environment, and the imminence of nuclear war.

Physical and biological technologies have alleviated pestilence and famine and many painful, dangerous, and exhausting features of daily life, and behavioral technology can begin to alleviate other kinds of ills. In the analysis of human behavior it is just possible that we are slightly beyond Newton's position in the analysis of light, for we are beginning to make technological applications. There are wonderful possibilities—and all the more wonderful because traditional approaches have been so ineffective. It is hard to imagine a world in which people live together without quarreling, maintain themselves by producing the food, shelter, and clothing they need, enjoy themselves and contribute to the enjoyment of others in art, music, literature, and games, consume only a reasonable part of the resources of the world and add as little as possible to its pollution, bear no more children than can be raised decently, continue to explore the world around them and discover better ways of dealing with it, and come to know themselves accurately and, therefore, manage themselves effectively. Yet all this is possible, and even the slightest sign of progress should bring a kind of change which in traditional terms would be said to assuage wounded vanity, offset a sense of hopelessness or nostalgia, correct the impression that "we neither can nor need to do anything for ourselves," and promote a "sense of freedom and dignity" by building "a sense of confidence and worth." In other words, it should abundantly reinforce those who have been induced by their culture to work for its survival.

An experimental analysis shifts the determination of behavior from autonomous man to the environment—an environment responsible both for the evolution of the species and for the repertoire acquired by each member. Early versions of environmentalism were inadequate because they could not explain how the environment worked, and much seemed to be left for autonomous man to do. But environmental contingencies now take over functions once attributed to autonomous man, and certain questions arise. Is man then "abolished"? Certainly not as a species or as an individual achiever. It is the autonomous inner man who is abolished, and that is a step forward. But does man not then become merely a victim or passive observer of what is happening to him? He is indeed controlled by his environment, but we must remember that it is an environment largely of his own making. The evolution of a culture is a gigantic exercise in self-control. It is often said that a scientific view of man leads to wounded vanity, a sense of hopelessness, and nostalgia. But no theory changes what it is a theory about; man remains what he has always been. And a new theory may change what can be done with its subject matter. A scientific view of man offers exciting possibilities. We have not yet seen what man can make of man.

QUESTIONS FOR CRITICAL READING

1. Define the key terms of the chapter: "autonomous man," "contingencies of reinforcement," "environment," "the individual." Are there other key terms that need definition?
2. Skinner has not provided much of the scientific data on which his views are based because he wishes to address a general audience, one that can profit from the results, rather than the process, of scientific research. Should he have provided more scientific data? Is his audience a general audience? Would you have liked more data, more experimental information?
3. What are the most important ideas set forth in this piece? How do they relate to the field of psychology?
4. What kinds of different environments does Skinner take into account in the chapter? He mentions physical and social environments in paragraph 48. Are there others?
5. Skinner believes that his view is scientific. Is he correct?

WRITING ASSIGNMENTS

1. One of the chief issues in the selection is concerned with the nature of the self. In an essay using Skinner's technique of the rhetorical question, answer the following question as carefully as he answers his: What is a self? Refer to paragraphs 32–34. Try to clarify Skinner's idea of the self and offer your own views as you do so.
2. Examine the selection for reference to character traits. By referring to specific quotations and analyzing them carefully in relation to one another, explain what Skinner means by "character traits." Is his analysis of this term reasonable? Is he convincing in suggesting that character traits may not be "permanent" or "basic" as had been thought?
3. Look around you for examples of contingencies of reinforcement. What kind of person does your environment seem to encourage you to be? What kinds of reinforcement are available in your immediate environment? Be as specific as possible in answering these questions.
4. Answer the question: Am I an autonomous agent? Use Skinner's strategy of first examining the environment in which you live, giving special attention to the contingencies of reinforcement you are aware

of. Then proceed to examine your own inner nature—insofar as that is possible—to see what that will contribute to your autonomy. Consider, as you answer this question, the issues of identity raised in paragraph 32 and thereafter. Does the process of answering this question help you to a better insight into your own identity?

5. Answer the question: Are my friends autonomous agents? Using Skinner's theories of contingencies of reinforcement, examine the behavior of two or three of your friends (or one in depth). Do they feel that they are free to do as they wish? Do you believe that they are aware of the limits on their freedom or of the degree to which they react to the reinforcements in their environment? To what extent is their behavior predictable by an outside observer?

6. In this selection, Skinner is basically predicting the death knell of the concept of the individual as an autonomous agent. What does he see as the alternative to this concept? Analyze closely the section from paragraph 45 to paragraph 55. What exactly is Skinner saying in these paragraphs? What will replace the concept of man as an autonomous agent? Is Skinner's view acceptable to you? How would you describe his vision of the future? Establish his thinking on the nature of the individual in the future.

7. **CONNECTIONS**   How would Freud or Jung regard Skinner's views? Skinner does not speak of "autonomous complexes," as Jung does, nor of the sexual origins of psychological problems, as Freud does with his "Oedipus complex" and "penis envy." To what extent might Freud or Jung agree with Skinner; on which issues would Freud or Jung be likely to disagree with him? As you think about this question, consider also whether Karen Horney would agree or disagree with Skinner.

IDEAS IN THE WORLD OF SCIENCE

CAN WE KNOW THE SECRETS
OF NATURE? HOW CAN WE MAKE
OUR KNOWLEDGE USEFUL?

Francis Bacon
Charles Darwin
Rachel Carson
Thomas S. Kuhn
Stephen Jay Gould

INTRODUCTION

THE WORD "SCIENCE" is etymologically related to *scire,* "to know." The scientist wants to know about the world of experience, both that which is within the grasp and perception of the individual and that which is beyond the individual's grasp. For that reason, at its root science has always been concerned with developing a true knowledge of the nature of things. All the writers in Part Four are preoccupied with how the world works, what the nature of nature is, and how we can take advantage of that knowledge. Some of the writers, such as Francis Bacon and Thomas Kuhn, are interested in basic theories of how we know and how we make discoveries. Others, such as Charles Darwin and Stephen Jay Gould, are interested in establishing what they feel is the truth about things. All are concerned with what we can know and whether we can trust our knowledge.

The problem with knowing anything in the sciences, as Francis Bacon reminds his readers in "The Four Idols," is that human beings already have heads filled with presumptions and with methods of inquiry that are not necessarily the best tools for scientific examination. This is an important essay because in it Bacon confronts some of the basic issues in the sciences: What casts of mind are essential to gain knowledge? What in our makeup prevents us from seeing clearly? In an age before the advent of sophisticated instruments that permitted scientists to see directly into the way nature works, it was essential to probe first into the way in which we conceived problems and then set about to solve these problems. At the time Bacon wrote, the most sophisticated scientific instruments were the five senses.

Charles Darwin, in "Natural Selection," proposed a theory that is still controversial. While on a voyage around South America in the *Beagle,* Darwin had the opportunity to observe impressive similarities in the structures of various animals. He had the advantages of a good education, a deep knowledge of the Bible and theology (he was trained as a minister), and a systematic and inquiring mind. He kept scientific samples of insects and flowers and other forms of life and studied them closely in order to detect their resemblances. To explain the significance of his findings, he developed his theories of evolution. Explaining the nature of nature—or one aspect of nature, at least—as it functioned in human experience formed an essential element of Darwin's work.

Rachel Carson's "Elixirs of Death," from *Silent Spring,* changed people's regard for the environment. Carson's analysis of the common pesticides that pollute the environment led to the passage of numerous laws, the formation of many ecological organizations, and the general elevation of public awareness of the effects science has on everyday life. Carson sounded an alarm that has continued ringing ever since she published this essay.

In "Anomaly and the Emergence of Scientific Discoveries," scientific historian Thomas S. Kuhn introduces us to the concept of paradigms, which he defines as "universally recognized scientific achievements that for a time provide model problems and solutions to a community of practitioners." In other words, a paradigm is a model for thought accepted by most people. Anything that strays from the model provides the opportunity for new knowledge. Take, for example, the principle of gravity: if something is on the earth we expect it to come to rest on the ground and not float endlessly above it. Were an object to begin floating in the air, we would have an anomaly—an unexpected exception. From such anomalies, Kuhn explains, come scientific discoveries. By explaining the importance of anomalies for scientific discovery, Kuhn establishes the value of paradigms.

Stephen Jay Gould, in "Nonmoral Nature," examines the results of the kind of thinking that Bacon had deplored in the seventeenth century but that nevertheless flourished in the nineteenth century. Interpreting the world of nature as if it were fashioned by someone with the same predilections as the Victorian scientist—who was usually, by the way, also a minister—naturally caused people to see good and evil in animal and insect behavior. Even today most of us see the world in such terms. To Gould, however, the world is the world; moral issues relate to people, not to dolphins or sharks. To learn that lesson is certainly difficult, but a scientific orientation should help us achieve the necessary detachment. The way we approach the evidence in front of our eyes, in other words, affects what we see just as much as what is observed. Gould wants us to give up anthropomorphic ways of interpreting evidence in favor of a more rational approach.

FRANCIS BACON
The Four Idols

*FRANCIS BACON, Lord Verulam (1561–1626), lived during some
of the most exciting times in history. Among his contemporaries were
the essayist Michel de Montaigne; the playwrights Christopher Mar-
lowe and William Shakespeare; the adventurer Sir Francis Drake; and
Queen Elizabeth I, in whose reign he held several high offices. He
became lord high chancellor of England in 1618, but fell from power
in 1621 through a complicated series of events, among which was his
complicity in a bribery scheme. His so-called crimes were minor, but
he paid dearly for them. His book of Essays (1597) was exceptionally
popular during his lifetime, and when he found himself without a proper
job, he devoted himself to what he declared to be his own true work,
writing about philosophy and science.*

His purposes in Novum Organum *(The New Organon), published in 1620, were to replace the old organon, or instrument of
thought, Aristotle's treatises on logic and thought. Despite the absolute
stranglehold that Aristotle held on sixteenth- and seventeenth-century
minds because his texts were used everywhere in schools and colleges,
Bacon thought that Aristotelian logic produced error. In* Novum Organum *he tried to set the stage for a new attitude toward logic and
scientific inquiry. He proposed a system of reasoning usually referred
to as induction. This quasi-scientific method involves collecting and
listing a great mass of observations from nature. Once a mass of observations is gathered and organized, Bacon believed, the truth about what
is observed will leap out at one.*

Bacon is often mistakenly credited with having invented the scientific

From *Novum Organum.*

method, but although he was on the right track with respect to collecting and observing, he was wrong about the outcome of that process. After all, one could watch an infinite number of apples (and oranges, too) fall to the ground without ever having the slightest sense of why they do so. What Bacon failed to realize—and he died before he could get close enough to scientific observation to realize it—is the creative function of the scientist as expressed in the hypothesis. The hypothesis—a shrewd guess about why something happens—is then tested by the kinds of observations Bacon approved.

Nonetheless, "The Four Idols" is a brilliant work. It does establish the requirements for the kind of observation that produces true scientific knowledge. Bacon despaired of any science in his own day, in part because no one paid any attention to the ways in which the idols strangled thought, observation, and imagination. He realized that the would-be scientist was foiled even before he began. Bacon was a farsighted man. He was correct about the failures of science in his time; and he was correct, moreover, in his assessment that scientific advance would depend on sensory perception and on aids to perception, such as microscopes and telescopes. The real brilliance of "The Four Idols" lies in Bacon's focus not on what is observed but on the instrument of observation, the human mind. Only when the instrument is freed of error can its observations be relied upon.

BACON'S RHETORIC

Bacon was trained during the great age of rhetoric, and his prose (even though in this case it is translated from Latin) shows the clarity, balance, and organization that characterize the prose writing of seventeenth-century England. The most basic device Bacon uses is enumeration: stating clearly that there are four idols and implying that he will treat each one in turn.

Enumeration is one of the most common and most reliable rhetorical devices. The listener hears a speaker say, "I have only three things I want to say today. . . ." And the listener is alerted to listen for all three, while feeling secretly grateful that there are only three. When encountering complex material, the reader is always happy to have such "road signs" as "The second aspect of this question is. . . ."

"The Four Idols," after a three-paragraph introduction, proceeds with a single paragraph devoted to each idol, so that we have an early definition of each and a sense of what to look for. Paragraphs 8–16 cover only the issues related to the Idols of the Tribe: the problems all people have simply because they are people. Paragraphs 17–22 consider the Idols of the Cave, those particular fixations individuals have because *of their special backgrounds or limitations. Paragraphs 23–26 address the questions related to Idols of the Marketplace, particularly those that deal with the way people misuse words and abuse definitions. The remainder of the selection treats the Idols of the Theater, which relate entirely to philosophic systems and preconceptions—all of which tend to narrow the scope of research and understanding.*

Enumeration is used within each of these groups of paragraphs as well. Bacon often begins a paragraph with such statements as "There is one principal . . . distinction between different minds" (para. 19). Or he says, "The idols imposed by words on the understanding are of two kinds" (para. 24). The effect is to ensure clarity where confusion could easily reign.

As an added means of achieving clarity, Bacon sets aside a single paragraph—the last—as a summary of the main points that have been made, and in the order in which they were made.

Within any section of this selection, Bacon depends upon observation, example, and reason to make his points. When he speaks of a given idol, he defines it, gives several examples to make it clearer, discusses its effects on thought, then dismisses it as dangerous. He then goes on to the next idol. Where appropriate, in some cases he names those who are victims of a specific idol. In each case he tries to be thorough, explanatory, and convincing.

Not only is this work a landmark in thought; it is also, because of its absolute clarity, a beacon. We can still profit from its light.

The Four Idols

The idols[1] and false notions which are now in possession of the human understanding, and have taken deep root therein, not only so beset men's minds that truth can hardly find entrance, but even after entrance obtained, they will again in the very instauration[2] of the sciences meet and trouble us, unless men being forewarned of the danger fortify themselves as far as may be against their assaults.

There are four classes of idols which beset men's minds. To

---

[1]*idols* By this term Bacon means phantoms or illusions (see note 21). The Greek philosopher Democritus spoke of *eidola,* tiny representations of things that impressed themselves on the mind.

[2]*instauration* Renewal; renovation.

these for distinction's sake I have assigned names—calling the first class *Idols of the Tribe*; the second, *Idols of the Cave*; the third, *Idols of the Marketplace*; the fourth, *Idols of the Theater*.

The formation of ideas and axioms by true induction[3] is no doubt the proper remedy to be applied for the keeping off and clearing away of idols. To point them out, however, is of great use; for the doctrine of idols is to the interpretation of nature what the doctrine of the refutation of sophisms[4] is to common logic.

The *Idols of the Tribe* have their foundation in human nature itself, and in the tribe or race of men. For it is a false assertion that the sense of man is the measure of things. On the contrary, all perceptions as well of the sense as of the mind are according to the measure of the individual and not according to the measure of the universe. And the human understanding is like a false mirror, which, receiving rays irregularly, distorts and discolors the nature of things by mingling its own nature with it.

The *Idols of the Cave* are the idols of the individual man. For everyone (besides the errors common to human nature in general) has a cave or den of his own, which refracts[5] and discolors the light of nature; owing either to his own proper and peculiar nature; or to his education and conversation with others; or to the reading of books, and the authority of those whom he esteems and admires; or to the differences of impressions, accordingly as they take place in a mind preoccupied and predisposed or in a mind indifferent and settled; or the like. So that the spirit of man (according as it is meted out to different individuals) is in fact a thing variable and full of perturbation,[6] and governed as it were by chance. Whence it was well observed by Heraclitus[7] that men look for sciences in their own lesser worlds, and not in the greater or common world.

There are also idols formed by the intercourse and association

4

---

[3]***induction***   Bacon championed induction as the method by which new knowledge is developed. As he saw it, induction involved a patient gathering and categorizing of facts in the hope that a large number of them would point to the truth. As a process of gathering evidence from which inferences are drawn, induction is contrasted with Aristotle's method, *deduction,* according to which a theory is established and the truth deduced. Deduction places the stress on the authority of the expert; induction places the stress on the facts themselves.

[4]***sophisms***   Apparently intelligent statements that are wrong; false wisdom.

[5]***refracts***   Deflects, bends back, alters.

[6]***perturbation***   Uncertainty, disturbance. In astronomy, the motion caused by the gravity of nearby planets.

[7]***Heraclitus (535?–475? B.C.)***   Greek philosopher who believed that there was no reality except in change; all else was illusion. He also believed that fire was the basis of all the world and that everything we see is a transformation of it.

of men with each other, which I call *Idols of the Marketplace,* on account of the commerce and consort of men there. For it is by discourse that men associate; and words are imposed according to the apprehension of the vulgar.[8] And therefore the ill and unfit choice of words wonderfully obstructs the understanding. Nor do the definitions or explanations wherewith in some things learned men are wont[9] to guard and defend themselves, by any means set the matter right. But words plainly force and overrule the understanding, and throw all into confusion and lead men away into numberless empty controversies and idle fancies.

Lastly, there are idols which have immigrated into men's minds from the various dogmas of philosophies, and also from wrong laws of demonstration.[10] These I call *Idols of the Theater;* because in my judgment all the received systems[11] are but so many stage-plays, representing worlds of their own creation after an unreal and scenic fashion. Nor is it only of the systems now in vogue, or only of the ancient sects and philosophies, that I speak; for many more plays of the same kind may yet be composed and in like artificial manner set forth; seeing that errors the most widely different have nevertheless causes for the most part alike. Neither again do I mean this only of entire systems, but also of many principles and axioms in science, which by tradition, credulity, and negligence, have come to be received.

But of these several kinds of idols I must speak more largely and exactly, that the understanding may be duly cautioned.   8

The human understanding is of its own nature prone to suppose the existence of more order and regularity in the world than it finds. And though there be many things in nature which are singular and unmatched, yet it devises for them parallels and conjugates and relatives[12] which do not exist. Hence the fiction that all celestial bodies move in perfect circles; spirals and dragons being (except in name) utterly rejected. Hence too the element of fire with its orb is brought in, to make up the square with the other three which the sense perceives. Hence also the ratio of density[13] of the so-called

---

[8]*vulgar*   Common people.

[9]*wont*   Accustomed.

[10]*laws of demonstration*   Bacon may be referring to Aristotle's logical system of syllogism and deduction.

[11]*received systems*   Official or authorized views of scientific truth.

[12]*parallels and conjugates and relatives*   A reference to the habit of assuming that phenomena are regular and ordered, consisting of squares, triangles, circles, and other regular shapes.

[13]*ratio of density*   The false assumption that the relationship of mass or weight to volume was ten to one. This is another example of Bacon's complaint, establishing

elements is arbitrarily fixed at ten to one. And so on of other dreams. And these fancies affect not dogmas only, but simple notions also.

The human understanding when it has once adopted an opinion (either as being the received opinion or as being agreeable to itself) draws all things else to support and agree with it. And though there be a greater number and weight of instances to be found on the other side, yet these it either neglects and despises, or else by some distinction sets aside and rejects; in order that by this great and pernicious predetermination the authority of its former conclusions may remain inviolate. And therefore it was a good answer that was made by one who when they showed him hanging in a temple a picture of those who had paid their vows as having escaped shipwreck, and would have him say whether he did not now acknowledge the power of the gods—"Ay," asked he again, "but where are they painted that were drowned after their vows?" And such is the way of all superstition, whether in astrology, dreams, omens, divine judgments, or the like; wherein men having a delight in such vanities, mark the events where they are fulfilled, but where they fail, though this happen much oftener, neglect and pass them by. But with far more subtlety does this mischief insinuate itself into philosophy and the sciences; in which the first conclusion colors and brings into conformity with itself all that come after, though far sounder and better. Besides, independently of that delight and vanity which I have described, it is the peculiar and perpetual error of the human intellect to be more moved and excited by affirmatives than by negatives; whereas it ought properly to hold itself indifferently disposed towards both alike. Indeed, in the establishment of any true axiom, the negative instance is the more forcible of the two.

The human understanding is moved by those things most which strike and enter the mind simultaneously and suddenly, and so fill the imagination; and then it feigns and supposes all other things to be somehow, though it cannot see how, similar to those few things by which it is surrounded. But for that going to and fro to remote and heterogeneous instances, by which axioms are tried as in the fire,[14] the intellect is altogether slow and unfit, unless it be forced thereto by severe laws and overruling authority.

The human understanding is unquiet; it cannot stop or rest, 12 and still presses onward, but in vain. Therefore it is that we cannot

---

a convenient regular "relative" or relationship.

[14]*tried as in the fire* Trial by fire is a figure of speech representing thorough, rigorous testing even to the point of risking what is tested. An axiom is a statement of apparent truth that has not yet been put to the test of examination and investigation.

conceive of any end or limit to the world, but always as of necessity it occurs to us that there is something beyond. Neither again can it be conceived how eternity has flowed down to the present day; for that distinction which is commonly received of infinity in time past and in time to come can by no means hold; for it would thence follow that one infinity is greater than another, and that infinity is wasting away and tending to become finite. The like subtlety arises touching the infinite divisibility of lines,[15] from the same inability of thought to stop. But this inability interferes more mischievously in the discovery of causes:[16] for although the most general principles in nature ought to be held merely positive, as they are discovered, and cannot with truth be referred to a cause; nevertheless, the human understanding being unable to rest still seeks something prior in the order of nature. And then it is that in struggling towards that which is further off, it falls back upon that which is more nigh at hand; namely, on final causes: which have relation clearly to the nature of man rather than to the nature of the universe, and from this source have strangely defiled philosophy. But he is no less an unskilled and shallow philosopher who seeks causes of that which is most general, than he who in things subordinate and subaltern[17] omits to do so.

The human understanding is no dry light, but receives an infusion from the will and affections;[18] whence proceed sciences which may be called "sciences as one would." For what a man had rather were true he more readily believes. Therefore he rejects difficult things from impatience of research; sober things, because they narrow hope; the deeper things of nature, from superstition; the light of experience, from arrogance and price, lest his mind should seem to be occupied with things mean and transitory; things not com-

---

[15]*infinite divisibility of lines*   This gave rise to the paradox of Zeno, the Greek philosopher of the fifth century B.C. who showed that it was impossible to get from one point to another because one had to pass the midpoint of the line determined by the two original points, and then the midpoint of the remaining distance, and then of that remaining distance, down to an infinite number of points. By using accepted truths to "prove" an absurdity about motion, Zeno actually hoped to prove that motion itself did not exist. This is the "subtlety" or confusion Bacon says is produced by the "inability of thought to stop."

[16]*discovery of causes*   Knowledge of the world was based on four causes: efficient (who made it?); material (what is it made of?); formal (what is its shape?); and final (what is its purpose?). The scholastics concentrated their thinking on the first and last, while the "middle causes," related to matter and shape, were the proper subject matter of science because they alone yielded to observation. (See paragraph 33.)

[17]*subaltern*   Lower in status.

[18]*will and affections*   Human free will and emotional needs and responses.

monly believed, out of deference to the opinion of the vulgar. Numberless in short are the ways, and sometimes imperceptible, in which the affections color and infect the understanding.

But by far the greatest hindrance and aberration of the human understanding proceeds from the dullness, incompetency, and deceptions of the senses; in that things which strike the sense outweigh things which do not immediately strike it, though they be more important. Hence it is that speculation commonly ceases where sight ceases; insomuch that of things invisible there is little or no observation. Hence all the working of the spirits[19] enclosed in tangible bodies lies hid and unobserved of men. So also all the more subtle changes of form in the parts of coarser substances (which they commonly call alteration, though it is in truth local motion through exceedingly small spaces) is in like manner unobserved. And yet unless these two things just mentioned be searched out and brought to light, nothing great can be achieved in nature, as far as the production of works is concerned. So again the essential nature of our common air, and of all bodies less dense than air (which are very many) is almost unknown. For the sense by itself is a thing infirm and erring; neither can instruments for enlarging or sharpening the senses do much; but all the truer kind of interpretation of nature is effected by instances and experiments fit and apposite;[20] wherein the sense decides touching the experiment only, and the experiment touching the point in nature and the thing itself.

The human understanding is of its own nature prone to abstractions and gives a substance and reality to things which are fleeting. But to resolve nature into abstractions is less to our purpose than to dissect her into parts; as did the school of Democritus,[21] which went further into nature than the rest. Matter rather than forms should be the object of our attention, its configurations and changes of configuration, and simple action, and law of action or motion; for forms are figments of the human mind, unless you will call those laws of action forms.

Such then are the idols which I call *Idols of the Tribe;* and which   16
take their rise either from the homogeneity of the substance of the human spirit,[22] or from its preoccupation, or from it narrowness,

---

[19]***spirits***   The soul or animating force.

[20]***apposite***   Appropriate; well related.

[21]***Democritus (460?–370? B.C.)***   Greek philosopher who thought the world was composed of atoms. Bacon felt such "dissection" to be useless because it was impractical. Yet Democritus's concept of the *eidola,* the mind's impressions of things, may have contributed to Bacon's idea of "the idol."

[22]***human spirit***   Human nature.

or from its restless motion, or from an infusion of the affections, or from the incompetency of the senses, or from the mode of impression.

The *Idols of the Cave* take their rise in the peculiar constitution, mental or bodily, of each individual; and also in education, habit, and accident. Of this kind there is a great number and variety; but I will instance those the pointing out of which contains the most important caution, and which have most effect in disturbing the clearness of the understanding.

Men become attached to certain particular sciences and speculations, either because they fancy themselves the authors and inventors thereof, or because they have bestowed the greatest pains upon them and become most habituated to them. But men of this kind, if they betake themselves to philosophy and contemplations of a general character, distort and color them in obedience to their former fancies; a thing especially to be noticed in Aristotle,[23] who made his natural philosophy[24] a mere bondservant to his logic, thereby rendering it contentious and well nigh useless. The race of chemists[25] again out of a few experiments of the furnace have built up a fantastic philosophy, framed with reference to a few things; and Gilbert[26] also, after he had employed himself most laboriously in the study and observation of the loadstone, proceeded at once to construct an entire system in accordance with his favorite subject.

There is one principal and, as it were, radical distinction between different minds, in respect of philosophy and the sciences, which is this: that some minds are stronger and apter to mark the differences of things, others to mark their resemblances. The steady and acute mind can fix its contemplations and dwell and fasten on the subtlest distinctions: the lofty and discursive mind recognizes and puts together the finest and most general resemblances. Both kinds however easily err in excess, by catching the one at gradations, the other at shadows.

There are found some minds given to an extreme admiration of antiquity, others to an extreme love and appetite for novelty; 20

---

[23]*Aristotle (384–322 B.C.)* Greek philosopher whose *Organon* (system of logic) dominated the thought of Bacon's time. Bacon sought to overthrow Aristotle's hold on science and thought.

[24]*natural philosophy* The scientific study of nature in general—biology, zoology, geology, etc.

[25]*chemists* Alchemists had developed a "fantastic philosophy" from their experimental attempts to transmute lead into gold.

[26]*William Gilbert (1540–1603)* An English scientist who studied magnetism and codified many laws related to magnetic fields. He was particularly ridiculed by Bacon for being too narrow in his researches.

but few so duly tempered that they can hold the mean, neither carping at what has been well laid down by the ancients, nor despising what is well introduced by the moderns. This however turns to the great injury of the sciences and philosophy; since these affectations of antiquity and novelty are the humors[27] of partisans rather than judgments; and truth is to be sought for not in the felicity of any age, which is an unstable thing, but in the light of nature and experience, which is eternal. These factions therefore must be abjured,[28] and care must be taken that the intellect be not hurried by them into assent.

Contemplations of nature and of bodies in their simple form break up and distract the understanding, while contemplations of nature and bodies in their composition and configuration overpower and dissolve the understanding: a distinction well seen in the school of Leucippus[29] and Democritus as compared with the other philosophies. For that school is so busied with the particles that it hardly attends to the structure; while the others are so lost in admiration of the structure that they do not penetrate to the simplicity of nature. These kinds of contemplation should therefore be alternated and taken by turns; that so the understanding may be rendered at once penetrating and comprehensive, and the inconveniences above mentioned, with the idols which proceed from them, may be avoided.

Let such then be our provision and contemplative prudence for keeping off and dislodging the *Idols of the Cave,* which grow for the most part either out of the predominance of a favorite subject, or out of an excessive tendency to compare or to distinguish, or out of partiality for particular ages, or out of the largeness or minuteness of the objects contemplated. And generally let every student of nature take this as a rule—that whatever his mind seizes and dwells upon with peculiar satisfaction is to be held in suspicion, and that so much the more care is to be taken in dealing with such questions to keep the understanding even and clear.

But the *Idols of the Marketplace* are the most troublesome of all: idols which have crept into the understanding through the alliances of words and names. For men believe that their reason governs words; but it is also true that words react on the understanding; and this it is that has rendered philosophy and the sciences sophistical and inactive. Now words, being commonly framed and applied according to the capacity of the vulgar, follow those lines of division

---

[27]**humors**   Used in a medical sense to mean a distortion caused by imbalance.
[28]**abjured**   Renounced, sworn off, repudiated.
[29]**Leucippus (fifth century B.C.)**   Greek philosopher; teacher of Democritus and inventor of the atomistic theory. His works survive only in fragments.

which are most obvious to the vulgar understanding. And whenever an understanding of greater acuteness or a more diligent observation would alter those lines to suit the true divisions of nature, words stand in the way and resist the change. Whence it comes to pass that the high and formal discussions of learned men end oftentimes in disputes about words and names; with which (according to the use and wisdom of the mathematicians) it would be more prudent to begin, and so by means of definitions reduce them to order. Yet even definitions cannot cure this evil in dealing with natural and material things; since the definitions themselves consist of words, and those words beget others: so that it is necessary to recur to individual instances, and those in due series and order; as I shall say presently when I come to the method and scheme for the formation of notions and axioms.[30]

The idols imposed by words on the understanding are of two   24
kinds. They are either names of things which do not exist (for as there are things left unnamed through lack of observation, so likewise are there names which result from fantastic suppositions and to which nothing in reality responds), or they are names of things which exist, but yet confused and ill-defined, and hastily and irregularly derived from realities. Of the former kind are Fortune, the Prime Mover, Planetary Orbits, Element of Fire, and like fictions which owe their origin to false and idle theories.[31] And this class of idols is more easily expelled, because to get rid of them it is only necessary that all theories should be steadily rejected and dismissed as obsolete.

But the other class, which springs out of a faulty and unskillful abstraction, is intricate and deeply rooted. Let us take for example such a word as *humid*; and see how far the several things which the word is used to signify agree with each other; and we shall find the word *humid* to be nothing else than a mark loosely and confusedly applied to denote a variety of actions which will not bear to be reduced to any constant meaning. For it both signifies that which easily spreads itself round any other body; and that which in itself is indeterminate and cannot solidize; and that which readily yields in every direction; and that which easily divides and scatters itself; and that which easily unites and collects itself; and that which readily flows and is put in motion; and that which readily clings to another

---

[30]***notions and axioms***   Conceptions and definitive statements of truth.

[31]***idle theories***   These are things that cannot be observed and thus do not exist. Fortune is fate; the Prime Mover is God or some "first" force; the notion that planets orbited the sun was considered as "fantastic" as these others, or as the idea that everything was made up of fire and its many permutations.

body and wets it; and that which is easily reduced to a liquid, or being solid easily melts. Accordingly when you come to apply the word—if you take it in one sense, flame is humid; if in another, air is not humid; if in another, fine dust is humid; if in another, glass is humid. So that it is easy to see that the notion is taken by abstraction only from water and common and ordinary liquids, without any due verification.

There are however in words certain degrees of distortion and error. One of the least faulty kinds is that of names of substances, especially of lowest species and well-deduced (for the notion of *chalk* and of *mud* is good, of *earth* bad);[32] a more faulty kind is that of actions, as *to generate, to corrupt, to alter;* the most faulty is of qualities (except such as are the immediate objects of the sense), as *heavy, light, rare, dense,* and the like. Yet in all these cases some notions are of necessity a little better than others, in proportion to the greater variety of subjects that fall within the range of the human sense.

But the *Idols of the Theater* are not innate, nor do they steal into the understanding secretly, but are plainly impressed and received into the mind from the play-books of philosophical systems and the perverted rules of demonstration.[33] To attempt refutations in this case would be merely inconsistent with what I have already said: for since we agree neither upon principles nor upon demonstrations, there is no place for argument. And this is so far well, inasmuch as it leaves the honor of the ancients untouched. For they are no wise disparaged—the question between them and me being only as to the way. For as the saying is, the lame man who keeps the right road outstrips the runner who takes a wrong one. Nay, it is obvious that when a man runs the wrong way, the more active and swift he is the further he will go astray.

But the course I propose for the discovery of sciences is such   28 as leaves but little to the acuteness and strength of wits, but places all wits[34] and understandings nearly on a level. For as in the drawing of a straight line or perfect circle, much depends on the steadiness and practice of the hand, if it be done by aim of hand only, but if with the aid of rule or compass, little or nothing; so is it exactly

---

[32]**earth bad**   Chalk and mud were useful in manufacture; hence they were terms of approval. *Earth* is used here in the sense we use *dirt,* as in "digging in the dirt."

[33]*perverted rules of demonstration*   Another complaint against Aristotle's logic as misapplied in Bacon's day.

[34]*wits*   Intelligence, reasoning powers.

with my plan. But though particular confutations[35] would be of no avail, yet touching the sects and general divisions of such systems I must say something; something also touching the external signs which show that they are unsound; and finally something touching the causes of such great infelicity and of such lasting and general agreement in error; that so the access to truth may be made less difficult, and the human understanding may the more willingly submit to its purgation and dismiss its idols.

Idols of the Theater, or of systems, are many, and there can be and perhaps will be yet many more. For were it not that now for many ages men's minds have been busied with religion and theology; and were it not that civil governments, especially monarchies, have been averse to such novelties, even in matters speculative; so that men labor therein to the peril and harming of their fortunes—not only unrewarded, but exposed also to contempt and envy; doubtless there would have arisen many other philosophical sects like to those which in great variety flourished once among the Greeks. For as on the phenomena of the heavens many hypotheses may be constructed, so likewise (and more also) many various dogmas may be set up and established on the phenomena of philosophy. And in the plays of this philosophical theater you may observe the same thing which is found in the theater of the poets, that stories invented for the stage are more compact and elegant, and more as one would wish them to be, than true stories out of history.

In general, however, there is taken for the material of philosophy either a great deal out of a few things, or a very little out of many things; so that on both sides philosophy is based on too narrow a foundation of experiment and natural history, and decides on the authority of too few cases. For the rational school of philosophers[36] snatches from experience a variety of common instances, neither duly ascertained nor diligently examined and weighed, and leaves all the rest to meditation and agitation of wit.

There is also another class of philosophers,[37] who having be-

---

[35]*confutations*   Specific counterarguments. Bacon means that he cannot offer particular arguments against each scientific sect; thus he offers a general warning.

[36]*rational school of philosophers*   Platonists who felt that human reason alone could discover the truth and that experiment was unnecessary. Their observation of experience produced only a "variety of common instances" from which they reasoned.

[37]*another class of philosophers*   William Gilbert (1540–1603) experimented tirelessly with magnetism, from which he derived numerous odd theories. Though Gilbert was a true scientist, Bacon thought of him as limited and on the wrong track.

stowed much diligent and careful labor on a few experiments, have thence made bold to educe and construct systems; wresting all other facts in a strange fashion to conformity therewith.

And there is yet a third class,[38] consisting of those who out   32 of faith and veneration mix their philosophy with theology and traditions; among whom the vanity of some has gone so far aside as to seek the origin of sciences among spirits and genii.[39] So that this parent stock of errors—this false philosophy—is of three kinds; the sophistical, the empirical, and the superstitious. . . .

But the corruption of philosophy by superstition and an admixture of theology is far more widely spread, and does the greatest harm, whether to entire systems or to their parts. For the human understanding is obnoxious to the influence of the imagination no less than to the influence of common notions. For the contentious and sophistical kind of philosophy ensnares the understanding; but this kind, being fanciful and tumid[40] and half poetical, misleads it more by flattery. For there is in man an ambition of the understanding, no less than of the will, especially in high and lofty spirits.

Of this kind we have among the Greeks a striking example in Pythagoras, though he united with it a coarser and more cumbrous superstition; another in Plato and his school,[41] more dangerous and subtle. It shows itself likewise in parts of other philosophies, in the introduction of abstract forms and final causes and first causes, with the omission in most cases of causes intermediate, and the like. Upon this point the greatest caution should be used. For nothing is so mischievous as the apotheosis of error; and it is a very plague of the understanding for vanity to become the object of veneration. Yet in this vanity some of the moderns have with extreme levity indulged so far as to attempt to found a system of natural philosophy on the first chapter of Genesis, on the book of Job, and other parts of the sacred writings; seeking for the dead among the living: which also makes the inhibition and repression of it the more important, because from this unwholesome mixture of things human and divine

---

[38]***a third class*** Pythagoras (580?–500? B.C.) was a Greek philosopher who experimented rigorously with mathematics and a tuned string. He is said to have developed the musical scale. His theory of reincarnation, or the transmigration of souls, was somehow based on his travels in India and his work with scales. The superstitious belief in the movement of souls is what Bacon complains of.

[39]***genii*** Oriental demons or spirits; a slap at Pythagoras, who traveled in the Orient.

[40]***tumid*** Overblown, swollen.

[41]***Plato and his school*** Plato's religious bent was further developed by Plotinus (A.D. 205–270) in his *Enneads*. Although Plotinus was not a Christian, his Neo-Platonism was welcomed as a philosophy compatible with Christianity.

there arises not only a fantastic philosophy but also an heretical religion. Very meet it is therefore that we be sober-minded, and give to faith that only which is faith's. . . .

So much concerning the several classes of Idols, and their equipage: all of which must be renounced and put away with a fixed and solemn determination, and the understanding thoroughly freed and cleansed; the entrance into the kingdom of man, founded on the sciences, being not much other than the entrance into the kingdom of heaven, whereunto none may enter except as a little child.

QUESTIONS FOR CRITICAL READING

1. Which of Bacon's idols is the most difficult to understand? Do your best to define it.
2. Which of these idols do we still need to worry about? Why? What dangers does it present?
3. What does Bacon mean by saying that our senses are weak (para. 14)? Is he correct in making that statement?
4. Occasionally Bacon says something in such a way that it seems a bit like an aphorism (see the introduction to Machiavelli, p. 33). Find at least one such expression in this selection. Upon examination, does the expression have as much meaning as it seems to have?
5. What kind of readers did Bacon expect for this piece? What clues does his way of communicating provide regarding the nature of his anticipated readers?

WRITING ASSIGNMENTS

1. Which of Bacon's idols most seriously applies to you as a person? Using enumeration, arrange the idols in order of their effect on your own judgment. If you prefer, you may write about which idol you believe is most important in impeding scientific investigation today.
2. Is it true, as Bacon says in paragraph 10, that people are in general more excited by affirmation than by negation? Do we really stress the positive and deemphasize the negative in the conduct of our general affairs? Find at least three instances in which people seem to gravitate toward the positive or the negative in various everyday situations. Try to establish whether or not Bacon has, in fact, described what is a habit of mind.
3. In paragraph 13, Bacon states that the "will and affections" enter into matters of thought. By this he means that our understanding of what we observe is conditioned by what we want and what we feel. Thus, when he says, "For what a man had rather were true he more readily

believes," he tells us that people tend to believe what they want to believe. Test this statement by means of observation. Find out, for example, how many older people are convinced that the world is deteriorating, how many younger people feel that there is a plot on the part of older people to hold them back, how many women feel that men consciously oppress women, and how many men feel that feminists are not as feminine as they should be. What other beliefs can you discover that seem to have their origin in what people want to believe rather than in what is true?

4. Establish the extent to which the Idols of the Marketplace are relevant to issues in modern life. In particular, study the language used in the newspapers (and important magazines) to discuss nuclear warfare. To what extent are official words (those uttered by governments) designed to obscure issues? In what sense are they misleading? Review the discussion in paragraph 23 and following paragraphs before answering this question. In what sense does Bacon's assertion that "words stand in the way and resist the change" apply to the debate on nuclear war? If you wish to substitute another major issue (e.g., abortion, improving secondary schools, social welfare services, taxation, prayer in the schools), feel free to do so.

5. Bacon's views on religion have always been questionable. He grew up in a very religious time, but his writings rarely discuss religion positively. In this work he talks about giving "to faith only that which is faith's." He seems to feel that scientific investigation is something quite separate from religion. Examine the selection carefully to determine what you think Bacon's view on this question is. Then take a stand on the issue of the relationship between religion and science. Should science be totally independent of religious concerns? Should religious issues control scientific experimentation? What does Bacon mean when he complains about the vanity of founding "a system of natural philosophy on the first chapter of Genesis, on the book of Job, and other parts of the sacred writings" (para. 34)? "Natural philosophy" means biology, chemistry, physics, and science in general. Are Bacon's complaints justified? Would his complaints be relevant today?

6. Bacon's purpose is to show how certain innate problems in our thinking can limit our ability to know the truth about the world of experience. He wants us to think scientifically. To what extent is Bacon's advice useful for thinking about experience that is other than science? Is he helpful in advising us how to think about religion, inner feelings, or spiritual awareness? How useful is the advice in "The Four Idols" for these areas of experience?

7. **CONNECTIONS**   Has the reception of Darwin's work been affected by a general inability of the public to see beyond Bacon's four idols? Read both Darwin's essay and that of Stephen Jay Gould. Which of those two writers is more concerned with the lingering effects of the four idols? Do you feel that the effects have seriously affected people's beliefs regarding Darwinian theory?

8. **CONNECTIONS**   Choose a writer from Part One of this book and

demonstrate the usefulness of Bacon's four idols for clarifying thought about underlying political realities. Niccolò Machiavelli may provide an especially useful essay in this regard. Bacon was always interested in clear thinking and in avoiding the idols that muddied thought. Do you think Machiavelli would agree with him?

CHARLES DARWIN

Natural Selection

CHARLES DARWIN (1809–1882) was trained as a minister in the
Church of England, but he was also the grandson of one of England's
greatest horticulturists, Erasmus Darwin. Partly as a way of putting
off ordination in the church, and partly because of his natural curiosity
and scientific enterprise, Darwin found himself performing the functions
of a naturalist on HMS Beagle, which was engaged in scientific explor-
ations around South America during the years 1831–1836. Darwin's
fascinating book Voyage of the Beagle (1839) details the experiences
he had and offers us some views of his self-education as a naturalist.

His experiences on the Beagle led him to take note of variations
in species of animals he found in various separate locales, particularly
between remote islands and the mainland. Varieties—his term for any
visible (or invisible) differences in markings, coloration, size or shape
of appendages, organs, or bodies—were of some peculiar use, he believed, for the animals in the environment in which he found them. He
was not certain just what the use of these varieties might be, and he
did not know whether the changes that created the varieties resulted from
the environment or from some chance operation of nature. Ultimately, he
concluded that varieties in nature were caused by three forces: (1) natural
selection, in which varieties occur spontaneously by chance but are then
"selected" for because they are aids to survival; (2) direct action of the

---

From *On the Origin of Species by Means of Natural Selection*. This text is from
the first edition, 1859. In the five subsequent editions, Darwin hedged more and
more on his theory, often introducing material in defense against objections. The
first edition is vigorous and direct; this edition jolted the worlds of science and
religion out of their complaisance. In later editions, this chapter was titled "Natural
Selection; or, Survival of the Fittest."

environment, in which nonadaptive varieties do not survive because of climate, food conditions, or the like; and (3) the effects of use or disuse of a variation (for example, the short beak of a bird in para. 9). Darwin later regarded sexual selection, which figures prominently in this work, as less significant.

The idea of evolution—the gradual change of species through some kind of modification of varieties—had been in the air for many years when Darwin began his work. The English scientists C. W. Wells in 1813 and Patrick Matthew in 1831 had both proposed theories of natural selection, although Darwin was unaware of their work. Alfred Russel Wallace (1823–1913), a younger English scientist, revealed in 1858 that he was about to propose the same theory of evolution as was Darwin. They jointly published brief versions of their theories in 1858, and the next year Darwin rushed the final version of his book On the Origin of Species by Means of Natural Selection *to press.*

Darwin does not mention human beings as part of the evolutionary process in the selection. Because he was particularly concerned about the probable adverse reactions of theologians, he merely promised later discussion of that subject. It came in The Descent of Man *(1871), the companion to* On the Origin of Species.

When Darwin returned to England after completing his researches on the Beagle, *he supplemented his knowledge with information gathered from breeders of pigeons, livestock, dogs, and horses. This research, it must be noted, was rather limited, involving relatively few samples, and was conducted according to comparatively unscientific practices. Yet, it corresponded with his observations of nature. The fact was that man could cause changes in species; it was Darwin's task to show that nature— through the process of natural selection—could do the same thing.*

Naturally, The Descent of Man *stirred up a great deal of controversy between the church and Darwin's supporters. Not since the Roman Catholic Church denied the fact that the earth went around the sun, which Galileo had proven scientifically in 1632 (being banished for his pains), had there been a more serious confrontation between science and religion. Darwin was ridiculed by ministers and doubted by older scientists; but his views were stoutly defended by younger scientists, many of whom had arrived at similar conclusions. In the end, Darwin's views were accepted by the Church of England, and when he died in 1882 he was lionized and buried at Westminster Abbey in London. Only recently has controversy concerning his work arisen again.*

DARWIN'S RHETORIC

Darwin's writing is fluent, smooth, and stylistically sophisticated. Yet, his material is burdensome, detailed, and in general not appealing.

Despite these drawbacks, he manages to keep the reader engaged. His rhetorical method depends entirely on the yoking of thesis and demonstration. He uses definition frequently, but most often he uses testimony, gathering information and instances, both real and imaginary, from many different sources.

Interestingly enough, Darwin claimed that he used Francis Bacon's method of induction in his researches. That involves gathering evidence of many instances of a given phenomenon, from which the truth—or a natural law—will emerge. In fact Darwin did not quite follow this path. Like most modern scientists, he established a hypothesis after a period of observation; then he looked for evidence that would confirm or refute the hypothesis. He was careful to include examples that argued against his view, but like most scientists, he emphasized the importance of the positive samples.

Induction plays a part in the rhetoric of this selection in that it is dominated by examples. There are examples taken from the breeding of birds, from the condition of birds in nature, from domestic farm animals and their breeding; and there are many, many examples taken from botany, including the breeding of plants and the interdependence of certain insects and certain plants. Erasmus Darwin was famous for his work with plants, and it is natural that such observations would play an important part in his grandson's thinking.

The process of natural selection is carefully discussed, particularly in paragraph 8 and thereafter. Darwin emphasizes its positive nature and its differences from selection by human breeders. The use of comparison, which appears frequently in the selection, is most conspicuous in these paragraphs. He postulates a nature in which the fittest survive because they are best adapted for survival, but he does not dwell on the fate of those who are unfit individuals. It was left to later writers, often misapplying his theories, to do that.

Natural Selection

How will the struggle for existence . . . act in regard to variation? Can the principle of selection, which we have seen is so potent in the hands of man, apply in nature? I think we shall see that it can act most effectually. Let it be borne in mind in what an endless number of strange peculiarities our domestic productions, and, in a lesser degree, those under nature, vary; and how strong the hereditary tendency is. Under domestication, it may be truly said that the whole organization becomes in some degree plastic.[1] Let it be borne in mind how infinitely complex and close-fitting are the mutual relations of all organic beings to each other and to their physical conditions of life. Can it, then, be thought improbable, seeing that variations useful to man have undoubtedly occurred, that other variations useful in some way to each being in the great and complex battle of life, should sometimes occur in the course of thousands of generations? If such do occur, can we doubt (remembering that many more individuals are born than can possibly survive) that individuals having any advantage, however slight, over others, would have the best chance of surviving and or procreating their kind? On the other hand, we may feel sure that any variation in the least degree injurious would be rigidly destroyed. This preservation of favorable variations and the rejection of injurious variations, I call Natural Selection. Variations neither useful nor injurious would not be affected by natural selection, and would be left a fluctuating element, as perhaps we see in the species called polymorphic.[2]

We shall best understand the probable course of natural selection by taking the case of a country undergoing some physical change, for instance, of climate. The proportional numbers of its inhabitants would almost immediately undergo a change, and some species might become extinct. We may conclude, from what we have seen of the intimate and complex manner in which the inhabitants of each country are bound together, that any change in the numerical proportions of some of the inhabitants, independently of the change of climate itself, would most seriously affect many of the others. If the country were open on its borders, new forms would certainly immigrate, and this also would seriously disturb the relations of some of the former inhabitants. Let it be remembered how powerful the influence of a single introduced tree or mammal has been shown to be. But in the case of an island, or of a country partly surrounded by barriers, into which new and better adapted forms could not freely enter, we should then have places in the economy of nature which would assuredly be better filled up, if some of the original inhabitants were in some manner modified; for, had the area been open to immigration, these same places would have been seized on by intruders. In such case, every slight modification, which in the course of ages chanced to arise, and which in any way favored the individuals of any of the species, by better adapting them to their

---

[1]*plastic*   Capable of being shaped and changed.
[2]*species called polymorphic*   Species that have more than one form over the course of their lives, such as butterflies.

altered conditions, would tend to be preserved; and natural selection would thus have free scope for the work of improvement.

We have reason to believe . . . that a change in the conditions of life, by specially acting on the reproductive system, causes or increases variability; and in the foregoing case the conditions of life are supposed to have undergone a change, and this would manifestly be favorable to natural selection, by giving a better chance of profitable variations occurring; and unless profitable variations do occur, natural selection can do nothing. Not that, as I believe, any extreme amount of variability is necessary; as man can certainly produce great results by adding up in any given direction mere individual differences, so could Nature, but far more easily, from having incomparably longer time at her disposal. Nor do I believe that any great physical change, as of climate, or any unusual degree of isolation to check immigration, is actually necessary to produce new and unoccupied places for natural selection to fill up by modifying and improving some of the varying inhabitants. For as all the inhabitants of each country are struggling together with nicely balanced forces, extremely slight modifications in the structure or habits of one inhabitant would often give it an advantage over others; and still further modifications of the same kind would often still further increase the advantage. No country can be named in which all the native inhabitants are now so perfectly adapted to each other and to the physical conditions under which they live, that none of them could anyhow be improved; for in all countries, the natives have been so far conquered by naturalized productions, that they have allowed foreigners to take firm possession of the land. And as foreigners have thus everywhere beaten some of the natives, we may safely conclude that the natives might have been modified with advantage, so as to have better resisted such intruders.

As man can produce and certainly has produced a great result 4 by his methodical and unconscious means of selection, what may not nature effect? Man can act only on external and visible characters; nature cares nothing for appearances, except in so far as they may be useful to any being. She can act on every internal organ, on every shade of constitutional difference, on the whole machinery of life. Man selects only for his own good; Nature only for that of the being which she tends. Every selected character is fully exercised by her; and the being is placed under well-suited conditions of life. Man keeps the natives of many climates in the same country; he seldom exercises each selected character in some peculiar and fitting manner; he feeds a long and a short beaked pigeon on the same food; he does not exercise a long-backed or long-legged quadruped in any peculiar manner; he exposes sheep with long and short wool to the same climate. He does not allow the most vigorous males to struggle for the females. He does not rigidly destroy all inferior animals, but protects during each varying season, as far as lies in his power, all his productions. He often begins his selection by some half-monstrous form; or at least by some modification prominent enough to catch the eye, or to be plainly useful to him. Under nature, the slightest difference of structure or constitution may well turn the nicely balanced scale in the struggle for life, and so be preserved. How fleeting are the wishes and efforts of man! how short his time! and consequently how poor will his products be, compared with those accumulated by nature during whole geological periods. Can we wonder, then, that nature's productions should be far "truer" in character than man's productions; that they should be infinitely better adapted to the most complex conditions of life, and should plainly bear the stamp of far higher workmanship?

It may be said that natural selection is daily and hourly scrutinizing, throughout the world, every variation, even the slightest; rejecting that which is bad, preserving and adding up all that is good; silently and insensibly working, whenever and wherever opportunity offers, at the improvement of each organic being in relation to its organic and inorganic conditions of life. We see nothing of these slow changes in progress, until the hand of time has marked the long lapse of ages, and then so imperfect is our view into long past geological ages, that we only see that the forms of life are now different from what they formerly were.

Although natural selection can act only through and for the good of each being, yet characters and structures, which we are apt to consider as of very trifling importance, may thus be acted on. When we see leaf-eating insects green, and bark-feeders mottled-grey; the alpine ptarmigan white in winter, the red-grouse the color of heather, and the black-grouse that of peaty earth, we must believe that these tints are of service to these birds and insects in preserving them from danger. Grouse, if not destroyed at some period of their lives, would increase in countless numbers; they are known to suffer largely from birds of prey; and hawks are guided by eyesight to their prey—so much so that on parts of the Continent[3] persons are warned not to keep white pigeons, as being the most liable to destruction. Hence I can see no reason to doubt that natural selection might be most effective in giving the proper color to each kind of grouse, and in keeping that color, when once acquired, true and

---

[3]***Continent***　European continent; the contiguous land mass of Europe, which excludes the British Isles.

constant. Nor ought we to think that the occasional destruction of an animal of any particular color would produce little effect; we should remember how essential it is in a flock of white sheep to destroy every lamb with the faintest trace of black. In plants, the down on the fruit and the color of the flesh are considered by botanists as characters of the most trifling importance; yet we hear from an excellent horticulturist, Downing,[4] that in the United States, smooth-skinned fruits suffer far more from a beetle, a curculio,[5] than those with down; that purple plums suffer far more from a certain disease than yellow plums; whereas another disease attacks yellow-fleshed peaches far more than those with other colored flesh. If, with all the aids of art, these slight differences make a great difference in cultivating the several varieties, assuredly, in a state of nature, where the trees would have to struggle with other trees and with a host of enemies, such differences would effectually settle which variety, whether a smooth or downy, a yellow or purple fleshed fruit, should succeed.

In looking at many small points of difference between species, which, as far as our ignorance permits us to judge, seem to be quite unimportant, we must not forget that climate, food, etc., probably produce some slight and direct effect. It is, however, far more necessary to bear in mind that there are many unknown laws of correlation[6] of growth, which, when one part of the organization is modified through variation and the modifications are accumulated by natural selection for the good of the being, will cause other modifications, often of the most unexpected nature.

As we see that those variations which under domestication appear at any particular period of life, tend to reappear in the offspring at the same period—for instance, in the seeds of the many varieties of our culinary and agricultural plants; in the caterpillar and cocoon stages of the varieties of the silkworm; in the eggs of poultry, and in the color of the down of their chickens; in the horns of our sheep and cattle when nearly adult—so in a state of nature, natural selection will be enabled to act on and modify organic beings at any age, by the accumulation of profitable variations at that age, and by their inheritance at a corresponding age. If it profit a plant to have its seeds more and more widely disseminated by the wind, I can see no greater diffi-   8

---

[4]*Andrew Jackson Downing (1815–1852)*   American horticulturist and specialist in fruit and fruit trees.

[5]*curculio*   A weevil.

[6]*laws of correlation*   In certain plants and animals, one condition relates to another, as in the case of blue-eyed white cats, which are always deaf; the reasons are not clear.

culty in this being effected through natural selection than in the cotton-planter increasing and improving by selection the down in the pods on his cotton-trees. Natural selection may modify and adapt the larva of an insect to a score of contingencies, wholly different from those which concern the mature insect. These modifications will no doubt effect, through the laws of correlation, the structure of the adult; and probably in the case of those insects which live only for a few hours, and which never feed, a large part of their structure is merely the correlated result of successive changes in the structure of their larvae. So, conversely, modifications in the adult will probably often affect the structure of the larva; but in all cases natural selection will ensure that modifications consequent on other modifications at a different period of life, shall not be in the least degree injurious: for if they became so, they would cause the extinction of the species.

Natural selection will modify the structure of the young in relation to the parent, and of the parent in relation to the young. In social animals it will adapt the structure of each individual for the benefit of the community; if each in consequence profits by the selected change. What natural selection cannot do is to modify the structure of one species, without giving it any advantage, for the good of another species; and though statements to this effect may be found in works of natural history, I cannot find one case which will bear investigation. A structure used only once in an animal's whole life, if of high importance to it, might be modified to any extent by natural selection; for instance, the great jaws possessed by certain insects, and used exclusively for opening the cocoon— or the hard tip to the beak of nestling birds, used for breaking the egg. It has been asserted that of the best short-beaked tumbler-pigeons, more perish in the egg than are able to get out of it; so that fanciers[7] assist in the act of hatching. Now, if nature had to make the beak of a full-grown pigeon very short for the bird's own advantage, the process of modification would be very slow, and there would be simultaneously the most rigorous selection of the young birds within the egg, which had the most powerful and hardest beaks, for all with weak beaks would inevitably perish; or, more delicate and more easily broken shells might be selected, the thickness of the shell being known to vary like every other structure.

Sexual Selection

Inasmuch as peculiarities often appear under domestication in one sex and become hereditarily attached to that sex, the same fact

---

[7]*fanciers* Amateurs who raise and race pigeons.

probably occurs under nature, and if so, natural selection will be able to modify one sex in its functional relations to the other sex, or in relation to wholly different habits of life in the two sexes, as is sometimes the case with insects. And this leads me to say a few words on what I call Sexual Selection. This depends, not on a struggle for existence, but on a struggle between the males for possession of the females; the result is not death to the unsuccessful competitor, but few or no offspring. Sexual selection is, therefore, less rigorous than natural selection. Generally, the most vigorous males, those which are best fitted for their places in nature, will leave most progeny. But in many cases, victory will depend not on general vigor, but on having special weapons, confined to the male sex. A hornless stag or spurless cock would have a poor chance of leaving offspring. Sexual selection by always allowing the victor to breed might surely give indomitable courage, length to the spur, and strength to the wing to strike in the spurred leg, as well as the brutal cock fighter,[8] who knows well that he can improve his breed by careful selection of the best cocks. How low in the scale of nature this law of battle descends, I know not; male alligators have been described as fighting, bellowing, and whirling round, like Indians in a wardance, for the possession of the females; male salmons have been seen fighting all day long; male stag-beetles often bear wounds from the huge mandibles[9] of other males. The war is, perhaps, severest between the males of polygamous animals,[10] and these seem oftenest provided with special weapons. The males of carnivorous animals are already well armed; though to them and to others, special means of defense may be given through means of sexual selection, as the mane to the lion, the shoulder-pad to the boar, and the hooked jaw to the male salmon; for the shield may be as important for victory as the sword or spear.

Among birds, the contest is often of a more peaceful character. All those who have attended to the subject believe that there is the severest rivalry between the males of many species to attract, by singing, the females. The rock-thrush of Guiana,[11] birds of paradise, and some others, congregate; and successive males display their gorgeous plumage and perform strange antics before the females, which standing by as spectators, at last choose the most attractive partner. Those who have closely attended to birds in confinement

[8]*brutal cock fighter*   Cockfights were a popular spectator sport in England, especially for gamblers; but many people considered them a form of horrible brutality.

[9]*mandibles*   Jaws.

[10]*polygamous animals*   Animals that typically have more than one mate.

[11]**Guyana**   Formerly British Guiana, on the northeast coast of South America.

well know that they often take individual preferences and dislikes: thus Sir R. Heron[12] has described how one pied peacock was eminently attractive to all his hen birds. It may appear childish to attribute any effect to such apparently weak means: I cannot here enter on the details necessary to support this view; but if man can in a short time give elegant carriage and beauty to his bantams,[13] according to his standard of beauty, I can see no good reason to doubt that female birds, by selecting, during thousands of generations, the most melodious or beautiful males, according to their standard of beauty, might produce a marked effect. I strongly suspect that some well-known laws with respect to the plumage of male and female birds, in comparison with the plumage of the young, can be explained on the view of plumage having been chiefly modified by sexual selection, acting when the birds have come to the breeding age or during the breeding season; the modifications thus produced being inherited at corresponding ages or seasons, either by the males alone, or by the males and females; but I have not space here to enter on this subject.

Thus it is, as I believe, that when the males and females of any 12 animal have the same general habits of life, but differ in structure, color, or ornament, such differences have been mainly caused by sexual selection; that is, individual males have had, in successive generations, some slight advantage over other males, in their weapons, means of defense, or charms; and have transmitted these advantages to their male offspring. Yet, I would not wish to attribute all such sexual differences to this agency: for we see peculiarities arising and becoming attached to the male sex in our domestic animals (as the wattle in male carriers, horn-like protuberances in the cocks of certain fowls, etc.), which we cannot believe to be either useful to the males in battle, or attractive to the females. We see analogous cases under nature, for instance, the tuft of hair on the breast of the turkey-cock, which can hardly be either useful or ornamental to this bird; indeed, had the tuft appeared under domestication, it would have been called a monstrosity.

Illustrations of the Action of Natural Selection

In order to make it clear how, as I believe, natural selection acts, I must beg permission to give one or two imaginary illustrations. Let

---

[12]*Sir Robert Heron (1765–1854)*   English politician who maintained a menagerie of animals.
[13]*bantams*   Cocks bred for fighting.

us take the case of a wolf, which preys on various animals, securing some by craft, some by strength, and some by fleetness; and let us suppose that the fleetest prey, a deer for instance, had from any change in the country increased in numbers, or that other prey had decreased in numbers, during that season of the year when the wolf is hardest pressed for food. I can under such circumstances see no reason to doubt that the swiftest and slimmest wolves would have the best chance of surviving, and so be preserved or selected, provided always that they retained strength to master their prey at this or at some other period of the year, when they might be compelled to prey on other animals. I can see no more reason to doubt this, than that man can improve the fleetness of his greyhounds by careful and methodical selection, or by that unconscious selection which results from each man trying to keep the best dogs without any thought of modifying the breed.

Even without any change in the proportional numbers of the animals on which our wolf preyed, a cub might be born with an innate tendency to pursue certain kinds of prey. Nor can this be thought very improbable; for we often observe great differences in the natural tendencies of our domestic animals; one cat, for instance, taking to catch rats, another mice; one cat, according to Mr. St. John,[14] bringing home winged game, another hares or rabbits, and another hunting on marshy ground and almost nightly catching woodcocks or snipes. The tendency to catch rats rather than mice is known to be inherited. Now, if any slight innate change of habit or of structure benefited an individual wolf, it would have the best chance of surviving and of leaving offspring. Some of its young would probably inherit the same habits or structure, and by the repetition of this process, a new variety might be formed which would either supplant or coexist with the parent-form of wolf. Or, again, the wolves inhabiting a mountainous district, and those frequenting the lowlands, would naturally be forced to hunt different prey; and from the continued preservation of the individuals best fitted for the two sites, two varieties might slowly be formed. These varieties would cross and blend where they met; but to this subject of intercrossing we shall soon have to return. I may add, that, according to Mr. Pierce,[15] there are two varieties of the wolf inhabiting the Catskill Mountains in the United States, one

---

[14]*Charles George William St. John (1809–1856)* An English naturalist whose book, *Wild Sports and Natural History of the Highlands,* was published in 1846 and in a second edition in 1848.

[15]*Pierce* Unidentified.

with a light greyhound-like form, which pursues deer, and the other more bulky, with shorter legs, which more frequently attacks the shepherd's flocks.

Let us now take a more complex case. Certain plants excrete a sweet juice, apparently for the sake of eliminating something injurious from their sap; this is effected by glands at the base of the stipules[16] in some Leguminosæ, and at the back of the leaf of the common laurel. This juice, though small in quantity, is greedily sought by insects. Let us now suppose a little sweet juice or nectar to be excreted by the inner bases of the petals of a flower. In this case insects in seeking the nectar would get dusted with pollen, and would certainly often transport the pollen from one flower to the stigma of another flower. The flowers of two distinct individuals of the same species would thus get crossed; and the act of crossing, we have good reason to believe (as will hereafter be more fully alluded to), would produce very vigorous seedlings, which consequently would have the best chance of flourishing and surviving. Some of these seedlings would probably inherit the nectar-excreting power. Those individual flowers which had the largest glands or nectaries, and which excreted most nectar, would be oftenest visited by insects, and would be oftenest crossed; and so in the long-run would gain the upper hand. Those flowers, also, which had their stamens and pistils[17] placed, in relation to the size and habits of the particular insects which visited them, so as to favor in any degree the transportal of their pollen from flower to flower, would likewise be favored or selected. We might have taken the case of insects visiting flowers for the sake of collecting pollen instead of nectar; and as pollen is formed for the sole object of fertilization, its destruction appears a simple loss to the plant; yet if a little pollen were carried, at first occasionally and then habitually, by the pollen-devouring insects from flower to flower, and a cross thus effected, although nine-tenths of the pollen were destroyed, it might still be a great gain to the plant; and those individuals which produced more and more pollen, and had larger and larger anthers,[18] would be selected.

When our plant, by this process of the continued preservation or natural selection of more and more attractive flowers, had been rendered highly attractive to insects, they would, uninten-   16

---

[16]*stipules* Spines at the base of a leaf.
[17]*stamens and pistils* Sexual organs of plants. The male and female organs appear together in the same flower.
[18]*anthers* An anther is that part of the stamen that contains pollen.

tionally on their part, regularly carry pollen from flower to flower; and that they can most effectually do this, I could easily show by many striking instances. I will give only one—not as a very striking case, but as likewise illustrating one step in the separation of the sexes of plants, presently to be alluded to. Some holly-trees bear only male flowers, which have four stamens producing rather a small quantity of pollen, and a rudimentary pistil; other holly-trees bear only female flowers; these have a full-sized pistil, and four stamens with shrivelled anthers, in which not a grain of pollen can be detected. Having found a female tree exactly sixty yards from a male tree, I put the stigmas[19] of twenty flowers, taken from different branches, under the microscope, and on all, without exception, there were pollen-grains, and on some a profusion of pollen. As the wind had set for several days from the female to the male tree, the pollen could not thus have been carried. The weather had been cold and boisterous, and therefore not favorable to bees; nevertheless every female flower which I examined had been effectually fertilized by the bees, accidentally dusted with pollen, having flown from tree to tree in search of nectar. But to return to our imaginary case: as soon as the plant had been rendered so highly attractive to insects that pollen was regularly carried from flower to flower, another process might commence. No naturalist doubts the advantage of what has been called the "physiological division of labor"; hence we may believe that it would be advantageous to a plant to produce stamens alone in one flower or on one whole plant, and pistils alone in another flower or on another plant. In plants under culture and placed under new conditions of life, sometimes the male organs and sometimes the female organs become more or less impotent; now if we suppose this to occur in ever so slight a degree under nature, then as pollen is already carried regularly from flower to flower, and as a more complete separation of the sexes of our plant would be advantageous on the principle of the division of labor, individuals with this tendency more and more increased, would be continually favored or selected, until at last a complete separation of the sexes would be effected.

Let us now turn to the nectar-feeding insects in our imaginary case: we may suppose the plant of which we have been slowly increasing the nectar by continued selection, to be a common plant; and that certain insects depended in main part on its nectar

---

[19]*stigmas* Where the plant's pollen develops.

for food. I could give many facts, showing how anxious bees are to save time; for instance, their habit of cutting holes and sucking the nectar at the bases of certain flowers, which they can, with a very little more trouble, enter by the mouth. Bearing such facts in mind, I can see no reason to doubt that an accidental deviation in the size and form of the body, or in the curvature and length of the proboscis,[20] etc., far too slight to be appreciated by us, might profit a bee or other insect, so that an individual so characterized would be able to obtain its food more quickly, and so have a better chance of living and leaving descendants. Its descendants would probably inherit a tendency to a similar slight deviation of structure. The tubes of the corollas[21] of the common red and incarnate clovers (Trifolium pratense and incarnatum) do not on a hasty glance appear to differ in length; yet the hive-bee can easily suck the nectar out of the incarnate clover, but not out of the common red clover, which is visited by humble-bees[22] alone; so that whole fields of the red clover offer in vain an abundant supply of precious nectar to the hive-bee. Thus it might be a great advantage to the hive-bee to have a slightly longer or differently constructed proboscis. On the other hand, I have found by experiment that the fertility of clover greatly depends on bees visiting and moving parts of the corolla, so as to push the pollen on to the stigmatic surface. Hence, again, if humble-bees were to become rare in any country, it might be a great advantage to the red clover to have a shorter or more deeply divided tube to its corolla, so that the hive-bee could visit its flowers. Thus I can understand how a flower and a bee might slowly become, either simultaneously or one after the other, modified and adapted in the most perfect manner to each other, by the continued preservation of individuals presenting mutual and slightly favorable deviations of structure.

I am well aware that this doctrine of natural selection, exemplified in the above imaginary instances, is open to the same objections which were at first urged against Sir Charles Lyell's noble views[23] on "the modern changes of the earth, as illustrative of geology"; but we now very seldom hear the action,

---

[20]***proboscis***   Snout.

[21]***corollas***   Inner set of floral petals.

[22]***humble-bees***   Bumblebees.

[23]***Sir Charles Lyell's noble views***   Lyell (1797–1875) was an English geologist whose landmark work, *Principles of Geology* (1830–1833), Darwin read while on the *Beagle*. The book inspired Darwin, and the two scientists became friends. Lyell was shown portions of *On the Origin of Species* while Darwin was writing it.

for instance, of the coast-waves, called a trifling and insignificant cause, when applied to the excavation of gigantic valleys or to the formation of the longest lines of inland cliffs. Natural selection can act only by the preservation and accumulation of infinitesimally small inherited modifications, each profitable to the preserved being; and as modern geology has almost banished such views as the excavation of a great valley by a single diluvial[24] wave, so will natural selection, if it be a true principle, banish the belief of the continued creation of new organic beings, or of any great and sudden modification in their structure.

---

[24]*diluvial*   Pertaining to a flood. Darwin means that geological changes, such as those which caused the Grand Canyon, were no longer thought of as being created instantly by flood (or other catastrophes), but were considered to have developed over a long period of time, as he imagines happened in the evolution of the species.

QUESTIONS FOR CRITICAL READING

1. Darwin's metaphor "battle of life" (para. 1) introduces issues that might be thought extraneous to a scientific inquiry. What is the danger of using such a metaphor? What is the advantage of doing so?
2. Many religious groups reject Darwin's concept of natural selection, but they heartily accept human selection. Why would there be such a difference between the two?
3. Do you feel that the theory of natural selection is a positive force? Could it be directed by divine power?
4. There is no reference to human beings in this work. Would you assume that the principles at work on animals would also be at work on people? Do you think that Darwin assumes so?
5. When this chapter was published in a later edition, Darwin added to its title "Survival of the Fittest." What issues or emotions does that new title raise that "Natural Selection" does not?

WRITING ASSIGNMENTS

1. In paragraph 13, Darwin uses imaginary examples. Compare the value of his genuine examples and these imaginary ones. How effective is the use of imaginary examples in an argument? What requirements would an imaginary example have to meet to be forceful in an argument? Do you find Darwin's imaginary examples to be strong or weak?
2. From paragraph 14 on, Darwin discusses the process of modification

of a species through its beginning in the modification of an individual. Explain, insofar as you understand the concept, just how a species could be modified by a variation occurring in just one individual. In your explanation, use Darwin's rhetorical technique of the imaginary example.

3. Write an essay that takes as its thesis statement the following sentence from paragraph 18: "Natural selection can act only by the preservation and accumulation of infinitesimally small inherited modifications, each profitable to the preserved being." Be sure to examine the work carefully for other statements by Darwin that add strength, clarity, and meaning to this one. You may also employ the Darwinian device of presenting "imaginary instances" in your essay.

4. A controversy exists concerning the Darwinian theory of evolution. Explore the *Readers' Guide to Periodical Literature* for up-to-date information on the creationist-evolutionist conflict in schools. Look up either or both terms to see what articles you can find. Define the controversy and take a stand on it. Use your knowledge of natural selection gained from this piece. Remember, too, that Darwin was trained as a minister of the church and was very concerned about religious opinion.

5. When Darwin wrote this piece, he believed that sexual selection was of great importance in evolutionary changes in species. Assuming that this belief is true, establish the similarities between sexual selection in plants and animals and sexual selection, as you have observed it, in people. Paragraphs 10–12 discuss this issue. Darwin does not discuss human beings, but it is clear that physical and stylistic distinctions between the sexes have some bearing on selection. Assuming that to be true, what qualities in people (physical and mental) are likely to survive? Why?

6. In the Middle Ages and earlier, the official view of the church was that the world was flat. Columbus proved that the world was round, and the church agreed not to argue with him. The official view of the church was that the sun went around the earth. When Galileo proved otherwise, he was forced to deny his observations and was then banished. Only later, in the face of overwhelming evidence, did the church back down. In Darwin's case, the church maintained its stance that all species were created on a specially appointed day and that, therefore, evolution was impossible. The Church of England and the Roman Catholic Church, after some struggle, seem to have accepted Darwin's views. Why is it still difficult for some religious organizations to do so? To answer this question, you may have to interview some people connected with a church that rejects Darwin's views. You may also find some religious literature attacking Darwin. If so, establish what are the concerns of some churches and other religious organizations. Make as clear an argument for their point of view as you can.

7. **CONNECTIONS** Which of Francis Bacon's four idols would have made it most difficult for Darwin's contemporaries to accept the theory

of evolution, despite the mass of evidence he presented? Do the idols interfere with people's ability to evaluate evidence?

8. **CONNECTIONS** Thomas S. Kuhn describes both the paradigms that guide scientists in their investigations and the anomalies that bring them to their discoveries. Examine Darwin's description of his method of work and try to establish the paradigm within which he conducted his investigation. What anomalies began to point him in a new direction of thought? Did Darwin's method depend more on induction or deduction for its results?

RACHEL CARSON
Elixirs of Death

R*ACHEL CARSON (1907–1964) was educated at the Pittsburgh College for Women and Johns Hopkins University, where she received a master's degree in biology in 1932. She continued her studies at the Marine Biological Laboratory of the Woods Hole Oceanographic Institute in Massachusetts. After teaching biology at the University of Maryland, Carson joined the United States Fish and Wildlife service in 1936 as editor of its publications. In 1951 her first best-selling book on science,* The Sea Around Us, *earned her, among many prizes, a Guggenheim Fellowship, which made it possible for her to leave government service in 1952 and devote all of her time to research and writing. She was elected to the British Royal Society of Literature and the American Institute of Arts and Letters.*

Rachel Carson was not herself a distinguished scientist, although she was frequently praised for her science writing in some of her articles. Clearly, her writing about science distinguished her from others in her field. For example, she won the George Westinghouse Science Writing Award for "Birth of an Island," which appeared in the Yale Review *in 1950. She was a painstaking writer who, by her own admission, wrote late into the night and subjected her work to many revisions. In addition to magazine articles, she wrote a number of books, including* Under the Sea-Wind: A Naturalist's Picture of Ocean Life *(1941),* The Sea Around Us *(1951),* Silent Spring *(1962), and* The Edge of the Sea *(1971).*

By the early 1960s, people had begun to notice that many common birds and insects no longer appeared on the landscape. The effect of DDT and other powerful insecticides had killed off not just the pests that hampered crop growth but also many desirable and beautiful animals that were part of the food chain depending on those insects. Silent

419

Spring, *in which "Elixirs of Death" appears, is an attack on the wholesale use of pesticides in farming and agriculture. Carson herself was unprepared for the book's reception: it not only sold over 500,000 copies but also shocked the public into awareness of the dangers of wholesale damage to the environment.*

One of the results of Carson's book was the instigation of a government investigation during the Kennedy administration that resulted in legislation attempting to reverse the effect of indiscriminate spraying and pesticide use. The ecological movement in full swing today was triggered in large part by the frightening picture of pesticides that Rachel Carson painted in Silent Spring.

"Elixirs of Death" is an unemotional, direct, scientific discussion of the most common forms of insecticides and herbicides in common use since World War II. As Carson points out, such poisons originated in chemical warfare experimentation. For example, variants of nerve gases commonly used for insect control were used during World War II in Germany for the mass murder of Jews, Gypsies, homosexuals, and political prisoners.

As Carson tells us, pesticides were virtually uncontrolled when they were first used, because their effects are usually long-term rather than immediate. Today, environmentalists strive to ensure that the use of pesticides remains controlled.

CARSON'S RHETORIC

Rachel Carson was praised immediately for her ability to communicate scientific truths to a wide audience. In college, she was an English major before she switched to biology; her style, while not specifically literary in this essay, is characterized by careful writing, vivid description, and metaphors designed to move her audience. In other words, she aims to affect her readers as well as to inform them.

Carson's descriptions are specific, unadorned, and functional, providing detailed information on the nature of the organic compounds that have been synthesized for use as industrial poisons. She begins by examining the carbon molecule whose versatility makes all the variants possible. Then, in what she calls a "Who's Who of pesticides," she names each of the major groups: arsenical poisons; chlorinated hydrocarbons (DDT); alkyl or organic phosphorus insecticides (parathion and malathion); systemic insecticides. She details the properties of each of these groups, naming the most familiar forms of each, and considers their lasting effects on the human body.

Rhetorically, one of her most important resources is her willingness to name and describe in detail. She offers quotations from experts in

*the field, such as Dr. W. C. Hueper of the National Cancer Institute
(para. 7), as well as other authorities working in government laboratories. In addition, she uses one of the most effective rhetorical weapons:
the example. In her rundown of each kind of pesticide, she lists examples
of the effects on individuals who have used the pesticide or have been
in the same environment in which it was used. Her examples are concrete
and specific; some of them are shocking.*

*In addition to providing numerous specific examples, Carson refers
to research on the human body, demonstrating that even small amounts
of toxic materials build up in the system and can prove harmful for
years after exposure. She points out that whether we like it or not,
whether we want it or not, we all carry toxic chemicals resulting from
the widespread use of pesticides in our bones and in our body tissues.
Until 1961, the world took little notice of this major problem; by the
mid-1990s, cleaning up the environment and protecting people from
the dangers of toxic chemicals had become a primary goal. It was Rachel
Carson who sounded the alarm in a way that helped bring about this
fundamental change in attitude.*

Elixirs of Death

For the first time in the history of the world, every human
being is now subjected to contact with dangerous chemicals, from
the moment of conception until death. In the less than two decades
of their use, the synthetic pesticides have been so thoroughly distributed throughout the animate and inanimate world that they occur
virtually everywhere. They have been recovered from most of the
major river systems and even from streams of groundwater flowing
unseen through the earth. Residues of these chemicals linger in soil
to which they may have been applied a dozen years before. They
have entered and lodged in the bodies of fish, birds, reptiles, and
domestic and wild animals so universally that scientists carrying on
animal experiments find it almost impossible to locate subjects free
from such contamination. They have been found in fish in remote
mountain lakes, in earthworms burrowing in soil, in the eggs of
birds—and in man himself. For these chemicals are now stored in
the bodies of the vast majority of human beings, regardless of age.
They occur in the mother's milk, and probably in the tissues of the
unborn child.

All this has come about because of the sudden rise and prodigious growth of an industry for the production of man-made or synthetic chemicals with insecticidal properties. This industry is a child of the Second World War. In the course of developing agents of chemical warfare, some of the chemicals created in the laboratory were found to be lethal to insects. The discovery did not come by chance: insects were widely used to test chemicals as agents of death for man.

The result has been a seemingly endless stream of synthetic insecticides. In being man-made—by ingenious laboratory manipulation of the molecules, substituting atoms, altering their arrangement—they differ sharply from the simpler inorganic insecticides of prewar days. These were derived from naturally occurring minerals and plant products—compounds of arsenic, copper, lead, manganese, zinc, and other minerals, pyrethrum from the dried flowers of chrysanthemums, nicotine sulphate from some of the relatives of tobacco, and rotenone from leguminous plants of the East Indies.

What sets the new synthetic insecticides apart is their enormous biological potency. They have immense power not merely to poison but to enter into the most vital processes of the body and change them in sinister and often deadly ways. Thus, as we shall see, they destroy the very enzymes whose function is to protect the body from harm, they block the oxidation processes from which the body receives its energy, they prevent the normal functioning of various organs, and they may initiate in certain cells the slow and irreversible change that leads to malignancy.

Yet new and more deadly chemicals are added to the list each year and new uses are devised so that contact with these materials has become practically worldwide. The production of synthetic pesticides in the United States soared from 124,259,000 pounds in 1947 to 637,666,000 pounds in 1960—more than a fivefold increase. The wholesale value of these products was well over a quarter of a billion dollars. But in the plans and hopes of the industry this enormous production is only a beginning.

A Who's Who of pesticides is therefore of concern to us all. If we are going to live so intimately with these chemicals—eating and drinking them, taking them into the very marrow of our bones— we had better know something about their nature and their power.

Although the Second World War marked a turning away from inorganic chemicals as pesticides into the wonder world of the carbon molecule, a few of the old materials persist. Chief among these is arsenic, which is still the basic ingredient in a variety of weed and insect killers. Arsenic is a highly toxic mineral occurring widely in association with the ores of various metals, and in very small amounts in volcanoes, in the sea, and in spring water. Its relations to man are varied and historic. Since many of its compounds are tasteless, it has been a favorite agent of homicide from long before the time of the Borgias to the present. Arsenic was the first recognized elementary carcinogen (or cancer-causing substance), identified in chimney soot and linked to cancer nearly two centuries ago by an English physician. Epidemics of chronic arsenical poisoning involving whole populations over long periods are on record. Arsenic-contaminated environments have also caused sickness and death among horses, cows, goats, pigs, deer, fishes, and bees; despite this record arsenical sprays and dusts are widely used. In the arsenic-sprayed cotton country of southern United States beekeeping as an industry has nearly died out. Farmers using arsenic dusts over long periods have been afflicted with chronic arsenic poisoning; livestock have been poisoned by crop sprays or weed killers containing arsenic. Drifting arsenic dusts from blueberry lands have spread over neighboring farms, contaminating streams, fatally poisoning bees and cows, and causing human illness. "It is scarcely possible . . . to handle arsenicals with more utter disregard of the general health than that which has been practiced in our country in recent years," said Dr. W. C. Hueper of the National Cancer Institute, an authority on environmental cancer. "Anyone who has watched the dusters and sprayers of arsenical insecticides at work must have been impressed by the almost supreme carelessness with which the poisonous substances are dispensed."

Modern insecticides are still more deadly. The vast majority 8 fall into one of two large groups of chemicals. One, represented by DDT, is known as the "chlorinated hydrocarbons." The other group consists of the organic phosphorus insecticides, and is represented by the reasonably familiar malathion and parathion. All have one thing in common. As mentioned above, they are built on a basis of carbon atoms, which are also the indispensable building blocks of the living world, and thus classed as "organic." To understand them, we must see of what they are made, and how, although linked with the basic chemistry of all life, they lend themselves to the modifications which make them agents of death.

The basic element, carbon, is one whose atoms have an almost infinite capacity for uniting with each other in chains and rings and various other configurations, and for becoming linked with atoms of other substances. Indeed, the incredible diversity of living creatures from bacteria to the great blue whale is largely due to this capacity of carbon. The complex protein molecule has the carbon atom as its basis, as have molecules of fat, carbohydrates, enzymes, and vitamins. So, too, have enormous numbers of nonliving things, for carbon is not necessarily a symbol of life.

Some organic compounds are simply combinations of carbon and hydrogen. The simplest of these is methane, or marsh gas, formed in nature by the bacterial decomposition of organic matter under water. Mixed with air in proper proportions, methane becomes the dreaded "fire damp" of coal mines. Its structure is beautifully simple, consisting of one carbon atom to which four hydrogen atoms have become attached:

H   H
 \\   /
    C
 /   \\
H   H

Chemists have discovered that it is possible to detach one or all of the hydrogen atoms and substitute other elements. For example, by substituting one atom of chlorine for one of hydrogen we produce methyl chloride:

Take away three hydrogen atoms and substitute chlorine and we have the anesthetic chloroform:

H   Cl
 \\   /
    C
 /   \\
Cl   Cl

Substitute chlorine atoms for all of the hydrogen atoms and the result is carbon tetrachloride, the familiar cleaning fluid:

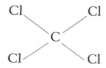

In the simplest possible terms, these changes rung upon the basic molecule of methane illustrate what a chlorinated hydrocarbon is. But this illustration gives little hint of the true complexity of the chemical world of the hydrocarbons, or of the manipulations by which the organic chemist creates his infinitely varied materials. For instead of the simple methane molecule with its single carbon atom, he may work with hydrocarbon molecules consisting of many carbon atoms, arranged in rings or chains, with side chains or branches, holding to themselves with chemical bonds not merely simple atoms of hydrogen or chlorine but also a wide variety of chemical groups. By seemingly slight changes the whole character of the substance is changed; for example, not only what is attached but the place of attachment to the carbon atom is highly important. Such ingenious manipulations have produced a battery of poisons of truly extraordinary power.

DDT (short for dichloro-diphenyl-trichloro-ethane) was first 12
synthesized by a German chemist in 1874, but its properties as an insecticide were not discovered until 1939. Almost immediately DDT was hailed as a means of stamping out insect-borne disease and winning the farmers' war against crop destroyers overnight. The discoverer, Paul Müller of Switzerland, won the Nobel Prize.

DDT is now so universally used that in most minds the product takes on the harmless aspect of the familiar. Perhaps the myth of the harmlessness of DDT rests on the fact that one of its first uses was the wartime dusting of many thousands of soldiers, refugees, and prisoners, to combat lice. It is widely believed that since so many people came into extremely intimate contact with DDT and suffered no immediate ill effects the chemical must certainly be innocent of harm. This understandable misconception arises from the fact that—unlike other chlorinated hydrocarbons—DDT *in powder form* not readily absorbed through the skin. Dissolved in oil, as it usually is, DDT is definitely toxic. If swallowed, it is absorbed slowly through the digestive tract; it may also be absorbed through the lungs. Once it has entered the body it is stored largely in organs rich in fatty substances (because DDT itself is fat-soluble) such as the adrenals, testes, or thyroid. Relatively large amounts are deposited in the liver, kidneys, and the fat of the large, protective mesenteries that enfold the intestines.

This storage of DDT begins with the smallest conceivable intake of the chemical (which is present as residues on most foodstuffs) and continues until quite high levels are reached. The fatty storage depots act as biological magnifiers, so that an intake of as little as $\frac{1}{10}$ of 1 part per million in the diet results in storage of about 10 to 15 parts per million, an increase of one hundredfold or more. These terms of reference, so commonplace to the chemist or the pharmacologist, are unfamiliar to most of us. One part in a million sounds like a very small amount—and so it is. But such substances are so potent that a minute quantity can bring about vast changes in the body. In animal experiments, 3 parts per million has been found to inhibit an essential enzyme in heart muscle; only 5 parts per million has brought about necrosis or disintegration of liver cells; only 2.5 parts per million of the closely related chemicals dieldrin and chlordane did the same.

This is really not surprising. In the normal chemistry of the human body there is just such a disparity between cause and effect. For example, a quantity of iodine as small as two ten-thousandths of a gram spells the difference between health and disease. Because these small amounts of pesticides are cumulatively stored and only slowly excreted, the threat of chronic poisoning and degenerative changes of the liver and other organs is very real.

Scientists do not agree upon how much DDT can be stored in 16 the human body. Dr. Arnold Lehman, who is the chief pharmacologist of the Food and Drug Administration, says there is neither a floor below which DDT is not absorbed nor a ceiling beyond which absorption and storage ceases. On the other hand, Dr. Wayland Hayes of the United States Public Health Service contends that in every individual a point of equilibrium is reached, and that DDT in excess of this amount is excreted. For practical purposes it is not particularly important which of these men is right. Storage in human beings has been well investigated, and we know that the average person is storing potentially harmful amounts. According to various studies, individuals with no known exposure (except the inevitable dietary one) store an average of 5.3 parts per million to 7.4 parts per million; agricultural workers 17.1 parts per million; and workers in insecticide plants as high as 648 parts per million! So the range of proven storage is quite wide and, what is even more to the point, the minimum figures are above the level at which damage to the liver and other organs or tissues may begin.

One of the most sinister features of DDT and related chemicals is the way they are passed on from one organism to another through all the links of the food chains. For example, fields of alfalfa are dusted with DDT; meal is later prepared from the alfalfa and fed to hens; the hens lay eggs which contain DDT. Or the hay, containing residues of 7 to 8 parts per million, may be fed to cows. The DDT will turn up in the milk in the amount of about 3 parts per million, but in butter made from this milk the concentration may run to 65 parts per million. Through such a process of transfer, what started out as a very small amount of DDT may end as a heavy concentration. Farmers nowadays find it difficult to obtain uncontaminated fodder for their milk cows, though the Food and Drug Administration forbids the presence of insecticide residues in milk shipped in interstate commerce.

The poison may also be passed on from mother to offspring.

Insecticide residues have been recovered from human milk in samples tested by Food and Drug Administration scientists. This means that the breast-fed human infant is receiving small but regular additions to the load of toxic chemicals building up in his body. It is by no means his first exposure, however: there is good reason to believe this begins while he is still in the womb. In experimental animals the chlorinated hydrocarbon insecticides freely cross the barrier of the placenta, the traditional protective shield between the embryo and harmful substances in the mother's body. While the quantities so received by human infants would normally be small, they are not unimportant because children are more susceptible to poisoning than adults. This situation also means that today the average individual almost certainly starts life with the first deposit of the growing load of chemicals his body will be required to carry thenceforth.

All these facts—storage at even low levels, subsequent accumulation, and occurrence of liver damage at levels that may easily occur in normal diets, caused Food and Drug Administration scientists to declare as early as 1950 that it is "extremely likely the potential hazard of DDT has been underestimated." There has been no such parallel situation in medical history. No one yet knows what the ultimate consequences may be.

Chlordane, another chlorinated hydrocarbon, has all these un-   20 pleasant attributes of DDT plus a few that are peculiarly its own. Its residues are long persistent in soil, on foodstuffs, or on surfaces to which it may be applied. Chlordane makes use of all available portals to enter the body. It may be absorbed through the skin, may be breathed in as a spray or dust, and of course is absorbed from the digestive tract if residues are swallowed. Like all other chlorinated hydrocarbons, its deposits build up in the body in cumulative fashion. A diet containing such a small amount of chlordane as 2.5 parts per million may eventually lead to storage of 75 parts per million of the fat of experimental animals.

So experienced a pharmacologist as Dr. Lehman has described chlordane in 1950 as "one of the most toxic of insecticides—anyone handling it could be poisoned." Judging by the carefree liberality with which dusts for lawn treatments by suburbanites are laced with chlordane, this warning has not been taken to heart. The fact that the suburbanite is not instantly stricken has little meaning, for the toxins may sleep long in his body, to become manifest months or years later in an obscure disorder almost impossible to trace to its origins. On the other hand, death may strike quickly. One victim who accidentally spilled a 25 percent industrial solution on the skin developed symptoms of poisoning within forty minutes and died before medical help could be obtained. No reliance can be placed on receiving advance warning which might allow treatment to be had in time.

Heptachlor, one of the constituents of chlordane, is marketed as a separate formulation. It has a particularly high capacity for storage in fat. If the diet contains as little as $1/10$ of 1 part per million there will be measurable amounts of heptachlor in the body. It also has the curious ability to undergo change into a chemically distinct substance known as heptachlor epoxide. It does this in soil and in the tissues of both plants and animals. Tests on birds indicate that the epoxide that results from this change is more toxic than the original chemical, which in turn is four times as toxic as chlordane.

As long ago as the mid-1930s a special group of hydrocarbons, the chlorinated naphthalenes, was found to cause hepatitis, and also a rare and almost invariably fatal liver disease in persons subjected to occupational exposure. They have led to illness and death of workers in electrical industries; and more recently, in agriculture, they have been considered a cause of a mysterious and usually fatal disease of cattle. In view of these antecedents, it is not surprising that three of the insecticides that are related to this group are among the most violently poisonous of all the hydrocarbons. These are dieldrin, aldrin, and endrin.

Dieldrin, named for a German chemist, Diels, is about 5 times as toxic as DDT when swallowed but 40 times as toxic when absorbed through the skin in solution. It is notorious for striking quickly, and with terrible effect at the nervous system, sending the victims into convulsions. Persons thus poisoned recover so slowly as to indicate chronic effects. As with other chlorinated hydrocarbons, these long-term effects include severe damage to the liver. The long duration of its residues and the effective insecticidal action make dieldrin one of the most used insecticides today, despite the appalling destruction of wildlife that has followed its use. As tested on quail and pheasants, it has proved to be about 40 to 50 times as toxic as DDT.

There are vast gaps in our knowledge of how dieldrin is stored or distributed in the body, or excreted, for the chemists' ingenuity in devising insecticides has long ago outrun biological knowledge of the way these poisons affect the living organism. However, there is every indication of long storage in the human body, where deposits may lie dormant like a slumbering volcano, only to flare up in periods of physiological stress when the body draws upon its

24

fat reserves. Much of what we do know has been learned through hard experience in the antimalarial campaigns carried out by the World Health Organization. As soon as dieldrin was substituted for DDT in malaria-control work (because the malaria mosquitoes had become resistant to DDT), cases of poisoning among the spraymen began to occur. The seizures were severe—from half to all (varying in the different programs) of the men affected went into convulsions and several died. Some had convulsions as long as *four months* after the last exposure.

Aldrin is a somewhat mysterious substance, for although it exists as a separate entity it bears the relation of alter ego to dieldrin. When carrots are taken from a bed treated with aldrin they are found to contain residues of dieldrin. This change occurs in living tissues and also in soil. Such alchemistic transformations have led to many erroneous reports, for if a chemist, knowing aldrin has been applied, tests for it he will be deceived into thinking all residues have been dissipated. The residues are there, but they are dieldrin and this requires a different test.

Like dieldrin, aldrin is extremely toxic. It produces degenerative changes in the liver and kidneys. A quantity the size of an aspirin tablet is enough to kill more than 400 quail. Many cases of human poisonings are on record, most of them in connection with industrial handling.

Aldrin, like most of this group of insecticides, projects a menacing shadow into the future, the shadow of sterility. Pheasants fed quantities too small to kill them nevertheless laid few eggs, and the chicks that hatched soon died. The effect is not confined to birds. Rats exposed to aldrin had fewer pregnancies and their young were sickly and short-lived. Puppies born of treated mothers died within three days. By one means or another, the new generations suffer for the poisoning of their parents. No one knows whether the same effect will be seen in human beings, yet this chemical has been sprayed from airplanes over suburban areas and farmlands. 28

Endrin is the most toxic of all the chlorinated hydrocarbons. Although chemically rather closely related to dieldrin, a little twist in its molecular structure makes it 5 times as poisonous. It makes the progenitor of all this group of insecticides, DDT, seem by comparison almost harmless. It is 15 times as poisonous as DDT to mammals, 30 times as poisonous to fish, and about 300 times as poisonous to some birds.

In the decade of its use, endrin has killed enormous numbers of fish, has fatally poisoned cattle that have wandered into sprayed orchards, has poisoned wells, and has drawn a sharp warning from at least one state health department that its careless use is endangering human lives.

In one of the most tragic cases of endrin poisoning there was no apparent carelessness; efforts had been made to take precautions apparently considered adequate. A year-old child had been taken by his American parents to live in Venezuela. There were cockroaches in the house to which they moved, and after a few days a spray containing endrin was used. The baby and the small family dog were taken out of the house before the spraying was done about nine o'clock one morning. After the spraying the floors were washed. The baby and dog were returned to the house in midafternoon. An hour or so later the dog vomited, went into convulsions, and died. At 10 P.M. on the evening of the same day the baby also vomited, went into convulsions, and lost consciousness. After that fateful contact with endrin, this normal, healthy child became little more than a vegetable—unable to see or hear, subject to frequent muscular spasms, apparently completely cut off from contact with his surroundings. Several months of treatment in a New York hospital failed to change his condition or bring hope of change. "It is extremely doubtful," reported the attending physicians, "that any useful degree of recovery will occur."

The second major group of insecticides, the alkyl or organic 32 phosphates, are among the most poisonous chemicals in the world. The chief and most obvious hazard attending their use is that of acute poisoning of people applying the sprays or accidentally coming in contact with drifting spray, with vegetation coated by it, or with a discarded container. In Florida, two children found an empty bag and used it to repair a swing. Shortly thereafter both of them died and three of their playmates became ill. The bag had once contained an insecticide called parathion, one of the organic phosphates; tests established death by parathion poisoning. On another occasion two small boys in Wisconsin, cousins, died on the same night. One had been playing in his yard when spray drifted in from an adjoining field where his father was spraying potatoes with parathion; the other had run playfully into the barn after his father and had put his hand on the nozzle of the spray equipment.

The origin of these insecticides has a certain ironic significance. Although some of the chemicals themselves—organic esters of phosphoric acid—had been known for many years, their insecticidal properties remained to be discovered by a German chemist, Gerhard Schrader, in the late 1930s. Almost immediately the German government recognized the value of these same chemicals as new and devastating weapons in man's war against his own kind, and the work on them was declared secret. Some became the deadly nerve gases. Others, of closely allied structure, became insecticides.

The organic phosphorus insecticides act on the living organism in a peculiar way. They have the ability to destroy enzymes—enzymes that perform necessary functions in the body. Their target is the nervous system, whether the victim is an insect or a warm-blooded animal. Under normal conditions, an impulse passes from nerve to nerve with the aid of a "chemical transmitter" called acetylcholine, a substance that performs an essential function and then disappears. Indeed, its existence is so ephemeral that medical researchers are unable, without special procedures, to sample it before the body has destroyed it. This transient nature of the transmitting chemical is necessary to the normal functioning of the body. If the acetylcholine is not destroyed as soon as a nerve impulse has passed, impulses continue to flash across the bridge from nerve to nerve, as the chemical exerts its effects in an ever more intensified manner. The movements of the whole body become uncoordinated: tremors, muscular spasms, convulsions, and death quickly result.

This contingency has been provided for by the body. A protective enzyme called cholinesterase is at hand to destroy the transmitting chemical once it is no longer needed. By this means a precise balance is struck and the body never builds up a dangerous amount of acetylcholine. But on contact with the organic phosphorus insecticides, the protective enzyme is destroyed, and as the quantity of the enzyme is reduced that of the transmitting chemical builds up. In this effect, the organic phosphorus compounds resemble the alkaloid poison muscarine, found in a poisonous mushroom, the fly amanita.

Repeated exposures may lower the cholinesterase level until   36
an individual reaches the brink of acute poisoning, a brink over which he may be pushed by a very small additional exposure. For this reason it is considered important to make periodic examinations of the blood of spray operators and others regularly exposed.

Parathion is one of the most widely used of the organic phosphates. It is also one of the most powerful and dangerous. Honeybees become "wildly agitated and bellicose" on contact with it, perform frantic cleaning movements, and are near death within half an hour. A chemist, thinking to learn by the most direct possible means the dose acutely toxic to human beings, swallowed a minute amount, equivalent to about .00424 ounce.

Paralysis followed so instantaneously that he could not reach the antidotes he had prepared at hand, and so he died. Parathion is now said to be a favorite instrument of suicide in Finland. In recent years the State of California has reported an average of more than 200 cases of accidental parathion poisoning annually. In many parts of the world the fatality rate from parathion is startling: 100 fatal cases in India and 67 in Syria in 1958, and an average of 336 deaths per year in Japan.

Yet some 7,000,000 pounds of parathion are now applied to fields and orchards of the United States—by hand sprayers, motorized blowers and dusters, and by airplane. The amount used on California farms alone could, according to one medical authority, "provide a lethal dose for 5 to 10 times the whole world's population."

One of the few circumstances that save us from extinction by this means is the fact that parathion and other chemicals of this group are decomposed rather rapidly. Their residues on the crops to which they are applied are therefore relatively short-lived compared with the chlorinated hydrocarbons. However, they last long enough to create hazards and produce consequences that range from the merely serious to the fatal. In Riverside, California, eleven out of thirty men picking oranges became violently ill and all but one had to be hospitalized. Their symptoms were typical of parathion poisoning. The grove had been sprayed with parathion some two and a half weeks earlier; the residues that reduced them to retching, half-blind, semiconscious misery were sixteen to nineteen days old. And this is not by any means a record for persistence. Similar mishaps have occurred in groves sprayed a month earlier, and residues have been found in the peel of oranges six months after treatment with standard dosages.

The danger to all workers applying the organic phosphorus   40 insecticides in fields, orchards, and vineyards, is so extreme that some states using these chemicals have established laboratories where physicians may obtain aid in diagnosis and treatment. Even the physicians themselves may be in some danger, unless they wear rubber gloves in handling the victims of poisoning. So may a laundress washing the clothing of such victims, which may have absorbed enough parathion to affect her.

Malathion, another of the organic phosphates, is almost as familiar to the public as DDT, being widely used by gardeners, in household insecticides, in mosquito spraying, and in such blanket attacks on insects as the spraying of nearly a million acres of Florida communities for the Mediterranean fruit fly. It is considered the least toxic of this group of chemicals and many people assume they may use it freely and without fear of harm. Commercial advertising encourages this comfortable attitude.

The alleged "safety" of malathion rests on rather precarious ground, although—as often happens—this was not discovered until the chemical had been in use for several years. Malathion is "safe" only because the mammalian liver, an organ with extraordinary protective powers, renders it relatively harmless. The detoxification is accomplished by one of the enzymes of the liver. If, however, something destroys this enzyme or interferes with its action, the person exposed to malathion receives the full force of the poison.

Unfortunately for all of us, opportunities for this sort of thing to happen are legion. A few years ago a team of Food and Drug Administration scientists discovered that when malathion and certain other organic phosphates are administered simultaneously a massive poisoning results—up to 50 times as severe as would be predicted on the basis of adding together the toxicities of the two. In other words, $\frac{1}{100}$ of the lethal dose of each compound may be fatal when the two are combined.

This discovery led to the testing of other combinations. It is now known that many pairs of organic phosphate insecticides are highly dangerous, the toxicity being stepped up or "potentiated" through the combined action. Potentiation seems to take place when one compound destroys the liver enzyme responsible for detoxifying the other. The two need not be given simultaneously. The hazard exists not only for the man who may spray this week with one insecticide and next week with another; it exists also for the consumer of sprayed products. The common salad bowl may easily present a combination of organic phosphate insecticides. Residues well within the legally permissible limits may interact.

The full scope of the dangerous interaction of chemicals is as yet little known, but disturbing findings now come regularly from scientific laboratories. Among these is the discovery that the toxicity of an organic phosphate can be increased by a second agent that is not necessarily an insecticide. For example, one of the plasticizing agents may act even more strongly than another insecticide to make malathion more dangerous. Again, this is because it inhibits the liver enzyme that normally would "draw the teeth" of the poisonous insecticide.

What of other chemicals in the normal human environment? What, in particular, of drugs? A bare beginning has been made on this subject, but already it is known that some organic phosphates

44

(parathion and malathion) increase the toxicity of some drugs used as muscle relaxants, and that several others (again including malathion) markedly increase the sleeping time of barbiturates.

In Greek mythology the sorceress Medea, enraged at being supplanted by a rival for the affections of her husband Jason, presented the new bride with a robe possessing magic properties. The wearer of the robe immediately suffered a violent death. This death-by-indirection now finds its counterpart in what are known as "systemic insecticides." These are chemicals with extraordinary properties which are used to convert plants or animals into a sort of Medea's robe by making them actually poisonous. This is done with the purpose of killing insects that may come in contact with them, especially by sucking their juices or blood.

The world of systemic insecticides is a weird world, surpassing the imaginings of the brothers Grimm—perhaps most closely akin to the cartoon world of Charles Addams. It is a world where the enchanted forest of the fairy tales has become the poisonous forest in which an insect that chews a leaf or sucks the sap of a plant is doomed. It is a world where a flea bites a dog and dies because the dog's blood has been made poisonous, where an insect may die from vapors emanating from a plant it has never touched, where a bee may carry poisonous nectar, back to its hive and presently produce poisonous honey. 48

The entomologists' dream of the built-in insecticide was born when workers in the field of applied entomology realized they could take a hint from nature: they found that wheat growing in soil containing sodium selenate was immune to attack by aphids or spider mites. Selenium, a naturally occurring element found sparingly in rocks and soils of many parts of the world, thus became the first systemic insecticide.

What makes an insecticide a systemic is the ability to permeate all the tissues of a plant or animal and make them toxic. This quality is possessed by some chemicals of the chlorinated hydrocarbon group and by others of the organophosphorus group, all synthetically produced, as well as by certain naturally occurring substances. In practice, however, most systemics are drawn from the organophosphorus group because the problem of residues is somewhat less acute.

Systemics act in other devious ways. Applied to seeds, either by soaking or in a coating combined with carbon, they extend their effects into the following plant generation and produce seedlings poisonous to aphids and other sucking insects. Vegetables such as peas, beans, and sugar beets are sometimes thus protected. Cotton seeds coated with a systemic insecticide have been in use for some time in California, where twenty-five farm laborers planting cotton in the San Joaquin Valley in 1959 were seized with sudden illness, caused by handling the bags of treated seeds.

In England someone wondered what happened when bees made 52 use of nectar from plants treated with systemics. This was investigated in areas treated with a chemical called schradan. Although the plants had been sprayed before the flowers were formed, the nectar later produced contained the poison. The result, as might have been predicted, was that the honey made by the bees also was contaminated with schradan.

Use of animal systemics has concentrated chiefly on control of the cattle grub, a damaging parasite of livestock. Extreme care must be used in order to create an insecticidal effect in the blood and tissues of the host without setting up a fatal poisoning. The balance is delicate and government veterinarians have found that repeated small doses can gradually deplete an animal's supply of the protective enzyme cholinesterase, so that without warning a minute additional dose will cause poisoning.

There are strong indications that fields closer to our daily lives are being opened up. You may now give your dog a pill which, it is claimed, will rid him of fleas by making his blood poisonous to them. The hazards discovered in treating cattle would presumably apply to the dog. As yet no one seems to have proposed a human systemic that would make us lethal to a mosquito. Perhaps this is the next step.

So far . . . we have been discussing the deadly chemicals that are being used in our war against the insects. What of our simultaneous war against the weeds?

The desire for a quick and easy method of killing unwanted 56 plants has given rise to a large and growing array of chemicals that are known as herbicides, or, less formally, as weed killers. The . . . question that here concerns us is whether the weed killers are poisons and whether their use is contributing to the poisoning of the environment.

The legend that the herbicides are toxic only to plants and so pose no threat to animal life has been widely disseminated, but unfortunately it is not true. The plant killers include a large variety of chemicals that act on animal tissue as well as on vegetation. They vary greatly in their action on the organism. Some are general poisons, some are powerful stimulants of metabolism, causing a fatal rise in body temperature, some induce malignant tumors either alone or in partnership with other chemicals, some strike at the genetic material of the race by causing gene mutations. The herbicides, then, like the insecticides, include some very dangerous chemicals, and their careless use in the belief that they are "safe" can have disastrous results.

Despite the competition of a constant stream of new chemicals issuing from the laboratories, arsenic compounds are still liberally used, both as insecticides (as mentioned above) and as weed killers, where they usually take the chemical form of sodium arsenite. The history of their use is not reassuring. As roadside sprays, they have cost many a farmer his cow and killed uncounted numbers of wild creatures. As aquatic weed killers in lakes and reservoirs they have made public waters unsuitable for drinking or even for swimming. As a spray applied to potato fields to destroy the vines they have taken a toll of human and nonhuman life.

In England this latter practice developed about 1951 as a result of a shortage of sulfuric acid, formerly used to burn off the potato vines. The Ministry of Agriculture considered it necessary to give warning of the hazard of going into the arsenic-sprayed fields, but the warning was not understood by the cattle (nor, we must assume, by the wild animals and birds) and reports of cattle poisoned by the arsenic sprays came with monotonous regularity. When death came also to a farmer's wife through arsenic-contaminated water, one of the major English chemical companies (in 1959) stopped production of arsenical sprays and called in supplies already in the hands of dealers, and shortly thereafter the Ministry of Agriculture announced that because of high risks to people and cattle restrictions on the use of arsenites would be imposed. In 1961, the Australian government announced a similar ban. No such restrictions impede the use of these poisons in the United States, however.

Some of the "dinitro" compounds are also used as herbicides. 60 They are rated as among the most dangerous materials of this type in use in the United States. Dinitrophenol is a strong metabolic stimulant. For this reason it was at one time used as a reducing drug, but the margin between the slimming dose and that required to poison or kill was slight—so slight that several patients died and many suffered permanent injury before use of the drug was finally halted.

A related chemical, pentachlorophenol, sometimes known as "penta," is used as a weed killer as well as an insecticide, often being sprayed along railroad tracks and in waste areas. Penta is extremely toxic to a wide variety of organisms from bacteria to man. Like the dinitros, it interferes, often fatally, with the body's source of energy, so that the affected organism almost literally burns itself up. Its fearful power is illustrated in a fatal accident recently reported by the California Department of Health. A tank truck driver was preparing a cotton defoliant by mixing diesel oil with pentachlorophenol. As he was drawing the concentrated chemical out of a drum, the spigot accidentally toppled back. He reached in with his bare hand to regain the spigot. Although he washed immediately, he became acutely ill and died the next day.

While the results of weed killers such as sodium arsenite or the phenols are grossly obvious, some other herbicides are more insidious in their effects. For example, the now famous cranberry-weed-killer aminotriazole, or amitrol, is rated as having relatively low toxicity. But in the long run its tendency to cause malignant tumors of the thyroid may be far more significant for wildlife and perhaps also for man.

Among the herbicides are some that are classified as "mutagens," or agents capable of modifying the genes, the materials of heredity. We are rightly appalled by the genetic effects of radiation; how then, can we be indifferent to the same effect in chemicals that we disseminate widely in our environment?

QUESTIONS FOR CRITICAL READING

1. Why are the "new synthetic insecticides" dangerous?
2. How does the human body react to new synthetic insecticides?
3. According to Carson, what quantities of pesticides are used in the United States?
4. What is the path of transmission of most pesticides from the field to human beings?
5. How does the body help fight against poisons such as the organic phosphorus insecticides?
6. Are you personally aware of any widespread use of pesticides? If so, what do you know about their results?
7. What pesticides do you regularly use at home? What chemical categories do they belong to? Do you know of any harmful effects from their use?

WRITING ASSIGNMENTS

1. Review the essay for examples of death or illness resulting from exposure to insecticides. How many examples are given in all? Is there one

for each kind of insecticide? Once you have collected them, assess each example's effectiveness in helping to convince you that pesticides are dangerous. Did you begin reading the essay thinking they were generally harmless, or were you already convinced of their danger? How has your attitude or behavior regarding these compounds been affected by Carson's essay?

2. Parathion and malathion are commonly used in suburban settings for lawn and garden control. Find out what kind of sprays are permitted in your community by contacting your town or city hall and asking to speak with someone in charge of environmental protection. Find out what precautions are called for in your community and ask whether or not there have been recent infractions. What have been the penalties for infractions?

3. Among your close acquaintances, do you notice a widespread difference in attitude toward the environment and its protection, or do most agree with your thinking? Do you perceive a difference of attitude in people older than you? In those younger than you? Do you feel the nation has come to appreciate fully the damage caused by spraying the kinds of insecticides Carson describes?

4. Using the *Readers' Guide to Periodical Literature* for the years 1962–1970, search for articles responding to Carson's alarm regarding the use of insecticides. Look under "Carson, Rachel" as well as "insecticide use," "DDT," "parathion," "malathion," and "crop spraying." Can you detect a change of attitude and behavior as a result of Carson's work? You may also find it useful to search the index of the *New York Times* or a local major newspaper for the same time period.

5. Do you accept the argument that the use of DDT and other powerful insecticides has made it possible for a small number of farmers to feed the world? The economic value of pesticides shows up in cheap grains, cereals, poultry, and meats. In the 1950s some experts were predicting widespread famine by the late 1970s or early 1980s. Yet no such famine has occurred. One reason is that pesticides have helped increase crop yield. Do you think restricting the use of pesticides could lead to famine? How do you balance the rewards of pesticides with their risks?

6. What is the current view of the Environmental Protection Agency regarding the use of pesticides? Consult the index of a major newspaper for recent articles and examine their content in light of Carson's essay. Do contemporary articles seem as enlightened about the use of pesticides as Carson would want them to be? Have contemporary attitudes eased up regarding insecticides?

7. **CONNECTIONS**   Examine the circumstances that confronted Carson when she began to study the use of pesticides. Would Thomas Kuhn describe the work that Carson did as upsetting the current paradigm concerning the safety and use of pesticides? Did she rely on anomalies in order to begin replacing the old paradigm with a new one? Examine Carson's work carefully in light of what Kuhn

says about the way scientific paradigms are replaced and the resistance that usually accompanies that event.

8. **CONNECTIONS**   Examine the Declaration of Independence in relation to Carson's warnings regarding the use of pesticides. What serious political issues are raised in Carson's discussion of how widespread use of pesticides was permitted before anyone truly understood their properties? What should politicians learn about technological advancements and their applications in the public sector? Whose independence is most in question in Carson's essay: the scientific business establishment's or the individual's?

THOMAS S. KUHN

Anomaly and the Emergence
of Scientific Discoveries

THOMAS S. KUHN (b. 1922) began his career as a research physicist but soon switched his focus to the history of science. His contributions
in that field have been striking and original. The Structure of Scientific Revolutions (1962; 1970; 2nd ed. 1964, 1982), from which
the following essay is taken, was a landmark in the history of science
because it established the patterns of progress in scientific thought. The
Copernican Revolution: Planetary Astronomy in the Development of Western Thought (1957), examines the effects of the Copernican scientific revolution; The Essential Tension: Selected Studies
in Scientific Tradition and Change (1977), a book of essays, looks
at our current scientific education.

Originally, The Structure of Scientific Revolutions was published as Volume 2 of the International Encyclopedia of Unified
Science (1962). Consequently, some of the demands for compression
expected in an encyclopedia are reflected in the essay presented here.
The work had its beginnings in a series of lectures, then grew in a
series of interactions with social scientists and natural scientists until
Kuhn began to regard his problems from a variety of perspectives. In
the preface he records some of his surprises in dealing with scientists
from other disciplines.

One of the most important insights Kuhn developed was the concept
of the scientific paradigm. The current widespread use of the word in
many intellectual areas can be traced back to The Structure of Scientific Revolutions. A paradigm is a pattern of thought built around
theory and expectation. Science works in terms of paradigms—accepted
beliefs—and, as Kuhn points out, normal science concentrates on exploring those beliefs and enlarging our understanding of them. But science
also develops in terms of one paradigm replacing another. For example,

for most biologists, the Darwinian paradigm of evolution has replaced an older paradigm that insisted on individual creation of species. In this case, we may underscore the word "most," since the Darwinian paradigm is seen as contradicting some religious views, and consequently some scientists reject it. Christopher Columbus is said to have accepted the paradigm of the flat earth, but, pressing westward, he began the investigations that utterly shattered that paradigm and replaced it with the paradigm of the round earth.

Paradigms are the accepted ways of thinking. Every scientist proceeds from a base of an accepted way of thought. Establishing from the outset that normal science aims to fill in particulars and extend our understanding of specific theories, Kuhn explains that clear, well-understood paradigms do not hinder discovery. Instead, they aid it by permitting the scientist to see the anomaly—the unexpected, unexplained exception to the paradigm's rules—more clearly. Anomalies are unexpected simply because they do not fit into the already established patterns of scientific thought. Scientific discoveries begin, explains Kuhn, with the observation of an anomaly and the efforts to explain it.

Kuhn uses several examples to show that discovery is a complicated concept. Oxygen, for example, was discovered by several people around the same time, but it is not entirely clear who discovered it first. Some chemists had isolated it not knowing what it was, only that it was something they did not expect. At that time gaseous elements such as nitrogen, oxygen, and hydrogen were unknown. Scientists had isolated some of them, but were quite unaware of what they had done.

Researches in chemistry were in such a state that the explanation of how combustion occurred demanded extraordinary ingenuity: the invention of an unseen, unexamined, imaginary element called phlogiston. Essentially, phlogiston was thought to be released in combustion, making fire possible. The paradigm of phlogiston chemistry was then replaced by the paradigm of oxygen chemistry—but only after nitrogen and oxygen had been "discovered" simultaneously by several scientists who were unaware of what they had found. Once discovered, the role of oxygen—in rapid oxidation—in fire was understood, and phlogiston chemistry was dead.

KUHN'S RHETORIC

Because this was originally an entry in an encyclopedia, the essay is dense and economical in style. The prose has a sense of urgency. In paragraph 2, Kuhn points to his technique: "examining selected discoveries" in order to show how scientific discoveries have been made. He chooses three examples. The first concerns the discovery of oxygen (paras. 3–6). The chemist Lavoisier, he explains, did not so much discover oxygen as "the oxygen theory of combustion." Because it replaced the existing paradigm, this example is exceptionally important. The second example concerns the discovery of X-rays (paras. 7–8) and the third the discovery of the Leyden jar (paras. 13–14), which, coated inside and out with tinfoil, acts as a condenser for temporary storage of an electrostatic charge.

Kuhn reminds us that although these three examples seem different on the surface, they share important qualities. For one, they were discoveries made while in pursuit of "normal science"—confirmation of existing theories—operating within the established paradigm of the moment. The anomalies that arose from the methods of normal science gave rise to examination that produced not only new knowledge but new paradigms of thought.

Kuhn summarizes the process of scientific discovery when he explains what the three examples have in common: "the previous awareness of anomaly, the gradual and simultaneous emergence of both observational and conceptual recognition, and the consequent change of paradigm categories and procedures often accompanied by resistance" (para. 15). The resistance is, naturally, a resistance to change. Both Priestley and Lavoisier found it impossible to change some of their thinking concerning their discoveries of oxygen, because they were thoroughly committed to a given paradigm and could not quickly replace it. Kuhn reminds us that paradigms are of inestimable value to the scientist, but that they also make it difficult for scientists to accept the discoveries they have made.

Anomaly and the Emergence
of Scientific Discoveries

Normal science . . . is a highly cumulative enterprise, eminently successful in its aim, the steady extension of the scope and precision of scientific knowledge. In all these respects it fits with great precision the most usual image of scientific work. Yet one standard product of the scientific enterprise is missing. Normal science does not aim at novelties of fact or theory and, when successful, finds none. New and unsuspected phenomena are, however, repeatedly uncovered by scientific research, and radical new theories have again and again been invented by scientists. History even suggests that the scientific enterprise has developed a uniquely pow-

erful technique for producing surprises of this sort. If this characteristic of science is to be reconciled with what has already been said,
then research under a paradigm[1] must be a particularly effective way
of inducing paradigm change. That is what fundamental novelties of
fact and theory do. Produced inadvertently by a game played under
one set of rules, their assimilation requires the elaboration of another
set. After they have become parts of science, the enterprise, at least
of those specialists in whose particular field the novelties lie, is
never quite the same again.

We must now ask how changes of this sort can come about,
considering first discoveries, or novelties of fact, and then inventions, or novelties of theory. That distinction between discovery
and invention or between fact and theory will, however, immediately prove to be exceedingly artificial. Its artificiality is an important
clue to several of this essay's main theses. Examining selected discoveries in the rest of this section, we shall quickly find that they are
not isolated events but extended episodes with a regularly recurrent
structure. Discovery commences with the awareness of anomaly,
i.e., with the recognition that nature has somehow violated the
paradigm-induced expectations that govern normal science. It then
continues with a more or less extended exploration of the area of
anomaly. And it closes only when the paradigm theory has been
adjusted so that the anomalous has become the expected. Assimilat-
ing a new sort of fact demands a more than addictive adjustment
of theory, and until that adjustment is completed—until the scientist
has learned to see nature in a different way—the new fact is not
quite a scientific fact at all.

To see how closely factual and theoretical novelty are intertwined in scientific discovery examine a particularly famous example, the discovery of oxygen. At least three different men have a
legitimate claim to it, and several other chemists must, in the early
1770s, have had enriched air in a laboratory vessel without knowing
it.[2] The progress of normal science, in this case of pneumatic chemistry, prepared the way to a breakthrough quite thoroughly. The
earliest of the claimants to prepare a relatively pure sample of the

---

[1]*paradigm*   See introduction to Kuhn, pp. 441–443.
[2]For the still classic discussion of oxygen's discovery, see A. N. Meldrum, *The
Eighteenth-Century Revolution in Science—the First Phase* (Calcutta, 1930), chap. v.
An indispensable recent review, including an account of the priority controversy,
is Maurice Daumas, *Lavoisier, théoricien et expérimentateur* (Paris, 1955), chaps. ii–iii.
For a fuller account and bibliography, see also T. S. Kuhn, "The Historical Structure
of Scientific Discovery," *Science*, CXXXVI (June 1, 1962), pp. 760–764. [Kuhn's
note]

gas was the Swedish apothecary, C. W. Scheele.[3] We may, however, ignore his work since it was not published until oxygen's discovery had repeatedly been announced elsewhere and thus had no effect upon the historical pattern that most concerns us here.[4] The second in time to establish a claim was the British scientist and divine, Joseph Priestley,[5] who collected the gas released by heated red oxide of mercury as one item in a prolonged normal investigation of the "airs" evolved by a large number of solid substances. In 1774 he identified the gas thus produced as nitrous oxide and in 1775, led by further tests, as common air with less than its usual quantity of phlogiston.[6] The third claimant, Lavoisier,[7] started the work that led him to oxygen after Priestley's experiments of 1774 and possibly as the result of a hint from Priestley. Early in 1775 Lavoisier reported that the gas obtained by heating the red oxide of mercury was "air itself entire without alteration [except that] . . . it comes out more pure, more respirable."[8] By 1777, probably with the assistance of a second hint from Priestley, Lavoisier had concluded that the gas was a distinct species, one of the two main constituents of the atmosphere, a conclusion that Priestley was never able to accept.

This pattern of discovery raises a question that can be asked about every novel phenomenon that has ever entered the consciousness of scientists. Was it Priestley or Lavoisier, if either, who first discovered oxygen? In any case, when was oxygen discovered? In that form the question could be asked even if only one claimant had existed. As a ruling about priority and date, an answer does not at all concern us. Nevertheless, an attempt to produce one will illuminate the nature of discovery, because there is no answer of the kind that is sought. Discovery is not the sort of process about which the question is appropriately asked. The fact that it is asked— the priority for oxygen has repeatedly been contested since the 1780s—is a symptom of something askew in the image of science that gives discovery so fundamental a role. Look once more at our

4

---

[3]*C. W. Scheele (1742–1786)*   Swedish chemist.

[4]See, however, Uno Bocklund, "A lost Letter from Scheele to Lavoisier," *Lychnos,* 1957–1958, pp. 39–62, for a different evaluation of Scheele's role. [Kuhn's note]

[5]*Joseph Priestley (1733–1804)*   English theologian and scientist.

[6]*phlogiston*   See introduction to Kuhn, p. 442.

[7]*Antoine Lavoisier (1743–1794)*   French chemist and physicist.

[8]J. B. Conant, *The Overthrow of the Phlogiston Theory: The Chemical Revolution of 1775–1789* ("Harvard Case Histories in Experimental Science," Case 2; Cambridge, Mass., 1950), p. 23. This very useful pamphlet reprints many of the relevant documents. [Kuhn's note]

example. Priestley's claim to the discovery of oxygen is based upon his priority in isolating a gas that was later recognized as a distinct species. But Priestley's sample was not pure, and, if holding impure oxygen in one's hands is to discover it, that had been done by everyone who ever bottled atmospheric air. Besides, if Priestley was the discoverer, when was the discovery made? In 1774 he thought he had obtained nitrous oxide, a species he already knew; in 1775 he saw the gas as dephlogisticated air, which is still not oxygen or even, for phlogistic chemists, a quite unexpected sort of gas. Lavoisier's claim may be stronger, but it presents the same problems. If we refuse the palm to Priestley, we cannot award it to Lavoisier for the work of 1775 which led him to identify the gas as the "air itself entire." Presumably we wait for the work of 1776 and 1777 which led Lavoisier to see not merely the gas but what the gas was. Yet even this award could be questioned, for in 1777 and to the end of his life Lavoisier insisted that oxygen was an atomic "principle of acidity" and that oxygen gas was formed only when that "principle" united with caloric, the matter of heat.[9] Shall we therefore say that oxygen had not yet been discovered in 1777? Some may be tempted to do so. But the principle of acidity was not banished from chemistry until after 1810, and caloric lingered until the 1860s. Oxygen had become a standard chemical substance before either of those dates.

Clearly we need a new vocabulary and concepts for analyzing events like the discovery of oxygen. Though undoubtedly correct, the sentence, "Oxygen was discovered," misleads by suggesting that discovering something is a single simple act assimilable to our usual (and also questionable) concept of seeing. That is why we so readily assume that discovering, like seeing or touching, should be unequivocally attributable to an individual and to a moment in time. But the latter attribution is always impossible, and the former often is as well. Ignoring Scheele, we can safely say that oxygen had not been discovered before 1774, and we would probably also say that it had been discovered by 1777 or shortly thereafter. But within those limits or others like them, any attempt to date the discovery must inevitably be arbitrary because discovering a new sort of phenomenon is necessarily a complex event, one which involves recognizing both *that* something is and *what* it is. Note, for example, that if oxygen were dephlogisticated air for us, we should insist without hesitation that Priestley had discovered it,

---

[9]H. Metzger, *La philosophie de la matière chez Lavoisier* (Paris, 1935); and Daumas, op. cit., chap. vii. [Kuhn's note]

though we would still not know quite when. But if both observation and conceptualization, fact and assimilation to theory, are inseparably linked in discovery, then discovery is a process and must take time. Only when all the relevant conceptual categories are prepared in advance, in which case the phenomenon would not be of a new sort, can discovering *that* and discovering *what* occur effortlessly, together, and in an instant.

Grant now that discovery involves an extended, though not necessarily long, process of conceptual assimilation. Can we also say that it involves a change in paradigm? To that question, no general answer can yet be given, but in this case at least, the answer must be yes. What Lavoisier announced in his papers from 1777 on was not so much the discovery of oxygen as the oxygen theory of combustion. That theory was the keystone for a reformulation of chemistry so vast that it is usually called the chemical revolution. Indeed, if the discovery of oxygen had not been an intimate part of the emergence of a new paradigm for chemistry, the question of priority from which we began would never have seemed so important. In this case as in others, the value placed upon a new phenomenon and thus upon its discoverer varies with our estimate of the extent to which the phenomenon violated paradigm-induced anticipations. Notice, however, since it will be important later, that the discovery of oxygen was not by itself the cause of the change in chemical theory. Long before he played any part in the discovery of the new gas, Lavoisier was convinced both that something was wrong with the phlogiston theory and that burning bodies absorbed some part of the atmosphere. That much he had recorded in a sealed note deposited with the Secretary of the French Academy in 1772.[10] What the work on oxygen did was to give much additional form and structure to Lavoisier's earlier sense that something was amiss. It told him a thing he was already prepared to discover—the nature of the substance that combustion removes from the atmosphere. That advance awareness of difficulties must be a significant part of what enabled Lavoisier to see in experiments like Priestley's a gas that Priestley had been unable to see there himself. Conversely, the fact that a major paradigm revision was needed to see what Lavoisier saw must be the principal reason why Priestley was, to the end of his long life, unable to see it.

Two other and far briefer examples will reinforce much that has just been said and simultaneously carry us from an elucidation

---

[10]The most authoritative account of the origin of Lavoisier's discontent is Henry Guerlac, *Lavoisier—the Crucial Year: The Background and Origin of His First Experiments on Combustion in 1772* (Ithaca, N.Y., 1961). [Kuhn's note]

of the nature of discoveries toward an understanding of the circumstances under which they emerge in science. In an effort to represent
the main ways in which discoveries can come about, these examples
are chosen to be different both from each other and from the discovery of oxygen. The first, X-rays, is a classic case of discovery
through accident, a type that occurs more frequently than the imper-
sonal standards of scientific reporting allow us easily to realize. Its
story opens on the day that the physicist Roentgen interrupted a
normal investigation of cathode rays because he had noticed that a
barium platinocyanide screen at some distance from his shielded
apparatus glowed when the discharge was in process. Further investigations—they required seven hectic weeks during which Roentgen
rarely left the laboratory—indicated that the cause of the glow came
in straight lines from the cathode ray tube, that the radiation cast
shadows, could not be deflected by a magnet, and much else besides.
Before announcing his discovery, Roentgen had convinced himself
that his effect was not due to cathode rays but to an agent with at
least some similarity to light.[11]

Even so brief an epitome reveals striking resemblances to the
discovery of oxygen: before experimenting with red oxide of mercury, Lavoisier had performed experiments that did not produce
the results anticipated under the phlogiston paradigm; Roentgen's
discovery commenced with the recognition that his screen glowed
when it should not. In both cases the perception of anomaly—of a
phenomenon, that is, for which his paradigm had not readied the
investigator—played an essential role in preparing the way for perception of novelty. But, again in both cases, the perception that
something had gone wrong was only the prelude to discovery.
Neither oxygen nor X-rays emerged without a further process
of experimentation and assimilation. At what point in Roentgen's
investigation, for example, ought we say that X-rays had actually
been discovered? Not, in any case, at the first instant, when all that
had been noted was a glowing screen. At least one other investigator
had seen that glow and, to his subsequent chagrin, discovered nothing at all.[12] Nor, it is almost as clear, can the moment of discovery
be pushed forward to a point during the last week of investigation,
by which time Roentgen was exploring the properties of the new

8

---

[11]L. W. Taylor, *Physics, the Pioneer Science* (Boston, 1941), pp. 790–794; and
T. W. Chalmers, *Historic Researches* (London, 1949), pp. 218–219. [Kuhn's note]

[12]E. T. Whittaker, *A History of the Theories of Aether and Electricity*, I (2nd ed.;
London, 1951), p. 358, n. 1. Sir George Thomson has informed me of a second
near miss. Alerted by unaccountably fogged photographic plates, Sir William
Crookes was also on the track of the discovery. [Kuhn's note]

radiation he had *already* discovered. We can only say that X-rays emerged in Würzburg between November 8 and December 28, 1895.

In a third area, however, the existence of significant parallels between the discoveries of oxygen and of X-rays is far less apparent. Unlike the discovery of oxygen, that of X-rays was not, at least for a decade after the event, implicated in any obvious upheaval in scientific theory. In what sense, then, can the assimilation of that discovery be said to have necessitated paradigm change? The case for denying such a change is very strong. To be sure, the paradigms subscribed to by Roentgen and his contemporaries could not have been used to predict X-rays. (Maxwell's electromagnetic theory had not yet been accepted everywhere, and the particulate theory of cathode rays was only one of several current speculations.) But neither did those paradigms, at least in any obvious sense, prohibit the existence of X-rays as the phlogiston theory had prohibited Lavoisier's interpretation of Priestley's gas. On the contrary, in 1895 accepted scientific theory and practice admitted a number of forms of radiation—visible, infrared, and ultraviolet. Why could not X-rays have been accepted as just one more form of a well-known class of natural phenomena? Why were they not, for example, received in the same way as the discovery of an additional chemical element? New elements to fill empty places in the periodic table were still being sought and found in Roentgen's day. Their pursuit was a standard project for normal science, and success was an occasion only for congratulations, not for surprise.

X-rays, however, were greeted not only with surprise but with shock. Lord Kelvin at first pronounced them an elaborate hoax.[13] Others, though they could not doubt the evidence, were clearly staggered by it. Though X-rays were not prohibited by established theory, they violated deeply entrenched expectations. Those expectations, I suggest, were implicit in the design and interpretation of established laboratory procedures. By the 1890s cathode ray equipment was widely deployed in numerous European laboratories. If Roentgen's apparatus had produced X-rays, then a number of other experimentalists must for some time have been producing those rays without knowing it. Perhaps those rays, which might well have other unacknowledged sources too, were implicated in behavior previously explained without reference to them. At the very least, several sorts of long familiar apparatus would in the

---

[13]Silvanus P. Thompson, *The Life of Sir William Thomson, Baron Kelvin of Largs* (London, 1910), II, p. 1125. [Kuhn's note]

future have to be shielded with lead. Previously completed work on normal projects would now have to be done again because earlier scientists had failed to recognize and control a relevant variable. X-rays, to be sure, opened up a new field and thus added to the potential domain of normal science. But they also, and this is now the more important point, changed fields that had already existed. In the process they denied previously paradigmatic types of instrumentation their right to that title.

In short, consciously or not, the decision to employ a particular piece of apparatus and to use it in a particular way carries an assumption that only certain sorts of circumstances will arise. There are instrumental as well as theoretical expectations, and they have often played a decisive role in scientific development. One such expectation is, for example, part of the story of oxygen's belated discovery. Using a standard test for "the goodness of air," both Priestley and Lavoisier mixed two volumes of their gas with one volume of nitric oxide, shook the mixture over water, and measured the volume of the gaseous residue. The previous experience from which this standard procedure had evolved assured them that with atmospheric air the residue would be one volume and that for any other gas (or for polluted air) it would be greater. In the oxygen experiments both found a residue close to one volume and identified the gas accordingly. Only much later and in part through an accident did Priestley renounce the standard procedure and try mixing nitric oxide with his gas in other proportions. He then found that with quadruple the volume of nitric oxide there was almost no residue at all. His commitment to the original test procedure—a procedure sanctioned by much previous experience—had been simultaneously a commitment to the non-existence of gases that could behave as oxygen did.[14]

Illustrations of this sort could be multiplied by reference, for example, to the belated identification of uranium fission. One reason why that nuclear reaction proved especially difficult to recognize was that men who knew what to expect when bombarding uranium chose chemical tests aimed mainly at elements from the upper end of the periodic table.[15] Ought we conclude from the frequency

12

---

[14]Conant, op. cit., pp. 18–20. [Kuhn's note]

[15]K. K. Darrow, "Nuclear Fission," *Bell System Technical Journal,* XIX (1940), pp. 267–289. Krypton, one of the two main fission products, seems not to have been identified by chemical means until after the reaction was well understood. Barium, the other product, was almost identified chemically at a late stage of the investigation because, as it happened, that element had to be added to the radioactive

with which such instrumental commitments prove misleading that science should abandon standard tests and standard instruments? That would result in an inconceivable method of research. Paradigm procedures and applications are as necessary to science as paradigm laws and theories, and they have the same effects. Inevitably they restrict the phenomenological field accessible for scientific investigation at any given time. Recognizing that much, we may simultaneously see an essential sense in which a discovery like X-rays necessitates paradigm change—and therefore change in both procedures and expectations—for a special segment of the scientific community. As a result, we may also understand how the discovery of X-rays could seem to open a strange new world to many scientists and could thus participate so effectively in the crisis that led to twentieth-century physics.

Our final example of scientific discovery, that of the Leyden jar, belongs to a class that may be described as theory-induced. Initially, the term may seem paradoxical. Much that has been said so far suggests that discoveries predicted by theory in advance are parts of normal science and result in no *new sort* of fact. I have, for example, previously referred to the discoveries of new chemical elements during the second half of the nineteenth century as proceeding from normal science in that way. But not all theories are paradigm theories. Both during preparadigm periods and during the crises that lead to large-scale changes of paradigm, scientists usually develop many speculative and unarticulated theories that can themselves point the way to discovery. Often, however, that discovery is not quite the one anticipated by the speculative and tentative hypothesis. Only as experiment and tentative theory are together articulated to a match does the discovery emerge and the theory become a paradigm.

The discovery of the Leyden jar displays all these features as well as the others we have observed before. When it began, there

---

solution to precipitate the heavy element for which nuclear chemists were looking. Failure to separate that added barium from the radioactive product finally led, after the reaction had been repeatedly investigated for almost five years, to the following report: "As chemists we should be led by this research . . . to change all the names in the preceding [reaction] schema and thus write Ba, La, Ce instead of Ra, Ac, Th. But as 'nuclear chemists,' with close affiliations to physics, we cannot bring ourselves to this leap which would contradict all previous experience of nuclear physics. It may be that a series of strange accidents renders our results deceptive" (Otto Hahn and Fritz Strassman, "Über den Nachweis und das Verhalten der bei der Bestrahlung des Urans mittels Neutronen entstehended Erdalkalimetalle," *Die Naturwissenschaften,* XXVII [1939], p. 15). [Kuhn's note] was no single paradigm for electrical research. Instead, a number of theories, all derived from relatively accessible phenomena, were in competition. None of them succeeded in ordering the whole variety of electrical phenomena very well. That failure is the source of several of the anomalies that provide background for the discovery of the Leyden jar. One of the competing schools of electricians took electricity to be a fluid, and that conception led a number of men to attempt bottling the fluid by holding a water-filled glass vial in their hands and touching the water to a conductor suspended from an active electrostatic generator. On removing the jar from the machine and touching the water (or a conductor connected to it) with his free hand, each of these investigators experienced a severe shock. Those first experiments did not, however, provide electricians with the Leyden jar. That device emerged more slowly, and it is again impossible to say just when its discovery was completed. The initial attempts to store electrical fluid worked only because investigators held the vial in their hands while standing upon the ground. Electricians had still to learn that the jar required an outer as well as an inner conducting coating and that the fluid is not really stored in the jar at all. Somewhere in the course of the investigations that showed them this, and which introduced them to several other anomalous effects, the device that we call the Leyden jar emerged. Furthermore, the experiments that led to its emergence, many of them performed by Franklin, were also the ones that necessitated the drastic revision of the fluid theory and thus provided the first full paradigm for electricity.[16]

To a greater or lesser extent (corresponding to the continuum from the shocking to the anticipated result), the characteristics common to the three examples above are characteristic of all discoveries from which new sorts of phenomena emerge. Those characteristics include: the previous awareness of anomaly, the gradual and simultaneous emergence of both observational and conceptual recognition, and the consequent change of paradigm categories and procedures often accompanied by resistance. There is even evidence that these same characteristics are built into the nature of the perceptual process itself. In a psychological experiment that deserves to be far better known outside the trade, Bruner and Postman asked experimental subjects to identify on short and controlled exposure

---

[16]For various stages in the Leyden jar's evolution, see I. B. Cohen, *Franklin and Newton: An Inquiry into Speculative Newtonian Experimental Science and Franklin's Work in Electricity as an Example Thereof* (Philadelphia, 1956), pp. 385–386, 400–406, 452–467, 506–507. The last stage is described by Whittaker, op. cit., pp. 50–52. [Kuhn's note]

a series of playing cards. Many of the cards were normal, but some were made anomalous, e.g., a red six of spades and a black four of hearts. Each experimental run was constituted by the display of a single card to a single subject in a series of gradually increased exposures. After each exposure the subject was asked what he had seen, and the run was terminated by two successive correct identifications.[17]

Even on the shortest exposures many subjects identified most of the cards, and after a small increase all the subjects identified them all. For the normal cards these identifications were usually correct, but the anomalous cards were almost always identified, without apparent hesitation or puzzlement, as normal. The black four of hearts might, for example, be identified as the four of either spades or hearts. Without any awareness of trouble, it was immediately fitted to one of the conceptual categories prepared by prior experience. One would not even like to say that the subjects had seen something different from what they identified. With a further increase of exposure to the anomalous cards, subjects did begin to hesitate and to display awareness of anomaly. Exposed, for example, to the red six of spades, some would say: That's the six of spades, but there's something wrong with it—the black has a red border. Further increase of exposure resulted in still more hesitation and confusion until finally, and sometimes quite suddenly, most subjects would produce the correct identification without hesitation. Moreover, after doing this with two or three of the anomalous cards, they would have little further difficulty with the others. A few subjects, however, were never able to make the requisite adjustment of their categories. Even at forty times the average exposure required to recognize normal cards for what they were, more than 10 percent of the anomalous cards were not correctly identified. And the subjects who then failed often experienced acute personal distress. One of them exclaimed: "I can't make the suit out, whatever it is. It didn't even look like a card that time. I don't know what color it is now or whether it's a spade or a heart. I'm not even sure now what a spade looks like. My God!"[18] . . . We shall occasionally see scientists behaving this way too.

Either as a metaphor or because it reflects the nature of the mind, that psychological experiment provides a wonderfully simple

16

---

[17]J. S. Bruner and Leo Postman, "On the Perception of Incongruity: A Paradigm," *Journal of Personality*, XVIII (1949), pp. 206–223. [Kuhn's note]

[18]Ibid., p. 218. My colleague Postman tells me that, though knowing all about the apparatus and display in advance, he nevertheless found looking at the incongruous cards acutely uncomfortable. [Kuhn's note]

and cogent schema for the process of scientific discovery. In science, as in the playing card experiment, novelty emerges only with difficulty, manifested by resistance, against a background provided by expectation. Initially, only the anticipated and usual are experienced even under circumstances where anomaly is later to be observed. Further acquaintance, however, does result in awareness of something wrong or does relate the effect to something that has gone wrong before. That awareness of anomaly opens a period in which conceptual categories are adjusted until the initially anomalous has become the anticipated. At this point the discovery has been completed. I have already urged that that process or one very much like it is involved in the emergence of all fundamental scientific novelties. Let me now point out that, recognizing the process, we can at last begin to see why normal science, a pursuit not directed to novelties and tending at first to suppress them, should nevertheless be so effective in causing them to arise.

In the development of any science, the first received paradigm is usually felt to account quite successfully for most of the observations and experiments easily accessible to that science's practitioners. Further development, therefore, ordinarily calls for the construction of elaborate equipment, the development of an esoteric vocabulary and skills, and a refinement of concepts that increasingly lessens their resemblance to their usual commonsense prototypes. That professionalization leads, on the one hand, to an immense restriction of the scientist's vision and to a considerable resistance to paradigm change. The science has become increasingly rigid. On the other hand, within those areas to which the paradigm directs the attention of the group, normal science leads to a detail of information and to a precision of the observation-theory match that could be achieved in no other way. Furthermore, that detail and precision-of-match have a value that transcends their not always very high intrinsic interest. Without the special apparatus that is constructed mainly for anticipated functions, the results that lead ultimately to novelty could not occur. And even when the apparatus exists, novelty ordinarily emerges only for the man who, knowing *with precision* what he should expect, is able to recognize that something has gone wrong. Anomaly appears only against the background provided by the paradigm. The more precise and far-reaching that paradigm is, the more sensitive an indicator it provides of anomaly and hence of an occasion for paradigm change. . . . By ensuring that the paradigm will not be too easily surrendered, resistance guarantees that scientists will not be lightly distracted and that the anomalies that lead to paradigm change will penetrate existing knowledge to the core. The very fact that a significant scientific novelty so often emerges simultaneously from several laboratories is an index both to the strongly traditional nature of normal science and to the completeness with which that traditional pursuit prepares the way for its own change.

QUESTIONS FOR CRITICAL READING

1. Examine the concept of the paradigm in science. How would you define it in terms of this essay?
2. What is the effect of a paradigm on our processes of observation?
3. What examples of common paradigms do you or your friends accept and live by?
4. In his final paragraph, Kuhn explains that a "received paradigm"—a paradigm accepted by virtually everyone—tends to make scientists resistant to change. Do you think Kuhn is correct? Are you aware of a resistance to change within yourself?
5. How useful is Bruner and Postman's experiment to Kuhn's argument? Does it help clarify the concept of the paradigm? What is its value to Kuhn's essay?
6. What is the anomaly in each of the three examples Kuhn presents?
7. What is Kuhn's argument regarding the use of standard tests and standard procedures in science (see para. 12)?
8. Which of the three examples—discovery of oxygen, X-rays, or the Leyden jar—is most powerful in explaining Kuhn's ideas?
9. In paragraph 6, Kuhn points out that not every discovery will necessitate a change in paradigm. Do his examples validate this view?

WRITING ASSIGNMENTS

1. Research the background of Priestley and Lavoisier's discovery of oxygen in light of Kuhn's description. What important details does Kuhn leave out? Do they affect the overall significance of the example? Try to explain the process of the discovery of oxygen with a view toward defining the existing scientific paradigms that Priestley and Lavoisier worked with. Use Henry Guerlac's book as a resource (see footnote 10).
2. Consult J. B. Conant's *The Overthrow of the Phlogiston Theory: The Chemical Revolution of 1775–1789* (Cambridge, 1950) and write an essay that clarifies the phlogiston theory and explains how it was discredited. In the process, examine what seem to have been the primary paradigms directing the research of the chemists involved in working with the theory.
3. In paragraph 11, Kuhn states that "consciously or not, the decision

to employ a particular piece of apparatus and to use it in a particular way carries an assumption that only certain sorts of circumstances will arise." Examine the validity of this statement. Construct an argument agreeing or disagreeing with Kuhn's statement by examining a specific apparatus and its use. Do people naturally accept certain limited assumptions when approaching the apparatus or when using it? Describe what those assumptions might be and how they represent a paradigm. If you have experience with scientific apparatuses, choose one.

4. The concept of the paradigm as a way of thinking about experience is useful in the social sciences as well as in the natural sciences. Examine the current paradigms that apply to reflections on the poor in society. What paradigms seem to exist? Have any of them been challenged recently? Have you found your paradigms regarding the poor changed by your education or your personal experience? Describe the changes, if any.

5. If you have a scientific background, add another example to Kuhn's. Describe the scientific situation of your example, clarify the existing paradigm of thought, and then describe the anomaly that demanded explanation. If possible, describe the efforts made to explain the anomaly and decide whether or not a new paradigm became essential after the discovery was made.

6. Explain to someone with a nonscientific background the importance of Kuhn's theory of paradigms. Use Kuhn's rhetorical method of examples and description.

7. **CONNECTIONS** Would the shift in attitude toward primitive cultures promoted by the researches of Franz Boas, Ruth Benedict, and Margaret Mead constitute a paradigm shift? Examine those passages in light of Kuhn's essay and answer the question in light of his position.

8. **CONNECTIONS** How could one apply Thomas S. Kuhn's concept of the paradigm to modern economics? Read John Kenneth Galbraith's "The Position of Poverty" and Robert Reich's "Why the Rich Are Getting Richer and the Poor, Poorer." Is there room for an application of paradigm theory in their essays? Do they seem to be aware of the possibility of such theory being introduced into their discussion? To what extent do Galbraith and Reich attempt to move toward a paradigm shift in general attitudes toward economics?

STEPHEN JAY GOULD
Nonmoral Nature

*S*TEPHEN *JAY GOULD (b. 1941) is professor of geology at Harvard University, where his field of interest centers on the special evolutionary problems related to species of Bahamian snails. He decided to become a paleontologist when he was five years old, after his father had taken him to the American Museum of Natural History in New York City, where he first saw reconstructed dinosaurs.*

Gould has become well known for his essays on science, essays not only written with the clarity needed to explain complex concepts to a general audience but also informed by a superb scientific understanding. His articles for Natural History *magazine have been widely quoted and also collected in book form. His books have won both praise and prizes. With works such as* Ever Since Darwin *(1977),* The Panda's Thumb *(1980),* The Mismeasure of Man *(1981),* The Flamingo's Smile *(1985),* Bully for Brontosaurus *(1992), and* Eight Little Piggies *(1993), Gould has constantly pointed to the significance of the work of the scientist he most frequently praises, Charles Darwin. His books have been celebrated around the world, and in 1981 Gould won a MacArthur Fellowship—a stipend of more than $38,000 a year for five years that permitted him to do any work he wished.*

"Nonmoral Nature" concerns itself with a highly controversial issue: the religious "reading" of natural events. Gould has frequently given testimony at legislative hearings in which creationists have insisted that the Bible's version of creation be taught in science courses as scientific fact. Gould opposes this position because he views the account of the creation in Genesis as religious, not scientific. He points out that Darwin (who was trained as a minister) did not think there was conflict between his theories and religious beliefs.

Gould's primary point in this selection is that the behavior of animals in nature—with ruthless and efficient predators inflicting pain on an essentially helpless prey—has presented theologians with very exacting problems. If God is good and if creation reveals his goodness, how does one account for the suffering of nature's victims?

Gould examines in great detail certain specific issues that plagued nineteenth-century theologians. One of these, the behavior of the ichneumon wasp, an efficient wasp that plants its egg in a host caterpillar or aphid, is his special concern. There are so many species of ichneumons that this could not be regarded as an isolated phenomenon. Gould describes the behavior of the ichneumon in detail to make it plain that the total mechanism of the predatory, parasitic animal is complex, subtle, and brilliant.

It is almost impossible to read this selection without developing a sense of respect for the predator, something that was extremely difficult, if not impossible, for nineteenth-century theologians to do. Their problem, Gould asserts, was that they anthropomorphized the behavior of these insects. That is, they thought of them in human terms. The act of predation was seen as comparable to the acts of human thugs who toy with their victims, or as Gould puts it, the acts of official, state-hired killers whose job in Renaissance England was to inflict as much pain as possible on traitors before killing them. This model is the kind of lens through which the behavior of predators was interpreted and understood. The ichneumon paralyzes its host and then eats it from the inside out; it takes great care not to permit a victim to die until the last morsel is consumed.

Instead of an anthropocentric—human-centered—view, Gould suggests a scientific view that sees the predators' behavior as sympathetically as that of the victims'. In this way, he asserts, one will come to view the ichneumon—and nature—as nonmoral, rather than thinking of the act of predation as evil. The concept of evil, he says, is limited to human beings. The world of nature is unconcerned with it, and if we apply morality to nature, we end up merely seeing nature as a reflection of our own beliefs and values. Instead, he wishes us to conceive of nature as he thinks it is, something apart from strictly human values.

GOULD'S RHETORIC

Gould's writing is distinguished for its clarity and directness. In this essay, he relies on the testimony of renowned authorities, establishing at once a remarkable breadth of interest and revealing considerably detailed learning about his subject. He explores a number of theories with sympathy and care, demonstrating their limits before offering his own views.

Since his field of interest is advanced biology, he runs the risk of losing the general reader. He might have oversimplified his subject in order to avoid doing this, but he does not: he does not shrink from using Latin classifications to identify his subject matter, but he defines each specialized term when he first uses it. He clarifies each opposing argument and demonstrates, in his analysis, its limitations and potential.

Interestingly, instead of using a metaphor to convince us of a significant fact or critical opinion, Gould "deconstructs" a metaphor that was once in wide use. In other words, he reveals the metaphor to us; he shows us how it has affected belief and then asks us to reject it in favor of seeing the world as it actually is. The metaphor is simple: the animal world is comparable to the human world with respect to ethical (normal) behavior. Since the behavior of animals is metaphorically like that of people, the ethical issue must be deep in the grain of nature. This view is mistaken, Gould says. Maintaining the metaphor is inviting and can be irresistible. Yet we must resist it.

Gould also makes widespread use of the rhetorical device of metonymy, in which a part of something stands for the whole. Thus, the details of nature, which is God's creation, are made to reflect the entirety, which is God. Therefore, the behavior of the ichneumon comes to stand for the nature of God; and because the ichneumon's behavior is adjudged evil by those who hold to the first metaphor, there is a terrible contradiction that cannot be rationalized by theological arguments.

Gould shows us just how difficult the problem of the theologian is. Then he shows us a way out. But it is a way out that depends on the capacity to think in a new way, a change that some may not be able to achieve.

Nonmoral Nature

When the Right Honorable and Reverend Francis Henry, earl of Bridgewater,[1] died in February, 1829, he left £8,000 to support a series of books "on the power, wisdom and goodness of God, as manifested in the creation." William Buckland,[2] England's first

---

[1] **Reverend Francis Henry, earl of Bridgewater (1756–1829)** He was the eighth and last earl of Bridgewater. He was also a naturalist and a Fellow at All Souls College, Oxford, before he became earl of Bridgewater in 1823. On his death, he left a fund to be used for the publication of the Bridgewater Treatises, essay discussions of the moral implications of scientific research and discoveries.

[2] **William Buckland (1784–1856)** An English clergyman and also a geologist. His essay "Geology and Mineralogy" was a Bridgewater Treatise in 1836.

official academic geologist and later dean of Westminster, was invited to compose one of the nine Bridgewater Treatises. In it he discussed the most pressing problem of natural theology: If God is benevolent and the Creation displays his "power, wisdom and goodness," then why are we surrounded with pain, suffering, and apparently senseless cruelty in the animal world?

Buckland considered the depredation of "carnivorous races" as the primary challenge to an idealized world in which the lion might dwell with the lamb. He resolved the issue to his satisfaction by arguing that carnivores actually increase "the aggregate of animal enjoyment" and "diminish that of pain." The death of victims, after all, is swift and relatively painless, victims are spared the ravages of decreptitude and senility, and populations do not outrun their food supply to the greater sorrow of all. God knew what he was doing when he made lions. Buckland concluded in hardly concealed rapture:

> The appointment of death by the agency of carnivora, as the ordinary termination of animal existence, appears therefore in its main results to be a dispensation of benevolence; it deducts much from the aggregate amount of the pain of universal death; it abridges, and almost annihilates, throughout the brute creation, the misery of disease, and accidental injuries, and lingering decay; and imposes such salutary restraint upon excessive increase of numbers, that the supply of food maintains perpetually a due ratio to the demand. The result is, that the surface of the land and depths of the waters are ever crowded with myriads of animated beings, the pleasures of whose life are co-extensive with its duration; and which throughout the little day of existence that is allotted to them, fulfill with joy the functions for which they were created.

We may find a certain amusing charm in Buckland's vision today, but such arguments did begin to address "the problem of evil" for many of Buckland's contemporaries—how could a benevolent God create such a world of carnage and bloodshed? Yet these claims could not abolish the problem of evil entirely, for nature includes many phenomena far more horrible in our eyes than simple predation. I suspect that nothing evokes greater disgust in most of us than slow destruction of a host by an internal parasite—slow ingestion, bit by bit, from the inside. In no other way can I explain why *Alien,* an uninspired, grade-C, formula horror film, should have won such a following. That single scene of Mr. Alien, popping forth as a baby parasite from the body of a human host, was both

sickening and stunning. Our nineteenth-century forebears maintained similar feelings. Their greatest challenge to the concept of a
benevolent deity was not simple predation—for one can admire
quick and efficient butcheries, especially since we strive to construct them ourselves—but slow death by parasitic ingestion. The
classic case, treated at length by all the great naturalists, involved
the so-called ichneumon fly. Buckland had sidestepped the major
issue.

The ichneumon fly, which provoked such concern among natu-   4
ral theologians, was a composite creature representing the habits
of an enormous tribe. The Ichneumonoidea are a group of wasps,
not flies, that include more species than all the vertebrates combined
(wasps, with ants and bees, constitute the order Hymenoptera; flies,
with their two wings—wasps have four—form the order Diptera).
In addition, many related wasps of similar habits were often cited
for the same grisly details. Thus, the famous story did not merely
implicate a single aberrant species (perhaps a perverse leakage from
Satan's realm), but perhaps hundreds of thousands of them—a large
chunk of what could only be God's creation.

The ichneumons, like most wasps, generally live freely as adults
but pass their larval life as parasites feeding on the bodies of other
animals, almost invariably members of their own phylum, Arthro-
poda. The most common victims are caterpillars (butterfly and
moth larvae), but some ichneumons prefer aphids and others attack
spiders. Most hosts are parasitized as larvae, but some adults are
attacked, and many tiny ichneumons inject their brood directly into
the egg of their host.

The free-flying females locate an appropriate host and then
convert it to a food factory for their own young. Parasitologists
speak of ectoparasitism when the uninvited guest lives on the surface
of its host, and endoparasitism when the parasite dwells within.
Among endoparasitic ichneumons, adult females pierce the host
with their ovipositor and deposit eggs within it. (The ovipositor,
a thin tube extending backward from the wasp's rear end, may be
many times as long as the body itself.) Usually, the host is not
otherwise inconvenienced for the moment, at least until the eggs
hatch and the ichneumon larvae begin their grim work of interior
excavation. Among ectoparasites, however, many females lay their
eggs directly upon the host's body. Since an active host would
easily dislodge the egg, the ichneumon mother often simultaneously
injects a toxin that paralyzes the caterpillar or other victim. The
paralysis may be permanent, and the caterpillar lies, alive but immobile, with the agent of its future destruction secure on its belly. The

egg hatches, the helpless caterpillar twitches, the wasp larva pierces and begins its grisly feast.

Since a dead and decaying caterpillar will do the wasp larva no good, it eats in a pattern that cannot help but recall, in our inappropriate, anthropocentric interpretation, the ancient English penalty for treason—drawing and quartering, with its explicit object of extracting as much torment as possible by keeping the victim alive and sentient. As the king's executioner drew out and burned his client's entrails, so does the ichneumon larva eat fat bodies and digestive organs first, keeping the caterpillar alive by preserving intact the essential heart and central nervous system. Finally, the larva completes its work and kills its victim, leaving behind the caterpillar's empty shell. Is it any wonder that ichneumons, not snakes or lions, stood as the paramount challenge to God's benevolence during the heyday of natural theology?

As I read through the nineteenth- and twentieth-century litera-   8 ture on ichneumons, nothing amused me more than the tension between an intellectual knowledge that wasps should not be described in human terms and a literary or emotional inability to avoid the familiar categories of epic and narrative, pain and destruction, victim and vanquisher. We seem to be caught in the mythic structures of our own cultural sagas, quite unable, even in our basic descriptions, to use any other language than the metaphors of battle and conquest. We cannot render this corner of natural history as anything but story, combining the themes of grim horror and fascination and usually ending not so much with pity for the caterpillar as with admiration for the efficiency of the ichneumon.

I detect two basic themes in most epic descriptions: the struggles of prey and the ruthless efficiency of parasites. Although we acknowledge that we witness little more than automatic instinct or physiological reaction, still we describe the defenses of hosts as though they represented conscious struggles. Thus, aphids kick and caterpillars may wriggle violently as wasps attempt to insert their ovipositors. The pupa of the tortoise-shell butterfly (usually considered an inert creature silently awaiting its conversion from duckling to swan) may contort its abdominal region so sharply that attacking wasps are thrown into the air. The caterpillars of *Hapalia*, when attacked by the wasp *Apanteles machaeralis*, drop suddenly from their leaves and suspend themselves in air by a silken thread. But the wasp may run down the thread and insert its eggs nonetheless. Some hosts can encapsulate the injected egg with blood cells that aggregate and harden, thus suffocating the parasite.

J. H. Fabre,[3] the great nineteenth-century French entomologist, who remains to this day the preeminently literate natural historian of insects, made a special study of parasitic wasps and wrote with an unabashed anthropocentrism about the struggles of paralyzed victims (see his books *Insect Life* and *The Wonders of Instinct*). He describes some imperfectly paralyzed caterpillars that struggle so violently every time a parasite approaches that the wasp larvae must feed with unusual caution. They attach themselves to a silken strand from the roof of their burrow and descend upon a safe and exposed part of the caterpillar:

> The grub is at dinner: head downwards, it is digging into the limp belly of one of the caterpillars. . . . At the least sign of danger in the heap of caterpillars, the larva retreats . . . and climbs back to the ceiling, where the swarming rabble cannot reach it. When peace is restored, it slides down [its silken cord] and returns to table, with its head over the viands and its rear upturned and ready to withdraw in case of need.

In another chapter, he describes the fate of a paralyzed cricket:

> One may see the cricket, bitten to the quick, vainly move its antennae and abdominal styles, open and close its empty jaws, and even move a foot, but the larva is safe and searches its vitals with impunity. What an awful nightmare for the paralyzed cricket!

Fabre even learned to feed some paralyzed victims by placing   12
a syrup of sugar and water on their mouthparts—thus showing that they remained alive, sentient, and (by implication) grateful for any palliation of their inevitable fate. If Jesus, immobile and thirsting on the cross, received only vinegar from his tormentors, Fabre at least could make an ending bittersweet.

The second theme, ruthless efficiency of the parasites, leads to the opposite conclusion—grudging admiration for the victors. We learn of their skill in capturing dangerous hosts often many times larger than themselves. Caterpillars may be easy game, but the psammocharid wasps prefer spiders. They must insert their ovipositors in a safe and precise spot. Some leave a paralyzed spider in its own burrow. *Planiceps hirsutus,* for example, parasitizes a California trapdoor spider. It searches for spider tubes on sand dunes, then

---

[3]*Jean-Henri Fabre (1823–1915)*   A French entomologist whose patient study of insects earned him the nickname "the Virgil of Insects." His writings are voluminous and, at times, elegant.

digs into nearby sand to disturb the spider's home and drive it out. When the spider emerges, the wasp attacks, paralyzes its victim, drags it back into its own tube, shuts and fastens the trapdoor, and deposits a single egg upon the spider's abdomen. Other psammo-charids will drag a heavy spider back to a previously prepared cluster of clay or mud cells. Some amputate a spider's legs to make the passage easier. Others fly back over water, skimming a buoyant spider along the surface.

Some wasps must battle with other parasites over a host's body. *Rhyssella curvipes* can detect the larvae of wood wasps deep within alder wood and drill down to its potential victims with its sharply ridged ovipositor. *Pseudorhyssa alpestris,* a related parasite, cannot drill directly into wood since its slender ovipositor bears only rudi-mentary cutting ridges. It locates the holes made by *Rhyssella,* inserts its ovipositor, and lays an egg on the host (already conveniently paralyzed by *Rhyssella*), right next to the egg deposited by its rela-tive. The two eggs hatch at about the same time, but the larva of *Pseudorhyssa* has a bigger head bearing much larger mandibles. *Pseudorhyssa* seizes the smaller *Rhyssella* larva, destroys it, and pro-ceeds to feast upon a banquet already well prepared.

Other praises for the efficiency of mothers invoke the themes of early, quick, and often. Many ichneumons don't even wait for their hosts to develop into larvae, but parasitize the egg directly (larval wasps may then either drain the egg itself or enter the devel-oping host larva). Others simply move fast. *Apanteles militaris* can deposit up to seventy-two eggs in a single second. Still others are doggedly persistent. *Aphidius gomezi* females produce up to 1,500 eggs and can parasitize as many as 600 aphids in a single working day. In a bizarre twist upon "often," some wasps indulge in polyem-bryony, a kind of iterated supertwinning. A single egg divides into cells that aggregate into as many as 500 individuals. Since some polyembryonic wasps parasitize caterpillars much larger than them-selves and may lay up to six eggs in each, as many as 3,000 larvae may develop within, and feed upon, a single host. These wasps are endoparasites and do not paralyze their victims. The caterpillars writhe back and forth, not (one suspects) from pain, but merely in response to the commotion induced by thousands of wasp larvae feeding within.

The efficiency of mothers is matched by their larval offspring.   16 I have already mentioned the pattern of eating less essential parts first, thus keeping the host alive and fresh to its final and merciful dispatch. After the larva digests every edible morsel of its victim (if only to prevent later fouling of its abode by decaying tissue), it may still use the outer shell of its host. One aphid parasite cuts a hole in the belly of its victim's shell, glues the skeleton to a leaf by sticky secretions from its salivary gland, and then spins a cocoon to pupate within the aphid's shell.

In using inappropriate anthropocentric language in this romp through the natural history of ichneumons, I have tried to emphasize just why these wasps became a preeminent challenge to natural theology—the antiquated doctrine that attempted to infer God's essence from the products of his creation. I have used twentieth-century examples for the most part, but all themes were known and stressed by the great nineteenth-century natural theologians. How then did they square the habits of these wasps with the goodness of God? How did they extract themselves from this dilemma of their own making?

The strategies were as varied as the practitioners; they shared only the theme of special pleading for an a priori doctrine[4]—they knew that God's benevolence was lurking somewhere behind all these tales of apparent horror. Charles Lyell[5] for example, in the first edition of his epochal *Principles of Geology* (1830–1833), decided that caterpillars posed such a threat to vegetation that any natural checks upon them could only reflect well upon a creating deity, for caterpillars would destroy human agriculture "did not Providence put causes in operation to keep them in due bounds."

The Reverend William Kirby,[6] rector of Barham and Britain's foremost entomologist, chose to ignore the plight of caterpillars and focused instead upon the virtue of mother love displayed by wasps in provisioning their young with such care.

> The great object of the female is to discover a proper nidus for her eggs. In search of this she is in constant motion. Is the caterpillar of a butterfly or moth the appropriate food for her young? You see her alight upon the plants where they are most usually to be met with, run quickly over them, carefully examining every leaf, and, having found the unfortunate object of her search, insert her sting into its flesh, and there deposit an egg. . . . The active

---

[4]*an a priori doctrine* A priori means beforehand, and Gould refers to those who approach a scientific situation with a preestablished view in mind. He is suggesting that such an approach prevents the kind of objectivity and fairness that scientific examination is supposed to produce.

[5]*Charles Lyell (1797–1875)* An English geologist who established the glacial layers of the Eocene (dawn of recent), Miocene (less recent), and Pliocene (more recent) epochs during his excavations of Tertiary period strata in Italy. He was influential in urging Darwin to publish his theories. His work is still respected.

[6]*The Reverend William Kirby (1759–1850)* An English specialist in insects. He was the author of a Bridgewater Treatise, *The History, Habits, and Instincts of Animals* (2 vols., 1835).

Ichneumon braves every danger, and does not desist until her
courage and address have insured subsistence for one of her future
progeny.

Kirby found this solicitude all the more remarkable because the   20
female wasp will never see her child and enjoy the pleasures of
parenthood. Yet her love compels her to danger nonetheless:

> A very large proportion of them are doomed to die before their
> young come into existence. But in these the passion is not extin-
> guished. . . . When you witness the solicitude with which they
> provide for the security and sustenance of their future young,
> you can scarcely deny to them love for a progeny they are never
> destined to behold.

Kirby also put in a good word for the marauding larvae, praising
them for their forbearance in eating selectively to keep their caterpillar prey alive. Would we all husband our resources with such care!

> In this strange and apparently cruel operation one circumstance
> is truly remarkable. The larva of the Ichneumon, though every
> day, perhaps for months, it gnaws the inside of the caterpillar,
> and though at last it has devoured almost every part of it except
> the skin and intestines, carefully all this time it avoids injuring
> the vital organs, as if aware that its own existence depends on
> that of the insect upon which it preys! . . . What would be the
> impression which a similar instance amongst the race of quadru-
> peds would make upon us? If, for example, an animal . . . should
> be found to feed upon the inside of a dog, devouring only those
> parts not essential to life, while it cautiously left uninjured the
> heart, arteries, lungs, and intestines—should we not regard such
> an instance as a perfect prodigy, as an example of instinctive
> forebearance almost miraculous? [The last three quotes come from
> the 1856, and last pre-Darwinian, edition of Kirby and Spence's
> *Introduction to Entomology*.]

This tradition of attempting to read moral meaning from nature
did not cease with the triumph of evolutionary theory after Darwin
published *On the Origin of Species* in 1859—for evolution could be
read as God's chosen method of peopling our planet, and ethical
messages might still populate nature. Thus, St. George Mivart,[7]
one of Darwin's most effective evolutionary critics and a devout
Catholic, argued that "many amiable and excellent people" had

---

[7]**St. George Mivart (1827–1900)**   English anatomist and biologist who examined the comparative anatomies of insect-eating and meat-eating animals. A convert
to Roman Catholicism in 1844, he was unable to reconcile religious and evolutionary
theories and was excommunicated from the church in 1900.

been misled by the apparent suffering of animals for two reasons. First, however much it might hurt, "physical suffering and moral evil are simply incommensurable." Since beasts are not moral agents, their feelings cannot bear any ethical message. But secondly, lest our visceral sensitivities still be aroused, Mivart assures us that animals must feel little, if any, pain. Using a favorite racist argument of the time—that "primitive" people suffer far less than advanced and cultured people—Mivart extrapolated further down the ladder of life into a realm of very limited pain indeed: Physical suffering, he argued,

> depends greatly upon the mental condition of the sufferer. Only during consciousness does it exist, and only in the most highly organized men does it reach its acme. The author has been assured that lower races of men appear less keenly sensitive to physical suffering than do more cultivated and refined human beings. Thus only in man can there really be any intense degree of suffering, because only in him is there that intellectual recollection of past moments and that anticipation of future ones, which constitute in great part the bitterness of suffering. The momentary pang, the present pain, which beasts endure, though real enough, is yet, doubtless, not to be compared as to its intensity with the suffering which is produced in man through his high prerogative of self-consciousness [from *Genesis of Species,* 1871].

It took Darwin himself to derail this ancient tradition—in that gentle way so characteristic of his radical intellectual approach to nearly everything. The ichneumons also troubled Darwin greatly and he wrote of them to Asa Gray[8] in 1860:

> I own that I cannot see as plainly as others do, and as I should wish to do, evidence of design and beneficence on all sides of us. There seems to me too much misery in the world. I cannot persuade myself that a beneficent and omnipotent God would have designedly created the Ichneumonidae with the express intention of their feeding within the living bodies of Caterpillars, or that a cat should play with mice.

---

[8]*Asa Gray (1810–1888)* America's greatest botanist. His works, which are still considered important, are *Structural Botany* (1879) [originally published in 1842 as *Botanical Text-Book*], *The Elements of Botany* (1836), *How Plants Grow* (1858), and *How Plants Behave* (1872). Gray was a serious critic of Darwin and wrote a great number of letters to him; but he was also a firm believer in Darwinian evolution. Since he was also a well-known member of an evangelical Protestant faith, he was effective in countering religious attacks on Darwin by showing that there is no conflict between Darwinism and religion.

Indeed, he had written with more passion to Joseph Hooker[9] 24 in 1856: "What a book a devil's chaplain might write on the clumsy, wasteful, blundering, low, and horribly cruel works of nature!"

This honest admission—that nature is often (by our standards) cruel and that all previous attempts to find a lurking goodness behind everything represent just so much absurd special pleading— can lead in two directions. One might retain the principle that nature holds moral messages for humans, but reverse the usual perspective and claim that morality consists in understanding the ways of nature and doing the opposite. Thomas Henry Huxley[10] advanced this argument in his famous essay on *Evolution and Ethics* (1893):

> The practice of that which is ethically best—what we call goodness or virtue—involves a course of conduct which, in all respects, is opposed to that which leads to success in the cosmic struggle for existence. In place of ruthless self-assertion it demands self-restraint; in place of thrusting aside, or treading down, all competitors, it requires that the individual shall not merely respect, but shall help his fellows. . . . It repudiates the gladiatorial theory of existence. . . . Laws and moral precepts are directed to the end of curbing the cosmic process.

The other argument, more radical in Darwin's day but common now, holds that nature simply is as we find it. Our failure to discern the universal good we once expected does not record our lack of insight or ingenuity but merely demonstrates that nature contains no moral messages framed in human terms. Morality is a subject for philosophers, theologians, students of the humanities, indeed for all thinking people. The answers will not be read passively from nature; they do not, and cannot, arise from the data of science. The factual state of the world does not teach us how we, with our powers for good and evil, should alter or preserve it in the most ethical manner.

Darwin himself tended toward this view, although he could not, as a man of his time, thoroughly abandon the idea that laws

---

[9]***Joseph Hooker (1817–1911)*** English botanist who studied flowers in exotic locations such as Tasmania, the Antarctic, New Zealand, and India. He was, along with Charles Lyell, a friend of Darwin and one of those who urged him to publish *On the Origin of Species*. He was the director of London's Kew Gardens from 1865 to 1885.

[10]***Thomas Henry Huxley (1825–1895)*** An English naturalist who, quite independent of organizations and formal support, became one of the most important scientists of his time. He searched for a theory of evolution that was based on a rigorous examination of the facts and found, in Darwin's work, the theory that he could finally respect. He was a strong champion of Darwin.

of nature might reflect some higher purpose. He clearly recognized that the specific manifestations of those laws—cats playing with mice, and ichneumon larvae eating caterpillars—could not embody ethical messages, but he somehow hoped that unknown higher laws might exist "with the details, whether good or bad, left to the working out of what we may call chance."

Since ichneumons are a detail, and since natural selection is a law regulating details, the answer to the ancient dilemma of why such cruelty (in our terms) exists in nature can only be that there isn't any answer—and that the framing of the question "in our terms" is thoroughly inappropriate in a natural world neither made for us nor ruled by us. It just plain happens. It is a strategy that works for ichneumons and that natural selection has programmed into their behavioral repertoire. Caterpillars are not suffering to teach us something; they have simply been outmaneuvered, for now, in the evolutionary game. Perhaps they will evolve a set of adequate defenses sometime in the future, thus sealing the fate of ichneumons. And perhaps, indeed probably, they will not.

Another Huxley, Thomas's grandson Julian,[11] spoke for this position, using as an example—yes, you guessed it—the ubiquitous ichneumons:

> Natural selection, in fact, though like the mills of God in grinding slowly and grinding small, has few other attributes that a civilized religion would call divine. . . . Its products are just as likely to be aesthetically, morally, or intellectually repulsive to us as they are to be attractive. We need only think of the ugliness of *Sacculina* or a bladderworm, the stupidity of a rhinoceros or a stegosaur, the horror of a female mantis devouring its mate or a brood of ichneumon flies slowly eating out a caterpillar.

It is amusing in this context, or rather ironic since it is too serious to be amusing, that modern creationists accuse evolutionists of preaching a specific ethical doctrine called secular humanism and thereby demand equal time for their unscientific and discredited views. If nature is nonmoral, then evolution cannot teach any ethical theory at all. The assumption that it can has abetted a panoply of social evils that ideologues falsely read into nature from their beliefs—eugenics and (misnamed) social Darwinism prominently among them. Not only did Darwin eschew any attempt to discover an antireligious ethic in nature, he also expressly stated his personal bewilderment about such deep issues as the problem of evil. Just a

---

[11]***Thomas's grandson Julian*** Julian Huxley (1887–1975), an English biologist and a brother of the novelist Aldous Huxley.

few sentences after invoking the ichneumons, and in words that express both the modesty of this splendid man and the compatibility, through lack of contact, between science and true religion, Darwin wrote to Asa Gray,

> I feel most deeply that the whole subject is too profound for the human intellect. A dog might as well speculate on the mind of Newton. Let each man hope and believe what he can.

QUESTIONS FOR CRITICAL READING

1. What does Gould reveal to us about the nature of insect life?
2. Scientifically speaking, what information does Gould provide that is most valuable in explaining how nature works?
3. What does it mean to anthropomorphize nature? What are some concrete results of doing so?
4. Do you find yourself bothered, annoyed, or disconcerted by the knowledge of how the ichneumon wasp parasitizes its host?
5. Does the behavior of the ichneumon wasp put at stake any genuine religious questions of today?
6. Does the existence of predatory insects and animals at all threaten religious belief?
7. Is it difficult to accept Gould's view that nature is nonmoral?

WRITING ASSIGNMENTS

1. In a brief essay, try to answer the question Gould examines in paragraph 1: "Why are we surrounded with pain, suffering, and apparently senseless cruelty in the animal world?"
2. Is the fact of such pain, suffering, and apparently senseless cruelty a religious issue? If so, in what way? If not, demonstrate why.
3. In paragraph 17, Gould describes natural theology as "the antiquated doctrine that attempted to infer God's essence from the products of his creation." Is this a reasonable description of natural theology as you understand it? What would a theology that based its claims in an observation of nature be able to claim about the essence of God? What kind of religion would be possible if all theology were based on the behavior of natural life, including ichneumons?
4. Gould points out that even after having established his theory of evolution, Darwin could not "thoroughly abandon the idea that laws of nature might reflect some higher purpose" (para. 27). Assuming that you agree with Darwin but also acknowledge the problems that Gould presents, clarify what the higher purpose of a nature such as Gould describes might be. Does Gould's description of the behavior

of the ichneumon (or any other) predator in any way compromise the idea that nature has a higher purpose? Does Gould hold that it has a higher purpose?

5. **CONNECTIONS**   Compare this essay with Francis Bacon's "The Four Idols." What intellectual issues do the two essays share? Is there common ground between them regarding their attitudes toward science and religion? What might Francis Bacon have decided about the ultimate ethical issues raised by a consideration of the ichneumon? Do you think that Bacon would have held the same views about the ichneumon's predatory powers as did the nineteenth-century theologians? That is, would he have conceived of nature in ethical/moral terms?

6. **CONNECTIONS**   Why would Gould's scientific subject matter involve issues of morality to a greater extent than, say, the subject matter of Francis Bacon, Charles Darwin, Rachel Carson? Is it possible that the study of physics or chemistry is less fundamentally concerned with moral issues than the study of biology is? One result of Darwin's concerns is the possibility that apes and humans are related. Is this point less worthy of consideration from a moral viewpoint than the behavior of the ichneumon wasp? What are the major moral issues in science that you observed from examining these writers?

IDEAS IN THE WORLD OF PHILOSOPHY

HOW CAN WE TELL THE GOOD FROM THE BAD? HOW CAN WE KNOW WHAT IS TRUE?

Siddhārtha Gautama, the Buddha

Plato

Aristotle

René Descartes

Friedrich Nietzsche

Mary Daly

INTRODUCTION

THE SELECTIONS in Part Five center on issues of moral behavior and remind us that the pursuit of wisdom is a natural human activity that leads us toward happiness. Although some of these pieces were written by members of religious orders—the Buddha, Descartes, and Mary Daly, for example—the essays are not limited to religious issues. More important, these writers recognize the question of whether there exists a path to lead us to wisdom, or enlightenment. Such a question involves all of us, no matter what our gender, our age, or our station.

The wisdom of Siddhārtha Gautama, the Buddha, directs our attention inward to the deepest resources of the individual. According to the Buddha, meditation is the path to enlightenment, revealing a moral life that follows an eightfold path and eventually provides spiritual peace. Anticipating Plato, the Buddha recommended freeing oneself from the bondage of the senses and seeking moderation. He also looked forward to the teachings of Descartes and the Christian church in reminding his disciples of their final spiritual goals. For the Buddha, meditation remained the way to the essential goal of enlightenment, which in turn led to the accomplishment of an ethical life.

Plato instructed that the first requirement of finding the proper ethical path lay in knowing how to avoid being fooled by false appearances. For Plato, ethical issues could be distorted by a mistaken materialism that assumed the world of the senses to be of primary importance. Materialism, he explained, is an illusion. The world of ideas is the only true world; it is the world of heavenly apprehension. Therefore, to achieve enlightenment, one must know how to choose properly. In other words, to choose the good, one must know the good. Plato insisted that the choices leading to the good led away from the world of matter. So the first ethical choice involved choosing to know the truth. This message, by the way, is repeated in different ways by many of these philosophers.

Aristotle, on the other hand, held that the good was not relegated to a Platonic spiritual realm but attained here on earth through a person's actions. Aristotle urges the pursuit of the ultimate good in this life, which he takes to be happiness. However, he cautions against assuming happiness to be synonymous with self-indulgence, since experience demonstrates that such happiness is not long-lasting. For Aristotle, the most profound, enduring happiness must include a commitment to "perfect virtue," because without virtue all happiness is temporary, a delusion. Aristotle's conclusions in this selection link ethical behavior to happiness in one of the most influential statements in philosophy.

René Descartes wrote in an age influenced by a revival of attention to Greek philosophers. His views parallel those of both Plato and Aristotle in one important way: he insisted upon gathering knowledge that he knew would produce certainty of understanding. Like Aristotle, Descartes wished to consider the most profound issues of philosophy. In the spirit of Plato, he cast doubt on the senses' information and began to meditate on questions that went beyond sensory experience to the kind of reasoning that Aristotle practices in the *Nichomachean Ethics*. His great dictum, "I think, therefore I am," provided him with a basis upon which to construct an argument leading him to the proof of the existence of God.

In "Apollonianism and Dionysianism," Friedrich Nietzsche explores issues that were difficult for the Greeks to resolve. Greek philosophers usually recommended that on the path to enlightenment a person should avoid extremes and practice moderation. But Apollonianism (the rational life associated with Apollo, god of music and poetry) and Dionysianism (the life of passion, personified by Dionysus, god of wine) are profound extremes that the Greeks regarded as forms of divine madness. Nietzsche asserted, then, that there is more than one appropriate path to pursue and that both are products of a special form of divinity.

These gods may be threatening to conventional thought, but Nietzsche argued that they are not immoral. He complicated the issue of morality by demanding consideration for the godliness of the individual and the virtues of inspiration. A divine madness is what he praised, something close to the ecstasy of the ancients, a path that he found more appealing than that of the Buddha.

In "The Qualitative Leap Beyond Patriarchal Religion," Mary Daly questions the basic patriarchal assumptions of most modern religions. Daly believes that adherence to imagery praising the masculine ideal and condemning the feminine as evil does not inevitably produce the best ethical behavior. In support of this belief she cites religious wars and acts of oppression that have been conducted under the guise of patriarchal morality. Her views lead her to propose a diarchy to replace the old-fashioned patriarchy, introducing a renovated image of women that allows the image of humanity to be celebrated universally.

Control is central in Mary Daly's essay, but she examines the implications of how the ethical behavior of an institution—the church—affects individuals. According to Daly, the patriarchy of Christianity introduces a key ethical question concerning its nature.

Because these essays concern themselves with ethical issues, they describe again and again the quest to perfect the self and to apply self-control as a means to achieve that perfection. Even when an essay explores varieties of divine madness and the value of loss of control, as in Friedrich Nietzsche's "Apollonianism and Dionysianism," the focus is still on questions of control, lack of control, and the benefits that can be derived from both.

These pieces are extraordinary for their differing attitudes toward the Good and the True. Ethical opinions can be complex and difficult to clarify—these writers demonstrate some of the reasons why. They also remind us that to be human is to continually consider the ethical alternatives available—and that humans remain the only creatures for whom such alternatives have moral implications.

SIDDHĀRTHA GAUTAMA, THE BUDDHA

Meditation:
The Path to Enlightenment

SIDDHĀRTHA GAUTAMA (563?–483? B.C.), known as the Buddha (Sanskrit for "enlightened one"), was born in Kapilavastu, the chief town of Kapila in what is now Nepal. His family was petty royalty, and he himself a minor prince. One of his names is Sakyamuni, "sage of the Sakya clan." Early texts state that he was protected from knowledge of the outside world so that when he was twenty-nine, after finally witnessing the pain and difficulties of the poor, he renounced his aristocratic position and his wife and family. He left his home and wandered, living the ascetic religious life, until he reached Bodh Gaya, where he spent his time in meditation until he achieved enlightenment.

His purpose in seeking enlightenment was to show the way to people so that they could relieve the misery of their own lives. In most versions of Buddhism, the Buddha is regarded as "Lord" Buddha. In other versions, he is regarded as a man who had reached a level of perfection that is possible for ordinary people to achieve. Some branches of Buddhism describe several Buddhas, or bodhisattvas—those who enter different spiritual stages at different times and may be viewed as either great teachers or as heavenly saviors.

In the religion that developed from the Buddha's teachings, the purpose of life is to achieve the enlightenment that will enable the individual to end samsāra—the wandering of the soul from one becoming (incarnation) to another—and reach nirvana, a peace that lies beyond human understanding. In the selection that follows, nirvana is referred to as the end of being.

Because Buddhists hope to achieve nirvana, they guide their lives

---

Translated by Edward Conze.

by firm precepts. They believe that the existence they now enjoy was shaped and formed by the soul in a previous existence and that since their present way of life shapes existences to come, they need to make their own karma. Karma *is a Sanskrit word for "making," translated sometimes as "action." Therefore, Buddhists have established eight principles of behavior for creating their karma called the noble eightfold Path:*

1. *Right views—the avoidance of delusion*
2. *Right aims—purposive intentions to achieve nirvana*
3. *Right speech—preferring the truth*
4. *Right conduct—being honest, true, pure in behavior*
5. *Right living—avoiding hurting all beings and thus preferring a vegetarian diet*
6. *Self-control—preferring disciplined behavior*
7. *Right-mindedness—being aware and alert*
8. *Right meditation—deep contemplation of life and the process of thought*

The ethical implications of Buddhism are evident in the eight admonitions of the noble eightfold Path.

The Buddhist scriptures, from which this passage comes, were not written by the Buddha, but gathered from his teachings by disciples such as his personal follower, Ānanda. The scriptures date from the fifth century B.C. *and were written down sometime in the seventh century* A.D. *by monks who were fearful that the teachings, because of intense persecution of Buddhists, might be lost. Buddhism is rare in India today—its adherents are located mainly in Sri Lanka—but it was transplanted to Tibet, China, and Japan, where it remains influential. Although Southeast Asia today is largely Buddhist, Buddhism coexists with many local religions, some of which contain quite opposing views.*

The volume of Buddhist scriptures—hundreds of thousands of pages—resulted from the contribution of many different schools of Buddhism, each with its own interpretation. In Japan, for example, several schools of Buddhism have been prominent. One is the Rinzai sect, a form of Buddhism that meditates on complex and baffling riddles, such as the question "What is the sound of one hand clapping?" Such a riddle, called a koan, *is especially difficult for the Western mind to comprehend. Another is the Soto sect, which dates from the thirteenth century* A.D. *and emphasizes quiet sitting—zazen—as a means to enlightenment. Both of these sects are still vital in modern Buddhism.*

Buddhist meditation, which originated from Zen Buddhism, depends on a willingness to remain quiet and suspend all logical thought, desire, and attachments. It is an extremely difficult discipline but is recognized by all Buddhists as the one true path to enlightenment, demanding the denial of the sensory world, of transitory events and values.

The following passage emphasizes the advantages of meditation as well as the advantages of introversion. The material world is seen as a distraction that incessantly robs people of their peace and their awareness of the truth about existence. Zen meditation is a radical technique for bringing the external world under the control of the spirit. However, it is closely related to Greek and Roman advice and therefore central to much that is basic to Western views concerning spiritual values in modern times.

B U D D H I S T   R H E T O R I C

The material in this selection is not only translated from a language and a tradition quite foreign to English but is also derived from several sources. "The Advantages of Meditation" comes from a scripture called Milindapanha *and is rendered in prose. "The Practice of Introversion," however, originates from another text,* Shantideva, *and is rendered in poetry. The third section, "The Progressive Steps of Meditation," is from the* Ashvaghosha, *yet another important Buddhist text. That these texts differ in age and in approach makes the rhetorical situation unusual.*

However, certain qualities are present in all the texts. All are "how-to" texts, offering a step-by-step examination of the nature of meditation, its benefits, characteristics, and results. Typical of many Buddhist texts is the technique of enumeration: listing eight noble paths, twenty-eight advantages to meditation, and so on. Such a technique is especially useful for instruction because of its clear, progressive approach.

However, there is a further problem that the translator must resolve. As Edward Conze, the translator of these texts, explains, "For Buddhists the founder of their religion is the 'Lord Buddha,' a godlike being who has transcended the conditions of ordinary life, and his words are not those of a mere man, but a voice issuing from another world. It is therefore quite inconceivable that the Buddha should speak as ordinary people do." Therefore, the text as translated employs an elevated diction in a tone that is formal and distant. We might consider it priestlike. We usually expect and appreciate conversational, direct prose. But in confronting material that is so serious, dignified, and spiritual, it seems more appropriate that the level of diction be high and the tone formal.

However, the material here remains accessible. The scriptures aim at clarity and immediacy and invite us to take part in a fascinating spiritual journey.

Meditation:
The Path to Enlightenment

1. The Advantages of Meditation

Secluded meditation has many virtues. All the Tathagatas[1] have won their all-knowledge in a state of secluded meditation, and, even after their enlightenment, they have continued to cultivate meditation in the recollection of the benefits it brought to them in the past. It is just as a man who has received some boon from a king, and who would, in recollection of the benefits he has had, remain also in the future in attendance on that king.

There are, in fact, twenty-eight advantages to be gained from secluded meditation, and they are the reason why the Tathagatas have devoted themselves to it. They are as follows: secluded medita- tion guards him who meditates, lengthens his life, gives him strength, and shuts out faults; it removes illfame, and leads to good repute; it drives out discontent, and makes for contentment; it removes fear, and gives confidence; it removes sloth and generates vigor; it removes greed, hate, and delusion; it slays pride, breaks up preoccupations, makes thought one-pointed, softens the mind, generates gladness, makes one venerable, gives rise to much profit, makes one worthy of homage, brings exuberant joy, causes delight, shows the own-being of all conditioned things, abolishes rebirth in the world of becoming, and it bestows all the benefits of an ascetic life. These are the twenty-eight advantages of meditation which induce the Tathagatas to practice it.

And it is because the Tathagatas wish to experience the calm and easeful delight of meditational attainments that they practice meditation with this end in view. Four are the reasons why the Tathagatas tend meditation: so that they may dwell at ease; on account of the manifoldness of its faultless virtues; because it is the road to all holy states without exception; and because it has been praised, lauded, exalted, and commended by all the Buddhas.

2. The Practice of Introversion

With his vigor grown strong, his mind should be placed in samadhi;[2] 4
For if thought be distracted we lie in the fangs of the passions.

---

[1]*Tathagata* One of the Buddha's titles. It means "he who has thus come."
[2]*samadhi* Trancelike concentration.

No distractions can touch the man who's alone both in his body
and mind.
Therefore renounce you the world, give up all thinking discursive!

Thirsting for gain, and loving the world, the people fail to renounce
it.
But the wise can discard this love, reflecting as follows:

Through stillness joined to insight true,
His passions are annihilated.
Stillness must first of all be found.
That springs from disregarding worldly satisfactions.

Shortlived yourself, how can you think that others, quite as fleeting, 8
are worthy of your love?
Thousands of births will pass without a sight of him you cherish
so.

When unable to see your beloved, discontent disturbs your samadhi;
When you have seen, your longing, unsated as ever, returns as
before.

Then you forfeit the truth of the Real; your fallen condition shocks
you no longer;
Burning with grief you yearn for reunion with him whom you
cherish.

Worries like these consume a brief life—over and over again to no
purpose;
You stray from the Dharma[3] eternal, for the sake of a transient
friend.

To share in the life of the foolish will lead to the states of woe; 12
You share not, and they will hate you; what good comes from
contact with fools?

Good friends at one time, of a sudden they dislike you,
You try to please them, quite in vain—the worldly are not easily
contented!

Advice on their duties stirs anger; your own good deeds they
impede;
When you ignore what they say they are angry, and head for a
state of woe.

Of his betters he is envious, with his equals there is strife;
To inferiors he is haughty, mad for praise and wroth at blame;
Is there ever any goodness in these foolish common men?

---

[3]**Dharma** Reality, divine law, virtue. This word has numerous meanings,
depending on its context.

Self-applause, belittling others, or encouragement to sin,   16
Some such evil's sure to happen where one fool another meets.

Two evils meet when fools consort together.
Alone I'll live, in peace and with unblemished mind.

Far should one flee from fools. When met, they should be won by
    kindness,
Not in the hope of intimacy, but so as to preserve an even, holy,
    mind.

Enough for Dharma's work I'll take from him, just as a bee takes
    honey from a flower.
Hidden and unknown, like the new moon, I will live my life.

The fools are no one's friends, so have the Buddhas taught us;   20
They cannot love unless their interest in themselves impels them.

Trees do not show disdain, and they demand no toilsome wooing;
Fain would I now consort with them as my companions.

Fain would I dwell in a deserted sanctuary, beneath a tree, or in a
    cave,
In noble disregard for all, and never looking back on what I left.

Fain would I dwell in spacious regions owned by no one,
And there, a homeless wanderer, follow my own mind,

A clay bowl as my only wealth, a robe that does not tempt the   24
    robbers,
Dwelling exempt from fear, and careless of my body.

Alone a man is born, and quite alone he also meets his death;
This private anguish no one shares; and friends can only bar true
    welfare.

Those who travel through Becoming should regard each incarnation
As no more than a passing station on their journey through
    Samsāra.[4]

So will I ever tend delightful and untroubled solitude,
Bestowing bliss, and stilling all distractions.

And from all other care released, the mind set on collecting my   28
    own spirit,
To unify and discipline my spirit I will strive.

3. The Progressive Steps
of Meditation

The restraint of the senses. By taking your stand on mindfulness
you must hold back from the sense-objects your senses, unsteady

---

[4]***Samsāra*** The world of being and becoming.

by nature. Fire, snakes, and lightning are less inimical to us than our own senses, so much more dangerous. For they assail us all the time. Even the most vicious enemies can attack only some people at some times, and not at others, but everybody is always and everywhere weighed down by his senses. And people do not go to hell because some enemy has knocked them down and cast them into it; it is because they have been knocked down by their unsteady senses that they are helplessly dragged there. Those attacked by external enemies may, or may not, suffer injury to their souls; but those who are weighed down by the senses suffer in body and soul alike. For the five senses are rather like arrows which have been smeared with the poison of fancies, have cares for their feathers and happiness for their points, and fly about in the space provided by the range of the sense-objects; shot off by Kama, the God of Love, they hit men in their very hearts as a hunter hits a deer, and if men do not know how to ward off these arrows they will be their undoing; when they come near us we should stand firm in self-control, be agile and steadfast, and ward them off with the great armor of mindfulness. As a man who has subdued his enemies can everywhere live and sleep at ease and free from care, so can he who has pacified his senses. For the senses constantly ask for more by way of worldly objects, and normally behave like voracious dogs who can never have enough. This disorderly mob of the senses can never reach satiety, not by any amount of sense-objects; they are rather like the sea, which one can go on indefinitely replenishing with water.

In this world the senses cannot be prevented from being active, each in its own sphere. But they should not be allowed to grasp either the general features of an object, or its particularities. When you have beheld a sight-object with your eyes, you must merely determine the basic element (which it represents, e.g., it is a "sight-object") and should not under any circumstances fancy it as, say, a woman or a man. But if now and then you have inadvertently grasped something as a "woman" or a "man," you should not follow that up by determining the hairs, teeth, etc., as lovely. Nothing should be subtracted from the datum, nothing added to it; it should be seen as it really is, as what it is like in real truth.

If you thus try to look continually for the true reality in that which the senses present to you, covetousness and aversion will soon be left without a foothold. Coveting ruins those living beings who are bent on sensuous enjoyment by means of pleasing forms, like an enemy with a friendly face who speaks loving words, but plans dark deeds. But what is called "aversion" is a kind of anger directed towards certain objects, and anyone who is deluded enough to pursue it is bound to suffer for it either in this or a future life.

Afflicted by their likes and dislikes, as by excessive heat or cold, men will never find either happiness or the highest good as long as they put their trust in the unsteady senses.

How the senses cause bondage.   A sense-organ, although it may have   32 begun to react to a sense-object, does not get caught up in it unless the mind conceives imaginary ideas about the object. Both fuel and air must be present for a fire to blaze up; so the fire of the passions is born from a combination of a sense-object with imaginations. For people are tied down by a sense-object when they cover it with unreal imaginations; likewise they are liberated from it when they see it as it really is. The sight of one and the same object may attract one person, repel another, and leave a third indifferent; a fourth may be moved to withdraw gently from it. Hence the sense-object itself is not the decisive cause of either bondage or emancipation. It is the presence or absence of imaginations which determines whether attachment takes place or not. Supreme exertions should therefore be made to bring about a restraint of the senses; for un-guarded senses lead to suffering and continued becomings. In all circumstances you should therefore watch out for these enemies which cause so much evil, and you should always control them, i.e., your seeing, hearing, smelling, tasting, and touching. Do not be negligent in this matter even for a moment. The onrush of sense-experiences must be shut out with the sluice-gate of mindfulness.

Moderation in eating.   Moreover you must learn to be moderate in eating, and eat only enough to remain healthy, and fit for trance. For excessive food obstructs the flow of the breath as it goes in and out, induces lassitude and sleepiness, and kills all valor. And as too much food has unfortunate consequences, so also starvation does not lead to efficiency. For starvation drains away the body's volume, luster, firmness, performance, and strength. You should take food in accordance with your individual capacity, neither too much, nor, from pride, too little. As somebody with a running sore puts healing ointment on it, so the man who seeks liberation should use food only to remove his hunger. As the axle of a chariot must be lubricated so that it may work properly, so the wise man employs food only to maintain his life. He takes care of his body, and carries it along with him, not because he has any affection for it, but simply because it enables him to cross the flood of suffering. The spiritual man offers food to his body merely to dispel hunger, and not from greed, or from any love for it.

The avoidance of sleep.   After he has passed his day in keeping his mind collected, the self-possessed man should shake off his sleepiness and spend also the night in the practice of Yoga.[5] When threatened with sleepiness you should constantly mobilize in your mind the factors of exertion and fortitude, of stamina and courage. You should repeat long passages from the Scriptures which you know by heart, expound them to others and reflect on them yourself. In order to keep awake all the time, wet your face with water, look round in all directions and fix your eyes on the stars. With your senses turned inwards, unmoved and well-controlled, with your mind undistracted, you should walk about or sit down at night. Fear, zest, and grief keep sleepiness away; therefore cultivate these three when you feel drowsy. Fear is best fostered by the thought of death coming upon you, zest by thinking of the blessings of the Dharma, grief by dwelling on the boundless ills which result from birth. These, and similar steps, my friend, you should take to keep awake. For what wise man would not regret sleeping away his life uselessly? In fact a wise man, who wants to be saved from the great danger, would not want to go to sleep while ignoring his faults, which are like vicious snakes that have crept into a house. Who would think of lying down to sleep undisturbed when the whole living world is like a house on fire, blazing with the flames of death, disease, and old age? Therefore you should recognize sleep as a darkening of your mind, and it would be unworthy of you to become absorbed in it while your faults are still with you and threaten you like enemies with their swords. The first three of the nine hours of the night you should spend in strenuous activity; then only should you rest your body, and lie down to sleep, but without relaxing your self-control. With a tranquil mind you should lie on your right side, you should look forward to the time when you will wake up and when the sun will shine again. In the third watch you should get up, and, either walking or sitting, with a pure mind and well-guarded senses, continue your practice of Yoga.

Full awareness of the postures, etc.   You are further asked to apply mindfulness to your sitting, walking, standing, looking, speaking, and so on, and to remain fully conscious in all your activities. The man who has imposed strict mindfulness on all he does, and remains as watchful as a gatekeeper at a city-gate, is safe from injury by the passions, just as a well-guarded town is safe from its foes. No defilement can arise in him whose mindfulness is directed on all that concerns his body. On all occasions he guards his thought, as

[4]*Yoga* Disciplined exercise designed to further self-control. A yogin is one who practices yoga.

a nurse guards a child. Without the armor of mindfulness a man is an easy target for the defilements, just as on a battlefield someone who has lost his armor is easily shot by his enemies. A mind which is not protected by mindfulness is as helpless as a sightless man walking over uneven ground without a guide. Loss of mindfulness is the reason why people engage in useless pursuits, do not care for their own true interests, and remain unalarmed in the presence of things which actually menace their welfare. And, as a herdsman runs after his scattered cows, so mindfulness runs after all the virtues, such as morality, etc., wherever they can be found. The Deathless is beyond the reach of those who disperse their attention, but it is within the grasp of those who direct their mindfulness on all that concerns the body. Without mindfulness no one can have the correct holy method; and in the absence of the holy method he has lost the true Path. By losing the true Path he has lost the road to the Deathless; the Deathless being outside his reach, he cannot win freedom from suffering. Therefore you should superintend your walking by thinking "I am walking," your standing by thinking "I am standing," and so on; that is how you are asked to apply mindfulness to all such activities.

The advantages of solitary meditation.   Then, my friend, you should 36 find yourself a living-place which, to be suitable for Yoga, must be without noise and without people. First the body must be placed in seclusion; then detachment of the mind is easy to attain. But those who do not like to live in solitude, because their hearts are not at peace and because they are full of greed, they will hurt themselves there, like someone who walks on very thorny ground because he cannot find the proper road. It is no easier to deny the urges of a man who has not seen the real truth, and who finds himself standing in the fairground of the sensory world, fascinated by its brightness, than it is to deny those of a bull who is eating corn in the middle of a cornfield. A brightly shining fire, when not stirred by the wind, is soon appeased; so the unstimulated heart of those who live in seclusion wins peace without much effort. One who delights in solitude is content with his own company, eats wherever he may be, lodges anywhere, and wears just anything. To shun familiarity with others, as if they were a thorn in the flesh, shows a sound judgment, and helps to accomplish a useful purpose and to know the taste of a happy tranquillity. In a world which takes pleasure in worldly conditions and which is made unrestful by the sense-objects, he dwells in solitude indifferent to worldly conditions, as one who has attained his object, who is tranquil in his heart. The solitary man then drinks the nectar of the Deathless, he becomes content in his heart, and he grieves for the world made wretched by its attachment to sense-objects. If he is satisfied with living alone for a long time in an empty place, if he refrains from dallying with the agents of defilement, regarding them as bitter enemies, and if, content with his own company, he drinks the nectar of spiritual exultation, then he enjoys a happiness greater than that of paradise.

Concentration, and the forsaking of idle thoughts.   Sitting cross-legged in some solitary spot, hold your body straight, and for a time keep your attention in front of you, either on the tip of the nose or the space on your forehead between the eyebrows. Then force your wandering mind to become wholly occupied with one object. If that mental fever, the preoccupation with sensuous desires, should dare to attack you, do not give your consent, but shake it off, as if it were dust on your clothes. Although, out of wise consideration, you may habitually eschew sense-desires, you can definitely rid yourself of them only through an antidote which acts on them like sunshine on darkness. There remains a latent tendency towards them, like a fire hidden under the ashes; this, like fire by water, must be put out by systematic meditation. As plants sprout forth from a seed, so sense-desires continue to come forth from that latent tendency; they will cease only when that seed is destroyed. When you consider what sufferings these sense-pleasures entail, by way of their acquisition, and so on, you will be prepared to cut them off at the root, for they are false friends. Sense-pleasures are impermanent, deceptive, trivial, ruinous, and largely in the power of others, avoid them as if they were poisonous vipers! The search for them involves suffering and they are enjoyed in constant disquiet; their loss leads to much grief, and their gain can never result in lasting satisfaction. A man is lost if he expects contentment from great possessions, the fulfilment of all his wishes from entry into heaven, or happiness from the sense-pleasures. These sense-pleasures are not worth paying any attention to, for they are unstable, unreal, hollow, and uncertain, and the happiness they can give is merely imaginary.

But if ill-will or the desire to hurt others should stir your mind, purify it again with its opposite, which will act on it like a wishing jewel on muddied water. Friendliness and compassionateness are, you should know, their antidotes; for they are forever as opposed to hatred as light is to darkness. A man who, although he has learned to abstain from overt immoral acts, still persists in nursing ill-will, harms himself by throwing dirt over himself, like an elephant after his bath. For a holy man forms a tender estimate of the true condition of mortal beings, and how should he want to inflict further suffering on them when they are already suffering enough from disease, death, old age, and so on? With his malevolent mind a man may cause damage to others, or he may not; in any case his own malevolent mind will be forthwith burned up. Therefore you should strive to think of all that lives with friendliness and compassion, and not with ill-will and a desire to hurt. For whatever a man thinks about continually, to that his mind becomes inclined by the force of habit. Abandoning what is unwholesome, you therefore ought to ponder what is wholesome; for that will bring you advantages in this world and help you to win the highest goal. For unwholesome thoughts will grow when nursed in the heart, and breed misfortunes for yourself and others alike. They not only bring calamities to oneself by obstructing the way to supreme beatitude, but they also ruin the affection of others, because one ceases to be worthy of it.

You must also learn to avoid confusion in your mental actions, and you should, my friend, never think even one single unwholesome thought. All the ideas in your mind which are tainted by greed, hate, and delusion deprive you of virtue and fashion your bondage. Delusion injures others, brings hardship to oneself, soils the mind, and may well lead to hell. It is better for you not to hurt yourself with such unwholesome thoughts! Just as an unintelligent person might burn precious aloe wood as if it were a piece of ordinary timber, so by not observing the correct method which leads to emancipation you would waste the rare opportunities offered by a human birth. To neglect the most excellent Dharma, and instead to think demeritorious thoughts, is like neglecting the jewels on a jewel-island and collecting lumps of earth instead. A person who has won existence as a human being, and who would pursue evil rather than good, is like a traveller to the Himalayas who would feed on deadly rather than on health-giving herbs. Having understood this, try to drive out disturbing thoughts by means of their appropriate antidotes, just as one pushes a wedge out of a cleft in a log with the help of a slender counterwedge.

How to deal with thoughts concerning family and homeland.   But if you   40
start worrying about the prosperity or difficulties of your relatives, you should investigate the true nature of the world of the living, and these ideas will disappear again. Among beings whom their Karma drags along in the cycle of Samsāra, who is a stranger, who a relation? Delusion alone ties one person to another. For in the past the person who is now one of your own people happened to

be a stranger to you; in the future the stranger of today will be one of your own people. Over a number of lives a person is no more firmly associated with his own people than birds who flock together at the close of day, some here, some there. Relatives are no more closely united than travellers who for a while meet at an inn, and then part again, losing sight of each other. This world is by nature split up into disjointed parts; no one really belongs to anyone else; it is held together by cause and effect, as loose sand by a clenched first. And yet, a mother will cherish her son because she expects that he will support her, and a son loves his mother because she bore him in her womb. As long as relatives agree with each other, they display affection; but disagreements turn them into enemies. We see relatives behave unkindly, while nonrelatives may show us kindness. Men, indeed, make and break affections according to their interests. As an artist becomes enamored of a woman he has himself painted, so the affection, which a person has for another with whom he feels at one, is entirely of his own making. As for him who in another life was bound to you by ties to kinship, and who was so dear to you then, what is he to you now or you to him? Therefore it is unworthy of you to allow your mind to become preoccupied with thoughts of your relatives. In the Samsaric world there is no fixed division between your own people and other people.

And if you should hit on the idea that this or that country is safe, prosperous, or fortunate, give it up, my friend, and do not entertain it in any way; for you ought to know that the world everywhere is ablaze with the fires of some faults or others. There is certain to be some suffering, either from the cycle of the seasons, or from hunger, thirst, or exhaustion, and a wholly fortunate country does not exist anywhere. Whether it be excessive cold or heat, sickness or danger, something always afflicts people everywhere; no safe refuge can thus be found in the world. And in all countries of the world people are greatly afraid of old age, disease, and death, and there is none where these fears do not arise. Wherever this body may go, there suffering must follow; there is no place in the world where it is not accompanied by afflictions. However delightful, prosperous, and safe a country may appear to be, it should be recognized as a bad country if consumed by the defilements. This world is smitten with countless ills, which affect both body and mind, and we cannot go to any country which is safe from them and where we can expect to live at ease.

Suffering is the lot of everyone, everywhere and all the time; therefore, my friend, do not hanker after the glittering objects of this world! And, once this hankering is extinct in you, then you will clearly see that this entire world of the living can be said to be on fire.

How to be mindful of death.   But if you should make any plans that do not reckon with the inevitability of death, you must make an effort to lay them down again, as if they were an illness which attacks your own self. Not even for a moment should you rely on life going on, for Time, like a hidden tiger, lies in wait to slay the unsuspecting. There is no point in your feeling too strong or too young to die, for death strikes down people whatever their circumstances, and is no respecter of youthful vitality. The body we drag along with us is a fertile soil for all sorts of mishaps, and no sensible person would entertain any firm expectation of well-being or of life. Who could ever be free from cares as long as he has to bear with this body which, as a receptacle of the four great elements, resembles a pot full of snakes at war with each other? Consider how strange and wonderful it is that this man, on drawing in his breath, can immediately afterwards breathe out again; so little can life be trusted! And this is another strange and wonderful thing that, having slept, he wakes up again, and that, having got up, he goes to sleep again; for many are the adversities of those who have a body. How can we ever feel secure from death, when from the womb onwards it follows us like a murderer with his sword raised to kill us? No man born into this world, however pious or strong he be, ever gets the better of the King of Death, either now, or in the past or the future. For when Death in all its ferocity has arrived on the scene, no bargaining can ward him off, no gifts, no attempt at sowing dissension, no force of arms and no restraint. Our hold on life is so uncertain that it is not worth relying on. All the time Death constantly carries people away, and does not wait for them to reach the age of seventy! Who, unless he be quite mad, would make plans which do not reckon with death, when he sees the world so unsubstantial and frail, like a water bubble?

The four holy truths.   Investigating the true nature of reality and 44 directing his mind towards the complete destruction of the Out-flows, the Yogin learns to understand correctly the four statements which express the four Truths, i.e., suffering, and the rest. First there is the ubiquitous fact of suffering, which can be defined as oppression; then the cause of suffering, which is the same as its origination; the extinction of suffering, which consists essentially in the definite escape from it; and finally the path which leads to tranquillity, and which has the essential function of saving. And those whose intellect has awakened to these four holy truths, and who have correctly penetrated to their meaning, their meditations shall overcome all the Outflows, they will gain the blessed calm, and no more will they be reborn. It is, on the other hand, through its failure to awaken to these four facts which summarize the essential nature of true reality, and through its inability to penetrate to their meaning, that the Samsaric world whirls round and round, that it goes from one becoming to another, and that it cannot win the blessed calm.

You should therefore, to explain it briefly, know with regard to the fact of ill, that birth is the basis of all the other misfortunes, like old age, and so on; for as all plants grow on the earth, so all calamities grow on the soil of birth. For the birth of a body endowed with sense-organs leads of necessity to manifold ills, and the production of a person's physical existence automatically implies that of death and sickness. As food, whether good or bad, far from sustaining us becomes merely destructive when mixed with poison, so all birth into this world, whether among animals, or above or below them, tends to ill and not to ease. The numerous afflictions of living beings, such as old age and so on, are unavoidably produced wherever there is Worldly Activity; but even the most frightful gales could not possibly shake trees that have never been planted. Where there is a body, there must also be such sufferings as disease, old age, and so on, and likewise hunger, thirst, wetness, heat, cold, etc. And the mind which is dependent on the body involves us in such ills as grief, discontent, anger, fear, etc. Wherever there is a psycho-physical organism, suffering is bound to take place; but for him who is liberated from it there can be no suffering, either now, or in the past, or the future.

And that suffering which we find bound up with Worldly Activity in this world is caused by the multitude of the defilements, such as craving, and the rest; but it is not due to a Creator, or Primordial Matter, or Time, or the Nature of things, or Fate, or Chance. And for that reason, i.e., because all Worldly Activity is a result of the defilements, we can be sure that the passionate and the dull will die, whereas those who are without passion and dullness will not be born again.

Therefore, once you have seen, my friend, that craving, etc., are the causes of the manifold ills which follow on birth, remove those causes if you want to be free from suffering; for an effect ceases when its cause has been stopped, and so also suffering becomes extinct when its cause has been quite exhausted. You must therefore come face to face with the holy, calm, and fortunate Dharma, which through dispassion has turned away from craving, which is the supreme place of rest, wherein all Worldly Activity is stopped, a shelter which abides eternally and which nothing can ever take away; that secure place which is final and imperishable, and where there is no birth, old age, death, or disease, no conjunction with unpleasant things, no disappointment over one's wishes, nor separation from what is dear. When the flame of a lamp comes to an end, it does not go anywhere down in the earth or up in the sky, nor into any of the directions of space, but because his defilements have become extinct he simply ceases to be disturbed.

The wise man who wishes to carry out the sacred precepts of tradition should, as a means for the attainment of this Dharma, develop the eightfold Path—three of its steps, i.e., right speech, right bodily action, and right livelihood concern morality; three, i.e., right views, right intentions, and right effort concern wisdom; two again, i.e., right mindfulness and right concentration promote tranquilizing concentration. As a result of morality the defilements no longer proliferate, as seeds no longer germinate after the right season for them has passed; for when a man's morality is pure, the vices attack his mind but halfheartedly, as if they had become ashamed. Concentration, in its turn, blocks the defilements, as a rock blocks the torrent of a mighty river; for the faults are unable to attack a man who is absorbed in trance, as if they were spellbound snakes immobilized by mantras. Wisdom, finally, completely destroys the defilements, as a river, which in the rainy season overflows its banks, sweeps away the trees that grow on them; consumed by wisdom, the faults cease to thrive and grow, like a tree burnt up by the fire which flares up after it has been struck by a thunderbolt. By entering on this eightfold path, which has morality, concentration, and wisdom for its three divisions, and which is holy, incorruptible, and straight, one forsakes those faults which are the causes of suffering, and one attains the state of absolute peace. Ten qualities are required of those who proceed along it: steadfastness, sincerity, self-respect, vigilance, seclusion from the world, contentment with little, simplicity of tastes, nonattachment, aversion to Worldly Activity, and patience. For he who discovers the true nature of ill, its origin and its cessation, can advance on the holy path, in the company of spiritual friends, towards Peace. It is like someone who correctly diagnoses a disease as a disease, and who correctly determines its cause and its cure; when treated by skilful friends he will soon be healthy again. You should therefore regard ill as a disease, the defilements as its cause, their cessation as the state of health, and the path as the remedy. What you must furthermore understand is that suffering is the same as Worldly Activity, and that it is kept going by the defilements; that their stopping is the same as inactivity, and that it is the path which leads to that. As though your turban or your clothes were on fire, so with a sense or urgency should you apply your intellect to the comprehension of the truths. It is because it fails to perceive the guidance given by these truths that the world of the living is being burnt alive. When therefore someone sees that this psycho-physical organism is something that ought to be extinguished, then he has the correct vision; in consequence of his correct insight he becomes disgusted with the things of the world; and as he is no longer drawn to them, his greed gradually exhausts itself. Solemnly I assure you that his mind is definitely liberated when passion and the hope of pleasure have become extinct; and that; once his mind is well freed of those two, there is nothing further that he has to do. For I proclaim it as a fact that the effective extinction of all the Outflows lies in seeing and discerning the own-being of the psychophysical personality, its cause and its disappearance.

QUESTIONS FOR CRITICAL READING

1. What does it mean to restrain the senses?
2. Do you think restraining the senses can produce the results that the Buddha desires?
3. In paragraphs 29–31, the Buddha complains about the unsteadiness of the senses. What does he mean? Are you aware of the unsteadiness of the senses?
4. What seem to be the primary advantages of meditation? Are the advantages obviously religious, or are they secular as well?
5. What is the Buddhist attitude toward the body? How does it seem to differ from Western culture's current attitudes?
6. The Buddha recommends constant mindfulness. What does this entail?
7. Why should meditation be solitary? Are you convinced that solitariness is essential?
8. What does enlightenment seem to mean for the Buddha? Do you feel that it is possible for you to achieve it?

WRITING ASSIGNMENTS

1. Follow the directions for meditation as closely as possible. Try to spend at least three days meditating for ten minutes a day or longer. Record your experiences and determine what for you are the advantages of meditation. Reread paragraph 37 closely before beginning this experiment.

2. In paragraph 37, we find the statement "Sense-pleasures are impermanent, deceptive, trivial, ruinous, and largely in the power of others;
avoid them as if they were poisonous vipers!" Obviously, this attitude
is not generally shared by Westerners. What is your position on the
sense-pleasures? Are they as evil as the Buddha suggests, or do they
possess value?

3. The Buddha suggests that greed, hate, and delusion actually lead people
into bondage. By referring to specific historical examples or examples
from your own experience, explain how this observation is true. What
is it about such ideas that makes them potentially so damaging to
those who hold them? Does the Buddha recommend ways to avoid
holding such ideas? Fashion an essay that examines these questions.

4. In paragraph 44, the Buddha states that suffering is universal. He
equates suffering with oppression. Examine his teachings on this question and relate the question of suffering to modern Western society.
Do you feel that oppression produces suffering today as it did in the
Buddha's time? Is there a sense in which the Buddha's suggestions for
the relief of suffering—implied in the techniques of meditation—would
alleviate the sufferings of oppressed people in our time?

5. The noble eightfold Path is discussed in paragraph 48 as well as in the
introduction to this selection. Determine its applicability to your life,
and take a stand on whether you believe your life would improve if
you were to follow this path. Be as specific as possible, referring to
definitve actions, either actual or potential, and particular relationhips,
either actual or potential, that would be altered in your life.

6. **CONNECTIONS** Compare the basic principles of "Meditation: The
Path to Enlightenment" with the views of Plato on the trustworthiness
of the senses. Does the Buddha seem to be in close agreement with
Plato? What distinctions make their approaches different?

7. **CONNECTIONS** Are Francis Bacon's Four Idols related to the Buddha's eightfold Path? Establish the distinctions and the similarities
between the two programs and decide whether they are basically
compatible or incompatible. Can the Buddha's Path be adapted to
questions of secular knowledge or can Bacon's four Idols be applied
to questions of spiritual knowledge?

8. **CONNECTIONS** To what extent are the philosophies of Lao-Tzu
and the Buddha parallel in their ultimate intentions regarding the
happiness of humankind? Do they have important connections that
identify them as products of Eastern thought? Can they be contrasted
with Western philosophers such as Aristotle and Descartes?

PLATO

The Allegory of the Cave

PLATO (428–347 B.C.) was born into an aristocratic Athenian family and educated according to the best precepts available. He eventually became a student of Socrates and later involved himself closely with Socrates' work and teaching. Plato was not only Socrates' finest student but also the student who immortalized Socrates in his works. Most of Plato's works are philosophical essays, in which Socrates speaks as a character in a dialogue with one or more students or listeners. Thus, Plato transmits a vision of Socrates written by one who knew him and listened carefully to what he said.

The times in which Plato lived were turbulent indeed. In 405 B.C. Athens was defeated by Sparta and its government taken over by tyrants. Political life in Athens became dangerous. Plato felt, however, that he could effect positive change in Athenian politics until, in 399 B.C., Socrates was tried unjustly for corrupting the youth of Athens and sentenced to death. After that, Plato withdrew from public life and devoted himself to writing and to the Academy he founded in an olive grove in Athens. The Academy endured for almost a thousand years, which tells us how greatly Plato's thought was valued.

Although it is not easy to condense Plato's views, he may be said to have held the world of sense perception to be inferior to the world of ideal entities that exist only in a pure spiritual realm. These ideals, or forms, are perceived directly by everyone before birth and then dimly remembered here on earth. But the memory, dim as it is, enables people to understand what the senses perceive, despite the fact that the senses are so unreliable and their perceptions so imperfect.

From *The Republic*. Translated by Benjamin Jowett.

This view of reality has long been important to philosophers because it gives a philosophical basis to antimaterialistic thought. It values the spirit first and frees people from the tyranny of sensory perception and sensory reward. In the case of love, Plato held that Eros leads individuals to revere the body and its pleasures; but the thrust of his teaching is that the body is a metaphor for spiritual delights. Plato maintains that the body is only a starting point, which can eventually lead both to spiritual fulfillment and to the appreciation of true beauty.

*On the one hand, "The Allegory of the Cave" is a discussion of politics—*The Republic, *from which it is taken, is a treatise on justice and the ideal government. On the other hand, it has long stood as an example of the notion that if we must rely upon our perceptions to know the truth about the world, then we actually know very little about it. We know what we perceive, but we have no way of knowing anything beyond that. Likewise, in order to live ethically, it is essential to know what is true and, therefore, what is important to us.*

Plato's allegory has been persuasive for centuries and remains at the center of thought that attempts to counter the pleasures of the sensual life. Most religions aim for spiritual refinement and praise the qualities of the soul, which lies beyond perception. Thus, it comes as no surprise that Christianity and other religions have not only praised Plato but have developed systems of thought that bear a close resemblance to his. Later refinements of his thought, usually called Neo-Platonism, have been influential even into modern times.

PLATO'S RHETORIC

Two very important rhetorical techniques are at work in the following selection. The first and more obvious—at least on one level—is the device of the allegory, a story in which the characters and situations actually represent people and situations in another context. It is a difficult technique to sustain, although Aesop's fables were certainly successful in using animals to represent people and their foibles. The advantage of the technique is that a complex and sometimes unpopular argument can be fought and won before the audience realizes that an argument is under way. The disadvantage of the technique is that the terms of the allegory may only approximate the situation it represents; thus, the argument may fail to be convincing.

The second rhetorical technique Plato uses is the dialogue. In fact, this device is a hallmark of Plato's work, since most of his writings are called dialogues. The Symposium, Apology, Phaedo, Crito, Meno, *and most of his famous works are written in dialogue form.*

Usually Socrates is speaking to a student or a friend about highly abstract issues, asking questions that require simple answers. Slowly, the questioning proceeds to elucidate the answers to the most complex issues.

This use of the question-and-answer technique basically constitutes the Socratic method. Socrates analyzes the answer to each question, examines its implications, and then asserts the truth. The method works partly because Plato believes that people do not learn things, they remember them. That is, people originate from heaven, where they knew the truth; they already possess knowledge and must recover it by means of the dialogue. Socrates' method is ideally suited to that purpose.

Beyond these techniques, however, we must look at Plato's style. It is true that he is working with very difficult ideas, but his style is so clear, simple, and direct that few people would have trouble understanding what he is saying at any given moment. Considering the influence this work has had on world thought and the reputation Plato had earned by the time he came to write The Republic, *it is remarkable that its style is so plain and so accessible. It is significant that such a great mind can express itself with such impressive clarity. Part of that capacity is due to Plato's respect for rhetoric and its proper uses.*

The Allegory of the Cave

SOCRATES, GLAUCON. The den, the prisoners: the light at a distance;

And now, I said, let me show in a figure how far our nature is enlightened or unenlightened:—Behold! human beings living in an underground den, which has a mouth open towards the light and reaching all along the den; here they have been from their childhood, and have their legs and necks chained so that they cannot move, and can only see before them, being prevented by the chains from turning round their heads. Above and behind them a fire is blazing at a distance, and between the fire and the prisoners there is a raised way; and you will see, if you look, a low wall built along the way, like the screen which marionette players have in front of them, over which they show the puppets.

I see.

the low
wall, and
the moving
figures of
which the
shadows
are seen
on the
opposite
wall of the
den.

And do you see, I said, men passing along the wall carrying all sorts of vessels, and statues and figures of animals made of wood and stone and various materials, which appear over the wall? Some of them are talking, others silent.

You have shown me a strange image, and they are   4
strange prisoners.

Like ourselves, I replied; and they see only their own shadows, or the shadows of one another, which the fire throws on the opposite wall of the cave?

True, he said; how could they see anything but the shadows if they were never allowed to move their heads?

And of the objects which are being carried in like manner they would only see the shadows?

Yes, he said.   8

And if they were able to converse with one another, would they not suppose that they were naming what was actually before them?

Very true.

The
prisoners
would
mistake the
shadows
for
realities.

And suppose further that the prison had an echo which came from the other side, would they not be sure to fancy when one of the passers-by spoke that the voice which they heard came from the passing shadow?

No question, he replied.   12

To them, I said, the truth would be literally nothing but the shadows of the images.

That is certain.

And now look again, and see what will naturally follow if the prisoners are released and disabused of their error. At first, when any of them is liberated and compelled suddenly to stand up and turn his neck round and walk and look towards the light, he will suffer sharp pains; the glare will distress him, and he will be unable to see the realities of which in his former state he had seen the shadows; and then conceive some one saying to him, that what he saw before was an illusion, but

And when
released,
they would
still persist
in main-
taining the
superior
truth of the
shadows.

that now, when he is approaching nearer to being and his eye is turned towards more real existence, he has a clearer vision—what will be his reply? And you may further imagine that his instructor is pointing to the objects as they pass and requiring him to name them,— will he not be perplexed? Will he not fancy that the shadows which he formerly saw are truer than the objects which are now shown to him?

Far truer.   16

And if he is compelled to look straight at the light, will he not have a pain in his eyes which will make him turn away to take refuge in the objects of vision which he can see, and which he will conceive to be in reality clearer than the things which are now being shown to him?

True, he said.

When dragged upwards, they would be dazzled by excess of light.

And suppose once more, that he is reluctantly dragged up a steep and rugged ascent, and held fast until he is forced into the presence of the sun himself, is he not likely to be pained and irritated? When he approaches the light his eyes will be dazzled, and he will not be able to see anything at all of what are now called realities.

Not all in a moment, he said.   20

He will require to grow accustomed to the sight of the upper world. And first he will see the shadows best, next the reflections of men and other objects in the water, and then the objects themselves; then he will gaze upon the light of the moon and the stars and the spangled heaven; and he will see the sky and the stars by night better than the sun or the light of the sun by day?

Certainly.

At length they will see the sun and understand his nature.

Last of all he will be able to see the sun, and not mere reflections of him in the water, but he will see him in his own proper place, and not in another; and he will contemplate him as he is.

Certainly.   24

He will then proceed to argue that this is he who gives the season and the years, and is the guardian of all that is in the visible world, and in a certain way the cause of all things which he and his fellows have been accustomed to behold?

Clearly, he said, he would first see the sun and then reason about him.

They would then pity their old companions of the den.

And when he remembered his old habitation, and the wisdom of the den and his fellow prisoners, do you not suppose that he would felicitate himself on the change, and pity them?

Certainly, he would.   28

And if they were in the habit of conferring honors among themselves on those who were quickest to observe the passing shadows and to remark which of them went before, and which followed after, and which were together; and who were therefore best able to draw conclusions as to the future, do you think that he would care for such honors and glories, or envy the possessors of them? Would he not say with Homer,

> Better to be the poor servant of a poor master,

and to endure anything, rather than think as they do and live after their manner?

Yes, he said, I think that he would rather suffer anything than entertain these false notions and live in this miserable manner.

Imagine once more, I said, such an one coming suddenly out of the sun to be replaced in his old situation; would he not be certain to have his eyes full of darkness?

To be sure, he said.   32

But when they returned to the den they would see much worse than those who had never left it.

And if there were a contest, and he had to compete in measuring the shadows with the prisoners who had never moved out of the den, while his sight was still weak, and before his eyes had become steady (and the time which would be needed to acquire this new habit of sight might be very considerable), would he not be ridiculous? Men would say of him that up he went and down he came without his eyes; and that it was better not even to think of ascending; and if any one tried to loose another and lead him up to the light, let them only catch the offender, and they would put him to death.

No question, he said.

The prison is the world of sight, the light of the fire is the sun.

This entire allegory, I said, you may now append, dear Glaucon, to the previous argument; the prison house is the world of sight, the light of the fire is the sun, and you will not misapprehend me if you interpret the journey upwards to be the ascent of the soul into the intellectual world according to my poor belief, which, at your desire, I have expressed—whether rightly or wrongly God knows. But, whether true or false, my opinion is that in the world of knowledge the idea of good appears last of all, and is seen only with an effort; and, when seen, is also inferred to be the universal author of all things beautiful and right, parent of light and of the lord of light in this visible world, and the immediate source of reason and truth in the intellectual; and that this is the power upon which he who would act rationally either in public or private life must have his eye fixed.

I agree, he said, as far as I am able to understand   36
you.

Moreover, I said, you must not wonder that those
who attain to this beatific vision are unwilling to descend
to human affairs; for their souls are ever hastening into
the upper world where they desire to dwell; which desire
of theirs is very natural, if our allegory may be trusted.

Yes, very natural.

Nothing extraordinary in the philosopher being unable to see in the dark.

And is there anything surprising in one who passes
from divine contemplations to the evil state of man,
misbehaving himself in a ridiculous manner; if, while
his eyes are blinking and before he has become accustomed to the surrounding darkness, he is compelled to
fight in courts of law, or in other places, about the images
or the shadows of images of justice, and is endeavoring
to meet the conceptions of those who have never yet
seen absolute justice?

Anything but surprising, he replied.   40

The eyes may be blinded in two ways, by excess or by defect of light.

Anyone who has common sense will remember that
the bewilderments of the eyes are of two kinds, and arise
from two causes, either from coming out of the light
or from going into the light, which is true of the mind's
eye, quite as much as of the bodily eye; and he who
remembers this when he sees anyone whose vision is
perplexed and weak, will not be too ready to laugh; he
will first ask whether that soul of man has come out of
the brighter life, and is unable to see because unaccustomed to the dark, or having turned from darkness to
the day is dazzled by excess of light. And he will count
the one happy in his condition and state of being, and
he will pity the other; or, if he have a mind to laugh at
the soul which comes from below into the light, there
will be more reason in this than in the laugh which greets
him who returns from above out of the light into the
den.

That, he said, is a very just distinction.

The conversion of the soul is the turning round the eye from darkness to light.

But then, if I am right, certain professors of education must be wrong when they say that they can put a
knowledge into the soul which was not there before,
like sight into blind eyes.

They undoubtedly say this, he replied.   44

Whereas, our argument shows that the power and
capacity of learning exists in the soul already; and that
just as the eye was unable to turn from darkness to

light without the whole body, so too the instrument of knowledge can only by the movement of the whole soul be turned from the world of becoming into that of being, and learn by degrees to endure the sight of being, and of the brightest and best of being, or in other words, of the good.

Very true.

And must there not be some art which will effect conversion in the easiest and quickest manner; not implanting the faculty of sight, for that exists already, but has been turned in the wrong direction, and is looking away from the truth?

Yes, he said, such an art may be presumed.   48

The virtue of wisdom has a divine power which may be turned either towards good or towards evil.

And whereas the other so-called virtues of the soul seem to be akin to bodily qualities, for even when they are not originally innate they can be implanted later by habit and exercise, the virtue of wisdom more than anything else contains a divine element which always remains, and by this conversion is rendered useful and profitable; or, on the other hand, hurtful and useless. Did you never observe the narrow intelligence flashing from the keen eye of a clever rogue—how eager he is, how clearly his paltry soul sees the way to his end; he is the reverse of blind, but his keen eyesight is forced into the service of evil, and he is mischievous in proportion to his cleverness?

Very true, he said.

But what if there had been a circumcision of such natures in the days of their youth; and they had been severed from those sensual pleasures, such as eating and drinking, which, like leaden weights, were attached to them at their birth, and which drag them down and turn the vision of their souls upon the things that are below— if, I say, they had been released from these impediments and turned in the opposite direction, the very same faculty in them would have seen the truth as keenly as they see what their eyes are turned to now.

Neither the uneducated nor the overeducated will be good servants of the State.

Very likely.   52

Yes, I said; and there is another thing which is likely, or rather a necessary inference from what has preceded, that neither the uneducated and uninformed of the truth, nor yet those who never make an end of their education, will be able ministers of State; not the former, because they have no single aim of duty which is the rule of all their actions, private as well as public; nor the latter, because they will not act at all except upon compulsion, fancying that they are already dwelling apart in the islands of the blessed.

Very true, he replied.

Then, I said, the business of us who are the founders of the State will be to compel the best minds to attain that knowledge which we have already shown to be the greatest of all—they must continue to ascend until they arrive at the good; but when they have ascended and seen enough we must not allow them to do as they do now.

What do you mean? 56

Men should ascend to the upper world, but they should also return to the lower.

I mean that they remain in the upper world: but this must not be allowed; they must be made to descend again among the prisoners in the den, and partake of their labors and honors, whether they are worth having or not.

But is not this unjust? he said; ought we to give them a worse life, when they might have a better?

You have again forgotten, my friend, I said, the intention of the legislator, who did not aim at making any one class in the State happy above the rest; the happiness was to be in the whole State, and he held the citizens together by persuasion and necessity, making them benefactors of the State, and therefore benefactors of one another; to this end he created them, not to please themselves, but to be his instruments in binding up the State.

True, he said, I had forgotten. 60

The duties of philosophers.

Observe, Glaucon, that there will be no injustice in compelling our philosophers to have a care and providence of others; we shall explain to them that in other States, men of their class are not obliged to share in the toils of politics: and this is reasonable, for they grow up at their own sweet will, and the government would rather not have them. Being self-taught, they cannot be expected to show any gratitude for a culture which they have never received. But we have brought you into the world to be rulers of the hive, kings of yourselves and of the other citizens, and have educated you far better and more perfectly than they have been educated, and you are better able to share in the double duty. Wherefore each of you, when his turn comes, must go down to

Their
obligations
to their
country
will induce
them to
take part in
her gov-
ernment.

the general underground abode, and get the habit of
seeing in the dark. When you have acquired the habit,
you will see ten thousand times better than the inhabitants of the den, and you will know what the several
images are, and what they represent, because you have
seen the beautiful and just and good in their truth. And
thus our State, which is also yours, will be a reality, and
not a dream only, and will be administered in a spirit
unlike that of other States, in which men fight with one
another about shadows only and are distracted in the
struggle for power, which in their eyes is a great good.
Whereas the truth is that the State in which the rulers
are most reluctant to govern is always the best and most
quietly governed, and the State in which they are most
eager, the worst.

Quite true, he replied.

And will our pupils, when they hear this, refuse to
take their turn at the toils of State, when they are allowed
to spend the greater part of their time with one another
in the heavenly light?

They will
be willing
but not
anxious to
rule.

Impossible, he answered; for they are just men, and   64
the commands which we impose upon them are just;
there can be no doubt that every one of them will take
office as a stern necessity, and not after the fashion of
our present rulers of State.

The
statesman
must be
provided
with a
better life
than that of
a ruler; and
then he will
not covet
office.

Yes, my friend, I said; and there lies the point. You
must contrive for your future rulers another and a better
life than that of a ruler, and then you may have a well-
ordered State; for only in the State which offers this,
will they rule who are truly rich, not in silver and gold,
but in virtue and wisdom, which are the true blessings
of life. Whereas if they go to the administration of public
affairs, poor and hungering after their own private advantage, thinking that hence they are to snatch the chief
good, order there can never be; for they will be fighting
about office, and the civil and domestic broils which
thus arise will be the ruin of the rulers themselves and
of the whole State.

Most true, he replied.

And the only life which looks down upon the life
of political ambition is that of true philosophy. Do you
know of any other?

Indeed, I do not, he said.   68

QUESTIONS FOR CRITICAL READING

1. What is the relationship between Socrates and Glaucon? Are they equal in intellectual authority? Are they concerned with the same issues?
2. How does the allegory of the prisoners in the cave watching shadows on a wall relate to us today? What are the shadows that we see and how do they distort our sense of what is real?
3. Are we prisoners in the same sense that Plato's characters are?
4. From a scientific point of view—taking into account the thought of Bacon, for example—what are the facts about our inabilities to perceive the reality of experience? Does the fact that the material world is dominated by the four Idols imply that we are in a position similar to those in Plato's cave?
5. If Plato is right that the material world is an illusion, how would too great a reliance on materialism affect ethical decisions?
6. What ethical issues, if any, are raised by Plato's allegory?
7. In paragraph 49, Plato states that the virtue of wisdom "contains a divine element." What is "a divine element"? What does this statement seem to mean? Do you agree with Plato?
8. What distinctions does Plato make between the public and the private? Would you make the same distinctions (see paras, 53–55)?

WRITING ASSIGNMENTS

1. Analyze the allegory of the cave for its strengths and weaknesses. Consider what it is meant to imply for people living in a world of the senses and what Plato implies lies behind that world. Consider the extent to which people are like (or unlike) the figures in the cave. Consider the extent to which the world we know is like the cave. Consider, too, the "revelations" implied in the allegory and its contemplation.
2. Socrates ends the dialogue by saying that after rulers of the state have served their term they must be able to look forward to a better life than that of being rulers. He and Glaucon agree that there is only one life that "looks down upon the life of political ambition"—"that of true philosophy." What is the life of true philosophy? Is it superior to that of being a ruler (or anything else)? How would you define its superiority? What would its qualities be? What would its concerns be? Would you be happy leading such a life?
3. In what ways would a dependence on the material world for one's highest moral values affect ethical behavior? What is the connection between ethics and materialism? Write a brief essay that defends or attacks materialism as a basis for ethical action. How can people aspire to the good if they root their greatest pleasures in the senses? What alternatives do modern people have if they choose to base their actions

on nonmaterialistic, or spiritual, values? What are those values? How can they guide our ethical behavior? Do you think they should?

4. In paragraph 61, Socrates outlines a program that would assure Athens of good rulers and good government. Clarify exactly what the program is, what its problems and benefits are, and how it could be put into action. Then decide whether or not the program would work. You may consider whether or not it would work for our time, for Socrates' time, or both. If possible, use examples (hypothetical or real) to bolster your argument.

5. Socrates states unequivocally that Athens should compel the best and the most intelligent young men to be rulers of the state. Review his reasons for saying so; consider what his concept of the state is; then take a stand on the issue. Is it right to compel the best and most intelligent young people to become rulers? If so, would it be equally proper to compel those well suited for the professions of law, medicine, teaching, or religion to follow those respective callings? Would an ideal society result if all people were forced to practice the calling for which they had the best aptitude?

6. **CONNECTIONS** Plato has a great deal to say about goodness as it relates to government. Compare his views with those of Lao-Tzu and Machiavelli. Which of those thinkers would Plato have agreed with most? Which do you feel he most emphatically influenced? In comparing these writers and their political views, consider the nature of goodness they required in a ruler. Do you think that we hold similar attitudes today in our expectations for the goodness of our government?

7. **CONNECTIONS** Examine Descartes's *Discourse Four.* Can we consider Descartes an inheritor of Plato's thought? What are the similarities between the allegory of the cave and Descartes's concerns for establishing an unassailable position from which to begin a process of reasoning? Does Descartes continue Plato's work?

8. **CONNECTIONS** Plato and Aristotle have traditionally been seen not just as teacher and student but as intellectual adversaries. Plato's view has questioned sensory evidence in reasoning, while Aristotle's view has given it credit. What debts to Plato are apparent in Aristotle's "The Aim of Man," and in what ways does Aristotle seem to differ from Plato's basic thought? In comparison with Aristotle, what makes Plato platonic?

ARISTOTLE

The Aim of Man

*A*RISTOTLE *(384–322* B.C.*) is the great inheritor of Plato's influence in philosophical thought. He was a student at the Academy of Plato in Athens from age seventeen to thirty-seven, and by all accounts he was Plato's most brilliant pupil. He did not agree with Plato on all issues, however, and seems to have broken with his master sometime around Plato's death (347* B.C.*). In certain of his writings he is careful to disagree with the Platonists while insisting on his friendship with them. In the* Nichomachean Ethics, *for example, the most difficult section (omitted here) demonstrates that Plato is not correct in assuming that the good exists in some ideal form in a higher spiritual realm.*

One interesting point concerning Aristotle's career is that when he became a teacher, his most distinguished student was Alexander the Great, the youthful ruler who spread Greek values and laws throughout the rest of the known world. Much speculation has centered on just what Aristotle might have taught Alexander about politics. The emphasis on statecraft and political goals in the Nichomachean Ethics *suggests that it may have been a great deal. A surviving fragment of a letter from Aristotle to Alexander suggests that he advised Alexander to become the leader of the Greeks and the master of the barbarians.*

The Nichomachean Ethics *is a difficult document. Aristotle may have written it with an eye to tutoring his son, Nichomachus, but it is also a document meant to be read by those who have thought deeply about human ethical behavior. "The Aim of Man" treats most of the basic issues in the entire document. It is difficult primarily because it is so thoroughly abstract. Abstract reason was thought to be the highest*

From the *Nichomachean Ethics*. Translated by Martin Ostwald.

form of reason, because it is independent of sensory experience and because only human beings can indulge in it. Aristotle, whose studies included works on plants, physics, animals, law, rhetoric, and logic, to name only some subjects, reminds us often of what we have in common with the animal and vegetable worlds. But because he values abstract thought so much, his reasoning demands unusual attention from contemporary readers.

Moreover, because he wrote so much on scientific subjects—and, unlike Plato, emphasized the role of sensory perception in scientific matters—he is careful to warn that reasoning about humankind cannot entail the precision taken for granted in science. That warning is repeated several times in this selection. The study of humankind requires awareness of people's differences of background, education, habit, temperament, and other, similar factors. Such differences will impede the kinds of precision of definition and analysis taken for granted in other sciences.

Aristotle reveals an interesting Greek prejudice when he admits that the highest good for humankind is likely to be found in statecraft. He tells us that the well-ordered state—the pride of the Greek way of life—is of such noble value that other values must take second place to it. Because current thought somewhat agrees with this view, Aristotle sounds peculiarly modern in this passage. Unlike the Christian theorists of the Middle Ages, the theorists of the Islamic insurgence, or the theorists of the Judaic Scriptures, Aristotle does not put divinity or godliness first. He is a practical man whose concerns are with the life that human beings know here on earth. When he considers the question, for instance, of whether a man can be thought of as happy before he has died (tragedy can always befall the happy man), he is thoroughly practical and does not point to happiness in heaven as any substitute for happiness on earth.

ARISTOTLE'S RHETORIC

Even though Aristotle is the author of the single most influential treatise on rhetoric, this document does not have as eloquent a style as might be expected, which has suggested to some that the manuscript was taken from lecture notes of a student. But, of course, he does use certain minor techniques that demonstrate his awareness of rhetorical effect. He makes careful use of aphorisms, for example, "One swallow does not make a spring" and "Perfect justice is noblest, health is best, / But to gain one's heart's desire is pleasantest" (para. 21).

In terms of style, Aristotle is at a disadvantage—or perhaps the modern world is—because he addresses an audience of those who have thought very deeply on the issues of human behavior, so that his style is elevated and complex. Fortunately, nothing he says here is beyond the grasp of the careful reader, although modern readers expect to be provided with a good many concrete examples to help them understand abstract principles. Aristotle purposely avoids using examples so as not to limit too sharply the truths he has to impart.

Aristotle's most prominent rhetorical technique is definition. His overall goal in this work is to define the aim of man. Thus, the first section of this work is entitled "Definition of the Good." In "Primacy of Statecraft" he begins to qualify various types of good. Later, he considers the relationship between good and happiness (paras. 8–9) and the various views concerning happiness and its definition (paras. 10–11). By then the reader is prepared for a "Functional Definition of Man's Highest Good" (paras. 12–18). He confirms his conclusions in the section entitled "Confirmation by Popular Beliefs" (paras. 19–22). After isolating happiness as the ultimate good, he devotes paragraphs 23–32 to its causes, its effects, and the events that will affect it, such as luck and human decision. The final section (paras. 33–39) constitutes an examination of the soul (the most human element) and its relationship to virtue; he begins that section by repeating, for the third time, his definition of happiness: "Happiness is a certain activity of the soul in accordance with perfect virtue."

It could be said that, rhetorically speaking, the body of the work is an exploration and definition of the highest good.

The Aim of Man

Definition of the Good

Every art and every "scientific investigation," as well as every action and "purposive choice," appears to aim at some good; hence the good has rightly been declared to be that at which all things aim. A difference is observable, to be sure, among the several ends: some of them are activities, while others are products over and above the activities that produce them. Wherever there are certain ends over and above the actions themselves, it is the nature of such products to be better than the activities.

As actions and arts and sciences are of many kinds, there must be a corresponding diversity of ends: health, for example, is the aim of medicine, ships of shipbuilding, victory of military strategy, and wealth of domestic economics. Where several such arts fall

under some one faculty—as bridle-making and the other arts concerned with horses' equipment fall under horsemanship, while this
in turn along with all other military matters falls under the head of
strategy, and similarly in the case of other arts—the aim of the
master art is always more choiceworthy than the aims of its subordinate arts, inasmuch as these are pursued for its sake. And this holds
equally good whether the end in view is just the activity itself or
something distinct from the activity, as in the case of the sciences
above mentioned.

Primacy of Statecraft

If in all our conduct, then, there is some end that we wish on
its own account, choosing everything else as a means to it; if, that
is to say, we do not choose everything as a means to something
else (for at that rate we should go on *ad infinitum*[1] and our desire
would be left empty and vain); then clearly this one end must be
the good—even, indeed, the highest good. Will not a knowledge
of it, then, have an important influence on our lives? Will it not
better enable us to hit the right mark, like archers who have a
definite target to aim at? If so, we must try to comprehend, in
outline at least, what that highest end is, and to which of the sciences
or arts it belongs.

Evidently the art or science in question must be the most abso- 4
lute and most authoritative of all. Statecraft answers best to this
description; for it prescribes which of the sciences are to have a
place in the state, and which of them are to be studied by the
different classes of citizens, and up to what point; and we find that
even the most highly esteemed of the arts are subordinated to it,
e.g., military strategy, domestic economics, and oratory. So then,
since statecraft employs all the other sciences, prescribing also what
the citizens are to do and what they are to refrain from doing, its
aim must embrace the aims of all the others; whence it follows that
the aim of statecraft is man's proper good. Even supposing the
chief good to be eventually the same for the individual as for the
state, that of the state is evidently of greater and more fundamental
importance both to attain and to preserve. The securing of even
one individual's good is cause for rejoicing, but to secure the good
of a nation or of a city-state[2] is nobler and more divine. This, then,

---

[1]**ad infinitum**   Endlessly; to infinity.
[2]***city-state***   Athens was an independent nation, a city-state *(polis)*. Greece
consisted of a great many independent states, which often leagued together in

is the aim of our present inquiry, which is in a sense the study of statecraft.

Two Observations
on the Study of Ethics

Our discussion will be adequate if we are content with as much precision as is appropriate to the subject matter; for the same degree of exactitude ought no more to be expected in all kinds of reasoning than in all kinds of handicraft. Excellence and justice, the things with which statecraft deals, involve so much disagreement and uncertainty that they come to be looked on as mere conventions, having no natural foundation. The good involves a similar uncertainty, inasmuch as good things often prove detrimental: there are examples of people destroyed by wealth, of others destroyed by courage. In such matters, then, and starting from such premises as we do, we must be content with a rough approximation to the truth; for when we are dealing with and starting out from what holds good only "as a general rule," the conclusions that we reach will have the same character. Let each of the views put forward be accepted in this spirit, for it is the mark of an educated mind to seek only so much exactness in each type of inquiry as may be allowed by the nature of the subject matter. It is equally wrong to accept probable reasoning from a mathematician and to demand strict demonstrations from an orator.

A man judges well and is called a good judge of the things about which he knows. If he has been educated in a particular subject he is a good judge of that subject; if his education has been well-rounded he is a good judge in general. Hence no very young man is qualified to attend lectures on statecraft; for he is inexperienced in the affairs of life, and these form the data and subject matter of statecraft. Moreover, so long as he tends to be swayed by his feelings he will listen vainly and without profit, for the purport of these [lectures] is not purely theoretical but practical. Nor does it make any difference whether his immaturity is a matter of years or of character: the defect is not a matter of time, but consists in the fact that his life and all his pursuits are under the control of his passions. Men of this sort, as is evident from the case of those we call incontinent,[3] do not turn their knowledge to any

---

confederations.
[3]***incontinent*** Uncontrolled, in this case by reason.

account in practice; but those whose desires and actions are controlled by reason will derive much profit from a knowledge of these matters.

So much, then, for our prefatory remarks about the student, the manner of inquiry, and the aim.

The Good as Happiness

To resume, then: since all knowledge and all purpose aims at   8
some good, what is it that we declare to be the aim of statecraft;
or, in other words, what is the highest of all realizable goods? As
to its name there is pretty general agreement: the majority of men,
as well as the cultured few, speak of it as happiness; and they would
maintain that to live well and to do well are the same thing as to
be happy. They differ, however, as to what happiness is, and the
mass of mankind give a different account of it from philosophers.
The former take it to be something palpable and obvious, like
pleasure or wealth or fame; they differ, too, among themselves,
nor is the same man always of one mind about it: when ill he
identifies it with health, when poor with wealth; then growing
aware of his ignorance about the whole matter he feels admiration
for anyone who proclaims some grand ideal above his comprehension. And to add to the confusion, there have been some philosophers who held that besides the various particular good things there
is an absolute good which is the cause of all particular goods. As
it would hardly be worthwhile to examine all the opinions that
have been entertained, we shall confine our attention to those that
are most popular or that appear to have some rational foundation.

One point not to be overlooked is the difference between arguments that start from first principles[4] and arguments that lead up
to first principles. Plato very wisely used to raise this question, and
to ask whether the right way is from or toward first principles—
as in the racecourse there is a difference between running from the
judges to the boundary line and running back again. Granted that
we must start with what is known, this may be interpreted in a
double sense: as what is familiar to us or as what is intelligible in
itself. Our own method, at any rate, must be to start with what is
familiar to us. That is why a sound moral training is required before
a man can listen intelligently to discussions about excellence and

---

[4]*first principles* Concepts such as goodness, truth, and justice. Arguments
that lead to first principles usually begin with familiar, less abstract evidence.

justice, and generally speaking, about statecraft. For in this field we must take as our "first principles" plain facts; if these are sufficiently evident we shall not insist upon the whys and wherefores. Such principles are in the possession of, or at any rate readily accessible to, the man with a sound moral training. As for the man who neither possesses nor can acquire them, let him hear the words of Hesiod:[5]

> Best is he who makes his own discoveries;
> Good is he who listens to the wise;
> But he who, knowing not, rejects another's wisdom
>   Is a plain fool.

Conflicting Views of Happiness

Let us now resume our discussion from the point at which we digressed. What is happiness, or the chief good? If it is permissible to judge from men's actual lives, we may say that the mass of them, being vulgarians, identify it with pleasure, which is the reason why they aim at nothing higher than a life of enjoyment. For there are three outstanding types of life: the one just mentioned, the political, and, thirdly, the contemplative. "The mass of men" reveal their utter slavishness by preferring a life fit only for cattle; yet their views have a certain plausibility from the fact that many of those in high places share the tastes of Sardanapalus.[6] Men of superior refinement and active disposition, on the other hand, identify happiness with honor, this being more or less the aim of a statesman's life. It is evidently too superficial, however, to be the good that we are seeking; for it appears to depend rather on him who bestows than on him who receives it, while we may suspect the chief good to be something peculiarly a man's own, which he is not easily deprived of. Besides, men seem to pursue honor primarily in order to assure themselves of their own merit; at any rate, apart from personal acquaintances, it is by those of sound judgment that they

---

[5] *Works and Days,* ll. 293–297. [Translator's note] Hesiod (eighth century B.C.) was a well-known Greek author. His *Works and Days* is notable for its portraits of everyday shepherd life and for its moralizing fables. His *Theogony* is a description of the creation, widely taken as accurate in his day.

[6] An ancient Assyrian king to whom is attributed the saying, "Eat, drink, and be merry: nothing else is worth a snap of the fingers." [Translator's note] Sardanapalus (d. 880 B.C.) was noted for his slothful and decadent life. When it was certain that he was to die—the walls of his city had been breached by an opposing army—he had his wives, animals, and possessions burned with him in his palace.

seek to be appreciated, and on the score of virtue. Clearly, then, they imply that virtue is superior to honor: and so, perhaps, we should regard this rather than honor as the end and aim of the statesman's life. Yet even about virtue there is a certain incompleteness; for it is supposed that a man may possess it while asleep or during lifelong inactivity, or even while suffering the greatest disasters and misfortunes; and surely no one would call such a man happy, unless for the sake of a paradox. But we need not further pursue this subject, which has been sufficiently treated of in current discussions. Thirdly, there is the contemplative life, which we shall examine at a later point.

As for the life of money-making, it is something unnatural. Wealth is clearly not the good that we are seeking, for it is merely useful as a means to something else. Even the objects above mentioned come closer to possessing intrinsic goodness than wealth does, for they at least are cherished on their own account. But not even they, it seems, can be the chief good, although much labor has been lost in attempting to prove them so. With this observation we may close the present subject.

Functional Definition
of Man's Highest Good

Returning now to the good that we are seeking, let us inquire   12
into its nature. Evidently it is different in different actions and arts: it is not the same thing in medicine as in strategy, and so on. What definition of good will apply to all the arts? Let us say it is that for the sake of which all else is done. In medicine this is health, in the art of war victory, in building it is a house, and in each of the arts something different, although in every case, wherever there is action and choice involved, it is a certain end; because it is always for the sake of a certain end that all else is done. If, then, there is one end and aim of all our actions, this will be the realizable good; if there are several such ends, these jointly will be our realizable goods. Thus in a roundabout way the discussion has been brought back to the same point as before; which we must now try to explain more clearly.

As there is evidently a plurality of ends, and as some of these are chosen only as means to ulterior ends (e.g., wealth, flutes, and instruments in general), it is clear that not all ends are final.[7] But

---

[7]*not all ends are final* By *ends* Aristotle means purposes. Some purposes are final—the most important; some are immediate—the less important. When a

the supreme good must of course be something final. Accordingly, if there is only one final end, this will be the good that we are seeking; and if there is more than one such end, the most complete and final of them will be this good. Now we call what is pursued as an end in itself more final than what is pursued as a means to something else; and what is never chosen as a means we call more final than what is chosen both as an end in itself and as a means; in fact, when a thing is chosen always as an end in itself and never as a means we call it absolutely final. Happiness seems, more than anything else, to answer to this description: for it is something we choose always for its own sake and never for the sake of something else; while honor, pleasure, reason, and all the virtues, though chosen partly for themselves (for we might choose any one of them without heeding the result), are chosen also for the sake of the happiness which we suppose they will bring us. Happiness, on the other hand, is never chosen for the sake of any of these, nor indeed as a means to anything else at all.

We seem to arrive at the same conclusion if we start from the notion of self-sufficiency; for the final good is admittedly self-sufficient. To be self-sufficient we do not mean that an individual must live in isolation. Parents, children, wife, as well as friends and fellow citizens generally, are all permissible; for man is by nature political. To be sure, some limit has to be set to such relationships, for if they are extended to embrace ancestors, descendants, and friends of friends, we should go on *ad infinitum*. But this point will be considered later on; provisionally we may attribute self-sufficiency to that which taken by itself makes life choiceworthy and lacking in nothing. Such a thing we conceive happiness to be. Moreover, we regard happiness as the most choiceworthy of all things; nor does this mean that it is merely one good thing among others, for if that were the case it is plain that the addition of even the least of those other goods would increase its desirability; since the addition would create a larger amount of good, and of two goods the greater is always to be preferred. Evidently, then, happiness is something final and self-sufficient, and is the end and aim of all that we do.

But perhaps it will be objected that to call happiness the supreme good is a mere truism, and that a clearer account of it is still needed. We can give this best, probably, if we ascertain the proper function of man. Just as the excellence and good performance of a flute

---

corporation contributes funds to Public Broadcasting, for example, its immediate purpose may be to fund a worthwhile program. Its final purpose may be to benefit from the publicity gained from advertising.

player, a sculptor, or any kind of artist, and generally speaking of anyone who has a function or business to perform, lies always in that function, so man's good would seem to lie in the function of man, if he has one. But can we suppose that while a carpenter and a cobbler each has a function and mode of activity of his own, man qua man[8] has none, but has been left by nature functionless? Surely it is more likely that as his several members, eye and hand and foot, can be shown to have each its own function, so man too must have a function over and above the special functions of his various members. What will such a function be? Not merely to live, of course: he shares that even with plants, whereas we are seeking something peculiar to himself. We must exclude, therefore, the life of nutrition and growth. Next comes sentient[9] life, but this again is had in common with the horse, the ox, and in fact all animals whatever. There remains only the "practical"[10] life of his rational nature; and this has two aspects, one of which is rational in the sense that it obeys a "rational principle," the other in the sense that it possesses and exercises reason. To avoid ambiguity let us specify that by "rational" we mean the "exercise or activity," not the mere possession, of reason; for it is the former that would seem more properly entitled to the name. Thus we conclude that man's function is an activity of the soul in conformity with, or at any rate involving the use of, "rational principle."

An individual and a superior individual who belong to the same class we regard as sharing the same function: a harpist and a good harpist, for instance, are essentially the same. This holds true of any class of individuals whatever; for superior excellence with respect to a function is nothing but an amplification of that selfsame function: e.g., the function of a harpist is to play the harp, while that of a good harpist is to play it well. This being so, if we take man's proper function to be a certain kind of life, viz. an activity and conduct of the soul that involves reason, and if it is the part of a good man to perform such activities well and nobly, and if a function is well performed when it is performed in accordance with its own proper excellence; we may conclude that the good of man is an activity of the soul in accordance with virtue, or, if there be more than one virtue, in accordance with the best and most perfect of them. And we must add, in a complete life. For one swallow does

16

---

[8]***man qua man***   Man as such, without reference to what he may be or do.
[9]***sentient***   Knowing, aware, conscious.
[10]***"practical"***   Aristotle refers to the actual practices that will define the ethical nature of the individual.

not make a spring, nor does one fine day; and similarly one day or brief period of happiness does not make a man happy and blessed.

So much, then, for a rough outline of the good: the proper procedure being, we may suppose, to sketch an outline first and afterwards to fill in the details. When a good outline has been made, almost anyone presumably can expand it and fill it out; and time is a good inventor and collaborator in this work. It is in just such a way that progress has been made in the various "human techniques,"[11] for filling in the gaps is something anybody can do.

But in all this we must bear constantly in mind our previous warning: not to expect the same degree of precision in all fields, but only so much as belongs to a given subject matter and is appropriate to a particular "type of inquiry." Both the carpenter and the geometer investigate the right angle, but in different ways: the one wants only such an approximation to it as will serve his work; the other, being concerned with truth, seeks to determine its essence or essential attributes. And so in other subjects we must follow a like procedure, lest we be so much taken up with side issues that we pass over the matter in hand. Similarly we ought not in all cases to demand the "reason why"; sometimes it is enough to point out the bare fact. This is true, for instance, in the case of "first principles"; for a bare fact must always be the ultimate starting point of any inquiry. First principles may be arrived at in a variety of ways: some by induction,[12] some by direct perception, some by a kind of habituation, and others in other ways. In each case we should try to apprehend them in whatever way is proper to them, and we should take care to define them clearly, because they will have a considerable influence upon the subsequent course of our inquiry. A good beginning is more than half of the whole inquiry, and once established clears up many of its difficulties.

Confirmation by Popular Beliefs

It is important to consider our ethical "first principle" not merely as a conclusion drawn from certain premises, but also in its relation to popular opinion; for all data harmonize with a true principle, but with a false one they are soon found to be discordant. Now it has been customary to divide good things into three classes:

---

[11]*"human techniques"* Arts or skills; in a sense, technology.

[12]*induction* A process of reasoning based on careful observation and collection of details upon which theories are based. "A kind of habituation" may refer to a combination of intellectual approaches characteristic of an individual.

external goods on the one hand, and on the other goods of the soul and goods of the body; and those of the soul we call good in the highest sense, and in the fullest degree. "Conscious actions," i.e., "active expressions of our nature," we take, of course, as belonging to the soul; and thus our account is confirmed by the doctrine referred to, which is of long standing and has been generally accepted by students of philosophy. . . .

We are in agreement also with those who identify happiness with virtue or with some particular virtue; for our phrase "activity in accordance with virtue" is the same as what they call virtue. It makes quite a difference, however, whether we conceive the supreme good as the mere possession of virtue or as its employment— i.e., as a state of character or as its active expression in conduct. For a state of character may be present without yielding any good result, as in a man who is asleep or in some other way inactive; but this is not true of its active expression, which must show itself in action, indeed in good action. As at the Olympic games it is not merely the fairest and strongest that receive the victory wreath, but those who compete (since the victors will of course be found among the competitors), so in life too those who carry off the finest prizes are those who manifest their excellence in their deeds.

Moreover, the life of those active in virtue is intrinsically pleasant. For besides the fact that pleasure is something belonging to the soul, each man takes pleasure in what he is said to love—the horse lover in horses, the lover of sights in public spectacles, and similarly the lover of justice in just acts, and more generally, the lover of virtue in virtuous acts. And while most men take pleasure in things which, as they are not truly pleasant by nature, create warring factions in the soul, the lovers of what is noble take pleasure in things that are truly pleasant in themselves. Virtuous actions are things of this kind; hence they are pleasant for such men, as well as pleasant intrinsically. The life of such men, therefore, requires no adventitious[13] pleasures, but finds its own pleasure within itself. This is further shown by the fact that a man who does not enjoy doing noble actions is not a good man at all: surely no one would call a man just who did not enjoy performing just actions, nor generous who did not enjoy performing generous actions, and so on. On this ground too, then, actions in conformity with virtue must be intrinsically pleasant. And certainly they are good as well as noble, and both in the highest degree, if the judgment of the good man is any criterion; for he will judge them as we have said.

20

---

[13]*adventitious*   Unnecessary; superfluous.

It follows, therefore, that happiness is at once the best and noblest and pleasantest of things, and that these attributes are not separable as the inscription at Delos[14] pretends:

> Perfect justice is noblest, health is best,
> But to gain one's heart's desire is pleasantest.

For our best activities possess all of these attributes; and it is in our best activities, or in the best one of them, that we say happiness consists.

Nevertheless, happiness plainly requires external goods as well; for it is impossible, or at least not easy, to act nobly without the proper equipment. There are many actions that can only be performed through such instruments as friends, wealth, or political influence; and there are some things, again, the lack of which must mar felicity, such as good birth, fine children, and personal comeliness: for the man who is repulsive in appearance, or ill-born, or solitary and childless does not meet the requirements of a happy man, and still less does one who has worthless children and friends, or who has lost good ones by death. As we have said, then, happiness seems to require the addition of external prosperity, and this has led some to identify it with "good fortune," just as others have made the opposite mistake of identifying it with virtue.

Sources of Happiness

For the same reason there are many who wonder whether happiness is attained by learning, or by habituation or some other kind of training, or whether it comes by some divine dispensation,[15] or even by chance. Well, certainly if the gods do give any gifts to men we may reasonably suppose that happiness is god-given; indeed, of all human blessings it is the most likely to be so, inasmuch as it is the best of them all. While this question no doubt belongs more properly to another branch of inquiry, we remark here that even if happiness is not god-sent but comes as a result of virtue or some kind of learning or training, still it is evidently one of the most divine things in the world, because that which is the reward as well as the end and aim of virtuous conduct must evidently be of supreme excellence, something divine and most blessed. If this is the case, happiness must further be something that can be generally

---

[14]***inscription at Delos***   Delos is the island that once held the Athenian treasury. It was the birthplace of Apollo, with whom the inscription would be associated.
[15]***divine dispensation***   A gift of the gods.

shared; for with the exception of those whose capacity for virtue has been stunted or maimed, everyone will have the ability, by study and diligence, to acquire it. And if it is better that happiness should be acquired in this way than by chance, we may reasonably suppose that it happens so; because everything in nature is arranged in the best way possible—just as in the case of man-made products, and of every kind of causation, especially the highest. It would be altogether wrong that what is greatest and noblest in the world should be left to the dispensation of chance.

Our present difficulty is cleared up by our previous definition   24 of happiness, as a certain activity of the soul in accordance with virtue; whereas all other sorts of good are either necessary conditions of, or cooperative with and naturally useful instruments of this. Such a conclusion, moreover, agrees with the proposition we laid down at the outset: that the end of statecraft is the best of all ends, and that the principal concern of statecraft is to make the citizens of a certain character—namely, good and disposed to perform noble actions.

Naturally, therefore, we do not call an ox or a horse or any other brute happy, since none of them is able to participate in conduct of this kind. For the same reason a child is not happy, since at his age he too is incapable of such conduct. Or if we do call a child happy, it is in the sense of predicting for him a happy future. Happiness, as we have said, involves not only a completeness of virtue but also a complete lifetime for its fulfillment. Life brings many vicissitudes and chance happenings, and it may be that one who is now prosperous will suffer great misfortunes in his old age, as is told of Priam[16] in the Trojan legends; and a man who is thus buffeted by fortune and comes to a miserable end can scarcely be called happy.

Happiness and the Vicissitudes of Fortune

Are we, then, to call no one happy while he lives? Must we, as Solon[17] advises, wait to see his end? And if we accept this verdict, are we to interpret it as meaning that a man actually becomes happy only after he is dead? Would not this be downright absurd, especially

---

[16]**Priam**   King of Troy in Homer's *Iliad.* He suffered a terrible reversal of fortune when Troy was defeated by the Greeks.

[17]**Solon (639–559 B.C.)**   Greek lawgiver and one of Greece's earliest poets. He was one of the Seven Sages of Athens.

for us who define happiness as a kind of vital activity? Or if we reject this interpretation, and suppose Solon to mean rather that it is only after death, when beyond the reach of further evil and calamity that a man can safely be said to have been happy during his life, there is still a possible objection that may be offered. For many hold that both good and evil may in a certain sense befall a dead man (just as they may befall a living man even when he is unconscious of them)—e.g., honors and disgraces, and the prosperity or misfortune of his children and the rest of his descendants. And this presents a further problem: suppose a man to have lived to a happy old age, and to have ended as he lived, there are still plenty of reverses that may befall his descendants—some of them will perhaps lead a good life and be dealt with by fortune as they deserve, others not. (It is clear, too, that a man's relationship to his descendants admits of various degrees.) It would be odd, then, if the dead man were to change along with the fortunes of his descendants, becoming happy and miserable by turns; although, to be sure, it would be equally odd if the fortunes of his descendants did not affect him at all, even for a brief time.

But let us go back to our earlier question,[18] which may perhaps clear up the one we are raising at present. Suppose we agree that we must look to the end of a man's life, and only then call him happy, not because he then *is* happy but because we can only then know him to have been so: is it not paradoxical to have refused to call him happy during just the period when happiness was present to him? On the other hand, we are naturally loath to apply the term to living men, considering the vicissitudes to which they are liable. Happiness, we argue, must be something that endures without any essential change, whereas a living individual may experience many turns of fortune's wheel. Obviously if we judge by his changing fortunes we shall have to call the same man now happy now wretched, thereby regarding the happy man as a kind of chameleon and his happiness as built on no secure foundation; yet it surely cannot be right to regard a man's happiness as wholly dependent on his fortunes. True good and evil are not of this character; rather, as we have said, although good fortune is a necessary adjunct to a complete human life, it is virtuous activities that constitute happiness, and the opposite sort of activities that constitute its opposite.

The foregoing difficulty [that happiness can be judged of only   28

---

[18]I.e., whether we are to call no one happy while he still lives. [Translator's note]

in retrospect] confirms, as a matter of fact, our theory. For none of man's functions is so permanent as his virtuous activities—indeed, many believe them to be more abiding even than a knowledge of the sciences; and of his virtuous activities those are the most abiding which are of highest worth, for it is with them that anyone blessed with supreme happiness is most fully and most continuously occupied, and hence never oblivious of. The happy man, then, will possess this attribute of permanence or stability about which we have been inquiring, and will keep it all his life; because at all times and in preference to everything else he will be engaged in virtuous action and contemplation, and he will bear the changes of fortune as nobly and in every respect as decorously as possible, inasmuch as he is truly good and "four-square beyond reproach."[19]

But the dispensations of fortune are many, some great, others small. Small ones do not appreciably turn the scales of life, but a multitude of great ones, if they are of the nature of blessings, will make life happier; for they add to life a grace of their own, provided that a man makes noble and good use of them. If, however, they are of an evil kind, they will crush and maim happiness, in that they bring pain and thereby hinder many of our natural activities. Yet true nobility shines out even here, if a multitude of great misfortunes be borne with calmness—not, to be sure, with the calmness of insensibility, but of nobility and greatness of soul.

If, as we have declared, it is our activities that give life its character, then no happy man can become miserable, inasmuch as he will never do what is hateful or base. For we hold that the truly good and wise man will bear with dignity whatever fortune sends, and will always make the best of his circumstances, as a good general makes the most effective use of the forces at his command, and a good shoemaker makes the best shoes out of the leather that is available, and so in the case of the other crafts. On this interpretation, the happy man can never become miserable—although of course he will not be blessed with happiness in the full sense of the word if he meets with such a fate as Priam's. At all events, he is not variable and always changing; for no ordinary misfortunes but only a multitude of great ones will dislodge him from his happy state, and should this occur he will not readily recover his happiness in a short time, but only, if at all, after a long period has run its course, during which he has achieved distinctions of a high order.

---

[19]A quotation from Simonides. [Translator's note] Simonides (556?–469 B.C.) was a Greek lyric poet who lived and wrote for a while in Athens. His works survive in a handful of fragments; this quotation is from fragment 5.

Is there any objection, then, to our defining a happy man as one whose activities are an expression of complete virtue, and who at the same time enjoys a sufficiency of worldly goods, not just for some limited period, but for his entire lifetime? Or perhaps we had better add the proviso that he shall be destined to go on living in this manner, and die as he has lived; for, whereas the future is obscure to us, we conceive happiness to be an end, something altogether and in every respect final and complete. Granting all this, we may declare those living men to be "blessed with supreme happiness" in whom these conditions have been and are continuing to be fulfilled. Their blessedness, however, is of human order.

So much for our discussion of this question.   32

Derivation of the Two Kinds
of Human Excellence

Since happiness is a certain activity of the soul in accordance with perfect virtue, we must next examine the nature of virtue. Not only will such an inquiry perhaps clarify the problem of happiness; it will also be of vital concern to the true student of statecraft, whose aim is to make his fellow citizens good and law-abiding. The Cretan and Spartan lawgivers,[20] as well as such others as may have resembled them, exemplify this aim. And clearly, if such an inquiry has to do with statecraft, it will be in keeping with our original purpose to pursue it.

It goes without saying that the virtue we are to study is human virtue, just as the good that we have been inquiring about is a human good, and the happiness a human happiness. By human virtue we mean virtue not of the body but of the soul, and by happiness too we mean an activity of the soul. This being the case, it is no less evident that the student of statecraft must have some knowledge of the soul, than that a physician who is to heal the eye or the whole body must have some knowledge of these organs; more so, indeed, in proportion as statecraft is superior to and more honorable than medicine. Now all physicians who are educated take much pains to know about the body. Hence as students of statecraft, too, we must inquire into the nature of the soul; but we must do so with reference to our own distinctive aim and only to

---

[20]***Cretan and Spartan lawgivers***   Both Crete and Sparta were noted for their constitutions, based on the laws of Gortyn in Crete. These laws were aristocratic, not democratic as in Athens; they promoted a class system and a rigid code of personal behavior.

the extent that it requires, for to go into minuter detail would be more laborious than is warranted by our subject matter.

We may adopt here certain doctrines about the soul that have been adequately stated in our public discourses:[21] as that the soul may be distinguished into two parts, one of which is irrational while the other possesses reason. Whether these two parts are actually distinct like the parts of the body or any other divisible thing, or are distinct only in a logical sense, like convex and concave in the circumference of a circle, is immaterial to our present inquiry.

Of the irrational part, again, one division is apparently of a   36
vegetative nature and common to all living things: I mean that which is the cause of nutrition and growth. It is more reasonable to postulate a vital faculty of this sort, present in all things that take nourishment, even when in an embryo stage, and retained by the full-grown organism, than to assume a special nutritive faculty in the latter. Hence we may say that the excellence belonging to this part of the soul is common to all species, and not specifically human: a point that is further confirmed by the popular view that this part of the soul is most active during sleep. For it is during sleep that the distinction between good men and bad is least apparent; whence the saying that for half their lives the happy are no better off than the wretched. This, indeed, is natural enough, for sleep is an inactivity of the soul in those respects in which the soul is called good or bad. (It is true, however, that to a slight degree certain bodily movements penetrate to the soul; which is the reason why good men's dreams are superior to those of the average person.) But enough of this subject: let us dismiss the nutritive principle, since it has by nature no share in human excellence.

There seems to be a second part of the soul, which though irrational yet in some way partakes of reason. For while we praise the rational principle and the part of the soul that manifests it in the case of the continent and incontinent man alike, on the ground that it exhorts them rightly and urges them to do what is best; yet we find within these men another element different in nature from the rational element, and struggling against and resisting it. Just as ataxic limbs,[22] when we choose to move them to the right, turn on the contrary to the left, so it is with the soul: the impulses of the incontinent man run counter to his ruling part. The only difference is that in the case of the body we see what it is that goes astray, while in the soul we do not. Nevertheless the comparison will doubtless

---

[21]*our public discourses*   Aristotle may be referring to speeches at which the public is welcome, as opposed to his lectures to students.
[22]*ataxic limbs*   Aristotle refers to a nervous disorder of the limbs.

suffice to show that there is in the soul something besides the rational element, opposing and running counter to it. (In what sense the two elements are distinct is immaterial.) But this other element, as we have said, seems also to have some share in a rational principle: at any rate, in the continent man it submits to reason, while in the man who is at once temperate and courageous it is presumably all the more obedient; for in him it speaks on all matters harmoniously with the voice of reason.

Evidently, then, the irrational part of the soul is twofold. There is the vegetative element, which has no share in reason, and there is the concupiscent,[23] or rather the appetitive element, which does in a sense partake of reason, in that it is amenable and obedient to it: i.e., it is rational in the sense that we speak of "having *logos* of" [paying heed to] father and friends, not in the sense of "having *logos* of" [having a rational understanding of] mathematical truths. That this irrational element is in some way amenable to reason is shown by our practice of giving admonishment, and by rebuke and exhortation generally. If on this account it is deemed more correct to regard this element as also possessing reason, then the rational part of the soul, in turn, will have two subdivisions: the one being rational in the strict sense as actually possessing reason, the other merely in the sense that a child obeys its father.

Virtue, too, is differentiated in accordance with this division of the soul: for we call some of the virtues intellectual and others moral: wisdom, understanding, and sagacity being among the former, liberality and temperance among the latter. In speaking of a man's character we do not say that he is wise or intelligent, but that he is gentle or temperate; yet we praise the wise man too for the disposition he has developed within himself, and praiseworthy dispositions we call virtues.

---

[23]*concupiscent*   Sexual; Aristotle corrects himself to refer to the general nature of desire.

QUESTIONS FOR CRITICAL READING

1. Define the following terms: "good," "virtue," "honor," "happiness," "truth," "soul," "body."
2. In the first paragraphs of the selection, Aristotle talks about aims and ends. What does he mean by these terms?
3. Do you feel that Aristotle's view of the relationship of virtue to happiness is as important today as he argued it was in his day?
4. What is Aristotle's attitude toward most people?

5. What characteristics can we assume about the audience for whom Aristotle writes?
6. In what senses is the selection modern? In what senses is it antique or dated?

WRITING ASSIGNMENTS

1. In his section on the primacy of statecraft, Aristotle makes a number of assertions regarding the relationship of the happiness of the individual to the welfare (or happiness) of the state. Clarify as much as possible the relationship of the individual's happiness to that of the state. How can a state be happy? Is the term relevant to anything other than an individual? Does Aristotle think that the individual's interests should be subservient to the state's?

2. In paragraph 15, Aristotle talks about the function of man. Relying on that discussion and other aspects of the work, write your own version of "The Function of Man." Be sure to use "man" as a collective term for both men and women. Once you have clarified the function of man, establish the connection between function and happiness. Is it true that the best-functioning person will be the happiest person? Aristotle implies that it is not enough to be, say, honorable or noble, but that one must act honorably or nobly. Is the implication true?

3. Take Aristotle's definition, "Happiness is a certain activity of the soul in accordance with perfect virtue." Define it in terms that are clear not only to you but also to your peers. Take care to include each part of the definition: "certain activity" (or lack of it), "soul" (which in modern terms may be "personality" or "psyche"), "in accordance with," "perfect virtue." You may rely on any parts of the selection that can be of help, but be sure to use the topic of definition to guide you through the selection. You certainly may disagree with Aristotle or amplify aspects of his definitions. In one sense, you will be defining "happiness" for yourself and your times.

4. In his "confirmation by popular beliefs" (para. 19 and following), Aristotle talks about the good. He mentions three classes of good, ranking them in order from lowest to highest: external goods, goods of the body, and goods of the soul. Using concrete examples, define each of these classes of good. Do you agree with Aristotle's order? Do you think that your peers agree with it? Where possible, give examples to help establish the validity of your opinion. Finally, do you think that our society in general puts the same value on these three classes of good that Aristotle does? Again, use examples where possible.

5. Analyze the following quotations from the selection, taking a stand on the question of whether or not Aristotle is generally correct in his assertion about the aim of man:

It is in our best activities, or in the best one of them, that we say happiness consists. (para. 21)

A man who does not enjoy doing noble actions is not a good man at all. (para. 21)

Even supposing the chief good to be eventually the same for the individual as for the state, that of the state is evidently of greater and more fundamental importance both to attain and to preserve. (para. 4)

In life . . . those who carry off the finest prizes are those who manifest their excellence in their deeds. (para. 20)

If, as we have declared, it is our activities that give life its character, then no happy man can become miserable, inasmuch as he will never do what is hateful or base. (para. 30)

6. **CONNECTIONS**   Aristotle's emphasis on the word *man* derives from his cultural experience in teaching only men, discoursing only with men, and assuming that his readers would be men. Consider Mary Daly's view that the symbolic images of an institution affect the members of the institution and decide whether or not Aristotle's advice is explicitly patriarchal. If you think it is patriarchal, do you think Mary Daly would feel empowered to disregard the messages Aristotle offers us? Would his messages perpetuate the conventional patriarchal structure that Daly argues against?

7. **CONNECTIONS**   Of the remaining philosophers in this section, which address ethical issues with a concern similar to that of Aristotle? Consider the basic issues of happiness and suggestions for ways of living. What fundamental differences do you see in their approaches?

RENÉ DESCARTES
Discourse Four

RENÉ DESCARTES *(1596–1650), credited with founding modern philosophy, was educated in Jesuit schools in France, beginning with Jesuit college at La Flèche, which was established by the king for the education of the brightest children of the upper classes. In time he came to reject certain principles of his education and developed his Method, the intellectual system expounded in his* Discourse on the Method of Rightly Conducting One's Reason and Seeking Truth in the Sciences *(1637). This work was followed by* Meditations on First Philosophy *(1641), which discuss the "first philosophy"—the nature of God.*

For many thinkers Discourse on Method *represents the beginning of the end of the domination of Aristotle and the scholastics. The scholastic philosophers (churchmen teaching throughout Europe) followed Aristotle and St. Thomas Aquinas in a rigid system governed by rules of logic. Although sensory evidence was sometimes relied upon, the final authority was the church. Descartes wished on the contrary to substitute the authority of his own reasoning in his investigations into the nature of truth.*

His discovery of Method came to him suddenly in 1619 in a "blinding flash" of insight. Seeing the need for a unity of thought in science, he realized that the step-by-step proofs used by geometricians could be employed in all aspects of science. In "Discourse Two" he explains the four rules of his Method and ends with a summary of his insight into geometry:

From *Discourse on the Method of Rightly Conducting One's Reason and Seeking Truth in the Sciences.* Translated by F. E. Sutcliffe.

The first was never to accept anything as true that I did not know to be evidently so: that is to say, carefully to avoid precipitancy and prejudice, and to include in my judgements nothing more than what presented itself so clearly and so distinctly to my mind that I might have no occasion to place it in doubt.

The second, to divide each of the difficulties that I was examining into as many parts as might be possible and necessary in order best to solve it.

The third, to conduct my thoughts in an orderly way, beginning with the simplest objects and the easiest to know, in order to climb gradually, as by degrees, as far as the knowledge of the most complex, and even supposing some order among those objects which do not precede each other naturally.

And the last, everywhere to make such complete enumerations and such general reviews that I would be sure to have omitted nothing.

These long chains of reasonings, quite simple and easy, which geometers are accustomed to using to teach their most difficult demonstrations, had given me cause to imagine that everything which can be encompassed by man's knowledge is linked in the same way, and that, provided only that one abstains from accepting any for true which is not true, and that one always keeps the right order to one thing to be deduced from that which precedes it, there can be nothing so distant that one does not reach it eventually, or so hidden that one cannot discover it.

Descartes insisted that if each step of the inquiry were free from error the darkest secrets of nature could be discovered. What he needed once he established this principle was an unassailable position from which to begin. That first point reached, his chain of reasoning could stretch to the stars; without it true knowledge was impossible. Descartes describes that point in the following selection, "Discourse Four." It contains the most famous catch-phrase in philosophy: "Cogito, ergo sum" (I think, therefore I am). After rejecting many other possible points of departure, Descartes hit upon the statement that was for him unassailable: if he thought about something, then he knew that he must exist, that he was a "thing that thinks," and that he could not be deceived about the fact that he thought. After establishing this basic truth, he moved toward a proof of the existence of God that did not depend on sensory evidence. It is sometimes described as an intuitive proof, because it depends on a chain of reasoning that starts neither from observation nor from an outside authority.

Descartes was influenced by the skepticism of Michel de Montaigne (1533–1592), who, in his essays, accepted the view that certainty was impossible because the senses were unreliable and the very existence of the individual unprovable. In the latter part of the sixteenth century, the discovery of important classical texts—especially Sextus Empiricus's translation of the work of the ancient Greek philosopher Pyrrho—was enormously influential in Europe because they cast doubt on all things. The fracturing of the Christian Church into several sects called into question the most authoritative truths of all, most notably when Martin Luther challenged the authority of the church on the question of the truth. Doubt and uncertainty were therefore part of a crisis in European thought. Descartes worked out his theories a hundred years after Luther, and with the publication of Discourse on Method he seemed to have begun to offer a way out of the crisis.

Ironically, Descartes's reliance on intuitive chains of reasoning did not work in his favor in scientific investigations of the kind we now rely upon. He was uncomfortable with evidence gathered by the senses—what is now called empirical evidence—and therefore made little contribution to the development of modern science. However, he did not hold science back. He especially admired Galileo (1564–1642), the most renowned scientist of his time.

Another legacy of Descartes is the body-mind split. He states in "Discourse Four" that he is aware of the distinctions between his body and his mind and sees them as different in certain essentials. Eventually, he postulates that the mind's existence may not depend on the body. Such a view was widely developed in poetry and literature and is for some critics a lamentable fact. However, Descartes remains a philosopher who confronted difficult problems in a very personal way. His "Discourse" records his personal development as a thinker, indulging at times in biographical detail that may seem superfluous. However, it is essential to his approach, since the individual, like him, must be in a position to acquire reliable knowledge in an effort to reach the truth.

Discourse Four

I do not know if I ought to tell you about the first meditations I pursued there, for they are so abstract and unusual that they will probably not be to the taste of everyone; and yet, so that one may judge if the foundations I have laid are firm enough, I find myself to some extent forced to speak of them. I had long ago noticed that, in matters relating to conduct, one needs sometimes to follow, just as if they were absolutely indubitable, opinions one knows to be very unsure, as has been said above; but as I wanted to concentrate solely on the search for truth, I thought I ought to do just the opposite, and reject as being absolutely false everything in which I could suppose the slightest reason for doubt, in order to see if there did not remain after that anything in my belief which was entirely indubitable. So, because our senses sometimes play us false, I decided to suppose that there was nothing at all which was such as they cause us to imagine it; and because there are men who make mistakes in reasoning, even with the simplest geometrical matters, and make paralogisms,[1] judging that I was as liable to error as anyone else, I rejected as being false all the reasonings I had hitherto accepted as proofs. And finally, considering that all the same thoughts that we have when we are awake can also come to us when we are asleep, without any one of them then being true, I resolved to pretend that nothing which had ever entered my mind was any more true than the illusions of my dreams. But immediately afterwards I became aware that, while I decided thus to think that everything was false, it followed necessarily that I who thought thus must be something; and observing that this truth: *I think, therefore I am,* was so certain and so evident that all the most extravagant suppositions of the sceptics were not capable of shaking it, I judged that I would accept it without scruple as the first principle of the philosophy I was seeking.

Then, examining attentively what I was, and seeing that I could pretend that I had no body and that there was no world or place that I was in, but that I could not, for all that, pretend that I did not exist, and that, on the contrary, from the very fact that I thought of doubting the truth of other things, it followed very evidently and very certainly that I existed; while, on the other hand, if I had only ceased to think, although all the rest of what I had ever imagined had been true, I would have had no reason to believe that I existed; I thereby concluded that I was a substance, of which the whole essence or nature consists in thinking, and which, in order to exist, needs no place and depends on no material thing; so that this 'I', that is to say, the mind, by which I am what I am, is entirely distinct from the body, and even that it is easier to know than the body, and moreover, that even if the body were not, it would not cease to be all that it is.

After this, I considered in general what is needed for a proposition to be true and certain; for, since I had just found one which I knew to be so, I thought that I ought also to know what this certainty consisted of. And having noticed that there is nothing at all in this, *I think, therefore I am,* which assures me that I am speaking

---

[1] *paralogisms* Illogical reasonings.

the truth, except that I see very clearly that in order to think one must exist, I judged that I could take it to be a general rule that the things we conceive very clearly and very distinctly are all true, but that there is nevertheless some difficulty in being able to recognize for certain which are the things we see distinctly.

Following this, reflecting on the fact that I had doubts, and that consequently my being was not completely perfect, for I saw clearly that it was a greater perfection to know than to doubt, I decided to inquire whence I had learned to think of some thing more perfect than myself; and I clearly recognized that this must have been from some nature which was in fact more perfect. As for the notions I had of several other things outside myself, such as the sky, the earth, light, heat, and a thousand others, I had not the same concern to know their source, because, seeing nothing in them which seemed to make them superior to myself, I could believe that, if they were true, they were dependencies of my nature, in as much as it had some perfection; and, if they were not, that I held them from nothing, that is to say that they were in me because of an imperfection in my nature. But I could not make the same judgment concerning the idea of a being more perfect than myself; for to hold it from nothing was something manifestly impossible; and because it is no less contradictory that the more perfect should proceed from and depend on the less perfect, than it is that something should emerge out of nothing, I could not hold it from myself; with the result that it remained that it must have been put into me by a being whose nature was truly more perfect than mine and which even had in itself all the perfections of which I could have any idea, that is to say, in a single word, which was God. To which I added that, since I knew some perfections that I did not have, I was not the only being which existed (I shall freely use here, with your permission, the terms of the School) but that there must of necessity be another more perfect, upon whom I depended, and from whom I had acquired all I had; for, if I had been alone and independent of all other, so as to have had from myself this small portion of perfection that I had by participation in the perfection of God, I could have given myself, by the same reason, all the remainder of perfection that I knew myself to lack, and thus to be myself infinite, eternal, immutable, omniscient, all-powerful, and finally to have all the perfections that I could observe to be in God. For, consequentially upon the reasonings by which I had proved the existence of God, in order to understand the nature of God as far as my own nature was capable of doing, I had only to consider, concerning all the things of which I found in myself some idea, whether it was a perfection or not to have them: and I was assured that none of those which indicated some imperfection was in him, but that all the others were. So I saw that doubt, inconstancy, sadness, and similar things could not be in him, seeing that I myself would have been very pleased to be free from them. Then, further, I had ideas of many sensible and bodily things; for even supposing that I was dreaming, and that everything I saw or imagined was false, I could not, nevertheless, deny that the ideas were really in my thoughts. But, because I had already recognized in myself very clearly that intelligent nature is distinct from the corporeal, considering that all composition is evidence of dependency, and that dependency is manifestly a defect, I thence judged that it could not be a perfection in God to be composed of these two natures, and that, consequently, he was not so composed; but that, if there were any bodies in the world or any intelligences or other natures which were not wholly perfect, their existence must depend on his power, in such a way that they could not subsist without him for a single instant.

I set out after that to seek other truths; and turning to the object of the geometers, which I conceived as a continuous body, or a space extended indefinitely in length, width, and height or depth, divisible into various parts, which could have various figures and sizes and be moved or transposed in all sorts of ways—for the geometers take all that to be in the object of their study—I went through some of their simplest proofs. And having observed that the great certainty that everyone attributes to them is based only on the fact that they are clearly conceived according to the rule I spoke of earlier, I noticed also that they had nothing at all in them which might assure me of the existence of their object. Thus, for example, I very well perceived that, supposing a triangle to be given, its three angles must be equal to two right angles, but I saw nothing, for all that, which assured me that any such triangle existed in the world; whereas, reverting to the examination of the idea I had of a perfect Being, I found that existence was comprised in the idea in the same way that the equality of the three angles of a triangle to two right angles is comprised in the idea of a triangle or, as in the idea of a sphere, the fact that all its parts are equidistant from its center, or even more obviously so; and that consequently it is at least as certain that God, who is this perfect Being, is, or exists, as any geometric demonstration can be.

But what persuades many people that it is difficult to know this, and even also to know what their soul is, is that they never lift their minds above tangible things, and that they are so accustomed not to think of anything except by imagining it, which is a mode of thinking peculiar to material objects, that everything which is not within the realm of imagination seems to them unintelligible. This is evident enough from the fact that even the philosophers hold as a maxim in the Schools, that there is nothing in the understanding which has not first been in the senses, in which, however, it is certain that ideas about God and the soul have never been; and it seems to me that those who wish to use their imagination to understand them are doing just the same as if, to hear sounds or smell odors, they attempted to use their eyes; except that there is still this difference, that the sense of light assures us no less of the truth of its objects than do the senses of smell and hearing, whereas neither our imagination nor our senses could ever assure us of anything, if our understanding did not intervene. Finally, if there are still men who are not sufficiently persuaded of the existence of God and of their soul by the reasons I have given, I would like them to know that all the other things of which they think themselves perhaps more assured, such as having a body, and that there are stars and an earth, and such like, are less certain; for, although we may have a moral assurance of these things, which is such that it seems that, short of being foolish, no one can doubt their existence, at the same time also, short of being unreasonable, when it is a question of a metaphysical certainty, one cannot deny that there are not sufficient grounds for being absolutely assured, when one observes that one can in the same way imagine, being asleep, that one has another body, and that one sees other stars and another earth, without there being anything of the sort. For how does one know that the thoughts which come while one dreams are false rather than the others, seeing that they are often no less strong and clear? And may the most intelligent men study this question as much as they please, I do not believe that they can give any reason which would be sufficient to remove this doubt, unless they presuppose the existence of God. For, firstly, even the rule which I stated above that I held, namely, that the things we grasp very clearly and very distinctly are all true, is assured only because God is or exists, and because he is a perfect Being, and because everything that is in us comes from him; whence it follows that our ideas and notions, being real things and coming from God, in so far as they are clear and distinct, cannot to this extent be other than true. Accordingly, if we often enough have ideas which contain errors, they can only be those which contain something confused and obscure, because in this they participate in nothingness, that is to say that they are in us in this confused way only because we are not completely perfect. And it is evident that it is no less contradictory that error or imperfection, as such, should proceed from God, than that truth or perfection should come from nothingness. But, if we did not know that all that is in us which is real and true comes from a perfect and infinite Being, we would have no reason which would assure us that, however clear and distinct our ideas might be, they had the perfection of being true.

But, after knowledge of God and of the soul has thus made us certain of this rule, it is a simple matter to understand that the dreams we imagine when we are asleep should not in any way make us doubt the truth of the thoughts we have when we are awake. For, even if it should happen that, while sleeping, one should have some quite distinct idea, as, for example, if a geometer were to discover some new demonstration, his being asleep would not prevent it from being true; and as for the most ordinary error of our dreams, which consists in representing to us various objects in the same way as our waking senses do, it does not matter that they give us occasion to doubt the truth of such ideas, because they can also lead us into error often enough without our being asleep, as when those who have jaundice see everything yellow, or when the stars or other very distant bodies seem to us much smaller than they are. For, finally, whether we are awake or asleep, we should never let ourselves be persuaded except on the evidence of our reason. And it is to be observed that I say: of our reason, and not: of our imagination or our senses. For, although we see the sun very clearly, we should not on that account judge that it is only as large as we see it; and we can well imagine distinctly a lion's head grafted on to the body of a goat, without concluding on that account that there is any such chimera in the world; for reason does not dictate that what we see or imagine thus is true, but it does tell us that all our ideas and notions must have some basis in truth, for it would not be possible that God, who is all perfect and true, should have put them in us unless it were so. And because our reasonings are never so clear or complete while we sleep as when we are awake, even though sometimes our imaginations are as vivid and distinct or even more so, reason tells us that, it not being possible that our thoughts should all be true, because we are not absolutely perfect, what truth there is in them will undoubtedly be found in those we have when we are awake rather than in those we have in our dreams.

QUESTIONS FOR CRITICAL READING

1. Do you perceive a difference between your thoughts when you are awake and your thoughts when you are asleep? Why does Descartes worry about this distinction?
2. Why did Descartes resolve "to pretend that nothing which had ever entered my mind was any more true than the illusions of my dreams" (para. 1)?
3. Why is "I think, therefore I am" a powerful statement guaranteeing certainty on the part of the person who says it?
4. In paragraph 2, Descartes realizes he "was a substance, of which the

whole essence or nature consists in thinking . . . so this 'I,' . . . the mind . . . is entirely distinct from the body." Do you perceive this to be true?

5. Why, in paragraph 4, does he inquire "of something more perfect than myself"?

6. How does Descartes prove the existence of God (paras. 4 and 5)?

7. Do you feel Descartes is right to be suspicious of information gathered through the senses? Under what conditions can the senses be deceiving?

WRITING ASSIGNMENTS

1. In paragraph 6, Descartes complains that the "philosophers hold as a maxim in the Schools, that there is nothing in the understanding which has not first been in the senses." Examine that statement for accuracy and then explain in a brief essay why it is important to Descartes's search for the truth.

2. Explain the way in which Descartes, according to his explanations in this "Discourse," proceeded to move toward certainty. He states that his quest is for truth and that in order to begin thinking truthfully he needs to have a statement whose validity is unquestionably true. Once he has that statement, what does he do?

3. One of the problems Descartes faced was the absence of an ironclad way to argue that one is not dreaming all the time. Common sense tells most people whether they are awake or dreaming, but it is certainly possible to dream that one is awake. Examine this question with an eye toward clarifying the issues. Can anyone know positively that he or she is not dreaming?

4. About the most important questions of certainty Descartes says, "Whether we are awake or asleep, we should never let ourselves be persuaded except on the evidence of our reason. And it is to be observed that I say: of our reason, and not: of our imagination or our senses" (para. 7). Explain what Descartes means (you may wish to point to his example, geometry), and then give an example of the process of establishing an important truth by using your reason and not your imagination or senses.

5. Examine Descartes's proof of the existence of God. Does Descartes depend on imagination and the senses, or does he depend only on reason? Is it possible to prove the existence of God using only reason? Would you find it easier to prove the existence of God if you also used your imagination and your senses?

6. **CONNECTIONS** What intellectual principles does Descartes share with Francis Bacon? You may want to consider the relationship of his four rules of Method—excerpted in the introduction to this piece— with Bacon's four idols. Would Bacon have felt at ease with Descartes's way of thinking, or has Descartes fallen into some of the traps that Bacon warns of?

FRIEDRICH NIETZSCHE
Apollonianism and
Dionysianism

*F*RIEDRICH NIETZSCHE *(1844–1900), one of the most influential modern thinkers, was concerned that the rise of science in the modern world and the changes in attitudes toward religion and the nature of God would leave people with a loss of purpose. Like many historians and philosophers of the day, he feared that modern civilization itself was somehow hanging in the balance, and that unless people struggled to reclaim the leadership that brought progress and prosperity, the foundations of society would collapse.*

His solution for the malaise that he felt was settling on modern society involved a search for meaning through a form of introspection and self-understanding that might well have been intelligible to Buddha, Plato, or Aristotle. For Nietzsche, self-mastery was the key to transcending the confusion of modern thought. Realizing that self-domination was not an easy state to achieve, he named that man who succeeded in mastering himself "superman," a man who could create his own values instead of blindly following conventional or societal standards.

Nietzsche's own personal life was rather difficult. He was the son of a minister, but his father died when he was four, and Nietzsche was raised by a gathering of family women. Some critics have felt that the antifemale tone in certain of his writings is a result of his upbringing, but may also be related to the possibility that he may have contracted syphilis from a prostitute when he was a young man.

He was a brilliant student, particularly of the classics, and he became a professor at the University of Basel at a very young age. His first book, The Birth of Tragedy from the Spirit of Music *(1872),*

From *The Birth of Tragedy from the Spirit of Music*. Translated by Francis Golffing.

is the result of his effort to clarify certain aspects of the music of Richard Wagner, the contemporary composer of the Ring Cycle of operas based on Scandinavian mythology. Nietzsche eventually broke with Wagner on philosophical matters, but his regard for Wagner's music remained strong. The insight on which the work rests, presented in the selection reprinted here, is an attempt to clarify the two basic psychological forces in humankind: Apollonian intellectuality and Dionysian passion. Both forces were present in ancient Greek society, which Nietzsche seems to take as a standard of high civilization, particularly in its Doric phase—a phase of clear, calm, beautiful works exemplified by the Parthenon in Athens. Although the Apollonian is opposed to the Dionysian, Nietzsche points out that the Greeks discovered the need for both forces to be present in a culture. The tragedy, he says, was the ground on which these forces were able to meet in ancient Greece. In Nietzsche's time—as he points out in a section not included here—they meet in the music of Richard Wagner.

The kind of behavior countenanced by these two gods is quite different, but each of them represents an aspect of divinity. The rational approximates the ideals of Plato and Aristotle, but the ecstatic qualities of Dionysianism come closer to the views of Mary Daly, who argues passionately against a hierarchy built on logic. Because these are psychological states of mind that can be experienced by the same person at different times, Nietzsche carefully describes the positive aspects of each kind of behavior.

Nietzsche relies on art to help him clarify the psychological types represented by each of these Greek gods. Apollo dominates intellectually. He demands clarity, order, reason, and calm. He is also the god of the individual. Dionysus, on the other hand, is the god of ecstasy and passion. Obscurity, disorder, irrational behavior, even hysteria are encouraged by Dionysus. He is the god of throngs and mobs. After reading this excerpt, we realize that most of us have both capacities within us and that one of the challenges of life is learning how to balance them.

NIETZSCHE'S RHETORIC

The most obvious rhetorical device Nietzsche uses is comparison and contrast. The Apollonian contrasts with the Dionysian; the Greek with the barbarian; the dream with the illusion; the god with the human; the individual with the group; the one with the many; even life with death. In this sense, the subject at hand has governed the basic shape of the work.

Nietzsche's task was to explain the different polarities, their form *of expression, and their effect. Since these terms were quite new to most readers when he wrote this work, it took him some time to clarify the nature of the Apollonian and the Dionysian. In a sense, the first paragraphs are spent in the task of definition. Some of the paragraphs explore the topic of circumstance, a survey of past time, particularly in regard to Greek society. Once each polarity is defined, Nietzsche goes on to explain its sphere of influence, what we can expect of it, and what its implications are. Insofar as those qualities are present in the rhetoric, the essay is itself Apollonian.*

There is a surprise in Nietzsche's use of rhetoric here, however. Through rhetorical techniques, he also illustrates some aspects of the Dionysian nature. There are passages in the selection, such as the discussion of Dionysus, in paragraph 5, which can best be described as ecstatic, poetic—and, if not irrational, certainly obscure and difficult to grasp. The Dionysian aspects of the passage are based on feeling. We all know that there are poems we read that we cannot break down into other words—or even explain to others. What we get from such poems is not an understanding but a feeling or an impression. The same is true of the passages we confront in this essay. They challenge us because we know that the general character of any essay must be Apollonian. When we are greeted by Dionysian verbal excursions, we are thrown off a bit. Yet that is part of Nietzsche's point: verbal artifacts (such as Greek tragedy) can combine both forces.

In fact, it may be that Nietzsche's most important point is that both forces yearn to be joined in some kind of artifact. For the ancients it was in the work of the Greek tragedians. For the Elizabethans it was in Shakespeare. For people of his own day it was in the Ring Cycle of Wagner. The ultimate effect of using the rhetorical device of comparison and contrast is to emphasize the fact that these two forces must be unified in the highest cultures. Diversity is everywhere in nature, as Nietzsche implies throughout, but that diversity has one deep longing: to be One with the One. As he says (para. 14), the eternal goal of the original Oneness is its redemption through illusion. Illusion is art, not just dream. The great psychologists who built twentieth-century theories understood both dream and illusion; they are projections of mental states and give access to the inner nature of humankind.

Apollonianism and
Dionysianism

Much will have been gained for esthetics once we have succeeded in apprehending directly—rather than merely *ascertaining*—
that art owes its continuous evolution to the Apollonian-Dionysiac
duality, even as the propagation of the species depends on the
duality of the sexes, their constant conflicts and periodic acts of
reconciliation. I have borrowed my adjectives from the Greeks,
who developed their mystical doctrines of art through plausible
embodiments, not through purely conceptual means. It is by those
two art-sponsoring deities, Apollo and Dionysos,[1] that we are made
to recognize the tremendous split, as regards both origins and objectives, between the plastic, Apollonian arts and the non-visual art of
music inspired by Dionysos. The two creative tendencies developed
alongside one another, usually in fierce opposition, each by its taunts
forcing the other to more energetic production, both perpetuating
in a discordant concord that agon[2] which the term *art* but feebly
denominates: until at last, by the thaumaturgy[3] of an Hellenic art
of will, the pair accepted the yoke of marriage and, in this condition,
begot Attic tragedy,[4] which exhibits the salient features of both
parents.

To reach a closer understanding of both these tendencies, let
us begin by viewing them as the separate art realms of *dream* and
intoxication, two physiological phenomena standing toward one another in much the same relationship as the Apollonian and Dionysiac. It was in a dream, according to Lucretius,[5] that the marvelous
gods and goddesses first presented themselves to the minds of men.
That great healing sculptor, Phidias,[6] beheld in a dream the entranc-
ing bodies of more-than-human beings, and likewise, if anyone had

---

[1]***Apollo and Dionysos (Dionysus)*** Apollo is the god of music, healing, and
archery, and, as Phoebus Apollo, is also regarded as the god of light. Dionysus is
the god of wine and drunkenness.

[2]*agon* A contest or opposition of forces.

[3]*thaumaturgy* A magical change. Nietzsche means that a powerful transformation was needed for Apollo and Dionysus to be able to join together.

[4]*Attic tragedy* Greek tragedy performed in Athens, in the Greek region of
Attica, sixth century–fourth century B.C.

[5]*Lucretius (100?–55 B.C.)* A Roman philosopher whose book on natural science was standard for more than a millennium.

[6]*Phidias (fl. 430 B.C.)* Greek sculptor who carved the figures of the gods and
goddesses on the Parthenon.

asked the Greek poets about the mystery of poetic creation, they too would have referred him to dreams and instructed him much as Hans Sachs[7] instructs us in *Die Meistersinger:*

> My friend, it is the poet's work
> Dreams to interpret and to mark.
> Believe me that man's true conceit
> In a dream becomes complete:
> All poetry we ever read
> Is but true dreams interpreted.

The fair illusion of the dream sphere, in the production of which every man proves himself an accomplished artist, is a precondition not only of all plastic art, but even, as we shall see presently, of a wide range of poetry. Here we enjoy an immediate apprehension of form, all shapes speak to us directly, nothing seems indifferent or redundant. Despite the high intensity with which these dream realities exist for us, we still have a residual sensation that they are illusions; at least such has been my experience—and the frequency, not to say normality, of the experience is borne out in many passages of the poets. Men of philosophical disposition are known for their constant premonition that our everyday reality, too, is an illusion, hiding another, totally different kind of reality. It was Schopenhauer[8] who considered the ability to view at certain times all men and things as mere phantoms or dream images to be the true mark of philosophic talent. The person who is responsive to the stimuli of art behaves toward the reality of dream much the way the philosopher behaves toward the reality of existence: he observes exactly and enjoys his observations, for it is by these images that he interprets life, by these processes that he rehearses it. Nor is it by pleasant images only that such plausible connections are made: the whole divine comedy of life, including its somber aspects, its sudden balkings, impish accidents, anxious expectations, moves past him, not quite like a shadow play—for it is he himself, after all, who lives and suffers through these scenes—yet never without giving a fleeting sense of illusion; and I imagine that many persons have reassured themselves amidst the perils of dream by calling out, "It is a dream! I want it to go on." I have even heard of people spinning

---

[7]**Hans Sachs**   The legendary singer-hero of Richard Wagner's opera *The Master-Singer;* the lines quoted are from that opera.

[8]***Arthur Schopenhauer (1788–1860)***   German philosopher who influenced Nietzsche. His books, *The World as Will and Idea* (1883–1886) and *On the Will in Nature* (1836; tr. 1889), emphasized the power of free will as a chief force in the world.

out the causality of one and the same dream over three or more successive nights. All these facts clearly bear witness that our innermost being, the common substratum of humanity, experiences dreams with deep delight and a sense of real necessity. This deep and happy sense of the necessity of dream experiences was expressed by the Greeks in the image of Apollo. Apollo is at once the god of all plastic powers and the soothsaying god. He who is etymologically the "lucent" one, the god of light, reigns also over the fair illusions of our inner world of fantasy. The perfection of these conditions in contrast to our imperfectly understood waking reality, as well as our profound awareness of nature's healing powers during the interval of sleep and dream, furnishes a symbolic analogue to the soothsaying faculty and quite generally to the arts, which make life possible and worth living. But the image of Apollo must incorporate that thin line which the dream image may not cross, under penalty of becoming pathological, of imposing itself on us as crass reality: a discreet limitation, a freedom from all extravagant urges, the sapient tranquility of the plastic god. His eye must be sunlike, in keeping with his origin. Even at those moments when he is angry and ill-tempered there lies upon him the consecration of fair illusion. In an eccentric way one might say of Apollo what Schopenhauer says, in the first part of *The World as Will and Idea,* of man caught in the veil of Maya:[9] "Even as on an immense, raging sea, assailed by huge wave crests, a man sits in a little rowboat trusting his frail craft, so, amidst the furious torments of this world, the individual sits tranquilly, supported by the *principium individuationis*[10] and relying on it." One might say that the unshakable confidence in that principle has received its most magnificent expression in Apollo, and that Apollo himself may be regarded as the marvelous divine image of the *principium individuationis,* whose looks and gestures radiate the full delight, wisdom, and beauty of "illusion."

In the same context Schopenhauer has described for us the 4 tremendous awe which seizes man when he suddenly begins to doubt the cognitive modes of experience, in other words, when in a given instance the law of causation seems to suspend itself. If we add to this awe the glorious transport which arises in man, even from the very depths of nature, at the shattering of the *principium individuationis,* then we are in a position to apprehend the essence of Dionysiac rapture, whose closest analogy is furnished by physical

---

[9]*Maya*   A Hindu term for the material world of the senses. The veil of Maya is the illusion hiding the reality that lies beneath material surfaces.

[10]*principium individuationis*   The principle of the individual, as apart from the crowd.

intoxication. Dionysiac stirrings arise either through the influence of those narcotic potions of which all primitive races speak in their hymns, or through the powerful approach of spring, which penetrates with joy the whole frame of nature. So stirred, the individual forgets himself completely. It is the same Dionysiac power which in medieval Germany drove ever increasing crowds of people singing and dancing from place to place; we recognize in these St. John's and St. Vitus' dancers the bacchic choruses[11] of the Greeks, who had their precursors in Asia Minor and as far back as Babylon and the orgiastic Sacaea.[12] There are people who, either from lack of experience or out of sheer stupidity, turn away from such phenomena, and, strong in the sense of their own sanity, label them either mockingly or pityingly "endemic diseases." These benighted souls have no idea how cadaverous and ghostly their "sanity" appears as the intense throng of Dionysiac revelers sweeps past them.

Not only does the bond between man and man come to be forged once more by the magic of the Dionysiac rite, but nature itself, long alienated or subjugated, rises again to celebrate the reconciliation with her prodigal son, man. The earth offers its gifts voluntarily, and the savage beasts of mountain and desert approach in peace. The chariot of Dionysos is bedecked with flowers and garlands; panthers and tigers stride beneath his yoke. If one were to convert Beethoven's "Paean to Joy"[13] into a painting and refuse to curb the imagination when that multitude prostrates itself reverently in the dust, one might form some apprehension of Dionysiac ritual. Now the slave emerges as a freeman; all the rigid, hostile walls which either necessity or despotism has erected between men are shattered. Now that the gospel or universal harmony is sounded, each individual becomes not only reconciled to his fellow but actually at one with him—as though the veil of Maya had been torn apart and there remained only shreds floating before the vision of mystical Oneness. Man now expresses himself through song and dance as the member of a higher community; he has forgotten how to walk, how to speak, and is on the brink of taking wing as he dances. Each of his gestures betokens enchantment; through him

---

[11]*bacchic choruses*   Bacchus was the god of wine (a variant of Dionysus); thus, this term means drunken choruses. The St. John's and St. Vitus's dancers were ecstatic Christian dancers of the Middle Ages. Their dance was a mania which spread to a number of major religious centers.

[12]*Sacaea*   A Babylonian summer festival for the god Ishtar. The point is that such religious orgies are ancient.

[13]*"Paean to Joy"*   This is Friedrich von Schiller's (1759–1805) poem, *Ode to Joy*, which Ludwig van Beethoven (1770–1827) set to music in the last movement of his Symphony no. 9, the Choral symphony.

sounds a supernatural power, the same power which makes the animals speak and the earth render up milk and honey. He feels himself to be godlike and strides with the same elation and ecstasy as the gods he has seen in his dreams. No longer the *artist,* he has himself become a *work of art:* the productive power of the whole universe is now manifest in his transport, to the glorious satisfaction of the primordial One. The finest clay, the most precious marble—man—is here kneaded and hewn, and the chisel blows of the Dionysiac world artist are accompanied by the cry of the Eleusinian mystagogues:[14] "Do you fall on your knees, multitudes, do you divine your creator?"

So far we have examined the Apollonian and Dionysiac states as the product of formative forces arising directly from nature without the mediation of the human artist. At this stage artistic urges are satisfied directly, on the one hand through the imagery of dreams, whose perfection is quite independent of the intellectual rank, the artistic development of the individual; on the other hand, through an ecstatic reality which once again takes no account of the individual and may even destroy him, or else redeem him through a mystical experience of the collective. In relation to these immediate creative conditions of nature every artist must appear as "imitator," either as the Apollonian dream artist or the Dionysiac ecstatic artist, or, finally (as in Greek tragedy, for example) as dream and ecstatic artist in one. We might picture to ourselves how the last of these, in a state of Dionysiac intoxication and mystical self-abrogation,[15] wandering apart from the reveling throng, sinks upon the ground, and how there is then revealed to him his own condition—complete oneness with the essence of the universe—in a dream similitude.

Having set down these general premises and distinctions, we now turn to the Greeks in order to realize to what degree the formative forces of nature were developed in them. Such an inquiry will enable us to assess properly the relation of the Greek artist to his prototypes or, to use Aristotle's expression, his "imitation of nature."[16] Of the dreams the Greeks dreamed it is not possible to speak with any certainty, despite the extant dream literature and

---

[14]***Eleusinian mystagogues***   Those who participate in the ancient Greek Eleusinian secret ceremonies celebrating life after death.

[15]***self-abrogation***   The reveler "loses" his self, his sense of being an individual apart from the throng.

[16]***"imitation of nature"***   A key term in Aristotle's theory of *mimesis,* the doctrine that art imitates nature and that the artist must observe nature carefully. Nietzsche emphasizes dreams as a part of nature and something to be closely observed by the artist.

the large number of dream anecdotes. But considering the incredible accuracy of their eyes, their keen and unabashed delight in colors, one can hardly be wrong in assuming that their dreams too showed a strict consequence of lines and contours, hues and groupings, a progression of scenes similar to their best bas-reliefs.[17] The perfection of these dream scenes might almost tempt us to consider the dreaming Greek as a Homer and Homer as a dreaming Greek; which would be as though the modern man were to compare himself in his dreaming to Shakespeare.

Yet there is another point about which we do not have to   8 conjecture at all: I mean the profound gap separating the Dionysiac Greeks from the Dionysiac barbarians. Throughout the range of ancient civilization (leaving the newer civilizations out of account for the moment) we find evidence of Dionysiac celebrations which stand to the Greek type in much the same relation as the bearded satyr,[18] whose name and attributes are derived from the he-goat, stands to the god Dionysos. The central concern of such celebrations was, almost universally, a complete sexual promiscuity overriding every form of established tribal law; all the savage urges of the mind were unleashed on those occasions until they reached that paroxysm of lust and cruelty which has always struck me as the "witches' cauldron" *par excellence*. It would appear that the Greeks were for a while quite immune from these feverish excesses which must have reached them by every known land or sea route. What kept Greece safe was the proud, imposing image of Apollo, who in holding up the head of the Gorgon[19] to those brutal and grotesque Dionysiac forces subdued them. Doric art has immortalized Apollo's majestic rejection of all license. But resistance became difficult, even impossible, as soon as similar urges began to break forth from the deep substratum of Hellenism itself. Soon the function of the Delphic god[20] developed into something quite different and much more limited: all he could hope to accomplish now was to wrest the destructive weapon, by a timely gesture of pacification,

---

[17]***bas-reliefs*** Sculptures projecting only slightly from a flat surface; they usually tell a story in a series of scenes.

[18]***satyr*** Greek god, half man, half goat; a symbol of lechery.

[19]***Gorgon*** Powerful monster in Greek mythology with serpents for hair. There were three Gorgons, all sisters, but only Medusa was not immortal. With the help of the goddess Athena, Perseus beheaded Medusa, whose very glance was supposed to turn men to stone. Later Perseus vanquished his enemies by exposing the head to them and turning them to stone.

[20]***Delphic god*** Apollo. The oracle at the temple to Apollo at Delphi, in Greece, was for more than 1,000 years a source of prophecies of the future. It was among the most sacred places in Greece.

from his opponent's hand. That act of pacification represents the most important event in the history of Greek ritual, every department of life now shows symptoms of a revolutionary change. The two great antagonists have been reconciled. Each feels obliged henceforth to keep to his bounds, each will honor the other by the bestowal of periodic gifts, while the cleavage remains fundamentally the same. And yet, if we examine what happened to the Dionysiac powers under the pressure of that treaty we notice a great difference: in the place of the Babylonian Sacaea, with their throwback of men to the condition of apes and tigers, we now see entirely new rites celebrated: rites of universal redemption, of glorious transfiguration. Only now has it become possible to speak of nature's celebrating an *esthetic* triumph; only now has the abrogation of the *principium individuationis* become an esthetic event. That terrible witches' brew concocted of lust and cruelty has lost all power under the new conditions. Yet the peculiar blending of emotions in the heart of the Dionysiac reveler—his ambiguity if you will—seems still to hark back (as the medicinal drug harks back to the deadly poison) to the days when the infliction of pain was experienced as joy while a sense of supreme triumph elicited cries of anguish from the heart. For now in every exuberant joy there is heard an undertone of terror, or else a wistful lament over an irrecoverable loss. It is as though in these Greek festivals a sentimental trait of nature were coming to the fore, as though nature were bemoaning the fact of her fragmentation, her decomposition into separate individuals. The chants and gestures of these revelers, so ambiguous in their motivation, represented an absolute *novum*[21] in the world of the Homeric Greeks; their Dionysiac music, in especial, spread abroad terror and a deep shudder. It is true: music had long been familiar to the Greeks as an Apollonian art, as a regular beat like that of waves lapping the shore, a plastic rhythm[22] expressly developed for the portrayal of Apollonian conditions. Apollo's music was a Doric architecture of sound—of barely hinted sounds such as are proper to the cithara.[23] Those very elements which characterize Dionysiac music and, after it, music quite generally: the heart-shaking power of tone, the uniform stream of melody, the incomparable resources of harmony—all those elements had been carefully kept at a distance as being inconsonant with the Apollonian norm. In the Dionysiac

---

[21]*an absolute novum*   A genuine novelty.

[22]*plastic rhythm*   Plastic in this sense means capable of being shaped, responsive to slight changes—not rigid.

[23]*cithara*   An ancient stringed instrument, the lyre, used to accompany songs and recitations.

dithyramb[24] man is incited to strain his symbolic faculties to the utmost; something quite unheard of is now clamoring to be heard: the desire to tear asunder the veil of Maya, to sink back into the original oneness of nature; the desire to express the very essence of nature symbolically. Thus an entirely new set of symbols springs into being. First, all the symbols pertaining to physical features: mouth, face, the spoken word, the dance movement which coordinates the limbs and bends them to its rhythm. Then suddenly all the rest of the symbolic forces—music and rhythm as such, dynamics, harmony—assert themselves with great energy. In order to comprehend this total emancipation of all the symbolic powers one must have reached the same measure of inner freedom those powers themselves were making manifest; which is to say that the votary of Dionysos[25] could not be understood except by his own kind. It is not difficult to imagine the awed surprise with which the Apollonian Greek must have looked on him. And that surprise would be further increased as the latter realized, with a shudder, that all this was not so alien to him after all, that his Apollonian consciousness was but a thin veil hiding from him the whole Dionysiac realm.

In order to comprehend this we must take down the elaborate edifice of Apollonian culture stone by stone until we discover its foundations. At first the eye is struck by the marvelous shapes of the Olympian gods who stand upon its pediments, and whose exploits, in shining bas-relief, adorn its friezes. The fact that among them we find Apollo as one god among many, making no claim to a privileged position, should not mislead us. The same drive that found its most complete representation in Apollo generated the whole Olympian world, and in this sense we may consider Apollo the father of that world. But what was the radical need out of which that illustrious society of Olympian beings sprang?

Whoever approaches the Olympians with a different religion in his heart, seeking moral elevation, sanctity, spirituality, loving-kindness, will presently be forced to turn away from them in ill-humored disappointment. Nothing in these deities reminds us of asceticism, high intellect, or duty: we are confronted by luxuriant, triumphant *existence,* which defies the good and the bad indifferently. And the beholder may find himself dismayed in the presence of such overflowing life and ask himself what potion these heady people must have drunk in order to behold, in whatever direction

---

[24]**Dionysiac dithyramb**   A passionate hymn to Dionysus, usually delivered by a chorus.

[25]**votary of Dionysos**   A follower of Dionysus; one devoted to Dionysian ecstasy.

they looked, Helen[26] laughing back at them, the beguiling image of their own existence. But we shall call out to this beholder, who has already turned his back: Don't go! Listen first to what the Greeks themselves have to say of this life, which spreads itself before you with such puzzling serenity. An old legend has it that King Midas[27] hunted a long time in the woods for the wise Silenus, companion of Dionysos, without being able to catch him. When he had finally caught him the king asked him what he considered man's greatest good. The daemon remained sullen and uncommunicative until finally, forced by the king, he broke into a shrill laugh and spoke: "Ephemeral wretch, begotten by accident and toil, why do you force me to tell you what it would be your greatest boon not to hear? What would be best for you is quite beyond your reach: not to have been born, not to *be,* to be *nothing.* But the second best is to die soon."

What is the relation of the Olympian gods to this popular wisdom? It is that of the entranced vision of the martyr to his torment.

Now the Olympian magic mountain opens itself before us,   12 showing us its very roots. The Greeks were keenly aware of the terrors and horrors of existence; in order to be able to live at all they had to place before them the shining fantasy of the Olympians. Their tremendous distrust of the titanic forces of nature: *Moira,*[28] mercilessly enthroned beyond the knowable world; the vulture which fed upon the great philanthropist Prometheus;[29] the terrible lot drawn by wise Oedipus; the curse on the house of Atreus which brought Orestes to the murder of his mother: that whole Panic philosophy,[30] in short, with its mythic examples, by which the gloomy Etruscans perished, the Greeks conquered—or at least hid

---

[26]*Helen*   The runaway wife of Menelaus, immortalized in Homer's *Iliad* as the cause of the ten-year Trojan War. She was not "good" or ascetic, but her intensity of living secured her a permanent place in history and myth.

[27]*King Midas*   Midas was a foolish king who kidnapped Silenus, a satyr (half man, half goat) who was a companion of Dionysus. Silenus, a daemon or spirit, granted Midas his wish to have everything he touched turn to gold. Because his food turned to gold, he almost died. Dionysus eventually saved him by bathing him in a sacred river.

[28]**Moira**   Fate personified; the figure who gives each person his fate.

[29]*Prometheus*   The god who gave men fire—thus, his generosity is philanthropy, the love of man. He was punished by the gods.

[30]*Panic philosophy*   Belief in fate. Oedipus's fate was to murder his father and marry his mother. He tried to escape it, but could not. Orestes murdered his mother, Clytemnestra, because she had murdered his father, Agamemnon. All of these were members of the cursed house of Atreus and provide examples of how fate works.

from view—again and again by means of this artificial Olympus. In order to live at all the Greeks had to construct these deities. The Apollonian need for beauty had to develop the Olympian hierarchy of joy by slow degrees from the original titanic hierarchy of terror, as roses are seen to break from a thorny thicket. How else could life have been borne by a race so hypersensitive, so emotionally intense, so equipped for suffering? The same drive which called art into being as a completion and consummation of existence, and as a guarantee of further existence, gave rise also to that Olympian realm which acted as a transfiguring mirror to the Hellenic will. The gods justified human life by living it themselves—the only satisfactory theodicy[31] ever invented. To exist in the clear sunlight of such deities was now felt to be the highest good, and the only real grief suffered by Homeric man was inspired by the thought of leaving that sunlight, especially when the departure seemed imminent. Now it became possible to stand the wisdom of Silenus on its head and proclaim that it was the worst evil for man to die soon, and second worst for him to die at all. Such laments as arise now arise over short-lived Achilles,[32] over the generations ephemeral as leaves, the decline of the heroic age. It is not unbecoming to even the greatest hero to yearn for an afterlife, though it be as a day laborer. So impetuously, during the Apollonian phase, does man's will desire to remain on earth, so identified does he become with existence, that even his lament turns to a song of praise.

It should have become apparent by now that the harmony with nature which we late-comers regard with such nostalgia, and for which Schiller has coined the cant term *naïve*,[33] is by no means a simple and inevitable condition to be found at the gateway to every culture, a kind of paradise. Such a belief could have been endorsed only by a period for which Rousseau's Émile was an artist and Homer just such an artist nurtured in the bosom of nature. Whenever we encounter "naïveté" in art, we are face to face with the ripest fruit of Apollonian culture—which must always triumph first over titans, kill monsters, and overcome the somber contemplation

---

[31]***theodicy*** Examination of the question whether the gods are just. Because the gods shared human life, they ennobled it; they suffered evil as well.

[32]***short-lived Achilles*** Achilles' fate was to lead the Greeks to victory at Troy, but to die by an arrow shot by Paris, who had taken Helen to Troy. Apollo guided the arrow so that it hit Achilles in the heel, his one vulnerable spot. Achilles, like many heroes, lived a brief but intense life.

[33]***naïve*** Schiller's *On the Naïve and the Sentimental in Poetry* (1795–1796) contrasted the classic (naïve) with the romantic (sentimental) in art. It is not the same as Nietzsche's distinction, but it is similar. Nietzsche uses "naïve" to refer to a kind of classical purity and temper.

of actuality, the intense susceptibility to suffering, by means of illusions strenuously and zestfully entertained. But how rare are the instances of true naïveté, of that complete identification with the beauty of appearance! It is this achievement which makes Homer so magnificent—Homer, who, as a single individual, stood to Apollonian popular culture in the same relation as the individual dream artist to the oneiric[34] capacity of a race and of nature generally. The naïveté of Homer must be viewed as a complete victory of Apollonian illusion. Nature often uses illusions of this sort in order to accomplish its secret purposes. The true goal is covered over by a phantasm. We stretch out our hands to the latter, while nature, aided by our deception, attains the former. In the case of the Greeks it was the will wishing to behold itself in the work of art, in the transcendence of genius; but in order so to behold itself its creatures had first to view themselves as glorious, to transpose themselves to a higher sphere, without having that sphere of pure contemplation either challenge them or upbraid them with insufficiency. It was in that sphere of beauty that the Greeks saw the Olympians as their mirror images; it was by means of that esthetic mirror that the Greek will opposed suffering and the somber wisdom of suffering which always accompanies artistic talent. As a monument to its victory stands Homer, the naïve artist.

We can learn something about that naïve artist through the analogy of dream. We can imagine the dreamer as he calls out to himself, still caught in the illusion of his dream and without disturbing it, "This is a dream, and I want to go on dreaming," and we can infer, on the one hand, that he takes deep delight in the contemplation of his dream, and, on the other, that he must have forgotten the day, with its horrible importunity, so to enjoy his dream. Apollo, the interpreter of dreams, will furnish the clue to what is happening here. Although of the two halves of life—the waking and the dreaming—the former is generally considered not only the more important but the only one which is truly lived, I would, at the risk of sounding paradoxical, propose the opposite view. The more I have come to realize in nature those omnipotent formative tendencies and, with them, an intense longing for illusion, the more I feel inclined to the hypothesis that the original Oneness, the ground of Being, ever-suffering and contradictory, time and again has need of rapt vision and delightful illusion to redeem itself. Since we ourselves are the very stuff of such illusions, we must view ourselves as the truly non-existent, that is to say, as a perpetual

---

[34]**oneiric** Pertaining to dreams.

unfolding in time, space, and causality—what we label "empiric reality."[35] But if, for the moment, we abstract from our own reality, viewing our empiric existence, as well as the existence of the world at large, as the *idea* of the original Oneness, produced anew each instant, then our dreams will appear to us as illusions of illusions, hence as a still higher form of satisfaction of the original desire for illusion. It is for this reason that the very core of nature takes such a deep delight in the naïve artist and the naïve work of art, which likewise is merely the illusion of an illusion. Raphael,[36] himself one of those immortal "naïve" artists, in a symbolic canvas has illustrated that reduction of illusion to further illusion which is the original act of the naïve artist and at the same time of all Apollonian culture. In the lower half of his "Transfiguration," through the figures of the possessed boy, the despairing bearers, the helpless, terrified disciples, we see a reflection of original pain, the sole ground of being: "illusion" here is a reflection of eternal contradiction, begetter of all things. From this illusion there rises, like the fragrance of ambrosia, a new illusory world, invisible to those enmeshed in the first: a radiant vision of pure delight, a rapt seeing through wide-open eyes. Here we have, in a great symbol of art, both the fair world of Apollo and its substratum, the terrible wisdom of Silenus, and we can comprehend intuitively how they mutually require one another. But Apollo appears to us once again as the apotheosis[37] of the *principium individuationis,* in whom the eternal goal of the original Oneness, namely its redemption through illusion, accomplishes itself. With august gesture the god shows us how there is need for a whole world of torment in order for the individual to produce the redemptive vision and to sit quietly in his rocking rowboat in mid-sea, absorbed in contemplation.

If this apotheosis of individuation is to be read in nominative terms, we may infer that there is one norm only: the individual—or, more precisely, the observance of the limits of the individual: *sophrosyne.*[38] As a moral deity Apollo demands self-control from his people and, in order to observe such self-control, a knowledge of self. And so we find that the esthetic necessity of beauty is

---

[35]*"empiric reality"*   The reality we can test by experience.

[36]*Raphael (1483–1520)*   A Renaissance artist. Raphael was influenced by classical forms, but his work became progressively more humanistic, in some cases tending to Schiller's "sentimental." *Transfiguration* (1517–1520), his last painting, points to the new age of baroque painting: an intense, emotional, ecstatic style.

[37]*apotheosis*   Godlike embodiment. Nietzsche is saying that Apollo is the god in whom the concept of the individual is best expressed.

[38]**sophrosyne**   Greek word for wisdom.

accompanied by the imperatives, "Know thyself," and "Nothing too much." Conversely, excess and *hubris*[39] come to be regarded as the hostile spirits of the non-Apollonian sphere, hence as properties of the pre-Apollonian era—the age of Titans[40]—and the extra-Apollonian world, that is to say the world of the barbarians. It was because of his Titanic love of man that Prometheus had to be devoured by vultures; it was because of his extravagant wisdom which succeeded in solving the riddle of the Sphinx[41] that Oedipus had to be cast into a whirlpool of crime: in this fashion does the Delphic god interpret the Greek past.

The effects of the Dionysiac spirit struck the Apollonian Greeks   16
as titanic and barbaric; yet they could not disguise from themselves the fact that they were essentially akin to those deposed Titans and heroes. They felt more than that: their whole existence, with its temperate beauty, rested upon a base of suffering and *knowledge* which had been hidden from them until the reinstatement of Dionysos uncovered it once more. And lo and behold! Apollo found it impossible to live without Dionysos. The elements of titanism and barbarism turned out to be quite as fundamental as the Apollonian element. And now let us imagine how the ecstatic sounds of the Dionysiac rites penetrated ever more enticingly into that artificially restrained and discreet world of illusion, how this clamor expressed the whole outrageous gamut of nature—delight, grief, knowledge— even to the most piercing cry; and then let us imagine how the Apollonian artist with his thin, monotonous harp music must have sounded beside the demoniac chant of the multitude! The muses presiding over the illusory arts paled before an art which enthusiastically told the truth, and the wisdom of Silenus cried "Woe!" against the serene Olympians. The individual, with his limits and moderations, forgot himself in the Dionysiac vortex and became oblivious to the laws of Apollo. Indiscreet extravagance revealed itself as truth, and contradiction, a delight born of pain, spoke out of the bosom of nature. Wherever the Dionysiac voice was heard, the Apollonian norm seemed suspended or destroyed. Yet it is equally

---

[39]**hubris**   Greek word for pride, especially dangerous, defiant pride.

[40]*age of Titans*   A reference to the gods who reigned before Zeus; an unenlightened age.

[41]*riddle of the Sphinx*   The sphinx, part woman and part beast, waited outside Thebes for years, killing all who tried to pass by but could not solve its riddle. Oedipus (see note 30) answered the riddle: "What walks on four legs in the morning, two legs in the day, and three legs in the evening?" The answer: man, who crawls in infancy, walks upright in his prime, and uses a cane in old age. The solution freed Thebes from its bondage to the Sphinx, but it brought Oedipus closer to his awful fate.

true that, in those places where the first assault was withstood, the prestige and majesty of the Delphic god appeared more rigid and threatening than before. The only way I am able to view Doric art and the Doric[42] state is as a perpetual military encampment of the Apollonian forces. An art so defiantly austere, so ringed about with fortifications—an education so military and exacting—a polity so ruthlessly cruel—could endure only in a continual state of resistance against the titanic and barbaric menace of Dionysos.

Up to this point I have developed at some length a theme which was sounded at the beginning of this essay: how the Dionysiac and Apollonian elements, in a continuous chain of creations, each enhancing the other, dominated the Hellenic mind: how from the Iron Age,[43] with its battles of Titans and its austere popular philosophy, there developed under the aegis of Apollo the Homeric world of beauty; how this "naïve" splendor was then absorbed once more by the Dionysiac torrent, and how, face to face with this new power, the Apollonian code rigidified into the majesty of Doric art and contemplation. If the earlier phase of Greek history may justly be broken down into four major artistic epochs dramatizing the battle between the two hostile principles, then we must inquire further (lest Doric art appear to us as the acme and final goal of all these striving tendencies) what was the true end toward which that evolution moved. And our eyes will come to rest on the sublime and much lauded achievement of the dramatic dithyramb and Attic tragedy, as the common goal of both urges; whose mysterious marriage, after long discord, ennobled itself with such a child, at once Antigone and Cassandra.[44]

---

[42]**Doric**   The Doric styles were unadorned, clear, intellectual rather than sensual. They represent purity and uprightness.

[43]**Iron Age**   An earlier age, ruled by sterner, less humane gods, the Titans.

[44]**Antigone and Cassandra**   Children in Greek tragedies; Antigone, daughter of Oedipus, defied the authorities in *Antigone* by Sophocles (496?–406 B.C.) and suffered; Cassandra, daughter of Priam, king of Troy, appears in Homer's *Iliad* and several tragedies by Aeschylus (525–456 B.C.) and Euripides (484?–406 B.C.). She had the gift of prophecy but was doomed never to be believed. She foresaw the destruction of Troy, and after its fall she was taken prisoner by Agamemnon. She and Antigone were both heroic in their suffering.

QUESTIONS FOR CRITICAL READING

1. Define "Apollonianism" and "Dionysianism." What kind of behavior does each word stand for?
2. What are the important distinctions between the self and the mob? Dream and illusion?
3. In paragraph 6, Nietzsche speaks of the "mystical experience of the collective." What does he mean by this phrase? Is there such a thing?
4. Which paragraphs in the selection are most obscure and difficult to understand? Do they seem to show Dionysian qualities?
5. Do you feel that any contemporary art unifies the Apollonian and the Dionysian? Would Nietzsche have thought a modern film could do so?
6. Do the distinctions Nietzsche makes give you useful insights into behavior?
7. What ethical issues might the Apollonian person and the Dionysian person interpret differently? Consider especially questions of law.
8. For which of these polarities of behavior is self-control more likely a virtue?

WRITING ASSIGNMENTS

1. Examine paragraph 6 carefully. How valid are Nietzsche's insights concerning the self and the "reveling throng"? Drawing on personal experience, contrast the behavior of yourself or a friend—first as an individual, then as a member of a large gathering of people. Are you (or your friend) "possessed" when a member of such an assemblage? Be as specific as possible in writing about this contrast.
2. Establish a principle of ethical behavior by which you feel the Apollonian can live. Then establish one for the Dionysian. Compare the two personalities to determine their differences and their similarities. What is it about the mental states represented by these polarities that makes their ethical systems different? On what would they agree? Is either of these polarities in danger of appearing unethical to people in general?
3. Music is the inspiration for this essay. Choose a piece of music that is very important to you. Consider it as an artifact and describe the qualities it has that you feel are Apollonian and Dionysian respectively. Is the range of the music—in terms of exciting or sustaining emotional response—narrow or great? Describe your emotional and intellectual reactions to the music and ask others about their responses to the same music. Is music an appropriate source for finding the conjunction of these two forces?
4. Examine aspects of our culture that reveal whether it is basically Apollonian or basically Dionysian. Be sure to consider political life; education; entertainment of various kinds, including literature, music, and sports; and any aspects of personal life in your immediate environment.

In considering these features of our culture, you have an opportunity to use Nietzsche's technique of comparison and contrast. For instance, you may find the Apollonian and Dionysian sides of, say, football as interesting contrasts, just as you may wish to contrast the games of chess and rugby, rock music and Muzak, or any other related pairs.

5. Which of these two polarities of behavior most resembles your own behavior? Are you Apollonian or Dionysian? Define your behavior with reference to Nietzsche. Ask others who have read this selection to comment on your character in terms of the Apollonian-Dionysian distinction. Do you think that you achieve the kind of control that enables you to realize yourself fully in terms of these polarities, or do you feel that control is not an issue?

6. **CONNECTIONS** How would Aristotle critique Nietzsche's proposals? What ethical issues might he find in Nietzsche's suggestions that the Apollonian and Dionysian extremes are desirable? What fault might Plato have found with Nietzsche's views? Do you find yourself convinced more by Plato and Aristotle or by Nietzsche?

7. **CONNECTIONS** Would it be fair to describe Mary Daly's essay on patriarchal religion as a result of Apollonianism or Dionysianism? Or is it neither of these? What problems would one have in establishing a connection between Nietzsche's approach to values and Mary Daly's approach to values?

8. **CONNECTIONS** Ruth Benedict relies on this essay of Nietzsche for her distinctions between cultures of Pueblo Indians and their neighbors. Examine "The Pueblos of New Mexico" and decide whether or not her representation of the distinctions between cultures as Apollonian and Dionysian seems to be an accurate interpretation of Nietzsche. Does she treat Nietzsche's ideas fairly and does she seem to apply them reasonably?

MARY DALY

The Qualitative Leap
Beyond Patriarchal Religion

MARY DALY *(b. 1928) is arguably the most prominent feminist philosopher in America. She was educated in Roman Catholic schools in the United States and later attended the University of Fribourg in Switzerland, where she received an St.D. in theology in 1963 and a Ph.D. in philosophy in 1965 (she holds a total of three doctorates). She is currently a professor in the Department of Theology at Boston College. She describes herself as a "PostChristian," a term designed to reflect her belief that the patriarchal underpinnings of all major religions have been damaging to all women. Her reputation as a radical feminist has often caused her difficulty in her academic career, but she has persisted in discussing the united goals of feminism, existentialism, and theology.*

Her work is controversial and marked by a level of ethical seriousness that is second to none. As she declares in "The Qualitative Leap Beyond Patriarchal Religion," some of the great injustices in the world have been supported by the church's patriarchal imagery and symbolism. In general, patriarchy is a social structure that favors men ("patriarchy" is derived from the Latin for "father"). The church patriarchs are the church fathers who have written virtually all of the documents that govern the church and serve to interpret its laws.

Daly believes that patriarchy has so structured the church that women really have no voice in what is done or how it is done. Moreover, she feels that the primary symbols of the Christian church, such as the concept of the Trinity, are transparently gender-based and designed to keep women second-class citizens. Some of her writings are among the most influential texts of modern religious social theory. Her works include Natural Knowl-

---

From *Quest: A Feminist Quarterly,* Vol. 1, No. 4, Spring 1975.

edge of God in the Philosophy of Jacques Maritain *(1966);* The Church and the Second Sex *(1968);* Beyond God the Father: Toward a Philosophy of Women's Liberation *(1973);* Gyn/Ecology: The Metaethics of Radical Feminism *(1978);* Pure Lust: Elemental Feminist Philosophy *(1984);* Websters' First New Intergalactic Wickedary of the English Language *(1987) [conjured in cahoots with Jane Caputi]; and* Outercourse: The Be-Dazzling Voyage *(1992). These works have placed her in the forefront of modern feminist theory.*

Her latest book incorporates many interesting discussions centering on words and in doing so reminds us, as does the essay included here, that language can be either a tool of oppression or a tool of liberation. She calls her discussion of language a "wickedary" because it supplies new meaning to words, such as witch, *that standard dictionaries define in a negative way. Daly suggests that a witch is a woman who is an advanced (read "radical") feminist in a society that will not tolerate her.*

One of the most interesting sections of "The Qualitative Leap Beyond Patriarchal Religion" begins at paragraph 43 with her discussion of the word androgyny, *the combination of male and female qualities. She brings care and skill to her analysis of the word. At one point, she considers turning the word around and spelling it "gynandry," with the female part of the word appearing first. In part, this reworking reorients us to the concepts that underlie the term; but it also reminds us that in dealing with the term on any level, we are dealing with male and female stereotypes that are socially structured rather than biologically determined.*

In another discussion of language, Daly discusses the words "God" and "Goddess." She regards the use of "God" language as a kind of intellectual prison from which both she and we need to break. For her, the concept of "Be-ing" seems closer to what others mean when they use the word God in a sense that is not linked to gender (if avoiding gender-based descriptions is at all possible).

For her, much of the problem lies in religious images such as the Trinity, which she describes as the "All Male Divine Family." Recognizing the problems that a religious image system involves, and that women must always emerge a distant second, she recommends that the concept of the transcendent become something other than a physical man, such as Jesus, and become instead an ontological force that reaches far beyond our traditional concepts. Such thinking is not foreign to religion, or even to Christianity. One of the most important of contemporary Christian theologians, Paul Tillich (1886–1965), wrote extensively in his book Dynamics of Faith *(1957) about the effect of symbolism in religion. Daly agrees with his proposal that the idea of the transcendent be detached from the emblem of a specific human figure. She believes that such a choice will help to rid religion of its oppressiveness.*

Underlying much of her discussion of language is her conviction that radical feminism cannot settle for a simple redistribution of masculine power. Feminism must create something quite new: an order of thought that is free of gender-based illusions and gender-based privilege, for these always reduce the women in the world to subservience.

One of her demands (paras. 29–34) is a "remythologization" of male institutions, starting with the concept of the procession (academic, religious, military—ceremonies of all kinds led by males). The idea of the procession was analyzed earlier by Virginia Woolf, the world-famous writer who was excluded from academic processions: specifically, the graduating class of a university. Because she was a woman, Woolf could not attend the university (she was overage when British universities finally admitted women) or even use the library of the university for her research. Because she was so excluded, Woolf began to question why she should support the professions that all depended on the procession of graduation. It was, as she said, a procession of the "sons of educated men." Woolf said, in Three Guineas, *"Nothing would induce the authorities encamped within the sacred gates to allow the women to enter. They said that God was on their side, Nature was on their side, Law was on their side, and Property was on their side. The college was founded for the benefit of men only; men only were entitled by law to benefit from its endowments." Daly interprets the male-controlled professions, "church, state, university, army," as gynocidal: death to women. But she also regards them as genocidal, implying death for men and women alike. Although she does not elaborate on this theme in this essay, she believes that the male stereotype of aggressive behavior is at the root of war and destruction.*

DALY'S RHETORIC

This essay was originally delivered as a paper at an international symposium to a primarily male audience of theologians and sociologists; later it appeared in this abridged form in Quest, *a feminist journal that is no longer published. Daly did not expect to change the minds of the conservative audience at the conference, nor to encounter serious resistance to her ideas from the readers of* Quest. *Thus, she does not employ a rhetorical strategy explicitly designed to "reason" the audience into agreement with her.*

In a manner reminiscent of Jefferson's Declaration of Independence, Daly begins by listing twenty-three items that must be addressed by women who are "becoming." This strategy is sometimes called enumeration and recalls not only Jefferson but also Francis Bacon, who enumerates four areas of discussion in "The Four Idols." The technique, useful for its clarity and its capacity to isolate issues for discussion, also possesses the quality of the pronunciamento, a tactic especially fitting for an essay on the oppression of a group of people because the items demand explication and expansion. For example, in item six Daly writes that the symbols of Christianity are essentially sexist and related to such godfathers as Vito Corleone, the fictional (and symbolic) head of the Mafia, a statement that requires further discussion.

Daly's rhetorical strategy is based on identifying a condition: the patriarchy of the church, as upheld by the patriarchal imagery and symbolism that have characterized the church from its beginning. Consequently, her definition of patriarchy and her representation of the symbolism remain critical to her position. For those who may not already agree with her position, her claims that the gender distinctions that exist in our society make it a "rapist society" may sound exaggerated. But a few days spent listening to TV or radio news or reading the newspapers of any major city ought to help anyone to understand her point.

Another aspect of her rhetorical strategy consists of her realization that she is unlikely to convince anyone to whom her cause is not already important. Many men may feel that the existing imagery and symbolism of the church are both appropriate and historically validated by the Bible. Therefore, Daly knows that her reasoning, no matter how effective, will not alter the male point of view. In her article After the Death of God the Father, *she holds out a specter for the church to consider: religion, if it does not rid itself of its oppressive tendencies, will "go out of business."*

The Qualitative Leap
Beyond Patriarchal Religion

Prolegomena

1. There exists a planetary sexual caste system, essentially the same in Saudi Arabia and in New York, differing only in degree.
2. This system is masked by sex role segregation, by the dual identity of women, by ideologies and myths.
3. Among the primary loci of sexist conditioning is grammar.
4. The "methods" of the various "fields" are not adequate to express feminist thought. Methodolatry requires that women perform Methodicide, an act of intellectual bravery.
5. All of the major world religions function to legitimate patriarchy. This is true also of the popular cults such as the Krishna movement and the Jesus Freaks.

6. The myths and symbols of Christianity are essentially sexist. Since "God" is male, the male is God. God the Father legitimates all earthly Godfathers, including Vito Corleone,[1] Pope Paul, President Gerald Ford, the Godfathers of medicine (e.g., the American Medical Association, of science (e.g., NASA), of the media, of psychiatry; of education, and of all the -ologies.
7. The myth of feminine evil, expressed in the story of the Fall, is reinforced by the myth of salvation/redemption by a single human being of the male sex. The idea of a unique divine incarnation in a male, the God-man of the "hypostatic union,"[2] is inherently sexist and oppressive. Christolatry is idolatry.
8. A significant and growing cognitive minority of women, radical feminists, are breaking out from under the sacred shelter of patriarchal religious myths.
9. This breaking out, facing anomy when the meaning structures of patriarchy are seen through and rejected, is a communal, political event. It is a revelatory event, a creative, political ontophany.[3]
10. The bonding of the growing cognitive minority of women who are radical feminists, commonly called *sisterhood,* involves a process of new naming, in which words are wrenched out of their old semantic context and heard in a new semantic context. For example, the "sisterhoods" of patriarchy, such as religious congregations of women, were really mini-brotherhoods. *Sisterhood* heard with new ears is bonding for women's own liberation.
11. There is an inherent dynamic in the women's revolution in Judeo-Christian society which is Antichurch, whether or not feminists specifically concern ourselves with churches. This is so because the Judeo-Christian tradition legitimates patriarchy—the prevailing power structure and prevailing world view—which the women's revolution leaves behind.
12. The women's revolution is not only Antichurch. It is a post-christian spiritual revolution.
13. The ethos of Judeo-Christian culture is dominated by The Most Unholy Trinity: Rape, Genocide, and War. It is rapism which spawns racism. It is gynocide which spawns genocide, for sexism (rapism) is fundamental socialization to objectify "the other."

---

[1] *Vito Corleone* The fictional Mafia character who founds the family "business" in Mario Puzo's novel *The Godfather.*
[2] *hypostatic union* The union of the divine and human aspects of Jesus Christ.
[3] *ontophany* Manifestation of being.

14. The women's revolution is concerned with transvaluation of values, beyond the ethics dominated by The Most Unholy Trinity.

15. The women's revolution is not merely about equality within a patriarchal society (a contradiction in terms). It is about *power* and redefining power.

16. Since Christian myths are inherently sexist, and since the women's revolution is not about "equality" but about power, there is an intrinsic dynamic in the feminist movement which goes beyond efforts to reform Christian churches. Such efforts eventually come to be recognized as comparable to a Black person's trying to reform the Ku Klux Klan.

17. Within patriarchy, power is generally understood as power *over* people, the environment, things. In the rising consciousness of women, power is experienced as *power of presence* to ourselves and to each other, as we affirm our own being against and beyond the alienated identity (non-being) bestowed upon us within patriarchy. This is experienced as *power of absence* by those who would objectify women as "the other," as magnifying mirrors.

18. The presence of women to ourselves which is *absence* to the oppressor is the essential dynamic opening up the women's revolution to human liberation. It is an invitation to men to confront non-being and hence affirm their be-ing.

19. It is unlikely that many men will accept this invitation willingly, or even be able to hear it, since they have profound vested (though self-destructive) interest in the present social arrangements.

20. The women's movement is a new mode of relating to the self, to each other, to men, to the environment—in a word—to the cosmos. It is self-affirming, refusing objectification of the self and the other.

21. Entrance into new feminist time/space, which is moving time/space located on the boundaries of patriarchal institutions, is active participation in ultimate reality, which is de-reified,[4] recognized as Verb, as intransitive Verb with no object to block its dynamism.

22. Entrance into radical feminist consciousness involves recogni-

---

⁴**de-reified**   Reify means to give a definite form to an abstraction; de-reify means to return that form to an abstraction. Thus, moving from the form of God as a man—reification of an abstraction—Daly wants to de-reify the concept of God as a man and substitute for it the concept of Verb. She wants to remove the concept of a human body from the idea of God.

tion that all male-dominated "revolutions," which do not reject the universally oppressive reality which is patriarchy, are in reality only reforms. They are "revolutions" only in the sense that they are spinnings of the wheels of the same senescent system.

23. Entrance into radical feminist consciousness implies an awareness that the women's revolution is the "final cause" (pun intended) in the radical sense that it is the cause which can move the other causes. It is the catalyst which can bring about real change, since it is the rising up of the universally and primordially objectified "Other," discrediting the myths which legitimate rapism. Rapism is by extension the objectification and destruction of all "others" and inherently tends to the destruction of the human species and of all life on this planet.

Radical feminism, the becoming of women, is very much an 24 Otherworld Journey. It is both discovery and creation of a world other than patriarchy. Some observation reveals that patriarchy is "everywhere." Even outer space and the future have been colonized. As a rule, even the more imaginative science fiction writers (seemingly the most foretelling futurists) cannot/will not create a space and time in which women get far beyond the role of space stewardess. Nor does this situation exist simply "outside" women's minds, securely fastened into institutions which we can physically leave behind. Rather, it is also internalized, festering inside women's heads, even feminist heads.

The journey of women *becoming,* then, involves exorcism of the internalized Godfather, in his various manifestations (His name is legion). It involves dangerous encounters with these demons. Within the Christian tradition, particularly in medieval times, evil spirits have sometimes been associated with the Seven Deadly Sins, both as personifications and as causes.[5] A "standard" and prevalent listing of the Sins is, of course, the following: pride, avarice, anger, lust, gluttony, envy, and sloth.[6] I am contending that these have all been radically misnamed, that is, inadequately and even perversely "understood" within Christianity. These concepts have been used to victimize the oppressed, particularly women. They are particularized expressions of the overall use of "evil" to victimize women.

---

[5]An elaborate historical study of the Sins is to be found in Morton W. Bloomfield, *The Seven Deadly Sins* (Michigan State University Press, 1952, 1967). [Daly's note]

[6]Bloomfield gives a variety of "listings" of Deadly Sins in different periods and cultures, with useful contextual information. [Daly's note]

The feminist journey involves confrontations with the demonic distortions of evil.

Why has it seemed "appropriate" in this culture that a popular book and film *(The Exorcist)* center around a Jesuit who "exorcises" a girl-child who is "possessed"? Why is there no book or film about a woman who exorcises a Jesuit?[7] Within a culture possessed by the myth of feminine evil, the naming, describing, and theorizing about good and evil has constituted a web of deception, a Maya. The journey of women becoming is breaking through this web— a Fall into free space. It is reassuming the role of subject, as opposed to object, and naming good and evil on the basis of our own intuitive intellection.

Breaking through the web of the Male Maya is both exorcism and ecstasy. These are two aspects of the same journey. Since women have been prohibited from real journeying, that is, from encountering the strange, the unknown, the women's movement is movement into uncharted territory. The process involves removal of the veils which prevent confrontation with the unknown. Let it be noted that "journey" is a multidimensional word and that the various meanings and images conjured up by the word are not sharply distinguishable. One thinks of mystical journeys, quests, adventurous travel, advancement in skills, in sports, in intellectual probing, in psychological integration and transformation. So also the "veils," the insulations against the unknown imposed upon women by male mediators, are multidimensional and intertwined. The veils are woven of religious myths (for example, the myth of the "good woman," the Virgin Mother who has only a Son, not a Daughter), legal restrictions, social customs, medical and psychoanalytic ideologies and practices, academic restrictions (withholding of access to "higher" education, to certain professions), grammatical conditioning ("he" supposedly includes "she"), economic limitations. The very process of exorcism, of casting off the blinding veils, is movement outside the patriarchally imposed sense of reality and identity. This demystification process, standing/moving outside The Lie, *is* ecstasy.

The process of encountering the unknown, of overcoming the 28 "protection" racket, also involves a continual conversion of the previously unknown into the familiar.[8] This requires the use of tools and instruments now in the possession of women's captors.

---

[7]See Dolores Bargowski's review of the film in *Quest: A Feminist Quarterly* I, No. 1, (Summer, 1974), pp. 53–57. [Daly's note]

[8]This idea is developed in a remarkable article. See Peggy Allegro, "The Strange and the Familiar," *Amazon Quarterly*, I, 1, pp. 29–41. [Daly's note]

Amazon expeditions into the male-controlled "fields" such as law, medicine, psychology, philosophy, theology, literature, history, sociology, biology, and physics are necessary in order to leave the Fathers' cave and live in the sun. A crucial problem has been to learn how to plunder righteously while avoiding being caught too long in the cave. In universities, and in virtually all of the professions, there are poisonous gases which are almost invisible and odorless, and which gradually stifle women's minds and spirits. Those who carry out the necessary expeditions run the risk of shrinking into the mold of the mystified Athena,[9] the twice-born who forgets and denies her Mother and Sisters. "Reborn" from the Father, she becomes Daddy's Girl, the mutant who serves the master's purposes. The token woman, who in reality is enchained, possessed, "knows" that she is free. She is a useful tool of the patriarchs, particularly against her sister Artemis who knows better, respects her womanself, bonds with her sisters, and refuses to sell her freedom, her original birthright, for a mess of respectability.

Exorcism, Processions, and Remythologization

What clues can we find concerning the "nature" and direction of the Other-world journey of radically feminist (i.e., conscious) women? Some important hints can be discovered in *Three Guineas,* an astonishing book published in the 1930s by a prophetic foremother. In that book Virginia Woolf links processions (e.g., academic, churchly, military, judicial) with professions and processions. She asks:

> What are these ceremonies and why should we take part in them? What are these professions and why should we make money out of them? Where, in short, is it leading us, the procession of the sons of educated men?[10]

Clearly, they are leading us to destruction of the human species and of the planet. The rigid, stylized, hierarchical, gynocidal and genocidal processions of male-controlled professions—of church, state, university, army—are all intimately interconnected. These

---

[9]***Athena***   Athena sprang full-grown and armed from the head of Zeus, the chief of Greek gods. She was born without the need of a mother and is therefore "Daddy's Girl," as Daly says.

[10]Virginia Woolf, *Three Guineas* (New York: Harcourt, Brace, and World, Inc., 1938, 1966), p. 63. [Daly's note]

processions capture and reify process. They are deadly. It is important to understand them in order to understand what feminist process/journeying is *not*.

Patriarchal processions both generate and reflect the archetypal image of "procession" from and return to God the Father. In Christian myth, this is a cyclic pattern: separation and return. Christians participate in the procession—they join the parade—through Baptism, which explicitly contains a rite of exorcism. This mythic symbolic procession toward "God," then, begins with belief in possession by evil forces ("possession" technically in a broad sense, of course), release from which requires captivity by the church. What is ultimately sought is reconciliation with the Father.

Clearly, the ultimate symbol of "procession" is the All Male   32 Trinity itself. In various abstruse ways theologians have elaborated upon the "mystery," or as some would say, the "symbol," of the Trinity. What is of great significance here is the fact that this is a myth of Father and Son (no Mother or Daughter involved) in total unity, so total that this "love" is expressed by the Third Person, the Holy Spirit. This is the epitome of male bonding, beyond the wildest dreams of Lionel Tiger.[11] It is (almost?) erotic male homosexual mythos, the perfect All Male Marriage, the All Male Divine Family. It is asymmetric patriarchy carried to the sublime absurdity of contradiction, christened "mystery." To the timid objections sometimes voiced by Christian women, the classic answer has been: "You're included. The Holy Spirit is feminine." The conclusion of this absurd logic arrives quickly if one asks: How then, did "he" impregnate the Virgin Mary?

Mere human males, of course, cannot fully identify with the divine Son. Perfect consubstantiality[12] with the Father, therefore, cannot be achieved. The earthly processions of the sons of men have as their basic paradigm[13] an attempted identification with the Father. (God the Father, the Godfather, the Oedipal Father.[14]) The junior statesman dreams of becoming The President. The academic junior scholar (disciple) dreams of becoming The Professor (Master). The acolyte dreams of becoming The Priest. And, as Woolf[15]

---

[11]*Lionel Tiger (b. 1937)*   At the time this piece was written, Tiger was regarded as a scholarly antagonist of the feminist movement. He wrote *Men in Groups* (1984).

[12]*consubstantiality*   Having the same essence and substance.

[13]*paradigm*   Model, example.

[14]*Oedipal Father*   Each of the three examples Daly gives is a model or paradigm for the idea of father. The Oedipal Father is the figure that, according to Freud, the male child wants to kill in order to have the mother all to himself (see the selection from Freud in Part Three of this book).

[15]*Virginia Woolf (1882–1941)*   British novelist and distinguished critic.

recognized, the death-oriented military processions reveal the real direction of the whole scenario, which is a funeral procession of the human species. God the Father requires human sacrifice.

Women becoming must indeed recognize the fact of having been possessed by the structures of evil. However, the solution is not "rebirth" or Baptism by the Father's surrogates, for it is this socialized "rebirth" which is the captivity from which we are trying to escape. Radical feminism is *not* reconciliation with the Father. It begins with saying "No" to the Father, who attempts to eradicate our Mother and to transform us into mutants by forcing "rebirth" (whether from the head of Zeus or from the rib of Adam or from baptismal "grace"). More than this: radical feminism means saying "Yes" to our original birth, the original movement-surge toward life. This is both a remembering and a rediscovering. Athena remembers and rediscovers her Mother. That which is generated between us is Sisterhood. We are then no longer confined by our identities as "Mother" or "Daughter." The Daughter is *not* obedient to the Mother "unto death." The Mother does not send her forth to be crucified for the sins of women or of men. Rather, they go forth as Sisters. Radical feminism releases the inherent dynamic in the Mother-Daughter relationship toward Sisterhood, which is thwarted within the Male-mastered system. The Mother does *not* demand self-sacrifice of the Daughter. Rather, both demand of each other affirmation of the self and of each other in an on-going personal/political process which is mythic in its depths—which is both an exorcising and a remythologizing process. The "sacrifice" that is required is not mutilation of the hands of men, but rather the discipline needed for action together, for self-defense and self-actualization on a planet dominated by the Reign of Terror which is the Reign of the Godfathers. It is important that we consider the actual conditions of this terrain through which we must make our journey.

The Land of the Fathers

As Phyllis Chesler[16] has pointed out, the story of the Virgin Mary, impregnated by God to bring forth his only Son, is classic patriarchal rape-incest myth. The Madonna has no Divine Daughter. Moreover, as the same author perceptively says, she foregoes

---

[16]**Phyllis Chesler**   An author who writes on feminist issues. Her works include *Women and Madness* (1972).

sexual pleasure, physical prowess, and economic and intellectual power in order to become a "mother" for her "divine" son.[17] And this is the primary role-model for women in our culture. This is the life that women are condemned to live out—an alienation which is personal, social, mythic—and which is all the deeper because unrecognized, unacknowledged.

In a society in which women are in fact *robbed* of physical   36 prowess, of economic and intellectual power, we live in a State of Siege.[18] As Jeanne Lafferty and Evelyn Clark wrote:

> Every female person knows the humiliation of being constantly harassed and solicited by males. Having her person talked at, whistled at, yelled at, grunted at, hooted and howled at, visually dismembered or stared and winked at by males everywhere—on the street, at work, at school, at home—everywhere.[19]

This is the very real condition of women in a rapist society. Moreover, the dismemberment is not always only visual. Male fetishism concerning women's bodies, the cutting into objectified parts which is the prime material of advertising and pornography, has as its logical outcome the brutal rape murders and actual physical dismemberments which take place in such a society. In a world ruled by God the Father this is not considered a serious problem. A feminist author wrote: "Rape is too personal and too terrible a crime to be left to the punishment of indifferent male law."[20]

In a society possessed by the sexual caste system, that is, in a rapist society, there is a deep struggle on the part of those designated "victims" to cast out the deception that warps the soul. The deception inflicted upon women is a kind of mindbinding comparable to the footbinding procedure which mutilated millions of Chinese women for a thousand years.[21] Just as footbinding destroyed the capacity for physical movement—walking, running, dancing—

---

[17]Phyllis Chesler, *Women and Madness,* (New York: Doubleday, 1972), pp. 24–26. [Daly's note]

[18]This expression was used by Emily Culpepper in an unpublished paper entitled "Reflections on Ethics and Self Defense: Establishing a Firm Stance." [Daly's note]

[19]"Self Defense and the Preservation of Females," in *The Female State: A Journal of Female Liberation,* Issue 4 (April, 1970), p. 96. [Daly's note]

[20]Elizabeth Gould Davis, author of *The First Sex* (New York: G. P. Putnam's Sons, 1971) wrote this in an article about her own devastating rape in *Prime Time,* June, 1974, p. 3. [Daly's note]

[21]The horrors of footbinding are recounted by Andrea Dworkin, *Woman Hating* (New York; Dutton, 1974), pp. 95–117. These "tiny feet" were malodorous, mutilated humps. Women fell from one to the other. These stumps were described in fantastically deceptive euphemistic language and were the objects of sadistic male fetishism. [Daly's note]

mindbinding damages the capacity for autonomous creativity, action, thinking, imaging, willing. Stripping away the mindbindings of lies that reduce women to the status of physical, mental, and spiritual rapes is the basic loving act in such a society.

The Qualitative Leap

Creative, living, political hope for movement beyond the gynocidal reign of the Fathers will be fulfilled only if women continue to make qualitative leaps in living our transcendence. A short-circuited hope of transcendence has caused many to remain inside churches, and patriarchal religion sometimes has seemed to satisfy the hunger for transcendence. The problem has been that both the hunger and the satisfaction generated within such religions have to a great extent alienated women from our deepest aspirations. Spinning in vicious circles of false needs and false consciousness, women caught on the patriarchal wheel have not been able to experience women's own experience.

I suggest that what is required is *ludic cerebration,* the free play of intuition in our own space, giving rise to thinking that is vigorous, informed, multi-dimensional, independent, creative, tough. *Ludic cerebration* is thinking out of experience. I do not mean the experience of dredging out All That Was Wrong with Mother, or of instant intimacy in group encounters, or of waiting at the doctoral dispensary, or of self-lobotomization in order to publish, perish, and then be promoted. I mean the experience of being. *Be-ing* is the verb that says the dimensions of depth in all verbs, such as intuiting, reasoning, loving, imaging, making, acting, as well as the couraging, hoping, and playing that are always there when one is really living.

It may be that some new things happen within patriarchy, but one thing essentially stays the same: women are always marginal beings. From this vantage point of the margin it is possible to look at what is between the margins with the lucidity of The Compleat Outsider. To change metaphors: the systems within the System do not appear so radically different from each other to those excluded by all. Hope for a qualitative leap lies in *us* by reason of that deviance from the "norm" which was first imposed but which can also be chosen on our own terms. This means that there has to be a shift from "acceptable" female deviance (characterized by triviality, diffuseness, dependence upon others for self-definition, low self-esteem, powerlessness) to deviance which may be unacceptable to others but which is acceptable to the self and is self-acceptance.

For women concerned with philosophical/theological questions, it seems to me, this implies the necessity of some sort of choice. One either tries to avoid "acceptable" deviance ("normal" female idiocy) by becoming accepted as a male-identified professional, or else one tries to make the qualitative leap toward self-acceptable deviance as ludic cerebrator, questioner of everything, madwoman, and witch.

I do mean witch. The heretic who rejects the idols of patriarchy is the blasphemous creatrix of her own thoughts. She is finding her life and intends not to lose it. The witch that smolders within every woman who cared and dared enough to become a philosophically/spiritually questing feminist in the first place seems to be crying out these days: "Light my fire!" The qualitative leap, the light of those flames of spiritual imagination and cerebral fantasy can be a new dawn.

On "Androgyny"[22]

Feminists have searched for a word to express the concept-reality of psychic wholeness, of integration, which we are just beginning to glimpse intuitively, experientially, as realizable. In this search for the right word we have experienced the poverty of the language bequeathed to us, and we have recognized the manner in which it constricts and even distorts our thought. In my book *Beyond God the Father,* I frequently use the word "androgyny" to express this intuition and incipient experience of wholeness, which transcends sex-role stereotyping—the societally imposed "eternal feminine" and "eternal masculine." Feminist ethicist Janice Raymond[23] has written perceptively of an "intuition of androgyny" as identical with the intuition of being.[24] Two young theologians, graduates of Harvard Divinity School, used the term to convey a feminist understanding of wholeness in a much discussed jointly published article.[25] Feminist poet Adrienne Rich[26] used the word in

---

[22]***Androgyny***   Possessing the qualities of both sexes.

[23]***Janice Raymond (b. 1943)***   Author of *A Passion for Friends: Toward a Philosophy of Female Affection.*

[24]"Beyond Male Morality," in *Women and Religion,* Revised Edition, edited by Judith Plaskow and Joan Romero, (Missoula, Montana: American Academy of Religion and The Scholars' Press, 1974), pp. 115–125. [Daly's note]

[25]Linda L. Barufaldi and Emily E. Culpepper, "Androgyny and the Myth of Masculine/Feminine," *Christianity and Crisis,* April 16, 1973, pp. 69–71. [Daly's note]

[26]***Adrienne Rich (b. 1929)***   One of America's most distinguished poets.

her poem "The Stranger," which concludes with the following lines:

> I am the androgyne
> I am the living mind you fail to describe
> in your dead language
> the lost noun, the verb surviving
> only in the infinitive
> the letters of my name are written under the lids
> of the newborn child.[27]

All of these authors now experience some hesitancy about using the word "androgyny" to express our vision(s). This hesitancy is at least in part due to an increasing understanding of the political use and abuse of language. This increased sophistication has resulted from some distressing misinterpretations of the word.

In speaking to audiences, I have sometimes had the impression that people hearing this term vaguely envisage two distorted halves of a human being stuck together—something like John Wayne and Brigitte Bardot scotch-taped together—as if two distorted "halves" could make a whole. That is, there is a kind of reification of wholeness, instead of recognition that what is being described is continual process. This non-understanding of "androgyny," which feminists have used when attempting to describe the *process* of integration, is also reflected in the assumption on the part of some women (and men) that a woman who is successful in a career on male terms (for example, a successful business executive) and at the same time a model housewife has achieved "androgyny." In fact, this career housewife as described fails to criticize radically either the "masculine" or the "feminine" roles/worlds. She simply compartmentalizes her personality in order to function within both, instead of recognizing/rejecting/transcending the inherent oppressiveness of such institutions as big business and the nuclear family.

When one becomes conscious of the political usages of language, she recognizes also that the term "androgyny" is adaptable to such mystifying usage as the expression "human liberation" has been subjected to. That is, it can easily be used to deflect attention from the fact that women and men at this point in history cannot simply "get together and work it out," ignoring the profound differences in socialization and situation within the sexual caste system. Both "androgyny" and "human liberation" function fre-

44

---

quently to encourage false transcendence, masking—even though unintentionally—the specific content of the oppression of women, and suggesting that wholeness depends upon identification with men. Some of us do still use the term "androgyny," of course, but less frequently, more circumspectly, and with some apprehension that we will be misunderstood.

Some feminists began to feel somewhat less comfortable with the word "androgyny" when the implications of a small terse fact surfaced to consciousness. That fact is etymological: the first part of the word obviously is derived from the Greek *aner, andros* (man), while the second part is from *gyne* (woman). This, of course, carries its own message. A first reaction was to employ the word "gynandry," which, from the perspective of women's becoming, is more appropriate. But it soon became evident that the priority problem in the etymology of the word was really symptomatic of deeper problems.

In fact, the term "androgyny" comes to us heavily fraught   48 with traditional associations, that is, associations of male-centered tradition(s). The image conveyed by the word is that of a "feminized" male. This fact has been brought home to me in public discussions with male Christian theologians who, confronted with the problem of the inherent oppressiveness of Christolatry, have responded earnestly that there really is no problem since "Jesus was androgynous." Whatever this may mean, it has little relevance to the problem of women's becoming *now*, and in fact it distracts from the real issues confronting us. Dressing up old symbols just will not work for women who are conscious of sexist religiosity.

"Gynandry" helps to shift images away from the traditional biases, but only to a limited degree. Placing the female part of the word first does not dissolve the inherent dependency of the word itself upon stereotypes in order that there be any meaningful content at all. To put it another way, in an "androgynous" or "gynandrous" society it would be senseless to speak of "androgyny" or "gynandry" since people would have no idea of the sex-stereotyped characteristics and/or roles referred to by the components of the terms. Use of these terms at this point in history is dysfunctional to the extent that it encourages on some level a perpetuation of stereotypes (as is the case with Jungian ideology of the "anima" and "animus"). "Gynandry" or "androgyny" *can* function in a liberating way if they are seen as "transitional" words, or, more precisely, as self-liquidating words. They should be understood as having a built-in planned obsolescence.[28]

---

[28]In a speech delivered at the Modern Language Association Forum, December, 1973, Cynthia Secor noted that there is no "Androgyne Quarterly"—most probably because there are no androgynes around to publish it. [Daly's note]

Wanted: "God" or "The Goddess"?

Feminist consciousness is experienced by a significant number of women as ontological becoming, that is, be-ing. This process requires existential courage, courage to be and to *see,* which is both revolutionary and revelatory, revealing our participation in ultimate reality as Verb, as intransitive Verb.

The question obviously arises of the need for anthropomorphic symbols for this reality. There is no inherent contradiction between speaking of ultimate reality as Verb and speaking of this as personal. The Verb is more personal than a mere static noun. However, if we choose to *image* the Verb in anthropomorphic symbols, we can run into a problematic phenomenon which sociologist Henri Desroche[29] calls "crossing." "Crossing" refers to a notable tendency among oppressed groups to attempt to change or adapt the ideological tools of the oppressor, so that they can be used *against* him and *for* the oppressed. The problem here is the fact that the functioning of "crossing" does not generally move far enough outside the ideological framework it seeks to undermine. In the "Black theology" of James Cone,[30] for example, we find a Black God and a Black Messiah, but this pigmentation operation does not significantly alter the behavior of Jahweh & Son. Cone's Black God is as revengeful and sexist as his White prototype. For feminist eyes it is clear that this God is at least as oppressive as the old (for black women as well as for white women). The message in the alteration of symbol is simply about *which* male-ruled racial group will be on top and which will be on the bottom. The basic presupposition of *hierarchy* remains unaltered: that is, the presupposition that there must be an "us" or a "them" on top, and a corresponding "them" or "us" on the bottom.

Some women religious leaders within Western culture in modern times have performed something like a "crossing" operation, notably such figures as Mary Baker Eddy[31] and Ann Lee,[32] in stressing the "maternal" aspect of the divinity. The result has been mixed. Eddy's "Father-Mother God" is, after all, the Christian God. Nor does Ann Lee really move completely outside the Christian frame-

52

---

[29]***Henri Desroche*** Author of *Religious Inspiration and Temporal Structures* (1948).

[30]***James Cone (b. 1938)*** Theologian and author of *Black Theology and Black Power* (1969).

[31]***Mary Baker Eddy (1821–1910)*** Author of *Science and Health, with Key to the Scriptures.* She is the founder of Christian Science.

[32]***Ann Lee (1736–1784)*** Religious leader know as "Mother Ann" who founded the Shaker communal religious sect in the American colonies. She preached celibacy and believed she embodied the female half of God's dual nature.

work. It is interesting that their writings lack the thirst for vengeance that characterizes Cone's all too Christian Black theology, which is certainly in their favor. But it is also necessary to note that their theologies lack explicit relevance to the concrete problems of the oppression of women. Intellection and spirituality remain cut off from creative political movement. In earlier periods also there were women within the Christian tradition who tried to "cross" the Christian all-male God and Christ to some degree. An outstanding example was Juliana of Norwich,[33] an English recluse and mystic who lived in the last half of the fourteenth century. Juliana's "God" and "Jesus" were—if language conveys anything—hermaphroditic constructs, with the primary identity clearly male. While there are many levels on which I could analyze Juliana's words about "our beloved Mother, Jesus, (who) feeds us with himself,"[34] suffice it to say here that this hermaphroditic image is somewhat less than attractive. The "androgynous" God and Jesus present problems analogous to and related to those problems which occur in connection with the use of the term "androgyny" to describe the direction of women's becoming. There is something like a "liberation of the woman within" the (primarily male) God and Jesus.

Indeed, it is harder to perform a transsexual operation on the Judeo-Christian divinity than a mere pigmentation operation. This is one reason, no doubt, why Cone is able to achieve a purely Black God and Black Messiah, rather than a Mulatto, whereas the Christian women mentioned brought forth hermaphrodites, with emphasis upon maleness. Indeed, they did something on the symbolic level which is analogous to "liberating the woman within the man." Since they went only this far, they accomplished little or nothing, in social or mythic terms, toward the genuine liberation of women.

One fact that stands out here is that these were women whose imaginations were still partially controlled by Christian myth. My contention is that they were caught in a contradiction (which is not the case in the work of Black *male* theologians). I am saying that there is a profound contradiction between the inherent logic of radical feminism and the inherent logic of the Christian symbol system. I would not have said this ten years ago, at the time of writing the original edition of *The Church and the Second Sex,* which

---

[33]*Juliana of Norwich (d. 1420?)*   A mystic whose *Revelations of Divine Love* (c. 1393) is based on sixteen visions of Jesus Christ. She is often referred to as Julian of Norwich, which illustrates Daly's point.

[34]Juliana of Norwich, *Revelations of Divine Love,* edited by Clifton Walters (Baltimore, Maryland: 1966), Ch. 61. [Daly's note]

expressed hope for reform of Christianity in general and Roman Catholicism in particular. Nor would some women today say this— women who still perceive their identity as both Christian and feminist.

Both the reformers and those who leave Judaism and Christianity behind are contributing and will contribute in different ways to the process of the becoming of women. The point here is not to place value judgments upon individual persons and their efforts— and there are heroic efforts at all points of the feminist spectrum. Rather, it is to disclose an inherent logic in feminism. The courage which some women have in affirming this logic comes in part from having been on the feminist journey for quite awhile. Encouragement comes also from knowing increasing numbers of women who have chosen the route of the logical conclusion. Some of these women have "graduated" from Christianity or religious Judaism, and some have never even been associated closely with church or synagogue, but have discovered spiritual and mythic depths in the women's movement itself. What we share is a sense of becoming in cosmic process, which I prefer to call the Verb, Be-ing, and which some would still call "God."

For some feminists concerned with the spiritual depth of the 56 movement, the word "God" is becoming increasingly problematic, however. This by no means indicates a movement in the direction of "atheism" or "agnosticism" or "secularism," as these terms are usually understood. Rather, the problem arises precisely because of the spiritual and mythic quality perceived in feminist process itself. Some use expressions such as "power of being." Some reluctantly still use the word "God" while earnestly trying to divest the term of its patriarchal associations, attempting to think perhaps of the "God of the philosophers" rather than the overtly masculist and oppressive "God of the theologians." But the problem becomes increasingly troublesome, the more the "God" of the various Western philosophers is subjected to feminist analysis. "He"—"Jahweh" still often hovers behind the abstractions, stunting our own thought, giving us a sense of contrived doublethink. The word "God" just may be inherently oppressive.

Indeed, the word "Goddess" has also been problematic, but for different reasons. Some have been worried about the problem of "crossing." However, that difficulty appears more and more as a pseudo-difficulty when it is recognized that "crossing" is likely to occur only when one is trying to work *within* a sexist tradition. For example, Christian women who in their "feminist liturgies" experiment with referring to "God" as "she" and to the Trinity as "The Mother, the Daughter, and the Holy Spirit," are still working within all the boundaries of the same symbolic framework and the same power structure. Significantly, their services are at the same place and time as "the usual," and are regarded by most of the constituency of the churches as occasional variations of "business as usual."

As women who are outside the Christian church inform ourselves of evidence supporting the existence of ancient matriarchy and of evidence indicating that the Gods of patriarchy are indeed contrived, pale derivatives and reversals of the Great Goddess of an earlier period, the fear of mere "crossing" appears less appropriate and perhaps even absurd. There is also less credibility allowable to the notion that "Goddess" would function like "God" in reverse, that is, to legitimate an oppressive "female-dominated" society, if one is inclined to look seriously at evidence that matriarchal society was not structured like patriarchy, that it was non-hierarchical.[35]

Would "Goddess" be likely to function oppressively, like "God"? Given the present situation of women, the danger is not imminent. "Would it function that way in the future?" My inclination is to think not, but it is not my intention to attempt to "prove" this point at this time. The question has a quality of "abstraction" and remoteness from the present social realities and it is, it seems to me, diversionary. When it is raised, and it is usually raised by men, one senses an "atmosphere" about the question, an aroma of masculine hysteria, a fear of invading hordes of "matriarchs" (read: female patriarchs) taking over the Man's world.

There are however, two points concerning the symbol "Goddess" which I think *are* relevant to the existing situation. First, it can at the very least be pointed out that whenever the pendulum has swung extremely in one direction (and it *has*—for millennia), it is psychologically/socially/ethically important to emphasize "the other side." The hermaphroditic[36] image hardly seems satisfactory for anyone. For an increasing minority of women—and even for some men[37]—"Goddess" is becoming more functional, meaningful, and loaded with healing associations. As this minority grows, Western society will be shaken by the presence of gynarchic symbolism in a new and potent way. It should be noted that women are inclined

---

[35]See Robert Briffault, *The Mothers,* (New York: Macmillan, 1927), Vol. I. See also J. J. Bachofen, *Myth, Religion and Mother-Right,* trans. by Ralph Manheim (Princeton: Princeton University Press, 1967). [Daly's note]

[36]***hermaphroditic***   The hermaphrodite possessed the sexual organs of both sexes and was therefore imaginary; however, the image persists.

[37]Kenneth Pitchford chooses Goddess imagery, which occurs frequently in his more recent poems. [Daly's note]

to speak and write of "The Goddess," whereas one seldom says "The God." In our culture it has been assumed that "goddesses" are many and trivial, whereas the "real" divinity *is* "God," who does not even require the definite article. The use of the expression, "The Goddess," is a way of confronting this trivialization, of exorcising the male "God," and of affirming a different myth/reality.

A second, and related, point has to do with the fact that the "self-transcending immanence," the sense of giving birth to ourselves, the sense of power of being within, which is being affirmed by many women, does not seem to be denoted, imaged, adequately pointed to, or perhaps even associated with the term "God." With her permission, I will relate a story told to me by a theologian for whose insights I have the greatest respect. This woman told me that in the past when riding in planes (and feeling fearful about the situation) she often conjured up images remembered from childhood of "God" as "having the whole world in his hands." Later, this image/prayer? became meaningless. When she was on a plane recently, the ride suddenly became extremely "bumpy" and rough. It occurred to her to "try on" the name/image "Goddess." The result, as she described it, was immediate, electrifying, consoling. She sensed a presence and had/heard? the thought: "Just let go. Just sit on the seat and sit on the air waves and ride." The ride, though as rough as before, became a joyful experience.[38]

Clearly, it would be inappropriate and arrogant to try to "explain" or "interpret" this experience of another person. I can only comment that many women I know are finding power of being within the self, rather than in "internalized" father images. As a philosopher, my preference has been for abstractions. Indeed I have always been annoyed and rather embarrassed by "anthropomorphic" symbols, preferring terms such as "ground and power of being" (Tillich), "beyond subjectivity and objectivity" (James), "the Encompassing" (Jaspers), or the commonly used "Ultimate Reality," or "cosmic process." More recently I have used the expression "Intransitive Verb." Despite this philosophical inclination, and also because of it, I find it impossible to ignore the realm of symbols, or to fail to recognize that many women are experiencing and participating in a remythologizing process, which is a new dawn.

It is necessary to add a few remarks about the functioning of the confusing and complex "Mary" symbol within Christianity. Through it, the power of the Great Goddess symbol is enchained,

---

[38]The story was told by Professor Nelle Morton of Drew Theological Seminary and paraphrased by myself. [Daly's note]

captured, used, cannibalized, tokenized, domesticated, tranquilized. In spite of this, I think that many women and at least some men, when they have heard of or imaged the "Mother of God," have, by something like a selective perception process, screened out the standardized, lobotomized, dull, derivative and dwarfed Christian reflections of a more ancient symbol; they have perceived something that might more accurately be described as the Great Goddess, and which, in human terms, can be translated into "the strong woman who can relate because she can stand alone." A woman of Jewish background commented that "Mother of God" had always seemed strange and contradictory to her. Not having been programmed to "know" about the distinctions between the "divine" and the "human" nature of "Christ," or to "know" that the "Mother of God" is less than God, this woman had been able to hear the expression with the ears of an extraenvironmental listener. It sounded, she said, something like "infinite plus one."[39] When this symbolic nonsense is recognized, it is more plausible simply to *think* "infinite," and to *image* something like "Great Mother," or "Goddess."

It may appear that the suffix "-ess" presents a problem, when   64 one considers other usages of that suffix, for example, in "poetess," or in "authoress." In these cases, there is a tone of depreciation, a suggestion that women poets and authors are in a separate and "inferior" category to be judged by different standards than their male counterparts. However, the suffix does not always function in this "diminishing" way. For example, there appear to be no "diminutive" overtones suggested by the word "actress." So also it seems that the term "Goddess"—or "The Goddess"—*is not only non-diminutive,* but very strong. Indeed, it calls before the mind images of a powerful and ancient tradition before, behind, and beyond Christianity. These are multi-dimensional images of women's present and future becoming/be-ing.

"Priests" or "Priestesses"?

I would suggest that "priestess" has diminutive connotations if it is applied within the framework of Christianity (Episcopalian priestesses?), since of course within the limitations of that framework the role "acted out" by women has to be seen as derivative. It is only when one considers the possibility that the Christian

---

[39]Comment of Linda Franklin, Boston College student. [Daly's note]

tradition is itself derivative from a far more ancient and woman-centered tradition, that one's perception of priesthood changes. For women to be priestesses then is no longer perceived simply as a derivative phenomenon, but as primary and authentic. But then neither is it a Christian phenomenon. The priesthood of women need not seek legitimation within Christian churches. Nor need it be seen as a title or office conferred upon certain officially designated women to the exclusion of others.

Moreover, there are impossible contradictions in the idea of woman-identified Christian priests. While it may be possible for a twice-born Athena to "say Mass," or to commit baptism "in the name of the Father and of the Son and of the Holy Ghost," this sort of behavior presents incredible problems, that is, problems of credibility. Moreover, as I have said, it is inconsistent simply to try to fit a "feminine" symbolism into these sclerotic vessels. The "form" would still be the message, with some alterations in "content."

Is it true, as Malcolm Boyd[40] has recently argued, that "when the (Christian) priest is a woman, even God is no longer a male?"[41] At one time, some years ago, I might have agreed with this. However, it is important to look at Protestant churches which have been ordaining women for years. Clearly, their God (and Gods) are still male. Large patriarchal institutions are still male. Large patriarchal institutions are still quite capable of absorbing a few tokens and in fact of profiting from this, appearing "liberal" while at the same time attracting women who are doubly devoted to the task of serving male Gods. I say "doubly devoted" because, as the cliche goes, a woman has to be twice as "good" as a man to get half as much recognition.

It is instructive to read the list of 110 Catholic signers who have called for the ordination of women "to the priesthood of the universal church."[42] Having read some writings of some of them, I question (1) whether they can possibly understand what the logic of feminism is all about (i.e., leaving behind and thus leaving to die the inherently oppressive structures of patriarchal religions; (2) whether they do "understand" what the logic of feminism is about and see "containment" as an important tactic for holding women in bondage as long as possible.

The women's movement is about refusal to be merely contained as well as refusal to be mere containers. It is about saying "Yes"

68

---

[40]***Malcolm Boyd (b. 1923)***   Author of *The Underground Church* (1968).

[41]*Ms.*, December, 1974. [Daly's note]

[42]Reported in *National Catholic Reporter*, November 8, 1974, p. 5. [Daly's note]

to ourselves, which is the deepest way of saying "Yes" to others. At some point in her history a woman may sincerely see ordination to the Christian priesthood as her way of saying this "Yes." It is my hope that such women will *continue* their journey. Ambition to "ordination" perhaps reaches a respectable altitude for the jet age, but it does not reach very far, I think, into feminist space/time. It is my hope that these sisters will raise their ambitions and their self-respect higher, immeasurably higher, that they will one day outgrow their books of common prayer and dream less common dreams.

QUESTIONS FOR CRITICAL READING

1. Is the imagery connected with the Trinity sexist in the way that Daly suggests?
2. Is it possible to approach Christianity in a nonsexist way and yet still adhere to its tenets? For example, is it possible to be Christian and still interpret the Trinity as Daly does?
3. According to Daly, what effects do patriarchal symbols have on a culture? Do you find yourself agreeing with her that ours is a rapist society?
4. What is the "myth of feminine evil"? Do you think it affects our society today?
5. Is there such a thing in our society as "The Most Unholy Trinity: Rape, Genocide, and War"?
6. Mary Daly believes that the women's movement is beginning to affect the fabric of society. Do you see evidence of such an influence?

WRITING ASSIGNMENTS

1. Describe the alternatives that religious people have to thinking about God as a man or as a woman. How could a religion renovate its symbolism and its beliefs in order to accommodate such a change in its position? In your opinion, would such a change make the religion more spiritual in character, or less spiritual?
2. In paragraph 16, Mary Daly writes, "Christian myths are inherently sexist." Is this statement true? How can its truth be demonstrated? How can its falseness be demonstrated? Examine our society for evidence that points in one direction or the other on this issue.
3. How do religious symbols function to promote a specific kind of belief? What religious symbols can you specifically point to that have had an effect on popular thought? What is it about symbols that make them powerful enough to affect the way people think? In what sense

are they substitutions for ideas or for independent thought? Are the religious symbols with which you are familiar coherent in their meaning, or do they sometimes seem contradictory? Choose three or four symbols and examine them carefully.

4. Write a brief response to Daly concerning her concept of the androgyne. Begin by looking the word up in an unabridged dictionary. Then look up the term in an encyclopedia of myth. The term is used in Plato's *Republic,* in his narration of a myth explaining the origins of sexuality. He states that originally people were both male and female, androgynes, and that our troubles began when the androgyne split into separate beings. What is your reaction to the concept of the androgyne? Do you feel it is desirable for people to try to relinquish gender role distinctions and encompass the qualities of both genders?

5. What are the ethical issues in this essay? Daly talks about "a society possessed by the sexual caste system, that is, . . . a rapist society" (para. 37). Do you accept her views on the nature of our society, and if so, do you feel that we are fully aware of the ethical consequences of male dominance?

6. Is there an ethical issue at stake in the phenomenon that Daly describes as "crossing"? (The term is defined and discussed beginning in paragraph 51). "Crossing" refers to adopting the position of the oppressor and practicing what amounts to self-oppression. Is this a genuine phenomenon? Do you think that women sometimes "cross" in the sense that Daly suggests? If so, do you think that there is an ethical question that should be raised regarding such women? Why should such a phenomenon concern us at all?

7. **CONNECTIONS** Compare Daly's concerns with those of some of the other philosophers in Part Five. Do any of the male philosophers discuss the relations between the sexes? Do any of them include feminist issues in their exhortations to ethical behavior? Is the feminist issue an ethical issue?

PART SIX

IDEAS IN THE WORLD OF ANTHROPOLOGY

HOW CAN ONE CULTURE
UNDERSTAND ANOTHER?
IS THERE SUCH A THING
AS AN OBJECTIVE ANALYSIS
OF OTHER CULTURES?

Franz Boas

Ruth Benedict

Margaret Mead

Claude Lévi-Strauss

Clifford Geertz

INTRODUCTION

THE BEGINNINGS of modern anthropology—the science of studying cultures other than one's own—date from the 1890s, when the field began to become popular in the United States and Europe through the efforts of pioneer teachers such as Franz Boas. Until the 1890s anthropology was often limited to the comparative examination of skulls in an effort to establish distinctions in human behavior on the basis of ethnic or racial differences. Geography was thought to contribute to the behavior of groups and to shape and form cultures. Both approaches, which were thought to be scientific, avoided the practice of spending time in the field living with people of other cultures as a means of coming to understand them. Professional anthropologists began such a practice following the example of Franz Boas, trained as a geographer, whose work with Eskimos on Baffin Island upset theories regarding the shaping effect of geography on culture. Bronislaw Malinowski (1884–1942), whose work is not represented here, was a Polish pioneer of fieldwork with cultures in the South Pacific. His work essentially corroborated Boas's discoveries concerning geography's effects on cultures, as did later anthropologists in the South Pacific: Ruth Benedict, Margaret Mead, and Clifford Geertz.

Living among a people while studying their culture seemed to offer the best means of learning about other cultures. Most of the anthropologists represented here learned the languages of the people they studied and lived with them for extensive periods of time as a means of learning to understand and think like those in the culture. Until recently most assumptions regarding their work were based on the premise that their methods permitted them to come to a reliable understanding of the cultures they studied. However, recent concerns have been raised regarding the capacity of an anthropologist—especially a European or American whose own tradition has been steeped in colonialism—to develop an objective view of another culture. Colonialism was based on the tacit assumption that European culture was superior to the cultures that it forced into subservience, and therefore it may be all but impossible to shed such views and truly understand another culture, especially one that is termed "savage" or "primitive," descriptions often used by anthropologists.

The nineteenth-century view of non-Western cultures was generally affected by colonial attitudes. Moreover, the concept of progress in the nineteenth century affected general attitudes toward culture and civilization. For example, it was generally assumed that cultures began as primitive and evolved into modern, civilized societies. The idea seemed obvious, especially given the support of the Darwinian metaphor of evolution. If animals evolve, then why not cultures?

Franz Boas, however, was instrumental in dispelling such ideas. Cultures may be styled as primitive in some senses and civilized in other senses, he argued, but all cultures have developed over thousands of years to their current levels of success. It is not self-evident that all primitive cultures wish to emulate so-called civilization. Changes in cultures usually occur because they are overrun by other cultures (as in the cases of wars or economic development), not because they recognize progress and decide to adopt it. On the other hand, changes sometimes occur because people see in another culture's habits an improvement they decide to emulate. Margaret Mead gives us an example of the latter phenomenon. The process of change in cultures depends largely on their interaction with other cultures. The more interaction, the faster the change.

That is one of the basic points of the first essay in this section, "Stability of Culture." In it, Franz Boas explains that archaeological digs reveal patterns of human behavior that have remained constant for thousands of years. However, the natural proliferation of people and the interaction of distinct cultures eventually produced changes and, with them, instability. Archaeology also reveals that the changes grew more rapid as populations increased and opportunities for interaction improved. Cultures, Boas insists, are shaped by the historical traditions they inherit; therefore, all cultures are not only unique but develop independently of their geographical surroundings and other environmental factors. In the late nineteenth century, when Boas begin to publish his findings, such an idea was almost revolutionary.

In her studies of the Pueblo Indians of New Mexico, Ruth Benedict began to explore ideas concerning the shaping of cultures. While she studied with Franz Boas, she developed her own concepts regarding the psychological makeup of cultures. Borrowing the terms *Apollonian* and *Dionysian* from Friedrich Nietzsche, she applied them to various peoples in and out of Pueblo culture. For example, she saw the Pueblo Zuñi as Apollonian—intellectual, cool, reserved—and the Kwakiutl of the Northwest, whom Boas had studied, as Dionysian—quick-tempered, intemperate, given to grand passion. On the other hand, she observed in the Dobu, a people she studied in the Pacific, a more sinister psychological quality—the schizophrenic.

Margaret Mead, a student of both Franz Boas and Ruth Benedict, learned seven languages in order to communicate with people in cultures in the South Pacific both before and after World War II. "Women, Sex, and Sin" is a study of attitudes toward women in the culture of the Manus, a people living on the largest of the Admiralty Islands northwest of what is today Papua New Guinea. She reveals a fascinating development in the culture caused largely by the wartime interaction of Manus men with men from Australia and with films from the United States. As she tells us, the men returned to the island of Manus and purposively restructured their society. Few anthropologists have the opportunity that Mead had to study the effects of such an overwhelming change in social behavior. In the process, however, she examines the effects of change on the women themselves and notes that underneath, much has remained the same.

Unlike Boas, Benedict, and Mead, the French anthropologist Claude Lévi-Strauss is not committed to extensive fieldwork among other cultures. He has spent time with Indian tribes along the Amazon in Brazil, but most of his work has derived from a limited experience in the field. He has, however, developed theories of structuralism examining underlying patterns of culture, which have been extremely influential on contemporary anthropologists. In his essay "A Little Glass of Rum," he discusses the enterprise of anthropology and the relationship of the culture under examination to the culture of the anthropologist. Surprisingly, his view is that anthropologists usually overvalue the culture being studied relative to their own. Lévi-Strauss's ideas raise basic questions concerning the way in which anthropologists examine other cultures.

Clifford Geertz reflects on the difficulty of ever being able to report on a culture "from the native's point of view." He establishes relatively quickly that such a venture is essentially impossible. However, he attempts to resolve the problem of how we can know another culture by suggesting that it is possible to study the "symbolic forms" of a culture, its "words, images, institutions, behaviors." He demonstrates what he means by reference to three cultures he has studied closely—Javanese, Balinese, and Moroccan. Each of these is different and each is instructive. In each case, Geertz discusses some key words in the local language in an effort to demonstrate the specificity of the symbolic forms he studied. His efforts offer us a method by which we can study not only other cultures, but also our own.

These essays exemplify the range of thought regarding the possibility of understanding other cultures. At the same time, they offer insight into the ways in which other people lived and continue to live, reminding us that we are part of a larger community of humanity, whose diverse cultures are in a constant state of interaction and change. In addition, the awareness anthropologists provide can help us understand ourselves as much as we hope to understand others.

FRANZ BOAS
Stability of Culture

FRANZ BOAS (1858–1942), born and educated in Germany, moved to the United States in 1887. By the time he left Germany, he had become a geographer and had spent time with the Eskimos on Baffin Island in the Arctic. His original studies and concerns were geographic, but after he encountered Eskimo culture he moved more and more firmly toward ethnology, the study of social groups. He eventually became a foremost expert on Native American cultures with a special interest in languages. The originality of his studies helped develop a new direction for the study of linguistics and the relationship between language and culture.

When he first settled in the United States, Boas was an assistant editor of the journal Science, but soon he found a post in anthropology at Clark University in Worcester, Massachusetts. At that time, anthropology was not a clearly defined field. Boas moved several times before becoming a professor at Columbia University in 1899, where he began to transform anthropology and create the discipline as it is understood by students today.

Boas published his monograph The Central Eskimo in 1888, but his most important early book was The Mind of Primitive Man (1911), which reshaped anthropology and reformed entirely the concept of culture. Before this book was published, anthropologists thought of culture as a fixed entity in which all societies participated to one degree or another. For them, culture was evolutionary, primitive peoples being at an early stage and more technically advanced peoples at a later stage. Consequently, anthropologists had spent much of their time taking physical measurements of people, collecting languages, and describing

From *Anthropology and Modern Life* (1928).

ceremonies and behaviors. Boas's great achievement was to establish that what anthropologists really needed to study were the differences between cultures and the ways in which various cultures developed in response to environment, circumstances, and local history. In other words, he redefined culture as a range of possibilities, dictated not so much by circumstances in a given place at a given time as by the specific historical inheritance of the people.

The importance of this new paradigm cannot be overstated. Prior to Boas, anthropologists typically spoke of groups of primitive people as backward rather than culturally distinct. Progress was assumed to be a cultural fact that was most evident in the technological West. Anthropologists before Boas believed that race played a powerful role in determining culture and that people of color were less culturally developed than whites; but after Boas published his ideas, race could no longer be represented as a determining feature of culture. Before Boas it was thought that the same environmental and geographical circumstances would produce more or less the same cultural results. After Boas, culture was seen as independent of geography, race, and environment. In Germany in the 1930s, Nazis publicly burned The Mind of Primitive Man *because it invalidated their racial theories.*

Boas demonstrated that each culture was formed by its unique history. The conformity of behavior that identifies different cultures resulted, he argued, from history and tradition, not from genetics or geography. People absorb their cultural patterns beginning in infancy, and the cultural patterns that seem inborn to the individuals themselves are actually inculcated by tradition. Thus, after Boas, culture—not heredity—became the determining factor for the study of anthropology.

Boas demonstrated that anthropologists must spend time in the field studying other cultures because each culture is distinct and can be understood only by reflection and examination. His own fieldwork with the Eskimos on Baffin Island was followed by extensive experience in the American Northwest with the Kwakiutl peoples, whose languages he learned and used. His students—among whom were Ruth Benedict, Margaret Mead, Ashley Montagu, and many other highly respected anthropologists—followed his lead by living with and studying primitive cultures whose languages they learned.

In "Stability of Culture" Boas attempts to define culture in historical terms, beginning with ancient cultures distinguished primarily in terms of the tools they developed. By examining changes in tools, he reveals patterns of change and interaction which begin slowly but increase rapidly through conquest and invasion. Today, changes in our culture are rapid, endless, and sometimes traumatic. Whereas older cultures were stable for long periods of time, modern cultures are in some ways less stable because of increasing interaction among differing groups.

BOAS'S RHETORIC

Boas did not assume a professional audience. Instead, he envisioned an audience of people who were interested in culture and believed that it was racially, geographically, and genetically determined. Therefore, he was patient and careful to establish his main concerns. In paragraph 13, for example, he says that "we are wont to measure the ability of a race by its cultural achievements." However, earlier, in paragraph 11, Boas had also pointed out that "Negroes of the United States" had experienced a rapidity of cultural change that was extraordinary. He points to distinctions that may exist among the races but sees them as a result of "social barriers" that have not been crossed.

Boas's method is to appear not to be arguing. This form of argument, sometimes described as Rogerian, appears neither threatening nor confrontational, but merely informative. Boas is gentle, nonthreatening, and cautious, but he is nonetheless constructing an argument. He often relies on conclusive paragraphs of only one or two sentences. For example, near the end of his discussion of instinctive and learned behavior he finishes his discussion of habits with an aphoristic one-sentence paragraph (24): "Whatever is acquired in infancy and childhood by unvarying habits becomes automatic." Boas expects the reader, upon reaching this paragraph, to be ready to accept the truth of the statement without further elaboration.

Among the more interesting examples in the essay are those of habitual behaviors that are second nature to most people in most cultures: table manners. Many people are intolerant of the eating habits of others. As he points out in his discussion of the "persecution of heretics" (para. 28), intolerance among social groups sometimes becomes violent. One of his conclusive paragraphs suggests a connection with some of Thomas Kuhn's views regarding paradigm shifts in science: "Even in science a similar intolerance may be observed in the struggle of opposing theories and in the difficulty of breaking down traditional viewpoints" (para. 30).

Culture, as Boas demonstrates, produces behavior that seems automatic and sometimes instinctive but is actually learned and transmitted to the individual. The conflict between tradition and change may be as fundamental to cultures as is automatic behavior. One result of reading this passage may be an increased sense of tolerance of the behavior of people from other cultures. Boas seems to have learned that lesson himself.

Stability of Culture

An isolated community that remains subject to the same environmental conditions, and without selective mating, becomes, after a number of generations, stable in bodily form. As long as there are no stimuli that modify the social structure and mental life the culture will also be fairly permanent. Primitive, isolated tribes appear to us and to themselves as stable, because under undisturbed conditions the processes of change of culture are slow.

In the very earliest times of mankind culture must have changed almost imperceptibly. The history of man, of a being that made tools, goes back maybe 150,000 years, more or less. The tools belonging to this period are found buried in the soil. They are stone implements of simple form. For a period of no less than 30,000 years the forms did not change. When we observe such permanence among animals we explain it as an expression of instinct. Objectively the toolmaking of man of this period seems like an instinctive trait similar to the instincts of ants and bees. The repetition of the same act without change, generation after generation, gives the impression of a biologically determined instinct. Still, we do not know that such a view would be correct, because we cannot tell in how far each generation learned from its predecessors. Animals like birds and mammals act not only instinctively; they also learn by example and imitation. Horses and dogs learn to react to calls or to the spoken word. English sparrows reared by canaries learn their song and call-notes. Parrots learn to imitate sounds. Apes even learn to use sticks or stones as tools.

It seems likely that conditions were the same in early man. Even in the earliest remains differences may be found. While in some areas the typical form of an implement was the flint blade, in others it was the cleaver or coup-de-point.[1] According to Menghin[2] a culture based on the use of bone originated in arctic Asia, another one based on the manufacture of flint blades in Eastern Asia, and one based on the flint cleaver in India.

The importance of the process of learning becomes more and 4 more evident the nearer we approach the present period. The tools become more differentiated. Not all localities show the same forms, and it seems likely that if we could examine the behavior of man in periods one thousand years apart that changes would be discovered.

---

[1]*coup-de-point* Hand-held stone edge.
[2]*Oswald Franz Ambrosius Menghin (1888–?)* A contemporary of Boas.

At the end of the ice age the differentiation in the forms of manufactured objects had come to be as great as that found nowadays among primitive tribes. There is no reason why we should assume the life of the people who lived towards the end of the ice age, the Magdalenians, to have been in any respect simpler than that of the modern Eskimo.

With the beginning of the present geological period the differentiation of local groups and of activities in each group was considerable. Changes which in the beginning required tens of thousands of years, later thousands of years, occurred now in centuries and brought about constantly increasing multiplicity of forms.

With the approach of the historic period the degree of stability of culture decreased still further and in modern times changes are proceeding with great rapidity, not only in material products of our civilization but also in forms of thought.

Since earliest times the rapidity of change has grown at an ever-increasing rate. 8

The rate of change in culture is by no means uniform. We may observe in many instances periods of comparative stability followed by others of rapid modifications. The great Teutonic migrations at the close of antiquity brought about fundamental changes in culture and speech. They were followed by periods of consolidation. The Arab conquest of North Africa destroyed an old civilization and new forms took its place. Assimilation of culture may also be observed among many primitive tribes, and, although we do not know the rate of change, there is often strong internal evidence of a rapid adjustment to a new level. In language the alternation between periods of rapid change and comparative stability may often be observed. The transition from Anglo-Saxon and Norman to English was rapid. The development of English since that time has been rather slow. Similar periods of disturbance have occurred in the development of modern Persian.

Changes of unusual rapidity are due to the influence of European civilization upon primitive cultures. When they do not completely disappear a new adjustment is reached with great rapidity. This is exemplified by the modern culture of the Indians of Mexico and Peru. Part of their ancient material culture survives. Under the veneer of catholicism and of other Spanish cultural forms old ideas persist, readjusted to the superimposed civilization. A blend has developed which does not yield until modern schools and a livelier participation in world affairs disturb the equilibrium. A remarkable example of adjustment between old and new is found among the Pueblo tribes of New Mexico who have consciously and as far as possible isolated themselves from the American life around them.

Their daily life has been modified by the use of products of American manufacture. Woven goods, glass windows and doors, agricultural implements, household furniture are in use; Catholic churches are attended on Sundays; the Saints' days are celebrated; and all this is assimilated to the older forms of life. The ancient house forms persist; in some Pueblos the former style of dress survives; as heretofore, corn is ground on the grinding stone; old types of Spanish ovens for baking bread continue to be used, and the ancient religious beliefs and ceremonials have been so adjusted that they continue, without serious inner conflicts, side by side with catholicism. The new equilibrium is disturbed only when the general conditions of life make continued isolation impossible and the younger generation finds a new adjustment to altered conditions.

Even more striking is the rapidity of change of culture among the Negroes of the United States. Since their introduction as slaves their language, their ancient customs and beliefs, have disappeared apace with their absorption in the economic life of America. Dr. Parsons, Dr. Herskovits, and Miss Zora Hurston[3] have shown that, as we proceed from south to north, from Dutch Guyana to the northern States, the survivals of Negro culture become less and less. The isolated Bush Negroes of Surinam are essentially African in culture. The Negro districts of the South retain some African elements, while the northern Negro city dweller is to all intents and purposes like his White neighbor, except in so far as social barriers tend to perpetuate one or the other peculiarity of behavior.

Notwithstanding the rapid changes in many aspects of our modern life we may observe in other respects a marked stability. Characteristics of our civilization are conflicts between the inertia of conservative tradition and the radicalism which has no respect for the past but attempts to reconstruct the future on the basis of rational considerations intended to further its ideals. These conflicts may be observed in education, law, economic theory, religion, and art. Discipline against freedom of control, subordination under the public weal against individual freedom, capitalism against socialism, dogma against freedom of belief, established art forms against esthetic expression subject only to individual whim, are some of these conflicts. They are possible only when in a rapidly changing culture the old and the new live side by side.

We are wont to measure the ability of a race by its cultural achievements which imply rapid changes. Those races among

12

---

[3]Talcott Parsons (1902–1979), Melville Jean Herskovits (1895–1963), and Zora Neale Hurston (1903–1960) were students of Boas. Hurston was important as a writer in the Harlem Renaissance.

whom the later changes have been most rapid appear, therefore, as most highly developed.

For these reasons it is important to study the conditions that make for stability and for change; and to know whether changes are organically or culturally determined.

Behavior that is organically determined is called instinctive. When the infant cries and smiles, when later on it walks, its actions are instinctive in this sense. Breathing, chewing, retiring from a sudden assault against the senses, approach towards desired objects are presumably organically determined. They do not need to be learned. Most of these actions are indispensable for the maintenance of life. We can never account for the reasons that prompt us to perform acts organically determined. The stimulus presents itself and we react at once, without conscious effort. Still, some of these reactions may be modified or even suppressed with impunity. Thus we may learn to overcome the reaction to fear. It is difficult to do so, but not impossible.

On the ground of this experience we are inclined to consider   16
every type of behavior that is marked by an immediate, involuntary reaction as instinctive. This is an error, for habits imposed upon us during infancy and childhood have the same characteristics. They determine the particular forms of our activities, even of those based on the structure of our organism. We must recognize that the specific *forms* of our actions are culturally determined.

We must eat in order to live. Arctic man is compelled by necessity to live on a meat diet; the Hindu lives on vegetal food by choice.

That we walk on our legs is organically conditioned. How we walk, our particular gait, depends upon the forms of our shoes, the cut of our clothing, the way we carry loads, the conformation of the ground we tread. Peculiar forms of motion may be, in part, physiologically determined, but many are due to imitation. They are repeated so often that they become automatic. They come to be the way in which we move "naturally." The response is as easy and as ready as an instinctive action, and a change from the acquired habit to a new one is equally difficult. When thoroughly established the level of consciousness of an automatic action is the same as that of an instinctive reaction.

In all these cases the *faculty* of developing a certain motor habit is organically determined. The particular *form* of movement is automatic, acquired by constant, habitual use.

This distinction is particularly clear in the use of language. The   20
faculty of speech is organically determined and should be called, therefore, instinctive. However, *what* we speak is determined solely

by our environment. We acquire one language or another, according to what we hear spoken around us. We become accustomed to very definite movements of lips, tongue and the whole group of articulating organs. When we speak, we are wholly unconscious of any of these movements and equally of the structure of the language we speak. We resent deviations in pronunciation and in structure. As adults we find it exceedingly difficult, if not impossible, to acquire complete mastery of new articulations and new structures such as are required in learning a foreign language. Our linguistic habits are not instinctive. They are automatic.

Our thoughts and our speech are accompanied by muscular movements—some people would even say they *are* our thoughts. The kinds of movements are not by any means the same everywhere. The mobility of the Italian contrasts strikingly with the restraint of the Englishman.

The human faculty of using tools is organically determined. It is instinctive. This, however, does not mean that the kind of tool developed is prescribed by instinct. Even the slightest knowledge of the development of tools proves that the special forms characteristic of each area and period depend upon tradition and are in no way organically determined. The choice of material depends partly upon environment, partly upon the state of inventions. We use steel and other artificially made materials; the African iron, others stone, bone, or shell. The forms of the working parts of the implements depend upon the tasks they are to perform, those of the handles upon our motor habits.

The same is ordinarily true of our likes and dislikes. We are organically capable of producing and enjoying music. What kind of music we enjoy depends for most of us solely upon habit. Our harmonies, rhythms, and melodies are not of the same kind as those enjoyed by the Siamese and a mutual understanding, if it can be attained at all, can be reached solely by long training.

Whatever is acquired in infancy and childhood by unvarying   24
habits becomes automatic.

There is a negative effect of automatism, no less important than the positive one which results in the ease of performance.

Any action that differs from those performed by us habitually strikes us immediately as ridiculous or objectionable, according to the emotional tone that accompanies it. Often deviations from automatic actions are strongly resented. A dog taught to give his hind paw instead of the front paw excites us to laughter. Formal dress worn at times when the conventions do not allow it seems ridiculous. So does the dress that was once fashionable but that has gone out of use. We need only think of the hoop skirt of the middle of the last century or of the bright colors of man's dress and the impression they would create to-day. We must also realize the resistance that we ourselves have to appearing in an inappropriate costume.

More serious are the resistances in matters that evoke stronger emotional reactions. Table manners are a good example. Most of us are exceedingly sensitive to a breach of good table manners. There are many tribes and people that do not know the use of the fork and who dip into the dish with their fingers. We feel this is disgusting because we are accustomed to the use of fork and knife. We are accustomed to eat quietly. Among some Indian tribes it is discourteous not to smack one's lips, the sign of enjoying one's food. What is nauseating to us is proper to them.

Still more striking is our reaction to breaches of modesty. We 28 have ourselves witnessed a marked change in regard to what is considered modest, what immodest. A comparative study shows that modesty is found the world over, but that the ideas of what is modest and what immodest vary incredibly. Thirty years ago woman's dress of to-day would have been immodest. South African Negroes greet a person of high rank by turning the back and bowing away from him. Some South American Indians consider it immodest to eat in view of other people. Whatever the form of modest behavior may be, a breach of etiquette is always strongly resented.

This is characteristic of all forms of automatic behavior. The performance of an automatic action is accompanied by the lowest degree of consciousness. To witness an action contrary to our automatic behavior excites at once intense attention and the strongest resistances must be overcome if we are required to perform such an action. Where motor habits are concerned the resistance is based on the difficulty of acquiring new habits, which is the greater the older we are, perhaps less on account of growing inadaptibility than for the reason that we are constantly required to act and have no time to adjust ourselves to new ways. In trifling matters the resistance may take the form of fear of ridicule, in more serious ones there may be dread of social ostracism. But it is not only the fear of the critical attitude of society that creates resistance, it rests equally in our own unwillingness to change, in our thorough disapprobation of the unconventional.

Intolerance of sharply divided social sets is often based on the strength of automatic reactions and upon the feeling of intense displeasure felt in acts opposed to our own automatism. The apparent fanaticism exhibited in the persecution of heretics must be explained in this manner. At a time when the dogma taught by the Church was imposed upon each individual so intensely that it became an automatic part of his thought and action, it was accompanied by a strong feeling of opposition, of hostility to any one who did not participate in this feeling. The term fanaticism does not quite correctly express the attitude of the Inquisition. Its psychological basis was rather the impossibility of changing a habit of thought that had become automatic and the consequent impossibility of following new lines of thought, which, for this very reason, seemed antisocial; that is, criminal.

We have a similar spectacle in the present conflict between nationalism and internationalism with their mutual intolerance.

Even in science a similar intolerance may be observed in the   32
struggle of opposing theories and in the difficulty of breaking down traditional viewpoints.

Both the positive and negative effect of automatically established actions implies that a culture replete with these must be stable. Every individual behaves according to the setting of the culture in which he lives. When the uniformity of automatic reaction is broken, the stability of culture will be weakened or lost. Conformity and stability are inseparably connected. Non-conformity breaks the force of tradition.

We are thus led to an investigation of the conditions that make for conformity or non-conformity.

Conformity to instinctive activities is enforced by our organic structure, conformity to automatic actions by habit. The infant learns to speak by imitation. During the first few years of life the movements of larynx, tongue, roof of the mouth, and lips are gradually controlled and finally executed with great accuracy and rapidity. If the child is removed to a new environment in which another language is spoken, before the time when the movements of articulation have become stable, and as long as a certain effort in speech is still required, the movements required by the new language are acquired with perfect ease. For the adult a change from one language to another is much more difficult. The demands of everyday life compel him to use speech, and the articulating organs follow the automatic, fixed habits of his childhood. By imitation certain modifications occur, but a complete break with the early habits is extremely difficult, for many well-nigh impossible, and probably in no case quite perfect. Unwonted movements reappear when, due to disease, the control of the central nervous system breaks down.

Early habits control also the movements of the body. In   36
childhood we acquire certain ways of handling our bodies. If these movements have become automatic it is almost impossible to change to another style, because all the muscles are attuned

to act in a fixed way. To change one's gait, to acquire a new style of handwriting, to change the play of the muscles of the face in response to emotion is a task that can never be accomplished satisfactorily.

What is true of the handling of the body is equally true of mental processes. When we have learned to think in definite ways it is exceedingly difficult to break away and to follow new paths. For a person who has never been accustomed as a young child to restrain responses to emotions, such as weeping, or laughing, a transition to the restraints cultivated among us will be difficult. The teachings of earliest childhood remain for most people the dogma of adult life, the truth of which is never doubted. Recently the importance of the impressions of earliest childhood has been emphasized again by psychoanalysts. Whatever happens during the first five years of life sets the pace for the reactions of the individual. Habits established in this period become automatic and will resist strongly any pressure requiring change.

It would be saying too much to claim that these habits are alone responsible for the reactions of the individual. His bodily organization certainly plays a part. This appears most clearly in the case of pathological individuals or of those unusually gifted in one way or another; but the whole population consists of individuals varying greatly in bodily form and function, and since the same forms and faculties occur in many groups, the group behavior cannot be deeply influenced by structure. Differences must be due to culturally acquired automatic habits and these are among the most important sources of conservatism.

QUESTIONS FOR CRITICAL READING

1. What does Boas imply about the rate of change in a culture?
2. What are the changes brought about by the influence of European culture on primitive cultures?
3. How does Boas describe "behavior that is organically determined" (para. 15)? Which of your behaviors are organically determined?
4. Boas makes a distinction between our activities and the *forms* of our activities. What is his point?
5. According to Boas, in what way are differences in our musical taste determined? Are those differences based on our faculties for perception or on our habits?
6. Is Boas correct in his assertion "Whatever is acquired in infancy and childhood by invarying habits becomes automatic" (para. 24)?

7. Are matters of dress or table manners especially emotional issues in modern American culture?

WRITING ASSIGNMENTS

1. To what extent do you feel that "the teachings of earliest childhood remain for most people the dogma of adult life, the truth of which is never doubted" (para. 37)? Do you know examples of people whose earliest teachings guide them today? Do the earliest teachings of most people stand them in good stead, or do they lead them into difficulties?
2. Boas describes the reactions that people in a given culture have to variations in dress. Boas calls them "deviations from automatic actions." What have you observed about people's way of dressing in your own culture? Do people react strongly to variations—deviations—from the norm? Do individuals try to stimulate reactions to their fashions on the part of others? What is the significance of those reactions to Boas's theories of culture?
3. Your own environment—that of a modern college—produces cultural expectations that may differ from your current cultural expectations at home or those you had when you were younger. Judging from your observations, would you defend or attack the view that most people actually share multiple cultural experiences rather than one? Use details from your observations of language, dress, eating habits, and expectations of behavior to prove your point. Do college students live in a culture distinct from that of adults or those who are not in a college?
4. Conformity and conservatism are linked together in Boas's analysis of culture. A conservative person will attempt to honor tradition and to bolster its importance in a community. To what extent is a conservative person likely to preserve cultural values? To what extent does your culture expect you to follow tradition? Is it difficult for the individual to follow another path?
5. **CONNECTIONS**   How do Boas's views regarding culture and automatic behavior fit in with B. F. Skinner's views on the conditioned behavior that we as "autonomous agents" take for granted as normal? Skinner feels we are products of environmental conditioning—and for him the environment includes our culture as well as our circumstances. Would Boas agree or disagree with him? Establish the points of agreement and disagreement that these two figures would most likely find with each other's views.
6. **CONNECTIONS**   Erich Fromm discusses the important differences between the psychological importance of environmental expectations and the subconscious forces built up in infancy as determining the mental health of the individual. What would Boas say about Fromm's theories?
7. **CONNECTIONS**   To what extent do the findings of Margaret Mead

in "Women, Sex, and Sin" support Boas's theories regarding the development of culture through history and tradition? Mead describes the Manus people who changed important patterns of behavior very rapidly after a period in which some Manus men lived with Australians and watched American films. How might Boas have reacted to Mead's findings?

RUTH BENEDICT

The Pueblos of New Mexico

RUTH BENEDICT *(1887–1948) studied anthropology at Columbia University under the direct supervision of Franz Boas and received
her Ph.D. there in 1923. She is renowned for her work with North
American Indians, and for her many distinguished books, such as* The
Concept of the Guardian Spirit in North America *(1923);* Tales
of the Cochiti Indians *(1931);* Patterns of Culture *(1935);* Race,
Science, and Politics *(1940); and* The Chrysanthemum and the
Sword *(1946). Like Boas, she insists that cultures are not determined
by race, biology, or geography but instead grow individually in response
to their own personal experiences and history, developing traditions
that make them distinct in behavior.*

*In her researches on southwestern Native Americans, Benedict
developed an interesting psychological model of cultures. She suggested
that the cultures she studied closely had developed psychological models
that correspond with certain well-known psychological types for individuals. For example, she uses the two general types that Friedrich
Nietzsche refers to in his essay "Apollonianism and Dionysianism."
For her the Zuñi of the Southwest are Apollonian—by which she
means that they are intellectual, rational, cool, and reserved. The
northwestern tribes of the Kwakiutl are, she felt, Dionysian—by which
she means given to intoxication, emotion, and celebration. She also
sees patterns of paranoia and schizophrenia in the "psychological personalities" of some cultures, such as the Dobu of Melanesia, whom she
also studied. The Dobu have an especially difficult time getting along
together because of ingrained distrust of their fellow Dobu.*

From *Patterns of Culture* (1934).

Benedict uses these psychological portraits drawn specifically from Nietzsche with the understanding that they should not be applied absolutely, but with respect for variations. Her point is that cultures develop much as individuals develop, in response to the historical tradition: "A culture, like an individual, is a more or less consistent pattern of thought and action. Within each culture there come into being characteristic purposes not necessarily shared by other types of society." Despite her use of the Nietzschean terms, Benedict felt that there is no way to establish a typology of cultures. The terms were designed only to establish a useful characterization to help understand the ways of the culture. Benedict believed, along with Boas and others, that one's own culture provides the lens through which one observes others. Consequently, Benedict warns us concerning our capacity to truly see and understand other peoples whose values and basic concepts are foreign.

Nonetheless, Benedict provides us with a view of the Zuñi that helps us gain some sense of their culture, particularly in terms of its distinctions. The question of whether we can truly understand other cultures always underlies her work. She understands our limitations but presses onward to give us what perspective we can gain. Her technique is to concentrate on clear exposition and description so that we see what is of importance to the culture.

Much of her emphasis is on the vision quest associated with religion and religious rites; she reminds us that religion and ritual are central to the culture of the American Indian; and she goes into great detail about both. "We cannot understand the Pueblo configuration of culture without a certain acquaintance with their customs," she explains. Benedict tells us a great deal about the distinctions between the Pueblo— or Zuñi—Indians and their surrounding neighbors, emphasizing that although Zuñi live extremely close to Indians in Mexico and New Mexico whose environments are essentially identical, the cultures are essentially distinct.

The distinction between the Apollonian and Dionysian becomes a convenient symbol for her to establish basic differences of attitude, especially toward the role of the individual in the society. In Zuñi, individualism is not promoted. The social group works together and devotes much of its energy to elaborate religious ceremonies that must be performed with letter-perfect accuracy to ensure their effectiveness. Other Indian cultures promote individualism in sometimes complex ways. For example, the emphasis on the vision quest—a solitary experience usually conducted in remote areas with the aid of natural drugs—is common among all the groups that surround Zuñi, but totally foreign to Zuñi. It is not part of their cultural heritage despite the fact that the drugs, such as peyote, are easily available.

BENEDICT'S RHETORIC

The passage reprinted here is marked by the use of comparison. At first Benedict compares the Zuñi with nearby tribes; then she introduces the Nietzschean terms that are themselves borrowed from Greek culture. The implied comparison with Greece is one of Benedict's subjects, but she soon moves back to the question of how the Zuñi compare with their neighbors.

Benedict's greatest skill as a writer is clarity. Her writing is concrete, with specific references to places and events. She is forced to write without naming individuals, a limitation that ordinarily cripples the style of many prose writers. But she sometimes introduces individuals through their activities, for example, preparing for marriage, setting out on a quest. The point of this strategy is to reduce our reliance on the individual as a measure of things. Zuñi does not rely on the individual and neither does Benedict. She attempts to show us the customs of the people so that we can come closer to understanding their culture.

By beginning with the description of experiences common to our own culture, such as courtship and marriage, Benedict helps not only to concretize her writing but also piques our interest immediately. However, Benedict soon moves on to describe events and concerns essentially exotic to our culture. The connection, for example, between drugs and the religious quest for visions that will guide the individual, and perhaps the group, for a lifetime is quite unlike any experience we are likely to have: our cultural use of drugs is either medicinal or recreational, not spiritual.

Finally, Benedict clarifies the issues behind the vision quest and those that separate the questers from Zuñi. She focuses clearly on the careful and accurate description of Zuñi customs. Her ability to remain concrete even in the face of her refusal to describe the individual experience of members of Zuñi is remarkable.

The Pueblos of New Mexico

No other aspect of existence seriously competes in Zuñi interest with the dances and the religious observances. Domestic affairs like marriage and divorce are casually and individually arranged. Zuñi is a strongly socialized culture and not much interested in those things that are matters for the individual to attend to. Marriage is arranged almost without courtship. Traditionally girls had few opportunities for speaking to a boy alone, but in the evening when all the girls carried the water-jars on their heads to the spring for water, a boy might waylay one and ask for a drink. If she liked him she gave it to him. He might ask her also to make him a throwing stick for the rabbit hunt, and give her afterwards the rabbits he had killed. Boys and girls were supposed to have no other meetings, and certainly there are many Zuñi women today who were married with no more preliminary sex experience than this.

When the boy decides to ask her father for the girl, he goes to her house. As in every Zuñi visit, he first tastes the food that is set before him, and the father says to him as he must say to every visitor, "Perhaps you came for something." The boy answers, "Yes, I came thinking of your daughter." The father calls his daughter, saying, "I cannot speak for her. Let her say." If she is willing, the mother goes into the next room and makes up the pallet and they retire together. Next day she washes his hair. After four days she dresses in her best clothes and carries a large basket of fine corn flour to his mother's house as a present. There are no further formalities and little social interest is aroused in the affair.

If they are not happy together, and think of separating, especially if they have no children that have lived, the wife will make a point of going to serve at the ceremonial feasts. When she has a tête-à-tête with some eligible man they will arrange a meeting. In Zuñi it is never thought to be difficult for a woman to acquire a new husband. There are fewer women than men, and it is more dignified for a man to live with a wife than remain in his mother's house. Men are perennially willing. When the woman is satisfied that she will not be left husbandless, she gathers together her husband's possessions and places them on the doorsill, in olden times on the roof by the hatchway. There are not many: his extra pair of moccasins, his dance skirt and sash, if he has them, his box of precious feathers for prayer-sticks, his paint-pots for prayer-sticks and for refurbishing masks. All his more important ceremonial possessions he has never brought from his mother's house. When he comes home in the evening he sees the little bundle, picks it up and cries, and returns with it to his mother's house. He and his family weep and are regarded as unfortunate. But the rearrangement of living-quarters is the subject of only fleeting gossip. There is rarely an interplay of deep feeling. Husbands and wives abide by the rules, and these rules hardly provide for violent emotions, either of jealousy or of revenge, or of an attachment that refuses to accept dismissal.

In spite of the casual nature of marriage and divorce, a very   4 large proportion of Zuñi marriages endure through the greater part of a lifetime. Bickering is not liked, and most marriages are peaceful. The permanence of Zuñi marriages is the more striking because marriage, instead of being the social form behind which all the forces of tradition are massed, as in our culture, cuts directly across the most strongly institutionalized social bond in Zuñi.

This is the matrilineal family, which is ceremonially united in its ownership and care of the sacred fetishes.[1] To the women of the household, the grandmother and her sisters, her daughters and their daughters, belong the house and the corn that is stored in it. No matter what may happen to marriages, the women of the household remain with the house for life. They present a solid front. They care for and feed the sacred objects that belong to them. They keep their secrets together. Their husbands are outsiders, and it is their brothers, married now into the houses of other clans, who are united with the household in all affairs of moment. It is they who return for all the retreats when the sacred objects of the house are set out before the altar. It is they, not the women, who learn the word-perfect ritual of their sacred bundle and perpetuate it. A man goes always, for all important occasions, to his mother's house, which, when she dies, becomes his sister's house, and if his marriage breaks up, he returns to the same stronghold.

This blood-relationship group, rooted in the ownership of the house, united in the care of sacred objects, is the important group in Zuñi. It has permanence and important common concerns. But it is not the economically functioning group. Each married son, each married brother, spends his labour upon the corn which will fill his wife's storeroom. Only when his mother's or sister's house lacks male labour does he care for the cornfield of his blood-relationship group. The economic group is the household that lives together, the old grandmother and her husband, her daughters and their husbands. These husbands count in the economic group, though in the ceremonial group they are outsiders.

For women there is no conflict. They have no allegiance of any kind to their husbands' groups. But for all men there is double allegiance. They are husbands in one group and brothers in another. Certainly in the more important families, in those which care for permanent fetishes, a man's allegiance as brother has more social weight than his allegiance as husband. In all families a man's position derives, not, as with us, from his position as breadwinner, but from his rôle in relation to the sacred objects of the household. The

---

[1]*fetishes*   Objects believed to have power for magic.

husband, with no such relationship to the ceremonial possessions of his wife's house to trade upon, only gradually attains to position in the household as his children grow to maturity. It is as their father, not as provider or as their mother's husband, that he finally attains some authority in the household where he may have lived for twenty years.

Economic affairs are always as comparatively unimportant in 8 Zuñi as they are in determining the family alignments. Like all the Pueblos, and perhaps in greater degree than the rest, Zuñi is rich. It has gardens and peach orchards and sheep and silver and turquoise. These are important to a man when they make it possible for him to have a mask made for himself, or to pay for the learning of ritual, or to entertain the tribal masked gods at the Shalako.[2] For this last he must build a new house for the gods to bless at house-warming. All that year he must feed the cult members who build for him, he must provide the great beams for the rafters, he must entertain the whole tribe at the final ceremony. There are endless responsibilities he must assume. For this purpose he will plan heavily the year before and increase his herd. He will receive help from his clan group, all of which he must return in kind. Riches used in this way are of course indispensable to a man of prestige, but neither he nor anyone else is concerned with the reckoning of possessions, but with the ceremonial rôle which he has taken. A "valuable" family, in native parlance, is always a family which owns permanent fetishes and a man of importance is one who has undertaken many ceremonial rôles.

All the traditional arrangements tend to make wealth play as small a part as possible in the performance of ritual prerogatives. Ceremonial objects, even though they are recognized personal property and attained by the expenditure of money and effort, are free to the use of anyone who can employ them. There are many sacred things too dangerous to be handled except by those who have qualified, but the tabus are not property tabus. Hunting fetishes are owned in the hunters' society, but anyone who is going hunting may take them for his use. He will have to assume the usual responsibilities for using holy things; he will have to plant prayer-sticks and be continent and benevolent for four days. But he pays nothing, and those who possess the fetishes as private property have no monopoly of their supernatural powers. Similarly a man who has

---

[2]**Shalako** A ritual ceremony honoring the *kachina,* ancestral spirits; often performed during the winter solstice and consisting of communal dances and chants.

no mask borrows one freely and is not thought of as a beggar or a suppliant.

Besides this unusual discontinuity between vested interests and the ownership of ceremonial objects in Zuñi, other more common arrangements make wealth of comparative unimportance. Membership in a clan with numerous ceremonial prerogatives outweighs wealth, and a poor man may be sought repeatedly for ritual offices because he is of the required lineage. Most ceremonial participation, in addition, is the responsibility of a group of people. An individual acts in assuming ritual posts as he does in all other affairs of life, as a member of a group. He may be a comparatively poor man, but the household or the kiva[3] acting through him provides the ceremonial necessaries. The group gains always from this participation because of the great blessing that accrues to it, and the property owned by a self-respecting individual is not the count on which he is admitted to or denied ceremonial rôles.

The Pueblos are a ceremonious people. But that is not the essential fashion in which they are set off from other peoples of North America and Mexico. It goes much deeper than any difference in degree in the amount of ritual that is current among them. The Aztec civilization of Mexico was as ritualistic as the Pueblo, and even the Plains Indians with their sun dance and their men's societies, their tobacco orders and their war rituals, had a rich ceremonialism.

The basic contrast between the Pueblos and the other cultures   12
of North America is the contrast that is named and described by Nietzsche in his studies of Greek tragedy. He discusses two diametrically opposed ways of arriving at the values of existence. The Dionysian pursues them through "the annihilation of the ordinary bounds and limits of existence"; he seeks to attain in his most valued moments escape from the boundaries imposed upon him by his five senses, to break through into another order of experience. The desire of the Dionysian, in personal experience or in ritual, is to press through it toward a certain psychological state, to achieve excess. The closest analogy to the emotions he seeks is drunkenness, and he values the illuminations of frenzy. With Blake,[4] he believes "the path of excess leads to the palace of wisdom." The Apollonian distrusts all this, and has often little idea of the nature of such experiences. He finds means to outlaw them from his conscious life. He "knows but one law, measure in the Hellenic sense." He

---

[3]*kiva*   Large one-room dwelling usually set aside for religious ceremonies.
[4]*William Blake (1757–1827)*   English mystic poet who had frequent visions.

keeps the middle of the road, stays within the known map, does not meddle with disruptive psychological states. In Nietzsche's fine phrase, even in the exaltation of the dance, he 'remains what he is, and retains his civic name.'

The Southwest Pueblos are Apollonian. Not all of Nietzsche's discussion of the contrast between Apollonian and Dionysian applies to the contrast between the Pueblos and the surrounding peoples. The fragments I have quoted are faithful descriptions, but there were refinements of the types in Greece that do not occur among the Indians of the Southwest, and among these latter, again, there are refinements that did not occur in Greece. It is with no thought of equating the civilization of Greece with that of aboriginal America that I use, in describing the cultural configurations of the latter, terms borrowed from the culture of Greece. I use them because they are categories that bring clearly to the fore the major qualities that differentiate Pueblo culture from those of other American Indians, not because all the attitudes that are found in Greece are found also in aboriginal America.

Apollonian institutions have been carried much further in the pueblos than in Greece. Greece was by no means as single-minded. In particular, Greece did not carry out as the Pueblos have the distrust of individualism that the Apollonian way of life implies, but which in Greece was scanted because of forces with which it came in conflict. Zuñi ideals and institutions on the other hand are rigorous on this point. The known map, the middle of the road, to any Apollonian is embodied in the common tradition of his people. To stay always within it is to commit himself to precedent, to tradition. Therefore those influences that are powerful against tradition are uncongenial and minimized in their institutions, and the greatest of these is individualism. It is disruptive, according to Apollonian philosophy in the Southwest, even when it refines upon and enlarges the tradition itself. That is not to say the Pueblos prevent this. No culture can protect itself from additions and changes. But the process by which these come is suspect and cloaked, and institutions that would give individuals a free hand are outlawed.

It is not possible to understand Pueblo attitudes toward life without some knowledge of the culture from which they have detached themselves: that of the rest of North America. It is by the force of the contrast that we can calculate the strength of their opposite drive and the resistances that have kept out of the Pueblos the most characteristic traits of the American aborigines. For the American Indians as a whole, and including those of Mexico, were passionately Dionysian. They valued all violent experience, all means by which human beings may break through the usual sensory routine, and to all such experiences they attributed the highest value.

The Indians of North America outside the Pueblos have, of course, anything but uniform culture. They contrast violently at almost every point, and there are eight of them that it is convenient to differentiate as separate culture areas. But throughout them all, in one or another guise, there run certain fundamental Dionysian practices. The most conspicuous of these is probably their practice of obtaining supernatural power in a dream or vision, of which we have already spoken. On the western plains men sought these visions with hideous tortures. They cut strips from the skin of their arms, they struck off fingers, they swung themselves from tall poles by straps inserted under the muscles of their shoulders. They went without food and water for extreme periods. They sought in every way to achieve an order of experience set apart from daily living. It was grown men, on the plains, who went out after visions. Sometimes they stood motionless, their hands tied behind them, or they staked out a tiny spot from which they could not move till they had received their blessing. Sometimes, in other tribes, they wandered over distant regions, far out into dangerous country. Some tribes chose precipices and places especially associated with danger. At all events a man went alone, or, if he was seeking his vision by torture and someone had to go out with him to tie him to the pole from which he was to swing till he had his supernatural experience, his helper did his part and left him alone for his ordeal.

It was necessary to keep one's mind fixed upon the expected visitation. Concentration was the technique above all others upon which they relied. "Keep thinking it all the time," the old medicine men said always. Sometimes it was necessary to keep the face wet with tears so that the spirits would pity the sufferer and grant him his request. "I am a poor man. Pity me," is a constant prayer. "Have nothing," the medicine men taught, "and the spirits will come to you."

On the western plains they believed that when the vision came it determined their life and the success they might expect. If no vision came, they were doomed to failure. "I was going to be poor; that is why I had no vision." If the experience was of curing, one had curing powers; if of warfare, one had warrior's powers. If one encountered Double Woman, one was a transvestite and took woman's occupations and habits. If one was blessed by the mythical Water Serpent, one had supernatural power for evil and sacrificed the lives of one's wife and children in payment for becoming a sorcerer. Any man who desired general strengthening or success in particular ventures sought visions often. They were necessary for warpaths and for curings and for all kinds of miscellaneous occasions; calling the buffalo, naming children, mourning, revenge, finding lost articles.

When the vision came, it might be visual or auditory hallucination, but it need not be. Most of the accounts tell of the appearance of some animal. When it first appeared it was often in human form, and it talked with the suppliant and gave him a song and a formula for some supernatural practice. As it was leaving, it turned into an animal, and the suppliant knew what animal it was that had blessed him, and what skin or bone or feathers he must get to keep as a memento of the experience and preserve for life as his sacred medicine bundle. On the other hand some experiences were much more casual. There were tribes that valued especially moments of intimacy with nature, occasions when a person alone by the edge of a river or following the trail felt in some otherwise simple event a compelling significance.

It might be from a dream that the supernatural power came to them. Some of the accounts of visions are unmistakable dream experiences, whether they occurred in sleep or under less normal conditions. Some tribes valued the dreams of sleep more highly than any other experiences. Lewis and Clark complained when they crossed the western plains in the early days that no night was fit for sleeping; some old man was always rousing to beat on his drum and ceremonially rehearse the dream he had just had. It was a valuable source of power.

In any case the criterion of whether or not the experience had power was necessarily a matter for the individual to decide. It was recognized as subjective, no matter what other social curbs were imposed upon its subsequent practice. Some experiences had power and some had not, and they distinguished by the flash of significance that singled out those that were valuable. If it did not communicate this thrill, an experience they had sought even with torture was counted valueless, and they dared not claim power from it for fear that the animal claimed as guardian spirit would visit death and disgrace upon them.

This belief in the power of a vision experience on the western plains is a cultural mechanism which gives a theoretically unlimited freedom to the individual. He might go out and get this supremely coveted power, no matter to what family he belonged. Besides this, he might claim his vision as authority for any innovation, any personal advantage which he might imagine, and this authority he invoked was an experience in solitude which in the nature of the case could not be judged by another person. It was, moreover, probably the experience of greatest instability that he could achieve.

It gave individual initiative a scope which is not easily equalled. Practically, of course, the authority of custom remained unchallenged. Even given the freest scope by their institutions, men are never inventive enough to make more than minute changes. From the point of view of an outsider the most radical innovations in any culture amount to no more than a minor revision, and it is a commonplace that prophets have been put to death for the difference between Tweedledum and Tweedledee. In the same way, the cultural license that the vision gave was used to establish, according to the instructions of the vision, a Strawberry Order of the Tobacco Society where before there had been a Snowbird Order, or the power of the skunk in warfare where the usual reliance was upon the buffalo. Other limitations were also inevitable. The emphasis might be placed upon trying out the vision. Only those could claim supernatural power for war who had put their vision to the test and had led a successful war party. In some tribes even the proposition to put the vision to the test had to go before the elders, and the body of elders was guided by no mystic communications.

In cultures other than those of the western plains these limitations upon Dionysian practices were carried much further. Wherever vested rights and privileges were important in any community the conflict occasioned by such a cultural trait as the vision is obvious enough. It is a frankly disruptive cultural mechanism. In tribes where the conflict was strong a number of things might happen. The supernatural experience, to which they still gave lip service, might become an empty shell. If prestige was vested in cult groups and in families, these could not afford to grant individuals free access to the supernatural and teach them that all power came from such contact. There was no reason why they could not still teach the dogma of the free and open vision, and they did. But it was an hypocrisy. No man could exercise power by any authority except that of succession to his father's place in the cult in which he had membership. Among the Omaha, although all power passed down strictly within the family line and was valued for the sorcery that it was, they did not revise their traditional dogma of absolute and sole dependence upon the solitary vision as a sanction for supernatural power. On the Northwest Coast, and among the Aztecs of Mexico, where prestige was also a guarded privilege, different compromises occurred, but they were compromises which did not outlaw the Dionysian values.

The Dionysian bent in the North American vision quest, how- 24 ever, did not usually have to make compromise with prestige groups and their privileges. The experience was often sought openly by means of drugs and alcohol. Among the Indian tribes of Mexico the fermented juice of the fruit of the giant cactus was used ceremonially to obtain the blessed state which was to them supremely religious. The great ceremony of the year among the related Pima, by means of which all blessings were obtained, was the brewing of this cactus beer. The priests drank first, and then all the people, "to get religious." Intoxication, in their practice and in their poetry, is the synonym of religion. It has the same mingling of clouded vision and of insight. It gives the whole tribe, together, the exaltation that it associated with religion.

Drugs were much commoner means of attaining this experience. The peyote or mescal bean is a cactus button from the highlands of Mexico. The plant is eaten fresh by the Indian tribes within pilgrimage distance, but the button is traded as far as the Canadian border. It is always used ceremonially. Its effect is well known. It gives peculiar sensations of levitation and brilliant colour images, and is accompanied by very strong affect, either ultimate despair or release from all inadequacy and insecurity. There is no motor disturbance and no erotic excitation.

The cult of the peyote among the American Indian is still spreading. It is incorporated as the Indian Church in Oklahoma and among many tribes the older tribal rituals have paled before this cult. It is associated everywhere with some attitude toward the whites, either a religious opposition to their influence, or a doctrine of speedy acceptance of white ways, and it has many Christian elements woven into its fabric. The peyote is passed and eaten in the manner of the sacrament, first the peyote, then the water, round and round, with songs and prayers. It is a dignified all-night ceremony, and the effects prolong themselves during the following day. In other cases it is eaten for four nights, with four days given up to the excitation. Peyote, within the cults that espouse it, is identified with god. A large button of it is placed upon the ground altar and worshipped. All good comes from it. "It is the only holy thing I have known in my life"; "this medicine alone is holy, and has rid me of all evil." And it is the Dionysian experience of the peyote trance that constitutes its appeal and its religious authority.

The datura or the jimson weed is a more drastic poison. It is more local, being used in Mexico and among the tribes of Southern California. In this latter region it was given to boys at initiation, and under its influence they received their visions. I have been told of boys who died as a result of the drink. The boys were comatose, and some tribes speak of this condition continuing for one day and some for four. The Mojave, the eastern neighbors of these tribes, used datura to get luck in gambling and were said to be unconscious for four days. During this time the dream came which gave them the luck they sought.

Everywhere among the North American Indians, therefore, except in the southern Pueblos, we encounter this Dionysian dogma and practice of the vision-dream from which comes supernatural power. The Southwest is surrounded by peoples who seek the vision by fasting, by torture, by drugs and alcohol. But the Pueblos do not accept disruptive experiences and they do not derive supernatural power from them. If a Zuñi Indian has by chance a visual or auditory hallucination it is regarded as a sign of death. It is an experience to avoid, not one to seek by fasting. Supernatural power among the Pueblos comes from cult membership, a membership which has been bought and paid for and which involves the learning of verbatim ritual. There is no occasion when they are expected to overpass the boundaries of sobriety either in preparation for membership, or in initiation, or in the subsequent rise, by payment, to the higher grades, or in the exercise of religious prerogatives. They do not seek or value excess. Nevertheless the elements out of which the widespread vision quest is built up are present: the seeking of dangerous places, the friendship with a bird or animal, fasting, the belief in special blessings from supernatural encounters. But they are no longer integrated as a Dionysian experience. There is complete re-interpretation. Among the Pueblos men go out at night to feared or sacred places and listen for a voice, not that they may break through to communication with the supernatural, but that they may take the omens of good luck and bad. It is regarded as a minor ordeal during which they are badly frightened, and the great tabu connected with it is that they must not look behind on the way home, no matter what seems to be following. The objective performance is much the same as in the vision quest; in each case, they go out during the preparation for a difficult undertaking—in the Southwest, often a foot-race—and make capital of the darkness, the solitariness, the appearance of animals. But the experience which is elsewhere conceived as Dionysian, among the Pueblos is a mechanical taking of omens.

Fasting, the technique upon which the American Indian most depended in attaining a self-induced vision, has received the same sort of reinterpretation. It is no longer utilized to dredge up experiences that normally lie below the level of consciousness; among the Pueblos it is a requirement for ceremonial cleanness. Nothing could be more unexpected to a Pueblo Indian than any theory of a connection between fasting and any sort of exaltation. Fasting is required during all priestly retreats, before participation in a dance, in a

28

race, and on endless ceremonial occasions, but is never followed by power-giving experience; it is never Dionysian.

The fate of the jimson-weed poisoning in the Southwest pueblos is much like that of the technique of fasting. The practice is present, but its teeth are drawn. The one-to-four-day jimson-weed trances of the Indians of Southern California are not for them. The drug is used as it was in ancient Mexico in order to discover a thief. In Zuñi the man who is to take the drug has a small quantity put into his mouth by the officiating priest, who then retires to the next room and listens for the incriminating name from the lips of the man who has taken the jimson weed. He is not supposed to be comatose at any time; he alternately sleeps and walks about the room. In the morning he is said to have no memory of the insight he has received. The chief care is to remove every trace of the drug and two common desacratizing techniques are employed to take away the dangerous sacredness of the plant: first, he is given an emetic, four times, till every vestige of the drug is supposed to be ejected; then his hair is washed in yucca suds. The other Zuñi use of jimson weed is even further from any Dionysian purpose; members of the priestly orders go out at night to plant prayer-sticks on certain occasions "to ask the birds to sing for rain," and at such times a minute quantity of the powdered root is put into the eyes, ears, and mouth of each priest. Here all connections with the physical properties of the drug are lost sight of.

Peyote has had an even more drastic fate. The Pueblos are close to the Mexican plateau where the peyote button is obtained, and the Apache and the tribes of the plains with which they came most in contact were peyote-eaters. But the practice gained no foothold in the pueblos. A small anti-government group in Taos, the most atypical and Plains-like of the Pueblos, has recently taken it up. But elsewhere it has never been accepted. In their strict Apollonian *ethos,* the Pueblos distrust and reject those experiences which take the individual in any way out of bounds and forfeit his sobriety.

This repugnance is so strong that it has even been sufficient to 32 keep American alcohol from becoming an administrative problem. Everywhere else on Indian reservations in the United States alcohol is an inescapable issue. There are no government regulations that can cope with the Indian's passion for whiskey. But in the pueblos the problem has never been important. They did not brew any native intoxicant in the old days, nor do they now. Nor is it a matter of course, as it is for instance with the near-by Apaches, that every trip to town, for old men or young, is a debauch. It is not that the Pueblos have a religious tabu against drinking. It is deeper than that. Drunkenness is repulsive to them. In Zuñi after the early introduction of liquor, the old men voluntarily outlawed it and the rule was congenial enough to be honored.

QUESTIONS FOR CRITICAL READING

1. What is the Zuñi attitude toward individualism? Do there seem to be contradictions implied in Benedict's description?
2. Do the marriage arrangements Benedict describes imply equality between the sexes?
3. What is the Zuñi attitude toward material possessions? What does it mean for Zuñi to be wealthy?
4. Explain what a matrilineal family is and how it compares with the family structure of your culture.
5. What is the attitude toward family in Zuñi?
6. Explain the different allegiances for men and women in Zuñi.

WRITING ASSIGNMENTS

1. Explain the important distinctions between the respective behaviors of the Apollonian and Dionysian cultures that Benedict describes. What are the most important distinctions, and how do they translate into terms that people in your culture can understand? Is it possible for you to come to a useful understanding of the cultural distinctions Benedict makes?
2. Benedict notes that using the psychological model of the Apollonian and Dionysian has certain inherent risks and problems. Write a brief essay that explores the risks Benedict takes in reducing cultures to psychological models. Decide as you do so whether or not Benedict is successful in her efforts or whether she falls victim to the problems of her approach.
3. Judging from the passage, what seem to be the gender roles appropriate for Zuñi? Do they differ markedly from those of other nearby Indian groups? Are gender roles specific, distinct, and preassigned? Are they rigid and firm, or do they imply flexibility depending on the individual? Can you compare the gender roles in Zuñi with those in your culture?
4. According to Benedict, "Apollonian institutions have been carried much further in the pueblos than in Greece" (para. 14). What does she mean? Analyze the extent to which the institutions have been carried in the behavior of the Pueblos. What are the key points, and why are they important to our developing an understanding of Zuñi?
5. Benedict describes the vision quest in some detail. Have you had a similar experience to those described? Is the vision quest—perhaps in an altered form—part of the rites or rituals of your culture? Benedict

tells us (para. 21) that the individual decides whether or not a specific
vision is truly religious and transforming enough to have a role in
shaping his life. Has your culture a similar attitude toward visions?
Could it have?

6. **CONNECTIONS**   Does Benedict's description of Zuñi support the
views of Franz Boas concerning the role of tradition in fashioning
culture, or do there seem to be genetic or environmental factors at
work that make Zuñi distinct? What role does tradition have in fashioning Zuñi culture?

7. **CONNECTIONS**   In paragraph 23, Benedict describes the vision
quest as "a frankly disruptive cultural mechanism." Her view is a
description of the politics of the vision quest. How might Thomas
Jefferson have reacted to the issues implied in the vision quest in his
efforts to shape a political entity in early America? Is the vision quest
included by implication in the Declaration of Independence? Would
Jefferson's Apollonian stance have caused him to ignore such a Dionysian experience?

8. **CONNECTIONS**   Examine the distinctions Nietzsche makes between the Apollonian and Dionysian and compare them with those
made by Benedict. How useful do you feel these distinctions are for
the purposes of our understanding Zuñi culture? Do you see similar
distinctions between cultures that you are familiar with?

MARGARET MEAD

Women, Sex, and Sin

MARGARET MEAD (1901–1978), a student of both Franz Boas
and Ruth Benedict, received her Ph.D in anthropology from Columbia
University in 1929. She is renowned for her fieldwork in the South
Pacific, and especially for her work on the island Manus in the Admiralty
Islands northwest of New Guinea. The fieldwork that she did in 1925
led to her doctoral dissertation and to the book that established her as
one of the most visible and readable modern anthropologists: Coming
of Age in Samoa: A Psychological Study of Primitive Youth
for Western Civilization (1928). Her work in the South Pacific in
the 1920s was extensive. She learned seven indigenous languages and
always used the languages of the people she lived with so that she could
think in ways close to the peoples she studied. Her experiences with
the Manus, which she discusses in this passage, span a period of twenty-
five years that included a disastrous world war. She first lived with
them in 1928, when she began the work that led her to write Growing
Up in New Guinea: A Comparative Study of Primitive Education (1930).

Her primary interests in research were in the patterns of education
of the young and the patterns of socialization of the women in different
communities. She became famous for her views on women and women's
sexuality, particularly on early sexual development. Mead asserted that
cultures are relative and that there are many ways of working out the
details of courtship, sex, marriage, and love. She consistently argued

From New Lives for Old (1966).

that there is no right way, suggesting rather that there are many ways, all of which are right for their individual culture.

Like Boas and Benedict, Mead emphasizes the psychological model of cultures, although the patterns she proposes are not quite comparable to the patterns of Apollonian, Dionysian, and paranoid that Benedict offers in her study of the American Southwest Pueblo cultures. However, she does make some efforts at typing the culture, such as her attempts in this passage to distinguish between feminine and masculine forms of behavior expected of Manus women. To the dismay of some anthropologists, Mead also emphasizes the social, traditional, and historical aspects of a culture without concerning herself with the biological or genetic. Recent critics of Mead have faulted her for this emphasis and have charged her with ignoring biological determinism in her researches (see Derek Freeman, Margaret Mead and Samoa [1983]); some of her critics have opposed her on the grounds that she is subjective—not scientifically detached—in her judgments; but others have opposed her largely because their own basic theories contradict hers.

"Women, Sex, and Sin" is remarkable for its discussion of profound changes in a primitive society. In 1928, the Manus were "a people without history, without any theory of how they came to be, without any belief in a permanent future life," but when Mead returned to the island in 1953 she was greeted by a community that had taken great pains to reinvent itself in the guise of a modern Western culture. She was startled by the astonishing changes they had made in such a short time.

Consequently, what she records in this passage are changes that were made to an entire culture of its own volition. She explains that the Manus "had taken their old culture apart piece by piece and put it together in a new way, in a way which they, who knew it best, thought would make it work to achieve their new goals." The work of changing the culture was essentially the work of one man, Pilau, who had returned to Manus after World War II with a vision of a new way to live. Because of a series of fortunate accidents, he was successful in implanting the "New Way," which is still adhered to by the Manus. The changes in the Manus culture demonstrate one of the ways—perhaps more drastic than usual—in which cultures alter themselves.

MEAD'S RHETORIC

Like Ruth Benedict, Mead writes in a clear, logical style. She entered college as an English major and shifted her interests only after she had studied with Franz Boas. Unlike Benedict, she writes about individuals with whom she lived or whom she remembered from her *earlier visit to the Manus. She names them and gives them an identity, so that the reader can develop a sense of understanding and personal concern.*

Her major rhetorical technique is to compare the old ways with the new ones. Mead constantly remembers things as they had been and contrasts them with the way things are in her second encounter. She records her surprise at the dimension and scope of change in the society and marvels that any people could absorb so much change in such a short time. In "Stability of Culture," Boas talks about the fact that cultures change more rapidly when they intersect or interrelate with other cultures; this is what happened to the Manus. Mead explains that the Manus men, who had gone off to work among the Australians and who had seen American films, returned with an entirely new model for relations between the sexes. They instigated change and transformed their society.

However, Mead also points out that the more things change, the more they remain the same. Her comparison gives way to an analysis in which she attempts to demonstrate that beneath the surface—which reflects so much change—are many of the same patterns, the same problems, the same deep cultural traditions. As she remarks at the very end of the essay, "So, in spite of their nominal emancipation, they still live in a world which in repudiating sex also repudiates women, and which in exalting fatherhood leaves less room for motherhood, except as a sort of delegated fatherhood."

Near the end of her life Margaret Mead was the most famous anthropologist in the United States. She was a media darling, writing a popular column in Redbook *magazine and frequent articles in other large-circulation magazines. She wrote more than twenty books and lectured widely to innumerable audiences. Her concerns centered on establishing the relativity of cultures, suggesting, for example, that on the basis of her work in the South Seas the angst of adolescence, which our culture takes as virtually a biological necessity, is tied into cultural expectations. The concept of the "teen-ager" is by no means universal, any more than the gender roles that our culture or any culture expects its men and women to follow. Mead was popular, but she was also a careful and devoted scientist. Her work on the South Pacific still stands as a major contribution to our knowledge of how different cultures deal with basic social issues.*

Women, Sex, and Sin

The Manus didn't know what to do with women twenty-five years ago, and they know almost as little today. The whole ethos is an essentially masculine one, in which the protective capacities of the male rather than the specifically maternal capacities of the female are the ones woven into the idea of parenthood. The ideal of personality is active, assertive, demanding, with great emphasis upon freedom of movement. There is likewise a very low interest in biological parenthood, in the breast-feeding tie between mother and child, or in any softness of feminine sex responsiveness which would yield too easily to evoke a measure of masculine anger.

Twenty-five years ago, the most valued women in the village were dominating women, even those who dominated their husbands, women who had strong clear minds, and who, as mediums, controlled a good part of the public affairs of the village. The woman who was regarded as the most dangerous woman in the village was a good-natured, easily responsive, slightly stupid widow, who was said to have been responsible for the deaths of six good men. Young women who were recalcitrant at marriage could be disciplined into shape, if necessary, as had been done in the case of one Peri wife who was finally shaped into compliancy on one of the smaller islands by a weekend of rape in which her husband and a group of his age mates participated. The pliant, the warm, the responsive were simply so many danger spots—girls who might be persuaded into running away or simply yielding to seduction. As daughters, as sisters, as wives, and as widows they were regarded as both dangerous and essentially unattractive.

In the long years between betrothal as a little girl of eight or ten and marriage, the girl of Old Peri was not being "good" in the sense that she was expected to be pure in heart and mind and never let her thoughts wander into areas of lust or even of desire, like the traditional expectation for unmarried Catholic girls in southern Europe. She was, it was true, expected to be circumspect, to obey the rules and avoidances, expected not to say her future husband's name, not to let herself get into any situation where property that had already been expended in her name would be jeopardized. Her virginity and reputation were rather like a sack of money which she was left to guard alone in the house, and out of loyalty to her relatives, fear of their anger and of the penalties which their Sir Ghosts[1] would exact, she guarded them. A theft, or even a slight

---

[1] *Sir Ghosts*   Powerful ghosts of ancestors.

defection which turned her head away from the main task for a moment would bring ruin on many people—perhaps death to one of her closest kin. Nor did her kin trust to her conscience; she was watched and chaperoned very severely; the slightest indiscretion brought down torrents of abuse and recrimination.

The young men were in a slightly different position. If one of 4 them had an affair, it would bring about an awful row between the Sir Ghost of their own household and that of the girl's kin; there would be expiations and payments, and perhaps someone would die in the end, but the attitude toward the young men was more that of indulgence toward a successful bandit. Failure to guard in the case of the girl was far more serious than success in breaking in on the part of the boy. Virginity was merely important as it affected the marriage arrangements. If the girl's lapse or the boy's lapse could be glossed over, expiatory payments made, ghosts and Sir Ghosts appeased, the mere technical matter of physical virginity did not matter very much.

To the young girl growing up in the village, the one person on whom her mind could not dwell, the one person about whom she could not daydream, give a sly, quick look or a provocative nudge in a crowd, was her fiancé. Toward him her relatives focused all the feeling they had shown earlier toward any failure of the girl to control her sphincters; his name, his appearance, everything about him was considered shame-evoking. The young girl's mother and all her older female relatives shared in this attitude toward him. Where she had been freer with her father than her mother could be, once betrothed she was again bound in with her mother because her father could no longer take her with him, and because of the taboos which she and her mother shared. Her materials for fantasy were the shame-arousing, unmentionable future marriage relationship, possibilities of seduction and rape which would only bring disaster in their train, and a conscious focus on the outward and visible forms of her present and future position—how many dog's teeth, how much shell money had been and would be given away in her name, how many strings of ornaments, how many money aprons would she wear as a bride, with how many canoe loads of sago[2] would she be fetched back home after the birth of her child.

Thus, all through girlhood the way was paved for married women to shrink from their husbands' advances and still conform to the moral code, avoiding out of sheer fear and not out of any compliancy the anger of their husbands' ghosts as they had avoided the anger of their own. They ran then, as they do today, the risk

---

[2]*sago* Edible part of the palm tree.

of being violently attracted by an extramarital adventure, which presented the contrast between the appeal of danger and the inhibitions of shame. Just as in the men's lives there was an overlay of careful continuous industriousness supported by ghostly sanctions, while underneath there was a far easier, more reckless self-confidence which was given very little scope, so also among the women a heavily sanctioned demand for circumspection and diligence screened a vigorous, reckless wilfulness, which only very, very heavy sanctions could prevent from coming into play. Meanwhile, at no point was there a chance to develop any gentleness associated with sex behavior in marriage itself.

Into this background of active, demanding babyhood and early childhood, inhibited and chaperoned girlhood set against the ever-present possibility of seduction and rape, and finally marriage—which was only made tolerable by emphasis upon the role of the economically successful woman who kept her husband's house and provided beadwork for her brother—came the first teaching of the Mission. Here one of the special aspects of Catholic as compared with Protestant missions came into play. When the Manus saw Catholic women, they saw nuns, not wives. For the little girls who went away to mission schools (there were two such women in Peri), sisters did not present an ideal to which they could ever aspire, but were rather earthly representatives of heavenly powers, intent, like the ghosts of old, upon making the girls quiet, obedient, and well-disciplined. They learned standards of personal neatness, learned to read and write, learned to sing, they had no models of Christian marriage which seriously challenged the models which they had learned in their youth.

Then, in 1946, came the emancipation of women by the New Way, the removal of all taboos, the disappearance of the old name avoidances, the prohibition of child betrothals, the permission of women to consent to their own seductions, the prohibition against fathers or brothers becoming angered by the behavior of daughters or sisters. There was the exhortation to young couples to behave in a way which was a mixture of work boys' memories of the marriages of Australian officials—in which husbands were protective of their wives, helped them on and off with their evening wraps, and hired servants to work for them, talked to them at meals, and kissed them on arrival and departure—and a model derived from American films—in which free choice of a mate and conspicuous, demonstrative public affection was felt to be the key to American marriage.

It was Manus men, and not Manus women, who had been work boys in Australian households, who had seen American films.

The emancipation of the women was presented to them by fiat; no more taboos—if you have a husband, speak his name. Explore freely if you are unmarried, and, once married, by choice, of course, publicly demonstrate your affection for your husband, and have as many children as possible so as to make the Manus, now so few, into many. As monarchs in Europe once ordered their people to follow them into baptism and membership in the Christian Church, so Manus men laid down the rules by which women in the New Way were to become emancipated and affectionate. There were to be no more taboos, girls and boys were to go to school together, young people to experiment in the choice of a mate. Having once been ordered to be compliant, to hide behind their avoidance mats and cloaks, to sit quietly and do beadwork, women were now ordered to be spontaneous, responsible, actively loving. And the men, modeling themselves on Australians, who had not expected their wives to care for children and do all the housework, having no servants, took over part of the care of even the very young babies.

The present results of this emancipation of women are both astonishing and depressing. Twenty-five years ago, the most conspicuous thing about Manus women was that they were deprived in those areas of affectionate domesticity which most societies permit to women and driven into continuous public economic participation. Today, the most conspicuous point is the extent to which they have been driven into a public display of a new form of personal relations, with little or no understanding or preparation for the new role. Manus women, twenty-five years ago, were singularly unattractive, angular, assertive, walking without any sense of the appeal of their own femininity, muting and constricting their femininity, emphasizing, with strident voice and sharp, unappealing gestures, that it might be possible to rape them, it might even be possible to seduce them—if enough risk attached—but what love and tenderness they had was already bespoken in formal terms by brothers. Manus women today are almost equally unattractive, but they look and act very differently. Where their contours were once sharp and angular, they are now softer, a little blurred. Where before, if one laid one's hands on a girl's shoulder, the muscles quivered like a taut bowstring, unused to gestures which were not menacing, stylized, and brittle, today they are heavier and slower, their bodies give a little beneath one's hand. The tense restiveness is gone, but no responsiveness has come to take its place. It is easy to see how husbands who once would have beaten them—as opponents in an unresolved contest—now beat them to get any response out of them at all. Whereas twenty-five years ago a husband's main complaints were about acts—a wife gossiped about him with her relatives or his brother's wife, a wife got up at night without her grass skirt when there were strangers sleeping in the house or was careless in feeding the baby—today the overwhelmingly most frequent complaint is that she "fastens her mouth." Some phrase, some slight act, will set her to brooding, and brooding she grows silent until her husband in a rage beats her, a beating which typically ends either in her running away or in a sexual reunion which has the elements of successful rape.

In the past, sex was something to be avoided by women in marriage, and in general; for men it was a reckless, brief adventure, usually accompanied by some kind of trouble. Women had grudged their husbands the brief encounters with captured prostituted stranger women, and did their best to spoil their husbands' pleasure by screeching taunts from a distance as they swung on bamboo swings far out over the lagoon, their laughter designed to echo into the men's house and make the men impotent. Today there are constant complaints both of sexual rejection and of wives who insist upon their husbands sleeping with them just to prove they haven't been with other women. "The one time you must have intercourse with your wife," say Peri men, "is if you have already been with another woman. Otherwise she is sure to find out and be angry." Counterpointed to this is the ideal extramarital affair which emphasizes choice—"She paid her half of the fine; she said she had chosen me," "This is really from the desire of both." But, even more important, the wonderful things about lovers is that you don't have to sleep with them. If either man or woman feels tired and disinclined toward love-making, the couple can simply sit and talk, and they need not have sex relations.

So, in spite of the apparent great change from a system in which women were the helpless pawns of complicated marriage exchanges, completely controlled by fathers, brothers, and husbands, to a system of marriage by choice and freedom of consent, the crucial position of sex has not changed very much. Sex is still associated with anger, with rights, with expression of or response to various sorts of resistance, and love is defined as a relationship in which sex can be ignored in favor of affection. As women once screamed their anger and jealousy because a man took a fish from his catch to his sister's house and sat quietly beside her fire, so they now rage over comparable incidents such as a husband bringing home a piece of cloth for his mistress, or his mother cooking him a meal. Quarrels in the village hinge not on the number of actual adulteries, but on the glances, tokens, and hints of adulteries long past, or perhaps never to come. The coincidence of two people

12

who have had an affair turning up in a distant village the same day, even though they hardly exchange a word there, gives the pair enormous pleasure and is guaranteed, if it is discovered, to throw their offended spouses into a rage.

In fact, there is a correspondence between the present chief requirement of a wife, that she should protect her husband's mind-soul from the sin of anger, and the chief enjoyment of illicit love, which is to tease and tantalize one's rivals. This teasing may go so far as, for example, Benedikta taking delight in getting her husband to buy her, with her own money, some conspicuous object, like a knife with a red handle, which she exhibited conspicuously, walking about, certain that her lover's wife would fall into the trap of thinking her lover had given it to her. Or two women whose lovers were friends would put on skirts of the same material, thus emphasizing the relationships and setting echoes going in the heads of the two wives who were their rivals. It is a game played by those who do not in any case expect satisfaction from sex, in whatever form it comes, and who get what satisfaction they can out of playing with dissatisfaction.

Appropriately enough, illicit love affairs and gambling were associated together. Men enjoyed giving women, their own or their friends' mistresses, money to gamble with; women enjoyed borrowing money from their lovers and lovers' friends, and gambling games were watched closely by hawk-eyed spouses alert for trouble. Among the occasional couples where both gambled, the style of the game was upset and inexplicable rows developed, as when Maria had a temper tantrum in "court" because her husband paid back his share of a debt to her with money she had lent a friend of his not knowing that part of it was for her own husband.

So women and sex remain associated with sin; where once they were associated with the punitive anger of ghosts, now they are associated with the jealous anger of men and women. Where once women were unwillingly circumspect and men grudgingly prudent, in order to prevent the ghost from visiting illness and death on them or their relatives because they had violated property rights or upset important economic affairs, today virtue consists in men and women leading quiet lives. Husbands and wives should reject overtures and opportunities so that there will be no anger between them, which might endanger the lives of their children, or anger concealed in the heart of the spouse, or in their own hearts because of the anger of the spouse. The responsiveness of men to resistance, either active or passive, the insistent demand of the jealous woman for sex expression, not for its own sake but as a symbol of her possession of her husband, keep this edge between sex and anger keen and sharp. From Christian teaching the Manus learned that sex was evil—a matter on which they were well convinced already—at least as far as women were concerned, but that sexual sins could be confessed and forgiven. From observation of Australian life, lightly reinforced by American films, they came to the conclusion that somehow Western white men seemed to manage their sex lives better, for there was so much less quarreling, and that this better management came from giving women more consideration, not beating them, helping them with their work, and giving them freedom of choice, and being mildly demonstrative in public. But the type of deeply responsible, tender marriage, which stands as the ideal of Catholic teaching, they never have had a chance to see.

For the woman who is intelligent, ambitious, and active, the   16
New Way, in spite of its nominal emancipation of women, offers no roles comparable to the part that women could play as mediums and entrepreneurs in the old system. The most that the wife of a member of the new bureaucracy is expected to do is to be a model for the rest of the community, keep her house and children in a modern way, and never embarrass her husband by being old-fashioned. This was the role played by the wife of Samol in Bunai; her baby received the most perfect infant care, her clothes were the most carefully chosen. Not until the Manus are introduced to the sort of women's clubs which have grown up around Port Moresby and in modern Samoa will the women have any glimpse of any sort of responsible public role again.

Meanwhile, there remains with them in the remembrance of gentleness received from old women, not mothers but grandmothers or aunts, who, freed from the tempestuousness of active sex lives, freed from quarreling with their husbands, were gentle and indulgent to small children. In the memories of the middle-aged men who are still dissatisfied with their marriages, who quarrel with their wives and beat them, the nostalgia for these kind old women can be heard, with its echo that some day their marriages, if they live long enough, will have in them women who are as kind and gentle as Pomat's Tchalolo grandmother or Kilipak's aunt, Isali. Something of the tenderness of these contacts used to survive in the relationship between brother and sister, and appeared again in the marriages of many years' standing, when the shame of speaking together and eating together had worn off. When husband and wife had cooperated in many enterprises, after she had borne him many children, as they came to the point of being grandparents, a gentleness could settle between them.

At present when people are still young, public opinion will

side strongly with the wife who is asked to do more than her share in supporting the household, but as they grow older, the case of the sickening husband with a wife who neglects him focuses the rage of the community, as it did when Christof, his arm shrunken and helpless, his legs mere sticks, was cut by his wife. When I arrived on this scene a few people were gathered around Christof. His wife, who had done the slashing, was sitting at a distance unconcernedly working on thatch. Suddenly their grown son, a great, husky creature, hurled himself through the room and began kicking his mother violently. People rushed to restrain him, and the councillor pontificated, "Don't add one trouble to another." His mother put on a dramatic, hysterical act to get attention from the bystanders, and even with this she received no sympathy. One of the gentlest of bystanders commented, "I am like that also, Piyap. If my mother didn't give food to my father, I'd fight her." And when I asked, "If your father would have fought your mother, would you have helped her?" I received an astonished, "Indeed, no!" One of the very young men summed it up: "I heard what it was about. They weren't giving Christof anything to eat. Yesterday he was angry, and he did not eat. Today they all went to the bush, and then they cooked food and gave him none. And he, is he a strong man? His arm and his leg are useless. He's just like a child [a great exaggeration]. Why don't they care for him? Now, Sepa [the daughter] wanted to give food to her father, and her mother was angry and cut her husband with a knife. Tomas heard this and he quarreled with his mother. His mother said, 'All right, beat me if you wish. This food, was it something you produced, so you have a right to talk?' Then Tomas said, 'Every day I bring sago, fish, and other things to you all, and I think you don't give any to my father.' Then Tomas was angry, and he attacked his mother."

The councillor's comment was that if the family decided to bring the matter to "court," Tomas would be in particular trouble because he had broken an important law of the New Way, the law that forbade one to get involved in one's relatives' quarrels.

When the case came to "court," the weight of disapproval was directed against the wife. This was a familiar pattern. If the blame could be firmly affixed to a woman, then any failure of the New Way among men need not be faced so directly. Women after all were still uneducated, illiterate, and undependable. For their part, the women felt many of the new procedures as traps. When they gave evidence it was written down and if, on being asked to repeat it, they gave a slightly different version, the whole weight of the "court" would come down upon them. The disapproval of indirect evidence also weighed heavily upon them, for when they would protest that they "knew" something was going on, the men would doggedly confront them with a "Did you see it with your eyes? Did you touch it with your hands?" So, in spite of their nominal emancipation, they still live in a world which in repudiating sex also repudiates women, and which in exalting fatherhood leaves less room for motherhood, except as a sort of delegated fatherhood.

QUESTIONS FOR CRITICAL READING

1. Of the Manus, Mead says their "whole ethos is an essentially masculine one" (para.1). What does she mean? How does her essay support this statement?
2. What impressed Mead about the women's behavior during her earlier stay with the Manus?
3. What was the preferred behavior of virgins in the earlier period Mead describes? Why did they guard their reputation and virginity?
4. Mead describes the shame associated with the husband's speaking to his wife. What seems to have been the form of communication between husband and wife under the Old Way?
5. What seems to have been the role of fear in the old society?
6. What were the characteristics of the emancipation of women that came about in 1946? What traditions of the old culture seem especially strange to you?
7. Mead feels that much that seems to have changed has not truly changed. What does she mean? Do you agree with her observations?

WRITING ASSIGNMENTS

1. Compare the new traditions of courtship and marriage with those you are familiar with in your own culture. What seem to be the ideals of the new Manus in respect to the desired behavior between men and women who have married?
2. Complete detachment is always impossible for an anthropologist, and Mead has sometimes been accused of injecting her personal views and values into her analysis. Go through the essay carefully to find passages in which Mead's personal opinions show through. How many such passages are there, and to what extent do they qualify or invalidate what Mead tells us about the Manus?
3. What is the attitude of the Manus toward personal property? Is property a major issue? Are women part of the property structure? Is sexuality an issue related to the property structure?
4. Describe the behavior of women toward husbands who have had affairs. Does their behavior have parallels in your own culture and

experience? If so, draw a careful comparison between both cultures and describe your culture in detail and with some of the same detachment that Mead uses.

5. In your opinion, is Mead's approach and general concern gender-based? Is her subject matter linked to her femaleness, or does she approach the study without gender bias?

6. **CONNECTIONS** How would Catharine MacKinnon regard the relationships between the sexes as practiced by the Manus? MacKinnon concerns herself with law and politics in discussing sexual harassment. Is it possible that she is trying to legislate new cultural traditions for her own culture? What light does Margaret Mead's study throw on MacKinnon's position?

7. **CONNECTIONS** Mary Wollstonecraft takes a very clear feminist view of the roles that women play in her society. How would Mead regard the cultural details that Wollstonecraft reveals about her society? What is anthropological about Wollstonecraft's essay? Would approaching her essay as a piece of anthropology change our view of what she has to say?

8. **CONNECTIONS** Clifford Geertz suggests that one characteristic of anthropologists is the likelihood of preferring the culture they study to the culture they themselves came from. Is there evidence in Mead's discussion that she has an overt preference for Manus culture as opposed to her own European-American culture? Is there evidence of her preference for her own culture? How might Mead react to Geertz's suggestions that anthropologists should study "symbolic forms" rather than immerse themselves in the culture in hopes of seeing things from the "native's point of view"?

CLAUDE LÉVI-STRAUSS
A Little Glass of Rum

CLAUDE LÉVI-STRAUSS (b. 1908) was born in Brussels, Bel-
gium, and studied philosophy and law at the Sorbonne in Paris. He
graduated in 1932 and began to redirect his attentions toward anthropology. In 1935 he accepted a post in Brazil as a professor at the University
of São Paulo. While there he visited the interior of the rain forest to
study a number of primitive groups; much of his research and writing
is based on the observations he made during these stays, which lasted
about a year and a half. In contrast to Boas, Lévi-Strauss did not
especially like fieldwork and took care to do as little of it as possible.
Nonetheless, his observations were keen, and his conclusions have inspired a generation of anthropologists.

"A Little Glass of Rum" comes from Tristes Tropiques (1955),
which was later translated as A World on the Wane (1961). The
book was the result of approximately two years of field studies among
the Bororo, the Nambikwara, and the Tupi people in central Brazil.
A highly personal book that has been described as both a travel book
and an autobiography, it was originally conceived as a novel; but
Lévi-Strauss soon decided to write it as nonfiction. The distinguished
American essayist Susan Sontag described the book as "one of the great
books of our century . . . rigorous, subtle and bold in thought"; and
Clifford Geertz, perhaps the most influential American anthropologist,
commented that it is "the best book ever written by an anthropologist."
Essentially, it is a book about the way the mind works in which Lévi-
Strauss permits his mind to explore numerous avenues of interest.

Among Lévi-Strauss's contributions to modern thought is his development of the concept of structuralism, which, although not easily

---

From Tristes Tropiques (1955; translated in 1961 as A World on the Wane).
Translated by John and Doreen Weightman.

summarized, is illustrated by his searches for patterns of mind that represent basic, repeatable structures. The essence of his anthropological thinking concerns the patterns and combinations of human actions that may express themselves in a bewildering number of forms but which, when analyzed in depth, can be recognized as manifestations of basic structures that repeat themselves across cultures. Some of his work following Structural Anthropology *(2 vols., 1958–1973) has developed these principles. For example,* The Raw and the Cooked *and* The Origin of Table Manners *(1964–1981), part of a multivolume project titled in English.*Introduction to the Science of Mythology, *examine the basic structures of cooking and serving food.*

"A Little Glass of Rum," which is the last chapter of Triste Tropiques, *avoids much of the complexity of structuralism that can make Lévi-Strauss's work difficult to understand at times. It is a summary chapter reflecting on the possibility of doing objective anthropology and on the question of how anthropologists see the relationship between their own culture and the culture they are studying. Lévi-Strauss suggests that some anthropologists undervalue their own culture and romanticize the culture they study, noting that "their allegiance is always given to the latter" (para. 2). Such a view may seem to run counter to the usual assumption that anthropologists consider their own culture the "norm" and treat other cultures with the disdain most people reserve for the exotic. In some ways it does, and that is part of the subject of Lévi-Strauss's argument.*

LÉVI-STRAUSS'S RHETORIC

Underlying much of Lévi-Strauss's writing is a fundamental dialectic, a posing of a question that begets an answer, albeit an answer that may be contradicted in the process of exploration. To an extent, this may remind us of Plato, whose method, although more openly question and answer, is similar to Lévi-Strauss's in that the view one is encouraged to accepted at one moment may well be unacceptable after reflection and analysis.

For example, Lévi-Strauss's analysis of cannibalism, which he introduces as a practice that "inspires the greatest horror and disgust" (para.11), has a number of surprises. For one thing, he qualifies the horror of cannibalism by suggesting that the phenomenon exists in some relatively benign forms. For example, there is cannibalism practiced as a result of famine, which Lévi-Strauss regards as essentially understandable because of the basic human need to eat. Then, as he says, "There remain those forms of cannibalism which can be termed positive" (para.

12), *such as religious or ritualistic cannibalism. The acceptability of these forms of cannibalism stands in dialectical opposition to the concept of horror with which he begins the discussion.*

He takes the point even further when he begins to compare our European culture with the cultures in which cannibalism is practiced. He asks us to stand outside our culture and our prejudices and look at them as cannibals might. He selects as an example our practice of constructing prisons to isolate criminals—something totally unheard of in primitive societies—and compares that practice with the behavior of the Nambikwara and other peoples he has studied. His conclusion forces us to consider that our cultural choices may be as cruel and seem as inhuman to cannibals as their cultural choices appear to us.

Lévi-Strauss reveals his deep interest in language when he connects his theories to those of Jean Jacques Rousseau (1712–1778), who discussed primitive social structures in his Social Contract *(1762). Rousseau was associated with the Romantic concept of the "noble savage," the view that humans living in a state of nature were somehow uncorrupted by the strains of the social order. Lévi-Strauss insists that Rousseau's views were quite opposed to such a simplification. He declares of Rousseau, "It was he who taught us that, after demolishing all forms of social organization, we can still discover the principles which will allow us to construct a new form" (para. 18). For Lévi-Strauss language, rather than organization, is the essential ingredient in forming the social bonds that Rousseau studied and anthropologists now study in their various cultural manifestations. But Lévi-Strauss is not a linguist—at least not in the sense that he would learn primitive languages (he did not). Rather, he is concerned with the role language plays in culture and sees it as the primary and quintessential mark of society. Without language there can be no society, and the existence of language naturally implied the existence of society.*

In his conclusion Lévi-Strauss produces another structuralist insight: the varieties of cultural expression lie within us. "What was done, but turned out wrong, can be done again" (para. 25). We have the potential to express ourselves in ways that cultures around the world do. In this sense, he is in agreement with the basic thought of Boas, Benedict, and Mead. We contain within ourselves the variety of humankind simply because we are human.

A Little Glass of Rum[1]

The only justification for the dramatic fable[2] described in the preceding chapter is that it illustrates the mental disorder to which the traveler is exposed through abnormal living conditions over a prolonged period. But the problem still remains: how can the anthropologist overcome the contradiction resulting from the circumstances of his choice? He has in front of him and available for study a given society—his own; why does he decide to spurn it and to reserve for other societies—which are among the most remote and the most alien—a patience and a devotion which his choice of vocation has deflected from his fellow-citizens? It is no accident that the anthropologist should rarely have a neutral attitude toward his own group. If he is a missionary or an administrator, we can infer from this that he has agreed to identify himself with a certain system, to the point of dedicating his life to its propagation; and when he practices his profession on a scientific or academic level, one can very probably discover in his past certain objective factors which show him to be ill-adapted to the society into which he was born. In assuming his role, he has tried to find either a practical means of reconciling his allegiance to a group and the reservations he feels with regard to it, or, quite simply, a way of turning to advantage an initial state of detachment which gives him an advantage in approaching different societies, since he is already halfway towards them.

But if he is honest, he is faced with a problem: the value he attaches to foreign societies—and which appears to be higher in proportion as the society is more foreign—has no independent foundation; it is a function of his disdain for, and occasionally hostility towards, the customs prevailing in his native setting. While often inclined to subversion among his own people and in revolt against the traditional behavior, the anthropologist appears respectful to the point of conservatism as soon as he is dealing with a society different from his own. This is more than just a bias. In fact, it is something quite different: I know some anthropologists who are conformists. But they are so in a derivative way, by virtue of a

---

[1]Traditionally, French criminals about to be guillotined were offered a last cigarette and a little glass of rum. The author is referring to the significance of rum as discussed in the chapter and to the possible fate of both the anthropologist and mankind as a whole. [Translator's note]

[2]*fable* Reference to a play that features an encounter of a man who is emperor with a man who has chosen to live in a state of nature.

kind of secondary assimilation of their society to the foreign ones they study. Their allegiance is always given to the latter, and the reason why they have abandoned their initial revolt against their own, is that they make the additional concession to foreign societies of approaching their own as they would like all societies to be approached. There is no way out of the dilemma: either the anthropologist adheres to the norms of his own group and other groups inspire in him no more than a fleeting curiosity which is never quite void of disapproval, or he is capable of giving himself wholeheartedly to these other groups and his objectivity is vitiated by the fact that, intentionally or not, he has had to withhold himself from at least one society, in order to devote himself to all. He therefore commits the very sin that he lays at the door of those who contest the exceptional significance of his vocation.

I was assailed by this doubt for the first time during the enforced stay in the West Indies that I described at the beginning of this book. In Martinique, I had visited rustic and neglected rum-distilleries where the equipment and the methods used had not changed since the eighteenth century. In Puerto Rico, on the other hand, in the factories of the company which enjoys a virtual monopoly over the whole of the sugar production, I was faced by a display of white enamel tanks and chromium piping. Yet the various kinds of Martinique rum, as I tasted them in front of ancient wooden vats thickly encrusted with waste matter, were mellow and scented, whereas those of Puerto Rico are coarse and harsh. We may suppose, then, that the subtlety of the Martinique rums is dependent on impurities the continuance of which is encouraged by the archaic method of production. To me, this contrast illustrates the paradox of civilization: its charms are due essentially to the various residues it carries along with it, although this does not absolve us of the obligation to purify the stream. By being doubly in the right, we are admitting our mistake. We are right to be rational and to try to increase our production and so keep manufacturing costs down. But we are also right to cherish those very imperfections we are endeavoring to eliminate. Social life consists in destroying that which gives it its savor. The contradiction seems to disappear when we move from the consideration of our own society to the study of foreign ones. We ourselves are caught up in the evolution of our own society and are, in a sense, interested parties. We are not in a position not to will those things which our situation forces us to carry into effect; when we are dealing with foreign societies, everything is different: the objectivity which was impossible in the first instance is freely granted to us. Since we are no longer agents but spectators of the transformations which are taking place, we are all the better able to compare and evaluate their future and their past, since these remain subjects for aesthetic contemplation and intellectual reflection, instead of being brought home to us in the form of mental anxiety.

By arguing as I have just done, I may have thrown light on   4
the contradiction; I have shown where it originates and how we manage to come to terms with it. But I have certainly not solved it. Is the contradiction, then, a permanent one? It has sometimes been said to be so, and the argument used as a condemnation of anthropologists. Since our vocation displays the predilection we feel for social and cultural structures very different from our own— overestimating the former at the expense of the latter—we are said to be guilty of a fundamental inconsistency; how could we proclaim the validity of the foreign societies, except by basing our judgment on the values of the society which has prompted us to engage in research? Since we are permanently unable to escape from the norms by which we have been conditioned, our attempts to put different societies, including our own, into perspective, are said to be no more than a shamefaced way of admitting its superiority over all the others.

Behind the reasoning of these specious critics, there is nothing but a bad pun: they try to pass off the mystification (in which they themselves indulge) as the reverse of mysticism (of which they wrongly accuse us). Archaeological or anthropological research shows that certain civilizations, whether contemporary or extinct, know, or used to know, how to solve certain problems better than we do, although we have endeavored to obtain the same results. To quote only one example: only during recent years have we discovered the material and physiological principles underlying Eskimo dress and the form of Eskimo houses, and how these principles, of which we were unaware, allow them to live in harsh climatic conditions, to which they are adapted neither by use nor by anything exceptional in their constitutions. So true is this that it also enables us to understand why the so-called improvement that explorers introduced into Eskimo dress proved to be less than useless, and in fact produced the opposite result to what was intended. The native solution was perfect; we could only realize this once we had grasped the theory on which it was based.

This is not where the difficulty lies. If we judge the achievements of other social groups in relation to the kind of objectives we set ourselves, we have at times to acknowledge their superiority; but in so doing we acquire the right to judge them, and hence to condemn all their other objectives which do not coincide with those we approve of. We implicitly acknowledge that our society with its customs and norms enjoys a privileged position, since an observer belonging to another social group would pass different verdicts on the same examples. This being so, how can the study of anthropology claim to be scientific? To reestablish an objective approach, we must abstain from making judgments of this kind. We must accept the fact that each society has made a certain choice, within the range of existing human possibilities, and that the various choices cannot be compared with each other: they are all equally valid. But in this case a new problem arises; while in the first instance we were in danger of falling into obscurantism, in the form of a blind refusal of everything foreign to us, we now run the risk of accepting a kind of eclecticism which would prevent us denouncing any feature of a given culture—not even cruelty, injustice and poverty, against which the very society suffering these ills may be protesting. And since these abuses also exist in our society, what right have we to combat them at home, if we accept them as inevitable when they occur elsewhere?

Behind the two divergent attitudes of the anthropologist who is a critic at home and a conformist abroad, there lies, then, another contradiction from which he finds it even more difficult to escape. If he wishes to contribute to the improvement of his own community, he must condemn social conditions similar to those he is fighting against, wherever they exist, in which case he relinquishes his objectivity and impartiality. Conversely, the detachment to which he is constrained by moral scrupulousness and scientific accuracy prevents him criticizing his own society, since he is refraining from judging any one society in order to acquire knowledge of them all. Action within one's own society precludes understanding of other societies, but a thirst for universal understanding involves renouncing all possibility of reform.

If the contradiction were insurmountable, the anthropologist 8 ought to have no hesitation about the alternative to opt for: he is an anthropologist, and chose to become one; he must therefore accept the mutilation inseparable from his vocation. He has preferred other societies and must suffer the consequences of his preference: his function will be simply to understand these other societies, in whose name he is unable to act, since the very fact that they are different prevents him thinking and taking decisions for them; such behavior would be tantamount to identifying himself with them. Furthermore, he will renounce all action within his own society, because he is afraid of taking a stand about values which could well recur in different societies, and therefore of allowing his thought to be colored by prejudice. Only the initial choice will remain, and for that he will admit no justification: it is a pure, unmotivated act, or if motivated at all, can be so only by external considerations connected with the character of life-history of the particular individual.

Fortunately, the situation is not quite as bad as that; after peering into the abyss which yawns in front of us, we may be allowed to look for a way of avoiding it. Such a way can be found, provided we are moderate in our judgments and break the difficulty down into two stages.

No society is perfect. It is in the nature of all societies to include a degree of impurity incompatible with the norms they proclaim and which finds concrete expression in a certain dosage of injustice, insensitiveness and cruelty. If it is asked how this dosage is to be evaluated, anthropological research can supply an answer. While it is true that comparison between a small number of societies makes them appear very different from each other, the differences diminish as the field of investigation widens. We then discover that no society is fundamentally good, but that none is absolutely bad; they all offer their members certain advantages, with the proviso that there is invariably a residue of evil, the amount of which seems to remain more or less constant and perhaps corresponds to a specific inertia in social life resistant to all attempts at organization.

This assertion will surprise readers of travelers' tales who recall with dismay the "barbarous" customs of some native community or other. Yet such superficial reactions cannot stand up to an accurate appreciation of the facts, once the latter have been set in a wider perspective. Let us take the case of cannibalism, which of all savage practices is no doubt the one that inspires the greatest horror and disgust. First, we must separate off its purely alimentary forms, that is those instances in which the appetite for human flesh is to be explained by the lack of any other animal food, as was the case in certain Polynesian islands. No society is morally protected from such hunger pangs: famine can force men to eat anything, as is proved by the recent example of the extermination camps.

There remain those forms of cannibalism which can be termed   12
positive, since they stem from a mystic, magic or religious cause: for instance, the consumption of a fragment of the body of a parent or of an enemy in order to ensure the incorporation of virtues or the neutralization of power; such rites are usually carried out very discreetly and involve only a small quantity of organic matter which is ground down or mixed with other foods, but even when they are practiced in more overt forms it has to be admitted that the moral condemnation of such customs implies either a belief in bodily resurrection (resurrection being jeopardized by the material destruction of the corpse), or the affirmation of a link between the soul

and the body, with a corresponding dualism; that is, in either case, convictions similar in nature to those underlying the practice of ritual consumption and which we have no reason to prefer to them. This is all the truer when we consider that the disrespect for the memory of the deceased which cannibals might be accused of is certainly no greater—far from it—than that tolerated by us on the dissecting table.

But above all, we should realize that certain of our own customs might appear, to an observer belonging to a different society, to be similar in nature to cannibalism, although cannibalism strikes us as being foreign to the idea of civilization. I am thinking, for instance, of our legal and prison systems. If we studied societies from the outside, it would be tempting to distinguish two contrasting types: those which practice cannibalism—that is, which regard the absorption of certain individuals possessing dangerous powers as the only means of neutralizing those powers and even of turning them to advantage—and those which, like our own society, adopt what might be called the practice of *anthropemy* (from the Greek *émein,* to vomit); faced with the same problem, the latter type of society has chosen the opposite solution, which consists in ejecting dangerous individuals from the social body and keeping them temporarily or permanently in isolation, away from all contact with their fellows, in establishments specially intended for this purpose. Most of the societies which we call primitive would regard this custom with profound horror; it would make us, in their eyes, guilty of that same barbarity of which we are inclined to accuse them because of their symmetrically opposite behavior.

Societies which seem savage to us in some respects may appear humane and kindly when considered from another angle. Let us take the case of the Plains Indians of North America, who are doubly significant in this connection, because they practiced certain moderate forms of cannibalism and at the same time offer one of the rare instances of a primitive community with an organized police system. It would never have occurred to their police (who were also a judicial body) to make the culprit's punishment take the form of a breaking of social ties. If a native had infringed the laws of the tribe, he was punished by having all his possessions destroyed, including his tent and horses. But at the same time, the police contracted a debt towards him: it was their duty to organize collective reparation for the losses sustained by the culprit as his punishment. This put him under an obligation to the group, and he had to show his gratitude to them by means of presents that the whole community—including the police—helped him to assemble, so that this once again reversed the relationships; and so on and so forth until, after a whole series of gifts and counter-gifts, the disorder introduced by the crime was gradually neutralized and there was a return to the pristine state of order. Not only are such customs more humane than ours, they are also more coherent, even if the problem is formulated in terms of modern European psychology; logically, the "infantilization" of the culprit implied by the notion of punishment demands that he should have a corresponding right to a reward, in the absence of which the initial procedure will prove ineffective and may even lead to results contrary to those that were hoped for. Our system is the height of absurdity, since we treat the culprit both as a child so as to have the right to punish him, and as an adult, in order to deny him consolation; and we believe we have made great spiritual progress because, instead of eating a few of our fellow-men, we subject them to physical and moral mutilation.

Analysis of this kind, if carried out sincerely and methodically, leads to two results: it introduces an element of moderation and honesty into our evaluation of customs and ways of life very remote from our own, without conferring on them the virtue of absoluteness, which exists in no society. And it removes from our own customs that air of inherent rightness which they so easily have for anyone unacquainted with other customs, or whose knowledge is partial and biased. Consequently, it is true that anthropological analysis tips the balance in favor of foreign societies and against the observer's own; in this sense, it is self-contradictory. But further reflection will show that the contradiction is more apparent than real.

It has sometimes been said that European society is the only 16 one which has produced anthropologists, and that therein lies its greatness. Anthropologists may wish to deny it other forms of superiority, but they must respect this one, since without it they themselves would not exist. Actually, one could claim exactly the opposite: Western Europe may have produced anthropologists precisely because it was a prey to strong feelings of remorse, which forced it to compare its image with those of different societies in the hope that they would show the same defects or would help to explain how its own defects had developed within it. But even if it is true that comparison between our society and all the rest, whether past or present, undermines the basis of our society, other societies will suffer the same fate. The general averageness I referred to above brings out by contrast the existence of a number of ogres, and it so happens that we are among them; not by accident, since if we had not been of their number and had not deserved first prize in this sorry competition, anthropology would not have been invented by us, because we would not have felt the need for it. The anthropologist is the less able to ignore his own civilization and to dissociate himself from its faults in that his very existence is incomprehensible except as an attempt at redemption: he is the symbol of atonement. But other societies too have been tainted with the same original sin; not very many perhaps, and they become increasingly fewer in number as we move down the scale of progress. I need only cite the example of Aztec culture, that open wound in the side of American history, whose maniacal obsession with blood and torture (a universal obsession, in fact, but overt in the case of the Aztecs in the *excessive form* that comparison allows us to define)—however explicable it may be through the need to overcome the fear of death—puts it on a level with ourselves, not because the Aztecs were the only people wicked in this way but because, like us, they were inordinately so.

Yet this condemnation of ourselves by ourselves does not imply that we are prepared to award a certificate of excellence to any particular society, past or present, situated at any specific point in time or space. To do so would be to commit a real injustice, since we should be failing to recognize the fact that, were we part of that society, we would find it intolerable: we would condemn it on the same grounds as we condemn our own society. Does this mean that we must inevitably criticize any form of social organization and glorify a state of nature which social organization can only corrupt? This was Diderot's[3] view when he wrote: "Beware of him who comes to impose order." He thought that "the abridged history" of humanity could be summarized as follows: "There existed a natural man; an artificial man was introduced into this natural man, and inside the cave there arose continuous warfare which lasts throughout life." This is an absurd conception. Man is inseparable from language and language implies society. Bougainville's Polynesians (Diderot put forward this theory in his *Supplément au voyage de Bougainville*) were just as much social beings as we are. To maintain any other point of view would be to run counter to anthropological analysis instead of moving in the direction which it encourages us to explore.

The more I consider these problems, the more I am convinced that they admit of no reply other than the one given by Rousseau:[4] Rousseau, who has been so maligned, who is more misunderstood

---

[3]***Denis Diderot (1713–1784)***   Father of the French encyclopedia and author of *Supplement to the Voyage of Bougainville* referred to later.

[4]***Jean Jacques Rousseau (1712–1778)***   Author of *The Social Contract*, a study of the structure of society, beginning with the neolithic family.

now than ever before and is preposterously accused of having glorified the state of nature—an error that can be attributed to Diderot but not to him—when in fact he said exactly the opposite and is the only thinker who can show us how to escape from the contradictions in which we are still floundering in the wake of his opponents; Rousseau, the most anthropological of the *philosophes*: although he never traveled to distant lands, his documentation was as complete as it could be for a man of his time and, unlike Voltaire,[5] he infused life into it by his warm-hearted curiosity about peasant customs and popular thought; Rousseau, our master and brother, to whom we have behaved with such ingratitude but to whom every page of this book could have been dedicated, had the homage been worthy of his great memory. We shall emerge from the contradiction inherent in the anthropologist's position only by repeating, on our own account, the procedure which allowed Rousseau to move on from the ruins left by the *Discours sur l'origine de l'inégalité [Discourse on the Origin of Inequality]*, to the ample structure of the *Contrat Social,* the secret of which is revealed in *Emile.* It was he who taught us that, after demolishing all forms of social organization, we can still discover the principles which will allow us to construct a new form.

Rousseau never fell into Diderot's error of idealizing natural man. He is never in any danger of confusing the natural state with the social state; he knows that the latter is inherent in man, but that it leads to evils; the only problem is to discover whether these evils are themselves inherent in the social state. This means looking beyond abuses and crimes to find the unshakable basis of human society.

To this quest, anthropological comparison can contribute in   20
two ways. It shows that the basis is not to be discovered in our civilization: of all known societies ours is no doubt the one most remote from it. At the same time, by bringing out the characteristics common to the majority of human societies, it helps us to postulate a type, of which no society is a faithful realization, but which indicates the direction the investigation ought to follow. Rousseau thought that the way of life now known as neolithic[6] offered the nearest approach to an experimental representation of the type. One may, or may not, agree with him. I am rather inclined to believe he was right. By neolithic times, man had already made most of the inventions necessary for his safety. We have already seen why

---

[5]*Françoise Marie de Arouet de Voltaire (1694–1778)*   French philosopher, dramatist, novelist, and satirist noted for his anti-church sentiments.
[6]*neolithic*   Referring to Stone Age culture.

writing can be excluded; to say that it is a double-edged weapon is not a sign of primitivism; this is a truth that has been rediscovered by contemporary cyberneticians.[7] In the neolithic period, man knew how to protect himself against cold and hunger; he had achieved leisure in which to think; no doubt there was little he could do against disease, but it is not certain that advances in hygiene have had any other effect than to transfer the responsibility for maintaining demographic equilibrium from epidemics, which were no more dreadful a means than any other, to different phenomena such as widespread famine and wars of extermination.

In that mythic age, man was no freer than he is today; but only his humanness made him a slave. Since his control over nature remained very limited, he was protected—and to some extent re-leased from bondage—by a cushioning of dreams. As these dreams were gradually transformed into knowledge, man's power increased and became a great source of pride; but this power, which gears us, as it were, to the universe, is surely little more than our subjective awareness of a progressive welding together of humanity and the physical universe, whose great deterministic laws, instead of re-maining remote and awe-inspiring, now use thought itself as an intermediary medium and are colonizing us on behalf of a silent world of which we have become the agents.

Rousseau was no doubt right to believe that it would have been better for our well-being had mankind kept to "a happy mean between the indolence of the primitive state and the irrepressible busyness of our self-esteem," that such a position was the "best for man" and that he only emerged from it through "some unhappy chance," this being, of course, the advent of mechanization, a dou-bly exceptional phenomenon, since it was both unique and of late occurrence. It nevertheless remains clear that this intermediary posi-tion is by no means a primitive state, since it presupposes and admits of a certain degree of progress; and that no known society offers an exceptionally accurate representation of it, even if "the example of the savages, who have almost all been found at this stage, would seem to confirm that the human race was intended always to remain in it."

The study of these savages leads to something other than the revelation of a Utopian state of nature or the discovery of the perfect society in the depth of the forest; it helps us to build a theoretical model of human society, which does not correspond to any observ-able reality, but with the aid of which we may succeed in distinguish-

---

[7]*cyberneticians* Those working with computers.

ing between "what is primordial and what is artificial in man's present nature and in obtaining a good knowledge of a state which no longer exists, which has perhaps never existed, and which will probably never exist in the future, but of which it is nevertheless essential to have a sound conception in order to pass valid judgment on our present state." I have already quoted this remark to bring out the significance of my study of the Nambikwara.[8] Rousseau's thought, which was always in advance of his time, does not dissociate theoretical sociology from research in the laboratory or in the field, which he recognized as being necessary. Natural man did not precede society, nor is he outside it. Our task is to rediscover his form as it is immanent in the social state, mankind being inconceivable outside society; this means working out a program of the experiments which "would be necessary in order to arrive at a knowledge of natural man" and determining "the means whereby these experiments can be made within society."

But the model—this is Rousseau's solution—is eternal and universal. Other societies are perhaps no better than our own; even if we are inclined to believe they are, we have no method at our disposal for proving it. However, by getting to know them better, we are enabled to detach ourselves from our own society. Not that our own society is peculiarly or absolutely bad. But it is the only one from which we have a duty to free ourselves: we are, by definition, free in relation to the others. We thus put ourselves in a position to embark on the second stage, which consists in using all societies—without adopting features from any one of them—to elucidate principles of social life that we can apply in reforming our own customs and not those of foreign societies: through the operation of a prerogative which is the reverse of the one just mentioned, the society we belong to is the only society we are in a position to transform without any risk of destroying it, since the changes, being introduced by us, are coming from within the society itself.

By taking as our inspiration a model outside time and place, we are certainly running a risk: we may be underestimating the reality of progress. It is as if we were asserting that men have always and everywhere undertaken the same task in striving towards the same objective and that, throughout history, only the means have differed. I confess that this view does not worry me; it seems to be the one most in keeping with the facts, as revealed by history and anthropology, and above all it appears to be more fruitful.

---

[8]***Nambikwara***   One of the tribes Lévi-Strauss studied in central Brazil.

Enthusiastic partisans of the idea of progress are in danger of failing to recognize—because they set so little store by them—the immense riches accumulated by the human race on either side of the narrow furrow on which they keep their eyes fixed; by underrating the achievements of the past, they devalue all those which still remain to be accomplished. If men have always been concerned with only one task—how to create a society fit to live in—the forces which inspired our distant ancestors are also present in us. Nothing is settled; everything can still be altered. What was done, but turned out wrong, can be done again. "The Golden Age, which blind superstition had placed behind [or ahead of] us, is *in us.*" The brotherhood of man requires a concrete meaning when it makes us see, in the poorest tribe, a confirmation of our own image and an experience, the lessons of which we can assimilate, along with so many others. We may even discover a pristine freshness in these lessons. Since we know that, for thousands of years, man has succeeded only in repeating himself, we will attain to that nobility of thought which consists in going back beyond all the repetitions and taking as the starting-point of our reflections the indefinable grandeur of man's beginnings. Being human signifies, for each one of us, belonging to a class, a society, a country, a continent, and a civilization; and for us European earth-dwellers, the adventure played out in the heart of the New World signifies in the first place that it was not our world and that we bear responsibility for the crime of its destruction; and secondly, that there will never be another New World: since the confrontation between the Old World and the New makes us thus conscious of ourselves, let us at least express it in its primary terms—in the place where, and by referring back to a time when, our world missed the opportunity offered to it of choosing between its various missions.

QUESTIONS FOR CRITICAL READING

1. Do you agree that the anthropologist rarely has a "neutral attitude toward his own group" (para. 1)?
2. In paragraph 2, Lévi-Strauss says that the anthropologist's "objectivity is vitiated by the fact that, intentionally or not, he has had to withhold himself from at least one society, in order to devote himself to all." Do you agree?
3. What seems to be the point of including the information about the mellowness resulting from impurities in Martinique rum as opposed to the coarseness of the pure Puerto Rican rum?

4. Are you convinced by Lévi-Strauss's argument about cannibalism and prisons? Did it change any of your opinions?
5. Examine the discussion of prejudice on the part of the anthropologist in paragraph 8. What must be the position of the anthropologist regarding values?
6. Why does our culture not practice the same kind of punishment toward criminals described in paragraph 14? If we were to follow the Plains Indian practices, what would be the results?
7. What would be the condition of the people "living in a state of nature"?

WRITING ASSIGNMENTS

1. Explore the statement "Social life consists in destroying that which gives it its savor" (para. 3). Find examples in your own experience that either bear out this dogmatic observation or contradict it. What is your culture currently attempting to destroy? Are those targets likely to give a special flavor to life?
2. In paragraph 16, Lévi-Strauss tells us, "It has sometimes been said that European society is the only one which has produced anthropologists, and that therein lies its greatness." Ignoring for the moment the question of greatness, explore the question of what it means for one society to spend its time studying another. Consider the issues of cultured comparison and the potential for the first culture to have power over the other. Is it possible that the production of anthropologists is an admission on the part of a culture of its basic weakness?
3. In some ways Lévi-Strauss pleads for the toleration of the practices of other cultures. He also reminds us that it is difficult to hold back from making judgments about cultures whose practices are quite different from ours. He points to "the example of Aztec culture, that open wound in the side of American history, whose maniacal obsession with blood and torture . . . puts it on a level with ourselves" (para. 16). Examine some of the history of Aztec culture and decide whether or not Lévi-Strauss is being sincere or ironic in this statement.
4. To what extent is Lévi-Strauss justified in claiming that "man is inseparable from language and language implies society" (para. 17)? Evaluate his statement by reflecting on the uses of language and the possibilities of a social structure without language. To what extent do you agree that language is the basic instrument of social formation?
5. In paragraphs 20–22, Lévi-Strauss reflects on the condition of neolithic man—essentially the cave dweller of fifteen or twenty thousand years ago. He said, "In that mythic age, man was no freer than he is today; but only his humanness made him a slave." What does this statement seem to mean? Do you agree with it, or would you qualify it? To what extent might primitive peoples be more or less free than we are?
6. **CONNECTIONS** Consider this passage in relation to the work of Franz Boas. Would he view its conclusions comfortably in relation

to his own theories? How would Boas have regarded Lévi-Strauss's tendency to reduce complexity to structural patterns?

7. **CONNECTIONS**   Consider Margaret Mead's study in light of Lévi-Strauss's discussion of the greater affection of anthropologists for the culture they study than for their own culture. Is there evidence in Mead's essay that would support Lévi-Strauss's thinking?

CLIFFORD GEERTZ

"From the Native's Point of View":
On the Nature of
Anthropological Understanding

CLIFFORD GEERTZ *(b. 1926), professor of social sciences at the Institute for Advanced Study at Princeton University, has become one of America's most visible anthropologists. Among his books are* The Religion of Java *(1976);* Interpretation of Cultures *(1977);* Kinship in Bali *(1978);* Negara: Theatre-State in Nineteenth-Century Bali *(1980);* Local Knowledge: Further Essays in Interpretive Anthropology *(1985), from which the passage included here comes; and* Works and Lives: The Anthropologist as Author *(1989). As in the case of "From the Native's Point of View," Geertz is especially effective as an anthropologist when he reflects on the role of the investigator responding to the entire enterprise of studying another culture. In* Works and Lives, *for example, Geertz seems to continue the work he began in "From the Native's Point of View" by examining the methods and results of important anthropologists such as Bronislaw Malinowski, Claude Lévi-Strauss, and Ruth Benedict.*

He begins this essay by pointing out that anthropologists are all too human. They have reactions and feelings, and they can run out of patience. In an example from Works and Lives, *Geertz reveals that Malinowski reported in his diary that once, when he wanted to photograph an important dance, he handed out plenty of tobacco as an incentive to get the natives to dance, only to watch them disappear once their share of tobacco was delivered. There was nothing Malinowski could do, and in his diary he records his frustration and tells himself that at that moment he would have voted to "exterminate the brutes." Geertz's point is that Malinowski's diary calls into question the objectivity of the*

From *Local Knowledge: Further Essays in Interpretive Anthropology.*

anthropologist and by implication raises the larger question of whether an anthropologist can ever understand a foreign culture. Everything, after all, is filtered through the anthropologist's own cultural assumptions and therefore distorted.

In the first part of his essay, Geertz explains the extent to which anthropologists are themselves aware of the difficulties of their work. He discusses two polarities of "experience-near" and "experience-distant" approaches. In the former, the anthropologist does everything to experience the culture as part of day-do-day life and to bring it as "near" as possible to his or her own culture. In the latter, the distance between the anthropologist's experience and the culture being studied is used to establish an objectivity that makes it possible to observe more dispassionately and, possibly, more accurately. Geertz says flatly, "The ethnographer does not, and, in my opinion, largely cannot, perceive what his informants perceive. What he perceives, and that uncertainly enough, is what they perceive 'with'—or 'by means of,' or 'through' . . . or whatever the word should be" (para. 7). The point is that the ethnographer cannot see beyond the primary culture by using informants because the informants necessarily remain lenses through which the ethnographer must see.

GEERTZ'S RHETORIC

Because he is writing for an audience knowledgeable about contemporary anthropology, Geertz does not pause either to explain who Malinowski is or to say why there should be a stir when his diary revealed that he was not without feelings and that he sometimes disliked and distrusted the very people he studied. Yet, assuming a level of knowledge typical of those familiar with the work of Malinowski and others, Geertz writes clearly and with structural care. He begins with an introduction, clarifying his feelings regarding Malinowski's methods and work.

He then sets out the conflict between the close and distant methods of studying cultures and states his own position. His aim is not to win his readers over right away but rather to enable them to draw their own conclusions. Geertz depends on what he considers possible: since he feels the anthropologist can neither be a member of another culture nor depend on an informant who is, he proposes that the ethnographer be content to study the signs of the culture.

Geertz then goes on to describe the results of his own work in three very different cultures: Javanese, Balinese, and Moroccan. His method, as he explains, was not to attempt to be like a native, nor to live intimately with the native culture. Instead, it was to study the "symbolic forms" of the culture. These "words, images, institutions, behaviors" (para. 8) are products of the culture and in many ways define the culture. They are the means by which people in the culture represent themselves to one another and then to the ethnographer. Geertz uses the term ethnographer to shift the emphasis from the study of man (a loose translation of the word anthropology) to the study of the signs or symbols (-graphy) produced by an ethnic group.

His rhetorical strategy is to break the experience into a pattern of three, a familiar scheme that usually works well for most readers. The first of his descriptions concerns his work in Java (para. 10), where he set about discovering the defining qualities of an individual and came up with a series of oppositions: "inside/outside" and "refined/vulgar" (para. 12). These are complex contrasts, rooted in Javanese religious experience. Geertz spends several pages describing, analyzing, and explaining these contrasts.

Geertz's research in Bali—for which he has become justly famous— centered on an examination of the theater culture. He emphasizes that the people of Bali stylize and ritualize their lives and that in many ways they go through life playing roles almost as if they were performers in a drama of life (paras. 17–19). Moroccan culture is so diverse that the language has developed to account for a great many ranges of relationship. Here Geertz explains the nisba, or terminology that defines people according to their locale, group, family, and many other details.

Finally, Geertz draws conclusions regarding the three cultures he observed. In the process he distinguishes himself from Malinowski and other anthropologists on either side of the "too close"–"too distant" controversy by defining himself as "a meanings-and-symbols ethnographer" (para. 32). In fact, other anthropologists, especially Malinowski, may be described in the same terms, but Geertz's strategy is not to offer such descriptions himself. Instead he permits the reader to do so. In this sense, the essay reveals itself to be an instrument of self-instruction. It is in the form of a lecture—not the type that fills the mind with knowledge, but the type that permits the audience to experience a change in attitude.

"From the Native's Point of View":
On the Nature of
Anthropological Understanding

Several years ago a minor scandal erupted in anthropology: one of its ancestral figures told the truth in a public place. As benefits an ancestor, he did it posthumously, and through his widow's decision rather than his own, with the result that a number of the sort of right-thinking types who are with us always immediately rose to cry that she, an in-marrier anyway, had betrayed clan secrets, profaned an idol, and let down the side. What will the children think, to say nothing of the layman? But the disturbance was not much lessened by such ceremonial wringing of the hands; the damn thing was, after all, already printed. In much the same fashion as James Watson's *The Double Helix*[1] exposed the way in which biophysics in fact gets done, Bronislaw Malinowski's[2] *A Diary in the Strict Sense of the Term* rendered established accounts of how anthropologists work fairly well implausible. The myth of the chameleon fieldworker, perfectly self-tuned to his exotic surroundings, a walking miracle of empathy, tact, patience, and cosmopolitanism, was demolished by the man who had perhaps done most to create it.

The squabble that arose around the publication of the *Diary* concentrated, naturally, on inessentials and missed, as was only to be expected, the point. Most of the shock seems to have arisen from the mere discovery that Malinowski was not, to put it delicately, an unmitigated nice guy. He had rude things to say about the natives he was living with, and rude words to say it in. He spent a great deal of his time wishing he were elsewhere. And he projected an image of a man about as little complaisant as the world has seen. (He also projected an image of a man consecrated to a strange vocation to the point of self-immolation, but that was less noted.) The discussion was made to come down to Malinowski's moral character or lack of it, and the genuinely profound question his book raised was ignored; namely, if it is not, as we had been taught

---

[1]**The Double Helix** This 1969 book by James Dewey Watson (b. 1928) revealed the infighting and competition among geneticists. Watson and Francis Crick (b. 1916) are credited with mapping the DNA molecule.

[2]***Bronislaw Malinowski (1884–1942)*** A Polish-American anthropologist noted for his important field studies in the South Pacific.

to believe, through some sort of extraordinary sensibility, an almost preternatural capacity to think, feel, and perceive like a native (a word, I should hurry to say, I use here "in the strict sense of the term"), how is anthropological knowledge of the way natives think, feel, and perceive possible? The issue the *Diary* presents, with a force perhaps only a working ethnographer can fully appreciate, is not moral. (The moral idealization of fieldworkers is a mere sentimentality in the first place, when it is not self-congratulation or a guild pretense.) The issue is epistemological.[3] If we are going to cling—as, in my opinion, we must—to the injunction to see things from the native's point of view, where are we when we can no longer claim some unique form of psychological closeness, a sort of transcultural identification, with our subjects? What happens to *verstehen* when *einfühlen*[4] disappears?

As a matter of fact, this general problem has been exercising methodological discussion in anthropology for the last ten or fifteen years; Malinowski's voice from the grave merely dramatizes it as a human dilemma over and above a professional one. The formulations have been various: "inside" versus "outside," or "first person" versus "third person" descriptions; "phenomenological" versus "objectivist," or "cognitive" versus "behavioral" theories; or, perhaps most commonly "emic" versus "etic" analyses, this last deriving from the distinction in linguistics between phonemics and phonetics, phonemics classifying sounds according to their internal function in language, phonetics classifying them according to their acoustic properties as such. But perhaps the simplest and most directly appreciable way to put the matter is in terms of a distinction formulated, for his own purposes, by the psychoanalyst Heinz Kohut, between what he calls "experience-near" and "experience-distant" concepts.

An experience-near concept is, roughly, one that someone—a   4 patient, a subject, in our case an informant—might himself naturally and effortlessly use to define what he or his fellows see, feel, think, imagine, and so on, and which he would readily understand when similarly applied by others. An experience-distant concept is one that specialists of one sort or another—an analyst, an experimenter, an ethnographer, even a priest or an ideologist—employ to forward their scientific, philosophical, or practical aims. "Love" is an experience-near concept, "object cathexis"[5] is an experience-distant one. "Social stratification" and perhaps for most peoples in the world

---

[3]*epistemological*   Referring to the study of knowledge.
[4]**verstehen**   Understanding. *Einfühlen* is German for "intuition."
[5]*object cathexis*   Transferring emotions to an object.

even "religion" (and certainly "religious system") are experience-distant; "caste" and "nirvana" are experience-near, at least for Hindus and Buddhists.

Clearly, the matter is one of degree, not polar opposition—"fear" is experience-nearer than "phobia," and "phobia" experience-nearer than "ego dyssyntonic."[6] And the difference is not, at least so far as anthropology is concerned (the matter is otherwise in poetry and physics), a normative[7] one, in the sense that one sort of concept is to be preferred as such over the other. Confinement to experience-near concepts leaves an ethnographer awash in immediacies, as well as entangled in vernacular.[8] Confinement to experience-distant ones leaves him stranded in abstractions and smothered in jargon. The real question, and the one Malinowski raised by demonstrating that, in the case of "natives," you don't have to be one to know one, is what roles the two sorts of concepts play in anthropological analysis. Or, more exactly, how, in each case, ought one to deploy them so as to produce an interpretation of the way a people lives which is neither imprisoned within their mental horizons, an ethnography of witchcraft as written by a witch, nor systematically deaf to the distinctive tonalities of their existence, an ethnography of witchcraft as written by a geometer.

Putting the matter this way—in terms of how anthropological analysis is to be conducted and its results framed, rather than what psychic constitution anthropologists need to have—reduces the mystery of what "seeing things from the native's point of view" means. But it does not make it any easier, nor does it lessen the demand for perceptiveness on the part of the fieldworker. To grasp concepts that, for another people, are experience-near, and to do so well enough to place them in illuminating connection with experience-distant concepts theorists have fashioned to capture the general features of social life, is clearly a task at least as delicate, if a bit less magical, as putting oneself into someone else's skin. The trick is not to get yourself into some inner correspondence of spirit with your informants. Preferring, like the rest of us, to call their souls their own, they are not going to be altogether keen about such an effort anyhow. The trick is to figure out what the devil they think they are up to.

In one sense, of course, no one knows this better than they do themselves; hence the passion to swim in the stream of their experience, and the illusion afterward that one somehow has. But

---

[6]*dyssyntonic* Ego disorder.
[7]*normative* Judgmental.
[8]*vernacular* The local language.

in another sense, that simple truism is simply not true. People use experience-near concepts spontaneously, unself-consciously, as it were colloquially; they do not, except fleetingly and on occasion, recognize that there are any "concepts" involved at all. That is what experience-near means—that ideas and the realities they inform are naturally and indissolubly bound up together. What else could you call a hippopotamus? Of course the gods are powerful, why else would we fear them? The ethnographer does not, and, in my opinion, largely cannot, perceive what his informants perceive. What he perceives, and that uncertainly enough, is what they perceive "with"—or "by means of," or "through" . . . or whatever the word should be. In the country of the blind, who are not as unobservant as they look, the one-eyed is not king, he is spectator.

Now, to make all this a bit more concrete, I want to turn for a moment to my own work, which, whatever its other faults, has at least the virtue of being mine—in discussions of this sort a distinct advantage. In all three of the societies I have studied intensively, Javanese, Balinese, and Moroccan, I have been concerned, among other things, with attempting to determine how the people who live there define themselves as persons, what goes into the idea they have (but, as I say, only half-realize they have) of what a self, Javanese, Balinese, or Moroccan style, is. And in each case, I have tried to get at this most intimate of notions not by imagining myself someone else, a rice peasant or a tribal sheikh, and then seeing what I thought, but by searching out and analyzing the symbolic forms— words, images, institutions, behaviors—in terms of which, in each place, people actually represented themselves to themselves and to one another.

The concept of person is, in fact, an excellent vehicle by means of which to examine this whole question of how to go about poking into another people's turn of mind. In the first place, some sort of concept of this kind, one feels reasonably safe in saying, exists in recognizable form among all social groups. The notions of what persons are may be, from our point of view, sometimes more than a little odd. They may be conceived to dart about nervously at night shaped like fireflies. Essential elements of their psyches, like hatred, may be thought to be lodged in granular black bodies within their livers, discoverable upon autopsy. They may share their fates with *doppelgänger*[9] beasts, so that when the beast sickens or dies they sicken or die too. But at least some conception of what a

8

---

[9]**doppelgänger**   A double; in this case, an animal who is the person's other self.

human individual is, as opposed to a rock, an animal, a rainstorm, or a god, is, so far as I can see, universal. Yet, at the same time, as these offhand examples suggest, the actual conceptions involved vary from one group to the next, and often quite sharply. The Western conception of the person as a bounded, unique, more or less integrated motivational and cognitive universe, a dynamic center of awareness, emotion, judgment, and action organized into a distinctive whole and set contrastively both against other such wholes and against its social and natural background, is, however incorrigible it may seem to us, a rather peculiar idea within the context of the world's cultures. Rather than attempting to place the experience of others within the framework of such a conception, which is what the extolled "empathy" in fact usually comes down to, understanding them demands setting that conception aside and seeing their experiences within the framework of their own idea of what selfhood is. And for Java, Bali, and Morocco, at least, that idea differs markedly not only from our own but, no less dramatically and no less instructively, from one to the other.

In Java, where I worked in the fifties, I studied a small, shabby inland county-seat sort of place; two shadeless streets of whitewashed wooden shops and offices, and even less substantial bamboo shacks crammed in helter-skelter behind them, the whole surrounded by a great half-circle of densely packed rice-bowl villages. Land was short, jobs were scarce, politics was unstable, health was poor, prices were rising, and life was altogether far from promising, a kind of agitated stagnancy in which, as I once put it, thinking of the curious mixture of borrowed fragments of modernity and exhausted relics of tradition that characterized the place, the future seemed about as remote as the past. Yet in the midst of this depressing scene there was an absolutely astonishing intellectual vitality, a philosophical passion really, and a popular one besides, to track the riddles of existence right down to the ground. Destitute peasants would discuss questions of freedom of the will, illiterate tradesmen discoursed on the properties of God, common laborers had theories about the relations between reason and passion, the nature of time, or the reliability of the senses. And, perhaps most importantly, the problem of the self—its nature, function, and mode of operation—was pursued with the sort of reflective intensity one could find among ourselves in only the most recherché[10] settings indeed.

---

[10]***recherché*** Refined.

The central ideas in terms of which this reflection proceeded, and which thus defined its boundaries and the Javanese sense of what a person is, were arranged into two sets of contrasts, at base religious, one between "inside" and "outside," and one between "refined" and "vulgar." These glosses are, of course, crude and imprecise; determining exactly what the terms involved signified, sorting out their shades of meaning, was what all the discussion was about. But together they formed a distinctive conception of the self which, far from being merely theoretical, was the one in terms of which Javanese in fact perceived one another and, of course, themselves.

The "inside"/"outside" words, *batin* and *lair* (terms borrowed,   12 as a matter of fact, from the Sufi tradition of Muslim mysticism, but locally reworked) refer on the one hand to the felt realm of human experience and on the other to the observed realm of human behavior. These have, one hastens to say, nothing to do with "soul" and "body" in our sense, for which there are in fact quite other words with quite other implications. *Batin,* the "inside" word, does not refer to a separate seat of encapsulated spirituality detached or detachable from the body, or indeed to a bounded unit at all, but to the emotional life of human beings taken generally. It consists of the fuzzy, shifting flow of subjective feeling perceived directly in all its phenomenological immediacy but considered to be, at its roots at least, identical across all individuals, whose individuality it thus effaces. And similarly, *lair,* the "outside" word, has nothing to do with the body as an object, even an experienced object. Rather, it refers to that part of human life which, in our culture, strict behaviorists limit themselves to studying—external actions, movements, postures, speech—again conceived as in its essence invariant from one individual to the next. These two sets of phenomena—inward feelings and outward actions—are then regarded not as functions of one another but as independent realms of being to be put in proper order independently.

It is in connection with this "proper ordering" that the contrast between *alus,* the word meaning "pure," "refined," "polished," "exquisite," "ethereal," "subtle," "civilized," "smooth," and *kasar,* the word meaning "impolite," "rough," "uncivilized," "coarse," "insensitive," "vulgar," comes into play. The goal is to be *alus* in both the separated realms of the self. In the inner realm this is to be achieved through religious discipline, much but not all of it mystical. In the outer realm, it is to be achieved through etiquette, the rules of which here are not only extraordinarily elaborate but have something of the force of law. Through meditation the civilized man thins out his emotional life to a kind of constant hum;

through etiquette, he both shields that life from external disruptions and regularizes his outer behavior in such a way that it appears to others as a predictable, undisturbing, elegant, and rather vacant set of choreographed motions and settled forms of speech.

There is much more to all this, because it connects up to both an ontology[11] and an aesthetic.[12] But so far as our problem is concerned, the result is a bifurcate conception of the self, half ungestured feeling and half unfelt gesture. An inner world of stilled emotion and an outer world of shaped behavior confront one another as sharply distinguished realms unto themselves, any particular person being but the momentary locus, so to speak, of that confrontation, a passing expression of their permanent existence, their permanent separation, and their permanent need to be kept in their own order. Only when you have seen, as I have, a young man whose wife— a woman he had in fact raised from childhood and who had been the center of his life—has suddenly and inexplicably died, greeting everyone with a set smile and formal apologies for his wife's absence and trying, by mystical techniques, to flatten out, as he himself put it, the hills and valleys of his emotion into an even, level plain ("That is what you have to do," he said to me, "be smooth inside and out") can you come, in the face of our own notions of the intrinsic honesty of deep feeling and the moral importance of personal sincerity, to take the possibility of such a conception of selfhood seriously and appreciate, however inaccessible it is to you, its own sort of force.

Bali, where I worked both in another small provincial town, though one rather less drifting and dispirited, and, later, in an upland village of highly skilled musical instruments makers, is of course in many ways similar to Java, with which it shared a common culture to the fifteenth century. But at a deeper level, having continued Hindu while Java was, nominally at least, Islamized, it is quite different. The intricate, obsessive ritual life—Hindu, Buddhist, and Polynesian in about equal proportions—whose development was more or less cut off in Java, leaving its Indic spirit to turn reflective and phenomenological,[13] even quietistic, in the way I have just described, flourished in Bali to reach levels of scale and flamboyance that have startled the world and made the Balinese a much more

---

[11]***ontology***   Philosophy of existence or being.
[12]***aesthetic***   Philosophy of art.
[13]***phenomenological***   Pertaining to a philosophy of consciousness.

dramaturgical people with a self to match. What is philosophy in Java is theater in Bali.

As a result, there is in Bali a persistent and systematic attempt   16 to stylize all aspects of personal expression to the point where anything idiosyncratic, anything characteristic of the individual merely because he is who he is physically, psychologically, or biographically, is muted in favor of his assigned place in the continuing and, so it is thought, never-changing pageant that is Balinese life. It is dramatis personae,[14] not actors, that endure; indeed, it is dramatis personae, not actors, that in the proper sense really exist. Physically men come and go, mere incidents in a happenstance history, of no genuine importance even to themselves. But the masks they wear, the stage they occupy, the parts they play, and, most important, the spectacle they mount remain, and comprise not the façade but the substance of things, not least the self. Shakespeare's old-trouper view of the vanity of action in the face of mortality—all the world's a stage and we but poor players, content to strut our hour, and so on—makes no sense here. There is no make-believe; of course players perish, but the play does not, and it is the latter, the performed rather than the performer, that really matters.

Again, all this is realized not in terms of some general mood the anthropologist in his spiritual versatility somehow captures, but through a set of readily observable symbolic forms: an elaborate repertoire of designations and titles. The Balinese have at least a half-dozen major sorts of labels, ascriptive, fixed, and absolute, which one person can apply to another (or, of course, to himself) to place him among his fellows. There are birth-order markers, kinship terms, caste titles, sex indicators, teknonyms,[15] and so on and so forth, each of which consists not of a mere collection of useful tags but a distinct and bounded, internally very complex, terminological system. When one applies one of these designations or titles (or, as is more common, several at once) to someone, one therefore defines him as a determinate point in a fixed pattern, as the temporary occupant of a particular, quite untemporary, cultural locus. To identify someone, yourself or somebody else, in Bali is thus to locate him within the familiar cast of characters—"king," "grandmother," "third-born," "Brahman"—of which the social drama is, like some stock company roadshow piece—*Charley's Aunt* or *Springtime for Henry*—inevitably composed.

---

[14]***dramatis personae***   Characters in the play.
[15]***teknonyms***   Names associated with one's profession.

The drama is of course not farce, and especially not transvestite farce, though there are such elements in it. It is an enactment of hierarchy, a theater of status. But that, though critical, is unpursuable here. The immediate point is that, in both their structure and their mode of operation, the terminological systems conduce to a view of the human person as an appropriate representative of a generic type, not a unique creature with a private fate. To see how they do this, how they tend to obscure the mere materialities—biological, psychological, historical—of individual existence in favor of standardized status qualities would involve an extended analysis. But perhaps a single example, the simplest further simplified, will suffice to suggest the pattern.

All Balinese receive what might be called birth-order names. There are four of these, "first-born," "second-born," "third-born," "fourth-born," after which they recycle, so that the fifth-born child is called again "first-born," the sixth "second-born," and so on. Further, these names are bestowed independently of the fates of the children. Dead children, even stillborn ones, count, so that in fact, in this still high-birthrate, high-mortality society, the names do not really tell you anything very reliable about the birth-order relations of concrete individuals. Within a set of living siblings, someone called "first-born" may actually be first, fifth, or ninth-born, or, if somebody is missing, almost anything in between, and someone called "second-born" may in fact be older. The birth-order naming system does not identify individuals as individuals, nor is it intended to; what it does is to suggest that, for all procreating couples, births form a circular succession of "firsts," "seconds," "thirds," and "fourths," an endless four-stage replication of an imperishable form. Physically men appear and disappear as the ephemerae they are, but socially the acting figures remain eternally the same as new "firsts," "seconds," and so on emerge from the timeless world of the gods to replace those who, dying, dissolve once more into it. All the designation and title systems, so I would argue, function in the same way: they represent the most time-saturated aspects of the human condition as but ingredients in an eternal, footlight present.

Nor is this sense the Balinese have of always being on stage a 20 vague and ineffable one either. It is, in fact, exactly summed up in what is surely one of their experience-nearest concepts: *lek*. *Lek* has been variously translated or mistranslated ("shame" is the most common attempt); but what it really means is close to what we call stage fright. Stage fright consists, of course, in the fear that, for want of skill or self-control, or perhaps by mere accident, on aesthetic illusion will not be maintained, that the actor will show through his part. Aesthetic distance collapses, the audience (and the actor) lose sight of Hamlet and gain it, uncomfortably for all concerned, of bumbling John Smith painfully miscast as the Prince of Denmark. In Bali, the case is the same: what is feared is that the public performance to which one's cultural location commits one will be botched and that the personality—as we would call it but the Balinese, of course, not believing in such a thing, would not—of the individual will break through to dissolve his standardized public identity. When this occurs, as it sometimes does, the immediacy of the moment is felt with excruciating intensity and men become suddenly and unwillingly creatural, locked in mutual embarrassment, as though they had happened upon each other's nakedness. It is the fear of faux pas,[16] rendered only that much more probable by the extraordinary ritualization of daily life, that keeps social intercourse on its deliberately narrowed rails and protects the dramatistical sense of self against the disruptive threat implicit in the immediacy and spontaneity even the most passionate ceremoniousness cannot fully eradicate from face-to-face encounters.

Morocco, Middle Eastern and dry rather than East Asian and wet, extrovert, fluid, activist, masculine, informal to a fault, a Wild West sort of place without the barrooms and the cattle drives, is another kettle of selves altogether. My work there, which began in the mid-sixties, has been centered around a moderately large town or small city in the foothills of the Middle Atlas, about twenty miles south of Fez. It's an old place, probably founded in the tenth century, conceivably even earlier. It has the walls, the gates, the narrow minarets rising to prayer-call platforms of a classical Muslim town, and, from a distance anyway, it is a rather pretty place, an irregular oval of blinding white set in the deep-sea-green of an olive grove oasis, the mountains, bronze and stony here, slanting up immediately behind it. Close up, it is less prepossessing, though more exciting: a labyrinth of passages and alleyways, three quarters of them blind,[17] pressed in by wall-like buildings and curbside shops and filled with a simply astounding variety of very emphatic human beings. Arabs, Berbers, and Jews; tailors, herdsmen, and soldiers; people out of offices, people out of markets, people out of tribes; rich, superrich, poor, superpoor; locals, immigrants, mimic Frenchmen, unbending medievalists, and somewhere, according to the official government census for 1960, an unemployed Jewish

---

[16]***faux pas*** Mistake.
[17]***blind*** Dead end.

airplane pilot—the town houses one of the finest collections of
rugged individuals I, at least, have ever come up against. Next to
Sefrou (the name of the place), Manhattan seems almost
monotonous.

Yet no society consists of anonymous eccentrics bouncing off
one another like billiard balls, and Moroccans, too, have symbolic
means by which to sort people out from one another and form an
idea of what it is to be a person. The main such means—not the
only one, but I think the most important and the one I want to
talk about particularly here—is a peculiar linguistic form called in
Arabic the *nisba*. The word derives from the triliteral root,
n-s-b, for "ascription," "attribution," "imputation," "relationship," "affinity," "correlation," "connection," "kinship." *Nsīb*
means "in-law"; *nsab* means "to attribute or impute to"; *munāsaba*
means "a relation," "an analogy," "a correspondence"; *mansūb*
means "belonging to," "pertaining to"; and so on to at least a
dozen derivatives, from *nassāb* ("genealogist") to *nīsbīya* ("[physical]
relativity").

Nisba itself, then, refers to a combination morphological,[18]
grammatical, and semantic process that consists in transforming a
noun into what we would call a relative adjective but what for
Arabs is just another sort of noun by adding *ī* (f., *īya*): *Sefru*/
Sefrou—*Sfruwī*/native son of Sefrou; *Sūs*/region of southwestern
Morocco—*Sūsī* /man coming from that region; *Beni Yazğa*/a tribe
near Sefrou—*Yazğī*/a member of that tribe; *Yahūd*/the Jews as a
people, Jewry—*Yahūdī*/a Jew; *'Adlun*/surname of a prominent Sefrou family—*'Adlūnī*/a member of that family. Nor is the procedure
confined to this more or less straightforward "ethnicizing" use, but
is employed in a wide range of domains to attribute relational
properties to persons. For example, occupation (*hrār*/silk—*hrārī*/
silk merchant); religious sect (*Darqāwā*/a mystical brotherhood—
Darqāwī/an adept of that brotherhood or spiritual status), (*'Ali*/The
Prophet's son-in-law—*'Alawī*/descendant of the Prophet's son-in-
law, and thus of the Prophet).

Now, as once formed, nisbas tend to be incorporated into   24
personal names—Umar Al-Buhadiwi/Umar of the Buhadu Tribe;
Muhammed Al-Sussi/Muhammed from the Sus Region—this sort
of adjectival attributive classification is quite publicly stamped onto
an individual's identity. I was unable to find a single case where an
individual was generally known, or known about, but his or her
nisba was not. Indeed, Sefrouis are far more likely to be ignorant

---

[18]*morphological*   Referring to form and structure of words.

of how well-off a man is, how long he has been around, what his personal character is, or where exactly he lives, than they are of what his nisba is—Sussi or Sefroui, Buhadiwi or Adluni, Harari or Darqawi. (Of women to whom he is not related that is very likely to be all that he knows—or, more exactly, is permitted to know.) The selves that bump and jostle each other in the alleys of Sefrou gain their definition from associative relations they are imputed to have with the society that surrounds them. They are contextualized persons.

But the situation is even more radical than this; nisbas render men relative to their contexts, but as contexts themselves are relative, so too are nisbas, and the whole thing rises, so to speak, to the second power: relativism squared. Thus, at one level, everyone in Sefrou has the same nisba, or at least the potential of it—namely, Sefroui. However, within Sefrou such a nisba, precisely because it does not discriminate, will never be heard as part of an individual designation. It is only outside of Sefrou that the relationship to that particular context becomes identifying. Inside it, he is an Adluni, Alawi, Meghrawi, Ngadi, or whatever. And similarly within these categories: there are, for example, twelve different nisbas (Shakibis, Zuinis, and so forth) by means of which, among themselves, Sefrou Alawis distinguish one another.

The whole matter is far from regular: what level or sort of nisba is used and seems relevant and appropriate (to the users, that is) depends heavily on the situation. A man I knew who lived in Sefrou and worked in Fez but came from the Beni Yazgha tribe settled nearby—and from the Hima lineage of the Taghut subfraction of the Wulad Ben Ydir fraction within it—was known as a Sefroui to his work fellows in Fez, a Yazghi to all of us non-Yazghis in Sefrou, an Ydiri to other Beni Yazghas around, except for those who were themselves of the Wulad Ben Ydir fraction, who called him a Taghuti. As for the few other Taghutis, they called him a Himiwi. That is as far as things went here, but not as far as they can go, in either direction. Should, by chance, our friend journey to Egypt, he would become a Maghrebi, the nisba formed from the Arabic word for North Africa. The social contextualization of persons is pervasive and, in its curiously unmethodical way, systematic. Men do not float as bounded psychic entities, detached from their backgrounds and singularly named. As individualistic, even willful, as the Moroccans in fact are, their identity is an attribute they borrow from their setting.

Now as with the Javanese inside/outside, smooth/rough phenomenological sort of reality dividing, and the absolutizing Balinese title systems, the nisba way of looking at persons—as though they were outlines waiting to be filled in—is not an isolated custom, but part of a total pattern of social life. This pattern is, like the others, difficult to characterize succinctly, but surely one of its outstanding features is a promiscuous tumbling in public settings of varieties of men kept carefully segregated in private ones—all-out cosmopolitanism in the streets, strict communalism (of which the famous secluded woman is only the most striking index) in the home. This is, indeed, the so-called mosaic system of social organization so often held to be characteristic of the Middle East generally: differently shaped and colored chips jammed in irregularly together to generate an intricate overall design within which their individual distinctiveness remains nonetheless intact. Nothing if not diverse, Moroccan society does not cope with its diversity by sealing it into castes, isolating it into tribes, dividing it into ethnic groups, or covering it over with some common-denominator concept of nationality, though, fitfully, all have now and then been tried. It copes with it by distinguishing, with elaborate precision, the contexts—marriage, worship, and to an extent diet, law, and education—within which men are separated by their dissimilitudes, and those—work, friendship, politics, trade—where, however warily and however conditionally, they are connected by them.

To such a social pattern, a concept of selfhood which marks public identity contextually and relativistically, but yet does so in terms—tribal, territorial, linguistic, religious, familial—that grow out of the more private and settled arenas of life and have a deep and permanent resonance there, would seem particularly appropriate. Indeed, the social pattern would seem virtually to create this concept of selfhood, for it produces a situation where people interact with one another in terms of categories whose meaning is almost purely positional, location in the general mosaic, leaving the substantive content of the categories, what they mean subjectively as experienced forms of life, aside as something properly concealed in apartments, temples, and tents. Nisba discriminations can be more specific or less, indicate location within the mosaic roughly or finely, and they can be adapted to almost any changes in circumstance. But they cannot carry with them more than the most sketchy, outline implications concerning what men so named as a rule are like. Calling a man a Sefroui is like calling him a San Franciscan: it classifies him, but it does not type him; it places him without portraying him.

It is the nisba system's capacity to do this—to create a framework within which persons can be identified in terms of supposedly immanent characteristics (speech, blood, faith, provenance,[19] and

---

[19]**provenance**   Origin.

28

the rest)—and yet to minimize the impact of those characteristics in determining the practical relations among such persons in markets, shops, bureaus, fields, cafés, baths, and roadways that makes it so central to the Moroccan idea of the self. Nisba-type categorization leads, paradoxically, to a hyperindividualism in public relationships, because by providing only a vacant sketch, and that shifting, of who the actors are—Yazghis, Adlunis, Buhadiwis, or whatever—it leaves the rest, that is, almost everything, to be filled in by the process of interaction itself. What makes the mosaic work is the confidence that one can be as totally pragmatic, adaptive, opportunistic, and generally ad hoc[20] in one's relations with others—a fox among foxes, a crocodile among crocodiles—as one wants without any risk of losing one's sense of who one is. Selfhood is never in danger because, outside the immediacies of procreation and prayer, only its coordinates are asserted.

Now, without trying to tie up the dozens of loose ends I have not only left dangling in these rather breathless accounts of the senses of selfhood of nearly ninety million people but have doubtless frazzled even more, let us return to the question of what all this can tell us, or could if it were done adequately, about "the native's point of view" in Java, Bali, and Morocco. Are we, in describing symbol uses, describing perceptions, sentiments, outlooks, experiences? And in what sense? What do we claim when we claim that we understand the semiotic means by which, in this case, persons are defined to one another? That we know words or that we know minds?

In answering this question, it is necessary, I think, first to notice the characteristic intellectual movement, the inward conceptual rhythm, in each of these analyses, and indeed in all similar analyses, including those of Malinowski— namely, a continuous dialectical tacking between the most local of local detail and the most global of global structure in such a way as to bring them into simultaneous view. In seeking to uncover the Javanese, Balinese, or Moroccan sense of self, one oscillates restlessly between the sort of exotic minutiae (lexical antitheses, categorical schemes, morphophonemic[21] transformations) that make even the best ethnographies a trial to read and the sort of sweeping characterizations ("quietism," "dramatism," "contextualism") that make all but the most pedestrian of them somewhat implausible. Hopping back and forth between the whole conceived through the parts that actualize it and

---

[20]***ad hoc*** Latin for "to this"; meaning one temporarily behaves toward another as that other would.

[21]***morphophonemic*** Forms of words.

the parts conceived through the whole that motivates them, we seek to turn them, by a sort of intellectual perpetual motion, into explications of one another.

All this is, of course, but the now familiar trajectory of what Dilthey called the hermeneutic circle,[22] and my argument here is merely that it is as central to ethnographic interpretation, and thus to the penetration of other people's modes of thought, as it is to literary, historical, philological, psychoanalytic, or biblical interpretation, or for that matter to the informal annotation of everyday experience we call common sense. In order to follow a baseball game one must understand what a bat, a hit, an inning, a left fielder, a squeeze play, a hanging curve, and a tightened infield are, and what the game in which these "things" are elements is all about. When an *explication de texte*[23] critic like Leo Spitzer attempts to interpret Keats's "Ode on a Grecian Urn," he does so by repetitively asking himself the alternating question "What is the whole poem about?" and "What exactly has Keats seen (or chosen to show us) depicted on the urn he is describing?," emerging at the end of an advancing spiral of general observations and specific remarks with a reading of the poem as an assertion of the triumph of the aesthetic mode of perception over the historical. In the same way, when a meanings-and-symbols ethnographer like myself attempts to find out what some pack of natives conceive a person to be, he moves back and forth between asking himself, "What is the general form of their life?" and "What exactly are the vehicles in which that form is embodied?," emerging in the end of a similar sort of spiral with the notion that they see the self as a composite, a persona, or a point in a pattern. You can no more know what *lek* is if you do not know what Balinese dramatism is than you can know what a catcher's mitt is if you do not know what baseball is. And you can no more know what mosaic social organization is if you do not know what a nisba is than you can know what Keats's Platonism is if you are unable to grasp, to use Spitzer's own formulation, the "intellectual thread of thought" captured in such fragment phrases as "Attic shape," "silent form," "bride of quietness," "cold pastoral," "silence and slow time," "peaceful citadel," or "ditties of no tone."[24]

In short, accounts of other peoples' subjectives can be built up without recourse to pretensions to more-than-normal capacities

---

[22]***hermeneutic circle***   Interpretive circle in which interpreting the part contributes to interpreting the whole.

[23]**explication de texte**   Critical, close reading of a text.

[24]**"*Attic . . . tone*"**   Quotations are from John Keats's "Ode on a Grecian Urn."

32

for ego effacement and fellow feeling. Normal capacities in these respects are, of course, essential, as is their cultivation, if we expect people to tolerate our intrusions into their lives at all and accept us as persons worth talking to. I am certainly not arguing for insensitivity here, and hope I have not demonstrated it. But whatever accurate or half-accurate sense one gets of what one's informants are, as the phrase goes, really like does not come from the experience of that acceptance as such, which is part of one's own biography, not of theirs. It comes from the ability to construe their modes of expression, what I would call their symbol systems, which such an acceptance allows one to work toward developing. Understanding the form and pressure of, to use the dangerous word one more time, natives' inner lives is more like grasping a proverb, catching an allusion, seeing a joke—or, as I have suggested, reading a poem—than it is like achieving communion.

QUESTIONS FOR CRITICAL READING

1. Geertz says Malinowski's diary shattered the myth of the chameleon fieldworker adapting to the society being studied. How does Geertz treat the myth? Have you felt its presence in other readings in this section?
2. How important is the distinction between "ethnographer" and "anthropologist"?
3. Does Geertz think empathy is necessary in anthropology?
4. Where do you stand on the question of experience-distant versus experience-close study of cultures (paras. 3–5)? Can you tell where Geertz stands?
5. What does it mean to see things "from the native's point of view"?
6. What is Geertz's own method of work in relation to other cultures? How does it differ from the methods he describes?
7. Is the Balinese attitude toward hierarchy and status understandable in terms of your own culture (paras. 17–20)? How does your culture express status?
8. Geertz spends a great deal of time discussing words specific to the languages of the cultures he describes. Why? Do his observations offer you special insights into the cultures?

WRITING ASSIGNMENTS

1. If you were to be "a meanings-and-symbols ethnographer," how would you go about examining your own culture? What symbolic forms would you center on in your examination? Geertz defines sym-

bolic forms as "words, images, institutions, behaviors." What are the patterns most characteristic of such symbolic forms? You might want to search for oppositions of the kind Geertz uses in his own studies.

2. Describe how "the Western conception of the person as a bounded, unique, more or less integrated motivational and cognitive universe" (para. 9) reveals itself in the culture you know best. How do people you know well regard themselves in relation to their individuality? Give a Geertzian portrait of the individual as you have observed it functioning in your society.

3. Clarify the distinctions between the inside and outside as Geertz uses the terms in describing the Javanese individual. Do Westerners have concepts that are in any way similar to these? Are you aware of having an inside and an outside to your character, personality, or self? How do such concepts manifest themselves? Do Westerners have contrasting aspects similar to the Javanese "refined/vulgar"?

4. In paragraph 14, Geertz talks about a split in personality, referring to "an inner world of stilled emotion and an outer world of shaped behavior." Examine his concept and explain it in your own words. Then go on to describe the instances in which such a description would apply to your own culture. When do people's actions hide their emotions? Under what conditions do their emotions go unexpressed? Do you recognize such moments as culturally determined? Are there special circumstances in your culture in which such a split is essential and expected?

5. Geertz describes Moroccans as "anonymous eccentrics bouncing off one another like billiard balls" (para. 22). In what ways are the individuals you know in your immediate environment like the Moroccans? Why is it possible for distinct and eccentric people to get along together? What are the conditions that make it work?

6. Which of the three cultures Geertz describes is closest in form to the culture you know best? What are the qualities that your culture shares with them?

7. In paragraph 27, Geertz describes the *nisba* way of looking at people "as though they were outlines waiting to be filled in." What does he mean? To what extent do you find a similar pattern in your own culture? Under what conditions does that approach most often seem to be used? Do institutions use that approach, or do individuals?

8. Examine the special symbolic forms of your own culture, with a special emphasis on your music. What are the cultural messages implicit in the music you hear and in the music that is played in homes, in auditoriums, on television, and in public places?

9. **CONNECTIONS**   Margaret Mead and Ruth Benedict both observed the cultures they studied from the "experience-near" point of view. Comment on the success or failure of their efforts to transmit to you a clear sense of these cultures. Do they indulge in any of the kinds of excess that Geertz comments on in the opening paragraphs of his essay? Would you have preferred them to use an "experience-distant" point of view in, say, the manner of Claude Lévi-Strauss?

WRITING ABOUT IDEAS

An Introduction to Rhetoric

WRITING ABOUT IDEAS has several functions. First, it helps make our thinking available to others for examination. The writers whose works are presented in this book benefited from their first readers' examinations and at times revised their work considerably as a result of such criticism. Writing about ideas also helps us to refine what we think—even without criticism from others—because writing is a self-instructional experience. We learn by writing in part because writing clarifies our thinking. When we think silently, we construct phrases and then reflect on them; when we speak, we both utter these phrases and sort them out in order to give our audience a tidier version of our thoughts. But spoken thought is difficult to sustain because we cannot review or revise what we said an hour earlier. Writing has the advantage of permitting us to expand our ideas, to work them through completely, and possibly to revise in the light of later discoveries. It is by writing that we truly gain control over our ideas.

GENERATING TOPICS FOR WRITING

Filled with sophisticated discussions of important ideas, the selections in this volume endlessly stimulate our responses and our writing. Reading the works of great thinkers can also be chastening to the point of making us feel sometimes that they have said it all and there is no room for our own thoughts. However, the suggestions that follow will assist you to write in response to the ideas of an important thinker.

Thinking critically: Asking a question.   One of the most reliable ways to start is to ask a question and then to anwer it. In many ways, that is what the writers in this book have done again and again. Karen Horney asked whether what Freud said about female psychology was true. Rachel Carson asked whether anyone knew for sure if the long-term effects of pesticides were known. She then asked whose interests were being served by the wholesale use of pesticides in the environment and discovered that only the chemical companies benefited. By asking these questions she changed the direction of the world's attention and shifted our gaze toward the protection of the environment. John Kenneth Galbraith asked questions about why poverty still existed in a prosperous economy. B. F. Skinner's "What Is Man?" poses questions about our deeper motivations. Even Aristotle asked himself what constituted ethical behavior. Such questioning is at the center of all critical thinking.

As a writer stimulated by other thinkers, you can use the same technique. For example, turn back to the Machiavelli excerpt annotated in "Evaluating Ideas: An Introduction to Critical Reading" (pp. 5–7). All of the annotations can easily be turned into questions. Any of the following questions, based on the annotations and our brief summary of the passage, could be the basis of an essay.

Should a leader be armed?

Is it true that an unarmed leader is despised?

Will those leaders who are always good come to ruin among those who are not good?

To remain in power, must a leader learn how not to be good?

One technique is to structure an essay around the answer to such a question. Another is to develop a series of questions and to answer each of them in various parts of an essay. Yet another technique is to use the question indirectly—by answering it, but not obviously. René Descartes, for example, structures *Discourse Four* around the question of whether it is possible to know anything with such certainty that that knowledge can be used as a basis upon which to build a philosophy. He finally answers the question with the statement "I think; therefore, I am." Once that proposal is accepted, the rest of his discourse follows. You can do the same kind of thing.

Many kinds of questions can be asked of a passage even as brief as the sample from Machiavelli. For one thing, we can limit ourselves to our annotations and go no further. But we can also reflect on the larger issues and ask a series of questions that would constitute a fuller inquiry. Out of that inquiry we can generate ideas for our own writing.

Two important ideas were isolated in our annotations. The first was that the prince must devote himself to war. In modern times, this implies that a president or other national leader must put matters of defense first—that all a leader's knowledge, training, and concerns must revolve around warfare. Taking that idea in general, we can develop other questions that, stimulated by Machiavelli's selection, can be used to generate essays.

Which modern leaders would Machiavelli approve?

Would Machiavelli approve of our current president?

Do military personnel make the best leaders?

Should our president have a military background?

Could a modern state survive with no army or military weapons?

What kind of a nation would we be if we did not stockpile nuclear weapons?

These questions derive from "The prince's profession should be war," the first idea that we isolated in the annotations. The next group of questions comes from the second idea, the issue of whether a leader can afford to be moral.

Can virtues cause a leader to lose power?

Is Machiavelli being cynical about morality, or is he being realistic (as he claims he is)? (We might also ask if Machiavelli uses the word "realistic" as a synonym for "cynical.")

Do most American leaders behave morally?

Do most leaders believe that they should behave morally?

Should our leaders be moral all the time?

Which vices can we permit our leaders to have?

Are there any vices we want our leaders to have?

Which world leaders behave most morally? Are they the ones we most respect?

Could a modern government govern well or at all if it were to behave morally in the face of immoral adversaries?

One of the reasons for reading Machiavelli is to help us confront large and serious questions. One of the reasons for writing about these ideas is to help clarify our own positions on such important issues.

Using suggestions for writing. Every selection in this book is followed by a number of questions and a number of writing assignments. The questions are designed to help clarify the most important issues raised in the piece. Unlike the questions derived from annotation, their purpose is to stimulate a classroom discussion so that you can benefit from hearing others' thoughts on these issues. Naturally, subjects for essays can arise from such discussion, but the discussion is most important for refining and focusing your ideas. The writing assignments, on the other hand, are explicitly meant to provide a useful starting point for producing an essay of 700 to 1,000 words.

A sample suggestion for writing about Machiavelli follows:

> Machiavelli advises the prince to study history and reflect on the actions of great men. Would you support such advice? Machiavelli mentions a number of great leaders in his essay. Which leaders would you recommend a prince should study? Do you think Machiavelli would agree?

Like most of the suggestions for writing, this one could be worked with in any one of several ways. It can be broken down into three parts. The first is the question of whether it is useful to study, as Machiavelli does, the performance of past leaders. If you agree, then the second part of the question asks you to name some leaders whose behavior you would recommend studying. If you do not agree, you can point to the performance of some past leaders and explain why their study would be pointless today. Finally, the third part of the question asks whether you think Machiavelli would agree with your choices.

To deal successfully with this suggestion for writing, you could begin by giving your reasons for recommending that a political leader study "the actions of great men." George Santayana once said, "Those who cannot remember the past are condemned to repeat it." That is, we study history in order not to have to live it over again. If you believe that a study of the past is important, the first part of an essay can answer the question of why such study could make a politician more successful.

The second part of the suggestion focuses on examples. In the sample from Machiavelli above, we omitted the examples, but in the complete essay they are very important for bringing Machiavelli's point home. Few things can convince as completely as examples, so the first thing to do is to choose several leaders to work with. If you have studied a world leader, such as Indira Gandhi, Winston Churchill, Franklin Delano Roosevelt, or Joseph Stalin, you could use that figure as one of your examples. If you have not done so, then the most appropriate procedure is to use the research library and—in the sections on history and politics—find books or articles on one or two leaders and read them with an eye to establishing their usefulness for your argument. The central question you would seek to answer is how a specific world leader could benefit from studying the behavior and conduct of a modern leader.

The third part of the suggestion for writing—whether Machiavelli would agree with you—is highly speculative. It invites you to look through the selection to find quotes or comments that indicate probable agreement or disagreement on Machiavelli's part. You can base your argument only on what Machiavelli says or implies, and this means that you will have to reread his essay to find evidence that will support your view.

In a sense, this part of the suggestion establishes a procedure for working with the writing assignments. Once you have clarified the parts of the assignment and have some useful questions to guide you, and once you have determined what research, if any, is necessary, the next step is to reread the selection with an eye to finding the most appropriate information to help you in writing your own essay. One of the most important activities in learning how to write from these selections is rereading, while you pay close attention to the annotations that you've made in the margins of the essays. It is one of the most important ways in which reading about significant ideas differs from reading for entertainment. Important ideas demand reflection and reconsideration. Rereading provides both.

DEVELOPING IDEAS IN WRITING

Every one of the selections, whether by Francis Bacon or Mary Daly, Frederick Douglass or Karl Marx, depends upon the use of specific rhetorical techniques that help the author communicate important ideas. Each introduction identifies the special rhetorical techniques used by the writer, partly to introduce you to the way in which such techniques are used. For example, Clifford Geertz provides an example of enumeration—the numbering of important sections of an essay—in his answer to the following rhetorical question: is it possible to see cultures from the native's point of view? In the course of this answer he enumerates three different cultures that he knows well: Javanese, Balinese, and Moroccan. Such techniques are invaluable for every writer. And they are not difficult to apply to your own writing. Some of the suggestions for writing that follow the passages encourage you to use the techniques by isolating and analyzing them.

"Rhetoric" is a general term used to discuss effective writing techniques. For example, one of the interesting rhetorical techniques

Machiavelli uses is that of illustration by example, usually to prove his points. Francis Bacon uses the technique of enumeration—partitioning his essay into four sections. Enumeration is especially useful when one wishes to be very clear or when one wishes to cover a subject point by point, using each point to accumulate more authority in the discussion. Martin Luther King, Jr., uses the technique of allusion, reminding his readers from the clergy that St. Paul also wrote similar letters to try to help early Christians better understand the nature of their faith. By alluding to the Bible and St. Paul, King effectively reminded his audience that they were all serving God.

A great many more rhetorical techniques may be found in these readings. Some of the techniques are familiar because many of us already use them naturally, but we study them to become aware of their value and to remind us to use them. After all, without using rhetorical techniques it is impossible to communicate the significance of even the most important ideas. Many of the authors in this book would surely admit that the effect of their ideas actually depends upon the way they are expressed, which is a way of saying that they depend upon the rhetorical methods used to express them.

Methods of Development

Most of the more specific rhetorical methods are discussed in the introductions to the individual selections. Several represent exceptionally useful general techniques. These are methods of development. They represent approaches to working up material; that is, developing ideas that contribute to the fullness and completeness of an essay. You may think of them as techniques that can be applied to any idea in almost any situation. They can enlarge upon the idea, clarify it, express it, and demonstrate its truth or effectiveness. Sometimes a technique may be direct, sometimes indirect. Sometimes it will call attention to itself; sometimes it will work behind the scenes. Sometimes it will be used alone, sometimes in conjunction with other methods. The most important techniques will be explained and then illustrated with examples from the selections in the book.

Development by definition.   Definition is essential for two purposes: the first is to make certain that you have a clear grasp of your concepts; the second is to make certain that you communicate a clear understanding to your reader. Definition goes far beyond the use of the dictionary in the manner of "According to Webster's . . . ." Such an approach is facile, because no complex idea is susceptible to a dictionary definition. A much better strategy is to offer an explanation followed by an example. Since some of the suggestions for writing that follow the selections ask you to use definition as a means of writing about ideas, some of the following tips should be kept in mind:

- Definition can be used to develop a paragraph, a section, or an entire essay.

- It considers questions of function, purpose, circumstance, origin, and implications for different groups.

- Explanations and examples make all definitions more complete and effective.

Many of the selections are devoted almost entirely to the act of definition. For example, in "The Position of Poverty," John Kenneth Galbraith begins by defining the two kinds of poverty that he feels characterize the economic situation of the poor: case poverty and insular poverty. He defines case poverty in this paragraph:

> Case poverty is commonly and properly related to some characteristic of the individuals so afflicted. Nearly everyone else has mastered his environment; this proves that it is not intractable. But some quality peculiar to the individual or family involved— mental deficiency, bad health, inability to adapt to the discipline of industrial life, uncontrollable procreation, alcohol, discrimination involving a very limited minority, some educational handicap unrelated to community shortcoming, or perhaps a combination of several of these handicaps—has kept these individuals from participating in the general well-being. (para. 9)

When he begins defining insular poverty, however, he is unable to produce a neat single-paragraph definition. He establishes that insular poverty describes a group of people alienated from the majority for any of many reasons. So, next he spends five paragraphs discussing what can produce such poverty—migration, racial prejudice, and lack of education. When working at the level of seriousness that characterizes his work, Galbraith shows us that definition works best when it employs full description and complex, detailed discussion.

Were we to write an essay on the annotated selection from Machiavelli we might want to define a number of key ideas. For example, if we suspect that Machiavelli might be cynical in suggesting that his prince would not hold power for long if he were to act morally, we would need to define what it means to be cynical. We might also need to define "moral behavior" in political terms.

When we argue any point, it is very important to spend time defining key ideas.

Martin Luther King, Jr., in "Letter from Birmingham Jail," takes time to establish some key definitions so that he can speak forcefully to his audience:

> Let us consider a more concrete example of just and unjust laws. An unjust law is a code that a numerical or power majority group compels a minority group to obey but does not make binding on itself. This is a *difference* made legal. By the same token, a just law is a code that a majority compels a minority to follow and that it is willing to follow itself. This is *sameness* made legal. (para. 17)

This is an adequate definition as far as it goes, but most serious ideas need more extensive definition than this passage gives us. And King does go further, providing what Machiavelli does in his essay: examples and explanations. Every full definition will profit from the extension of understanding that an explanation and example will provide. Consider this paragraph from King:

> Let me give another explanation. A law is unjust if it is inflicted on a minority that, as a result of being denied the right to vote, had no part in enacting or devising the law. Who can say that the legislature of Alabama which set up that state's segregation laws was democratically elected? Throughout Alabama all sorts of devious methods are used to prevent Negroes from becoming registered voters, and there are some counties in which, even though Negroes constitute a majority of the population, not a single Negro is registered. Can any law enacted under such circumstances be considered democratically structured? (para. 18)

King makes us aware of the fact that definition is complex and capable of great subtlety. It is an approach that can be used to develop a paragraph or an essay.

Development by comparison. Comparison is a natural operation of the mind. We rarely talk for long about any topic without resorting to a comparison with something else. We are always fascinated with comparisons between ourselves and others, and we realize that we come to know ourselves better as a result of such comparisons. Machiavelli, for example, compares the armed with the unarmed prince and shows us, by means of examples, the results of being unarmed.

Comparison usually includes the following:

- A definition of two or more elements to be compared.
- Definition may be by example, explanation, description, or any combination of these.
- Discussion of the qualities the elements have in common.
- Discussion of the qualities the elements have in distinction from one another.
- A clear reason for making the comparison.

Ruth Benedict's comparison of the Apollonian Pueblo Indians with other western tribes she regards as Dionysian itself begins with a comparison of the Pueblo Zuñi with the Greeks, who devised the Appollonian concept that Benedict borrows. Her comparison permits her to define her terms while at the same time making useful distinctions:

> Apollonian institutions have been carried much further in the Pueblos than in Greece. Greece was by no means as single-minded. In particular, Greece did not carry out as the Pueblos have the distrust of individualism that the Apollonian way of life implies, but which in Greece was scanted because of forces with which it came in conflict. Zuñi ideals and institutions on the other hand are rigorous on this point. The known map, the middle of the road, to any Apollonian is embodied in the common tradition of his people. To stay always within it is to commit himself to precedent, to tradition. Therefore those influences that are powerful against tradition are uncongenial and minimized in their institutions, and the greatest of these is individualism. It is disruptive, according to Apollonian philosophy in the Southwest, even when it refines upon and enlarges the tradition itself. That is not to say that the Pueblos prevent this. No culture can protect itself from additions and changes. But the process by which these come is suspect and cloaked, and institutions that would give individuals a free hand are outlawed. (para. 14)

Benedict defines Apollonianism in terms of its rejection of individualism. In other words, the Apollonian distrusts individualistic behavior and prefers behavior that reinforces tradition, the ways of the people. Even the Greeks, Apollonian though they sometimes were, did not go as far as the Zuñi in this matter. Benedict thus shows that there is a manifest difference between the Greek and Zuñi cultures in an important area.

Benedict's general strategy in the essay is comparison. She distinguishes between the Apollonian and Dionysian much as Friedrich Nietzsche does, although she focuses explicitly on the behavior of cultures rather than of individual people; in the process she reveals a great deal about the Zuñi and their neighbors. As with all comparisons, this one helps us sharpen our understanding and awareness of each of the components of the discussion. That is one function of good comparison.

Development by example.   Examples make abstract ideas concrete. When Clifford Geertz finishes his generalizations about the study of anthropology through an examination of the "symbolic struc-tures" of "words, images, institutions, behaviors," he turns to examples "to make this all a bit more concrete." He then chooses specific instances from three cultures—Javanese, Balinese, and Moroccan—that help make his theory explicit. These examples are the most convincing part of his discussion. When Machiavelli talks about looking at history to learn political lessons, he actually cites specific cases and brings them to the attention of his audience, the prince. Every selection in this book offers examples as a way of convincing us of the truth of a proposition or as a way of deepening our understanding of a statement.

Examples need to be chosen carefully because the burden, not only of proof but of explanation and clarity, often depends on them. The sample suggestion given earlier for writing on Machiavelli's essay obviously implies the use of carefully chosen examples when it asks who among world leaders Machiavelli might have approved. For that reason, when doing research for an essay, it is very im-portant to be sure that the example or examples you settle on really suit your purposes.

Examples can be used in several ways. One is to do as Darwin does and present a large number of examples that force one to a given conclusion. This is a somewhat indirect method and is some-times time-consuming. However, the very weight of numerous examples will be unusually effective. A second method, such as Machiavelli's, can also be effective. One makes a statement that is controversial or questionable and that can be tested by example. If you provide the right example, then your audience must draw a reasonable conclusion.

When using examples, keep these points in mind:

- Choose a few strong examples that support your point.
- Be concrete and specific, naming names, citing events, giving details where necessary.
- Develop each example as fully as possible, being sure to point out its relevance to your position.

In some selections, such as Charles Darwin's discussion of natu-ral selection, the argument hinges entirely on examples, and we find Darwin citing one example after another. Stephen Jay Gould shows how a particular example, that of the ichneumon fly, causes certain philosophical difficulties to theologians studying biology, and therefore to anyone who wishes to look closely at nature. The problem with the ichneumon is that it attacks caterpillars, which have earned sympathy from people, whereas the ichneumon is ugly and seems evil. As he tells us, one result is that we dislike the parasite and approve of its victim. But there is another side to this, a second theme.

> The second theme, ruthless efficiency of the parasites, leads to the opposite conclusion—grudging admiration for the victors. We learn of their skills in capturing dangerous hosts often many times larger than themselves. Caterpillars may be easy game, but the psammocharid wasps prefer spiders. They must insert their ovipositors in a safe and precise spot. Some leave a paralyzed spider in its own burrow. *Planiceps hirsutus,* for example, parasitizes a California trapdoor spider. It searches for spider tubes on sand dunes, then digs into nearby sand to disturb the spider's home and drive it out. When the spider emerges, the wasp attacks, paralyzes its victim, drags it back into its own tube, shuts and fastens the trapdoor, and deposits a single egg upon the spider's abdomen. Other psammocharids will drag a heavy spider back to a previously prepared cluster of clay or mud cells. Some amputate a spider's legs to make the passage easier. Others fly back over water, skimming a buoyant spider along the surface. (para. 13)

Gould's example demonstrates that there are two ways of thinking about the effectiveness of the parasitic psammocharid. The wasp does not always make its life easier by attacking defenseless prey; instead, it goes after big game spiders. Gould's description technique, emphasizing the wasp's risk of danger, forces the reader to respect the daring and ingenuity of the parasite even if at first one would not think to do so.

Development by analysis of cause and effect. People usually express an interest in causes. If something happens, we often ask what causes it, as if understanding the cause or causes could somehow help us accept the results. Yet dealing with cause and effect is rather subtle. In the case of definition, comparison, and examples, we can point to something specific and feel that the connections between it and our main points are reasonable. In the case of cause and effect, we must recognize that the cause of something has to be reasoned out. Be warned that the use of cause and effect must be conducted with real attention to the terms and situations you write about. It is easy to be wrong about causes and effects. Their relationship must be worked on thoughtfully. After an event has already occurred, it may only be possible to offer a hypothesis of a theory for its cause. In the same sense, if no effect has yet been obtained, it may only be possible to speculate on what it will be if a given plan of action is followed. In both cases, reasoning and imagination must be employed to establish the relationship of cause and effect.

The power of the rhetorical method of development through cause and effect is such that you will find it in every section of this book, in the work of virtually every author. Some suggestions to keep in mind when using it to develop your own thinking are:

- Clearly establish in your own mind the cause and the effect you wish to discuss.

- Develop a good line of reasoning that will demonstrate the relationship between the cause and the effect.

- Be sure that the cause-effect relationship is real and not merely apparent.

And, subtle though the method of development by cause and effect is, it is quite natural to our general way of thinking. One of the most important points of Franz Boas's general discussion of the stability of culture concerns the causes of cultural behavior. He tries to explain behavior in terms of choice and instinct—thus using comparison to a degree—with an emphasis on choice, which as he explains becomes habitual and therefore virtually automatic in its implementation. He spends several paragraphs on this development:

> On the ground of this experience we are inclined to consider every type of behavior that is marked by an immediate, involuntary reaction as instinctive. This is an error, for habits imposed upon us during infancy and childhood have the same characteristics. They determine the particular *forms* of our activities, even of those based on the structure of our organism. We must recognize that the specific forms of our actions are culturally determined.
>
> We must eat in order to live. Arctic man is compelled by necessity to live on a meat diet; the Hindu lives on vegetal food by choice.
>
> That we walk on our legs is organically conditioned. How we walk, our particular gait, depends upon the forms of our shoes, the cut of our clothing, the way we carry loads, the conformation of the ground we tread. Peculiar forms of motion may be, in part, physiologically determined, but many are due to imitation. They are repeated so often that they become automatic. They come to be the way in which we move "naturally." The

response is as easy and as ready as an instinctive action, and a change from the acquired habit to a new one is equally difficult. When thoroughly established the level of consciousness of an automatic action is the same as that of an instinctive reaction.

In all these cases the *faculty* of developing a certain motor habit is organically determined. The particular *form* of movement is automatic, acquired by constant, habitual use. (paras. 16–19)

Boas is basically asking what causes us to behave as we do. His answer is that it is not instinct but habit, tradition, the way we were taught in infancy. The answer to his question is fundamental to the rest of his argument in "Stability of Culture."

Everywhere in this collection authors rely on cause and effect to develop their thoughts. Thomas Jefferson establishes the relationship between the abuses of the British and the need for America to sever its colonial ties. Karl Marx establishes the capitalist economic system as the cause of the oppression of the workers who produce the wealth that the rich enjoy. The Buddha regards spiritual fulfillment as the result of the practice of meditation. John Kenneth Galbraith is concerned with the causes of poverty, which he feels is an anomaly in modern society. Henry David Thoreau establishes the causes that demand the effect of civil disobedience.

Development by analysis of circumstances. Everything we want to discuss exists as certain circumstances. Traditionally, the discussion of circumstances has had two parts. The first is an examination of what is possible or impossible in a given situation. Whenever you are trying to convince your audience that a specific course of action should be taken, it is helpful to show that, given the circumstances, no other course is possible. On the other hand, people may intend to follow a specific course of action because none other seems possible. If you disagree with that course of action, you may have to demonstrate that another is indeed possible.

The second part of this method of development is the analysis of what has been done in the past. If something has been done in the past, then it may be possible to do it again in the future. Therefore, it is often true that a historical survey of a situation is a form of examination of circumstances.

When using the method of examination of circumstances to develop an idea, keep in mind the following tips:

- Clarify the question of possibility and impossibility.

- Review past circumstances so that future ones can be determined.

- Suggest a course of action based on an analysis of possibility and past circumstances.
- Establish the present circumstances, listing them if necessary. Be detailed; concentrate on facts.

In "The Qualitative Leap Beyond Patriarchal Religion" Mary Daly investigates the nature of the institution of the church, looking back to its early structure. She sees that the church is based on a patriarchy that in some instances has had very negative effects on women. Even the symbols and imagery of the church are masculine. Daly claims that the patriarchal bias injures not only women but everyone. The male-controlled professions, she asserts, are in a complex way genocidal and must change. She reminds us that it is possible for an institution such as the church to alter its imagery and its stance, and when it does so it will be the better for it.

Machiavelli is also interested in the question of possibility, since he is trying to encourage his ideal prince to follow a prescribed pattern of behavior. As he constantly reminds us, if the prince does not do so it is possible that he will be deposed or killed. Taken as a whole, "The Qualities of the Prince" is a recitation of the circumstances that are necessary to guarantee success in politics. Machiavelli establishes this in a single paragraph.

> Therefore, it is not necessary for a prince to have all of the above-mentioned qualities, but it is very necessary for him to appear to have them. Furthermore, I shall be so bold as to assert this: that having them and practicing them at all times is harmful; and appearing to have them is useful; for instance, to seem merciful, faithful, humane, forthright, religious, and to be so; but his mind should be disposed in such a way that should it become necessary not to be so, he will be able and know how to change to the contrary. And it is essential to understand this: that a prince, and especially a new prince, cannot observe all those things by which men are considered good, for in order to maintain the state he is often obliged to act against his promise, against charity, against humanity, and against religion. And therefore, it is necessary that he have a mind ready to turn itself according to the way the winds of Fortune and the changeability of affairs require him; and, as I said above, as long as it is possible, he should not stray from the good, but he should know how to enter into evil when necessity commands. (para. 23)

This is the essential Machiavelli, the Machiavelli who is often thought of as a cynic. He advises his prince to be virtuous but says that it is not always possible to be so. Therefore, the prince must learn how not to be good when "necessity commands." The circumstances, he tells us, always determine whether it is possible to be virtuous. The most charitable reading of this passage can only conclude that his advice is amoral.

Many of the essays in this collection rely on an analysis of circumstances. Frederick Douglass examines the circumstances of slavery and freedom. When Karl Marx reviews the changes in economic history in *The Communist Manifesto,* he examines the circumstances in which labor functions:

> The feudal system of industry, under which industrial production was monopolized by closed guilds, now no longer sufficed for the growing wants of the new market. The manufacturing system took its place. The guild-masters were pushed on one side by the manufacturing middle-class: division of labor between the different corporate guilds vanished in the face of division of labor in each single workshop. (para. 14)

The capitalist economist John Maynard Keynes devotes considerable attention to a number of important circumstances affecting contemporary economic progress. One of them is population, about which he says, "The time has already come when each country needs a considered national policy about what size of Population, whether larger or smaller than at present or the same, is most expedient" (para. 13).

Development by analysis of quotations.   Not all the essays in this collection refer to or quote other writers, but a good many of them do. And often they point to writers who are held in esteem by their audience. Sometimes the authors do not quote directly but allude to texts that support their views. This is what Martin Luther King, Jr., does when he reminds his audience of certain important passages in the Bible.

When you use quotations some pointers to remember are:

- Quote accurately and do not distort the context of the original source.
- Choose quotations that are most representative of your author.
- Unless the quotation is absolutely self-evident in importance, offer your own clarifying comments and analysis.
- Make your audience understand why you chose to quote your author: establish clearly the function of the quote.

Erich Fromm is careful to use quotations effectively and to remind us that it is possible for people to accept slogans and simple saying as substitutes for serious thought or genuine feeling:

> Modern man is actually close to the picture Huxley describes in
> his *Brave New World:* well fed, well clad, satisfied sexually, yet
> without self, without any except the most superficial contact with
> his fellow men, guided by the slogans which Huxley formulated
> so succinctly, such as "When the individual feels, the community
> reels"; or "Never put off till tomorrow the fun you can have
> today," or, as the crowning statement: "Everybody is happy
> nowadays." (para. 6)

Fromm continues to examine the quotation, fitting it into his larger
discussion, which focuses on the alienation of "modern man." In
pointing to Huxley, Fromm points to a powerful ally, whose view
in *Brave New World* was similar to his own.

The uses of quotation can be rich and various. The most obvious
technique is to place a large chunk of quotation into the discussion,
setting it off much as I have done above and will do again below.
But there are other ways. For example, B. F. Skinner, in "What
Is Man?" sometimes invokes a flurry of quotations as a means of
explaining. Examine the following paragraph for its gathering of
relevant comments from writers whose primary fame comes from
their concerns for humanistic values.

> The picture which emerges from a scientific analysis *is* not
> of a body with a person inside, but of a body which is a person
> in the sense that it displays a complex repertoire of behavior. The
> picture is, of course, unfamiliar. The man thus portrayed is a
> stranger, and from the traditional point of view he may not seem
> to be a man at all. "For at least one hundred years," said Joseph
> Wood Krutch, "we have been prejudiced in every theory, includ-
> ing economic determinism, mechanistic behaviorism, and relativ-
> ism, that reduces the stature of man until he ceases to be man at
> all in any sense that the humanists of an earlier generation would
> recognize." Matson has argued that "the empirical behavioral
> scientist . . . denies, if only by implication, that a unique being,
> called Man, exists." "What is now under attack," said Maslow,
> "is the 'being' of man." C. S. Lewis put it quite bluntly: Man is
> being abolished. (para. 34)

Skinner has almost no time to comment on these quotations.
There are a great many of them in one paragraph—for some people's
taste, too many. But each of the quotations amasses an argument.
Skinner includes them because he is arguing against them, and he
wants us to feel that he recognizes the seriousness of his argument
and the weight of opinion that is against him. In this sense, the
paragraph is successful. Skinner is the first to admit that he must
account for the opinions of such worthies as Krutch, Maslow, and
Lewis if he is to convince us that his new view of the nature of
man is accurate.

Skinner comments on these quotations (and indirectly on many more as well) in subsequent paragraphs. He is arguing for a new view of man throughout the essay, and by quoting judiciously he can accommodate many positions that he well knows are opposed to his.

In your own writing you will find plenty of opportunity to cite passages from an author whose ideas have engaged your attention. In writing an essay in response to Machiavelli, B. F. Skinner, Ruth Benedict, or any of the authors in the book, you may find yourself quoting and commenting in some detail on specific lines or passages. This is especially true if you find yourself in disagreement with a point. Your first job, then, is to establish what you disagree with—and usually it helps to quote, which is essentially a way of producing evidence.

Finally, it must be admitted that only a few important points concerning the rhetorical methods used by the authors in this book have been discussed here. Rhetoric is a complex art that needs fuller study. But the points raised above are important because they are illustrated in many of the texts you will read, and by watching them at work you can begin to learn to use them yourself. By using them you will be able to achieve in your writing the fullness and purposiveness that mark mature prose.

A SAMPLE ESSAY

The following sample essay is based on the first several paragraphs of Machiavelli's "The Qualities of the Prince" that were annotated in "Evaluating Ideas: An Introduction to Critical Reading" (pp. 5–7). The essay is based on the annotations and the questions that were developed from them:

Should a leader be armed?

Is it true that an unarmed leader is despised?

Will those leaders who are always good come to ruin among those who are not good?

To remain in power, must a leader learn how not to be good?

Not all these questions are dealt with in the essay, but they serve as a starting point and a focus. The methods of development that are discussed above form the primary rhetorical techniques of the essay. Marginal notes identify each method as it is used simply to show in detail its effectiveness. The sample essay does two things simultaneously: it attempts to clarify the meaning of Machiavelli's advice, and then it attempts to apply that advice to a contemporary circumstance. Naturally, the essay could have chosen to discuss only the Renaissance situation that Machiavelli described, but to do so would have required unusual knowledge of that period. In this sample essay the questions prompted by the annotations serve as the basis of the discussion.

The Qualities of the President

Intro-duction   Machiavelli's essay, "The Qualities of the Prince," has a number of very worrisome points. The ones that worry me most have to do with the question of whether it is reasonable to expect a leader to behave virtuously. I think this is connected to the question of whether the leader should be armed. Machiavelli emphasizes that the prince must be armed or else face the possibility that someone will take over the government. When I think about how that advice applies to modern times, particularly in terms of how our president should behave, I find Machiavelli's position very different from my own.

Circum-stance   First, I want to discuss the question of being armed. That is where Machiavelli starts, and it is an important concern. In Machiavelli's time, the late fifteenth and early sixteenth centuries, it was common for men to walk in the streets of Florence wearing a rapier for protection. The possibility of robbery or even attack by rival political groups was great in those days. Even if he had a bodyguard, it was still important for a prince to know how to fight and to be able to defend himself. Machiavelli seems to be talking only about self-defense when he recommends that the prince be armed. In our time, sadly, it too is important to think about protecting the president and other leaders.

Examples   In recent years there have been many assassination attempts on world leaders, and our president, John F. Kennedy, was killed in Dallas in 1963. His brother Robert was killed when he was campaigning for the presidency in 1968. Also in 1968 Martin Luther King, Jr., was killed in Memphis because of his beliefs in racial equality. In the

1980s Pope John Paul II was shot by a would-be assassin, as
was President Ronald Reagan. They both lived, but Indira
Gandhi, the leader of India, was shot and killed in 1984.
This is a frightening record. Probably even Machiavelli
would have been appalled. But would his solution--being
armed--have helped? I do not think so.

Cause/
Effect For one thing, I cannot believe that if the pope had a gun
he would have shot his would-be assassin, Ali Acga. The
thought of it is almost silly. Martin Luther King, Jr., who
constantly preached the value of nonviolence, logically
could not have shot at an assailant. How could John F.
Kennedy have returned fire at a sniper? Robert Kennedy
had bodyguards, and both President Reagan and Indira
Gandhi were protected by armed guards. The presence of
arms obviously does not produce the desired effect:
security. The only thing that can produce that is to reduce
the visibility of a leader. The president could speak on
television or, when he must appear in public, use a
bulletproof screen. The opportunities for would-be
assassins can be reduced. But the thought of an American
president carrying arms is unacceptable.

Com-
parison The question of whether a president should be armed is
to some extent symbolic. Our president stands for America,
and if he were to appear in press conferences or state
meetings wearing a gun, he would give a symbolic message to
the world: look out, we're dangerous. Cuba's Fidel Castro
usually appears in a military uniform with a gun, and when
he spoke at the United Nations, he was the first, and I think
the only, world leader to wear a pistol there. I have seen
pictures of Benito Mussolini and Adolf Hitler appearing in
public in military uniform, but never in a business suit.
The same is true of Libyan leader Muammar al-Qaddafi and
Iraq's Saddam Hussein. Today when a president or a head of
state is armed there is often reason to worry. The current
leaders of Russia usually wear suits, but Joseph Stalin
always wore a military uniform. His rule in Russia was

marked by the extermination of whole groups of people and
the imprisonment of many more. We do not want an armed
president.

Use of
quotations   Yet, Machiavelli plainly says, "among the other bad
effects it causes, being disarmed makes you despised . . .
for between an armed and an unarmed man there is no comparison
also   whatsoever" (para. 2). The problem with this statement is
Com-
parison   that it is more relevant to the sixteenth century than the
twentieth. In our time the threat of assassination is so
great that being armed would be no sure protection, as we
have seen in the case of the assassination of President Sadat
of Egypt, winner of the Nobel Peace Prize. On the other hand,
the pope, like Martin Luther King, Jr., would never have
appeared with a weapon, and yet it can hardly be said they
were despised. If anything, the world's respect for them
is enormous. President Clinton also commands the world's
respect, as does John Major, prime minister of Great
Britain. Yet neither would ever think of being armed. If
what Machiavelli said was true in the early 1500s, it is
pretty clear that it is not true today.

Defini-
tion   All this basically translates into a question of whether
a leader should be virtuous. I suppose the definition of
virtuous would differ with different people, but I think of
it as holding a moral philosophy that you try to live by. No
one is ever completely virtuous, but I think a president
ought to try to be so. That means the president ought to tell
the truth, since that is one of the basic virtues. The
cardinal virtues--which were the same in Machiavelli's
time as in ours--are justice, prudence, fortitude, and
temperance. In a president, the virtue of justice is
absolutely a must, or else what America stands for is lost.
We definitely want our president to be prudent, to use good
judgment, particularly in this nuclear age, when acts of
imprudence could get us blown up. Fortitude, the ability
to stand up for what is right, is a must for our president.
Temperance is also important; we do not want a drunk for

a president, nor do we want anyone with excessive bad
habits.

Con-
clusion It seems to me that a president who was armed or who
emphasized arms in the way Machiavelli appears to mean
would be threatening injustice (the way Stalin did) and
implying intemperance, like many armed world leaders.
When I consider this issue, I cannot think of any vice that
our president ought to possess at any time. Injustice,
imprudence, cowardice, and intemperance are, for me,
unacceptable. Maybe Machiavelli was thinking of deception
and lying as necessary evils, but they are a form of
injustice, and no competent president--no president who was
truly virtuous--would need them. Prudence and fortitude
are the two virtues most essential for diplomacy. The
president who has those virtues will govern well and uphold
our basic values.

The range of this essay is controlled and expresses a viewpoint
that is focused and coherent. This is a brief essay, about 1,000
words. It illustrates each of the methods of development discussed
in the text and shows how it helps further the argument. The writer
takes issue with an aspect of Machiavelli and presents an argument
based on personal opinion, but it is bolstered by reference to example
and to an analysis of current political conditions as they compare
with those of Machiavelli's time. A longer essay could have gone
more deeply into any of the issues raised in any single paragraph,
and it could have studied more closely the views of a specific president, such as Ronald Reagan, who opposed stricter gun control
laws even after he had been shot.

The range of the selections in this volume is great. They
represent a considerable breadth and constitute a significant introduction to thought in many areas. They are especially useful for
stimulating our own thought and ideas. Obviously, there are no
absolute rules for how to do this. But observing how serious writers
work and how they apply rhetorical methods in their writing is
one of the ways to begin our own development as writers. The
suggestions for essays following each selection provide guides that
can be useful for learning from these writers, who encourage our
learning and reward our study.

Acknowledgments (continued from page iv)

Mary Daly, "The Qualitative Leap Beyond Patriarchal Religion." Originally appeared in *Quest* Magazine, Vol. I, No. 4, Spring 1975. Reprinted by permission of the author.

René Descartes, "Discourse Four" and excerpt from "Discourse Two." From Descartes's *Discourse on Method and the Meditations,* translated by F. E. Sutcliffe. Reprinted by permission of Penguin Books Ltd., UK.

Sigmund Freud, "Infantile Sexuality." From *The Basic Writings of Sigmund Freud,* translated and edited by Dr. A. A. Brill. Copyright 1938; copyright © renewed 1965 by Gioia B. Berheim and Edmund R. Brill. Reprinted by permission. Originally from *Three Essays on the Theory of Sexuality* (1905).

Erich Fromm, "Love and Its Disintegration in Contemporary Western Society." From *The Art of Loving* by Erich Fromm. Copyright © 1956 by Erich Fromm. Reprinted by permission of HarperCollins Publishers Inc.

John Kenneth Galbraith, "The Position of Poverty." From *The Affluent Society,* Fourth Edition, by John Kenneth Galbraith. Copyright © 1958, 1969, 1976, 1984 by John Kenneth Galbraith. Reprinted by permission of Houghton Mifflin Co. All rights reserved.

Clifford Geertz, "From the Native's Point of View: On the Nature of Anthropological Understanding." Copyright © 1957 by The Antioch Review, Inc. First appeared in *The Antioch Review,* Vol. 17, No. 4 (Winter 1957/58). Reprinted by permission of the Editors.

Stephen Jay Gould, "Nonmoral Nature." With permission from *Natural History,* Vol. 91, No. 2. Copyright © by the American Museum of Natural History, 1982.

Karen Horney, "The Distrust Between the Sexes." Speech read before the Berlin-Brandenburg Branch of the German Women's Medical Association on November 20, 1930, as "Das Misstrauen zwischen den Geschlechtern." *Die Ärztin,* VII (1931), pp. 5–12. Reprinted in translation with the permission of the Karen Horney Estate.

Carl Jung, "Anima and Animus." From *Aspects of the Feminine,* translated by R. F. C. Hull. Bollingen Series 20, Vol. 27. Copyright © 1982 by Princeton University Press. Excerpt, pp. 85–100, reprinted with permission of Princeton University Press.

John Maynard Keynes, "The End of Laissez-Faire." Extract from Vol. 9, *Essays in Persuasion* in *Collected Writings* by John Maynard Keynes. Reprinted by permission of the Royal Economic Society and Macmillan, London and Basingstoke.

Martin Luther King, Jr., "Letter from Birmingham Jail" (April 16, 1963). From *Why We Can't Wait* by Martin Luther King, Jr. Reprinted by arrangement with the heirs to the Estate of Martin Luther King, Jr., c/o Joan Daves Agency as agent for the proprietor. Copyright © 1963, 1964 by Martin Luther King, Jr.; copyright renewed 1991 by Coretta Scott King.

Thomas S. Kuhn, "Anomaly and the Emergence of Scientific Discoveries." From *The Structure of Scientific Revolutions.* Permission granted by the University of Chicago Press and the author.

Lao-Tzu, "Thoughts from the *Tao-te Ching.*" Excerpted from *Tao Te Ching,* translated by D. C. Lau. (Viking Penguin; London, 1978). Reprinted by permission of Viking Penguin, Ltd., London.

Claude Lévi-Strauss, "A Little Glass of Rum" from *Tristes Tropiques* by Claude Lévi-Strauss. Copyright © 1955 by Librarie Plon. English translation copyright © 1973 by Jonathan Cape Limited. Reprinted by permission of Georges Borchardt, Inc.

Niccolò Machiavelli, excerpts from "The Prince." From *Portable Machiavelli* by Peter Bondanella and Mark Musa. Copyright © 1979 by Viking Penguin, Inc. Used by permission of Viking Penguin, a division of Penguin Books USA, Inc.

Catharine A. MacKinnon, "Sexual Harassment and Sexual Politics." Reprinted by permission of the publishers from *Feminism Unmodified: Discourse on Life and*

INDEX OF
RHETORICAL TERMS

To the Student

We regularly revise the books we publish in order to make them better. To do this well we need to know what instructors and students think of the previous edition. At some point your instructor will be asked to comment on *A World of Ideas,* Fourth Edition; now we would like to hear from you.

Please take a few minutes to rate the selections and complete this questionnaire. Send it to Bedford Books of St. Martin's Press, 29 Winchester Street, Boston, Massachusetts 02116. We promise to listen to what you have to say. Thanks.

School _____

School Location (city, state) _____

Course title _____

Instructor's name _____

	Definitely Keep	Probably Keep	Uncertain	Drop	Not Assigned
Part One					
Lao-Tzu					
Machiavelli					
Jefferson					
Wollstonecraft					
Douglass					
Thoreau					
King					
MacKinnon					
Part Two					
Marx					
Veblen					
Keynes					
Galbraith					
Weil					
Reich					
Part Three					
Freud					
Jung					
Horney					
Fromm					
Skinner					
Part Four					
Bacon					
Darwin					
Carson					
Kuhn					
Gould					

	Definitely Keep	Probably Keep	Uncertain	Drop	Not Assigned
Part Five					
Buddha	____	____	____	__	____
Plato	____	____	____	__	____
Aristotle	____	____	____	__	____
Descartes	____	____	____	__	____
Nietzsche	____	____	____	__	____
Daly	____	____	____	__	____
Part Six					
Boas	____	____	____	__	____
Benedict	____	____	____	__	____
Mead	____	____	____	__	____
Lévi-Strauss	____	____	____	__	____
Geertz	____	____	____	__	____

Did you find the introductions to each selection helpful? How can we improve them? (Please use additional paper if necessary.)

_____

_____

_____

_____

Did your instructor assign the general introduction to the text? If so, did you find it useful?

_____

_____

_____

_____

Any general comments?

_____

_____

_____

_____

Name _____ Date _____

Address _____

_____